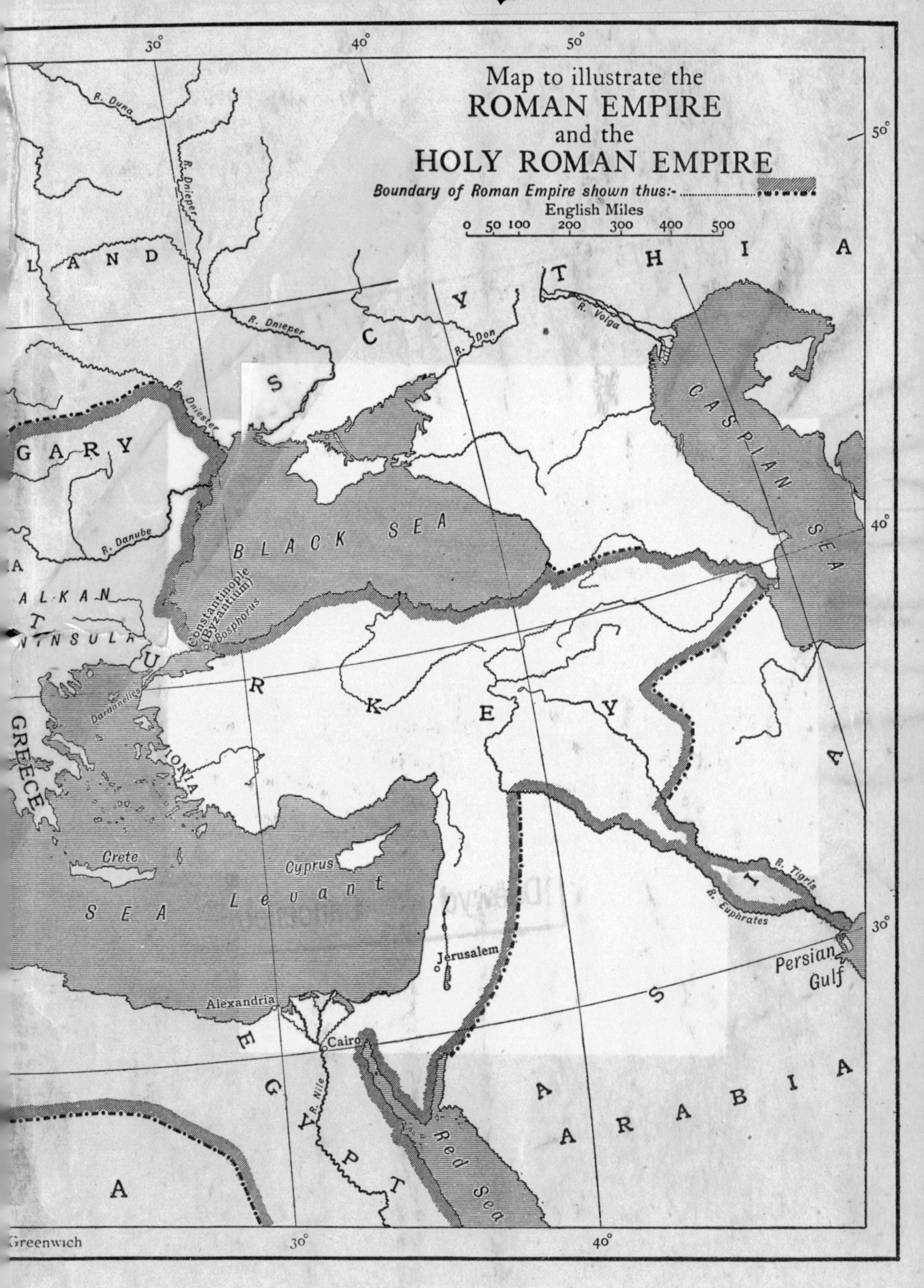

Map to illustrate the
ROMAN EMPIRE
and the
HOLY ROMAN EMPIRE
Boundary of Roman Empire shown thus:-
English Miles
0 50 100 200 300 400 500
R. Duna
R. Dnieper
R. Volga
R. Don
R. Dniester
R. Danube
SCYTHIA
CASPIAN SEA
BLACK SEA
Constantinople (Byzantium)
Bosphorus
Dardanelles
TURKEY
GREECE
IONIA
Crete
Cyprus
Levant
SEA
Jerusalem
Alexandria
Cairo
R. Nile
EGYPT
Red Sea
ARABIA
PERSIA
Persian Gulf
R. Tigris
R. Euphrates
Greenwich

FIDE ET VIRTUTE
W. E. Gladstone
St. Deiniol's Library
Hawarden, Clwyd
Founded by
The Rt. Hon. W. E. Gladstone

CIVITAS DEI

THE COMMONWEALTH OF GOD

CIVITAS DEI

THE COMMONWEALTH OF GOD

BY

LIONEL CURTIS

MACMILLAN AND CO., LIMITED
ST. MARTIN'S STREET, LONDON
1938

First Edition of Book I March 1934
Reprinted May 1934
First Edition of Book II June 1937
First Edition of Book III October 1937

PRINTED IN GREAT BRITAIN
BY R. & R. CLARK, LIMITED, EDINBURGH

THIS book is dedicated to friends, too many to name, for the most part members of the Round Table, Chatham House and All Souls College, in grateful acknowledgment of the help they have rendered by criticising the Studies upon which this attempt to discover a guiding principle in politics and how to apply it to the world situation is based.

This book is dedicated to friends, too many to name, to the constant members of the Round Table, Chatham House and All Souls College, in grateful acknowledgment of the help they have rendered by criticising the studies upon which this attempt to discover a guiding principle in politics and how to apply it to the world situation is based.

PREFACE

Since the Great War the world has relapsed into a growing confusion comparable only to that which St. Augustine was facing when he published his *De Civitate Dei*, at a time when Graeco-Roman civilisation was relapsing into the Dark Ages. I believed that this modern descent of human affairs into chaos could be stayed and reversed, but only by men with some reasoned idea in their minds of the goal at which civilisation should aim; but unless we conceive a clear idea of the goal we are trying to reach, we are moving at random, devoid of a guiding principle.

In the volume published in 1934 I was trying to see what the goal of human endeavour should be, as the clue to a guiding principle in public affairs. Having published this volume, called *Civitas Dei*, I then tried to work out in another how I thought the principle suggested should be applied to the world situation with which we are faced. The first draft of this further volume was privately printed and then submitted to a large circle of friends for their comments.

In preparing this draft I had come to realise the need of having in mind a picture of the facts to which I was trying to apply the principle, and also of allowing my readers to see what the picture was. So while the draft of my final volume was in the hands of my friends, I essayed the task of describing in an intermediate volume the world situation as I saw it. This led me to see that 'the present' is something which does not in fact exist. It becomes the past before one has written words to describe it. *The present is really the sum of the past*. In order to grasp it, I must have in mind some idea as to how it came out of the past, and must try to present that idea to my readers in narrative form. I therefore set out to prepare such a narrative, from the point where the story stopped in the volume published in 1934. In this breathless race from Plantagenet times to catch up with the present I found myself in December 1936 dealing with news in the daily papers, and closed my story at the end of that year.

I was thus led to work on the widest canvas which the framework of human records will support; but with no such equipment of historical training or reading as the task required. I must here thank readers and reviewers who have brought to my notice the mistakes I made. In the volume as now reprinted I have done my best to correct them.

When this narrative volume had gone to the printers, I was then free to consider the comments made by my friends on the first draft of the third and last volume. There was also a mass of valuable criticisms in reviews of the first volume. My first draft of the final volume was rewritten in the light of all this comment and criticism, and published in October 1937. It is here reprinted with a number of further corrections, which again I owe to the help of friends and reviewers.

These three volumes are thus republished, after careful revision, as Books I., II. and III. of a single volume, entitled *The Commonwealth of God*. Attempts to change the pronunciation of Latin, as taught in English schools from Tudor times till the present century, have led to such general confusion that my publishers found that booksellers and their customers are often too shy to pronounce Latin words so familiar and generally understood as *Civitas Dei*. It has, therefore, been thought necessary to publish this book in its final form under an English title.

L. CURTIS

ALL SOULS COLLEGE, OXFORD
7th March 1938

CONTENTS

BOOK I

AN ATTEMPT TO DISCOVER A GUIDING PRINCIPLE IN PUBLIC AFFAIRS

CHAPTER I

CHAPTER II

CHAPTER III

CHAPTER IV

CHAPTER V

CHAPTER VI

CHAPTER VII

CHAPTER VIII

CHAPTER IX

CHAPTER X

CHAPTER XI

CHAPTER XII

CHAPTER XVII

CHAPTER XXIII

CHAPTER XXIV

CHAPTER XXV

CHAPTER XXXII

CHAPTER XXXIII

BOOK II

AN ATTEMPT TO SHOW HOW THE PAST HAS LED TO THE PRESENT POSITION IN WORLD AFFAIRS

CHAPTER I

CHAPTER II

CHAPTER III

CHAPTER IV

CHAPTER V

CHAPTER VI

CHAPTER VII

CHAPTER VIII

CHAPTER IX

CHAPTER X

PAGE

CHAPTER XVIII

CHAPTER XIX

CHAPTER XX

CHAPTER XXVII

CHAPTER XXVIII

CHAPTER XXXVII

CHAPTER XXXVIII

CHAPTER XLV

CHAPTER XLVI

CHAPTER LXII

CHAPTER LXIII

CHAPTER LXIV

CHAPTER LXVIII

CHAPTER LXIX

CHAPTER LXX

* * * * * *

CHAPTER III

CHAPTER IV

CHAPTER V

CHAPTER VI

CHAPTER XI

CHAPTER XII

BOOK I

AN ATTEMPT TO DISCOVER A GUIDING PRINCIPLE IN PUBLIC AFFAIRS

CHAPTER I

INTRODUCTORY

THE art of writing, which made it possible for men to record events and their feelings about them, was only invented in the last few thousand years. A progressive improvement in these records has enabled historians to frame an ever fuller account of human activities. For this latest period of human existence the outline of its story can be gathered from witnesses, though circumstantial evidence is used to check their testimony and to fill in the details. We have thus been led to think of society as a whole, to see the problems by which we are faced and to study their solution. But when we ask how such problems were first set the historians fail us, because they arose in an age when men were unable to record what they saw or heard. Our knowledge of this age is derived from circumstantial evidence only. From ever-increasing material the anthropologists and archaeologists are slowly compiling the preface to history, and this, at least, we know with certainty, that the preface covers a period greater than the human mind had ever conceived until recent years.

The exact length of the prehistoric age is, of course, a matter of weighing and valuing inadequate evidence. According to a recent computation our ancestors were assuming a human character somewhere short of a million years ago.[1] One branch of the primitive half-human stock described as Pithecanthropus, though now extinct, was still living in Java about 200,000 years ago. Other species, definitely human, developed later. One, the Neanderthal stock, whose remains were first discovered in Germany, is thought to have branched off some 300,000 years ago. Two other species, whose bones have been found at Piltdown in Sussex and in Rhodesia, separated later.

These three species seem to have perished, but a fourth survived to become the progenitor of all the races that now inhabit the earth. From this surviving stock offshoots found their way to the habitable parts of the globe and so for long ages lost sight of each other. In the course of those ages their bodies and minds were responding to the physical conditions of the country and climate in which they lived. In tropical climates, for instance, the colour of the skin darkened to blackness and the absence of cold gave little incentive to continuous exertion. In temperate zones complexions whitened. Continuous exertion was the price of existence in the colder and damper climates of the north. In order to live through the winter, food, clothing, fuel and shelter had to be provided in the warmer months. The necessity for continuous work tended to method in working. In the temperate zones was developed a more vigorous physique, a higher sense of the value of time and a greater capacity for sustained and methodical action.

The great families of mankind have thus grown for many generations in separate worlds to be what they now are. The varieties of country and climate in which they developed have reacted on their physical structure and still more on their habits of life and thought. Yet all these races can still mix their blood with each other; for, as in the countries they inhabit, there remains beneath all these diversities a nature common to them all. In the course of a few brief centuries they were brought into contact, made to depend on each other and merged in the framework of a single society.

Till a few generations ago it was commonly supposed that the life of man on the earth began about

4000 B.C., as the dates printed in editions of the Bible which are not very old continue to remind us. The Christian world was long taught to believe that its end would come in a sudden cataclysm, which might be expected at any moment. The idea of society as something recent and essentially transient has profoundly influenced political thought for eighteen centuries. As noticed in the opening paragraph of this chapter, we now have to think of men as living their lives on this earth aeons before the few thousand years of which we have record.[2] Yet this change in our estimate of the past is of minor importance when compared with the change that the recent growth of our knowledge has wrought in our estimate of the future. We now have reason to believe, as firmly as we are able to believe anything for practical purposes, that the aeons in front of us are immeasurably greater than those behind us. Astronomers and physicists encourage us to assume that our earth will continue to support human life for millions of years. Yet political thinking is still slow to absorb the idea that human society is yet in its infancy, with vast spaces of time in which to fulfil the destiny that awaits it.

While astronomers and physicists regard this as probable, they are also able to predict with certainty that an age, however distant, must come when this planet will cease to support any form of life. The cold face of the moon is there, like the mummied corpse at Egyptian feasts, to remind us of a time when human history, however prolonged and however glorious, will be as a tale that is told, with no one to tell it and no one to hear it.

NOTES

[1] Keith, *The Antiquity of Man*, p. 714 (1925 edition).
[2] *Ibid.* p. 560.

CHAPTER II

THE GENESIS OF THE STATE

FROM bones and teeth discovered in the floors of caves it is clear that the people who lived in these natural shelters obtained their food by hunting and fishing. That they gathered the berries, leaves and roots of wild plants which they found to be wholesome may be also assumed. In these conditions human life, like that of the lower animals, was confined to the places where natural conditions provided the necessary food and shelter. The dawn of civilisation opened as men discovered how to cultivate edible plants, to tame and breed animals and birds and construct for themselves shelters other than caves. As these arts were acquired the regions where human beings could live were extended, and their numbers must have increased. They spread to the countries in which both soil and climate were suited to agriculture. Where land was brought under cultivation families clustered together for mutual help and protection. They were thus able to provide their food with a greater economy of time than was possible for families living in caves by hunting and fishing. They had leisure to develop such crafts as the making of pottery, spinning and weaving; crafts which led on to the decorative arts and finally to writing. Their power of providing for the future by storing preservable foods was increased.

The land within reach of one centre would only support a certain number of villagers. When their numbers had exceeded this limit new villages would naturally be formed in the neighbourhood. A certain number of such villages could be held together by a sense of kinship. The head of the senior family would be recognised as chief. In a tribal society the basis of authority is in theory parental.

In the village community subsisting on agriculture a variety of questions affecting the relations of the various families in the settlement and their rights to the land would begin to arise, creating the need for some kind of government. The village assembly was the natural outcome, for the heads of families could easily gather and try to discuss a settlement of questions at issue. In his famous book Sir Henry Maine has described these village communities as infant republics. That the principle of the commonwealth has its roots in village meetings and tribal assemblies is certainly true, but the process by which they developed into genuine organs of government was exceedingly slow. When a number of people meet to discuss some question at issue between them, they naturally assume that a settlement must be based on agreement of all concerned. This assumption governed Homeric assemblies and those of the Celtic, German and Slavonic tribes. It still prevails in the families of China, in the gatherings of North American Indians and in the Pitsos and Indabas of the Bantu races. It survived in the Polish Diet till the eighteenth century, to the ruin of Poland, and still survives in the English jury, as litigants sometimes find to their cost.

It is needless to dwell on the difficulty of basing a system of government on assemblies which decide nothing till all are agreed. Unanimous decisions are possible only where the issues in question are simple, where peace or war is to be declared, or the heir of a dead ruler to be recognised as chief. Even so, such decisions must usually be reached by coercing the minority or shouting them down. The supposed unanimity is often unreal.

Experience is the food by which commonwealths

are nourished; and until decisions can be freely made the growth of experience is fatally clogged. The assumption that a number of persons can decide nothing except in so far as they all agree is mainly responsible for arresting the natural development of popular government in primitive societies. With us the habit of dividing a meeting and allowing the majority to decide is now so confirmed that we scarcely realise how difficult it was for our ancestors even to conceive the idea.

The village community based on agriculture was the nucleus of political society. In Europe it was destined to act as the seed-bed for commonwealths. At an earlier period in Asia and Egypt it served as the brick from which monarchies were built on foundations of agricultural revenue.

By learning to cultivate grain and to breed domesticated cattle and birds, men ceased to live from hand to mouth. But this new power of making provision for the future was fraught with trouble. The accumulated wealth of a village or group of villages was a natural temptation to the predatory instincts of more powerful neighbours. As tribes began to raid each other, capacity for leadership in chiefs became a factor of importance. The prizes would fall to the chief with the greatest talent for organising his clansmen. Amongst such conquerors the more intelligent would realise the folly of massacring the people of a conquered village or of leaving them to starve—of killing the goose that laid the eggs. The expedient of blackmail appeared. The conquered villages were suffered to live and retain their lands in return for a share in the produce to be paid each year to the conqueror. The shrewder conquerors realised their own interest in maintaining some kind of authority and justice. Life and property in the village community thus tended to become safer than under a merely tribal regime.

By the crude process of conquest, the state in its primitive form of a kingdom began to replace a form of society which was merely tribal.

This process was not confined to the conquest of its neighbours by a stronger agricultural tribe. There were large areas of the earth's surface where climatic conditions were not suited to the methods of primitive agriculture, but would none the less support herds of camels, donkeys, horses, cattle and sheep. The steppes of Siberia and the deserts of Arabia are regions of this nature, where a pastoral society developed which was utterly different from that which grew up in the belts suited for agriculture. The sparse vegetation was sufficient to support animals so long as they moved over vast areas. So their owners travelled in tribes on camels, donkeys or horses, driving their herds to wherever pasture could be found. As they lived for the most part on the milk and flesh of their herds, their commissariat moved about with them on its own hooves. Intensely mobile and warlike, these nomadic tribes were constantly fighting each other to retain or acquire the best pastures. Their manner of life inured them to extremes of hunger and thirst, heat and cold. Nomadic society was naturally fertile in military leaders.

From time to time these wandering tribes outgrew the capacity of the steppes or deserts to support them. Their cattle were also liable to wholesale destruction by storms or droughts. On the steppes a blizzard would wipe out a great part of their herds in a few hours. In periods of scarcity due to these causes they naturally turned their hungry eyes on the stores of food garnered and herded in the villages of the agricultural regions. Apart from periods of unusual scarcity, the comparative wealth of the cultivated regions was a standing temptation to the formidable nomads of the desert and the steppe. Kingdoms created by one agricultural tribe conquering a number of others were thus liable to conquest in turn by pastoral hordes. A group of kingdoms would be thus conquered and made subject to tribute by some nomad chief whose genius for leadership had enabled him to organise a number of pastoral tribes. By this process were created autocracies in the form of great empires, which in one case, that of Genghis-Khan, covered nearly the whole of Asia and eastern Europe.

That tribal societies were merged into states by the process of conquest is undoubtedly true. But while brute force can change or destroy, it creates nothing of permanence without the aid of a moral idea. As Bismarck said in his famous aphorism, "You can do almost anything with bayonets, but sit on them". In tribal society the authority of the chief is in theory parental. The authority of one conquering chief over a number of subject tribes cannot be based on a fiction of parentage. Kings by virtue of conquest, or at any rate their heirs, were driven in course of time to find some moral authority for the power they exercised. The maintenance of such power depended, of course, in the long run on the ruler's ability to afford his subjects the security which enabled them to produce and so also to pay him the taxes he levied. But the theory that political power was based on deliberate contract between the king and his subjects is now generally recognised as a figment. "Men cannot live by bread alone", and the bonds which unite human beings in a state, however primitive its form, can never be explained merely in terms of material interests.

Archaeologists, helped by the spades of industrial excavators, have now shown that belief in a world other than that which men touch and see is older than some geological formations. The manner of burials made aeons ago proves no less. The spirits of the dead were held to survive and to punish or reward their descendants. In the fury of a storm or convulsions of an earthquake, so suggestive of human passion, the primitive mind saw the rage of invisible persons, not the blind energy of mechanical forces. So also with floods, droughts and plagues. The natural calamities that visit mankind were attributed to conscious and malignant powers. The first reaction of men to things they perceive without understanding is fear. As primitive man came to think of his life as controlled by forces other than those of nature, he ascribed his misfortunes to malignant spirits and ceremonies were devised to appease their wrath. It is only at a later stage in human development that gods are thought of as capable of goodness; and even so through long ages they were still regarded as beings whose will to do good to men must be excited by offerings of food. Fear of power not understood is the ruling motive in primitive society. Power, even when exercised by men, was readily assumed to be vested with supernatural sanctions.

A conqueror able to enforce obedience from his subjects was thus regarded by them as the agent of spiritual powers. That the ruler himself should accept the idea, and believe in it, was natural enough. It provided a moral basis for the absolute power he desired to wield. As the agent of supernatural authority there were no limits to his right to exact obedience. And the ultimate faculty of knowing what was right or wrong in matters of government was naturally confined to himself. For, if Heaven entrusted him with absolute power, it was logical to suppose that Heaven would also inform him with knowledge how it should be used. The organisation of society in states began before men had learned to study the working of their own minds. They thought of knowledge no less than of power as derived from supernatural sources. The priest or seer, like the king, was a man in touch with invisible powers, who was told by them what ordinary mortals could not know. It was, in a word, the age of authority, in which it was impious even to examine the basis on which authority rested. A state of society in which a large number of human beings obeyed the authority of a single ruler was the natural outcome of this attitude of mind. A power divinely bestowed and inspired is from its nature unlimited. In the primitive and absolute kingship such a right to obedience was deemed to exist. The state in fact comes to exist in so far as its members accept an authority which is, in principle, without limits. The idea of sovereignty was from the first implicit in the state.

The effects of conquest in creating a state could acquire no permanence without some belief to justify the claim of a ruler to his subjects' obedience. The connection of power with supernatural sanctions in the mind of the primitive world provided the conqueror with a moral claim to collect taxes and enforce the order without which the surplus wealth required for taxation cannot be raised. An administrative system, however simple, is highly precarious so long as it depends on orders given by word of mouth. The state in its crudest form could not be established over wide areas or with any degree of stability before the invention of writing.

We now know that ages before the invention of agriculture primitive men had been able to depict with masterly skill things which they saw, especially animals. In the better security afforded by agriculture villagers were contriving to use pictures to record their thoughts, their judgement of things which had happened, and also measures of quantity. To put the matter in another way, they learned to convey meaning, not merely by sounds which vanished the moment they were uttered, but by signs and marks visible to the eye which were also capable of remaining visible for long periods.

The art of writing was developed in Asia and Egypt, and was only conveyed at a much later date by Asiatics to tropical Africa. This fact of itself is sufficient to explain why political society developed in Asia and Egypt so long before tropical Africa began to emerge from tribal conditions.

The instinct of a conqueror must often have been to take from the conquered villages whatever he could get. But conquerors found that they could not hope to obtain a share of the village produce year after year unless they agreed to leave the villagers enough to support themselves and their families. So long as such agreements existed only in the memories of the ruler, of his officers and of his subjects, they were utterly precarious. There was nothing to prevent a rapacious officer from plundering a village till the cultivators starved, nor yet to secure that the ruler received his legitimate share of the produce. No real system of public finance was possible until the art of recording accounts was invented. And the same principle applies to the whole field of administration. Government was possible only within restricted areas and on very rudimentary lines until rulers were able to convey their orders and receive the reports of their officers in writing. We can therefore assume that states in the real sense of the word could scarcely be organised before the art of writing was known. Scribes were the necessary condition of states. They could also record for our knowledge what happened to those states. For this reason the history of states is coincident with the period of recorded history. The art which made a political organisation possible also enables its beginnings to be seen by evidence which is other than circumstantial.

CHAPTER III

SOUTH-EASTERN ASIA

When the period of recorded history opened the greater part of humanity was living in south-eastern Asia. Then, as now, India and China were enormous reservoirs of population.

In India the tropical sun and torrential rains produced by the trade winds combine to multiply human beings and then sweep them away by millions. Fear of invisible powers which besets the primitive mind is here at its highest. The mass of the people have always lived dangerously near to the margin of subsistence: yet their aggregate wealth has constantly attracted invaders from the north.

The country was peopled by Dravidians, a submissive, industrious and intelligent race with exceedingly dark complexions. In the neighbourhood of the Baltic were a vigorous people with the lightest of all complexions, who, for want of a better name, have been known as the Aryans. Some thousands of years before the Christian era they were set in motion by some social or economic disturbance. From their home in north-western Europe migrations began to move to the south and the east. In course of time some of them reached as far as India. They seem to have overrun the peninsula, conquering, dominating and perhaps enslaving the Dravidian people wherever they came. It is probable that most of their women perished by the way. The light-skinned invaders found themselves mates from the dark-skinned peoples they conquered.

This was much what happened when, in the seventeenth century, Europeans first came to South

Africa and began to make their homes in the country. The males, who were largely in excess of the females, began to mate with African women. Their children, who were darker than their fathers, were none the less disposed to look down on pure-bred members of the subject race with skins blacker than their own. While the white man does not like to associate with the Cape-boy or Griqua, as these mixed races are called, the half-breed in turn holds himself aloof from the Kaffir and Hottentot.

The first result of contact between a northern and tropical race is thus to produce three castes, the white, the black and the half-breed between them. But the process of stratification continues, for the reason that some half-breeds are lighter than others. In families born from the same parents one child will be almost white and another nearly as black. The half-breed girl is usually anxious to mate with a husband as light as herself. Half-breeds with skins of the same shade thus incline to marry each other. In course of time they are thus stratified into castes which try to avoid intermarriage. This process is also at work in the coloured communities of North America.

In India the process of stratification has continued for thousands of years, and Hindu society is now divided into more than two thousand castes. At the top of the scale are the Brahmins, whose skins are sometimes no darker than those of the French. The Aryans who invaded India brought with them a joyous creed. Their hymns, recorded in a later age, reflect the gladness of life in a temperate climate. But their outlook was presently coloured by the gloom of the Indian jungle and the withering heat of the tropical sun. The demon-worship of their subjects and wives began to affect them, much as the Hebrew tribes were affected when in Canaan they came into contact with beliefs less pure than their own. So also the Christian Church absorbed the beliefs of the older paganism. In India the result was Hinduism, a system which finds room for almost every grade of religious practice and thought, from the profession of a lofty philosophy to the cults of primitive animism. But Hinduism is more than a religion. It is a whole system of life in which the purest remnant of white invaders are held by the darker strains to be the repository of knowledge and power. The twice-born Brahmin is a man who knows how the ill-will of the powers behind nature may be avoided or appeased. This belief has given the Brahmin caste an influence in Hindu society greater than any hereditary class has ever acquired elsewhere.

Below this powerful hierarchy were the castes identified with professions, the warriors, the scribes, the bankers and so on. The practice of crafts was abandoned to castes which could claim some slight intermixture with the conquering race. To the pure Dravidian was left the removal of filth and other unsavoury tasks. They were treated as people necessary to Hindu society, but beyond its pale.

The religious belief of the Hindu grew out of this social structure. The caste into which one is born is determined by conduct in a previous existence. The virtuous man when he dies will be born to a higher caste, the impious man to a lower. Through an infinite series of successive rebirths the balance of merit and reward is established. The final goal is conceived as deliverance from birth by absorption into the infinite. For behind the whole system lies the conception that the visible world and the life men lead in it are evil rather than good. Hence the idea of asceticism which permeates Hindu thought. In the Hindu mind pain, and especially self-inflicted pain, is the road to merit and spiritual power.

To the north-east of the Indian peninsula is a belt of

almost impenetrable mountains, forests and deserts. Beyond this barrier is China, a country designed by nature to seclude an important section of the human race from the rest of mankind. This country was thickly inhabited by people of Mongolian origin, whose peculiar physique and outlook on life was formed, so anthropologists think, in the stress of combat with nature on the steppes before they invaded China and took to agriculture. Though subject to intense heat in the summer, China for its latitude is the coldest of all countries in winter, a fact which may have helped to preserve the vigorous nature of a race bred in the steppes. Whatever the reason may be, this fact at any rate is sure, that the natural outlook on life of the Chinese is as different as anything can be from that of the Indians. They are certainly not disposed to regard the good things of this life as illusory or unreal. They show more than the average capacity of men for cheerfulness and vigour in the presence of disaster. At one period they outdistanced the rest of the world in the standard of civilisation they reached. They produced for themselves a notable philosophy, but no great religion. They are, by general acceptance, the least religiously minded of people, and, for that reason perhaps, were susceptible to religious influence from without. Ideas are more portable than goods and, through barriers difficult for commerce to penetrate, religious conceptions bred in the climate of India spread to China and beyond it to Japan. The conception of life, not as something worthy of improvement but rather as something to escape from, travelled to the east and coloured the outlook of communities larger and more vigorous than those of India.

This explains why the vast mass of the human race congregated in south-eastern Asia reached the level of civilisation which is capable of philosophic reflection, and also of religion in the real sense of the word, and then failed for a long period to advance beyond that level. It is obvious enough that no great community will go on to improve its manner of life so long as it accepts the belief that the world about it is without value and without reality. The idea that the universe and the life men lead in it are real and valuable was destined to come from fragments of the human race which found their home to the west of India.

CHAPTER IV

ISRAEL

We have seen in the last chapter how an offshoot of the stock which was destined to people Europe found its way to the Indian peninsula. In an earlier age, say 25,000 years ago,[1] another group from the same primitive stock had found its way to the regions washed by the Mediterranean, the Persian Gulf and the Red Sea. Where the soil was fertilised by rain, wells or the waters of rivers like the Tigris and Euphrates, they developed the life of an agricultural people; and as in India, these settlements furnished material for the structure of monarchies at a later date. The fertile countries were a narrow fringe surrounding great areas of desert, where tribes lived a migratory life, subsisting partly on flocks and partly by carrying goods produced in the settled communities. They thus developed an aptitude for commerce, which in course of time sought for an outlet beyond the seas. Trading villages grew on the coast to become vast emporia like the Tyre and Sidon of historical times. In these maritime settlements their zest for trade led the Semites to acquire the habits of a seafaring people. The Greeks described these sailors as Phoenicians or red-skins, an adjective latinised in the form 'Punic', names under which they figure in classical history. Their traffic spread through the Mediterranean and beyond as far as the British and Canary Isles. Towards the close of the ninth century B.C., a colony was founded in the Gulf of Tunis called Kirjath Hadeshath (the Semitic equivalent of Naples or Newtown). It was known to the Greeks as Carchedon and to the Romans as Carthage.

In the deserts which extend from Syria and Mesopotamia to the Red Sea wandering tribes continued to lead a life different from that led in the settled areas, and in violent contrast to the busy, varied and luxurious life of the town. From these wastes, where nature defies human control and society can exist only in a simple and primitive form, have emerged prophets with a deeper insight into ultimate truths than is given to men in less awful surroundings. From the age of the Patriarchs to the present day the religious revivals of the Semite world are largely connected with desert life. The message of Moses was delivered in the desert. It runs through the stories of Elijah and John the Baptist. Even Jesus, who came 'eating and drinking', withdrew to the wilderness to prepare for his mission. St. Paul retired for some years to Arabia after his conversion. The reforms of Mahomet were conceived in those regions.

There was thus developed from the desert a puritan outlook which condemned the ritual practised in the agricultural regions and in cities. We can see this attitude in the story of Sodom and Gomorrah. It runs through the book of Joshua and partly explains the evil repute of Tyre and Sidon at a later age. We can see it to-day in the attitude of Wahabi fanatics towards Medina and Mecca.

The tribes of Arabia have thus been moved by religious and moral feelings, as well as by economic motives, to conquer the settled areas beyond their desert home, whenever a leader emerged whose genius enabled them to combine in numbers sufficient for the purpose. In the Semite world, as elsewhere, monarchies were founded by pastoral chiefs, and their titles were based on a claim to divine right in its clearest and most definite shape. So long as each tribe or nation was held to have gods of its own there were limits to the pious duty of conquest. But as one nation came to believe in its own god as the universal deity, the duty of conquest was deprived of all theoretical limits. Universal dominion was the necessary dream of a people who held such beliefs as Israel held at the Christian era, and as Islam adopted centuries later. We must therefore study in some detail the gradual growth of this potent idea.

Some seventeen hundred years before Christ, Egypt seems to have been conquered by Semitic hordes from the deserts of Arabia. The rulers they placed on the throne are known as the Hyksos or Shepherd Kings. From two to three centuries later the Egyptians rose under native leaders and enslaved or expelled the invaders. It is natural to suppose that the return of some of these nomads to the desert occasioned the stories we read in the book of Exodus.

At Kadesh, which lies some eighty miles north of the Gulf of Akabah, a number of these tribes were collected by Moses. From him they acquired religious ideas which gave them a sense of unity so close that after-generations explained it on the theory of common descent from a single ancestor. They learned to regard themselves as a people standing alone and apart, not merely from alien breeds like those of Egypt, but even from the kindred tribes of the Semite world. Their God Yahwe, so Moses taught them, was their only God, a spiritual being to be worshipped in the form of no visible image. He was to be served, not in shrines by priests offering sacrifices, human or animal, but by the faithful observance of moral laws, which Moses enunciated in a brief code.[2] Their relation to this national God was conceived as a covenant, by which he was bound to save them in war from their enemies so long as they kept his law.

The first commandment delivered by Moses to the children of Israel was "I am the Lord thy God.

Thou shalt have no other gods before me." Somewhere back in the twilight of history this idea that they had one God and one only served to unite the tribes of Israel wandering in the desert of Sinai. It raised their minds from superstitions which divide the world to spiritual truths which bind it together.

Polytheism arises by the personification of natural forces. Sunlight, thunder or pestilence are conceived as the work of invisible beings. Monotheism arises from an effort, whether conscious or otherwise, to explain by hypothesis a psychological fact—the sense men have of a difference between right and wrong. In a world saturated by polytheism the idea could only occur to a mind of exceptional power. The children of Israel, when they had grasped it, assumed that Yahwe must have revealed the secret of his nature to Moses in the wilderness.

As compared with the heathen gods and goddesses Yahwe was a spiritual and ethical conception. He was never to be worshipped in the form of an idol or with rites tainted with any kind of obscenity. The God of purity, he was also the God of justice. Righteousness was conceived as the will of God. As Yahwe was the God of Israel, so Israel was the people of Yahwe. Other nations had their gods and goddesses of whom Yahwe was jealous, and against whom they fought under his leadership, as a war God. For Israelites to yield to a primitive craving and to worship the idols of surrounding tribes was not merely a crime against Yahwe but treachery to the national idea. As the jurisdiction of Yahwe was coincident with the territory of Israel, so to conquer and exterminate heathen nations was to extend that jurisdiction, an act in which piety and patriotism were combined. They spoke of victory in battle as 'the day of Yahwe'.

When in after-ages the Hebrew legends and law were recorded in scriptures, the name of Yahwe was deemed too sacred for ordinary lips to pronounce. In order to remind those reading aloud to substitute the word Adonai (Lord), the vowels in Yahwe were omitted. At a later date the vowels of Adonai were inserted beneath the consonants, and, in ignorance of this, the Christian scholars who learned Hebrew read the name as Jehovah.[3] This erroneous form became familiar in English translations, and now suggests to our minds the tremendous attributes which the Hebrews learned to associate with a word that they dared not pronounce. To them in course of time Yahwe came to imply the one universal God, and that is the idea which Jehovah conveys to our minds. To us the name Yahwe suggests a Semitic God who stands some way removed from the level of Baal or Chemosh. The value of a word should be judged, first and foremost, by its power of conveying ideas. Attempts to force our lips to pronounce what can never be more than a bad imitation of the sounds made by those who first uttered them will, if they succeed, impoverish a living tongue. The scholars who shortened the first syllable of Satan did more to diminish his terrors than the sceptics who questioned his very existence. In these pages we shall follow the tradition of the Bible and Milton, and refer to the God of Israel as Jehovah.

The native Pharaohs, after ousting the Shepherd Kings, had conquered Canaan. By the fourteenth century they were losing their hold on the country. In letters found at Tell-el-Amarna, the captains of hard-pressed garrisons report an inroad from the desert of tribes called Habiru. The date of these letters is about 1350 B.C., and according to philologists "the equation of Habiru with 'Ibhrim or Hebrews is perfect".[4]

Canaan was the causeway, easily traversed because fertile, which connected Asia with Egypt and Africa. As in China and India, a people who live by tilling the soil are apt to develop elaborate cults. As the Hebrew nomads conquered the country and took to agriculture they began to temper the severity of the creed which Moses had taught, and copied practices followed by their Canaanite neighbours and serfs. They adopted their elaborate rites and learned to propitiate Jehovah by the sacrifice of animals and even of men, women and children. At times they worshipped their god in the form of a calf, a relic, as with the Brahmins, of an age when herds had furnished their means of subsistence. The superstitions of Canaan were thus grafted onto the teaching of Moses. Judah and Benjamin in the barren south were less exposed to such influence than the tribes which had conquered the fertile country to the north.

The adoption of ritual presently led to the development of an organised priesthood. In course of time the priests became a professional caste with a vested interest in ceremonial. There were seldom wanting, however, successors of Moses, who raised their voices against these practices. The priests, who figured as the guardians of established custom, were in frequent opposition to the prophets, whose sanctuary was often the desert.

But for the prophets, the teaching of Moses might have been buried as deeply in paganism as the teaching of Gautama is now buried in some sects of Buddhism, or the teaching of Jesus in some of the Christian Churches. In course of time they brought their people to abandon the worship of Jehovah in the form of an idol. The story of how God first commanded and then once for all forbade Abraham to sacrifice Isaac, his son, records their success in weaning Israel from a horrible rite. But animal sacrifice and a vast fabric of Canaanite ritual remained as an integral factor in Hebrew religion until the Romans destroyed the temple.

In an age when priests had begun to prepare

manuals of worship, these rites were ascribed to Moses himself. The idea that God could be pleased with the smell of an animal's blood and of its roasting flesh became a part of the national faith. To the last there were prophets who openly condemned such beliefs.

In course of time Hebrew ascendency in Canaan was threatened by a Cretan people who had settled on the coast opposite their island home. The pressure of Philistine armies forced the tribes of Israel to unite under one military leader. Saul of the tribe of Benjamin for a time rolled back the invaders. Later on he was beaten and perished in battle; but the fortunes of Israel were presently retrieved by David, a shepherd of the tribe of Judah. In the course of his reign he stormed the citadel still held by a Canaanite tribe in the country of Judah and made it his capital.

To unite the tribes by building a great shrine at Jerusalem was an obvious expedient; but David seems to have shrunk from a step which suggested that Jehovah could inhabit a house made with hands like a pagan deity. His powerful son Solomon had no such scruples. With the aid of Phoenician craftsmen he raised a temple to Jehovah, which also included shrines for the gods of his foreign seraglio.

Had the kingdom as founded by David and enlarged by Solomon endured, its history would scarcely have differed from that of other Semitic autocracies. Original thought would have languished under its rule and the Hebrew prophets might never have emerged to change the course of human destiny. But the centralised policy of Solomon had overstrained the national loyalty of the northern tribes. They grudged the revenues drawn from their richer country to embellish the capital in the sterile south. So after his death they seceded and established for themselves a separate monarchy with its seat at Samaria. The house of David continued to rule over Judah and Benjamin. The two Hebrew kingdoms were often at war with each other. When the monarchies of Mesopotamia and Egypt, strong in the wealth of their great riverine systems, came into conflict the Hebrew tribes were like grain between millstones. But foreign oppression may strengthen and purify native religion. In the debris of national ruin the fire which Moses had lit burst into flame from the hearts of the prophets.

The revolt of Israel from Judah seems to have occurred in the tenth century before Christ. The Phoenicians were now actively pushing their trade through the Mediterranean, and Carthage was founded in the ninth century. Damascus needed an outlet to the sea south of Phoenicia. Syrian armies invaded Israel, and in this struggle emerged Elijah, the central link in the chain which connects Moses with the prophets. In the cleft of Horeb where Moses was said to have talked with God, Elijah learned to divine his purpose for Israel in the quiet promptings of conscience, and not in the loud forces of nature.

> And behold, the Lord passed by, and a great and strong wind rent the mountains, and brake in pieces the rocks before the Lord; but the Lord was not in the wind: and after the wind an earthquake; but the Lord was not in the earthquake: and after the earthquake a fire; but the Lord was not in the fire: and after the fire a still small voice. And it was so, when Elijah heard it, that he wrapped his face in his mantle, and went out, and stood in the entering in of the cave.[5]

With the rise of empires, which was now beginning, the Syrian kingdom was swept aside. First Nineveh and then Babylon aspired to dominate the Nile and Mesopotamia. In the eighth century Israel became an Assyrian province, and military colonies were planted to hold down the Hebrew peasants. The leaders were removed to another part of the empire; hence the legend that the ten tribes were exiled and lost.

Judah was overrun and her shrines destroyed, all save the temple which Solomon had built. The walls of Jerusalem alone resisted the onset of Assyrian armies; but her kings had to render tribute to Nineveh. Towards the close of the seventh century, as Nineveh began to weaken, the patriots of Judah raised their heads. Under the rule of the young Josiah they sought to make Jerusalem the centre of national worship, not only for Judah, but also for Israel. In 612 B.C. Nineveh was destroyed by a combination of Babylon with the Medes and Scythians. Pharaoh, hastening to the help of his suzerain, seized and executed Josiah at Megiddo, but was presently crushed by Nebuchadrezzar. So Judah became a province of Babylon. In 588 B.C. Pharaoh Hophra drew Judah into rebellion. They were both crushed. The armies of Babylon sacked Jerusalem and burned the temple. Zedekiah, the last king of the house of David, was deported to Babylon with some of his subjects. Those chosen for deportation were of course leading spirits, and included the party who had sought to make the worship of Jehovah in the temple on Mount Moriah the axis of Jewish life. Exile strengthened the instinct to crystallise their creed into codes and hold themselves aloof from people not of their blood. But even so, they acquired certain ideas from the Babylonian myths. The belief in angels is probably due to this source.

Among the exiles, however, was a school more influenced by prophetic than by priestly thought, who did not regard the temple in Jerusalem with its organised ritual as essential to the faith. Jews of this way of thinking were freer to follow their instinct for trade. In the ports of the Mediterranean Jewish communities began to collect. No doubt they attracted some of their kindred from Palestine. For their public worship they established meeting-houses, which, as they adopted the Greek language, were called synagogues. They were not shrines or places for sacrifice, but centres of teaching as little adapted for dramatised worship as a Methodist chapel.

To the east of Mesopotamia was Persia, which was partly inhabited by vigorous nomads. While the Jews were in exile an Aryan leader, Cyrus the Great, emerged from these regions, and conquered the kingdoms west of Persia as far as the Black Sea and the Mediterranean. About 539 B.C. Babylon was subdued and incorporated in his empire, which his son Cambyses afterwards completed by conquering Egypt.

The Persians were followers of Zoroaster, who conceived the principle of goodness as one, though opposed in secular conflict to the principle of evil. This explains the sympathy which Cyrus clearly felt for the monotheist exiles from Palestine, and why he allowed those who regarded Jerusalem as the necessary centre of worship to return and rebuild their city and temple. By 444 B.C. the work was complete. The Jews had abandoned idolatry, but a shrine arose once more where the unseen God was supposed to dwell. An altar smoked to Jehovah and an organised corps of priests enacted a highly dramatised ritual.

The restoration of the temple and its worship revived the old antagonism of Israel and Judah, and the northern Israelites established another centre of worship on Mount Gerizim. This estrangement was still acute in the time of Christ. To this very day Samaritan worship with blood sacrifice is practised on Mount Gerizim.

NOTES

[1] Keith, *The Antiquity of Man*, p. 40.
[2] *The People and the Book*, p. 236.
[3] Moore, *Old Testament and Semitic Studies* (1908), i. p. 145.
[4] *The People and the Book*, p. 123.
[5] 1 Kings xix. 11-13.

CHAPTER V

THE LAW AND THE PROPHETS

Before the exile the priests of the temple had reduced to writing the traditional ceremonies together with a number of social ordinances. These writings came to be known as 'the law'. It is needless to argue that civilisation could never have passed certain points without the invention first of writing and also of printing. But none the less real progress has often been hampered or embarrassed by both. Time and again the fluid ideas and customs of a primitive age have been cast by scribes into rigid moulds and forged into chains for after-generations. Writing, moreover, like printing, has a curious psychological influence. Even educated people will sometimes support a statement they have made by adding that they have seen it in print. The influence of letters on a primitive community was infinitely greater. The ideas and usages of the Mosaic age, when written out, acquired a sanctity which tended to increase rather than diminish with time. Moses was believed to have taken them down at the dictation of Jehovah himself. The books of the law prescribed in minute detail the manner in which the God of Israel was to be served. And as they were inspired, so every sentence was equally important—the directions for sacrifice and ceremonial cleansing not less than the ten commandments. In time they came to be regarded as containing not merely truth but the whole of the truth. An attempt to add anything which was not implicit in those writings was blasphemous presumption. The priestly caste which recorded the law had an obvious interest in fostering such notions.

That Israel was none the less able to produce a long line of successors to Moses, who, like him, were profound and original thinkers, was due to its struggle for existence in the conflicts between Egypt and the northern and eastern despotisms. The ideas through which genuine religion has been gradually freed from primitive superstitions rooted in fear came from these prophets. Though prophets were sometimes found working in alliance with the priesthood, the two callings were profoundly opposed. The teachings of the prophets when written down came to be regarded, like the law, themselves as sacred and inspired. After a time the priests contrived to terminate the nuisance. They encouraged the idea that the age of the true prophets was finally ended, so that Israel had merely to obey the law and the prophets as they stood. By this process the 'canon was closed' and the Scriptures confined to the library known to the Christian world as the Old Testament.

The inveterate hostility of priests to prophets is recorded in a passage inserted by a priestly hand somewhere about 160 B.C. into the book of Zechariah (xiii. 2-5):

> I will cause the prophets and the unclean spirit to pass out of the land. And it shall come to pass that, when any shall yet prophesy, then his father and his mother that begat him shall say unto him, Thou shalt not live; for thou speakest lies in the name of the Lord: and his father and his mother that begat him shall thrust him through when he prophesieth. And it shall come to pass in that day, that the prophets shall be ashamed every one of his vision, when he prophesieth; neither shall they wear a hairy mantle to deceive: but he shall say, I am no prophet, I am a tiller of the ground; for I have been made a bondman from my youth.

The hereditary priesthood in Jerusalem regarded the prophets, who often sprang from the peasant class, with the jealousy of a cultured and privileged nobility. Jerusalem was a place dangerous to prophets.

Up to and during the period of the exile the prophets were patriots who believed intensely in the moral nature of the God of Israel. They thought out the consequences of that premise up to certain limits and arrived at results from which those who followed them reached far wider conclusions. They passed from the Mosaic stage of regarding Jehovah as the one God of Israel to the conception of Jehovah as the only God of the universe. "Thou shalt have none other gods before me" of the Mosaic law becomes in the prophets "There are no other gods than I".

On the other hand, their view of the life which awaited men after death had not emerged from that stage of paganism which is closely connected with ancestor-worship.[1] The souls of the dead were conceived as continuing some kind of ghostly existence in a place called Sheol under the earth. It was very like Hades as depicted by Homer, when he tells how Odysseus went down to it to visit the soul of Achilles. "Sooner would I be the slave of a landless man on earth than king in the realm of shadows" is the best that Achilles can say of the lot beyond death which awaits even the hero. So Sheol was a place of ghosts where good and evil alike met a fate faintly removed from annihilation. They had there no relations with God. "For Sheol cannot praise thee, Death cannot celebrate thee; they that go down into the pit cannot hope for thy truth."[2] These early prophets were not looking beyond the grave. The life in communion with God, the only life worth considering, was the life of the nation and not the life of the individual. It was to be lived not merely by punctilious observance of the minutiae of the law, as the priests taught, but by purity of life, righteous dealing, mercy to the weak, humbleness of heart.[3]

The people of Israel had been chosen by God to fulfil his will upon earth, and if they were faithless and disobedient God would destroy them.[4] This was the message of Amos (*circa* 760 B.C.), a shepherd who came from the edge of the desert to the south of Jerusalem. 'The day of Jehovah', he warned Israel, would mean destruction not to their enemies, but to themselves.[5] So also the first Isaiah in the closing years of the eighth century.[6] In this last prophet there is one concession to the popular hope that in the end Jehovah will pardon and restore his people.[7]

The second half of the seventh century was the era of the great reforms carried out by Josiah in the kingdom of Judah after it had survived the destruction of the northern kingdom. In consequence we find a different note in Nahum, Habakkuk and Zephaniah, the prophets of this period. The people of Judah are now regarded by these prophets as a righteous people in contrast with the wickedness of the heathen, who are doomed to destruction. Henceforward the habit develops of distinguishing Judah as the righteous and the Gentiles as the wicked. The destruction of the Gentiles in 'the day of the Lord' appears as a feature in Jewish conceptions of the future. In Nahum and Habakkuk the enemies of Judah are to be destroyed. In Zephaniah the idea of Jehovah as the one universal God of the earth has advanced a stage further. His judgement will apply to all the nations alike. At the close of it will be saved a righteous remnant of Israel.[8]

So far the prophets had thought of the 'day of Jehovah', the day of judgement, as applying to the nation as a whole. The idea that a remnant will be saved marks a change. Separation of the righteous from the wicked as the consequence of judgement implies that the prophet is beginning to consider the fate of the individual as distinguished from the fate of the nation. This idea comes strongly to the front in Jeremiah, who lived to see the fall of Jerusalem in 586 B.C., and also in Ezekiel, who went into exile in Babylon. The destruction of the Hebrew state forced the prophets to consider the fate of the individual Hebrew. But as their thoughts scarcely extended to a future life, the hopes of the individual are encouraged by a promise that the Hebrew state will witness a glorious revival. A new and regenerate Israel is to result from rewards and punishments assigned to individual Hebrews.

In one passage Jeremiah foretells that a scion of the royal house will govern the restored kingdom:

> Behold, the days come, saith the Lord, that I will raise unto David a righteous Branch, and he shall reign as king and deal wisely, and shall execute judgement and justice in the land. In his days Judah shall be saved, and Israel shall dwell safely.[9]

So, in the minds of this primitive and tortured Semitic community, ground between the millstones of Nineveh, Babylon and Egypt, was born the dream of a righteous kingdom established by God himself, a dream destined to influence the course of history and to mould human society for over two thousand years.

In the view of Jeremiah the Gentiles will be admitted to the Kingdom of God if they repent.[10] In the view of Ezekiel salvation is only for the righteous in Israel. For the Gentiles there is no room for repentance. They must either perish or, at best, survive as helots in the Kingdom of God.[11] Both Jeremiah and Ezekiel had arrived at absolute monotheism. But Jeremiah had divined that if there be one righteous God of the whole universe there must be room for repentance for all peoples of the earth, for the Gentiles as well as for the Jews. Ezekiel asserts that spirit of exclusion, which led the Jews to hold themselves aloof from other civilised nations, as they came in touch with them. In his view the Kingdom of God is for Hebrews alone. In Jeremiah the Kingdom of God is open to all, to Gentiles no less than to Jews. His idea led on to Christianity. The soul of Ezekiel issued in Judaism.

In the mind of that age there was no distinction between natural and supernatural events. In rain or droughts, in famine or plenty, in victory or defeat, they saw the direct and conscious working of Jehovah. God was the final reality, the absolute master of forces natural and human. For the prophets the only question was how far Israel could realise this truth and act upon it. Their future prosperity depended on obedience to the unseen spirit of righteousness who governed the laws of the universe. But as yet that conception was not fully thought out to all its conclusions. After death the righteous and the wicked alike passed to Sheol, a place beyond the divine jurisdiction.

The Kingdom of God for which they were looking was in fact an earthly kingdom established in Canaan with its centre in Jerusalem, such as had once been realised in the golden age of David. Its ruler would be Jehovah, issuing his edicts from his seat in the temple, though, perhaps, through a visible ruler descended from David. This kingdom would be everlasting. Its citizens would enjoy it, but only for their natural lives.

But what of the righteous in Israel who had died before the day of Jehovah and the final establishment of his kingdom? In answer to this question the prophets began to conceive the idea that the righteous would be raised to life from their graves to experience in the flesh the benefits of the Kingdom of God. His justice seemed to require no less, and the miracle involved was no difficulty to their minds. Thus came into being that strange idea that, in the day of Jehovah, the day of judgement, the bodies of the dead would rise from their graves and live once more.

> Thus saith the Lord God: Behold, I will open your graves, and cause you to come up out of your graves, O my people; and I will bring you into the land of Israel.[12]

The vision of Ezekiel in the valley of dry bones was in process of time to pass into dogma.

> And at that time thy people shall be delivered, every one that shall be found written in the book. And many of them that sleep in the dust of the earth shall awake, some to everlasting life, and some to shame and everlasting contempt.[13]

The reference to the book was no metaphor, for it seems that priests actually kept in a roll the names of those entitled to rank as members of Israel.[14] The tremendous privileges claimed for the people of God in contrast with the Gentiles required no less. This roll was known as the book of life. In the day of judgement it would be opened, and the names of those entitled to inherit the kingdom of God would be found in its pages.

By slow degrees the Hebrew seers were destined to realise that the facts of life could not be reconciled with the righteousness of God, so long as the relations of God to man were limited to physical life on this earth. The wicked not seldom prosper, while the righteous are found begging their bread. There is in this life no adequate adjustment of merit to reward. Jeremiah admits but cannot explain this. Ezekiel, with his narrower outlook, ignores the evident facts by assuming that in this life the righteous will be blessed and the wicked be punished, as they deserve.

Some centuries later the problem was faced with superlative courage. A nameless poet took for his hero a powerful sheik on the border of Edom and Arabia. The attention of Satan is drawn by God to the perfect virtue of the prosperous Job. To this Satan replies with a sneer that Job does not 'fear God for nought'. He is good because he is prosperous. The challenge is accepted and God authorises Satan to test the virtue of Job by taking away all his prosperity, sparing only his life. So Job is reduced to beggary, his children perish, and he himself is afflicted with leprosy. In the depths of his misery he is visited by friends who, true to the doctrine of Ezekiel, exhort Job to admit that he must have sinned to deserve such pain. Job, conscious of integrity, calls on God to justify his treatment of one whom he knows to be innocent. He is answered by God out of the whirlwind. The Creator of all things asks Job to consider whether he can explain the earth and heaven; the alternation of night and day, the order of the seasons, or the animal kingdom. If the human mind can grasp so little of the ways of God in the natural world, why then expect that the ways of God in the spiritual world can be fathomed? In a few closing words Job humbly admits the force of this argument, and falls back upon sheer faith in the justice of God, though it seems contrary to the facts of life.

The book of Job is a milestone in the progress of thought. It shows the Semitic mind approaching the truth reached by Socrates that if virtue and happiness, sin and pain are accurately balanced, in this life, as Ezekiel assumes, then virtue and sin lose their essential qualities. The Satanic sneer would remain unanswered.

The conception of reality as a spirit creative, righteous and existing beyond time and space, could not in the end be sustained without a further hypothesis. The souls of the righteous must also be assumed to be capable of inheriting the qualities of the spirit from which their being is derived. They also must know an existence beyond the limits of time and space, an existence in which such temporal conditions as pleasure and pain would have no relevance, where righteousness would need no extrinsic reward. For a moment this conception seems to have flashed through the mind of the poet, but only for a moment.

> But I know that my avenger liveth, And that at the last he will appear above my grave: And after my skin hath been thus destroyed, Without my body shall I see God: Whom I shall see for myself, And mine eyes shall behold, and not another.[15]

This idea which had thus begun to dawn on the Hebrew mind was utterly different from the notion mentioned above, that the bodies of righteous men would rise from their graves and live on the earth once more. This last idea was a product of folk-lore. The idea of the soul as immortal was a genuine product of thought. A confusion between them in creeds and liturgies continues to darken the popular mind.

In the Hebrew prophets we can thus discern great philosophic ideas emerging in a tangle of notions generated by the history of the Hebrew polity mixed with folk-lore. The idea of a righteous God, of society ordered in accordance with his laws, and of that society as subsisting beyond time, hypotheses which have vitalised civilisations, grew out of ideas of a Hebrew kingdom ruled from Jerusalem by a son of David, of a day of judgement at which it is initiated and a book of life in which the names of his subjects are enrolled. So from fields choked by the superstitions of astrologers, alchemists and magicians came the truths of astronomy, chemistry and physics. The wheat and the tares must grow together to be separated at the harvest.

This process is nowhere more evident than in the opening chapter of Genesis, beyond all question the work of a Hebrew exile in Babylon. The writer accounts for the universe by adapting for the purpose one from a number of Babylonian legends. In Mesopotamia he had obviously met and disputed with people whose minds were tinged with the pessimism of the further east.

> Nowhere as in India has the idea of the impermanence of the transient and the unreality of the phenomenal entered so deeply into the national soul, and become, even for the uneducated, an unconscious presupposition of a practical philosophy for everyday life.[16]

At this period, as Streeter shows, Hindu paganism was undergoing a reform analogous to that which Christianity afterwards produced in the Jewish religion. Its essential idea was cleared by Gautama of polytheism and also of rites by which the favour of deities could be won. This reforming process served to emphasise the idea native to India that "all things material, all the ordinary activities of daily life . . . are essentially maya or illusion", and therefore worthless. "The real is the unchanging." The best hope for the human soul is escape from the world where things happen, to merge like a dew-drop and lose its identity in the infinite ocean where nothing can happen.

To the north of India the Persian Zoroaster had founded another religion, based on a dualism which identified goodness with spirit and matter with evil. In the Indian view the world of sense was without value, in the Persian positively bad.

To anyone who holds this in mind it is clear that the Hebrew exile who wrote the first chapter of Genesis had in the great emporium of Babylon met and disputed with people whose minds were possessed by conceptions of the universe which came from India or Persia. At each of the stages of creation he meets those views with aggressive contradiction. Six times he asserts, "God saw that it was good", and when all is complete, he declares "And God saw everything that he had made, and, behold, it was very good". The origin of evil he relates in a legend but cannot explain any more than we in these days can explain it. Faced by a mystery, he reverts like Job to an attitude of faith in the goodness of God and therefore of his works. If reality, as the prophets had taught him, was a spirit creatively righteous, then the life he created was essentially good. We in this age may go a step further and say it is something in which the work of creation is worth continuing. Did the spirit of God really rest after his labours; or did he not rather call the beings he made in his likeness to join in his work? Is the age in which we are living not really the greatest of all the days of creation?

Gautama, who reformed and purified the Hindu religion, was perhaps contemporary with the Hebrew exile who wrote the opening chapters of Genesis. In the course of centuries Gautama's teaching penetrated the great barriers to the north-east of India and China adopted a religion which this cheerful people would certainly never have produced for themselves. In the view of Dr. Hu Shih, the greatest of living Chinese philosophers, the genius of China was diverted by Buddhism from its natural course.[17] This vast section of human society was taught by India to regard the world of sense as illusory, at best worthless, and something from which to escape. The conception of life which could vitalise man's creative energy and make it continuous was a product of Hebrew thought, proclaimed on the first page of the book which Europe learned to accept as the manual of truth.

The riverine systems of Egypt and Mesopotamia were the natural homes of powerful monarchies based on agricultural revenue. In the country between them, where these monarchies met and fought, lay the Hebrew kingdoms. Here was nothing to develop political society except in its primitive form of monarchy. In the books of the prophets we can see how the institutions under which they lived reacted on their minds. They thought of Jehovah as the King of Kings and of righteousness as a law enacted by him. They conceived the ideas which they gave to the world as oracles of God revealed through their lips, and not as the products of human thought. They accepted without question the view that truths which govern human existence are revealed to man by God through supernatural means, and not otherwise.

The first people who dared to question the principle of authority were the Greeks. Truth, as they came to perceive, is discovered by human intelligence applied to the facts of life. In the word intelligence is included the faculty of imagination. Our perceptions enable us to observe a certain number of facts, which we then try to explain. We imagine a possible explanation, and conceive what the Greeks called an hypothesis; and then in the course of time we proceed to observe how the facts fit the hypothesis. If they do not fit it, we try to think of some new theory to explain the facts. So in course of time certain ideas, the fruits of a vivid imagination, are established as truths. In the physical world many theories are finally accepted as truths. For example, all educated people who are normal accept the Copernican view of the earth as a ball revolving in space round the sun.

In the metaphysical field we can never expect this degree of certainty. If we say that ultimate reality is made of the same stuff as our minds, rather than of the same stuff as our bodies, we cannot expect all reasonable people to agree, as when we assert that the earth is a sphere. The facts of the spiritual world cannot be measured and weighed like the facts of the natural world. The idea of the earth as a sphere is merely a high probability. A physicist would advise us to act on it with unquestioning faith. But our practical conduct depends even more on the view we take of metaphysical truths. A people who think that right and wrong are valid distinctions will develop one kind of society and those who deny the distinction will develop another. "In the long run", wrote Bishop Gore at the close of his life, "what any society is to become will depend upon what it believes, or disbelieves, about the eternal things."[18] Whether we like it or not, we must form an hypothesis as to the nature of things beyond those that we touch and see. But here like Job we are driven to adopt beliefs which do not satisfy everyone, which do not satisfy even ourselves. We choose what seems, in spite of difficulties, the wisest basis for human existence. As we recognise the limits of our own minds, we are led to rely on faith to a greater extent than we have to rely on it in the natural world. As Mark Rutherford says:

> God vouchsafes to Job no revelation in order to solve the mystery with which he was oppressed. There is no promise of immortality, nothing but an injunction to open the eyes and look abroad over the universe. Whatever help is to be obtained is to be had, not through an oracle, but by the exercise of Job's own thought.[19]

The author of Job was in fact approaching the point which the Greeks in his time had begun to reach. As to whether ideas were already passing from the Greek to the Semite world we can only conjecture.

In its long struggle with kindred races Israel had won its way to monotheism cumbered and obscured by a mass of pagan traditions and beliefs. The impact of these ideas on Graeco-Roman civilisation was to shape the life of the modern world; and though Greece and Rome conquered Judea, the race was not always to the swift, nor the battle to the strong.

NOTES

[1] Charles, *Eschatology: Hebrew, Jewish and Christian*, chapter i.
[2] Isaiah xxxviii. 18.
[3] Hosea vi. 4-11.
[4] Amos iii. 1, 2.
[5] Amos v. 18-20.
[6] Isaiah xxix. 6.
[7] Isaiah i. 24-27.
[8] Zephaniah iii. 12, 13.
[9] Jeremiah xxiii. 5, 6.
[10] Jeremiah xvi. 19-21 and xii. 16, 17.
[11] Ezekiel xxxviii., xxxix.
[12] Ezekiel xxxvii. 12.
[13] Daniel xii. 1, 2.
[14] Charles, *Eschatology*, p. 165.
[15] *Ibid.* p. 71; Job xix. 25-27.
[16] Streeter, *The Buddha and the Christ*, p. 43.
[17] Hu Shih, *Religion and Philosophy in Chinese History*.
[18] Gore, *Jesus of Nazareth*, p. 250.
[19] Mark Rutherford, "Notes on the Book of Job", p. 197, in *The Deliverance* as reprinted by Jonathan Cape, 1927.

CHAPTER VI

HELLAS

WHEN the Aryan invaders descended on India some other hordes of this restless race seem to have moved on south-eastern Europe. The village communities on the coasts and islands of the eastern part of the Mediterranean had already achieved a definite civilisation of their own. They also were mastered by those forceful invaders; but the racial difference between them was not wide enough to establish any permanent system of caste. Conquerors and conquered blended as thoroughly as, in a later age, Saxons with Celts or Normans with English.

The mixture of bloods was in varying proportions. The southern race was a maritime people, who were best able to hold their own where they rested on the sea. In coastal regions they absorbed their conquerors as thoroughly as the native Irish afterwards absorbed Norman invaders. On the shores and islands of the Aegean the Mediterranean stock prevailed, and hence a more versatile genius marked the Ionian branch of the Greeks. The Dorian branch was produced in the inland communities where the mixture of northern blood was richer. This process of fusion in various proportions was already complete in the Greek world as revealed in the *Iliad* and *Odyssey* of Homer. In its village communities there are headmen whose office is hereditary. They have priestly functions and are called kings. But the village meeting is a definite factor which rulers know that they cannot ignore.

In Hebrew literature we are always conscious of pressure from without. On one side is Egypt, on the other Damascus, Nineveh or Babylon. In the poems of Homer this feeling of pressure is absent. There was nothing to force the Greek communities, as the Hebrews were forced in the time of Saul, to submit to a government common to them all. In Hebrew writings the ocean is noticed but little. In Homer it dominates everything with its strange paradoxical power to divide and connect. The village communities of Greece on the shores of a sea dotted with islands, though self-contained, are in constant touch with each other. As their products are readily exchanged they are less dependent than the Hebrews on agriculture. They speak the same language and follow the same habits of life. They appear as a nation except in this, that they have not achieved a national government. The idea of the state is confined to the village communities and develops within those limits.

The Homeric poems were probably composed by minstrels and placed on record at a later age. They show us what Greece was at the time when David was ruler of Israel. When four centuries later the Greek world can be seen once more in the pages of Herodotus, a change has occurred of which the Greeks themselves were unconscious.

The village meeting has already been noticed as a natural product of village life. In a village the heads of families can gather to discuss their common affairs, in the hope that discussion may lead to agreement. But conference seldom leads to agreement when the parties are more than two or three. So long as a general agreement is assumed to be necessary it cannot develop as a means of creating or establishing order or of enforcing justice, and it cannot, therefore, compete with any form of autocracy.

So far as we are able to judge from the poems of Homer, the village assemblies of that age in Greece were no exceptions to this rule. When the pages of accurate history open we find that Greek assemblies have in the interval hit on the novel device of taking a vote, and also of accepting the decisions of majorities as binding. They have ceased to be mere gatherings for discussion and have grown into organs capable of government.

In the Greek world as revealed in the pages of Herodotus, the hereditary rule of kings like Agamemnon, Menelaus, Achilles or Odysseus has almost vanished. The kind of government which has grown out of village meetings varies according to circumstances. The villages have grown into city-states, a growth aided by other causes than birth-rate, by captives in war reduced to slavery and by immigration from neighbouring states. The families which constituted the village community in the time of Homer are now in the position of an aristocracy surrounded by a larger number of inferior people. In some cases the heads of those families which formed the original village meeting have succeeded in reserving the government to themselves. In others, they have had in various degrees and by varying means to admit the newer and larger populace to a share in the government.

The inland cities were most dependent on agriculture for subsistence and on military organisation for defence. The older families were thus able to retain the power in their own hands. In coastal cities it was otherwise. Subsisting largely on trade, they attracted immigrants in larger numbers. For the purpose of defence the seafaring citizens were at least as important as the soldiers supplied by the landed families. These coastal communities were largely Ionian, a product of the mixture in which the versatile Mediterranean stock prevailed. The Dorian race, more largely derived from the northern invaders, prevailed in the inland communities. So in Dorian states political power was generally limited to the few. The bolder development of popular government was achieved in Ionian cities.

No system of government can be based on a meeting until it has learned the art of reaching decisions by taking a vote. A system in which decisions are made by a single autocrat is always far easier to work. In Greek communities the failure of experiments in popular government often led to a seizure of power by one leader supported by an organised party of armed followers. Such a government, based on force, with no sanction in custom or law, was described as a 'tyranny'. The idea of a monarchy based on divine right had no hold on the Greeks of that age. To them a tyranny was a government devoid of all moral foundations.

Such, in brief, were political conditions in the age when the Greek communities began to experience that pressure from without which had tortured Israel for centuries. The great riverine monarchies which oppressed Israel were now themselves conquered and absorbed by the Persian Empire. The pressure on the country between these monarchies was thus relieved. A remnant of Jews was restored to its home, and their heritage of thought, the fruit of long anguish, was saved for mankind. But in Hebrew monotheism the God of purity and righteousness, of mercy and truth, was also conceived as the King of Kings. It implied no threat to the principle of monarchy. With Greece it was otherwise. The ideas which inspired their civilisation were a challenge to the monarchy which had now united in one vast empire the countries known to the Greeks as Asia.

CHAPTER VII

THE PRINCIPLES OF MONARCHY AND OF THE COMMONWEALTH CONTRASTED

As Herodotus tells us in his opening paragraph, the theme of his history is the conflict of Europe with Asia. By Europe he means Greece and her civilisation; by Asia the kingdoms which Cyrus had absorbed in the vast empire of Persia.

For Asia, with all the various tribes of barbarians that inhabit it, is regarded by the Persians as their own; but Europe and the Greek race they look on as distinct and separate.[1]

The conflict was not in reality racial. The issue at stake arose from a struggle between two systems of society, which is still in progress and cannot be ended till one of them has completely destroyed the other. The first of these systems came from Asia, the second from Europe. But the secular struggle of Europe with Asia is blurred by the fact that the principle of monarchy, first developed in Asia, for ages mastered Europe itself, whilst the principle of the commonwealth which first sprang from Greece is now profoundly affecting Asia.

In Chapter II. we have seen how the first need of the village community based on agriculture was security. A village meeting where nothing was decided till all were agreed was powerless to meet this need. It was no match for the military conqueror, who found that it paid him to provide some security for the conquered villages, and inevitably based his right to rule on a claim to divine authority. Kingship based on religious sanctions in fact provided a degree of security for life and property much in advance of any security possible in a merely village or tribal society. It thus made possible a definite advance in arts and crafts, and finally led to the all-important invention of writing. With a system of record it was possible for rulers to organise states on a firmer basis and for larger areas. So recorded history opens with the story of great monarchies and greater empires in Egypt and Asia.

The theory of divine right enabled men to obey some motive higher than their own desires, and to this extent was based on reality. To this element of truth is due the contribution which monarchy has made to human progress. To its vast unrealities is traceable its ultimate failure to keep men moving along that path. For the ruler who thinks of himself as clothed with divine knowledge as well as authority is likely to lose his sense of proportion. The belief that his own ideas are inspired tempts him to reject the counsels of experienced advisers. His personal will, mistaken for divine intuition, is of more importance than the manifest wishes of his subjects. He becomes a prey to passion and caprice and learns to regard the people as well as the land he governs as his personal estate. In India to-day there are princes of native states who frankly adopt that view. The word 'state' is a remnant of this notion in royal minds. The monarch comes to think of his dominions, however vast, as the appanage of his throne rather than of the throne as their administrative axis. Crowns felt to be worn by right unfit the wearers for the duties they impose. Decadence is the ultimate trend of hereditary rule.

The mark of a sound political system is capacity to renew its own vigour, or else to render itself unnecessary. Autocracy is wanting in both these qualities. The doctrine of divine right disposes the minds of rulers and subjects alike to regard power over others as a good in itself, indeed as the object of human existence. It mistakes a necessary means for an end, and so directs human endeavour to a false destination, which proves when it is reached not worth the effort to attain it. A ruler who believes that his power is of God, because it is power, regards its extension as an act of piety. The subjects added to his rule by conquest come to accept his power to govern them as proof of his claim. Time and space are the only limiting factors, the amount of business which one human being can transact, and the physical difficulty of controlling his officers at a distance.

Of greater importance is the effect of this principle of authority on the people to whom it is applied. In a village community no progress is possible without some external protection for life and property. In the Greek communities the mountains and seas afforded security sufficient for the purpose; but this was a very exceptional case. With nomadic tribes, life is devoted to conquest or defence. In any case the energies of a people are mainly absorbed in the struggle for existence. The rule of a dynasty imposed upon village communities, until it becomes wholly corrupted, relieves this pressure. The instinct to decorate begins to have play, and a monarch desires not only revenue to defray the costs of government, but objects of beauty to grace his court and excite idolatry of his person. But progress in civilisation will sooner or later come to a standstill where laws are regarded as based on divine authority, and not on experience of facts apprehended and construed by human intelligence. The principles which govern human relations come to be grasped only when the task of adjusting them is thrown on the shoulders of ordinary men. They must realise that true knowledge is gained in the process of handling the facts of nature and life by an effort of mind. Creative thought is denied to those who believe only what they are told.

The idea of divine right thus presumes that the ordinary man is incapable of learning what is best for himself in public affairs. His whole duty is one of obedience to rulers to whom this knowledge is reserved. Independence of thought will tend to impair that spirit of obedience. A system of authority therefore tends to restrict freedom of choice not only in public but also in private matters. It does little to develop in those who live under it a skill in reading the meaning of facts, still less their sense of duty to each other. It stunts the growth of mind and character by accustoming men to lead their lives in accordance with fixed rules and prescribed ceremonies without examining the reasons which underlie them.

By enabling their village communities to reach decisions, the Greeks were destined to release man kind from this vicious circle. They were making it possible for ordinary men to read the lessons of experience in public life. Let us think, for a moment, how a man reads the lessons of experience in his private life. He deals with facts, makes decisions, acts upon them and in course of time sees the results. In the light of experience, though often unconsciously, he grasps the principles which govern the facts. It is for this reason that some men grow wiser as they grow older and develop a sense of responsibility. They have made decisions and acted upon them. A man artificially relieved from the necessity of making practical decisions remains with the mind of a child to the end. The mere physical growth of the brain is stunted for want of exercise, just as the muscles of a hand which is never used fail to develop. A certain amount can of course be learned from the experience of others, but only in so far as we are able to compare their experience with our own. Experience based on verified guesses lies at the root of all practical knowledge. It is thus that men learn to distinguish right from wrong in the actual cases which rise for decision. That suffering is not the ultimate punishment of error, but only a guide to wisdom, is a truth to be learned from the discipline of nature. In that school and in no other can its pupils discover that a preference for justice is the final good and a preference for injustice the absolute evil.

In a village community the heads of families begin to be faced by public questions which each cannot decide for himself, but which none the less call for decision. Where men have learned to grow most of their food in fields this situation becomes acute. There is only so much land within reach of the village, and no family can decide how much land to cultivate without affecting the welfare of others. Questions like these must be decided together, and may, for the purpose of mere village life, be decided by general agreement in a village meeting. But, as we have seen, communal development is arrested at a certain point when decisions are limited to those cases in which general agreement has proved possible. Such a polity is no match against a band of pastoral invaders who all accept the rapid decisions of a tribal chief. The villages are absorbed into a monarchy, in which political decisions are largely made over the heads of the people by an individual ruler, and come to be regarded as made by divine authority. In greater matters of public life the people are then too cowed to think, decide and act for themselves. The process of learning by experience, by mistakes which they themselves have made, is arrested. Nor do they come to regard the state as a living thing to which they themselves are imparting life.

The practice developed by some of the Greek

villages of accepting a majority vote enabled decisions to be reached whenever occasion called for decision. Laws have their origin in custom, and custom binds like a framework of iron where it cannot be changed, unless everyone, including the least progressive elements in the community, agrees to change it. But if ever a stage is reached when minorities are prepared to accept the decisions of majorities, the community will begin to grow like grass where a heavy stone has been lifted from the roots. Their decisions involve public discussion and, therefore, an appeal to reason. In the private decisions we have to make in our daily lives, we are conscious that reason will carry us to a certain point and no further. We have then to act, see what happens, and correct our methods by the results obtained. Life is one long process of correcting by trial the best guess we can make. Thought and action are alike indispensable, and success in life depends largely on a right adjustment of one to the other. And this also applies to a public assembly which is trying to compose matters too large for its individual members to decide for themselves. An assembly like the old Polish Diet, which can decide nothing until every member agrees, has no power of adjusting action to thought. The device of reaching decisions by a vote of the majority enables a public assembly to do what the individual does in his private life. By putting a period to argument, it enables hypothesis to be tested by action and wisdom to be drawn from experience of facts as gold from ore.

If these considerations were held in mind, less time might be wasted in debating the moral right of a majority to decide. *Vox populi vox Dei*, the favourite gibe of those who dislike popular government, is a covert appeal to the creed that guidance in public affairs is really a matter of divine inspiration. The principle of decision by counting heads is based on the fact that all decisions are essentially human and, as such, liable to error. No course of action can be said with certainty to be right or wrong until it has been tried and the people who have made the decision have experienced the results.

The principle of majority rule is justified by the fact that so and not otherwise can a public meeting function as an engine of government. But its operation in practice implies more than an intellectual capacity in the members of the meeting to recognise this fact. In a commonwealth a citizen often knows that some decision made in the general interest means ruin and possibly death to himself. If self-interest or self-preservation are the strongest instincts of human nature, what reason can the citizen have to accept and obey such decisions? In fact human nature is capable of responding to another and higher instinct; for members of free communities constantly accept and obey laws ruinous to themselves. Majority rule can operate only in so far as citizens have come to recognise the interests of the commonwealth as above their own, and in fact to treat that interest as their highest good. The axiom which explains all others, but cannot be explained, is this, that a man's highest good is to use himself for the benefit of others. Imperfect as they are, human beings are capable of loving their neighbours as themselves and will come to do so the more they are called upon to exercise this faculty. Such mutual devotion, which finds its expression in a sense of duty, is the ultimate bond which unites society. The end and object of all political measures should be to strengthen that bond.

The commonwealth is a state whose members have acquired the faculty of making decisions for themselves and obeying them as laws. Its essential feature is the sovereignty of law based on its own reading of facts. But citizens cannot be allowed to obey the laws only when each is willing to do so. There will always be those who fail to see their own interest in that of others. Unless they are constrained, the law will cease to operate at all, and the decisions upon which it rests lose their effect. If the commonwealth is to exist, it must call upon those who recognise their duty to obey it to enforce its decisions on those who do not. The basis of law is devotion, not force, but a commonwealth must use that devotion to enforce its law.

This does not mean that the whole duty of a citizen to the state is comprehended in obedience to law. The community is composed of human beings liable to error, even in the things which most concern themselves. A loyal citizen may find a law so fatal to his fellows who have passed it that in loyalty to them he must set it at naught. Beyond comparison such decisions are the gravest that a member of a commonwealth can be called upon to take. A man must indeed be sure of himself before he presumes to judge that the true interests of his fellow-citizens are best served by resisting their will and by breaking their laws. In the last resort, however, there is no external authority, not even that of a law made by general consent, which a man may accept as overriding his own conscience. The commonwealth rests on the principle that in the last resort each man must decide for himself between right and wrong. For its end and object is to render them fitter for such decisions.

In a commonwealth the safety of life and property, and the power of the state to secure such safety, are not treated as ends in themselves. They are necessary means to the ultimate end, which is a continuous growth in the characters and minds of the citizens, a continuous improvement in their sense of devotion to each other and also in capacity to judge rightly of measures which tend to the general welfare. It was this which the Greeks meant by saying that the state existed for the sake of goodness ; for by goodness they meant a growing excellence in the character of the citizens. They had grasped the profound truth that the growth of character and mind depends, not merely on individual nature, nor even on teaching as applied to that nature, but also on a form of society which calls on its members to exert their faculties in the public interest as well as in their own. They had seen this happening in the limited circle of their tiny commonwealths, states so small that all the citizens could meet in the market-place to elect officers, enact laws and make even executive decisions. To them it was inconceivable that a system based on the principle of the commonwealth could ever be applied to larger communities. They never arrived at the principle of representation, and a commonwealth embracing Greece as a whole was therefore impossible.

The principle of a commonwealth closely connects the citizens who compose it with the land they live in, more closely than the subjects of a despotism based on the theory of divine right. A commonwealth must coincide with a definite section of the earth's surface or else with the whole of it. A ruler who claims an authority based on divine right may also claim that his edicts operate without reference to particular territories. The importance of this will be seen in later chapters of this inquiry.

The city of Athens was the state in which the principle of the commonwealth reached its fullest expression in Greece. It was here that poets, historians and philosophers came to interpret its meaning. The civilisation of Greece reached its highest development in Athens. It was she by her leadership that saved that civilisation when Asia threatened to overwhelm it. The names of Europe and Asia stand for ideas as well as for continents. The vast territories which extend eastwards as far as the Pacific were destined in time to inherit the name of Asia. The world owes it to Athens that the name of Europe was preserved and extended to the shores of the Atlantic.

NOTE

[1] Herodotus, i. 4 (Rawlinson's translation).

CHAPTER VIII

THE PERSIAN WARS

HELLAS in all its political varieties was a model of Europe, as we see it to-day, on a miniature scale. Its numerous states, though deeply conscious of a civilisation common to them all, were acutely jealous of their separate sovereignties. The Greek communities were unable to achieve a national government for the race as a whole. Some states were of course more powerful than others, notably Sparta, which by means of a highly militarised system based on conservative institutions had attained a recognised primacy at the period when Cyrus was creating the Persian Empire.

Athens, the leading Ionian city, was next in authority. The foundations of her constitutional government had been laid by Solon in the opening years of the sixth century. In 560 B.C. the supreme power in the state was seized by an able tyrant, Peisistratus. In 510 B.C. the sons of Peisistratus were expelled by Cleisthenes, who headed a popular revolution. Under his leadership the people of Athens re-established their commonwealth and carried the principle of responsible government to limits which could only be exceeded when centuries later the device of representation was conceived and applied in the British Isles. As many citizens were admitted to the sovereign assembly as could gather in the great market of Athens and listen before they voted to the arguments of their leaders.

> For forms of government let fools contest;
> Whate'er is best administered is best.

How different was the view taken by the father of history may be seen from his comments on these events:

> Thus did the Athenians increase in strength. And it is plain enough, not from this instance only, but from many everywhere, that freedom is an excellent thing; since even the Athenians, who, while they continued under the rule of tyrants, were not a whit more valiant than any of their neighbours, no sooner shook off the yoke than they became decidedly the first of all. These things show that, while undergoing oppression, they let themselves be beaten, since then they worked for a master; but so soon as they got their freedom, each man was eager to do the best he could for himself. So fared it now with the Athenians.[1]

In his opening pages Herodotus tells us how Cyrus, at the head of his Persian army, conquered the whole of Asia Minor. The Ionian cities on its western shores were submerged in these conquests. Their free institutions were suppressed. They were placed under native tyrants, supported by Persian troops and tributary to the King of Kings. By 545 B.C. their subjugation was almost complete.

In 539 B.C. Babylon fell to the arms of Cyrus, and in 538 B.C. he allowed the Jews to return to Jerusalem. In 528 B.C. Cyrus was succeeded by his son Cambyses, who added Egypt to the Persian Empire.

Since the age of which Homer tells us, the Greeks had founded prosperous colonies in Sicily and the south of Italy, an extension afterwards known to the Romans as Magna Grecia. The Greek communities of Europe were now confronted by the greatest empire which Asia had yet produced, a despotism which controlled the resources not only of Persia and Asia Minor, of Mesopotamia and Egypt, but also the maritime power of Phoenicia.

In 521 B.C. Cambyses died by his own hand. A usurper who seized the throne was quickly removed and his place taken by Darius, who belonged to a younger branch of the family of Cyrus.

About 512 B.C. Darius crossed the Bosphorus with an army, conquered Thrace and Macedonia, and then, after bridging the Danube, attempted to subdue the tribes of the Russian steppes. Darius was the first to experience the perils which beset the would-be conquerors of Russia. He retreated in time, but only with the remnants of his vast army, to find his power in Asia Minor seriously shaken. In 499 B.C. the Ionic cities revolted and appealed to Sparta and Athens for support. Sparta 'abode in her breaches', but Athens came to their aid with ships. In a few years Darius had organised new armies from the obedient millions of his vast empire. The free cities of the mainland collapsed at their approach. The islands of the Aegean resisted so long as their ships were able to retain command of the sea against those of the Tyrian Semites who were subject to Persia. A Phoenician crew was no match for a ship manned by resourceful Greeks fighting for the freedom of their own city. But the ships from these numerous cities were unable to establish and recognise a united command for their fleet as a whole. In 494 B.C. they joined battle at Lade and collapsed before the combined tactics of the Tyrian admiral. The islands of the Aegean were swept by the troops of Darius and incorporated in his empire.

Darius was now in a position to prepare an attack on Athens herself. In 492 B.C. an army and fleet, led by his nephew Mardonius, were ordered to move on to Greece by way of the Thracian coast. In rounding the promontory of Mount Athos the fleet was destroyed by a storm. Mardonius and the army had then to retreat. Warned by this failure, Darius decided to send a fleet across the Aegean with an army on board to invade Attica from the sea. In 490 B.C. Datis and Artaphernes, who commanded this armament, succeeded in landing at Marathon, on the east coast of Attica, troops greatly outnumbering the citizens of Athens who opposed their advance. They were swept from the shore by one brilliant charge of the civic militia led by Miltiades. The Persians hastened by sea to Athens, hoping to land their reserves and seize the defenceless city. But Miltiades rapidly crossed the peninsula, and the Persians reached Piraeus to find ranged on the shore the same spears which a few days before had heaped the sands of Marathon with dead. They returned to Asia to report their failure.

The defeat of his army in a land battle by one puny Greek city was an insult which the Persian despot could scarcely afford to accept. He determined to mobilise the naval and military resources of his empire for the destruction of Athens and the conquest of Greece. He planned therefore to invade Greece by land with an army so large that it would have to be fed by sea. His fleets were organised and reserved for that purpose. He died, however, in 485 B.C. After some hesitation his son Xerxes resolved to persist in the enterprise. According to Herodotus his motives were explained in the following words:

> Once let us subdue this people, and those neighbours of theirs who hold the land of Pelops the Phrygian, and we shall extend the Persian territory as far as God's heaven reaches. The sun will then shine on no land beyond our borders; for I will pass through Europe from one end to the other, and with your aid make of all the lands which it contains one country. For thus, if what I hear be true, affairs stand: The nations whereof I have spoken, once swept away, there is no city, no country left in all the world, which will venture so much as to withstand us in arms. By this course then we shall bring all mankind under our yoke, alike those who are guilty and those who are innocent of doing us wrong.[2]

His plans for the conquest of all Greece were based on a strategy widely conceived. He arranged (so it seems) for Carthage to attack the Greek communities in Sicily from the west, while the Persian army and fleet were advancing on Greece from the east. For this purpose was assembled an army, the largest which had ever been mustered for a single campaign. The Hellespont was bridged and the danger of rounding Mount Athos avoided by cutting a canal through the isthmus which joins it to the mainland. In 480 B.C. the hosts of Xerxes crossed into Europe and advanced down the coasts of Thrace, Macedon and Thessaly, drawing their supplies from the Persian fleets.

Sparta at length realised that the Peloponnesus itself was doomed unless the advance of the Persian host could be stayed. She despatched a force under Leonidas to hold the narrow defile of Thermopylae, between Mount Oeta and the Maliac Gulf, through which the Persian host must pass before it could deploy for battle in Boeotia, overrun Attica and attack the isthmus of Corinth. The Persians, however, got round his flank and surrounded Leonidas. At the head of three hundred Spartans he died, leaving a name for valour rather than generalship. The Persian host swept through the pass, and occupied Athens. The citizens took refuge on the island of Salamis protected by their ships and those of their allies. In the sea fight which followed the Persian fleet was utterly destroyed.

On the same day (so runs the story) the rulers of Syracuse and Agrigentum, Gelon and Theron, vanquished the immense army of the Carthaginian general Hamilcar, son of Mago, at Himera so completely, that the war was thereby terminated, and the Phoenicians, who by no means cherished at that time the project of subduing the whole of Sicily on their own account, returned to their previous defensive policy.[3]

With the Greeks in command of the sea the Persian hosts encamped in Attica could no longer be fed, so Xerxes retired in haste to Asia, leaving behind him in Greece a force small enough to live on the country. In 479 B.C. the Greeks, led by the Spartan Pausanias, destroyed this force at Plataea, together with its leader, Mardonius. In the meantime the Athenians had crossed the Aegean and landed in Asia Minor with a number of allies. On the same day that Plataea was fought they defeated a Persian army at Mycale. A number of Ionian cities in Asia were thus relieved from the Persian yoke.

NOTES

[1] Herodotus, v. 78.
[2] *Ibid.* vii. 8.
[3] Mommsen, *History of Rome*, vol. i. pp. 330-31.

CHAPTER IX

RISE OF THE ATHENIAN EMPIRE

In the course of this struggle the Greeks had received more effective leadership from Athens than Sparta. For a little the victory of Plataea restored the Spartan prestige, and Pausanias was placed in command of the Greek fleets organised for the purpose of freeing the cities still subject to Persia. Athens supplied the largest contingent, in command of Cimon, son of Miltiades, the victor of Marathon, and of Aristeides, whose return from exile at a critical moment had largely contributed to the victory of Salamis.

In 478 B.C. Pausanias sailed in command of the Greek fleet to Cyprus, which lay opposite the coast of Phoenicia, upon which the naval power of Persia was based. The Greek cities of the island were freed from Persian control and re-established as outposts on the southern flank of the Greek world. Pausanias then left with the fleet to accomplish a similar task in the north. Passing through the Straits of the Hellespont into the sea of Marmora, he besieged Byzantium and took it.

Pausanias had now conceived the idea of achieving the mastery of Greece for himself, and offered to betray her cause to Xerxes in return for the hand of his daughter in marriage. The Ionians got wind of his purpose and secured his recall to Sparta. His proven treachery was a final blow to her waning prestige. The leadership of the fleets passed to the Athenian commanders.

Aristeides, who was recognised as the most disinterested man of his time, was entrusted with the task of organising a league to defend the states more immediately threatened by Persia, those on the islands and eastern coast of the Aegean. He devised a scheme under which the states, members of the league, should contribute men, ships and money to the common defence. A synod was then convened in the island of Delos, to which delegates to the number of at least two hundred were sent by the member states. The synod adopted his scheme and the cash contributions were lodged in the temple of Delos, in the hands of ten 'stewards of the Greeks' who were as a matter of fact Athenians. For some years the synod continued to meet and discuss the affairs of the league under the presidency of Athens. In the meantime the combined forces of the league completed the work of freeing the Greek cities from Persian rule, under the leadership of Cimon.

In opposition to the growing power of Athens a Peloponnesian league was formed under the leadership of Sparta which included most of the states on the mainland of Greece. Of these many had colonies on the islands and eastern coast of the Aegean which were now the unwilling subjects of Athens.

The numerous states of Hellas were thus ranged into two leagues. Those on the mainland of Greece, which were largely Dorian, followed the leadership of Sparta. Opposed to these were the island states, and those on the northern and eastern shores of the Aegean, whose normal communications with the mainland of Greece were across that sea. Behind the racial and military rivalry of Dorian land power and Ionian sea power was a deep political issue. In each city the older families were averse to sharing the government of the state with the growing population. Such growth was of course greatest in commercial and maritime cities, like Athens herself, and in those ranged under her leadership. In the mainland cities which followed Sparta political power was usually confined to the older families, who guarded that power by reserving to themselves the use of the heavier armour and weapons. In Ionian cities which followed Athens there were often a group of powerful citizens ready to side with Sparta, if ever she were strong enough to establish them in power over the populace. In Dorian states like Corcyra the populace was sometimes ready to enlist the aid and help of Athenian forces in expelling a native oligarchy. The league headed by Sparta thus stood for the principle of confining political power to leading citizens, while the league headed by Athens stood for the principle of extending it to as many citizens as possible, though not to women or children, aliens or slaves.

By a paradox, strange as any in history, the city of Athens, which stood for the principle of democracy, became the tyrant of Greece. As the Persian menace receded, the members of the league turned once more to domestic affairs and left the control of its general policy to Athens. Chios, Lesbos and Samos continued to furnish their quota of ships; but the rest preferred to commute this arduous service for payments of money. The delegates failed to attend at Delos, the synod faded out of existence and Athens remained in undisputed control. The league forces were used to coerce Naxos and Thasos when those states withheld their contributions and claimed the right to secede. In 454 B.C., when the synod had ceased to assemble in Delos, the treasury was removed to Athens for greater security from Persian attack. Henceforward the revenues of the league were spent not only on the fleet, but were also used for adorning Athens and providing doles for her sovereign voters. By imperceptible stages the confederacy of Delos had become the Empire of Athens.

CHAPTER X

THE GREEK COMMONWEALTH AS VIEWED BY CONTEMPORARIES

In 431 B.C., the mainland states led by Sparta determined to challenge the growing power of Athens. In the long struggle known as the Peloponnesian War nearly all the cities of Greece were involved. It was ended in 405 B.C., when Athens, defeated at sea, accepted the terms dictated by Sparta. Its story is told by Thucydides, an Athenian general, who was banished from Athens in 424 B.C. and devoted his exile to writing the history of this war. In brief and pregnant words he stated the point of view which has since governed all genuine historical writing.

> The absence of romance in my history will, I fear, detract somewhat from its interest; but if it be judged useful by those inquirers who desire an exact knowledge of the past as an aid to the interpretation of the future, which in the course of human things must resemble if it does not reflect it, I shall be content. In fine, I have written my work, not as an essay which is to win the applause of the moment, but as a possession for all time.[1]

Like Herodotus before him, Thucydides saw the characters of the combatants as profoundly influenced by their institutions. The Spartan and Athenian characters are contrasted in a speech which he puts into the mouth of Corinthian envoys who were trying to persuade Sparta to declare war.

> The Athenians are addicted to innovation, and their designs are characterised by swiftness alike in conception and execution; you have a genius for keeping what you have got, accompanied by a total want of invention, and when forced to act you never go far enough. Again, they are ad-

venturous beyond their power, and daring beyond their judgment, and in danger they are sanguine; your wont is to attempt less than is justified by your power, to mistrust even what is sanctioned by your judgment, and to fancy that from danger there is no release. Further, there is promptitude on their side against procrastination on yours; they are never at home, you are never from it: for they hope by their absence to extend their acquisitions, you fear by your advance to endanger what you have left behind. They are swift to follow up a success, and slow to recoil from a reverse. Their bodies they spend ungrudgingly in their city's cause; their intellect they jealously husband to be employed in her service. A scheme unexecuted is with them a positive loss, a successful enterprise a comparative failure. The deficiency created by the miscarriage of an undertaking is soon filled up by fresh hopes; for they alone are enabled to call a thing hoped for a thing got, by the speed with which they act upon their resolutions. Thus they toil on in trouble and danger all the days of their life, with little opportunity for enjoying, being ever engaged in getting: their only idea of a holiday is to do what the occasion demands, and to them laborious occupation is less of a misfortune than the peace of a quiet life. To describe their character in a word, one might truly say that they were born into the world to take no rest themselves and to give none to others.[2]

This theme is more fully developed in the speech which Pericles, the greatest of Athenian statesmen, delivered at the burial of the first Athenians who lost their lives in the Peloponnesian War.

Our government is not copied from those of our neighbours: we are an example to them rather than they to us. Our constitution is named a democracy, because it is in the hands not of the few but of the many. But our laws secure equal justice for all in their private disputes, and our public opinion welcomes and honours talent in every branch of achievement, not for any sectional reason but on grounds of excellence alone. And as we give free play to all in our public life, so we carry the same spirit into our daily relations with one another. We have no black looks or angry words for our neighbour if he enjoys himself in his own way, and we abstain from the little acts of churlishness which, though they leave no mark, yet cause annoyance to whoso notes them. Open and friendly in our private intercourse, in our public acts we keep strictly within the control of law. We acknowledge the restraint of reverence; we are obedient to whomsoever is set in authority, and to the laws, more especially to those which offer protection to the oppressed and those unwritten ordinances whose transgression brings admitted shame. . . .

We are lovers of beauty without extravagance, and lovers of wisdom without unmanliness. Wealth to us is not mere material for vainglory but an opportunity for achievement; and poverty we think it no disgrace to acknowledge but a real degradation to make no effort to overcome. Our citizens attend both to public and private duties, and do not allow absorption in their own various affairs to interfere with their knowledge of the city's. We differ from other states in regarding the man who holds aloof from public life not as 'quiet' but as useless; we decide or debate, carefully and in person, all matters of policy, holding, not that words and deeds go ill together, but that acts are foredoomed to failure when undertaken undiscussed. For we are noted for being at once most adventurous in action and most reflective beforehand. Other men are bold in ignorance, while reflection will stop their onset. But the bravest are surely those who have the clearest vision of what is before them, glory and danger alike, and yet notwithstanding go out to meet it. . . .

In a word I claim that our city as a whole is an education to Greece, and that her members yield to none, man by man, for independence of spirit, many-sidedness of attainment, and complete self-reliance in limbs and brain. . . .

Such then is the city for whom, lest they should lose her, the men whom we celebrate died a soldier's death: and it is but natural that all of us, who survive them, should wish to spend ourselves in her service. That, indeed, is why I have spent many words upon the city. I wished to show that we have more at stake than men who have no such inheritance, and to support my praise of the dead by making clear to you what they have done. For if I have chanted the glories of the city it was these men and their like who set hand to array her. . .

We survivors may pray to be spared their bitter hour, but must disdain to meet the foe with a spirit less triumphant. Let us draw strength, not merely from twice-told arguments—how fair and noble a thing it is to show courage in battle—but from the busy spectacle of our great city's life as we have it before us day by day, falling in love with her as we see her, and remembering that all this greatness she owes to men with the fighter's daring, the wise man's understanding of his duty, and the good man's self-discipline in its performance—to men who, if they failed in any ordeal, disdained to deprive the city of their services, but sacrificed their lives as the best offerings on her behalf. So they gave their bodies to the commonwealth and received, each for his own memory, praise that will never die, and with it the grandest of all sepulchres, not that in which their mortal bones are laid, but a home in the minds of men, where their glory remains fresh to stir to speech or action as the occasion comes by. For the whole earth is the sepulchre of famous men; and their story is not graven only on stone over their native earth, but lives on far away, without visible symbol, woven into the stuff of other men's lives.[3]

We have here a picture of life actually lived on a plane which no community had before reached: and no one has questioned the substantial truth of the portrait. The object for which the Athenian had learned to feel this intense devotion was not some vague abstraction, nor yet the place in which he lived, but the fellow-citizens who dwelt in that place with himself. "The people not the buildings are the city." "Neither tower nor ship are anything apart from the people who live in them."[4]

Amongst those who listened to the statesman and poet was a man greater than either, who was able to see what this kind of devotion implied. Portraits of Socrates have been drawn by two of his disciples, Xenophon the soldier, and Plato the incomparable literary artist. Early in life he embraced poverty in order to devote himself wholly to the task of helping his fellow-citizens to live according to reason. This as he conceived was possible only in so far as they would use their minds to grasp the principles of right living. In Socrates the Greek instinct to leave nothing unquestioned is seen at its highest. Profoundly religious, he attacked the current theology which represented the gods as beings capable of immoral conduct. His conception of God as one spirit, all-knowing and wholly just, was contrary to the ideas of orthodox Greeks, who believed in a number of gods and goddesses. They readily interpreted his ideas as atheism. Perceiving that men must find in their own sense of duty the final criterion of private or public morality, he ruthlessly exposed the contradictions which underlie the accepted canons of conduct. To conventional minds he seemed to be attacking morality. Their self-content was irritated by his ceaseless questions: they voted the questioner a highbrow and a bore. The constructive principles of conduct and belief which came in view when the rubbish was cleared from their minds were revealed only to a band of disciples who hung on his words.

The expression of those principles in his own life and death was a factor which gave permanence to his teaching. As a soldier in many campaigns he showed in the highest degree the courage and endurance ascribed to Athenians by friends and foes. On two occasions he refused to become the agent of illegal proceedings at the risk of his life. The first was in 406 B.C., when in an official position he refused, in response to popular clamour, to submit, contrary to law, a motion for the execution of certain generals. Some two years later, when the Tyrants established by the Spartans in Athens proscribed their opponents and ordered Socrates to arrest one of their victims, he defied their orders.

In 399 B.C. he was brought to trial and condemned to death on the charge of not believing in the gods of the city and of corrupting the youth. By promising his judges to keep silence in future he might have avoided this sentence. He refused to give this undertaking on the ground that "an unexamined life is not worth living". The commonwealth and law have their root in truth, and when law is used to stifle the search for truth it may be the duty of a citizen to break the law. Dying as a rebel, Socrates proved his supreme loyalty to Athens. And yet at the moment of his death he placed the duty of obedience to law higher than it has ever been put before or since. His friends had arranged his escape from prison. The reasons he gave them for refusing to accept their good offices are recorded by Plato:

SOCRATES. Consider it this way. Suppose the laws and the commonwealth were to come and appear to me as I was preparing to run away (if that is the right phrase to describe my escape) and were to ask, "Tell us, Socrates, what have you in your mind to do? What do you mean by trying to escape, but to destroy us the laws, and the whole city, as far as in you lies? Do you think that a state can exist and not be overthrown, in which the decisions of law are of no force, and are disregarded and set at nought by private individuals?" How shall we answer questions like that, Crito? Much might be said, especially by an orator, in defence of the law which made judicial decisions supreme. Shall I reply, "But the state has injured me: it has decided my cause wrongly?" Shall we say that?

CRITO. Certainly we will, Socrates.

SOCRATES. And suppose the laws were to reply, "Was that our agreement? Or was it that you would submit to whatever judgements the state should pronounce?" And if we were to wonder at their words, perhaps they would say, "Socrates, wonder not at our words, but answer us; you yourself are accustomed to ask questions and to answer them. What complaint have you against us and the city, that you are trying to destroy us? Are we not, first, your parents? Through us your father took your mother and begat you. Tell us, have you any fault to find with those of us that are the laws of marriage?" "I have none", I should reply. "Or have you any fault to find with those of us that regulate the nurture and education of the child, which you, like others, received? Did we not do well in bidding your father educate you in music and gymnastic?" "You did", I should say. "Well, then, since you were brought into the world and nurtured and educated by us, how, in the first place, can you deny that you are our child and our slave, as your fathers were before you? And if this be so, do you think that your rights are on a level with ours? Do you think that you have a right to retaliate upon us if we should try to do anything to you? You had not the same rights that your father had, or that your master would have had, if you had been a slave. You have no right to retaliate upon them if they ill-treat you, or to answer them if they reviled you, or to strike them back if they struck you, or to repay them evil with evil in any way. And do you think that you may retaliate on your country and on its laws? If we try to destroy you, because we think it right, will you in return do all that you can to destroy us, the laws, and your country, and say that in so doing you are doing right, you, the man, who in truth thinks so much of virtue? Or are you too wise to see that your country is worthier, and more august, and more sacred, and holier, and held in higher honour both by the gods and by all men of understanding, than your father and your mother and all your other ancestors; and it is your bounden duty to reverence it, and to submit to it, and to approach it more humbly than you would approach your father, when it is angry with you; and either to do whatever it bids you to do or to persuade it to excuse you; and to obey it in silence if it orders you to endure stripes or imprisonment, or if it send you to battle to be wounded or to die? That is what is your duty. You must not give way, nor retreat, nor desert your post. In war, and in the court of justice, and everywhere, you must do whatever your city and your country bid you do, or you must convince them that their demands are unjust. But it is against the law of God to do violence to your father or to your mother; and much more so is it against the law of God to use violence to your country."[5]

In the speech of Pericles and the argument of Socrates begin to appear the qualities which distinguished the Greek commonwealth from anything which had gone before it. We see here a society based on the assumption that all its members are called upon to contribute to its well-being the whole of their faculties, and if necessary life itself. That society is so constituted as to call for the exercise of those faculties to the utmost, and so develop them in the process. It seeks to increase the devotion of each to all by making the utmost demands upon it. The task of making decisions is thrown as completely as possible on the citizens themselves. And those decisions reduced to law are the final authority in the state, an authority as binding on the citizens as the edicts of a Persian king on his subjects. But the laws are not unchangeable like those of the Medes and Persians. They are subject to revision in the light of experience; but the duty of reading the experience and making the change rests on the citizens themselves. Their faculty for doing these things is developed by exercise. The commonwealth is thus a system of society which is capable of continuous growth, because it develops the mind and character of the members of whom it is composed. It calls into constant and active expression the capacity in men for putting the interests of others before their own. And in doing so it stimulates their mental capacity for conceiving and initiating the means whereby each service can best be rendered.

The Greek word for a city is πόλις. To the Greeks that word also connoted a state. The political history of mankind may be said to open with the development of the commonwealth in its miniature form by the Greeks. Based on the duty of each to all, it was something which differed in kind from monarchies in which any number of subjects are united in a common duty of implicit obedience to one ruler claiming divine authority and also knowledge divinely inspired and beyond the reach of ordinary men. Monarchy and commonwealth are alike based on a moral principle, on belief in the spiritual basis of things. They differ in this that the commonwealth puts its trust in reason and therefore must in the end prevail. What the Greeks described as 'tyranny' is a form of government based on no moral principle at all, a government which treats the conception of right as a figment, and sees in force the only reality. Tyranny is the necessary outcome of materialism, of the view that ultimate reality is of the nature of our bodies and not of our minds and souls.

The question which distracted the Greek commonwealths, as to how far government was to rest in the hands of the few or the many, was one which commonwealths have always to face. The commonwealth is a polity which recognises that power should be shared not by all its members, but at any rate by those who are fit for the task. No commonwealth has ever existed in which the suffrage was universal. The vote has never been given to children, and seldom if ever to recognised criminals. The commonwealth in which political power is too widely extended ceases to have a government, ceases to be a state, and therefore ceases to be a commonwealth at all. The end and object of a commonwealth is to increase by exercise the sense of duty which each of its members feels to the body as a whole, and also to increase his capacity for discharging that duty. But a commonwealth in which too many of the voters are deficient in their sense of this duty, or, like children, in the knowledge how to discharge it, falls into utter disorder. The more the voters, the greater the difficulty of practical government. Where those who exercise power are few it is for the moment easier to govern and maintain order. So those who recognise the vital importance of order are disposed to limit power to the few. But in doing so they are apt to forget that they leave unexercised and undeveloped the sense of devotion in the many to the state as a whole. The wise democrat is one ready to risk immediate order to a certain degree in order to cultivate in a larger number of citizens that loyalty and knowledge of public affairs upon which in the long run the structure of the state can alone rest in security.

We have dwelt here on the difference of principle which distinguished a commonwealth from a monarchy, and both from a tyranny; and also on the question which confronts each commonwealth as to how far it is safe to restrict or extend political power amongst the citizens, because those issues, which emerged in ancient Hellas, are exactly the same as those which mankind is now facing on the wider stage of the whole habitable earth.

The speech of Pericles is the earliest recorded expression of the principle of the commonwealth, clearer and simpler than anything we can quote from the literature of classical Greece. It is generally accepted that the thoughts recorded by Thucydides, in this particular speech, are those of Pericles himself, not those of the writer put into the mouth of the orator. It is likely that Thucydides listened to the speech, and even made notes of what Pericles said. Apart from this speech our ideas of the Greek commonwealth are largely derived from Plato and Aristotle, and from the history of Thucydides himself. Great as these masters of thought were, their minds were inevitably clouded by the ultimate victory of Sparta and the loss of her empire by Athens. We are some of us old enough to remember the respect which everything German commanded from 1872 to 1918. The speech of Pericles was delivered in an atmosphere as yet unclouded by disasters which might never have happened if he himself had survived to direct the counsels of Athens.

The theme of Thucydides is the failure of Athenian democracy to grasp the principles implicit in their own constitution, as expounded in the speech of Pericles, and apply them in the wider field of external relations. In dealing with the other cities of Greece and their own allies they relied on a doctrine, the negation of the principle of the commonwealth, the doctrine that society is founded on force, that might is right, that the weaker lies at the mercy of the stronger, that law is valid only where parties to a controversy are equals in strength.

NOTES

[1] Thucydides, i. 22 (Crawley's translation).
[2] *Ibid.* i. 70.
[3] Thucydides, ii. 37-43 (Zimmern's translation in his *Greek Commonwealth*, pp. 200-205).
[4] Sophocles, *Oedipus Tyrannus*, line 55.
[5] Plato, *The Crito* (Church's translation).

CHAPTER XI

FALL OF THE ATHENIAN EMPIRE

IN the earlier stages of the Peloponnesian War the advantage gained by Athens was such that, in 423 B.C., the Spartans asked for and obtained a truce, which was followed by a treaty of peace and indeed of alliance in the following year. This peace was never a reality. The fact that Sparta had sued for it led the Athenians to suppose that her power might now be safely ignored, and they dreamed of including the whole of Greece in their empire. One Dorian colony on the Island of Melos had throughout maintained a position of neutrality. In 416 B.C. the Athenians required them to join their confederacy and pay the tribute. The story is dramatised by Thucydides in the form of a dialogue between Athenian envoys and the Melian government.[1] One sentence from the argument of the Athenian envoys will suffice to reveal the moral and political philosophy which was now inspiring the policy of their state:

> You know as well as we do that right, as the world goes, is only in question between equals in power, while the strong do what they can and the weak suffer what they must.

The Melians refused to accept this argument, and hoping for aid from Peloponnese, tried to defend their city. Their hopes were in vain:

> some treachery taking place inside, the Melians surrendered at discretion to the Athenians, who put to death all the grown men whom they took, and sold the women and children for slaves, and subsequently sent out five hundred colonists and inhabited the place themselves.

Since the truce of 423 B.C. the Athenians had dreamed of mastering the Greek colonies of Sicily and Italy, and of then using the resources of the west for the conquest of the Peloponnese. In 415 B.C. the strongest expedition ever despatched by a Greek state was sent to attack Syracuse, a Corinthian colony and the largest city in Sicily. Another, but little inferior in strength, was despatched in the following year. In 413 B.C. these fleets and armies were captured and destroyed by the Syracusans led by a Spartan general Gylippus.

This enormous disaster encouraged the allies to revolt from Athens. She herself was distracted by revolution and at times fell under the control of an oligarchy. The marvel is that a city so stricken could continue the struggle for eight years after the loss of her armaments in Sicily. Eventually the Spartans made an alliance with Persia, and with foreign gold constructed fleets strong enough to challenge the power of Athens on the sea. In 405 B.C. the Spartans destroyed the last Athenian fleet in the Hellespont. Athens was then at her mercy. Her walls were dismantled, and her empire dissolved.

To the conquerors in this war we owe the idea crystallised in the adjective 'Spartan' and little besides in the field of ideas. To Athens our debt is beyond calculation, and indestructible. We owe her those things which perish only to yield an increasing harvest of life. That Athens could give to the world poets like Aeschylus, Sophocles or Euripides, an artist like Pheidias, a statesman like Pericles, a teacher like Socrates or a thinker like Plato, while victorious Sparta continued sterile, was no mere accident. This amazing originative power was, as her own historians felt, something released by a system which laid the tasks of government on the largest possible number of citizens, on the largest number then possible, and in doing so raised, not only their faculties, but also their sense of mutual devotion to a higher power than ever before. Amongst these faculties was the gift of expression in permanent literary form. Time and again nations will fail in the task of establishing order for themselves, yielding to monarchies which claim divine inspiration, or tyrannies which deny the validity of anything but organised force. But so long as the literature which sprang from Athens remains, so long will the sense of freedom survive, to develop once more a system of society based on the infinite duty of each to all.

How comes it, then, that in this protracted struggle the Athenians appear as exponents of the opposite doctrine that right is a figment "only in question between equals in power, while the strong do what they can and the weak suffer what they must"? In answering that question it will help us to remember that Hebrew literature leaves the impression of a people time and again reverting to the worship of idols and human sacrifice. Yet will anyone seriously question that the vision of one God as the spiritual essence of all goodness and love was the special gift of the Hebrew race to the world? So a visitor to Russia or China, to India, Ireland or even the self-governing Dominions might receive the impression that they find in England a standing opponent to the right each nation claims to manage its own affairs. Yet in history England will figure as the foremost champion of that right.

The essential achievement of Greece was the realisation of a state, however small, in which the unlimited duty of each to all was reduced to a practical system of government and so developed by continuous exercise. By accepting the vote of majorities as binding, the village meeting had acquired the faculty of reaching decisions, had become the genuine government of the village. So, even when the village had grown to a city, the citizens could gather to discuss its affairs, to vote taxes and express their will in the form of laws. Such a system, so Aristotle said, was possible only where all the citizens could listen to the voice of a single orator. In Athens, the greatest city of Greece, it had reached its limits. So far as the Greeks and the wisest amongst them were able to see, the principle of the commonwealth was capable of realisation only in cities. It was not capable of realisation on the national scale, even for Hellas with its common language and civilisation. Yet the time had arrived when the mountains and seas no longer afforded sufficient protection for Greece as a whole. Her own inventiveness in the arts of shipbuilding, which nations to the south and east had copied, had exposed her cities to maritime invasions. Intrinsic efficiency in her cities and their citizens, developed by the habit of governing themselves, had just enabled them to repel the onset of Asia. But to hold Asia at bay some authority which could organise the forces of Greece as a whole was clearly necessary. The confederacy of Delos was an effort in that direction. It was doubtless intended that the synod at Delos should direct its policy. We only know that the synod failed; but it is not difficult to conjecture the reason. It is fairly safe to assume that delegates refused to agree to necessary measures proposed without further instructions from the several cities. It thus was found impossible to obtain decisions when decisions were urgently necessary for the public safety. The leaders of Athens, as the dominant partner in the league, then took the decisions and, fearing the menace of Persia, the allied cities accepted the results. The proceedings of the synod lost their reality and presently its members ceased to attend. The allies, by leaving the initiative and control in the military and maritime field to Athens, were in time obliged to accept her decisions. Allies in name, they became her subjects in fact, and as the menace of Persia receded, developed the outlook of subjects and hated their Athenian masters in spite of their kinship. No device had been found for realising the principle of the commonwealth in the wider field of the national life. In maintaining some kind of government for Greece, the Athenians, without realising it, were led to act on its very negation, to adopt that negation as the basis of their rule, and in doing so compassed their own destruction.

NOTE

[1] Thucydides, v. 85-116.

CHAPTER XII

ALEXANDER THE GREAT

NOTHING in her history became Sparta so much as her clemency to Athens in the hour of victory. She refused to condone the proposal of her allies that the people of Athens should be treated as they themselves had treated the people of Melos. Her walls were demolished, but the people were suffered to remain in their city, and even when shorn of all military power retained their predominance in the field of ideas. Some fifteen years later the walls were rebuilt, and by 377 B.C. Athens had emerged once more at the head of a maritime league.

The military power of Sparta was now being challenged by Epaminondas, a soldier of genius, who was arming and organising the citizen forces of Thebes on a new model. His methods were studied by Philip, a Macedonian prince, who in 367 B.C. was sent as a hostage to Thebes. In the course of his sojourn in Greece Philip fell under the spell of Hellenic culture, the recognised focus of which was Athens. When called to the throne of Macedon in 359 B.C. he used and developed the methods he had learned from Epaminondas to organise a regular army strong enough to cope with the citizen forces of Greece. No effort was spared to assimilate his barbarous subjects to the culture of Hellas, except of course in the field of government. With this object in view he brought Aristotle from the schools of Athens to act as tutor to Alexander, his son by an Albanian mother. At the age of eighteen this youth was leading the left wing of his army when in 338 B.C. Philip broke the combined forces of Thebes and

Athens at Chaeronea. To Thebes he showed no mercy. Athens he treated with clemency as the centre of Greek civilisation. He then convened a conference at Corinth, which Sparta alone refused to attend, and there combined the rest of Greece in a league to settle the long-standing accounts of Hellas with Persia, with himself as its military leader.

In 336 B.C. Philip was murdered by one of his own guard and the throne of Macedon with the military leadership of Greece passed to his son Alexander at the age of twenty. In 334 B.C. Alexander crossed the Hellespont and freed the cities of Ionia, substituting popular governments in the place of the tyrants and oligarchies established by Persia. He next proceeded to conquer the whole coast of the Levant. In 333 B.C. he destroyed in Tyre the heart of the Persian sea power. He then occupied Palestine and, by settling Greek communities in the heart of Judaism, this daemonic youth set in train events destined to shake the world and change the course of human history, as the writer of Daniel dimly divined.[1]

Through Palestine Alexander hastened to the conquest of Egypt. On the coast west of the Delta he founded a city which he called after himself. It was peopled partly with Greek settlers, partly with 100,000 Jews brought from Palestine. By 331 B.C. the conquest of Egypt was completed. The Persian monarchy was thus deprived of the last strip of coast from which ships could be launched in Mediterranean waters. Alexander was now free to strike at its heart, and on September 20, 331 B.C., he attacked and destroyed the armies of Darius near Nineveh. Ascending the throne of the fallen monarch, he reduced to obedience the distant satrapies which Darius had ruled in name rather than in fact. In achieving this object he marched to the furthest boundaries of the Persian Empire as far north as the Caspian, eastwards beyond the Jaxartes and past Kabul into the Punjab to the valley of the Indus. A mutiny of his troops in 326 B.C. alone prevented him from pushing his conquests further. On the Indus he built a fleet which carried part of his forces back to the Persian Gulf, he himself leading the rest by a route near the coast to Susa, which he reached in 324 B.C. His superhuman vitality, which a number of wounds must have impaired, was now reaching its limits. In 323 B.C. he died at Babylon.

His father and he had imposed on Hellas a unity never achieved since the struggle with Xerxes, and under his leadership the Greeks had conquered the Persian Empire to its utmost limits. His amazing capacity as a soldier was merely one side of a greatness revealed in the field of creative ideas.[2] In the view of his master Aristotle the world was made up of Greeks and barbarians, "the lesser breeds without the law". The essential feature of Greek civilisation was the state, through the medium of which the fullest development of human faculties was alone attainable. But in Aristotle's mind such a state must be limited to the people of one city. To the Greek, no less than the Jew, the way of life for which he stood was limited to people of his own race. There is little in history more astonishing than the fact that the youthful pupil of Aristotle was able to transcend limitations from which an intellect so powerful as that of his master was unable to escape. In his schemes for ordering the world he had mastered Alexander deliberately set himself to destroy the idea that Greeks and barbarians were divided by a gulf which could never be bridged. Centuries later St. Paul was to picture a social order in which "there cannot be Greek or Jew, circumcision and uncircumcision, barbarian, Scythian, bondman, freeman".[3] This river of thought, if traced to its springs, will bring us, in the Hebrew world, to the prophet

Jeremiah, in the Greek to the youthful conqueror of Persia.

The world over which Alexander had ruled was divided after his death by his Macedonian companions and their successors. Macedon and the leadership of Greece fell to the house of Antigonus, Egypt to the Ptolemies, and the rest of the Persian Empire to the house of Seleucus.

By the conquests of Alexander Greek civilisation was so thoroughly established on the east coast of the Mediterranean that it lasted for more than a thousand years. Its influence extended even to India, and to-day sculptures can be noticed in the gardens of Peshawar which would not look out of place in the Greek galleries of the British Museum. But the empires of Seleucus and Ptolemy rapidly moved from the political traditions of Greece to those of Asia. In the Greek settlements the citizens continued to control their municipal affairs, but, in matters wider than those, learned to obey dynasties of their own race, who none the less claimed to derive their authority from Heaven, as frankly as their Persian predecessors had done. Though Greek manners and thought survived in these regions for some generations, they had no permanent effect on the structure of eastern society. The political traditions of Asia were impressed on the Greek monarchies, infected the Roman Empire which absorbed them, and through that empire have profoundly influenced the political development of Europe.

By his conquest of Palestine and Egypt Alexander had brought the Greek and Jewish communities into sudden and intimate contact. In Palestine he and his successors planted a number of Greek colonies. In Egypt, as we have seen, he created at the mouth of the Nile an entirely new city which was colonised partly by Greeks and partly by Jews. Throughout the Mediterranean Jewish and

Greek civilisation flourished for centuries side by side in separate and coequal communities. Except in Judea and Mesopotamia, the Jews acquired the Greek language and forgot their own. So a Greek translation of the Hebrew Scriptures had to be prepared to meet their needs. The Jewish mind which regarded these Scriptures as the word of God in the literal and absolute sense had a craving to feel that the Greek word was no less inspired than the Hebrew original. A legend was presently developed to satisfy this craving. Centuries later it was placed on record by St. Augustine and is worth quoting at length because it shows how this Jewish idea as to the means by which the eternal verities can be known to men fastened itself on the Graeco-Roman Empire, and through that empire on the Christian world.

§ 42. By what dispensation of God's providence the sacred Scriptures of the Old Testament were translated out of Hebrew into Greek, that they might be made known to all the nations.

One of the Ptolemies, kings of Egypt, desired to know and have these sacred books. For, after Alexander of Macedon, who is also styled the Great, had by his most wonderful, but by no means enduring power, subdued the whole of Asia, yea, almost the whole world, partly by force of arms, partly by terror, and, among other kingdoms of the East, had entered and obtained Judea also, on his death his generals did not peaceably divide that most ample kingdom among them for a possession, but rather dissipated it, wasting all things by wars. Then Egypt began to have the Ptolemies as her kings. The first of them, the son of Lagus, carried many captive out of Judea into Egypt. But another Ptolemy, called Philadelphus, who succeeded him, permitted all whom he had brought under the yoke to return free; and, more than that, sent kingly gifts to the temple of God, and begged Eleazar, who was the high priest, to give him the Scriptures, which he had heard by report were truly divine, and therefore greatly desired to have in that most noble library he had made. When the high priest had sent them to him in Hebrew, he afterwards demanded interpreters of him, and there were given him seventy-two, out of each of the twelve tribes six men, most learned in both languages, to wit, the Hebrew and Greek; and their translation is now by custom called the Septuagint. It is reported, indeed, that there was an agreement in their words so wonderful, stupendous, and plainly divine, that when they had sat at this work, each one apart (for so it pleased Ptolemy to test their fidelity), they differed from each other in no word which had the same meaning and force, or in the order of the words; but, as if the translators had been one, so what all had translated was one, because in very deed the one Spirit had been in them all. And they received so wonderful a gift of God, in order that the authority of these Scriptures might be commended not as human but divine, as indeed it was, for the benefit of the nations who should at some time believe, as we now see them doing.[4]

It was through this translation that the Hebrew Scriptures came to exercise their influence on the Greek and Roman Empires.

NOTES

[1] Daniel xi. 2-4.
[2] Tarn, *Cambridge Ancient History*, vol. vi. p. 437.
[3] Colossians iii. 11.
[4] *De Civitate Dei*, Book XVIII.

CHAPTER XIII

ROME

THE intrusion of northern tribes on Mediterranean society and its effect in producing a new system of life had not been limited to the shores of the Aegean. Somewhere north of the Alpine and Balkan ranges the migratory hordes had thrown off a second stream which eventually had made its way to the centre of Italy. There, as in Greece, they imposed their language on the composite race into which they merged. When, three centuries before the Christian era, their descendants came into contact once more, a thousand years of separation would amply serve to account for the difference of Greek and Latin.

The Latin peoples more nearly resembled the Dorian than the Ionian branch of the Greeks. It may well be that in Italy, as in the Peloponnese, the proportion of northern invaders was larger than that which came to stay in the village communities on the shores of the Aegean. They were less versatile than Ionian Greeks, slower to imagine and invent, but more stable in character and patient of detail. With a higher sense of discipline they knew better how to administer a system than how to change or interpret it. When Rome had become the centre of government for the whole Mediterranean, vast hordes of slaves were recruited from all its shores, especially from those of Asia Minor and Syria. The dark hair and complexion of the Latin races must be due in part to a large and continuous movement from the Levant. It need not surprise us, therefore, that the Romans on their first appearance should seem to resemble in character the nations of northern Europe rather than those of the south.

The political development of the village communities was closely parallel to that of the Greeks. The resemblance alone is enough to prove the nearness of their kinship. About the same period they abolished the paternal government of chiefs or kings. When they first emerged in the light of history a hatred of dynastic rule was the strongest element in Roman tradition. The fact that their officers were elected and their laws approved in public assemblies showed that they, like the Greeks, had grasped and applied the principle of decision by majorities. The citizens assembled in the forum were the ultimate source of all authority, though they never applied it to the details of government to anything like the same extent as the people of Athens. On the other hand, they evolved two leading ideas to which they adhered with singular tenacity. The object of Roman devotion, as with the Greeks, was the whole body of fellow-citizens and their successors. The general welfare implied by the word *respublica* supplied the motive of their public conduct. Side by side with this idea was the conception contained in the words *majestas populi Romani*, the sovereign authority of the Roman people, to which the citizen felt his obedience was due. The Greek had no word for obedience other than one which meant that his reason had been convinced. To the Roman mind the duty of obeying the law was prior to his right to share in framing it. The Greek was prone to forget that government is a condition precedent to self-government. For centuries the government of Rome was directed by a senate of hereditary elders by whom the traditions of public policy were handed on from one generation to another. The general assembly of citizens was content to elect officers and ratify laws submitted by the senate.

As in Greek cities, a number of slaves acquired

their freedom, and immigrants were attracted in growing numbers. In course of time this newer population aspired to share in the government of the state. The older families who tried to resist this claim became a nobility. The republican history of Rome is a long series of struggles by more recent and numerous immigrants for inclusion in the privileged circle of citizens. The principle that all power resided in the people of Rome was never in doubt, though the question as to who were to count as the Roman people was always at issue. But the party worsted in these struggles more rarely than in Greece made cause with the enemies of their city. In the story of Coriolanus we see what Rome thought of political emigrants.

The thoroughness of the Romans in all practical matters was reflected in their military organisation. When Alexander died in 323 B.C. the Roman republic was the dominant power in central Italy, and in course of time mastered the whole peninsula. The sovereignty was still vested in the citizens who could gather in the Roman forum; but Rome could marshal the whole manhood of Italy. Her resources in war were thus greater than any other power in the Mediterranean. Her commerce competed with that of the Greeks and Phoenicians. In the western Mediterranean Greek traders had founded cities like that at Massilia; but Carthage was the dominant power. Since Tyre had been absorbed in the Persian Empire her colony in the west had become the leading centre of Phoenician enterprise. Through colonies of her own on the coasts of Spain and Africa she guarded the Straits of Gibraltar and preserved her monopoly of the Atlantic trade.

In Hebrew, Greek and Roman literature the Phoenicians appear as a people with minds set on the possession of wealth, and their gift for creating it by production and trade was highly developed.

In their civilisation ideas played a lesser part than with any of their neighbours in the Mediterranean world. Their manner of life, and therefore their civil and military policy, reveal a tendency to measure all things by material values.

Granting that it is right to have regard not only to merit but also to affluence as a means of securing leisure, we may still censure the arrangement by which at Carthage the highest offices of State, viz. the Kingship and Generalship, are put up to sale. The effect of such a law is that wealth is more highly esteemed than virtue, and the whole State is avaricious. Whenever the ruling class regards a thing as honourable, the opinion of the citizens generally is sure to follow suit.[1]

As appears in this passage, the Carthaginians of historical times had abolished hereditary kingship. When Aristotle wrote, their institutions were influenced by the Greek and Latin republics with which they traded rather than inspired by their spirit. Wealth was regarded as a better title to authority than devotion to the public interest. The genius of Hannibal failed to command the support which Rome readily accorded to leaders of greatly inferior talent. By the merchant princes of Carthage war was conceived as a branch of commerce. Their armies were mainly composed of contingents hired from subjects and allies. The idea that the gods themselves give nothing except in return for value received helps to explain their retention of human sacrifice when other civilised races had abandoned the practice. As men rise to genuine religion they realise that the relation of God to man contains no element of barter. The Phoenicians were still in the clutch of a gross and primitive superstition when they lost their name and vanished from history.

Phoenician enterprise, none the less, was the main factor by which the civilisation of the eastern Mediterranean had in the age of Alexander spread to the whole of its shores, and beyond to those of the Atlantic. The Greek, Roman and Phoenician world had grown to be one economic unit. The premature death of Alexander and the absorption of his successors in the task of maintaining their various dynasties left Rome and Carthage to decide this phase of the long struggle between eastern and western ideas. As in the previous struggle of Greece with Persia, the issue was really decided by the relative merits of the two social systems. In the Roman polity the idea that a citizen owed more to the public interest than to himself was still uppermost, and stronger even than the passion for individual wealth. When all was lost the Carthaginians rose to heights of heroism, and, true to the tradition of the Semite race, they fought like lions when driven to their lair. With the total destruction of Carthage in 146 B.C. Rome was left with no serious rival in the Mediterranean.

Some fifty years before this time Rome had come into collision with Philip, a successor of Alexander in his Macedonian kingdom. At Cynoscephale in Thessaly the Romans defeated Philip in 197 B.C., and next year at the Isthmian games proclaimed the freedom of Greece from the Macedonian dominion. Now, as ever, the Greek cities proved incapable of maintaining stable relations between themselves, and Rome ere long was compelled to assume the office of constable from which she had ejected the Macedonian monarch. Her relations to the Greeks were marred by acts of cruelty, of which the destruction of Corinth, due to the jealousy of Roman merchants, was the most conspicuous. But, generally speaking, the relations of Greeks and Romans were in marked contrast to the relations of either people to the Semitic races with whom they came in contact. To the Semites both reacted as aliens, to each other as closely kindred peoples. The instinct of the Romans was not only to preserve the life, institutions and civilisation of the Greeks, so far as was compatible with the maintenance of order, but even to make them their own. The cities were left to govern themselves, though not of course to make war on each other. The institutions of self-government were thus reduced from the political to the municipal scale. The historians and poets of Rome, who wrote in Latin, followed the Greek models and metres; but Greek was recognised as the language of culture. The plastic arts of Greece were simply adopted by Rome as they stood. The city of Athens was treated with special tenderness and respect, and became the university where young Romans completed their training.

In less than a hundred years from the fall of Carthage the Roman republic had mastered the entire basin of the Mediterranean, the west of Europe from the Rhine to the Atlantic, and the whole Greek world including most of the conquests of Alexander, that is to say, Egypt, Syria and Asia as far as the Euphrates. The civilisation imposed on this vast area was neither Greek nor Latin but a fusion of both, Greek elements prevailing in the east and Latin in the west.

After the Persian wars the Athenian commonwealth had organised the cities of the Aegean in one political system by the simple expedient of rendering them all subject to her sovereignty. In two generations the system collapsed, to the ruin of Athens. In like manner the Roman commonwealth imposed its will on the vast congeries of heterogeneous peoples surrounding the Mediterranean. The system she created lasted for centuries, long enough to enable the principles of Graeco-Roman civilisation to take permanent root in the life of mankind. How she achieved so much and at what cost to her own institutions remained to be seen. The sovereignty of Rome was exercised by the citizens assembled in the forum, though the general transaction of business was left to the senate. The overmastering idea of *respublica*, the general interest, as something to which private ambitions and interests must in the last resort yield, enabled the illogical system to work for centuries. The hereditary capacity of the senators, and the continuous tradition of policy they maintained, enabled Rome first to conquer and then to master the whole shore of the Mediterranean. To the senate, however, the idea of the general interest was still that of the city of Rome, or rather of their own order. The popular assembly which met in the forum was largely composed of elements more recent than the senatorial families. The assembly, however, was really narrower in outlook than the senate, and interpreted the general interest as equivalent to its own. In early days the popular assembly which elected the officers and ratified laws was mainly composed of the same men who, enrolled in the legions, had marched from Rome for the conquest of Italy. But this was no longer possible when the armies were employed in long campaigns in Spain, Africa, Syria, Greece or Asia. And these armies were recruited to an ever-increasing degree from the fighting races outside Italy. They and the Roman generals who led them were little inclined to see their labours exploited either by the oligarchy which met in the senate house or the rabble which gathered in the forum at Rome.

When Rome had mastered the Mediterranean, the citizens who could gather in the forum represented the communities they controlled no more, and indeed less, than the citizens of Athens in the ecclesia represented the cities combined in the confederacy of Delos. They, like the people of Athens, failed to conceive the idea of representation. With their practical minds they disliked civil disorder more than the Greeks: so they solved the problem by entrusting the general interest to the one man able to maintain order, who could be no other than the leader whom the legions were willing to obey. When Rome had conquered the world the reality of power had passed from bodies which could gather in Rome to the conquering armies and the general they obeyed.

The long revolution which transformed Rome from a city republic to a world empire was consummated by Caesar. He was in fact a tyrant in the Greek sense of the word, in that he used force to destroy the existing forms of law. The selection of officers and the ratification of laws by popular vote ceased, except in form. Henceforward the official appointments were the choice and the laws enacted the edicts of a monarch. But these appointments and enactments were still influenced by the conception of the general interest extended from the city republic of Rome to include the whole of the people governed by the Empire. Emperors like Caligula were of course blind to the notion, but the marvellous succession of public-spirited rulers who administered the Empire in the course of three centuries, several of whom were not even Italian, attest the potency of the idea which the city republics had bequeathed to a society too large to be capable of direct government by its own citizens.

An essential feature in the principle of the commonwealth was the rule of law as the Greeks had divined. For this momentous discovery the Romans did what in our own time mechanicians, of whom Marconi is the greatest, have done in the realm of physics. In laboratories researchers like Clerk-Maxwell had recognised the existence, apart from the air, of something they called ether through the medium of which waves of electric energy can be passed. Marconi and others used this discovery to construct mechanism by which signals could be sent through the ether, and finally the words of a human voice. So the Romans adopted the supremacy of law, as conceived by Pericles, Socrates and Plato, from their reading of Greek experience, and constructed a practical system of law, applicable to the Empire as a whole, by which the daily life of a great part of the modern world is now ordered. The despotic power of the emperors enabled them to do this; but the element which distinguishes Roman jurisprudence from any previous system of law was derived from the city-state, which conceived law as the reasoned experience of the people who obeyed it, and not as the edicts of a monarch divinely inspired.

To men like Caesar, Augustus, Trajan, Hadrian and the Antonines the general interest of the whole civilised world was the end and object of public policy. As things were, the only possible way to preserve it was to entrust its maintenance to the master of the legions. But then, as always, the minds of men refused to accept a theory of government based on nothing but physical force. Quickly the idea developed that the emperor wielded his power by divine right, and was in fact himself divine. In a world which accepted polytheism the idea presented no difficulties, and throughout the Empire temples rose and altars smoked to the genius of Caesar. The magistrates and officers of the Empire relied on the theory in much the same way as officials and lawyers of the British Commonwealth rely on the theory of sovereignty of the Crown. As Kitchener imposed the oath of allegiance to Edward VII. on Cape rebels as a test of loyalty, so Pliny in Asia Minor imposed on Christians the duty of sacrifice as a test of loyalty to Trajan. But Pliny mistook the man Trajan for a god no more than Kitchener supposed that King Edward was the actual ruler of the British Dominions.

To the masses of Asia conquered by Alexander, organised by Seleucus as an empire and annexed by Rome, the idea of the emperor as divine was a living reality. In these regions the western culture imposed by the Greek conquerors was a veneer. Asiatic ideas of divine right were accepted as fundamental. They gradually mastered the Roman Empire itself until, in its later stages, there was little to distinguish it from the typical despotisms of Asia. The Christian Church absorbed the idea from the Empire, and Church and Empire together are largely responsible for its survival in Europe to the present age. Slowly but surely the idea of government by divine right destroyed the conception of the general interest which the best of the Roman emperors inherited from the city republics of Rome and Greece. The idea was the fruit of a system by which the people of a village community had learned to control their own public affairs, and in doing so had contracted a sense of devotion to the public welfare which was new to the world. The Roman Empire afforded a breathing-space in which a system of law and administration directed to the public interest could be developed. But the principle of authority which made this possible destroyed the springs from which the sense of devotion in individuals to the public interest had grown. Had migratory hordes from the north not appeared to destroy it, the Roman Empire would still have collapsed for lack of subjects with the public spirit to hold it together.

NOTE

[1] Aristotle, Book II. chap. xi. (trans. Welldon).

CHAPTER XIV

INTERACTIONS OF JEWISH, GREEK AND ROMAN HISTORY

"It was not the Romans that spred upon the World; But it was the World, that spred upon the Romans: And that was the sure way of Greatnesse."[1] The world of ideas which spread itself on Rome was a world created by Greek and Hebrew.

In the earlier records of Greece and Rome we meet the Phoenician traders everywhere scattered along the coasts of the Mediterranean. But after the fall of Carthage they seem to fade from the pages of history. Before the time of Caesar we meet the Jews in every part of the Graeco-Roman world, filling the place which the Phoenicians once occupied in the commercial life of the Mediterranean. Paul in his journeys finds a settlement of his countrymen in almost every city which he visits.

The explanation is fairly obvious. So long as Carthage remained the greatest centre of Semitic life, the mistress of Greek cities in Sicily and the formidable rival of Rome, the Phoenicians wherever they lived and traded boasted their race and their name. The splendour and wealth of Carthage covered the monstrous religion of which she was the centre with a cloak of respectability. But when Carthage was wiped from the map the cloak fell off and the Phoenicians in the Graeco-Roman world learned to be ashamed of human sacrifice practised in its most revolting form.

Carthage fell in 146 B.C. It so happened that their near kindred, the Jews, at that very moment had reached a stage in their history which recalled the days of the house of David.

In 175 B.C. Seleucus IV. was murdered by his minister Heliodorus, who hoped to govern in the name of his infant son. Antiochus, the brother of Seleucus, had for some years lived at Athens, and was indeed elected to the chief office in the city republic. He now managed to frustrate the designs of Heliodorus and seized the throne of his brother at Antioch.

With a natural bias in favour of Greek culture, he thought to unite the many and various races of the Seleucid Empire by a general adoption of Greek rites, manners and customs. Indeed he seems to have gone so far as to extend the self-governing powers of the leading cities on Greek lines. At this period Greek culture had acquired the same kind of prestige as European culture acquired in Bengal in the first half of the nineteenth century. His policy seems to have met with general acceptance outside Judea. But even in Jerusalem hellenisation, since the conquest of Alexander, had begun to exercise a marked influence, especially in priestly circles. Judea was by no means a rich country, but the Temple had become the repository of fabulous wealth annually furnished by the piety of the Jews, whose trading colonies now spread from Spain to Mesopotamia. Like the Vatican in the fifteenth century, the Levitical hierarchy of the Temple was tending to become rich, luxurious and sceptical and readily absorbed the fashionable side of Greek culture. There were noble exceptions, like the Maccabees and the sons of Zadok who seceded to Damascus in the time of Herod the Great and later on, in all probability, joined the Christians. But, generally speaking, the priests represented the pagan elements in Judaism and may be identified with the Sadducee party. In their view of a future existence they never advanced beyond the pagan idea of Sheol; religion was a question of securing the favour of Jehovah by appropriate ritual during men's lives.

The champions of the Jewish faith and law were drawn for the most part from the peasants and poorer classes. From these elements was formed about 200 B.C. a small sect called the Chasidim, who opposed the spread of Greek culture with the heroism and devotion of their race. The Epistle to the Hebrews refers to them as people who

> were beaten to death, not accepting their deliverance; that they might obtain a better resurrection: and others had trial of mockings and scourgings, yea, moreover of bonds and imprisonment: they were stoned, they were sawn asunder, they were tempted, they were slain with the sword: they went about in sheepskins, in goatskins; being destitute, afflicted, evil entreated (of whom the world was not worthy), wandering in deserts and mountains and caves, and the holes of the earth.[2]

The history of the Chasidim bears an interesting resemblance to that of our own nonconformists. The religious developments of the two centuries before Christ described in the next chapter were mainly, if not entirely, their work.

The sect of the Pharisees, which was presently to play so important a part, was an offshoot of the Chasidim. Its organisation was far less close than that of the Sadducees to which it was opposed. They stood for resistance to foreign influence. The name Pharisee implies separation, devotion to the idea of a people separated from all others as the people of Jehovah. In accordance with the teaching of the prophet Jeremiah, they included in this people all who accepted the Law of Moses, irrespective of natural descent.

This explains the missionary activities of Judaism in the period between the exile and the destruction of Jerusalem in A.D. 70. Behind this anxiety of the Pharisees to make proselytes was the motive which inspires the Christian missions of to-day. They were also responsible for organising synagogues, which discharged the functions of both churches and schools.

Though ardent exponents of the Law, they held, at least in their earlier stage, that God's will must be read from the course of history. When numbers of faithful Jews were massacred by Antiochus, they drew the conclusion that these martyrs of righteousness would be raised to life in the day of judgement to take their place in the Kingdom of God. It was thus that they came to teach a doctrine denied by the Sadducees.

In the view of the Pharisees God was their real King. No human ruler was entitled to obedience except as the mouthpiece of God. While the Sadducees held that the books of the Law as they stood were sufficient, the Pharisee scribes undertook to interpret the Law. In course of time their logical deductions from the text developed a mass of minute provisions, which some of them treated as of higher importance than the Law itself. The denunciations of Jesus were directed against this legalism, which had grown more oppressive than the Law as administered by the priests. But the Pharisee movement as a whole is no more to be judged by these later developments than the Protestant movement is to be judged by the fundamentalists and the rigid deductions they have drawn from Scripture.

With these explanations we may now return to the thread of our narrative.

Antiochus IV. naturally supported the priestly party which favoured hellenisation. He appointed one Jesus or Joshua as high priest, and authorised him to convert Jerusalem into a Greek city. He changed his name from Joshua to Jason, as a Jew nowadays will change the name of Levi into Lewis. A Greek gymnasium was established, for which the priests forsook the Temple. The young priests adopted the garb of the Greeks. The Chasidim were driven into fierce opposition. They resented the athletics and hats of the Greeks, just as the Moslems of Afghanistan resented the western clothes and habits of King Amanullah.

The cultural aims of Antiochus IV. were reinforced by the desire to possess himself of the vast treasures accumulated in the Temple. In 170 B.C. he plundered the Temple, massacred numbers of Jews, ordered the nation to adopt the polytheistic rites of Greece, and sacrificed swine to Zeus on the altar sacred to Jehovah. The sanctuary was dedicated to Zeus Olympius, and the Samaritan shrine on Mount Gerizim to Zeus Xenius. The rites of Judaism and the observance of the Sabbath were proscribed, and the Greeks in Palestine ordered to enforce the proscription. An Athenian missionary was introduced to direct the ceremonies of Greek worship. The first book of the Maccabees tells how matters came to a head. The story may be summarised as follows. When the king's officers reached the city of Modin to insist on the performance of a pagan sacrifice, Mattathias, the descendant of one Hasmon, an aged priest, moved to frenzy by the sight of an apostate Jew performing the rites, cut him down and slew the king's officer. He then fled with his five sons to the mountains and raised a rebellion, which was joined by the Chasidim. The third son of Mattathias, Judas, proved himself a brilliant military leader and acquired the Aramaic title of 'Maggaba', or 'the Hammer' (like Charles Martel). The name was shared by his brothers, who came to be known as the Maccabees.

Antiochus IV. died in 164 B.C. After his death the Seleucid Empire was so weakened by internal dissensions that the Maccabees were able to establish the virtual independence of Judea. They entered into friendly relations with Rome, and were able to extend their dominions over regions wider than Solomon had ruled. In 143 B.C. Simon, the last of the brothers, was invested with the office of high priest and clothed with absolute powers as ruler of the nation. The combined offices of priest and ruler were declared to be hereditary in his family. Simon was murdered by his son-in-law Ptolemy in 135 B.C. But Simon's son, John Hyrcanus, succeeded in seizing the high priesthood and, in doing so, lost the support of the Chasidim. He extended his father's conquests and died in 104 B.C. His son Aristobulus assumed the title of king. The office of high priest and king were thus combined in his person. Aristobulus conquered Galilee, a region occupied at this period by the normal Syrian mixture of Phoenician, Philistine, Hittite and Greek elements,[3] a people who had not as yet adopted the Jewish faith. They were suffered to remain in Galilee only on condition of submitting to circumcision. The majority appear to have accepted the condition and so to have joined the Jewish community, which, unlike the Samaritan sect, looked to Jerusalem as its centre. But their non-Jewish origin explains the contempt with which Galilee was regarded in Judea.[4]

From the moment when Simon in 143 B.C. assumed the high priesthood the worship of Jehovah in the Temple and the rigid enforcement of the Mosaic law was once more observed. Jerusalem acquired the place from which Tyre and Carthage had both fallen as the leading centre of Semitic civilisation. The monotheistic worship of which it was the seat was as much above the level of Graeco-Roman polytheism as the worship of Baal was below that of Athens and Rome. The numerous colonies of Jews dispersed from Babylon to Spain proudly regarded Jerusalem as the centre of their faith. The aim and hope of every Jew was, at least once in his life, to visit Jerusalem, to say his prayers and offer his sacrifice at the altar of Jehovah. Vast revenues flowed to the treasury of the Temple in the form of voluntary offerings collected by the synagogues in every commercial centre from the shores of the Atlantic to those of the Persian Gulf.

The Jews proudly viewed themselves as the people to whom the God of the universe had chosen to reveal not only his nature but the ritual and law by which men ought to live. Believing this, it was natural that, under Pharisee influence, they should wish to convert others to their faith. Their readiness at this stage of their history 'to compass sea and land to make one proselyte' is a well-established historical fact. The edict of Hadrian forbidding circumcision, at least of proselytes, was needed to quench it. With Jerusalem in her glory and Carthage in ruins the scattered Phoenician traders with their close racial affinity to the Jews were likely to be the readiest converts. From the time of Plato a certain drift towards monotheism had begun to affect the thought of the Graeco-Roman world. The Greeks and Romans viewed the religion of Jehovah with involuntary respect, and until the fall of Jerusalem regular provision was made by Roman emperors for sacrifice to be offered in the Temple on their behalf. The Jewish communities in Rome and elsewhere were allowed to lead their separate life and accorded certain privileges. Except in Judea and Mesopotamia they had generally adopted the Greek language, and after the fall of Carthage the Phoenician traders no doubt followed suit. They had thus every motive as well as every facility for abandoning the worship of Baal, with its hideous and barbarous rites, for that of Jehovah and for merging themselves in the Jewish communities. The process was gradual, and we know from Tertullian that up to the time of Tiberius they were still suspected of reverting to the practice of child sacrifice.

The upshot was that after the fall of Carthage the

Jews replaced the Phoenicians as the champions of Semitic culture in opposition to Graeco-Roman civilisation. The issues were postponed by the fact that the Maccabees sought the protection of the Roman republic against the Seleucids and became involved in the struggles of Roman parties and generals which ended in the establishment of the Empire. When Pompey was organising the Roman ascendency in the east he was called upon to settle between two Hasmonean princes, Hyrcanus and Aristobulus, their claims to the throne and high priesthood of Jerusalem. Pompey decided in favour of Hyrcanus, who was guided by the counsels of Antipater, an Edomite. As the followers of his rival refused to accept the award, Pompey besieged them in the Temple, slew some 12,000, and forcing his way into the Holy of Holies was astounded to find no image of Jehovah. This was in 65 B.C. When after the battle of Pharsalus in 48 B.C. Pompey had fled to Egypt, Caesar, who followed hard in pursuit, arrived to find that Pompey had been murdered on landing. Lured by the charms of Queen Cleopatra, the conqueror of the world got involved in a squalid local embroglio, and found himself entrapped with a mere handful of his men in the fortress of Alexandria. Antipater was mainly instrumental in extricating Caesar from his predicament, by inducing the vast Jewish population to take his side, and by marshalling for his rescue large forces from Syria and Arabia. The Jews found their reward in the privileges which Caesar accorded to their colonies at Rome and elsewhere throughout the Roman dominions. The payment of tribute by Jewish colonies to the Temple was legalised. Judea was relieved of any obligation to pay taxes to Rome. Antipater was appointed as Procurator. His son, Herod the Great, became king of a powerful monarchy under Roman protection. The high priesthood was now separated from the kingship and rendered subordinate to it. The high priests were in fact appointed by the king.

NOTES

[1] Bacon, *The Greatnesse of Kingdomes.*
[2] Hebrews xi. 35-38.
[3] My authority for this statement is Col. Lawrence.
[4] Bevan, *The House of Seleucus*, vol. ii. p. 256.

CHAPTER XV

THE KINGDOM OF GOD. TRANSCENDENTAL AND REALIST CONCEPTIONS

In an earlier chapter we have traced Jewish ideas as to their future and that of the Gentiles up to the period when a remnant returned from exile in Babylon, rebuilt the Temple in Jerusalem and re-established the Law of Moses in all its rigour. The writings of certain prophets as well as the books of the Law were recognised as divinely inspired. But the priests had endeavoured to end the disturbing influence of prophets by establishing the belief that the age of divine revelation was now terminated once for all. The prophecies of Amos, Hosea, Isaiah, Micah, Nahum, Habakkuk, Zephaniah, Jeremiah, Ezekiel, Haggai, Zechariah and Joel had been recorded in their own names. This obscure remnant of Israel was still to produce books like Daniel, Job, Jonah and Ecclesiastes, which remain as landmarks in literature. Some of them won their way into the canon with books previously recognised as inspired. But this was only because their real authors were able to pass them off as the work of historic or legendary prophets of an earlier age. To such devices we owe Daniel and many of the finest chapters in the prophecy of Isaiah. The first nineteen verses of Isaiah xxvi. are no earlier than the time of Alexander the Great. Messianic passages were freely interpolated in the older prophets. Many of the Psalms belong to this date. For a number of centuries the literature of the Jews was either anonymous or else given to the world under the names of men who had never existed or had died centuries before the books ascribed to them were written.

The old prophets were primarily interested in the future of Israel in this world. But the question of the future which awaited the individual, not merely the Israelite but also the Gentile, had been gradually forcing itself to the front. In the sufferings which Israel continued to endure after the exile some of the conclusions which follow from the postulate of one eternal, omnipotent and righteous God were dimly reached. Jewish thinkers had come to see that if Jehovah was indeed eternal, omnipotent and righteous, the life of the individual in God, that is to say the moral life, could not be limited to life in the flesh. The existence of the righteous must be eternal as that of the God by reason of whom all righteousness is. Life in God could not be ended by physical death.

A solution of the problem was attempted by combining into one picture the national restoration of Israel foretold by the prophets with the promise to righteous individuals of eternal life. In this picture 'the day of Jehovah', originally conceived as a day of battle, is now becoming a day of judgement. In that day God will appear as ruler of the universe to sift out the righteous from the wicked. His kingdom on earth will be constituted from the righteous in Israel. The thinkers who followed Jeremiah as opposed to Ezekiel did not exclude from this kingdom the Gentiles who turned to God. This kingdom would be everlasting, as the prophets had foretold. But leaders of thought who came after the exile had advanced beyond the prophets, and now held that the righteous included in the kingdom would live for ever. As noticed in Chapter V., this led them to ask what would happen to the righteous who had died on the earth before the day of the Lord had come? The answer to this question was supplied by the theory that they would rise from their graves on that day and live for ever in the Kingdom of God. The miracle required to produce this result presented no difficulty to the Jewish mind.

In the earlier conceptions the wicked are simply to perish; eternal blessedness in the kingdom is the proper reward of the righteous. The consummation of life for the individual was thus represented as inseparable from the consummation of life for the nation. By their own peculiar road these Jewish thinkers had arrived at a point little removed from that reached by Plato and Aristotle. To the Greek thinkers the state existed for the sake of goodness. A full development of goodness in the citizens was inconceivable apart from a full development of the state. So minds far removed from each other, who have groped their way to a truth, reach it and find themselves face to face.

In later Jewish conceptions the wicked as well as the righteous dead are to rise, and all the wicked are then adjudged to eternal punishment, often described as fiery torments. The vindictive side of the picture was accentuated by the miseries inflicted on the Jews by the persecution of Antiochus Epiphanes. In the last century before the Christian era the valley of Hinnom, or Gehenna, is fully developed as a place of torment for the wicked, where the worm dieth not and the fire is not quenched. In the *Assumption of Moses*, by an author contemporary with Jesus, the anguish of the wicked will serve to enhance the joys of the righteous: "and thou shalt look from on high and see thy enemies in Gehenna, and thou shalt recognise them and rejoice, and thou shalt give thanks and confess thy creator".[1] We shall presently find Tertullian preaching the same idea.

In the second century B.C., while the nation had leaders of genius in the first Maccabees, the yearning for a coming Messiah fell into the background. But when, in the next century, their successors began to oppress the Chasids, that yearning revived. By some of them Messiah was conceived as a supernatural being. But others who returned to the study of the Scriptures revived the idea that a son of David would appear to inaugurate the Kingdom of God.

In the gathering calamities of that age a further change took place in this compound of folk-lore with genuine philosophy. The Jewish quietists had begun to feel that no blessed future for the righteous was possible on this earth. According to chapters in the book of Enoch, composed between 94–64 B.C., Jehovah will appear and with him the Messiah, who is variously described as 'the Christ', 'the Righteous One', 'the Elect One', and 'the Son of Man'.[2]

The whole conception had thus reached the transcendental stage for those capable of such ideas. But a large proportion of the Jews reached these more spiritual conceptions with difficulty or not at all. To the Sadducee priesthood, who still adhered to the old pagan conception of Sheol, the transcendental view of the kingdom was of course impossible. To them the Kingdom of God could only mean what it meant to the old prophets, the restoration of an earthly kingdom. As a class their position was too comfortable to make them anxious to treat such projects as a question of immediate or practical politics. There were no such motives to curb the fanaticism of the proletariat which battened in the lanes of Jerusalem on the pilgrim traffic, or the proselyte ardour of the peasants who tilled the soil of Galilee and Judea.

Side by side with the spiritual conception of the Kingdom of Heaven, the crude nationalist idea that a day was at hand when God would send a scion of David to restore the kingdom to Israel maintained its hold on a large section of the people. As the project of a world empire came into view, the Jewish idea inevitably assumed wider proportions. From the moment that Pompey stormed Jerusalem and entered the Holy of Holies, there were Jews who kept in their hearts the dream of a day when a prince of the house of David, backed by the power of Jehovah, would transfer the dominion of the world from the Capitol to the Temple and teach the nations to exchange the laws of Rome for the laws of Moses.

It must always be held in mind that the great Jewish community settled in Mesopotamia was not at this time subject to Rome. In 248 B.C. the Parthian kingdom had broken off from the empire of Seleucus. The Romans themselves, after conquering that empire, had been unable to subdue the Parthians. In 53 B.C. these Iranian nomads had utterly destroyed Crassus and his army at the battle of Carrhae, after which Mesopotamia and Babylon remained in the hands of the Parthians till the time of Trajan. At the period with which we are now dealing this Parthian Empire was the spear-head of the Asiatic reaction against Graeco-Roman civilisation. Its frontiers were not very distant from Galilee and Judea and the famous disaster to Roman arms was vividly present to the minds of the Zealots.

We are here approaching the climax of history, when diverse materials of human experience smelted in a furnace were to yield elements of indestructible truth. A patient sifting of the ashes will for ever continue to uncover grains of gold which past generations have missed in their search. We must pause, therefore, to examine the forces which were seething in the human oven of which Jerusalem with its Temple was the mouth.

Masefield traces the catastrophes of Shakespeare to obsessions of the mind, to some blindness to truth, some passionate belief that things are thus when in fact they are otherwise. If so, then Shakespeare was handling the absolute stuff of human life, for obsession is the key to the tragedies of history. Apprehension of one truth so vivid as to make it appear as the whole and final truth is such an obsession. And round the luminous spot where the mind is focussed there presently gathers a cloud of phantasies. The conception of one righteous God which came to the people of Israel in the deserts of Sinai has appealed to the minds and consciences of men as a real intuition. But this intuition the people of Israel saw as a special revelation vouchsafed to themselves alone as the favourite people of God. The series of legends which purported to show how the ruler of the universe had made this special revelation to his chosen race were accepted as historical fact.

The conception of one righteous God raised their ideas of the conduct which ought to be expected of men. In time those ideas were reduced to a code which was in advance of the standards observed in that age by the rest of mankind. The code was reduced to writing, and ere long was believed to have been graven by God on tablets of stone. But the process did not stop there. The pagan rites by which they worshipped Jehovah, and the tedious and elaborate ceremonies developed during their settled life, were presently placed in the same category. The manuals in which their national customs and rites were recorded by the priesthood were believed to have been dictated by Jehovah himself and to have been taken down by Moses in the kloofs of Horeb. And so developed the creed that Jehovah was to be served only by their punctual observance.

None the less, the Hebrew gift of spiritual insight was from time to time revived from the deserts. 'Prophets arose' who dared to announce that Jehovah was not to be satisfied by burnt offerings, by elaborate washings and by the payment of dues to the priests, but rather by righteous dealing and mercy to the meek. Tradition tells that such prophets were fated to perish at Jerusalem, to die at the hands of priests and scribes whose profession it was to administer the rites and interpret the Law.

The same obsession coloured their view of history and determined their political outlook. Their minds dwelt on the brief period when the house of David had ruled from north of Damascus to the confines of Egypt. They thought of its founder as the chosen and anointed of God. Their Scriptures were saturated with prophecies that a scion of David's house, the Lord's anointed, was destined to be born and rule the whole earth in the name of Jehovah. This was the orthodox national belief of the Jewish communities throughout the world. Generally, no doubt, it was held as a dream to be kept in the background of their minds, but not permitted to interfere with the business of daily life. Not so with the poor and pious of Judea. There the belief possessed their minds and was one for which they were ready to die. The wealthy and cynical rulers of the Temple had always to reckon with it.

Twin are the gates to the impalpable land of dreams, these made from horn and those of ivory. Dreams that pass by the pale carven ivory are irony, cheats with a burden of vain hope: but every dream which comes to a man through the gate of horn forecasts the future truth.[3]

NOTES

[1] *Assumption of Moses*, x. 10 (Charles' translation).
[2] Charles, *Eschatology*, pp. 265-6.
[3] Homer, *Odyssey*, xix. 560 (trans. by Lawrence).

CHAPTER XVI

THE IVORY GATE

On the death of Herod in 4 B.C. the Emperor Augustus divided his kingdom between three of his sons. Philip received the northern portion south of Damascus and west of the lake of Gennesareth, including the Greek cities of Decapolis, east of the Jordan. To Antipas was assigned Galilee and the regions east of the Jordan inhabited by Jews. To each was assigned the title of Tetrarch. Samaria, Judea and Idumaea (Edom, the native country of the Herods) were assigned to Archelaus, with the title of Ethnarch. The Herods, though conforming to Judaism, were in open sympathy with Greek culture, and the nationalist party of the Jews never forgot their Edomite origin. At the Passover following the death of Herod the Great the mob in Jerusalem clamoured for the Ethnarch to eject pagans from Jerusalem, and also to dismiss the high priest appointed by his father. Archelaus quelled the disorder in blood and started for Rome. The outraged Jews thereupon sent a deputation of fifty delegates after him to oppose his appointment as Ethnarch. Augustus received them in the temple of Apollo, to which they were escorted by 8000 of the Jewish colony in Rome. The deputation perhaps included the moderate leaders and also spokesmen of the priestly caste who preferred the rule of Rome from a distance to that of an Edomite prince on the spot.

While matters were still in suspense at Rome, the nationalists in Judea broke loose and attacked the Roman garrison. The whole country was in fact the scene of a dangerous rising, and the Roman legions had to be called out by Varus, the governor of Syria, to suppress it. Augustus decided in favour of Archelaus. He proved so worthless a ruler, however, that in A.D. 6 Augustus deposed him and Coponius was appointed to rule as procurator of a Roman province under Publius Sulpicius Quirinius, the Prefect of Syria. These officials were responsible for maintaining the peace; this of course involved the presence of a Roman garrison and the levying of taxes to meet the cost.

In Jerusalem a wide jurisdiction was allowed to the native authorities. The human agency through which Jehovah was supposed to regulate the affairs of his people had developed before the age of the Maccabees. Like the constitution of Carthage it was influenced by the form rather than by the spirit of Greek models. It consisted of a council of elders called the Sanhedrin, a Semitic form of the Greek *συνέδριον*.

The presidency in it was held by the high priest, whom each ruler of the land, if he was not possibly himself high priest, appointed for the time. To the college belonged the former high priests and esteemed experts in the law. This assembly, in which the aristocratic element preponderated, acted as the supreme spiritual representative of the whole body of Jews, and, so far as this was not to be separated from it, also as the secular representative in particular of the community of Jerusalem. It is only the later Rabbinism that has by a pious fiction transformed the Synhedrion of Jerusalem into a spiritual institute of Mosaic appointment. It corresponded essentially to the council of the Greek urban constitution, but certainly bore, as respected its composition as well as its sphere of working, a more spiritual character than belonged to the Greek representatives of the community. To this Synhedrion and its high priest, who was now nominated by the procurator as representative of the imperial suzerain, the Roman government left or committed that jurisdiction which in the Hellenic subject communities belonged to the urban authorities and the common councils. With indifferent shortsightedness it allowed to the transcendental Messianism of the Pharisees free course, and to the by no means transcendental land-consistory—acting until the Messiah should arrive—tolerably free sway in affairs of faith, of manners, and of law, where Roman interests were not directly affected thereby. This applied in particular to the administration of justice. It is true that, as far as Roman burgesses were concerned in the matter, justice in civil as in criminal affairs must have been reserved for the Roman tribunals even already before the annexation of the land. But civil justice over the Jews remained even after that annexation chiefly with the local authority. Criminal justice over them was exercised by the latter probably in general concurrently with the Roman procurator; only sentences of death could not be executed by it otherwise than after confirmation by the imperial magistrate.[1]

From this account it is easy to see why the cynical realists of the Temple hierarchy preferred the distant rule of Rome to that of a local prince professing the Jewish religion. To the people of Israel God was their king and the Temple his dwelling. The hereditary caste which administered the Temple and controlled the vast and increasing revenues which poured into its coffers from all parts of the world naturally aspired to rule in the name of the invisible king. In their hearts they preferred the control of Seleucid emperors to that of the Maccabees, even though its founders were of their own order. A subordinate Roman official was easier to manage than a Herod.

The recognised leader at this juncture was Annas, a Sadducee who held the office of high priest. In A.D. 7 he persuaded the Roman governor to reappoint him to that office. He held it for seven years till the death of Augustus, but for long after was usually able to secure the appointment either of one of his sons or of some near relative like his son-in-law Caiaphas. In fact the appointment was kept in his family almost without interruption for fifty years.

The struggles in which the Roman republic had foundered were finally closed at the battle of Actium in 31 B.C. From that moment the motive which governed the policy of Augustus and Tiberius was to tranquillise the provinces. Magnificent gifts were made to the Temple treasury, and the Emperor paid for the daily sacrifice of a bullock and two lambs to the 'Supreme God'. Detachments detailed for garrison service at Jerusalem were ordered to leave the effigies of the Emperor at Caesarea. The most sacred robes of the high priest, which the Romans had kept in the citadel, were now restored to the Temple. There is clear evidence that the government was concerned not only to conciliate the hierarchy, but also to remove whatever might excite the fanaticism of the people. There were things, however, which no government at Rome could accomplish. It tried to restrain, but could never wholly prevent, failures in tact, lack of patience, or even rapacity in its local officials. Still less could it wholly exempt a province directly subject to Roman rule from the payment of taxes to the central treasury. Such taxes were far lighter than those levied by native princes with courts to support. With the best of goodwill the Roman government in suppressing the rule of native princes could not have avoided this issue. But inevitably it brought a system based on realities into conflict with the fundamental Jewish obsession.

Quirinius proceeded to frame the assessments of property necessary for levying the taxes. The wealthy classes were with difficulty persuaded by the high priest himself to swallow their resentment. But there sprang into being a party beyond the control of the priests and propertied classes—a party which believed in nothing but physical force. Its founder was Judas of Gamala, a Galilean. He raised a rebellion which was quickly suppressed, and Judas was nailed to a cross. This execution was the first scene in a tragedy which in two generations reached a climax, the horrors of which make those which attended the fall of Carthage seem faint and pale.

From the ashes of Judas there sprang a sect known to the Jews as Zealots. By the Romans they were known as *sicarii* or men of the knife. In these days the word 'gunmen' would express the significance of the term. They are best described in the words of a contemporary, Josephus:

> They said that God would not otherwise be assisting to them, than upon their joining with one another in such counsels as might be successful, and for their own advantage; and this especially, if they would set about great exploits, and not grow weary in executing the same; so men received what they said with pleasure, and this bold attempt proceeded to a great height. All sorts of misfortunes also sprang from these men, and the nation was infected with this doctrine to an incredible degree; one violent war came upon us after another, and we lost our friends, who used to alleviate our pain; there were also very great robberies and murders of our principal men. This was done in pretence indeed for the public welfare, but in reality for the hopes of gain to themselves; whence arose seditions, and from them murders of men, which sometimes fell on those of their own people, (by the madness of these men towards one another, while their desire was that none of the adverse party might be left,) and sometimes on their enemies; a famine also coming upon us, reduced us to the last degree of despair, as did also the taking and demolishing of cities; nay, the sedition at last increased so high, that the very temple of God was burnt down by their enemy's fire. Such were the consequences of this, that the customs of our fathers were altered, and such a change was made, as added a mighty weight toward bringing all to destruction, which these men occasioned by thus conspiring together; for Judas and Sadduc, who excited a fourth philosophic sect among us, and had a great many followers therein, filled our civil government with tumults at present, and laid the foundation of our future miseries, by this system of philosophy, which we were before unacquainted withal; concerning which I shall discourse a little, and this the rather, because the infection which spread thence among the younger sort,

who were zealous for it, brought the public to destruction. . . .

These men agree in all other things with the Pharisaic notions; but they have an inviolable attachment to liberty; and they say that God is to be their only Ruler and Lord. They also do not value dying any kinds of death, nor indeed do they heed the deaths of their relations and friends, nor can any such fear make them call any man Lord; and since this immovable resolution of theirs is well known to a great many, I shall speak no further about that matter; nor am I afraid that anything I have said of them should be disbelieved, but rather fear, that what I have said is beneath the resolution they shew when they undergo pain; and it was in Gessius Florus's time that the nation began to grow mad with this distemper, who was our procurator, and who occasioned the Jews to go wild with it by the abuse of his authority, and to make them revolt from the Romans.[2]

In countries ruled by foreigners whose views are in fundamental conflict with those of their subjects, political factions tend to develop on similar lines. The rulers enter into relations with such of the native race as are willing to act as their agents. They naturally endeavour to make this section feel that its interests are identical with their own, and, with this object in view, often entrust them with extensive powers. The people at large view with disfavour those of their race who are helping the foreigner to rule them. The native agents themselves regard with suppressed dislike the foreigners whose authority it is their interest to maintain. The best friends of the foreign authority are usually to be found in the classes more interested in business than politics. They fear disorders which any attempt to eject the foreigner will necessitate. On the other hand, they are chafed by the failures and abuses from which no government is exempt. They seek reforms without revolution, but are seldom satisfied with such reforms as are actually made.

There is, also, the party mainly drawn from the young and the poorer classes who, with little to lose but their lives and with no experience of administrative problems, mistrust all measures for reform which are not based on physical force. If inseparable from the system there is some condition which continues to outrage their ideals, there comes a time when they are willing to kill and also to be killed rather than endure it. If once blood begins to flow, the line which separates fighting from murder, war from banditry, or resistance to authority from wholesale crime, begins to vanish. These exponents of physical force come to regard terror as the only bond which unites society. To maintain unity amongst themselves they resort to murdering one another.

These three typical groups existed in Judea, and there, as in other countries moving towards revolution, they overlapped, and were sometimes combined in action by a hatred of the foreigner common to them all. The disturbance in which Pilate slaughtered a number of Galileans is a case in point. The inflammatory state of Judea was partly the result of unhealthy social conditions. The districts surrounding Jerusalem were barren and incapable of supporting so large a city. Its wealth was in fact the product of the dispersion. In every commercial centre of the civilised world were Jews making proselytes, gathering wealth and pouring it into the coffers of the Temple. In the general prosperity created by Augustus these contributions must have increased by leaps and bounds. The hierarchy, to which Augustus in A.D. 6 conceded such wide powers, had vast revenues at their disposal, a portion of which no doubt found its way into their private purses. They were not disposed to deplete the treasury by embarking on public works, such as Herod had freely undertaken. But this rapidly growing resort of pilgrims was in need of an adequate supply of potable water. To the Roman official with his orderly western mind, like that of an Indian civil servant, the filth and insanitary condition of the town was intolerable. His budget upon which the garrisons and his own establishment were charged was not intended to meet the cost of municipal services. The need of water in the city was created by the hordes of pilgrims attracted to the Temple, and was therefore a proper charge on its treasury. And so, says Josephus:

Pilate undertook to bring a current of water to Jerusalem, and did it with the sacred money, and derived the origin of the stream from the distance of two hundred furlongs. However, the Jews were not pleased with what had been done about this water; and many ten thousands of the people got together, and made a clamour against him, and insisted that he should leave off that design. Some of them also used reproaches, and abused the man, as crowds of such people usually do. So he habited a great number of his soldiers in their habit, who carried daggers under their garments, and sent them to a place where they might surround them. So he bade the Jews himself go away; but they boldly casting reproaches upon him, he gave the soldiers that signal which had been beforehand agreed on; who laid upon them much greater blows than Pilate had commanded them, and equally punished those that were tumultuous, and those that were not, nor did they spare them in the least; and since the people were unarmed, and were caught by men prepared for what they were about, there were a great number of them slain by this means, and others of them ran away wounded; and thus an end was put to this sedition.[3]

The construction of a great aqueduct must have meant the employment of numerous workmen and can scarcely have been an unpopular measure. The handful of wealthy priests were the only people who, on grounds of self-interest, were likely to resent the action of Pilate in challenging the exclusive right to control the wealth banked in the Temple. They had, as we have seen, material reasons for supporting the settlement made by Augustus. But some of them at any rate were unable to bridle their anger or resist the temptation to teach Pilate that the Temple treasure could not be touched with impunity. A hint of sacrilege spread through the whispering galleries of the great city would suffice to inflame the fanaticism of the Zealots. Men to whom human life was of no account were unlikely to consider the benefit done to a multitude of workers, still less the sanitary needs of the city. A handful of knife-men amongst the gangs could create a tumult and bring the works to a standstill. In the vain hope of composing the dispute, Pilate appeared on the spot with a guard dressed as civilians but with arms concealed beneath their cloaks. But the crowd, coerced by the knife-men, refused to take up their tools. The parley developed into a tumult. Pilate's suite drew their swords, and in the slaughter which followed there perished with the knife-men numbers of workers who would have been only too glad to have been left at peace to earn their wages.

The contributions which came from the trading communities were not the only or perhaps the largest stream of wealth which enriched Jerusalem. In the course of the year countless pilgrims came to pay their vows and offer their sacrifice. A bazaar where the offerings could be purchased was established in the courts of the Temple. And, as at Benares or Mecca, the performance of rites involved the payment of fees to priests. We have reason to know that the ceremonies attracted streams of pilgrims from Persia, Mesopotamia, Asia Minor, Egypt, Cyrene, Crete, Arabia and from Rome itself.[4]

Catering for pilgrims was the industry upon which Jerusalem had grown to affluence. A large proportion of the permanent residents no doubt lived by it. The political geography of the civilised world must have been as familiar in Jerusalem as in Athens or Rome. No man of intelligence interested in public affairs who lived in Judea at this period could have failed to know the outstanding facts of the Roman Empire. A great part of the known world was now subject to Rome. So much at least was familiar even to the peasants and bandits from whose ranks the Zealots were drawn. But by minds like these the facts of life were seen only through the coloured windows of the national legend. It was they who worshipped the one true God, whose chosen abode was the shrine at Jerusalem. The only authority they acknowledged was his, until he saw fit to send them a visible king of the lineage of David, anointed like him with the holy oil. But the days were long gone when the sovereignty of God could be limited to the narrow frontiers of David and Solomon. Not the Romans and their emperor, but the Jews and their king, were destined to govern the earth under the authority of Jehovah himself. The Kingdom of God was at hand. He was calling his chosen people to action, and whatever was lacking in organised force his miraculous power would supply.

A people whose mind is largely nourished with a legendary past are a grave menace to themselves and the world. Ideas are portable, and this fatal fanaticism could not be confined to the hotbed in which it was brewed. From a centre of pilgrimage like Jerusalem it was certain to spread to the Jewish settlements throughout the Empire. It infected even the Christian churches, and both Peter and Paul, in writing to churches in Rome and Asia, found it necessary to insist on the duty of civil obedience.[5]

Elsewhere in the Roman Empire troops were recruited from the local inhabitants. In Syria, Spain or Gaul, the most spirited youths were thus placed under strict discipline. Careers were opened to their talents which more than once led men of ability from the ranks to the throne. The discipline of a soldier's life was not compatible with the observance of the Sabbath, and one of the numerous privileges granted to the Jews was exemption from military service. Jews who were young, poor and ambitious were thus freed from discipline and also had closed to them military careers, open elsewhere to soldiers of ability and courage. The blood of Judas thus fell like seed on a soil peculiarly ready for its growth.

As imperial prestige declined in the hands of Caligula, Claudius and Nero, the growing unrest rapidly moved towards open revolution. But even so the hierarchy, which had everything to lose by rebellion, continued to play with fire. We have evidence of this from the pen of an eye-witness. In the year A.D. 57, Paul, a Pharisee by birth, had made up his mind to visit Jerusalem, where he was regarded as a dangerous schismatic. His friends at Caesarea besought him with tears to desist from his project; but he persevered, and his visit to the Temple led to a riot. Paul was with difficulty rescued by the officer in command of the Roman garrison, and was sent for trial heavily guarded before the Sanhedrin. There Paul dexterously raised the burning issue of the resurrection, and so enlisted the sympathy of the Pharisee members against the priests. So great was the uproar that the Roman officer removed him to the citadel. The knife-men approached the leaders of the priestly faction, who undertook to secure a further trial before their court, in the course of which these assassins were to overpower the guard and kill Paul. Claudius Lysias, the Roman officer, got wind of the plot and despatched Paul by night to be tried by Felix at Caesarea. The formidable nature of the plot is shown by the fact that the Roman commandant thought it necessary to provide an escort of 400 infantry and 70 cavalry.

Felix was succeeded by Porcius Festus, who died within two years of assuming office. He seems to have been the only honest and competent procurator appointed to Judea from the death of Tiberius till the siege of Jerusalem. The seat of Roman government was at Caesarea, where Greeks were as numerous as Jews. In Jerusalem the Roman authority was only represented by a garrison in the citadel under the command of a military officer. The rural districts were gradually abandoned to the knife-men, though during the brief period of his office Festus did what he could to round them up. The mass of the people, who wished only to be left alone, were terrorised by a handful of youthful fanatics. Their creed was war to the knife with Rome. Any Jew suspected of compromise on that point was marked for destruction at their hands. They seized whatever they needed in the national cause. The stage had been reached when everything which distinguished brigands and patriots had gone by the board.

The work begun by Festus was quickly undone by his two successors, Albinus and Florus. The friends of knife-men imprisoned by Festus secured their release by bribing Albinus. Florus seems to have found a speedier way to wealth by tapping the coffers of public corporations. His success on these lines in the north developed in his mind the dangerous ambition of seizing the fabled treasures of the Temple, and, with that object in view, he entered Jerusalem with a couple of cohorts. Such, however, was the fury of the populace that his courage failed him, and he retired, leaving one small detachment in the citadel of Antonia.

Agrippa, a prince of the house of Herod, at this juncture visited Jerusalem in the hope of allaying the popular excitement. He explained to the mob the strength of the Roman Empire, and argued that its power could not have been established except in accordance with the providence of God. Their belief that Jehovah would intervene to enable Jewish fanaticism to overcome Roman efficiency was a dangerous madness. His intervention seems to have restored the ascendency of the moderate party for the moment.

Florus, however, was supported by his senior officer Cestius Gallus, the Governor of Syria, who tried to bring home to the frivolous mind of Nero the formidable nature of the situation. In A.D. 65 he asked the priests, for the information of the Emperor, to compute the number of people collected in Jerusalem at the time of the Passover. The priests reported that there had been 256,500 Paschal suppers, at each of which at least ten persons would attend. From this they inferred that at least 2,700,200 were present at the suppers. But this did not include foreigners and persons debarred from attendance by ceremonial impurities. The arithmetic as reported by Josephus is confused, and the total incredible. It is difficult to see how 3,000,000 people could be fed in a place not open to water-borne traffic. It is clear, however, that vast multitudes were collected annually in this centre seething with religious fanaticism, and were recognised as a danger to the peace of the Empire.

Fanaticism, bred by a national obsession, is never confined to one class, and breaks out in the least expected quarters. It was suddenly realised that Eleazar, the son of the High Priest Ananias, had thrown in his lot with the revolution. As captain of the Temple he stopped the sacrifice endowed by Augustus which was daily offered on behalf of the Roman Empire. It was even as when Caesar ordered his army to cross the Rubicon, Washington decided on independence, or the mob of Paris stormed the Bastille. For the Jewish revolution was reserved a fate other than theirs. So devouring was the spirit of anarchy which possessed it, that its children consumed each other.

The high priests and moderate leaders withdrew their party to the upper city, and despatched messengers imploring Florus and Agrippa to send troops to assist them in restoring order. The Zealots, however, stormed their stronghold, burned the houses of Ananias and Agrippa, and besieged the Roman garrison in the tower of Antonia. At this juncture another band of Zealots led by Manahem, son of Judas the founder of zealotry (two other of his sons had been crucified by the Romans), entered the city and joined the siege. Storming part of the citadel, they allowed the party sent by Agrippa and others who were Jews to depart. Three of the towers were still held by a remnant of the Roman detachment. Next day Ananias the father and Hezekiah the brother of Eleazar fell into the hands of Manahem and were butchered. Eleazar now turned on Manahem, defeated his band and tortured him to death.

Eleazar then promised to spare the Roman garrison if they would surrender their arms. They accepted the promise, but no sooner had the Zealots taken their arms than they slaughtered them all with the single exception of Metelius, the officer in command, who agreed to be circumcised. So was the stage prepared for the long orgy of blood in which Zealot bands divided their time between fighting the Romans, massacring the starving people and doing each other to death in and about the sanctuary of God.

Jerusalem was thus overwhelmed by the anarchy which had long reigned in the country districts. It began to react on cities where the Greeks outnumbered the Jews. On the same day that the Roman garrison was butchered (August 6, A.D. 66), the Greeks in Caesarea rose and massacred the Jews. The thirst for carnage then spread, till the towns of the Levant from Antioch to Alexandria were running with blood.

The challenge thrown down by Eleazar could not be ignored by the Roman governor of Syria. In

September he entered the outer walls of Jerusalem with an army of 20,000 legionaries and 13,000 auxiliary troops. The inner city, including the Temple and palace, was held by the Zealots. The moderates secretly offered to admit Cestius, but, mistrusting their overtures, he endeavoured to storm the walls. On the first failure of the assault he lost his nerve and determined to retreat to Caesarea. As the whole country rose around him the retreat became a rout. The baggage and artillery were abandoned, and the Roman army only escaped destruction by leaving its rearguard to be slaughtered.

The rebellion now spread through the whole country up to the regions where Greeks outnumbered the Jewish population. A few of the moderate leaders escaped to Caesarea. They were sent by Cestius to tell Nero what had happened and to throw the blame on Florus. Nero had gone to Greece to compete for prizes in a vast programme of public games. But the news from Judea convinced him that serious measures were needed, and he chose for the task the ablest of his generals, Titus Flavius Vespasianus, who had done good service in Britain and elsewhere. The old general was made of that stuff which so long enabled Rome to survive the rule of emperors like Nero. He had been in disfavour for not pretending to admire the Emperor's singing, and actually thought, when the imperial messengers were announced, that they came to order his execution. He instantly left for the east with his son Titus and Mucianus, who was sent to supersede Cestius Gallus.

Meanwhile the moderates who remained in Jerusalem lost their heads and threw in their lot with the revolution. For the moment the Zealots accepted the direction of men like Ananus, the son of Annas, who controlled the high priesthood in the days of Pilate. The notables were allowed to organise the defence of Judea and Galilee and administer the country.

In March A.D. 67 Vespasian set out with his legions from Antioch and proceeded to crush the rebellion in Galilee and Judea. Towns where Greeks or law-abiding Jews were able to open their gates were alone spared and left with garrisons to defend them. The wilder spirits escaped to Jerusalem, expecting to see from its walls the Angel of the Lord smite the legions, as according to Scripture he had once smitten the armies of Sennacherib. They were there joined by Edomite hordes from the south. Local leaders of various bands fought like wolves for the mastery of the city. The moderate leaders were incapable of controlling the situation. Their government collapsed like a house of cards. In the early days of A.D. 68 several of its leaders including Ananus were ruthlessly butchered. Burial was denied to the bodies, an outrage, in Jewish ideas, infinitely worse than murder itself. Fully apprised of this state of affairs, Vespasian decided to allow the defenders of Judaism leisure to massacre each other, and employed the time in reducing the cities and villages of Judea.

Events were in train elsewhere which postponed and enhanced the final catastrophe. The scandal of Nero's frivolities in Greece had finally destroyed his authority in the provinces. He reluctantly agreed to return to Rome, and on reaching Naples in March learned that Vindex had raised a revolt in northern Gaul. The revolt was crushed by the army on the Rhine, which, however, threw off its allegiance to Nero. In Spain the legions saluted Galba as Emperor, and the senate hastened to confirm the election. In June Nero put an end to his life. The news reached Vespasian just as he was marshalling his legions to advance on Jerusalem. He resolved to await events, and withdrew them to Caesarea. Civil war raged in the west. Galba and Otho—another candidate for the purple—perished in the struggle, and in January A.D. 69 Vitellius was placed on the throne by his German legions. This determined the army of Syria to propose for the purple a candidate of their own. At Caesarea in July A.D. 69 the Syrian legions proclaimed Vespasian as Emperor. Mucianus was sent to deal with Vitellius. The siege of Jerusalem was entrusted to Titus, while Vespasian watched and directed from Egypt. Vitellius was defeated and slain, and by July A.D. 70 Vespasian was ruling as Emperor in Rome.

In April A.D. 70 Titus and his army arrived before Jerusalem on the eve of the Passover. The doomed city was crowded with pilgrims to its utmost capacity. In the frightful convulsions which followed the fall of Nero, people in the east thought they were witnessing the death throes of Rome. To the Jewish mind it was clear that the Kingdom of God was at hand. It is likely that the pilgrimage of A.D. 70 was swelled by thousands who hoped to witness the long-expected appearance of Messiah.

Events conspired to prepare the stage for one of the great tragedies of history. Behind ramparts almost impregnable, three parties of Zealots fought with each other like wild beasts. The helpless masses huddled in the city were plundered and massacred by their own countrymen. The altars of the sanctuary smoked to God, and blood from the sacrifice ran down its steps mingled with that of the worshippers, while the Roman rams thundered against the walls. In one narrow circle were concentrated the worst horrors of a civil revolution and a foreign war. The Jewish historian who watched these events from the camp of Titus imputes to the Zealots every kind of depravity: greed, cruelty, treachery, dissension, murder and lust. But he does not conceal their implacable courage. To Roman science and discipline they opposed prodigies of valour.

Titus combined the method of circumvallation

with that of assault. His offers to spare the city, its people and defenders, were met, first by treachery, and then with derision. As provisions failed, the Zealots ravened like dogs through the city, seizing for themselves whatever remained. In this reign of terror multitudes were butchered and left unburied. Still larger numbers perished of hunger, till the streets and houses were piled with corpses. Some thousands who tried to escape through the gates were caught by the Romans and nailed to crosses in sight of the walls, till trees and the space in which to plant them were both exhausted. In the end the walls were breached and the battle raged through the precincts of the Temple till it reached the Holy of Holies. By this time the infuriated soldiers had fired the cedar roofs, and a fabric, gorgeous as any that human hands have raised, vanished in a welter of blood and flame. Overwhelmed in this furnace, there perished a crowd which had flocked to the Temple, impelled by the belief that Jehovah would wait till his enemies had entered his shrine to destroy them. A whole people were led to their ruin by prophecies fatal as those of the witches who hailed Macbeth on the blasted heath.

To reduce the city and collect the captives was now only a matter of days. By September 8, A.D. 70, the struggle was over. Of the prisoners many were slaughtered, the greater part were sold into slavery, some, more unhappy than the rest, were distributed throughout the cities of the Empire, to be burned or torn by beasts as a spectacle in the theatres. So vast was the treasure seized in the Temple that gold fell to half its normal value in Syria. The veil of the Temple, its golden vessels and ornaments were reserved for the triumph of Titus. The famous candlestick with its seven lights may be seen sculptured on the Arch of Titus to-day. The city itself was demolished and the walls surrounding it, all but three towers. A legion was left encamped on the site to prevent resettlement. The focus of Jewish theocracy was finally destroyed. That tribute which the clemency of Caesar had allowed the priesthood to collect from the Jewish communities they were now ordered to remit to Rome for the service of Jupiter. In order to extinguish the line a sentence of death was announced against every Jew claiming descent from David. The story is told how certain great-nephews of Jesus who had settled east of the Jordan were arrested and brought to Domitian. The Emperor spared them when he saw what simple and mystic folk they were.

The conflict of Jewish theocracy with Graeco-Roman civilisation was renewed in the next generation. In A.D. 116, in the reign of Trajan, the Jews rose in Cyprus and Egypt to expel the Romans and Greeks. The Gentiles were massacred wholesale. The rising spread to the banks of the Euphrates, and required two of the ablest generals of the Empire to suppress it.

Thereafter Hadrian, who had governed Syria under Trajan and succeeded him as Emperor, went so far as to forbid the practice of circumcision. Judaism, threatened with extinction, prepared itself for one final struggle for existence. In A.D. 130 Hadrian visited Palestine and ordered a Roman city to be built from the ruins of Jerusalem under the name of Aelia Capitolina, which no Jew was permitted to enter under pain of death. A furious rebellion broke out in Judea headed by a priest Eleazar and one Simon, surnamed Bar-Kokeba ('Son of the Star of Messianic prophecy'), who claimed to be the anointed of God. The Jews defended a large number of subterranean strongholds. The Romans stormed as many as fifty of these. More than half a million Jews are said to have perished in the struggle. Nearly every village in

Judea had to be occupied by troops. When order was at length restored, the name of the country was changed to Syria Palestina (the land of the Philistines), and for close on eighteen centuries Judaism was deprived of its local habitation. In the end, the edict forbidding circumcision was confined to proselytes, and Judaism, accepting the compromise, became the least propagandist of all religions which have since been practised in Europe. The vision of a monarch sprung from the root of Jesse, administering to a Gentile world the laws given by Jehovah to Moses, was lost to the Jews in the dark ages. It had entered their dreams through the ivory gate.

NOTES

[1] Mommsen, *The Provinces of the Roman Empire*, vol. ii. pp. 187-8.
[2] Josephus, *Antiquities of the Jews*, Book XVIII. chap. i. (Whiston's translation), pp. 376-7.
[3] Josephus, *op. cit.* Book XVIII. chap. iii. p. 379.
[4] Acts ii. 9, 10.
[5] 1 Peter ii. 13-17; Romans xiii. 1-7.

CHAPTER XVII

CONTACT OF JEWISH AND GREEK IDEAS IN PALESTINE

As our minds dwell on the tragedy described in the previous chapter we are apt to forget how small was the theatre in which it was staged. The south-eastern portion of England from Hull in the north to Brighton in the south, and from Oxford, Leicester and Nottingham east to the North Sea, represents an area approximately equal to that covered by Galilee, Samaria and Judea. To the north was Syria, in which Greek civilisation was firmly established with its centre at Antioch. Jerusalem with the country surrounding it was the fortress of Judaism. In and about Galilee Greek and Semitic civilisation intermingled and overlapped. Like Ireland or the Balkans in modern times, this region was fertile in militant movements. West of the lake of Gennesareth was a population forcibly converted to Judaism by the Maccabees a century before the Christian era, who had come to regard their adopted religion with the zeal of proselytes. The shores of the lake were dotted by Greek colonies. East and south of it were the cities of Decapolis.

This term denoted, not a homogeneous stretch of country, but a league of Greek cities. Each of these had its own territory, stretching in some cases over a considerable area; each its own constitution, its rights, and privileges. Their boundaries would be settled by tradition or by definite deed and grants. They might have acquired, by treaty, rights of water or pasturage. They were associated with one another by common interests and obligations. But the different cities did not necessarily march with one another, and they were separated by territory which belonged to the tetrarchy.

The majority of these cities had been founded in the early days of the Macedonian conquest, they had suffered from the religious zeal of the Maccabees, and they most of them owed their freedom to Pompey, from whose expedition they dated their era. A league of Greek cities in the midst of a barbarian and unsympathetic population, they were bound together by their common Hellenism, by Hellenic culture, life, and religion.

The cities of the Decapolis were Scythopolis, the ancient Bethshan on the western side of the Jordan, guarding the entrance to the Plain of Esdraelon; on the eastern side Hippus, Gadara, and Pella, whose territories were contiguous; on the road which ran south from Pella were Dium, Gerasa, and Philadelphia—the ancient Rabbath Ammon; on the road west from Gadara, Raphana and Kanatha, which lay at the foot of the Jebel Hauran; finally, to the north was Damascus.

The sites of these cities are remarkable at the present day for the striking ruins of the empire that they preserve. Their theatres, their amphitheatres, their temples still stand in ruined magnificence; their aqueducts stretch for miles across the country; their bridges and their roads survive as memorials of a past when the country was civilized; their great columned streets may still be traced; at Gerasa there are still 200 columns standing. One may wander still among the side streets, and see the remains of shop and store and private dwelling-place.

They were strongholds of Hellenism in a Jewish land. Their gods were Greek—Zeus and Pallas, Heracles, Dionysus, Artemis; their language was Greek; they were the homes of men famous in Greek literature. From Gadara came Philodemus the epicurean, Meleager the epigrammatist, Menippus the satirist, Theodorus the rhetorician. Galilee, says Josephus, was surrounded by foreign nations. It is not without significance that within sight of the Sea of Galilee, on the hills above the valley of the Jordan, might be seen the signs of the religion and culture of the Greek world, and that Greek language and thought were permeating even Jewish life.[1]

From Scythopolis or Gadara to Nazareth, near the centre of Galilee, the distance is about twenty miles, less than from Oxford to Reading. Hippus is ten miles from Capernaum. From that town or from Tiberias a boat could reach the Greek city in an afternoon. Another comparison from the British Isles will help us to keep the topography in mind. Make a transparent tracing of Ireland and superimpose it on Palestine, with Lough Neagh exactly over Gennesareth. The Lough will fit the lake like an oblong frame round an oval mirror. Tyrone will rest on the hills of Galilee, while Antrim and Down will roughly cover the region of Decapolis. The name of Dublin will be read about ten miles south of Jerusalem. The one is eighty miles south of Lough Neagh, the other seventy miles south of Gennesareth.

The Zealot movement had sprung from Galilee. Its founder Judas had aspired to emulate his namesake 'the Hammer', and Jesus was old enough to remember his death on the cross. His blood, like that of the Maccabees, had nourished the seeds of the revolt; and as Jesus grew to manhood, the Zealot movement was fermenting in and about Nazareth. 'The Kingdom of God' was its whispered watchword. Amongst his friends were in all probability youths who hoped to see it accomplished, or at least to suffer and die for the cause. We know that a Zealot called Simon was converted by Jesus to peaceful ways and numbered amongst the apostles.

Greek culture and paganism, protected by Rome on the shores of Gennesareth, was a constant irritant to the Jews of Galilee, and they to the Greeks. A region where opposite systems of life are approaching their conflict is a hotbed of ideas. In such a society first principles are eagerly canvassed by young and old, and by all classes. A typical discussion of this kind was in 1891 published by Professor Firth under the auspices of the Camden Society. It consists of the shorthand notes of a debate held at Putney on October 25, 1647, between

Ireton, Cromwell and the Levellers of the Puritan army. It is worth consulting by a reader who does not happen to have listened to ordinary men discussing the first principles of society in the crisis of a revolution.[2]

We are safe in assuming that the principles and merits of Jewish and Greek civilisation were the chief subject of discussion in Galilee during the first thirty years of the Christian era. Conventional pictures of Jesus, calmly maturing his thoughts in the quiet and retirement of rustic seclusion, are at variance with obvious facts. Such conditions could no more exist in the Galilee of that time than they could in our own, in Tyrone or Fermanagh. From the rising of Judas to the fall of Jerusalem the valleys where Jesus spent his youth were a furnace of revolution. He analysed life and studied its elements in a crucible white with heat.

"And in those days cometh John the Baptist, preaching in the wilderness of Judea, saying, Repent ye; for the Kingdom of Heaven is at hand." A typical ascetic of the East, John "had his raiment of camel's hair and a leathern girdle about his loins; and his food was locusts and wild honey". According to Josephus, John

> was a good man, and commanded the Jews to exercise virtue, both as to righteousness towards one another, and piety towards God, and so to come to baptism; for that the washing would be acceptable to him, if they made use of it, not in order to the putting away of some sins but for the purification of the body: supposing still that the soul was thoroughly purified beforehand by righteousness. Now when others came to crowd about him, for they were greatly moved by hearing his words, Herod, who feared lest the great influence John had over the people might put it into his power and inclination to raise a rebellion, (for they seemed ready to do anything he should advise,) thought it best, by putting him to death, to prevent any mischief he might cause, and not bring himself into difficulties, by

sparing a man who might make him repent of it when it should be too late.[3]

In the Gospel narratives we find nothing to justify the fears and suspicions of Herod. Like the prophets before him, John was preaching a moral and spiritual reform. The divine kingdom was not to be realised by priests exploiting a costly ritual or by bandits committing the wildest excesses in the name of God. His own mission, he announced, was limited to these preparatory reforms. The nation when reformed would be led to its goal by another.

"The voice crying in the wilderness" drew Jesus from his home in Galilee to the Jordan valley, and the prophet saw in his young disciple the leader for whom he was looking. The son of a humble mechanic was presented by the teacher of his choice, and the foremost man of his time, to followers drawn from the finest elements in the country, as the leader predestined to fulfil the promise of ages.

In discussing first principles with friends of his age it is likely that Jesus had grown to be conscious of his own exceptional powers. He had probably realised his capacity for handling the revolutionary movement, if he chose to do so, a genius for leadership which his calm, cheerful and balanced nature had perhaps obscured from his own family. A time had now come when he felt himself called to tasks other than those of a joiner. But with knowledge of his own powers was coupled an unusual sense of responsibility as to their use. Before adopting the rôle of leader his mind was intent on defining the cause to which he would ask others as well as himself to devote their lives. To one who saw no virtue in hatred the Kingdom of God, as conceived by men destined to involve the whole nation in ruin, might well give pause. That subterranean fire was to end by choking its own crater in ashes. The ardour which Jesus brought to his task was calm as sunlight and as pregnant with life. He was none the less of an age when a man's passions and intellect, both fully developed, raise his ambitions to the spring tide. He knew himself able to make the most of the career opening before him. A time was to come when John felt some doubts on the subject. While perceiving the greatness of his young disciple, the ascetic did not perhaps understand the depths of a nature which could leave nothing unquestioned. To a mind so constituted it was necessary to know the end and be sure of knowing it before concerting the means. The end in truth must determine the means. So Jesus withdrew to the desert to consider in communion with God what course to pursue—to face the crisis of a great decision. "And straightway", writes our oldest authority, Mark, "the Spirit driveth him forth into the wilderness and he was in the wilderness forty days tempted of Satan; and he was with the wild beasts; and the angels ministered unto him".[4]

NOTES

[1] Headlam, *Life and Teaching of Jesus Christ*, pp. 73-5.

[2] Quoted by A. D. Lindsay, LL.D., Master of Balliol, in *The Essentials of Democracy*, pp. 11, 12.

[3] Josephus, *Antiquities of the Jews*, Book XVIII. chap. v. § 2.

[4] Mark i. 12, 13.

CHAPTER XVIII

THE GATE OF HORN

THE evangelist Matthew, who was not satisfied with the highly abbreviated narrative of Mark, has reproduced the version quoted at the end of the previous chapter; but before the last words he inserted a story which he evidently felt must also be placed on record:

> Then was Jesus led up of the Spirit into the wilderness to be tempted of the devil. And when he had fasted forty days and forty nights, he afterward hungered. And the tempter came and said unto him, If thou art the Son of God, command that these stones become bread. But he answered and said, It is written, Man shall not live by bread alone, but by every word that proceedeth out of the mouth of God. Then the devil taketh him into the holy city; and he set him on the pinnacle of the temple, and saith unto him, If thou art the Son of God, cast thyself down: for it is written, He shall give his angels charge concerning thee: And on their hands they shall bear thee up, Lest haply thou dash thy foot against a stone. Jesus said unto him, Again it is written, Thou shalt not tempt the Lord thy God. Again, the devil taketh him unto an exceeding high mountain, and sheweth him all the kingdoms of the world, and the glory of them; and he said unto him, All these things will I give thee, if thou wilt fall down and worship me. Then saith Jesus unto him, Get thee hence, Satan: for it is written, Thou shalt worship the Lord thy God, and him only shalt thou serve. Then the devil leaveth him; and behold, angels came and ministered unto him.[1]

It is now recognised by scholars that we have in this story, as recorded by Matthew and again by Luke, a parable in which Jesus had tried to convey to his followers the nature of the spiritual conflict through which he had passed in these weeks of retirement. To himself and his hearers Satan was a very real person, and indeed continued as such to Christians till far on in the nineteenth century. So the parable was long accepted as a record of a real adventure which had taken place between Satan and Jesus in the hungry desert. When its real character is recognised as a parable, in which Jesus was trying to explain a spiritual conflict, and when we hold in mind the political conditions, described in the previous chapters, in which that conflict was taking place, we shall see in this story material for genuine biography.

Jesus had grown to manhood in Galilee in the heart of the Zealot movement, in frequent contact with fanatics who believed with all the ardour of youth that their people were destined to rule the world. Some of them had died, and more were willing to die, for that cause. He thought of the kingdoms of the world and the glory of them, all united in subjection to Romans and Greeks. He had always been taught to regard them as 'lesser breeds without the law', usurping the heritage destined by God for his chosen people, but denied them as yet by reason of their sins. Judea was only the nucleus of a race spread through the whole Empire, with vast financial resources and powerful allies beyond its confines. The elements of a great movement were there ready for a leader to combine and direct them; but Israel had produced no leader of its own since the days of the Maccabees. The carpenter's son was conscious of gifts higher than theirs. He must have reflected that the founder of the dynasty which inspired the hopes of his people had tended sheep on the hills of Judea.

Humility is a question of knowing the truth about oneself, and history has proved that the estimate made by this humblest of men of his own powers was right. His judgement of himself is final proof of this amazing capacity which Jesus had of seeing things as they really are.

Gifts like these devoted to leading the Jewish revolt against Graeco-Roman civilisation would have changed the current of history—how far we can only conjecture. The relations of Europe and Asia to each other and the rest of the world would be other than they now are. In the forty years which had yet to pass till Jerusalem lay a heap of ruins and Judea desolate of her people, some massacred by the Romans, more by each other, the survivors deported to the cities of the Empire as slaves on the public works, as prostitutes in the stews, as victims for slaughter in the amphitheatres, the Jewish revolution was not destined to produce anyone deserving the name of leader. No one appeared who was capable of realising the latent resources of Judaism, in the counsels of state or the field of war. With a single exception the actors in this tragedy are known only by students of history. If the name of Josephus the apostate is more widely remembered, it is only because it was blown through the great trumpet which he himself made for that purpose. The qualities conspicuously lacking in the bandits whose violence worked the ruin of their cause, and in priests, whose right hands ministered to Rome while their left trafficked with the Zealots, were exactly those which distinguished the character of Jesus—a freedom from superstition amazing in that age, a sense of realities, the knowledge that faith is wiser than treachery, that love is a bond stronger than fear; intuition, with that coolness of judgement which together mean rapid and right decision; a perfect control of his own passions; inexhaustible patience, and infinite capacity for loyalty to a cause. His courage was finer than that of the Zealots: with lesser gifts Hannibal had shaken the foundations of Rome; and Jerusalem enshrined ideals higher than those of Carthage. It offered an ideal centre from which to organise a people whose colonies had penetrated the civilised world from east to west.

The great temptation is no idle phantasm, but a picture of the truth drawn by the hand of an artist. The conflict fought in that hungry waste was great as the mind which faced and settled it. Its positive issues were destined in time to affect the whole development of human reason. But that is not all. The negative issues, the great refusal to lead the impending revolution, vitally affected the events of history from that moment.

What enabled this young Galilean to reject a career which was noble as measured by every standard of his time, which the world would still feel was heroic, which Napoleon would have chosen without any struggle? We can only infer that his mind was endowed with a sense of values finer than that given to anyone else who, before or since, has been called to play so great a part in human affairs. He evidently asked himself what end would in fact be achieved, even if the forces of Jewish enthusiasm, disciplined and directed by himself, succeeded in imposing orthodox Judaism on civilised society. In declaring the unity of God, Judaism had given the world the most vital of truths. It was now telling the world that the will of God could only be fulfilled by the observance of an ever-increasing system of rules and rites, a routine which deadened the conscience and blinded the soul. It presented God in a false relation to men, and did little to suggest the vital importance of human relations, of the attitude of men one to another. They were taught to think of these rules and this ritual as instituted and ordained by divine authority. Men had yet to realise that each has for himself in his conscience a continuous revelation of the will of God, of right and wrong, which is dulled by neglect and brightened by exercise. Human nature, to grow to its fullness, must learn to draw on its own resources. The priests and Pharisees were for ever elaborating new rules and binding on men burdens too grievous to be borne. To call upon men to discard these rules and to begin thinking and acting for themselves was the task to which Jesus decided to devote his powers. He felt himself able to enunciate the principles upon which any order of society which really deserved to be called the Kingdom of God must be based.

From the parable recorded by Matthew and Luke it is clear that Jesus had in his youth felt himself drawn to throw in his lot with the Zealot movement. The story also records his deliberate and final renouncement of that idea. The Kingdom of God on earth as conceived by the Zealots was a nightmare from which he awoke. He also had dreams, dreams which had entered his brain through the gate of horn, that common material which in Homer's mind had stood for realities and sober sense.

NOTE

[1] Matthew iv. 1-11.

CHAPTER XIX

THE GATE OF HORN (*continued*)

THE story suggests another and no less amazing renouncement. Jesus of Nazareth moved in a world which assumed that original truths are divinely revealed and cannot be found for itself by the human mind. The Mosaic law derived its authority from the unquestioned belief that its actual words had been learned by Moses from the lips of God. The prophets were inspired. The truths they uttered were breathed into their minds. The underlying assumption was that vital truths could only be known in the first instance by supernatural means. It was natural to suppose, therefore, that God would also employ supernatural signs to indicate the messengers of his choice. They must be expected to show their credentials by affording ocular proof of miraculous powers. The working of miracles was a necessary credential.

In discussing this all-important matter, I must be at pains to show what I mean by the word 'miracle' even at the cost of a lengthy digression. A miracle implies an effect produced by mind on matter beyond the limits of normal experience. The mind can set in motion the limbs of the body and direct their action. We know that in doing this it acts through the brain, nerves and muscles. But how that spiritual reality, the mind, acts on the matter of the brain we can never know till mind is able to explain itself, which is in the nature of things impossible. From the point at which the matter of the brain receives the spiritual impulse and transmits it through the nerves to the muscles, the process is one susceptible of study and inquiry. Cause and effect appear to operate as in physical nature. By studying these causes and effects the spirit of man has altered the state of this earth to what it now is, as contrasted from what it would be if it did not contain animals capable of reasoned thought.

This effect of spirit on the matter of the brain is not described as a miracle because, though it cannot be explained, we know by experience that it happens. We also know the limits within which it occurs, and whatever is outside those limits is described as a miracle. I know by experience that if my mind so wills, my hand can remove a molehill. I also know that large hills, if not actual mountains, have been removed at will by the use of explosives and machinery, agencies designed and created for the purpose through knowledge acquired by long study of cause and effect. The thing may be seen happening in American towns like Seattle, where large hills have been bodily removed and thrown into the neighbouring sea. But if one individual had accomplished their removal by a mere exercise of will, such as enables him to move his hand, the removal would properly be described as miraculous.

In an age when the causes of physical phenomena, earthquakes and storms, eclipses and plagues, were not understood, it was natural to suppose that God acted in this way upon nature. It was equally natural to suppose that he conferred on his human agents powers of acting on matter by a mere exercise of the will, and, indeed, would do so to mark them as such. One has merely to recall one's own childhood to realise the extent to which ideas of this order fascinate the natural mind. A modern child in his day-dreams weaves plans for building cities, creating fleets of ships, driving tunnels or erecting bridges, and thinks of prodigious results brought to pass by a mere exercise of will more easily than he makes a castle on the sand with his hands. In the same way the author of the Apocalypse sees vast cosmic forces set in motion merely by an exercise of will, without the slightest idea of interposing between the thing as willed and accomplished a laborious chain of cause and effect.

Before men acquired the habit of studying the facts of nature, the occurrence of miracles was accepted as a matter of course, and still is where that habit has not been acquired or is simply ignored. The further nature is studied the more does its course seem to follow a sequence of cause and effect. To such an extent has this happened that the whole system of civilised society is now based on the assumption that miracles do not in fact occur. If a court were asked by a witness to accept some occurrence as a miracle and therefore by nature beyond explanation, the judge would refuse to believe him, or if he believed him would be superseded by higher authority as unfit for his office. To an ever-increasing extent our existence is based on the assumption that, given certain conditions, gas, heat or electric current will behave in a certain way, and yield constant results. An accident arising from apparent failure in those results is accepted as proof of some variation in the previous conditions. Inquiry is instituted as to what the variation was and how it occurred, with the practical object of controlling its recurrence. The intricate machinery, by virtue of which alone masses of men now work and eat their daily bread, is the fruit of an infinite number of such inquiries all based on the assumption that nature follows a regular sequence of cause and effect.

So vast is the cumulative evidence on this matter that the onus of proving a miracle must rest on those who believe it to have happened. In dealing with miracles recorded in all sincerity by an ancient writer, the historian observes the same principles as the judge in a modern court. He may use it as evidence of something normal which really happened, as when Rawlinson attributes the destruction of Sennacherib's army before Jerusalem to an outbreak of plague. He may quote it to explain a view taken by the author or by the actors in the events he describes. He would never allow that something had happened outside or contrary to the order of nature. He applies to ancient events exactly the same standards as are used by judges in analysing evidence of recent events.

The practice of methodical inquiry which has led to this attitude of mind originated with the Greeks. It had, however, made little impression on the Jewish society in which Jesus moved. When the nature of his teaching was realised in its fatal effect on current belief, his opponents instantly claimed that he should prove his authority by working a miracle.

> And the Pharisees and Sadducees came, and tempting him asked him to shew them a sign from heaven. But he answered and said unto them, When it is evening, ye say, It will be fair weather: for the heaven is red. And in the morning, It will be foul weather to-day: for the heaven is red and lowring. Ye know how to discern the face of the heaven; but ye cannot discern the signs of the times. An evil and adulterous generation seeketh after a sign; and there shall no sign be given unto it, but the sign of Jonah.[1]
>
> *i.e.* As Jonah preached repentance to the Gentiles with success, so a time will come when the Gentiles will hear and accept the Gospel, while Israel will reject it.[2]

These beliefs, however, were not confined to the hierarchy. They were so universal and engrained in the minds of all about him that his followers continued to assume that the validity of his teaching must be attested by wondrous works. The records from which we have now to discover what the real nature of that teaching was were preserved and collected by people whose minds were saturated with these views. They perceived in their hearts, as we also perceive, that here was one uttering priceless truths. They assumed, however, as we have no right to assume, that he must as a matter of course have miraculous powers.

It is clear that the person of Jesus commanded in those not biased by prejudice or interest against his teaching an unparalleled measure of devotion and reverence. Unlike Socrates, he impressed, not only a small circle of disciples, but whole multitudes in this way, and to such an extent that the enthusiasm they showed often endangered his safety with the civil authorities. To-day in the east, a teacher who makes this kind of impression not seldom acquires a reputation for miraculous power without desiring to do so. Indeed a teacher in whom was combined profound wisdom and purity of life with all the magnetic gifts of a leader would find himself powerless to arrest the growth of such legends. The writer has seen the thing happen to the saintliest woman it was ever his privilege to meet. Her story was told me by her son, a gifted and cultured Indian with whom I had formed an intimate friendship in the western hemisphere. For some time after her marriage his mother had remained childless. At length, in the anguish of her mind she recalled a picture of the crucified Christ circulated by Jesuit missionaries, which she happened to have seen. It occurred to her mind that a suffering God might grant what her own deities had denied, so she prayed to this unknown deity that a child might be given her, vowing that if her prayers were answered, the child should be dedicated to his service. Presently my friend was born, and she found herself faced by the question in what manner to fulfil her vow, cut off as she was from the world by all the restrictions that surround a high-caste woman in purdah. So determined, however, was the lady that her vow should not go unfulfilled that one day, in the absence of her husband, she escaped with the child in her arms, and made her way alone into the house of a Methodist missionary who lived in the English lines. The mental anguish involved in such a proceeding can only be understood by those who know what the restrictions of purdah in Indian families mean.

The missionary, to whom she explained her case, properly hesitated to baptize the child without the knowledge and consent of his father. But such was the urgency of the mother that at length he yielded, and baptized the child in his own house. The mother then wrote to her husband confessing what she had done. On receiving her letter, he instantly returned from a great distance and employed Brahmins to perform the elaborate and expensive ceremonies which were necessary to restore his son to the caste destroyed by initiation to another religion.

His mother, however, felt that her vow must be kept in the spirit as well as the letter. As the child grew she taught him to regard himself as dedicated to the God of suffering, and herself adopted the Christian religion. By the sheer force of her own conviction she eventually converted her husband. So my friend's brothers and sisters were also brought up in the Christian faith.

Some years after my friend had told me this story, I joined him in India at the place where he then lived with his family. I had to face with him a highly distasteful task, and as we set out to keep our appointment he told me that his mother was devoting the day to prayer that our work might be fruitful of good. When the task upon which we were bent was done he took me to his home, where I met his mother, for the first and only time, together with her husband and the rest of the family. In the few hours that I spent with them she was mainly busied with graceful duties of hospitality, but none the less she created an impression that here was a soul in continuous communion with God. When the time came for me to go, she signified the wish that I should go to a room apart with herself and her son for prayer.

Some months later, when a guest at the house of the Metropolitan, I found myself sitting next a bishop of one of those ancient Syrian churches in southern India which look to St. Thomas himself as their founder, a striking figure in a simple cassock of pure white. I addressed him with respect, and he soon impressed me as a person of great culture and profound sincerity. It presently appeared that the lady referred to in the last paragraph was well known to him. After emphasising the sanctity of her character he added quite simply, "She performs miracles, as you doubtless know". I replied that I had not heard this, and he then told me that some religious friends had happened to wait on her when by chance there was no food in the house. Quite undisturbed by the fact, she placed a pot on the coals, and when it boiled and the lid was removed it was found to be filled with rice ready to be eaten. This gifted and cultivated Indian bishop had no more doubts on the subject than Mark when he first recorded the story of the loaves and fishes as told him by Peter.

I have not published this story without submitting the proofs to my Indian friend. On reading the proofs he assured me with invincible sincerity that the Indian bishop was perfectly right. "We often had no food in the house; but my mother was never perturbed. She simply filled a vessel with water, put it on the fire, and when it had boiled and the lid was removed, food for her family was there." My own explanation of his statement is that the lady was always careful to keep reserves unknown to the family. When the time for the meal arrived her children found food in the pot though they knew of none in the house and ascribed to their wonderful mother miraculous powers without her knowing that they thought she had worked a miracle.

Such anecdotes could be multiplied to any extent from the experiences of those who have sojourned in Asia. They show how absurd it is to impute conscious invention or fraud to those who ascribe miraculous acts to teachers they love and revere. We have only to turn to the New Testament books to see such stories in course of development. As compared with the other evangelists, Mark, the earliest of the four, seems to attach more importance to the miracles than to the teaching of Jesus. The story of how Jesus sent two disciples to prepare for the last supper is told in a manner which suggests that he had supernatural knowledge.[3] The author of Matthew's gospel, in copying Mark's narrative, omits all such suggestions.[4] More striking still is the story of Eutychus as told by Luke,[5] because here the writer was himself an eye-witness of the incident he relates. Eutychus fell from a window, and when he was picked up came to his senses in the arms of Paul. But Luke is so sure that the great apostle is a worker of miracles that he says that Eutychus was actually dead. With naïve fidelity to truth he records that when Eutychus opened his eyes Paul said, "Make ye no more ado; for his life is in him". And so in the story of the shipwreck, when the snake leapt out of a bundle of sticks and seized Paul by the hand, the natives assumed that he must presently swell and fall down dead. But when he shook the snake off into the fire and took no hurt they presently thought he was a god. The habits of the snake described by Luke are exactly those of the coronella, a tree snake which lurks in bundles of sticks. Though perfectly harmless it has the terrifying habit of leaping from its lair and seizing the hands of people who are gathering firewood. It is well known in the New Forest, and is found in Malta.

Like country folk elsewhere the natives of Malta believed all snakes to be venomous.

In recent years medical science has come to recognise how largely the physical health of a patient is affected by the state of his mind. A power which some great physicians have of influencing the minds of their patients is regarded as a side of their professional equipment. There are recognised practitioners who specialise in the treatment of health by working on the mind. There are people with strong serene personalities who have the faculty of improving health by influencing sufferers to forget themselves and ailments which are not really organic, but which might become so if a state of distress were allowed to continue. The cures undoubtedly worked in cases of this kind by M. Coué, a simple and kindly French apothecary, if done in the east, would quickly breed a whole cycle of legends. It is clear from the records that Jesus had a power of self-control, a calmness of mind and a joy in life and sympathy with others developed in marked contrast to the tragic and high-strung people amongst whom he moved. They always thought of his teaching as a gospel, that is to say, good news, and as they listened to it forgot their ailments, and thought themselves healed by miraculous power. Such stories would grow by leaps and bounds as they passed from mouth to mouth, till wide circles came to believe that he had given sight to men born blind and restored the dead to life.

It is usual to draw a sharp distinction between miracles ascribed to Jesus, and acts of magic such as that told of Elisha when he is said to have made iron to float, and so reversed the evident physical law that a body must sink so long as its weight is greater than the body of water it displaces. The story of Jesus walking on the water involves a reversal of natural laws equally great. And so do the stories of raising the dead to life. It is possible to restore life when the lungs and even the heart have ceased to act, if an impulse sufficient to restart their action can be given in time. But unless this is done quickly the arteries empty and the blood solidifies in the veins which connect them with the heart. The restoration to life of a man who has really died several hours before, involves magical changes in physical conditions just as crude as the floating of iron in water, but more multifarious.

When in plain and gracious words Jesus expressed truths which went to the root of human problems, multitudes of simple folk felt them as such. So ordinary men recognise poetry and music in so far as they themselves are in a measure poets and musicians. The divine intuitions of Jesus were seen to be such, because in the minds of average men is implanted a sense of divine intuition. Their hearts were stirred as the strings of an instrument vibrate to the tones of a mighty voice. But they could not escape the traditional belief that as truths so striking could only be revealed to a teacher by supernatural means, he must be expected to display supernatural powers. They remarked the amazing influence that he exercised on others, especially in calming troubled and disordered minds, and related them as miracles of healing. As they passed from mouth to mouth such stories grew beyond all recognition, and the same process applied to striking examples of practical ability and foresight, such as Jesus showed when he thoughtfully provided for the feeding of crowds who had followed him to a lonely place to listen to his teaching.

The idea that a spiritual truth can be proved by a physical miracle was itself the deepest and most comprehensive of all superstitions, and one which persists to our own time. That right differs from wrong, the most fundamental of all truths, involves the hypothesis that the souls of men exist independent of time and space and are indestructible as matter itself. That belief is implicit in the teaching of Jesus. He said that the return of one from the dead would not of itself avail to convince the world of such truths. A little reflection will show that the return to life of any number of dead men would in no way prove the immortality of the soul. An age which knows that this earth will in time be unable to support any form of life has less excuse for persisting in such beliefs.

The story of the temptation shows that Jesus, before he embarked on his public career, had consciously made up his mind to resist the ingrained belief of his hearers that the truths he taught must be proved by miracles. From first to last the appeal that he made was to the conscience of ordinary men and to that alone. The theory of Renan that in practice he found it necessary to establish his position by conscious pandering to the current belief that he worked miracles, in fact by a few conjuring tricks, is contrary to evidence contained in the records. His public career was amazingly brief and covered at most some two and a half years. Its events and his sayings were not written down as we now have them till some thirty-five years after his death; for his followers believed that he had promised to return to them during their lives. The stories were told and retold till a whole generation had passed without his return. The circle of those interested in his life and teaching vastly increased, while those who had seen and heard him dwindled in number. A demand naturally developed for some record, and Mark, who shared to the full the predisposition of his race and age to believe in miracles, reduced to writing his own understanding of what Peter had told him. His gospel was probably written at Rome. When his work was read in the churches of Syria it was realised that Mark had omitted a great body of teaching which was there remembered. This teaching was added, and in order to make room for it in a roll of papyrus of the usual length, the stories of Mark were freely condensed. And so appeared the gospel issued under the name of Matthew. Luke, who had met the apostles at Jerusalem, and had spent two years at Caesarea with Paul, repeated the process. He used the writings of Mark and Matthew, but added a large body of tradition collected by himself from other sources. The fourth gospel was composed at or near Ephesus, on the lowest computation not earlier than two generations after the death of Jesus, a work in which dramatic and poetic elements are uppermost, and narrative is subordinated to the doctrines which the evangelist is writing to establish.

Earlier even than Mark are fragmentary statements contained in the epistles of Paul. Not one of these writers, not even Paul, one of the greatest of thinkers, was able to escape from the prepossession of the age in which they lived, or to see, as their Master had seen, that conceptions of ultimate truth cannot be supported by ocular proof, that they are of the nature of postulates, hypotheses necessary to account for our sense of the worth and meaning of life, that they are of the nature of faith which proves itself by practical effect.

Yet no one can read these records without realising how perfectly sincere not only the writers were, but also those whose memories had preserved the things they wrote. The best proof of this is the constant recurrence of sayings which they did not realise were contrary to beliefs so deeply imbedded in their own minds that they could not help imputing them to their great teacher. They repeatedly tell us how Jesus adjured those whom his influence had brought to a better state of health not to publish the fact abroad. If he really agreed with his followers that his mission was proved by his mighty works, it was surely his duty and theirs that these works should 'shine before men'. But when we remember the story of the temptation, which must have been told them by himself, and his condemnation of the demand that he should prove his mission by signs, his injunctions of silence can be only interpreted as a conscious effort on his part to prevent the good he was able to do to the health of overwrought followers from being noised abroad and exaggerated into stories that he proved his teaching by an exercise of magical powers. We know that he failed, and his early death, and its circumstances, clearly contributed to the failure.

I have no doubt in my own mind that Jesus believed, not only in miracles, but in his own power to cure the sick by miraculous means. In that age it could scarcely be otherwise. His refusal to prove his mission by 'signs' shows that he had seen that moral truths cannot be proved like physical truths by any phenomena. Such truths can only be recognised by each for himself in his own conscience. The belief that our choice between right and wrong is fraught with consequences which have no limit, that the world of spirit is indestructible and exists outside the limits of time, in a word, that souls are immortal, cannot be proved by evidence that a man has risen from the dead. Such evidence can prove only that the human spirit can continue in time for some period after the body is dead. By the irony of fate his followers believed that the doctrine of immortality could only be proved by a man rising from his grave or in some way convincing the senses of living friends that his personality was still in existence. A great body of Christians are to this day in the clutch of that fallacy.

I read the story of the temptation as recorded by Matthew and Luke as meaning that Jesus, believing in miracles and in his own power to work them, had felt himself tempted to appeal to these powers as proving the truths which he had to utter. The parable of his struggle with Satan in the desert records his conquest of that temptation.

NOTES

[1] Matthew xvi. 1-4.
[2] *A New Commentary on Holy Scripture.* Note on Matthew xii. 39.
[3] Mark xiv. 13-16.
[4] Matthew xxvi. 18, 19.
[5] Acts xx. 9, 10.

CHAPTER XX

THE COMMONWEALTH OF GOD

AMONG them that are born of women there hath not arisen a greater than John the Baptist: yet he that is but little in the kingdom of heaven is greater than he. And from the days of John the Baptist until now the kingdom of heaven suffereth violence, and men of violence take it by force.[1]

We have seen how the Jewish world in the time of Jesus was possessed by the notion that the Kingdom of God was at hand. We have also seen how differently the nature of this kingdom was conceived. The Zealots were looking for subversion of the Roman Empire by physical force, aided perhaps by a miracle, and the final establishment of Judaism as a world power. Herod, misled by his own fears, had seen in John a possible leader for this dangerous movement. The words we have quoted above suggest that the Zealot idea of a kingdom to be won by physical force was gaining ground.

It is also clear from these words that the Kingdom of Heaven, as conceived by Jesus, was something different from the Kingdom of Heaven as conceived by John, and that Jesus was now aware of this difference. We know that John and his followers were also aware of this difference. Like the Essenes they taught and practised asceticism,[2] a practice which Jesus openly renounced. He was seen enjoying the pleasures of life with all sorts and conditions of men. He said of himself that he "came eating and drinking", while John had abstained even from bread and wine. This was probably the reason why John had sent two of his disciples to ask Jesus, "Art thou he that should come, or do we look for another?"[3] He consciously and deliberately discarded the asceticism practised by John, and in so doing rejected the whole system of thought which regards matter, and therefore the sense of matter, and pleasure in things of sense as evil. The notion that merit can be earned merely by suffering pain is the necessary consequence of that view. Indifference to pain endured by others is a further corollary. He rejected in terms the belief that things material, whether touched or tasted, could of themselves defile the soul. Such teaching was an open challenge to the Jewish law which governed the intimate details of life.

Without some time spent in the east it is difficult to realise how deeply the view that matter and sense are evil permeates thought in those regions. In adopting a life contrary to that view Jesus was erecting the most stubborn of obstacles to his own acceptance in eastern society as a teacher of truth. More than any other thing that we know of him it shows how great was his courage and capacity for original thought. As one of his own race has said in these days, "a greater than Aristotle" is here.[4] So much importance was attached in his mind to this view that he ended by making the simple act of breaking bread and drinking wine the only ordinance which he asked his followers to observe. Food was the substance of flesh, drink of the blood which flowed in the veins. He bade his followers revere their bodies as good in themselves, as the temple of God.

Things of the sense are for enjoyment; yet such is the paradox of life that the happiness open to men is largely frustrated by regarding these things as its object. The joy of living is marred by overanxiety about them—a thought clothed in words destined to give us the most perfect sentence in English prose:

Consider the lilies of the field, how they grow; they toil not, neither do they spin: and yet I say unto you, that even Solomon in all his glory was not arrayed like one of these.[5]

Food, clothing, home, whatever makes for loveliness and joy would 'be added' if men but learned to seek first the Kingdom of God. They must realise the nature of God in order to know what his kingdom is.

The idea of God which he placed before them was the purified essence of Hebrew thought. The Jews had first given to the world their idea of the one and only God who is also perfectly righteous. They had first seen his relation to men as that of a king to his subjects. Hosea and Jeremiah had seen it as that of a father to sons. But even they still thought of Jehovah as the god of retributive justice. The Jewish conception of God as a father was still limited by the thought of themselves as the children of God, of the Gentiles as somewhere outside that relation. By Jesus God was conceived as a father whose love for his children had no limits. It included the Gentiles as well as the Jews, and indeed all sentient creatures:

Are not two sparrows sold for a farthing? and not one of them shall fall on the ground without your Father.[6]

The essential bond of society which unites men to each other and God is not primarily righteousness, as the prophets had taught, or justice, as Plato had assumed, but the love which results in righteousness and justice. To speak of God as a father, and of men as his children and therefore brethren, was the best image he could draw from physical life to express a spiritual truth. As letters of the alphabet are in origin pictures, so words are images chosen to convey ideas. Our tendency is to overlook the ideas, to dwell on the symbols and reason from them. By so doing, theology has spun the intricate webs which now make it so hard for us to see the significance of the images chosen by Jesus to convey his thoughts.

There is no evidence in our records that Jesus consciously attempted to harmonise eastern with western ideas. In fact he did it by force of an insight which perceived the truths implicit in both; for truths are by their nature consistent. Questioned by one of the scribes:

What commandment is the first of all? Jesus answered, The first is, Hear, O Israel; The Lord our God, the Lord is one; and thou shalt love the Lord thy God with all thy heart, and with all thy soul, and with all thy mind, and with all thy strength. The second is this, Thou shalt love thy neighbour as thyself. There is none other commandment greater than these.[7]

Our word 'love', as used in this context, is somewhat spoiled by its sentimental associations. The attitude of God to men as conceived by Jesus is as an infinite desire to do them good. Of this the most perfect image he could find in nature is the feeling that a parent should have for his own children, and they to him and to one another. An infinite desire to serve God was the attitude proper to men, and this they could only attain by serving each other, by desiring to render such service and placing that desire before all others. In order to develop this desire, men must first see what God is, and also what their neighbour is in his eyes. To love beauty, goodness and truth, is to love God and become like him. In so doing the Kingdom of God will be realised and his will fulfilled. The two ideas are inseparably linked in the prayer he taught his followers: "Thy kingdom come, thy will be done on earth as it is in heaven". This Kingdom of God is a definite system of society to be realised on earth. He did not profess to originate or invent it.

Being asked by the Pharisees, when the kingdom of God cometh, he answered them and said, The kingdom of God cometh not with observation: neither shall they say, Lo, here! or, There! for lo, the kingdom of God is in the midst of you.[8]

The desire of men to serve each other was already existent and capable of infinite expansion. "Ye therefore shall be perfect, as your heavenly Father is perfect."[9] This presumption of the infinite duty owed by men to each other was no idle illusion. He saw it as destined to be realised and made the operative principle of human society. That vital principle, partially realised in the minds of a limited number, is in fact what enables civilised society to exist at all. He compared it to leaven, the tiny ingredient which transforms masses of dough into wholesome bread, or to salt which preserves meat from corruption. Hence the importance that such minorities should be careful to keep their intrinsic property. Let them look to quality and ignore quantity.

On the other hand, the few inspired by these principles must never think of the divine commonwealth as something confined to themselves. For

the kingdom of heaven is like unto a net, that was cast into the sea, and gathered of every kind: which, when it was filled, they drew up on the beach; and they sat down, and gathered the good into vessels, but the bad they cast away.[10]

And he adds, "So shall it be in the consummation of the age". The principle of the commonwealth by its own operation sorts out the good from the bad, preserves the one and discards the other. Trust to experience. Let survival of the fittest operate in the sphere of human institutions. The same idea is reflected in the parable of the wheat and the tares. Beware of thinking that we can at the first glance distinguish the good from the bad. Cast the net, drive the plough, scatter the seed, be tireless in production. In the last resort the good and useful in men and things will survive by its own virtue, and the evil and useless will perish by its own vice and futility. To be tireless in service is also to be patient of results. Over-anxiety for the future, as to whether the work in hand is of permanent value, is expense of spirit and a waste of strength. Serenity is the temper which begets the finest quality in action. The Kingdom of Heaven in its small beginnings has the property of life which spreads without limit.

It is like a grain of mustard seed, which, when it is sown upon the earth, though it be less than all the seeds that are upon the earth, yet when it is sown, groweth up, and becometh greater than all the herbs, and putteth out great branches; so that the birds of the heaven can lodge under the shadow thereof.[11]

It is also a cause to which men will desire to give themselves wholly as they come to realise its nature.

The kingdom of heaven is like unto a treasure hidden in the field; which a man found, and hid; and in his joy he goeth and selleth all that he hath, and buyeth that field,[12]

and

Again, the kingdom of heaven is like unto a man that is a merchant seeking goodly pearls: and having found one pearl of great price, he went and sold all that he had, and bought it.[13]

This theory of an infinite obligation owed by each to all as the bond which unites human society and makes it a living thing, even when realised in part by the few, has nothing in common with the social contract of Hobbes and Rousseau. Attempts to exhibit society as held together by a balance of interests could only succeed if society were static. But in fact it lives and moves; the interests change and the balance is destroyed. To seek your own good is to miss it. As in the system propounded by

Socrates, the rights of men have here no place. But the thoughts of Jesus were conceived at a spot on the map of human society which was in certain respects more central than Athens or Rome. The infinite duty which Socrates conceived as due from himself to his city-state and its members, Jesus conceived as due to a society which included all classes and races of men, to the weak and the young, to the poor and also the rich, to the beggars, outcasts and criminals, to Gentiles no less than Jews:

> They shall come from the east and west, and from the north and south, and shall sit down in the kingdom of God.[14]

And the rules by which their lives are to be ordered are not to be gathered from laws, precedents and traditions, interpreted by kings or priests, regarded as channels of truth divinely ordained. Essential truth is revealed only to those who approach it with minds fresh and receptive as a child's, and as free from preconceived ideas. To be sure that you know is a fatal bar to the growth of knowledge. The real leaders are those who serve and are not afraid to make mistakes by which others as well as themselves will learn. They cannot rule in the Kingdom of God who shrink from responsibility for action; for the truth is only discovered in action and by contact with facts, and when discovered prevails.

The Kingdom of Heaven as Jesus conceived it consisted of men serving God by serving each other, the desire to serve increasing by exercise,[15] and depending for guidance on experience of facts interpreted by reason and conscience. For so and not otherwise could reason and conscience be made to grow, and with their growth the inclusion of all men in one society would become possible. These were the principles which Jesus propounded in the course of a public career which led to his death at the age of thirty. It is idle to speculate as to what he would have said if another thirty years had been given him in which to expound what these principles would mean when applied to the political structure of human society. The profitable task is to see for ourselves, in the light of all the experience gained since his time, how the structure of society must be designed if the principles he stated are to operate in practice. There are certain observations which will help us in this task. We can see, to begin with, that a community, a sufficient proportion of whose members had realised to a certain degree a capacity for putting the interest of others on a level with their own, could govern itself. A community consisting of people all clever as Iago could never govern themselves so long as they maintained his attitude to others. A convict settlement ruled by a governor with the powers of an autocrat would alone restrain them from mutual destruction. On the other hand, an island peopled by Humphry Clinker would begin by governing themselves, and would quickly advance in culture and intelligence. Self-government is primarily a question of character, and the ultimate problem of politics is how to develop that character. A commonwealth is simply the sermon on the mount translated into political terms.

A further observation may be added. A community in which the goodness necessary for self-government is sufficiently developed will lose that goodness unless its structure is organised on the principle of the commonwealth. If forced to submit to autocracy its virtue will decay. This certainly is a lesson of history which points to a practical conclusion. The members of such a society must labour to change its structure to that of a commonwealth. Under real autocracy a society may advance for a time, but will presently come to a standstill, and finally begin to decline. A continuous advance in the welfare of society depends upon a continuous increase of responsibility assumed by its members for controlling their mutual relations. The effect of institutions on those who live under them is immeasurable. Religious and secular teachers have their part to play, and it is an important part. But the claim of churches and schools to be answerable in the first degree for forming the character of a people, a claim supported not seldom by politicians and public officials, is a dangerous fallacy. The most potent factor in raising or lowering the character of a people, in increasing or diminishing their sense of duty to each other, is the structure of the society in which they live. Politics is the art of so adapting that structure as to raise the sense of duty in each to all. All policies and all measures, however commonplace, can be ultimately tested by this criterion. To engender in men a desire to serve each other is the end and object of human existence. Teaching and preaching are necessary to the process, but they yield in the end a harvest of cynicism unless the actual power of men to serve each other is continuously increased as they can bear it.

The application of this criterion cannot be limited to politics in the stricter sense of the term. We have reached an age when human welfare depends as directly on industrial and commercial combinations as on those of the state. At the moment efficiency seems to depend on confining their control to a handful of directors. But we have to remember how recent and novel these combinations are, when viewed in comparison with the ages through which society has come to be what it is. Their permanence and stability will depend upon how far the whole mass of workers can be rendered answerable to society for the services they render. To compass this in the field of commerce and industry is a far more difficult task than to extend responsibility in the field of politics. In the end it will prove to be no less vital; for though personal hope of gain may help to hold together the members of these combinations, it cannot avail to keep them in stable relations to each other or to the whole society of which they are organs. Freedom is in fact the social product of a capacity in individual men to control their desires and direct their conduct to unselfish ends in every aspect of life. The world's problem is how to increase that self-control. Its solution can in fact be found by patient and continuous study of human experience. "Seek, and ye shall find; knock, and it shall be opened unto you." [16] "The price of freedom is eternal vigilance."

The principles of society which Jesus propounded on the hills of Galilee were those of a commonwealth, not of a kingdom. From the nature of the case he had nothing to say as to the mechanism by which those principles had been applied in the past, or might again be applied in the future. A language, moreover, is limited by the ideas of those who use it, and the Jews like other races in the east had no idea what a commonwealth meant. An eminent scholar, the late Dr. Cowley, has informed the writer that the only word to express 'the state' in Aramaic, the language Jesus used, is the equivalent of a 'kingdom', *malkutha*. (The root is the same as in Moloch and also in Malek Rik, the name by which Richard Cœur de Lion was known to the Saracens.) When, some decades after the death of Jesus, the oral traditions which preserved his teaching were recorded in Greek, the Aramaic *malkutha* was translated into the Greek *βασιλεία*, which also means kingdom. But the kind of state which Jesus described would have been properly rendered by the word *πόλις*, of which *civitas* is the Latin equivalent. It was so rendered by St. Augustine in the title of his great treatise *De Civitate Dei*, which was taken as an argument in favour of assimilating the Empire to the Church. Just as in eastern language equivalents of the word *kingdom* had to be used to express a commonwealth, so, under the Roman Empire, *civitas* came to be used to express an autocracy. If regard be had to the meaning which Jesus sought to convey, the words used in our own version of the gospels should be rendered 'the Commonwealth of God'.

The world has agreed to accept Jesus as the founder of a religion with a highly developed theology. In our records of the teaching which was clearly his, his religion is implicit rather than expressed, and is too simple and profound to form the basis of a theological system. His interest centred on men not only in themselves, but in their relations to one another. To him, as to the Greeks, life was a thing of surpassing beauty and value. The key to that value he drew from the faith of his own race. It explained the relation of brotherhood which men were destined to realise. It also supplied a basis for the permanence of life, of its indestructible quality, without which we cannot account for a sense of its worth. In discerning the principles upon which it was based the intuitive perception of Jesus was greater than any mind has ever possessed. So complete was his sense of life as a whole that he never parcelled it out into ethics, politics and religion. He was merely concerned to consider how men should live. The principles he enunciated were on that plane which cannot alter with time or place. And no one will ever succeed in reconciling that teaching with authority, which seeks to balance society like a pyramid on its apex. Society, as conceived by Jesus, is made to stand with its base on the ground of experience as interpreted by the mind and conscience of man, with its point to heaven.

NOTES

[1] Matthew xi. 11, 12.
[2] Mark ii. 18.
[3] Matthew xi. 1-3.

[4] Simkhovitch, *Towards the Understanding of Jesus*, p. 58.
[5] Matthew vi. 28, 29.
[6] Matthew x. 29.
[7] Mark xii. 28-31.
[8] Luke xvii. 20, 21. Marginal reading.
[9] Matthew v. 48.
[10] Matthew xiii. 47, 48.
[11] Mark iv. 31, 32.
[12] Matthew xiii. 44.
[13] Matthew xiii. 45, 46.
[14] Luke xiii. 29.
[15] Matthew xxv. 14-30. The parable of the Talents.
[16] Matthew vii. 7.

CHAPTER XXI

JESUS IN CONFLICT WITH JUDAISM

ACCOUNTS of the new teaching and of its popular reception in the north reached Jerusalem and occasioned uneasiness in official circles. Emissaries sent to look into the matter reported to the Sanhedrin that the young reformer was challenging the authority of the scribes and indeed that of Moses himself. He was questioning principles which to Pharisees and Sadducees alike were the basis of Judaism. The Sadducee priests were opposed to all popular movements which might threaten to disturb the existing regime; for it gave them more power than they could hope to enjoy under any king, whether native or foreign. As things were going it looked as though Jesus would soon have the people behind him and come into collision with the Roman authorities. A member of the Sanhedrin had evidently said that means must be found to 'remove' him. Some scruples were expressed, but the High Priest brushed them aside with the remark that it was better that one man should die than that the whole people should perish, as they would, if led into conflict with the Roman power.

The object which Jesus had in view was to purify Judaism and, through Judaism, the larger society in which it was everywhere intermingled. There was everything to lose and nothing to gain by provoking a controversy between Judaism and the Roman Empire. Such a project was practical, though it called for infinite patience and self-command. The Jewish conception of one righteous God was attracting converts in growing numbers. But the force of this great conception was maimed by the limiting doctrine that God was interested in Israel only. The stubborn adherence of its spiritual leaders to tradition and authority, and the vested interests which the priesthood had developed at its centre, were a fatal bar to any real conquest by Judaism of the Graeco-Roman world. If once the relations of God to man as seen by the Jews had been based by them on conscience and reason, on the principles enunciated in the teaching of Jesus, Graeco-Roman society would have spread on such Judaism as the world had spread on Greece and Rome.[1]

With this object in view Jesus was bound to respond to the crowds in Galilee who were calling on him to accept the position of national leader, however little they might understand what that position meant to himself. He could only lead them in the right direction by accepting their wish to follow him. In order to effect his purpose he would have to challenge not only the hierarchy, but also the authority of the scribes and Pharisees as the national teachers. With such far-reaching objects in view he could do no less than claim for himself the position of national leader. Nay, rather he must claim the position of that supreme leader of whom his people had dreamed, and claim it, not merely in Galilee and Judea, but from that greater body of Israelites dispersed throughout the civilised world. But this could only be done by challenging the established authorities at Jerusalem at a time when the great annual feast had drawn to that centre pilgrims from every Jewish community in Europe and Asia. This, as he well knew, would be done at imminent risk to his own safety. But the movement could make no further advance unless he was ready to take that risk.

As was afterwards shown in the case of Paul, the priests were capable of employing assassins. So, avoiding the main stream of the pilgrimage, he approached Jerusalem by a route east of the Jordan, with a mere handful of intimate followers. They knew of his intentions but misunderstood them, and were beside themselves with grief when he warned them of the fate which might overtake him. The notion that somehow or other he must make himself king possessed their minds. A legend that he sprang from the lineage of David had created itself. He had openly combated the idea, arguing that David himself could not have thought that the Messiah would spring from his own family.[2] So great is the power of a fixed idea that his own disciples failed to grasp the significance of words which they faithfully transmitted. In the same gospels which record them were inserted genealogies tracing his descent from David through Joseph, though elsewhere they affirm that Joseph was not his physical father. In the mind of Paul his lineage from David was a fixed belief.[3]

In sight of Jerusalem he disclosed his presence to the stream of pilgrims arriving from Galilee. By them he was hailed as the national leader and publicly escorted through the gates of the city to the Temple. At the time of the feast the Procurator moved his quarters from Caesarea to the palace of Herod at Jerusalem to watch for and deal with any disturbance. That Pilate had seen nothing to fear in the conduct of Jesus on his public entry is plain from his attitude at the subsequent trial. Escorted by his followers he entered the Temple. No one building has ever counted for so much to a people as the Temple at Jerusalem to the Jews. Though prayer and worship might reach Jehovah at a distance, the offerings due from his people must be brought to the Temple. The priests had reason to regard as a mortal enemy anyone who called these ideas in question. From the story of his talk with the woman of Samaria it would seem that Jesus had openly challenged them.

The hour cometh, when neither in this mountain (Gerizim), nor in Jerusalem, shall ye worship the Father. . . . But the hour cometh, and now is, when the true worshippers shall worship the Father in spirit and truth: for such doth the Father seek to be his worshippers. God is spirit: and they that worship him must worship in spirit and truth.[4]

A leaf from the pages of a German scholar enables us to picture the kind of scenes in the Temple which Jesus witnessed in the course of that day:

But copious as those *public sacrifices* no doubt were, they still seem but few when compared with the multitudes of *private* offerings and sacrifices that were offered. It was the vast number of these latter—so vast in fact as to be well-nigh inconceivable—that gave its peculiar stamp to the worship at Jerusalem. Here day after day whole crowds of victims were slaughtered and whole masses of flesh burnt; and when any of the high festivals came round, there was such a host of sacrifices to dispose of that it was scarcely possible to attend to them all notwithstanding the fact that there were thousands of priests officiating on the occasion. But the people of Israel saw in the punctilious observance of this worship the principal means of securing for themselves the favour of their God.[5]

The inner courts where this wholesale slaughter went on must for all their marble and gilt have had the appearance of a knacker's yard. The idea that men could worship God by killing countless oxen and sheep, offering him their blood and by burning their fat, can only have repelled a mind that dwelt on the lilies of the field and loved to consider how they grew. But whatever pity he felt was turned into wrath by the things which he saw in the outer courts. In the precincts of the Temple itself dealers were licensed to sell the victims and in various ways to exploit the wealth which the pilgrims brought to Jerusalem:

And when he had looked round about upon all things, it being now eventide, he went out unto Bethany with the twelve.[6]

In the course of this night he seems to have resolved on an act which would bring home to the world of Judaism the degrading character of the priestly regime. Like the modern Vatican this vast establishment had guards of its own.

According to Philo, there were keepers in his day not only at the entrances to the inner court, but likewise at the gates of the outer one as well, one of their principal duties being to see that the prohibition in question was rigidly complied with. In addition to these there were watchmen patrolling all round by night and by day to make sure that nothing of an unseemly character was going on anywhere.[7]

When Jesus appeared in the Temple next morning and assumed the right to control what went on there, the priests and their guards must have seen that the vast concourse of pilgrims were ready to support him in anything he did. Resistance, however, was shown by the traders, and some force had to be used in clearing them out. We are told that

he made a scourge of cords, and cast all out of the temple, both the sheep and the oxen; and he poured out the changers' money, and overthrew their tables; and to them that sold the doves he said, Take these things hence; make not my Father's house a house of merchandise.[8]

He would not suffer that any man should carry a vessel through the temple. And he taught, and said unto them, Is it not written, My house shall be called a house of prayer *for all the nations*? but ye have made it a den of robbers. And the chief priests and the scribes heard it, and sought how they might destroy him: for they feared him, for all the multitude was astonished at his teaching.[9]

There was symbolism in his act. The bazaar was established in the court of the Gentiles, the only part of the Temple to which the world at large was admitted. This also, to him, was an integral part of the house of God, no less than the inner sanctuaries.

We know the effect which the growing abuses at

Rome came to have in the Middle Ages on the minds of pilgrims from northern Europe. Had Wycliffe or Luther appeared there at the head of a following strong enough to have purged the Vatican, they would probably have perished, but from their blood the Reformation would have drawn a wider momentum than it actually acquired. For the next few days Jesus was able to use the Temple as a centre from which to attack the whole fabric of orthodox Judaism. Unlike Paul thirty years later, he refrained from any attempt to conciliate the Pharisees or enlist their support in his struggle with the priests. Their blind attachment to the principle of authority and the rigid legalism of their scribes was a worse, because less obvious, evil than the greed and corruption of the hierarchy. They were stifling the growth of conscience and reason by leading men to think that life, whether private or public, must be governed by rules. The Sadducees at any rate were content with those embodied in the law which Moses was held to have received from God. But the Pharisee scribes had deduced from the written code a body of minute and trivial rules, which people were taught to regard as their necessary guide in every detail of life. The system is one which destroys all power of initiative and capacity for accepting responsibility in those who live under it. Its effects can be studied to-day in the sphere of public administration, especially in the east. In our Indian administration duties assigned to subordinate officers are governed by volumes of rules which seek to specify in all circumstances what the officer is to do and to leave nothing to his own judgement. With little justice we tax native officials trained in this way for backwardness in accepting responsibility. The effect of this system in depriving soldiers of initiative is common knowledge. By the Pharisee it was extended to the whole sphere of conduct and life. The rules they formulated were as frivolous in kind as they were infinite in number. They were treated as of greater importance than the written law, and the fact that these rules existed only in the memory of the scribes enhanced the position of their order. Jesus attacked these legalists in terms more scathing than any he used of the priests. Both Pharisees and Sadducees saw that their prestige would be permanently shaken unless they could either discredit or destroy him before the pilgrims dispersed.

Counting on Pharisee support the priests took the initiative. Their first idea was to undermine his influence with the crowd by making him show his hand on the burning political issue of the day. Not wishing to be openly involved in such controversies they arranged for some Pharisees and members of Herod's party to ask him in the presence of his followers whether he thought that tribute should be paid to Rome. It was difficult to see how he could frame an answer to this question which would neither involve his immediate arrest by the Procurator nor arouse the nationalist fury of the Galileans and turn his own followers against him. But the answer he gave them shows how far they had underrated the hold he had got on the popular party. He made his questioners show him a coin and then asked them:

> Whose is this image and superscription? And they said unto him, Caesar's. And Jesus said unto them, Render unto Caesar the things that are Caesar's, and unto God the things that are God's. And they marvelled greatly at him.[10]

He thus boldly advised the paying of tribute, openly renouncing the most certain appeal which any leader could make to the passions of Judaism. His opponents had failed, as politicians so often fail, to realise the part which moral courage and sincerity play in the leadership of men. The latter part of the answer was a reference to the tribute which the pilgrims brought at the Passover from the distant Jewish communities. It raised the dangerous question how far these vast revenues really accrued to the service of God in the hands of the priests.

This failure to alienate the affection of the people for their leader had to be recognised. The priests now set themselves to discover where he spent the night outside the walls, in order to arrest him while the pilgrims slept. They succeeded in corrupting Judas, one of his immediate followers, who guided their police to a garden to which Jesus had withdrawn for prayer together with Peter, James and John and some other disciples, who were all seized with panic and fled when the temple guards arrested him. He was then led to Jerusalem to the house of Annas,[11] the real head of the hierarchy, who had managed to keep the high priesthood in the hands of his own family for a series of years. Meanwhile his son-in-law, Caiaphas, had the members of the Sanhedrin roused and collected at his own house. In the small hours of the morning the prisoner was brought to them for trial.

These movements were watched in the darkness by Peter, who, trying to master his terror, had managed to mix with the throng when it entered the gates of Caiaphas. Challenged by a servant and betrayed by his northern brogue, Peter's courage again failed him. He escaped by denying all connection with Jesus, a denial which tortured his mind till the day of his death.

The charge formulated against Jesus was clear and accurately stated the matter at issue between the heads of the Jewish polity and the popular leader:

And there stood up certain, and bare false witness against him, saying, We heard him say, I will destroy this temple that is made with hands, and in three days I will build another made without hands. And not even so did their witness agree together.[12]

As to the exact words which a prisoner has used witnesses seldom agree, unless they have taken shorthand notes. The principles enunciated by Jesus led to a practical conclusion clearly expressed in the statement made by the witnesses. He had boldly declared his intention of destroying the institutions of which the Temple was the pivot, in order to clear the ground for a system based on the verities of life. The thought was his, though his own followers were unable to face its full implications. The evangelists were less near to the truth than the evidence they branded as false.

No attempt was made by Jesus to deny the charge. He refused to plead, and in fact treated the Sanhedrin, as he had treated the classes from which they were drawn when he met them in the Temple, as rulers who had forfeited the right to rule. Secretly arrested when his followers were asleep and deprived of their protection, he still confronted the Sanhedrin as the real national leader. By unanimous consent of those present Caiaphas pronounced the sentence of death.

To execute the sentence was not in their power. That lay with the Procurator, who had to be convinced that the prisoner had deserved it. The Sanhedrin realised that the reasons for which they had sentenced Jesus were scarcely likely to appeal to Pilate. When day dawned a further meeting was held to decide how best they could handle the matter in the Procurator's court where they must appear not as judges but as accusers. Their best plan lay in the open assertion made by Jesus of his claim to the position of national leader. They hoped to persuade Pilate that this implied a seditious intention, as it had done in the case of Judas the Zealot. Against this was the stand he had taken in the Temple against the Zealot movement and in favour of tribute. But men like Annas and Caiaphas, who had kept the appointment of the high priesthood in their family for years, knew how to apply political pressure. The position of Pilate, stubborn as he was, must have been permanently weakened when he was forced to remove the standards from his own palace to Caesarea.

Pilate must have known about Jesus long before he saw him in court; for the first duty of a Roman governor was to keep an eye on popular movements. He had evidently seen that Jesus was turning the mind of his countrymen from the dangerous dream of a rupture with Rome to the wholesome and practical project of setting their own household in order. He must have felt that sympathy with the movement which an English administrator cannot help feeling for the non-Brahmin movement in India.

It is equally clear that Jesus had read the character of his judge and had made up his mind that Pilate's goodwill to himself would yield to the persistence of the hierarchy the sacrifice of justice which their interests required. He stood before Pilate as the national leader well knowing that the Governor saw in his position no menace to the *pax Romana*. The Sanhedrin spoiled their case by asserting that Jesus had not only claimed the position of national leader (which was true), but had ordered the public to refuse the tribute to Rome (which was false). After questioning the prisoner, Pilate bluntly rejected the second charge and told the Sanhedrin that they had no case upon which to proceed in his court. He evidently knew that Jesus had openly enjoined the payment of tribute since he came to Jerusalem. His accusers tried to counter this by asserting that in Galilee he had preached sedition. This gave Pilate a possible loophole; for Galilee was outside his jurisdiction. It so happened that the native prince who ruled there had come to Jerusalem for the feast, just as Hindu princes go to Benares on similar occasions. So he sent him to Herod, who accepted the compliment, but was far too astute to incur the hostility of the Jewish hierarchy. He ridiculed Jesus as a pretentious impostor and returned him as such to the Procurator. Pilate tried to act on this view of the matter by first flogging Jesus and then telling the Sanhedrin that after inflicting this punishment he proposed to release him. The hierarchy evidently knew that if Jesus once came back into personal contact with the pilgrims their own position would be finally ruined. The ill-treatment he had met at their hands and at those of Herod and Pilate would merely enhance his influence. So they angrily protested against Pilate's decision by concentrating on the fact that the crowds had hailed him as Messiah and insisting that Jesus, in accepting this position, was assuming the political status of a king.

Pilate, though deeply alarmed, still shrank from judicial murder and thought of a way in which he might turn the tables against those who were hinting disloyalty against himself.

In the east it is customary for rulers to signalise great occasions by granting their subjects a boon, and the Romans had been in the habit of showing their clemency at this feast by pardoning a political prisoner. A certain Barabbas, who had taken part in some insurrection, had been chosen for the purpose.

It occurred to Pilate as an excellent plan to execute a man convicted of murder and sedition, and release in his stead a leader from whom the hierarchy had everything and the Romans nothing to fear. He might certainly have effected the exchange on his own authority. But he could not resist the temptation of turning the tables on the priests, who had openly hinted a charge of disloyalty against himself. For if they demanded the release of Barabbas it would not afterwards lie in their mouths to accuse the Governor of favouring a rebel. So he chose to allow the crowd in his court to say whether Jesus or Barabbas should be pardoned and released. In all these hurried proceedings the initiative lay with the priests, who had certainly seen that Pilate's court should be filled with their own supporters. The traders and other parasites of the Temple were available for the purpose. A court, even in the open air, would not contain the mass of pilgrims, whose presence in the Temple on previous days had helped and protected Jesus. So when Pilate made his proposal, it was met with a violent outcry for Barabbas, with renewed suggestions that Pilate was trying to protect a rival to the throne of his imperial master. His courage and resource finally failed him and he sent Jesus to be crucified with a couple of criminals already condemned.

In one direction, at any rate, the Romans had followed the example of Carthage rather than of Greece. They had studied the practice of cruelty in the terrible school of the Punic wars. The Phoenicians had invented crucifixion as a punishment for slaves. They were thought of as 'hands', and the nailing of hands to a cross was meant to express that the slave had finally failed in the only function for which he existed. In suppressing the revolt of Spartacus, Crassus had crucified thousands of his followers. Roman governors were expected to provide gladiators for the games, and had found it easier to obtain recruits when criminals realised that crucifixion was the only alternative.

To this fearful and lingering death Jesus was now legally condemned, in the hands of a Roman guard and beyond the reach of popular rescue. The real situation is revealed by the fact that Pilate thought it necessary to order the entire garrison, a whole cohort of five hundred men under a centurion, to escort the prisoner to the place of execution outside the walls.[13] "And there followed him a great multitude of the people, and of women who bewailed and lamented him."[14]

It is clear that the officer in command of the guard had seen in the verdict and sentence a gross miscarriage of justice. What little he could do to lighten its severity he did. The timber to be used in the execution was usually carried by the victim himself. The centurion saw that Jesus, exhausted by mental anguish and torn by the scourge, was unequal to the burden, and requisitioned one Simon, a pilgrim from Cyrene, to carry the cross. His sons Alexander and Rufus were evidently known to Mark and the readers for whom he wrote as members of the Christian community. When the place of execution was reached a potion of wine drugged with myrrh was offered to Jesus and refused. He was then nailed to the cross, and the cross planted in the ground with those of the bandits on either side of him.

It is known that crucified men often survived the slow process of exhaustion for several days. All the authorities agree in stating that Jesus succumbed at the end of six hours. It is natural to suppose that he passed to unconsciousness through a state of delirium, in which words are the mere reflex of physical conditions. In response to his cry of thirst one of the soldiers in mercy saturated a sponge with drink and held it to his mouth at the end of a stick. We are then told that Jesus having drunk the wine in the sponge "gave up the ghost".

NOTES

[1] See note 1 to Chapter XIV.
[2] Mark xii. 35-37.
[3] Romans i. 3.
[4] John iv. 21-24.

[5] Schürer, *The Jewish People in the Time of Jesus Christ*, Division ii. vol. i. p. 298.

Upon this description a distinguished Indian civilian has written the following comment: "This description of the temple reminds me of the Hindu temple to Devi at ——, and the priests must have been just as big scoundrels as the pandits who officiated and still officiate at ——. Once when inspecting officially I had to wade ankle deep in buffalo and goats' blood while in the precincts dealers were licensed to sell the victims and exploit the wealth of the pilgrims."

[6] Mark xi. 11.

[7] Schürer, Division ii. vol. i. p. 266.

[8] John ii. 15-16.

[9] Mark xi. 16-18.

[10] Mark xii. 16, 17.

[11] Streeter, *The Four Gospels*, pp. 381-2.

[12] Mark xiv. 57-59.

[13] Mark xv. 16.

[14] Luke xxiii. 27.

CHAPTER XXII

THE STORY OF THE RESURRECTION

We have here to do with events which more than all others have affected the course of human affairs. The writers who tell us about them certainly believed what they wrote, but do not agree in their various accounts of the miracles they relate. We have, therefore, to think for ourselves what probably happened, in the light which modern research has thrown on these records.[1]

The death of Jesus in six hours on the eve of the Sabbath confronted the priests with a difficulty they had not foreseen. In the law it was written:

> And if a man have committed a sin worthy of death, and he be put to death, and thou hang him on a tree; his body shall not remain all night upon the tree, but thou shalt surely bury him the same day; for he that is hanged is accursed of God; that thou defile not thy land which the Lord thy God giveth thee for an inheritance.[2]

On hearing that Jesus was dead, members of the Sanhedrin hurried to Pilate and urged him to authorise the immediate burial of the corpse. Their demand naturally raised the question as to what should be done with the two criminals who still survived, but might also die before the Sabbath was over. So the cruel suggestion was made that their legs should be broken to prevent all chance of escape. It is difficult to avoid the idea that this was preliminary to removing them dead or alive to their graves, though it must be remembered that burial alive was perhaps less painful than a lingering death on the cross.

According to Mark, Joseph of Arimathea, a member of the Sanhedrin, had a tomb prepared for his own burial in the rocks not far from the place where the crosses were planted. His offer to remove the body of Jesus to this tomb, before the Sabbath began with sunset, was accepted.

It is safe to assume that members of the Sanhedrin took no further step in the matter before the Sabbath was ended at sunset on the following day. That a special place was reserved for the bodies of executed criminals we know. It is possible, therefore, and indeed probable, that the Sanhedrin intended to remove the body of their victim to the less honourable place of burial when the Sabbath was over. As to whether they did so in fact we have no information.

Simon Peter and the other Galileans who had been with their Lord at Gethsemane had fled from Jerusalem. Peter, we know, was tortured by the sense of his own cowardice in refusing to admit any knowledge of his master, when challenged on the subject in the hall of Caiaphas. In their homes round the Lake of Gennesareth they presently recovered from the panic and despair which had overtaken them in the murderous atmosphere of Jerusalem. Those exquisite shores must have recalled to their minds the words at once powerful and tranquil by which they were drawn to Jesus in the earlier days of his ministry. The love which his person had inspired was refreshed, and with it the faith in his mission which his sudden and violent fate had almost destroyed. Their minds rejected the idea of his life as ended and done with, which indeed it was not. They recalled his attitude to physical death as a necessary step in the spiritual life. He had constantly dwelt on the soul in God as immune from decay. To the Sadducees he had said that God is not the God of the dead, but of the living. He had asked his disciples to believe that his death would not end the reality of his presence amongst them. "Lo, I am with you alway even unto the end of the world." So vivid were these memories to Peter and so powerful the emotions they awaked, that he saw in a vision the glorified presence of his Lord.

From the Gospel of Mark we know that Peter believed that he had seen Jesus during his lifetime on a lonely mountain "transfigured . . . his raiment . . . shining, exceeding white as snow; so as no fuller on earth can white them",[3] talking with Moses and Elijah. As to the vision of Jesus which Peter saw after his death we have evidence which is even more trustworthy. In after-years Peter was intimate with Paul, and the statement written by Paul to the Church in Corinth may be taken to represent what Peter himself believed and had told him.

> For I delivered unto you first of all that which also I received, how that Christ died for our sins according to the scriptures; and that he was buried; and that he hath been raised on the third day according to the scriptures; and that he appeared to Cephas; then to the twelve; then he appeared to above five hundred brethren at once, of whom the greater part remain until now, but some are fallen asleep; then he appeared to James; then to all the apostles; and last of all, as unto one born out of due time, he appeared to me also.[4]

As to the vision which Paul himself had seen we have here the statement of the writer himself. In the Acts we have fuller accounts of this vision recorded by Luke, who must often have listened to the story as told by Paul.

In this the earliest and most authentic account of the resurrection the appearances seen by Peter, by the other apostles, by more than five hundred disciples and also by James are placed on exactly the same footing as the vision seen by the writer himself. There is no suggestion that the body of

Jesus emerged from the tomb to eat and drink with his followers, and even to be touched by their loving hands.

That rational men and women, whose emotions have been deeply aroused, have believed that they saw and conversed with supernatural beings is a fact entirely beyond dispute. The most critical student of history can find no difficulty in thinking that Peter believed that his Lord had appeared to him in Galilee, or that this belief had revived his courage and inspired the thought that his master had returned to convince his followers that death meant change to a higher life, at any rate for those who accepted his message and followed his teaching. The revival of Peter's faith spread to the other disciples in Galilee. They shared his emotions and passed through the same religious experience. A number of them also came to believe as firmly as Peter himself that the person of their Lord had been made known to them in visible shape. Together they resolved to return to Jerusalem, to brave its perils, and discharge the task which their Lord had bequeathed to them of conveying his message to the world.

On reaching Jerusalem they told their story to the followers of Jesus in that city. Amongst them were women who had also a story to tell. On the morning of the third day, the day, that is, after the Sabbath, which followed the day of the crucifixion, they had sought the tomb where Jesus was laid, in the hope of giving to his body the rites of an honourable burial. They had gone to the sepulchre which they thought was his and found it open. Within was a young man who told them that the body of Jesus was not there. They were so overwhelmed by this failure that they had told no one about it, until they met Peter and his friends and had heard the marvellous and inspiring story of the visions they had seen in Galilee.

It is natural to suppose that as soon as the Sabbath

was over the Sanhedrin had lost no time in removing the body from the tomb which Joseph of Arimathea had made for himself to the common grave allotted to criminals. It is also possible that the women had hit on the wrong grave in the cemetery, a slope in the limestone formation honeycombed with tombs. A young man, working in the tomb, had simply told them that the body they were looking for was not there. Discouraged by this failure these distracted women had then abandoned the search.

The story told by Peter and his friends, coupled with that told by the women, gave rise to a new train of ideas. The doctrine which Jesus had preached to them, that human personality survived the fact of physical death, had been preached by the Chasidim. In Chapter XV. we have seen how the Pharisees had taught that the bodies of the righteous would rise from their graves to live once more in this world. These two ideas, though entirely distinct, were capable of confusion in an age when this physical world about us was thought to be permanent, however subject to change by supernatural means. If the actual facts were somewhat as those outlined above, a belief was certain to develop that the body of Jesus itself had risen, and issued from the tomb in some glorified shape, and in that shape had appeared to his followers.

A comparison of the earliest account, which is given by Mark, of the visit to the tomb by the women with later accounts given by Matthew, Luke and John, and also the story of the ascension given in the Acts, will show how the legend developed in response to various motives. Men readily believe what they wish to believe. The idea, conceived by the Pharisees and denied by the Sadducees, that the righteous would rise in the flesh from their graves, made it easy to believe that the body of Jesus had so risen. The young man who had told the women that the body was not in the tomb was the nucleus of the story of one or more angels, messengers of God, sent to announce that the Son of Man had risen from the dead. The legend of his final ascension to heaven grew up to explain why his corporate presence was no longer amongst them. They saw in Jesus the Messiah foretold by the prophets, and especially the suffering servant of Isaiah. So grew belief in his lineage from David, in miracles connected with his birth and in the story told by John how the soldiers pierced his side. "They shall look on him whom they pierced."[5]

These accounts, it is further suggested, were influenced by one of the earliest controversies which distracted the Christian Church. The Docetists were teaching that the Christ, the Messiah of prophecy, was a being who existed through all eternity. This supernatural being had been somehow immanent in the man Jesus during his lifetime on earth. The man Jesus had died on the cross, but not the immanent Christ.[6] The idea that the body of Jesus had risen from the tomb was thus contrary to the teaching of Docetists who held that the Christ had appeared to his followers after the crucifixion, but not the man Jesus who had died on the cross. The opponents of this doctrine had thus a motive for asserting that the actual body of Jesus had risen in the flesh. In the heat of the controversy they came to believe that Jesus had eaten and drunk with his followers. In time the story developed how the doubts of Thomas were removed by seeing the wounds in the risen body of his Lord. Such stories, readily believed by those who denied the Docetist doctrine, were incorporated in the later gospels, to become the foundation of the orthodox creed. It is easy to see how the visions recorded by Paul led the followers of Jesus to see in him the Messiah promised to their race by the prophets of old, the ruler descended from David and clothed with supernatural powers. Belief in his resurrection was of itself enough to create the atmosphere in which stories of the miracles he had wrought in his lifetime came to be told and widely accepted.

By his Jewish followers Jesus was thus recognised as the Christ foretold by their Scriptures. Presently, as their teaching spread beyond Palestine, it began to absorb ideas which, as modern research has shown, were deeply embedded in the folk-lore of the races inhabiting the eastern Mediterranean. In Egypt, in Asia Minor and Greece were primeval legends of a god incarnate in human form who after meeting a violent death would return to life as the destined saviour of suffering humanity. In Egypt this naturalistic idea was expressed in the legend of Isis and Osiris. In Greek mythology it is traceable in the stories of Adonis and Hyacinth. In all probability such ideas had their source in the commonest facts of nature, in the beauty of flowers scorched and withered by the sun, in their seed falling, to lie in the earth for a season and to blossom once more in the following spring. The light of the moon obscured for three days before the new crescent begins to appear is perhaps another element in this folk-lore. The idea of the god returning to life on the third day is traced to this source. The belief that Jesus had risen from his grave was in the course of years inevitably seen through the medium of primitive legends like these.

The belief that God could be pleased by the slaying of animals and birds, and by offerings of their flesh and their blood, had clearly no place in the mind of Jesus. Christianity broke once for all with sanctified butchery, a habit of paganism to which Judaism clung till the Romans destroyed the Temple in which it was practised. Yet so deeply was the sacrificial idea ingrained in the minds of the disciples that they came to regard the death of their master on the cross as a sacrifice to God superseding all others. The Mosaic ritual of the scapegoat, and the pagan ideas of a slaughtered god returning to life and redeeming humanity from its fate, combined to develop a body of doctrine in which genuine religion and growing accretions from pagan folk-lore were closely mingled. These ideas were transferred to the meal which Jesus had instituted as expressing the attitude which man should assume to material comforts, to things of the sense. This meal from its first institution was connected with the Passover ceremony and therefore the sacrifice of a lamb. They thought of their slaughtered master as the lamb. As the wine of the last supper suggested his blood, the bread was taken as a symbol of his flesh. In course of time a belief developed that, by a continuing miracle, the wine became his blood and the bread his flesh. These were transmuted materials through which the nature of Jesus entered the souls of his followers through their bodies. The eucharist was regarded not merely as a sacrifice but also as a meal, at which worshippers partook of the actual blood and body of God.

So rapidly sprung the weeds of paganism in fields which Jesus had sown with truth and enriched with his blood. The tares and the wheat were for ordinary mortals hard to distinguish till they yielded their fruit. In the time of harvest let reapers gather first the tares, and bind them in bundles to burn them: "but gather the wheat into my barn".[7] Already the fields are white for the harvest.

NOTES

[1] In this chapter the reverent and scholarly analysis of the evidence made by Professor Kirsopp Lake, M.A.(Oxon), Professor of New Testament Exegesis and Early Christian Literature in the University of

Leiden, has been largely followed. His book, *The Historical Evidence for the Resurrection of Jesus Christ*, is published by Williams and Norgate in the Crown Theological Library.

[2] Deut. xxi. 22, 23.
[3] Mark ix. 1-10.
[4] 1 Corinthians xv. 3-8.
[5] Ps. xxii. 16, 17; Zech. xii. 10.
[6] Kirsopp Lake, pp. 155-6.
[7] Matthew xiii. 30

CHAPTER XXIII

REVERSION OF THE CHURCH TO THE BASIS OF AUTHORITY

THE living contact of Jesus with his followers was a short one. As to how far he would have succeeded in purging their minds of the pagan ideas which infected Judaism, if sufficient time had been given him for the task, must always remain a matter of conjecture. With two vital aspects of his teaching they were seized. He had taught them to regard life as an episode of eternity. Now for the first time in history the idea that life must be lived as a phase of experience not to be ended by death began to influence increasing multitudes of ordinary men and women. He had further got into the minds of his followers the idea that the Father of all men must be served by the manner of life which his children adopted in relation to each other, as well as to himself. People from the lowest strata of society were inspired to practise the standards of personal conduct which Jesus had enunciated in the sermon on the mount. In eating and drinking, and above all in sexual relations, they learned to regard their bodies and those of others with the reverence due to temples where dwelt the spirit of God. They were taught to render not merely justice to each other, but an active solicitude, a desire in each to meet the needs of his fellows rather than his own.

It is safe to say that no person in history has ever so changed the current of human affairs by his life and death as Jesus of Nazareth. It is equally certain that the startling rapidity of this change was due to the belief in the minds of his followers that Jesus himself had risen from the grave, had conquered death, and that those who followed his teaching would share with their master eternal life. Every book in the New Testament shows that the impetus which enabled a movement, beginning in the humblest orders of society, presently to absorb the structure of the Roman Empire itself was a fervent belief in this miracle. It certainly enabled masses of people to grasp, in a form however crude, the essential conception which Jesus had taught of life on this earth, of the attitude of mind in which it should be led. But none the less, this belief that Jesus had returned from the grave to revive the faith of his followers obscured other aspects of his teaching which were no less important. "If they hear not Moses and the prophets, neither will they be persuaded, if one rise from the dead."[1] It is difficult to read these words without feeling that an intellect of the first order had at last transcended desires and superstitions deeply embedded in the human mind, and revealed to men the essential nature of spiritual truth. Ultimate verities cannot be proved by manifestations in the world of phenomena. Intercourse with the dead may convince us that the spirit is capable of surviving the flesh: as to whether the spirit is still indestructible it offers no proof. It cannot convince us that the issues of right and wrong affect an existence which has no limits in time or space. To us who know, as we now know, that experience of life on this earth, though extended by millions of years, must sooner or later be wiped out by physical forces, it matters little how many the millions be. Nothing less than permanence, apart from physical change, can satisfy the instinct that tells us that the difference of right conduct from wrong is a difference of infinite importance. That instinct, if genuine, drives us back on the view that the universe is of the nature of our minds rather than of our bodies, and that personality is not subject to the utter destruction which sooner or later overtakes the form of all bodily things. But, if this be so, the resurrection, even in the visions recorded by Paul, is no more necessary to faith in the message of Jesus than the virgin birth which former generations have held as a dogma. Insistence on belief in a supernatural event as necessary to prove the teaching of Jesus is in fact fatal to the principle of faith in the true sense of that word.

If supernatural events are really a necessary basis of belief in doctrines of fundamental importance, why then should the Father of men have left his children any reason to doubt that such supernatural events have occurred. He must surely have so ordered such events that their actual occurrence would have been beyond question, not only by men at the time when they happened, but also by all men in ages to come. The claims of authority, however tremendous, must always submit in the last resort to the judgement of the individual conscience and mind.

This belief that Jesus had returned from the grave and been manifest to the senses of his followers had the effect of throwing them back on the basis of authority from which he had been trying to reclaim their minds. The effect of this on the growth of the Church will be seen in the subsequent chapters of this inquiry. It led his followers to forget the special conception he had tried to convey in his use of the term 'Kingdom of Heaven'. His ultimate aim was, beyond question, the perfection of human character. "Be ye perfect as your father also is perfect." In order to attain this perfection his followers must think of God as their Father, and of all men as brethren. The importance of personal religion and conduct he emphasised to the full, so fully indeed that it is now almost a heresy to suggest that the teaching of Jesus had political aspects. But the growth of character depends upon more than religious observance and instruction in personal conduct. It depends to an even greater extent on environment. As the Greeks had divined, the most important aspect of environment is the structure of society in which the life of its members is led. Our Lord had realised that the souls of men cannot grow to perfection unless the structure of society itself is ordered in accordance with the laws of God, that is to say, founded on verities. To him the ultimate verity was goodness personified—God, whose nature is expressed, however imperfectly, in his creatures. The cardinal factor in human nature, as he saw it, was the instinct in men to serve each other. By strengthening that instinct, and not otherwise, was it possible to develop the nature of God in men. He realised that in ordinary men this instinct will develop only in so far as it is exercised and that men's relations one to another must be so organised as to prompt them to exercise this sense of duty in the highest possible degree. Such a system could not be founded on authority, on some revelation of divine direction expressed through a supernatural medium or attested by a miracle in the physical world. It must in the last resort depend on the revelation which God has implanted in the conscience and mind of all his children. The task he entrusted to men was that of ordering their mutual relations in such manner as to exercise to the utmost their sense of duty one to another, and also their minds in learning from experience how that sense of duty could best be rendered. I believe that he said, "The Kingdom of Heaven is within you". I believe that he also said, "The Kingdom of Heaven is amongst you".

These two aspects of truth, the divine nature as realised in each member of society and also in the structure of society which governs our relations one to another, are equally true, and inseparable, therefore, the one from the other.

The belief that their master had returned from the grave to attest the verity of his teaching, and that this miracle was the final proof of its verity, could scarcely do otherwise than swing back the minds of his followers to the basis of authority to which human nature instinctively clings. He was taken from them before he had had time to conquer their prepossessions. There was in the structure of the Roman Empire, as then developed, especially in its eastern regions, so little to exemplify what he meant. With us it is different in a world which has since done something to show how society can be made to rest on the mind and conscience of ordinary men. Happily for us, his followers remembered sayings and parables in which Jesus was expressing ideas less intelligible to them than they are to us in the light of our longer experience. In loving reverence they preserved many of his words much as he uttered them and, in their simplicity of mind, failed to perceive that these genuine truths could not be reconciled with much else that they came to attribute to Jesus and in all sincerity believed that he had said and done. The legend of his miraculous birth and of all the wonders he had wrought in his life was thus the natural corollary of the belief in the great miracle which had closed his career on earth.

The power of this idea was the greater because it led them to fit their master into the great national tradition and to see in his career the fulfilment of prophecy. In their belief he had lain dead in the grave for more than twenty-four hours, had returned to life and, after staying amongst them long enough to inspire them with unquenchable hopes, had withdrawn from their sight. They were comforted for his absence by remembering how he had told them that he would always be with them, though no longer visible to their eyes. These impressions shaped their ideas. His body having died and come to life again was no longer subject to death. Exempted from all the laws of matter and no longer subject to age and decay, he had withdrawn for a time to heaven, which they pictured almost as a place in the physical universe. But presently he would appear again in his glorified body, no longer as the humble mechanic and preacher, but in such manner as would render his sovereign power and position clear beyond all dispute. When he came again it would be as the ruler of the world. He would have no need to appeal to physical force. One side of their master's teaching had entered their minds so deeply as to render them immune from the madness of the Zealots. When Christ returned to rule the world as heavenly king, his power would be such that all men would recognise and obey him. He would put an end to sin and death. Those who had loved him and believed on him would lose all desire to sin. They would cease like him to be subject to death, and enjoy the presence of their master for ever. But those who had refused to recognise him and had rejected his teaching would be driven from his presence. The belief quickly developed that the most terrible miseries awaited them, miseries which included physical tortures without end. They could not escape the idea of reward and punishment deeply embedded in the human mind, which pervaded the religions of Jew and Gentile alike. But to earn the rewards it was necessary to believe not only on Christ, but also to live, as he himself had lived, in accordance with his teaching. So his followers formed themselves into societies, the members of which were to live the life which he had prescribed, and to persuade others to do so in preparation for his second coming. Their view was insensibly coloured by the Jewish tradition in which they were bred. His death on the cross they interpreted as a supreme sacrifice, superseding and ending the necessity for sacrifice in the Temple. His escape from death was the sure promise of immortal life for themselves. Their master had left them the task of warning all men that the Kingdom of God was at hand, and bidding them prepare to inherit its blessings. The master himself would return to inaugurate the kingdom by a miracle as great as that which had happened in the first creation of the world. The wicked would then be banished from his kingdom for ever. The meek alone would inherit the earth, and Christ at his second coming would inaugurate a regime in which evil would have no place and righteousness would wholly prevail. The conception of Jesus as the Messiah who had actually come, who was with them still and would presently establish the Kingdom of Heaven on earth, occupied their minds. He had come to fulfil and not to destroy the Law and the prophets. They still thought of God as mainly, if not exclusively, interested in the Jewish race. Before Gentiles could be included in the promised kingdom they must, as a matter of course, be circumcised as well as baptized.

NOTE

[1] Luke xvi. 31.

CHAPTER XXIV

JUDAISM FREED FROM ITS LIMITATIONS

THE doctrine that Messiah had actually come in the person of Jesus was an insult to orthodox Judaism. Its leaders who had planned and accomplished his death were presently aware that his followers had recovered their courage and enthusiasm. The movement centred in Jerusalem, where its members had copied the communistic ideas of the Essenes. We are told in the Gospels that the family of Jesus had not been in sympathy with his teaching. After his death one of his brothers, James, had come to believe in him, and presently appears as a kind of caliph at the head of the Church in Jerusalem.

The Sanhedrin did not again attempt the difficult task of persuading the Roman authorities to execute the leaders, but at times availed themselves of the violence of the mob. The stoning of Stephen was a case in point. In these proceedings their chief agent was Saul, a zealous and able young Pharisee, born and bred amongst Greek surroundings at Tarsus, a centre of those Greek mystery religions, the language of which is clearly reflected in his letters. He found, however, that his efforts to suppress the sect in Jerusalem were driving its members to distant cities where they made converts and created schisms in the local synagogues. So he furnished himself with letters from the high priest to the rulers of the synagogue in Damascus, and set out to suppress the sect in the north. We can scarcely doubt that the future author of the Epistles had argued at length with his prisoners, especially Stephen, and that what they had said to him haunted his mind. On the way to Damascus he passed through some great mental experience. What happened is best described by himself.

For I make known to you, brethren, as touching the gospel which was preached by me, that it is not after man. For neither did I receive it from man, nor was I taught it, but it came to me through revelation of Jesus Christ. For ye have heard of my manner of life in time past in the Jews' religion, how that beyond measure I persecuted the church of God, and made havock of it: and I advanced in the Jews' religion beyond many of mine own age among my countrymen, being more exceedingly zealous for the traditions of my fathers. But when it was the good pleasure of God, who separated me, even from my mother's womb, and called me through his grace, to reveal his Son in me, that I might preach him among the Gentiles; immediately I conferred not with flesh and blood: neither went I up to Jerusalem to them which were apostles before me: but I went away into Arabia; and again I returned unto Damascus. Then after three years I went up to Jerusalem to visit Cephas, and tarried with him fifteen days. But other of the apostles saw I none, save James the Lord's brother. Now touching the things which I write unto you, behold, before God, I lie not. Then I came into the regions of Syria and Cilicia. And I was still unknown by face unto the churches of Judaea which were in Christ: but they only heard say, He that once persecuted us now preacheth the faith of which he once made havock; and they glorified God in me. Then after the space of fourteen years I went up again to Jerusalem with Barnabas, taking Titus also with me.[1]

After the manner of his race Saul withdrew for a time to the wilderness to consider the tremendous idea which had entered his mind. The conception of Jesus as the Messiah who had come already and would presently return to inaugurate the Kingdom of God came easily to one of his Pharisee training. But he went beyond some of the personal followers of Jesus, as well as the Pharisees, in conceiving that the Kingdom of Messiah was intended for the benefit of the Gentiles no less than of the Jews. For Saul was a Roman-citizen-born and proud of the status it gave him, as well as of being a Jew by race. He looked on himself as the instrument ordained to convey this message to the whole Empire, and naturally aspired to begin this work in the country of his birth. Before setting out for Asia Minor he wished to hear more of the teaching of Jesus from those who had heard it. So he visited Jerusalem, saw Peter, and doubtless discussed the conclusions he had reached during his sojourn in Arabia. For the next fourteen years he was preaching in Cyprus, Asia, Thrace, Macedonia and Greece, and often found a more ready hearing in streets than in synagogues. For the rest of his life he was known by a latinised nickname, Paulus, the little man, a reference to the smallness of his body in contrast with the greatness of the soul it contained. Facing the question whether Jesus would have refused Gentiles as followers unless they submitted to the painful and, to them, degrading ordinance of circumcision, he answered it in the negative, and reached the conception that his teaching was intended to supersede the Mosaic law with its tedious and costly ritual.

The destruction of the Temple at Jerusalem, where this ritual had centred, finally established the movement initiated by Paul. The Christian Churches which observed the Mosaic law were thereafter limited to Palestine and died out in the course of a few generations.

For centuries before, the thoughts of Xenophanes, Socrates and Plato had been slowly leavening the Graeco-Roman world. The popular belief in a number of gods and goddesses with a standard of morality lower than that of the best human beings had been undermined. Judaism with its conception of one righteous God was attracting proselytes in growing numbers. But Judaism insisted that the one God must be served by the ritual prescribed in the Law of

Moses. This belief, founded only on Jewish tradition and contrary to reason, was a fatal obstacle to the general adoption of Judaism as a world religion. In Christianity, as interpreted by Paul, the creed of monotheism was freed from this parasitic condition. It appeared no longer as a sect of Judaism, but as a separate faith which Gentiles could adopt more easily than the Jews themselves. The destruction of Jerusalem in A.D. 70 settled the issue. Paul had started Christianity on the road which led to its adoption as the official religion of the Empire within three centuries.

The mind of Paul was none the less completely possessed by another side of the Jewish tradition. He viewed Jesus, whom he had not known in the flesh, through the medium of the Messianic idea in its supernatural form. His course was determined by the thought that Jesus would reappear to inaugurate the Kingdom of God for those who had accepted his teaching, and that this would happen as soon as his followers had conveyed his message to every part of the civilised world. His mission in life was to fulfil this condition and so hasten the second coming. Italy had already received the message. The great Jewish community in Rome sent thousands of pilgrims to Jerusalem, some of whom must have seen Jesus or listened to his followers after his death. It is quite unnecessary to suppose that the Church to which Paul addressed his great epistle was founded by missionaries sent by the churches in Palestine. We know that Paul was fired by the idea of hastening the coming of his Lord by announcing the message to the countries east and west of Italy.

The idea of human society, based on the infinite duty of men to each other, and so organised in harmony with the will of God, was thus viewed through the medium of Jewish legend and transferred to the supernatural plane.

Our earliest Christian records are the letters of Paul written while many of the personal followers of Jesus were living. In these letters we see how confidently they expected to see him return and change the order of the universe by a miracle as stupendous as that of the creation described in Genesis. They continually repeated their stories of what he had said, done and suffered in Galilee and Judea, and some of their hearers who wished to spread the good news to others may have made notes for their own use. But the need of comprehensive and authoritative accounts of his life and teaching was not felt in the first generation, which expected to see him return in the lifetime of some who had previously known him. As, one by one, those who had seen his face and listened to his words passed away, a demand for authoritative records began to arise and was presently met. The first biography of Jesus was produced by Mark, shortly before the time of the great upheaval which led to the fall of Jerusalem. Peter, in whom Jesus had recognised qualities which distinguished him from the rest of his followers, seems to have used Mark as a secretary. It is likely that Peter and Paul both perished at Rome in the massacre ordered by Nero, and that Mark then hastened to put into writing his version of the stories which Peter must very often have told in his hearing. His account was largely embodied and amplified in the two biographies issued some decades later under the names of Matthew and Luke. In any case the statements contained in these three gospels had been constantly repeated and handed from mouth to mouth for a number of years before they were written down. Every middle-aged man must have noticed how a story told by the same person over a long period gradually changes and takes its colour from the mind of the teller, however truthful. The change is of course far more rapid when the story is passed from mouth to mouth. But even when deeply coloured and freely embellished by repetition it often preserves the essential point. The sayings and doings of Jesus were subject to this process for a whole generation before they were placed on record. For several decades they lived on the tongues of simple followers inspired by a personal devotion which has never been equalled; and during that time were steeped in the very ideas he had tried to combat. These ideas, moreover, were greatly strengthened by the belief that his dead body had been raised to life. We thus have detailed accounts of what Jesus said and did, encrusted with legend and often distorted by the crust, side by side with stories which are all crust and with no genuine truth inside. It is only by breaking the crust and examining the contents that we find the truths and see how completely their living tissues differ from the composition of the legendary shell.

NOTE

[1] Gal. i. 11-24, ii. 1.

CHAPTER XXV

THE CHURCH MILITANT

To begin with, the Christians were regarded by the Gentile world as the most obnoxious sect of the Jews. In the cities they offended the mob by their puritan morality and their open condemnation of idols and also of the public games. They were treated as atheists, as Socrates had been. In time of public calamity the gods were thought to be visiting their anger on a world which allowed their very existence to be questioned. As Tertullian puts it:

> If the Tiber rises too high or the Nile does not rise high enough, or if there be drought or earthquake or famine, or pestilence, then straightway the Christians to the beasts.[1]

The mob were pleased to see these spoil-sports made to furnish the spectacles they denounced, and the Jews, in their hatred of the Christians, were only too ready to excite their passions. In A.D. 64 Nero gratified the rabble by torturing and burning the Christians in Rome. Meanwhile the doctrines of Paul, the destruction of Jerusalem and the open hatred of the Jews were having their effect. By the reign of Domitian the Churches had lost even the appearance of a Jewish sect, and with it the privileges which the Romans had accorded to the Jewish religion.

After the manner of despotisms the Empire was suspicious of private associations. It had tried to suppress pagan cults which attempted to practise secret rites. The existence of the Churches was in principle contrary to the spirit of its laws. The refusal of Gentile Christians to render divine honours to the emperors brought them into open conflict with the civil authorities. Merely to profess Christianity was an act of rebellion against the Empire. The magistrates had thus a legal excuse for gratifying the popular lust for blood, whenever they felt disposed to do so, by exposing Christians as victims at the games.

For nearly three centuries the Churches were the object of persecution, never so persistent as to destroy them, but severe enough, so long as they were active, to purge their ranks of all but people of the highest courage and noblest purpose. The metal of which they were wrought was extracted in a furnace and forged to steel on the terrible anvils of the amphitheatres.

This conviction that they were a *people—i.e.*, the transference of all the prerogatives and claims of the Jewish people to the new community as a new creation which exhibited and realized whatever was old and original in religion—this at once furnished adherents of the new faith with a *political and historical* self-consciousness. Nothing more comprehensive or complete or impressive than this consciousness can be conceived. Could there be any higher or more comprehensive conception than that of the complex of momenta afforded by the Christians' estimate of themselves as "the true Israel", "the new people", "the original people", and "the people of the future", *i.e.*, of eternity? This estimate of themselves rendered Christians impregnable against all attacks and movements of polemical criticism, while it further enabled them to advance in every direction for a war of conquest. Was the cry raised, "You are renegade Jews"—the answer came, "We are the community of the Messiah, and therefore the true Israelites". If people said, "You are simply Jews", the reply was, "We are a new creation and a new people". If, again, they were taxed with their recent origin and told that they were but of yesterday, they retorted, "We only seem to be the younger People; from the beginning we have been latent, we have always existed, previous to any other people; we are the original people of God". If they were told, "You do not deserve to live", the answer ran, "We would die to live, for we are citizens of the world to come, and sure that we shall rise again".[2]

Their sufferings at the hands of the Roman Empire naturally disposed the Christians to regard it as the kingdom of Satan. They held themselves aloof from its civil and military life and made no attempt to improve its polity. As Tertullian said, "No interest concerns us so little as that of the state".[3] To Christians, their Church was the Kingdom of Heaven in embryo. The more they endured the more earnestly they looked for the second coming of Christ to inaugurate its miraculous birth. This idea assumed in the minds of some of them a form alien to the spirit of their founder. Tertullian looked forward

with fierce exultation to the glorious gains of the day of judgement, when we shall see (and that full soon) gods and deified emperors, philosophers and poets, actors and jockeys, all burning together in the fires of hell at Christ's triumphant coming. These are *our* games; where is the praetor that can show us their like?[4]

Messianic ideas in their supernatural aspect had a strong hold on Paul. To this extent Judaism has continued to influence Christianity to the present day. It led the followers of Jesus to interpret the Kingdom of Heaven as propounded by him in the light of their national traditions, and to look for miraculous events which have never happened and are not destined to happen. Their master had taught that men must no longer look to the Mosaic law as interpreted by priests, Pharisees or scribes, as the source of truth, but to their own conscience and reason purified by direct intercourse with God. When, after his death, they had come to conceive him as a supernatural being, as divine rather than human, they thought of him as the only source of truth. He had said that God would bestow his spirit on those able to receive it. He had also said that his spirit would still be with them when they no longer saw him in the flesh. The spirit of God which descended on Christ and by him could be given to themselves was conceived in their minds as an essence and finally as an actual person. Truth was a matter of revelation vouchsafed to apostles, prophets and elders who had received the Holy Spirit from Christ himself.

In its early days the Church thus reverted to the same principle of authority which Jesus had attacked. The centralised organisation, ruled by a hierarchy, which it presently developed, was the natural result of regarding truth as finally revealed by God through Christ to men. The apostles, who had known Jesus and received his message, had clearly a right to prior authority; though, even in their day, there was Paul claiming to stand on the same footing by virtue of a special revelation vouchsafed to himself. His example was presently followed by various sectaries inspired by the old eastern idea of associating goodness with mind and evil with matter. On the basis of dualism they constructed a great variety of fantastic beliefs which they spoke of as 'science' (gnosis). But this science, as they claimed, was not the fruit of study or learning, but specially inspired by divine revelation. The Church was undoubtedly right in holding that the dualism of the Gnostics was contrary to the teaching of Jesus; but arguing the matter on the basis of authority rather than reason it was forced to deny the claim of the Gnostics to direct inspiration, and therefore to restrict the right of interpreting the teaching of Jesus to the apostles and to those ordained for the purpose by the apostles and their authorised successors. In the second century the Church was thus developing a hierarchy which claimed to prescribe to Christians not only what they should do but also what they must think.

In their earliest form the churches were schismatic congregations of Jews who recognised in Jesus the

Messiah or Christ, and were separated by that fact from the synagogues where orthodox Jews refused to accept him as such. Amongst Greek-speaking Jews who were also Christians their congregation was known as *κυριακὸν δῶμα*, the house of the Lord, a term which survives as *Kirche* in German and in English as church. Amongst western Gentiles the term used was often *ἐκκλησία*, a word which recalled the sovereign assembly of a city-state. The French *église* is derived from this word. As the Catholic movement developed, the name of 'church' was broadened to cover the larger organisation in which the local congregations were embodied.

It is safe to assume with Streeter that in their earlier stages a certain variety of organisation existed in the various churches.[5] In Jerusalem James the brother of the Lord seems to have been accorded a great measure of personal authority. In western churches the use of the word *ἐκκλησία* suggests that more democratic ideas prevailed. Generally speaking, the churches were ruled by bodies of elders or presbyters. Of these one was usually appointed as *ἐπίσκοπος* or overseer to manage the corporate property. He thus became the chief administrative officer, and also the channel through whom one church corresponded with another. The office would tend to be filled by the ablest of the presbyters and also to be continued for life where he proved himself as such. In the second century these overseers appear as the virtual rulers of the local church, though still assisted by councils of elders. From this time the office begins to assume the monarchical functions we have come to associate with the title of bishop. The sacraments were now filling the same place in Christian worship as the mysteries in pagan or the sacrifices in Jewish religion. The clergy required to administer them were almost as necessary to intercourse with God as the priests of the older faith. They received their commissions from the bishops, who in turn were held to receive their authority from the apostles through their successors.

The bishops were thus the living repositories of the truth as delivered to the apostles. When they differed on points of doctrine or discipline, gatherings or synods were held to settle their differences. The areas from which bishops were gathered were often those of the Roman provinces. The bishop of the leading city presided and acquired a certain primacy under the title of 'metropolitan'. In the Latinised western provinces the Bishop of Rome came to be recognised as superior to the others, the lineal successor of Peter and the Vicar of Christ, at whose hands the rest of the bishops received their commissions. As Christians thought of themselves as a separate people, they came to regard their church as the Kingdom of God to be finally established at the second coming of Christ. It was to them an organised state, more permanent than the Empire, with a higher claim to their loyalty. In moulding its institutions they were deeply influenced by those of the Empire, and especially by the discipline of the Roman army, of which the Emperor was head. From this early period date the military terms which have found their way into Christian language, 'the sword of the spirit', 'the church militant' and such-like; expressions to us worn so threadbare that we almost forget their origin.

> Suffer hardship with me, as a good soldier of Christ Jesus. No soldier on service entangleth himself in the affairs of this life; that he may please him who enrolled him as a soldier.[6]

The Salvation Army has more in common with the primitive Church than General Booth perhaps realised.

By Marcus Aurelius the Church was seen as a movement fatal to Greek culture and the Roman

Empire. In seeking to destroy it he had called the philosophy of Greece to the aid of imperial authority. At his death in A.D. 180, the Church, though widely diffused, still embraced but a fraction of his subjects. By A.D. 250 its numbers and the strength of its organisation had grown to such an extent that it openly described itself as a third race in distinction from pagans and Jews. The Emperor Decius declared that:

He would hear of a rival prince being set up against himself with far more patience and equanimity than of a priest of God being appointed in Rome.[7]

The Emperor had learned to regard the Bishop of Rome as a dangerous rival. Barbarian armies threatening its frontiers were no greater menace to the Emperor than an organisation which claimed an authority higher than his own, and attracted to its service the best of his subjects. As Celsus wrote to Origen:

If all men were to do as you do, nothing would prevent the Emperor from being deserted, and all things . . . falling into the power of . . savages.[8]

It ceased to be a question of punishing the Christians for breaking the law as Trajan had done. Decius was resolved to extinguish the Church by requiring all Christians on pain of torture and death to recognise the gods of the Empire. To begin with these measures secured more apostates than martyrs and looked like succeeding. But presently the example of the few who preferred to die rather than yield revived the fainting spirit of the Church. Prisons and arenas were glutted with victims and within ten years the persecution which Decius began was abandoned by his successor. Purged of her weaklings, the Church emerged with enhanced prestige and rapidly increased the roll of her converts.

In some of the provinces, and especially in Asia, the pagans scarcely outnumbered the Christians at the close of the century.

Diocletian was called to the purple in A.D. 284. His vigorous methods restored the discipline of the army and the fortunes of the Empire. In A.D. 293 he called to his aid three colleagues, Maximian and Constantius in the west, and Galerius in the east. The anxiety aroused in their minds by the growing power of the Church can be read in the edict issued by Galerius when the last and most formidable effort of the Empire to crush its rival had failed.

> Amongst our other efforts for the public good we formerly desired so to reform the state in accordance with the old laws and public discipline of the Romans, that the Christians also, who had given up the manner of life laid down by their own ancestors, might return to a better mind. For these Christians had reasoned so strangely, and become so possessed with self-will and folly, that they were not following those institutes of the ancients which perhaps their own ancestors had first established, *but were making laws for themselves after their own good-will and pleasure and by divers means collecting assemblies of divers peoples.*[9]

In A.D. 303 the emperors resolved on one final attempt to extinguish the Church. At the instigation of Maximian and Galerius, Diocletian condemned its buildings to destruction and its Scriptures to be burned. Christian officials were ordered to renounce their religion, or else to be stripped of their offices, and also of all civil rights and to be sold as slaves.

Two fires occurred in the palace which Diocletian attributed to Christian officials. Inflamed with fury he authorised a policy of general massacre. But the state could no longer count on the hatred of the mobs which a century before had clamoured for the Christians to be thrown to the lions. By A.D. 311 the attempt to exterminate the Church had palpably failed. It was ended by an edict issued by Galerius on his death-bed some words of which have been quoted above.

NOTES

[1] Tertullian, *Apology*, 40.

[2] Harnack, *The Mission and Expansion of Christianity*, vol. i. pp. 240-41.

[3] Tertullian, *Apology*, 38.

[4] Gwatkin, *Early Church History*, vol. i. p. 178.

[5] Streeter, *The Primitive Church*.

[6] 2 Tim. ii. 3, 4.

[7] Cyprian, Ep. LV. 9.

[8] Origen VIII. 68, quoted by Glover in his *Conflict of Religions in the Roman Empire*, p. 256.

[9] Gwatkin, *Early Church History*, vol. ii. p. 346.

CHAPTER XXVI

THE CHURCH TRIUMPHANT

THE division of the imperial power which Diocletian had made naturally led to a conflict between his colleagues or their heirs, from which the son of Constantius emerged as Emperor. In A.D. 313 Constantine proclaimed the principle of religious liberty and legalised the position of the Church in the edict of Milan. It was now, as he saw, the most vital element in the system of the Empire. Having made it his policy to enlist its support, he sought to strengthen it by composing its internal dissensions. In A.D. 325 he summoned at Nicaea a council of bishops from the whole Empire and gave to its decision the force of law. By the institution of the Ecumenical Council the principle of authority thus acquired its appropriate vehicle.

Under Theodosius (A.D. 379–395) orthodox Christianity, as defined at Nicaea, was finally established as the sole official religion of the Empire. Heathenism was now proscribed, and the relative positions which pagan and Christian worship had filled before Constantine were reversed. The emperors abandoned their claim to divinity, but not their claim to derive their authority from God. Henceforth they ruled as vicegerents of Christ pending his return finally to establish the Kingdom of God upon earth.

Constantine moved his capital to Byzantium, and gave it the name of Constantinople. He died in A.D. 337. The burden of government again proved too heavy for a single ruler, and in A.D. 364 was divided between two emperors, one at Constantinople and the other at Rome.

It was reunited by Theodosius in A.D. 379, and divided once more on his death. In A.D. 395 Honorius became Emperor in the west. Alarmed by the Gothic invasion of Italy, he left Rome in A.D. 404 and retired for safety behind the marshes which surround Ravenna. Henceforward Rome saw little of its emperors. In A.D. 410 it was stormed and sacked by the Goths under Alaric, who had served in the Roman army and had learned its technique.

The like had not happened since the days of Brennus. Italy lay at the mercy of northern barbarians. Nobles and landowners fled from her shores, leaving their property behind them. The poverty of these emigrants revealed to the provinces how low the majesty of Rome had fallen. Pagans saw in the catastrophe the vengeance of the gods whom the Empire had abandoned.

At this period an exchange of letters took place between Volusian, the pro-consul of Africa, a pagan of lofty character who had shown an intelligent interest in Christian teaching, and Augustine, the Bishop of Hippo. Volusian had expressed doubts whether Christianity could be reconciled with the loyalty which he felt for the Empire. Augustine was thus led, in A.D. 413, to survey the whole problem in a treatise entitled *De Civitate Dei*, issued from time to time in a series of books and finally completed in A.D. 426.[1]

The general argument of this monumental work may best be described in his own words:

> Rome having been stormed and sacked by the Goths under Alaric their king, the worshippers of false gods, or pagans, as we commonly call them, made an attempt to attribute this calamity to the Christian religion, and began to blaspheme the true God with even more than their wonted bitterness and acerbity. It was this which kindled my zeal for the house of God, and prompted me to undertake the defence of the city of God against the charges and misrepresentations of its assailants. . This great under-

taking was at last completed in twenty-two books. Of these, the first five refute those who fancy that the polytheistic worship is necessary in order to secure worldly prosperity, and that all these overwhelming calamities have befallen us in consequence of its prohibition. In the following five books I address myself to those who admit that such calamities have at all times attended, and will at all times attend, the human race. . . . In these ten books, then, I refute these two opinions, which are as groundless as they are antagonistic to the Christian religion.

But that no one might have occasion to say, that though I had refuted the tenets of other men, I had omitted to establish my own, I devote to this object the second part of this work, which comprises twelve books. . . . Of these twelve books, the first four contain an account of the origin of these two cities—the city of God, and the city of the world. The second four treat of their history or progress; the third and last four, of their deserved destinies. And so, though all these twenty-two books refer to both cities, yet I have named them after the better city, and called them The City of God.[2]

In the opening pages of Book XI. St. Augustine accepts divine revelation as the necessary basis of his system.

Since the mind itself, though naturally capable of reason and intelligence, is disabled by besotting and inveterate vices not merely from delighting and abiding in, but even from tolerating His unchangeable light, until it has been gradually healed, and renewed, and made capable of such felicity, it had, in the first place, to be impregnated with faith, and so purified. And that in this faith it might advance the more confidently towards the truth, the truth itself, God, God's Son, assuming humanity without destroying His divinity, established and founded this faith, that there might be a way for man to man's God through a God-man. For this is the Mediator between God and man, the man Christ Jesus. For it is as man that He is the Mediator and the Way. Since, if the way lieth between him who goes, and the place whither he goes, there is hope of his reaching it; but if there be no way, or if he know not where it is, what boots it to know whither he should go? Now the only way that is infallibly secured against all mistakes, is when the very same person is at once God and man, God our end, man our way.

3. *Of the authority of the canonical Scriptures composed by the Divine Spirit*

This Mediator, having spoken what He judged sufficient, first by the prophets, then by His own lips, and afterwards by the apostles, has besides produced the Scripture which is called canonical, which has paramount authority, and to which we yield assent in all matters of which we ought not to be ignorant, and yet cannot know of ourselves.[3]

In Book XV. the origin of the two polities is described. They were latent in society from the time of Adam and Eve.

Of these two first parents of the human race, then, Cain was the first-born, and he belonged to the city of men; after him was born Abel, who belonged to the city of God. . . . Accordingly, it is recorded of Cain that he built a city, but Abel, being a sojourner, built none. For the city of the saints is above, although here below it begets citizens, in whom it sojourns till the time of its reign arrives, when it shall gather together all in the day of the resurrection; and then shall the promised kingdom be given to them, in which they shall reign with their Prince, the King of the ages, time without end.[4]

Thus the founder of the earthly city was a fratricide. Overcome with envy, he slew his own brother, a citizen of the eternal city, and a sojourner on earth. So that we cannot be surprised that this first specimen, or, as the Greeks say, archetype of crime, should, long afterwards, find a corresponding crime at the foundation of that city which was destined to reign over so many nations, and be the head of this earthly city of which we speak. For of that city also, as one of their poets has mentioned, "the first walls were stained with a brother's blood", or, as Roman history records, Remus was slain by his brother Romulus.[5]

For practical purposes the earthly city is identified with the Roman Empire.

Babylon, like a first Rome, ran its course along with the city of God, which is a stranger in this world. But the things proper for insertion in this work in comparing the two cities, that is, the earthly and heavenly, ought to be taken mostly from the Greek and Latin kingdoms, where Rome herself is like a second Babylon.[6]

Later on we are told that the malignant demons rule that city, whose eternal punishment is to be shared by it.[7]

Miserable, therefore, is the people which is alienated from God. Yet even this people has a peace of its own which is not to be lightly esteemed, though, indeed, it shall not in the end enjoy it, because it makes no good use of it before the end. But it is our interest that it enjoy this peace meanwhile in this life; for as long as the two cities are commingled, we also enjoy the peace of Babylon. For from Babylon the people of God is so freed that it meanwhile sojourns in its company. And therefore the apostle also admonished the Church to pray for kings and those in authority, assigning as the reason, "that we may live a quiet and tranquil life in all godliness and love".[8]

The whole of Book XXI. is devoted to discussing the ultimate fate of the earthly city.

I propose with such ability as God may grant me, to discuss in this book more thoroughly the nature of the punishment which shall be assigned to the devil and all his retainers, when the two cities, the one of God, the other of the devil, shall have reached their proper ends through Jesus Christ our Lord, the Judge of quick and dead.[9]

In contrast with this awful prospect the reader is asked to

survey the progress of the city of God from the era of the patriarch Abraham, from whose time it begins to be more conspicuous, and the divine promises which are now fulfilled in Christ are more fully revealed.[10]

The Church founded by Christ is in fact

the city of the great King.[11] Yet because the churches are also full of those who shall be separated by the winnowing as in the threshing-floor, the glory of this house is not so apparent now as it shall be when every one who is there shall be there always.[12]

The final constitution of the City of God awaits the return of Christ.

That the last judgement, then, shall be administered by Jesus Christ in the manner predicted in the sacred writings is denied or doubted by no one, unless by those who, through some incredible animosity or blindness, decline to believe these writings, though already their truth is demonstrated to all the world. And at or in connection with that judgement the following events shall come to pass, as we have learned: Elias the Tishbite shall come; the Jews shall believe; Antichrist shall persecute; Christ shall judge; the dead shall rise; the good and the wicked shall be separated; the world shall be burned and renewed. All these things, we believe, shall come to pass; but how, or in what order, human understanding cannot perfectly teach us, but only the experience of the events themselves. My opinion, however, is, that they will happen in the order in which I have related them.[13]

In this work St. Augustine formulated and placed on record the outlook on life developed by the Church in the course of the four centuries which followed the life and death of Jesus. It shows how far the new Judaism, freed by Paul of nationalist and exclusive limitations, assimilated to the Roman Empire and rendered applicable to all human society, effaced the principles which inspired the Greek and Roman commonwealths. The spiritual conquest of Rome by the Greeks was surpassed by the grip which Jewish ideas had slowly acquired in the Roman world through the medium of the Church. Theocracy, in its transcendental form, had ousted the principle of the commonwealth, excluding the tests of conscience, reason and experience, asserting supernatural authority as the final basis of truth. The pen of Augustine was mighty as those that reduced to writing the laws of Manu, of Moses or of Rome. It crystallised the Jewish idea as refined in the crucibles of the Christian Church. In the depths of that crystal the Christian world was to read its destiny.

In the pages of St. Augustine the sermon on the mount is submerged and lost in the Jewish Scriptures. From ideas so rooted in supernatural sanctions some kind of monarchy was bound to spring. And the first and noblest exponent of a spiritual autocracy was at hand. In one of his letters[14] Augustine refers to an acolyte Leo who was very likely the Leo who ten years after his death became Bishop of Rome in A.D. 440. A Roman by birth, of lofty character and powerful mind, he raised the position of his see from *primus inter pares* to an absolute monarchy, claiming obedience in matters spiritual from the whole Church. In suppressing heretics, not only in Rome but in Spain and Gaul, he was supported by the Emperor Valentinian III., who in A.D. 445 ordained that nothing should be done in Gaul contrary to ancient usage without the authority of the Bishop of Rome, and that the decree of the apostolic see should henceforth be law.

But the claims of Leo went far beyond this. In his sermons he propounded the doctrine that the apostles Peter and Paul had given to Rome a dominion in spiritual matters which extended beyond the regions she actually governed to the whole world. He laid the foundations of a new and wider authority, at the very moment when the political sovereignty of Rome was about to collapse. The fifth century was one of those epochs when central Asia, stricken perhaps by a period of drought, was discharging its hordes on China, Persia, India and Europe. In A.D. 452 Attila stormed Aquileia, massacred the garrison, and was marching on Rome when Leo met him on the banks of the Mincio, and, by sheer force of his personality, persuaded the terrible Mongol to retreat. Three years later he saved Rome from massacre at the hands of the Vandal Gaiseric. It is not to be wondered that henceforward a quaking civilisation looked for leadership to the Bishop of Rome rather than to any of the nine puppets who jostled each other on the throne of Ravenna in the next twenty-one years.

Their end was nigh. In A.D. 476 the barbarian auxiliaries of the Empire claimed for themselves one-third of the lands in Italy. When their claim was refused their leader, Odoacer, dethroned the boy emperor, Romulus Augustulus, and, acknowledging the titular sovereignty of the Emperor at Constantinople, agreed to rule Italy as its king.

In A.D. 527 Justinian became Emperor in Constantinople. Before his death in A.D. 565 he had reconquered Africa, Italy and Sicily, and was governing Italy through an exarch stationed in Ravenna.

Since the time of Leo the Italians had learned to think of the Bishop of Rome as their virtual leader. The tradition that entitled the populace of Rome to live at the public expense was older than the Empire, and, when it fell, the task of feeding the proletariat was assumed by the Church. When threatened with spoliation by barbarian invaders thousands of landowners made over their property to the Church which could hold the conquerors in awe. The Church was thus furnished with revenues to meet the growing demands of charity. When Gregory was elected Pope in A.D. 590 he found himself called upon to administer estates which are estimated to have covered no less than 1800 square miles. So vast an ownership was inseparable from political power.

Italy was now in the throes of the Lombard invasion. Rome was cut off from Ravenna by their armies. We find Gregory issuing orders to the cities within his reach and giving directions for their defence as their recognised ruler in political no less than in spiritual matters.

Gregory, the greatest man who ever sat in the Chair

of St. Peter, largely completed the work begun by Leo in establishing the authority of the Papacy in western Christendom. The Visigoth kings of Spain had abandoned the Arian heresy and recognised the spiritual authority of Rome no less than France. That part of the British Isles which is now called England had been lost to the Church in the earlier decades of the fifth century when the Roman legions had left its shores to the mercy of the Anglo-Saxon invaders. Under Gregory the Church accomplished the often repeated process of a spiritual conquest. In A.D. 597 Ethelbert and most of his nobles and people were converted to Christianity by Augustine, the missionary sent to England by Gregory. With the enthusiasm of recent converts the Saxons became protagonists of the papal authority. It was Wynfrith, a native of Devonshire and trained at Exeter, who under the name of Boniface inspired and led the missionaries who converted a great part of Germany to the Christian faith and organised the German Church in obedience to Rome.

NOTES

[1] *De Civitate Dei* (Dod's translation), vol. i. p. viii.
[2] *Ibid.* p. vii.
[3] *Ibid.* p. 438.
[4] *Ibid.* vol. ii. pp. 50-51.
[5] *Ibid.* p. 54.
[6] *Ibid.* p. 219.
[7] *Ibid.* p. 313.
[8] *Ibid.* p. 341.
[9] *Ibid.* p. 413.
[10] *Ibid.* p. 124.
[11] *Ibid.* p. 172.
[12] *Ibid.* p. 281.
[13] *Ibid.* p. 411.
[14] St. Augustine, Ep. 104.

CHAPTER XXVII

ISLAM

In the north, the Teutonic destroyers of the Empire were fast submitting to the Bishop of Rome. In the south, Christendom was presently to be threatened by invaders armed with a sword tempered to match the spiritual weapons of the Church.

The Kingdom of God upon earth, as conceived by Judaism, lay buried in Jerusalem. Over her ruins a Roman city, peopled by Greeks, had been raised by Hadrian. In the sixth century the smouldering hostility of Asia to Graeco-Roman civilisation was showing signs of renewed activity in the oldest crater of the Semite world. Arabia had always been skirted by Greek and Roman armies alike. In deserts inviolate to phalanx and legion tribal society had remained as it was in the age of Abraham and Job. At the period now reached in our narrative the desert was devouring its own children. Whether by reason of exceptional drought or the natural increase of the people, their numbers had reached and exceeded the margin of subsistence. The proclivity of the clans to prey on each other was accentuated by hunger. To the north, east and west of Arabia fertile and thickly inhabited regions lay inviting the ravages of starving nomads; but the crumbling defences of the Roman Empire were as yet protected from Arab invasion by the internecine feuds of the tribes.

In this arid peninsula life naturally centres round isolated places where wells, or some local condition of rainfall, provide the moisture necessary for vegetable growth. In certain oases the springs are strong enough to supply the needs of considerable towns like Mecca and Medina. Before the age of mechanical transport communication between these centres of tribal life depended for the most part on camels, which of all the beasts of burden can travel furthest without the necessity of drinking and can also transport food and water for the Arab cavalry. By means of the camel the tribes have always been able to pillage as well as to trade with each other. Their natural mobility has also enabled them to keep in touch with civilisations beyond the deserts. From the earliest times caravans have connected Mecca and Medina with the shores of the Mediterranean.

At the period under review a few Christian and a large number of Jewish communities had settled in Arabia. At Medina the Jews had made a number of proselytes but in general the Arabs were still in the clutch of a primitive paganism. As usually happens with a people in this condition, they worshipped idols which were often rude inanimate objects, like the meteoric stone which Ephesians in the time of St. Paul revered as the Goddess Diana. Of all the Arabian sanctuaries the most distinguished was a kind of rectangular hut at Mecca which was called the Ka'ba or Cube which contained the figure of a god. The city of Mecca had long been the centre of an annual pilgrimage. In the walls of the Ka'ba was a black stone which the pilgrims came to adore.

In this city of Mecca Mahomet was born about A.D. 570. As a young man he entered the service of a prosperous widow, by name Khadijah. About the time when Augustine was landing in Kent Mahomet went as her agent with the caravans which were trading with Syria. On returning to Mecca he married Khadijah and for several years after prospered in trade.

The question whether Mahomet could read or write is of little importance, for the strength of his mind and his personality are beyond dispute. No youth of his calibre could visit a place like Damascus and discuss round the camp-fire what he there had seen and heard without obtaining some general knowledge of ideas current in the Empire ruled from Byzantium. In Syrian towns he probably felt as a trader from central Asia feels when he sojourns for a time in Peiping or in one of the Treaty Ports. He must have been conscious that Arabia was regarded in the Graeco-Roman Empire as a cultural backwater. From his contact with the Jewish and Christian world he had clearly grasped the idea of monotheism. He had also seen that it could not be reconciled with the worship of images.

The ideas of the Arabs were narrowly tribal. What seemed best for the tribe was right for its members, including vengeance on a hostile tribe. Along with monotheism Mahomet inbibed the idea it implies of a moral law which is universal, and propounded the duty of forgiving injuries instead of avenging them. He accepted the further conclusions which Hebrew prophets had gradually drawn from their notion that the ultimate reality behind the universe is a spirit of righteousness. Like others in the stage of paganism, the Arabs conceived the dead as surviving only in the shadowy form of wraiths. Mahomet adopted the Jewish and Christian conception of a future existence in its cruder form: the body itself would rise from the grave. His conceptions of Heaven and Hell were derived from those which were current in Christian literature; with this difference, that joys which were physical as well as spiritual were promised to believers.

Ere long these ideas secured such a hold on his mind that he turned from trade to the project of lifting his people from superstition to the plane of religion. He retained, however, to the end the practical shrewdness of a man trained in affairs. To begin with, at any rate, he sought to reform rather than abolish the paganism of his people, exhorting them to worship, not the image in the Ka'ba, but 'the Lord of the House', the god of Mecca, as one with the God of the Jews and Christians, the one universal deity. At first he encouraged his followers to turn in prayer to Jerusalem.

In all this were points of resemblance with the movements initiated by Hindus and Buddhists who have realised that the impact of western ideas cannot be met by mere negation. Such reforms are in these days taking the line of interpreting the national religion on lines conformable to Christian teaching.[1]

That Mahomet's ideas were largely imbibed from Jewish and Christian teaching is scarcely in doubt. That he and his followers thought that God had directly revealed them to Mahomet himself is equally clear. He recognised Moses and Jesus as prophets to whom God had revealed some of his truths; but the final revelation was reserved for Mahomet himself. After his death his teaching was placed on record in the Koran, which came to be regarded as a final and unalterable statement of truth. The new religion was epitomised in the dogma, "There is one God and Mahomet is his prophet". It was this which brought Islam into conflict with both the creeds from which it was derived. In the Christian religion, at any rate, the Greek idea that human knowledge of realities must be found in the mind and conscience of man, as revealed and verified in experience, has always been dormant like seed, ready to germinate again in favourable conditions. The revelation of Mahomet as recorded in the Koran left little room for further development and has therefore sterilised thought wherever his creed has prevailed. The boasted science of the Moslems in Spain is no real exception to this rule, for its source was the science of the Greeks introduced by Christians whom these least intolerant of Moslems employed.

The political results were tremendous, for the principle of authority asserted by Mahomet in its absolute and most uncompromising form enabled the tribes of Arabia to achieve, for a time, the structure of a state. This principle of authority was not limited in its range, as it was with the Jews, by a spirit of nationalism. Islam, as projected by its founder, was capable of becoming a world theocracy, in which all nations and kindreds and tongues could unite in common and equal obedience to the God of the universe. As a project of government for mankind, Christendom, begotten of the Greek and Roman Empires by Judaism, was at last confronted with a formidable rival.

To begin with, Mahomet had no political thoughts in his mind. In Mecca he formed groups of the people about him who held their meetings in privacy and engaged in prayer under the guidance of the prophet himself. They were pledged to renounce infanticide and other immoral practices and also to control the lusts of the flesh. Much stress was laid on 'surrender' to the will of God. Islam is the Arabic word for 'surrender'. The term Moslem means 'one who surrenders himself' to God.

The movement quickly aroused the antagonism which reformers who challenge established ideas and vested interests must always expect. Mahomet encountered the obstacles which had hampered the mission of Jesus, and barely avoided a similar fate.

> Some members of his own family . . . bitterly opposed him. . . . It would be a mistake to suppose that the enemies of the new faith were actuated by religious fanaticism. They were, for the most part, simply men of the world who, proud of their social position, objected to recognising the claims of an upstart and dreaded any sweeping change as likely to endanger the material advantages which they derived from the traditional cult. To the majority of the citizens Mahomet appeared a madman. . . . That he had to endure many affronts was quite natural, but actual

violence could not have been employed against him without risk of a blood-feud, which the Meccans were always most anxious to avoid.[2]

Like Jesus before him, he turned from the people who lived in the Holy City to the pilgrims who came to it. As noticed above, Medina was largely settled by Jews and was, therefore, a centre where the monotheistic idea was already familiar. In and about this populous centre the Arabian tribes were at war with each other and the peace of the place was constantly threatened by their feuds. Pilgrims who met Mahomet at Mecca conceived the idea that this prophet of monotheism with his masterful personality might command obedience and establish peace between the discordant factions that centred in and about Medina. Mahomet, whose life was in jeopardy from the Meccans, listened to these overtures. In A.D. 622 he and his followers escaped from Mecca and took refuge in Medina.

Thus was accomplished the great event known as the Emigration (*hijra*, distorted by Europeans into *hegira*) which forms the starting-point of the Moslim era.[3]

The claim of Mahomet to unique and final authority as the prophet of God brought him into conflict with the Jewish community of Medina. This antagonism is shown by the fact that in A.D. 624 Mahomet commanded his followers to turn in prayer to Mecca instead of to Jerusalem.

His mind was now concentrated on the task of welding the Arab clans who obeyed him into one organised community. These clans were forbidden to make war on each other and any matter at issue between them was to be brought for settlement to "God and Mahomet". They were all to unite to defend Medina. By the logic of events he was led to issue a stream of edicts which are now embodied in the Koran. They prescribed the ceremonies which

Moslems should observe in religion, their civil and criminal relations to each other and also the principles governing their military organisation, including conscription. They also created a system of public finance. Though in all probability he did not realise it, Mahomet was, in fact, creating a state.

Ere long Mahomet was able to make war on his enemies in Mecca, and an early though trifling engagement with superior numbers secured to him the credit of miraculous powers. This victory is ascribed in the Koran to the intervention of angels. He was now strong enough to expel from Medina the Jews who, as usual, were weakened in the face of an enemy by their own intestine dissensions.

A small expedition despatched to the north in A.D. 629 was signally defeated near the Dead Sea by the Byzantine Empire. This was, in all probability, a raid projected to satisfy the Arab propensity for pillage. By A.D. 630 his main forces were encamped within sight of Mecca. Its people, who realised that further resistance was futile, abandoned their weapons and retired to their houses. Mahomet then entered the city in triumph. He proclaimed an amnesty, but hastened to destroy images wherever he found them and defaced paintings which adorned the walls of the Ka'ba. A concession to paganism was made, however, in the case of the black stone, which Mahomet declared had been placed there by Abraham. The custom of adoring the stone, which from ancient times had attracted pilgrims to Mecca, was sanctioned and incorporated in Moslem worship. This concession to paganism, though resented by some of his followers, availed to conciliate the traditions and interests of the Meccans.

The new power established in Mecca as well as Medina was felt as a threat to their independence by the Bedouin tribes of the desert. Again Mahomet was victorious in a battle which established his authority over regions now covered by the modern kingdom of Hedjaz.

In A.D. 631 he issued a proclamation excluding all unbelievers from the pilgrimage to Mecca and the cult of the Ka'ba. In the following year he conducted the pilgrimage in person and finally settled its ritual. Henceforward this pilgrimage, pagan in origin and in some of its rites, was the visible bond which united Moslems throughout the world.

In A.D. 632 Mahomet was busy preparing an expedition against the Byzantine Empire when he suddenly died.

The death of the prophet was the signal for a further conflict between the Islamic state and the outlying tribes who clung to paganism. But Mahomet had left behind him followers who had grasped his ideas, and also a political organisation sufficiently developed to serve as their instrument. They realised that the dominating fact was a hunger which could never be satisfied so long as the tribes of Arabia preyed on each other. The obvious remedy was for all these tribes to unite in invading the fertile and populous countries beyond the deserts.

The faith of Islam provided the necessary bond, the theocracy which centred in Medina, the means required for effective action. A raid into Mesopotamia was quickly followed by an organised attack on the Syrian dominions of the Emperor Heraclius. The Semite inhabitants in these regions had been alienated by his crushing taxation. In the field of ideas the weeds of paganism had largely smothered the seed which Jesus had sown six centuries before. The doctrine of the Trinity was dangerously near to polytheism in minds too simple to follow the gymnastics of metaphysicians. The worship of images was not merely sanctioned but directly enjoined by the Church. Islam, asserting that God was one and not to be worshipped in visible form, was now confronting the eastern Church as a genuine reform in the sphere of religion.

Like Israel before them, the tribes of Arabia were drawn by the lure of the fertile belt. A similar creed had enabled Moses to unite the Hebrew tribes for the conquest of Canaan. By A.D. 636 the Byzantine armies were finally defeated and Damascus was taken. Jerusalem fell in A.D. 638 and Caesarea, which Heraclius could provision from the sea, was betrayed to the Arabs in A.D. 640.

In the course of the Syrian campaign the Arabs had realised the difficulty of seizing and holding the fertile lands on the coast while the enemy, however feeble on land, commanded the sea. The Byzantine Empire had some of its principal shipyards at the mouths of the Nile. The desert, moreover, was hungry for corn from Egypt, that unfailing supply which grew on its irrigated lands. In A.D. 640 the Arab cavalry invaded Egypt. By A.D. 642 Alexandria was occupied and Egypt was organised as a province of the Arabian Empire. Reversing the strategy which Pausanias had followed in 478 B.C., the Arabs attacked and seized the naval base of the Greek Empire in Cyprus in A.D. 649.

The Arabs were now in a position to attack the heart of the Byzantine Empire on the Bosphorus by land and sea. But the Arab invasion broke in vain on the walls of Constantinople. The tremendous defences which Constantine and his successors had thrown round the eastern gate of Europe were inviolate to Asia for more than eight centuries.

The Arabs were thus impelled by the logic of events to attack Europe from its western flank.

The invasion of Africa opened in 642 B.C. was a necessary sequel to the conquest of Egypt by the Arabs. The basic population of the African littoral was Berber. No stranger to desert life, the Berber had more in common with the Arab than with the

Latin or Greek colonist of the towns on the coast. They were not, however, so near akin to the Arabs as the Semite inhabitants of Syria, nor so easily detached from the Empire and religion of Constantinople and Rome. The process of absorbing the Berbers into Islam took longer. To the last the Arab power was weakened by racial dissension between themselves and the Berbers. The fall of Carthage and the conquest of Africa was only completed in A.D. 708.

Gibraltar still preserves the name of Tarik (Gebel Tarik, *i.e.* Mount Tarik), the leader who crossed the Straits in A.D. 711 with a mixed force of Arabs and Berbers and defeated Roderick, king of the Goths. The large Jewish population, whom the Goths had persecuted without mercy, at once made common cause with the Semite invaders. In six years the Arabs were masters of Spain and ready to attempt the invasion of France.

At the time when the western Empire was extinguished in Rome, Clovis, grandson of Merovech, king of the Franks, was extending his conquests in northern Gaul. In the hope of securing the support of the bishops he accepted baptism on Christmas Day in A.D. 496. His capital was established at Paris on an island in the Seine, and before he died in A.D. 511 his dominions extended to the Loire. The French kings looked back on Clovis as the founder of their monarchy; but the House of the Merovings followed the course which is usual with dynasties. Enfeebled by luxury, the descendants of Clovis allowed their authority to be exercised by powerful nobles. At the time of the Arab invasion, a mayor of the palace called Charles, a name which signified courage, was ruling the realm in the name of the Meroving monarch.

By A.D. 717 the Arabs and Berbers were crossing the Pyrenees. Their onset was opposed with varying fortunes by Eudo, the duke who ruled Aquitaine. In A.D. 732 a host of Arab horsemen were led by 'Abd-ar-Rahman, a fanatical Amir, across the passes. The Amir defeated Eudo and chased him north till he took refuge at Tours, behind the ranks of an army led by Charles. Day after day waves of the Arab horse broke on the shields of the Frankish warriors. 'Abd-ar-Rahman fell in one of these charges and his leaderless hosts fled in confusion, leaving their camp and baggage in the hands of Charles. His soldiers gave him the name of the Hammer, which, centuries before, a Semitic leader had won when he saved his people from the tyranny of the Greeks. The Franks might better have called their leader the Anvil; for the Arab squadrons had hammered on his infantry till they broke into pieces and were scattered to the wind. So the great onslaught on Christendom, which Mahomet had inspired in the heart of Arabia, was at length turned and broken in the centre of France exactly a century from the day of his death.

NOTES

[1] *Vide* Farquhar's *Crown of Hinduism.*

[2] *The Cambridge Mediaeval History*, vol. ii. p. 310. In chapters x., xi. and xii. of this volume the results of modern research into the early history of Islam are brilliantly summarised by Professor Bevan and Dr. Becker. In this chapter their statement of facts has been closely followed, though not always the conclusions they draw from them.

[3] *Ibid.* p. 313.

CHAPTER XXVIII

THE HOLY ROMAN EMPIRE

THE prestige which Charles Martel, the competent leader of the bravest army in Europe, won for his house as well as for himself, was, perhaps, the most far-reaching result of his victory at Tours. A glance at the map is sufficient to show that the Arab failure to conquer Christendom from the west was mainly due to the facts of geography. The real danger lay on the eastern flank. Europe had been saved from subjection to the Arabs when in A.D. 717 Leo the Isaurian had finally broken their attack on Constantinople by land and sea.

As so often happens, the victor was launched by his very success on a sea of troubles. In the course of the struggle Leo had felt the moral disadvantage at which he was placed, as the champion of Christendom, by the Arab claim that Islam was a faith purer and higher than his own. He resolved, therefore, to purge the Church from the taint of idolatry. In Italy his attempts to enforce this reform met with a fierce resistance. Gregory III. accused him of heresy and excommunicated iconoclasts in Rome.

The Arab wars had emptied the treasury of the Empire, so Leo ordered the exarch of Ravenna to levy tribute in Italy. The revenues of the Papacy were touched and the Pope joined with the people in resisting the levy. There was also Liutprand, king of the Lombards, seeking to extend his power in Italy at the Emperor's expense. In A.D. 727 Liutprand besieged Ravenna.

The Lombard king and the Pope, though opposed to the Emperor, were, none the less, at odds with each other. In Rome itself the Pope was now the temporal ruler, and in various parts of Italy claimed the revenues of vast landed estates. These claims in fact barred the hopes which the Lombard monarchy entertained of uniting Italy under their rule, just as those of the Pope in the nineteenth century were opposed to the projects of the Piedmont dynasty. Then, as now, the weapons of the monarchy were those of a government backed by its own national armies, while those of the Papacy were a spiritual influence which extended beyond the limits of Italy.

For the moment the Lombard king bowed to the ghostly authority of Gregory II., but, enraged by the intrigues of his successor, Gregory III., threatened Rome with his armies in A.D. 739. In this predicament the Pope adopted the expedient of using his spiritual influence in Europe to redress his political weakness in Italy. He appealed to Charles Martel to cross the Alps and act as the champion of the Church against the aggressions of a Lombard monarchy.

For the moment this attempt to make the two Teutonic kingdoms fight each other failed, for their courts and nobles were in cordial relations and Charles Martel refused to stir.

In A.D. 741 Charles Martel died, leaving his sons, Carloman and Pepin, as joint mayors of the palace. In A.D. 747 Carloman retired to a monastery which he founded on Mount Soracte. Changes were soon to follow which placed Pepin under deep obligations to the papal chair. In A.D. 749

Burchard, Bishop of Würzburg, and Folrad the chaplain were sent to Pope Zacharias to ask concerning the kings in Frank-land who at that time had no royal power, whether this was good or no. And Pope Zacharias commanded Pippin that it would be better that *he* should be called king who had the power, rather than he who was remaining without any royal power. That order might not be disturbed, by his apostolic authority he ordered that Pippin should be made king.

Pippin, according to the manner of the Franks, was elected king, and anointed by the hand of archbishop Boniface of holy memory, and he was raised to the kingdom by the Franks in the city of Soissons. But Hilderic, who was falsely called king, was tonsured and sent into a monastery.[1]

The election was according to Teuton custom, the anointing a Jewish rite prescribed by the Church as the symbol of divine authority. The coronation of Pepin took place in A.D. 750. When, in A.D. 749, Aistulf had succeeded to the Lombard throne, the conflict with Rome on the question of the papal estates became acute. Pope Stephen II., who succeeded Zacharias in A.D. 752, fled to the court of Pepin. By A.D. 756 Pepin had invaded Italy, restored the Pope to his see, and placed him in possession of the papal estates. He also transferred to him that territory which the eastern emperors had ruled through the exarch at Ravenna.

In A.D. 758 Pepin was succeeded by his son Charles the Great, who in A.D. 773-4, on the invitation of Pope Hadrian I., invaded Italy, dethroned Desiderius, king of the Lombards, annexed his dominions and recognised the Pope's sovereignty over two-thirds of the Italian peninsula.

Before the end of the century Charles had thrust the Saracens out of France, had conquered Spain up to the Ebro, Germany to the Elbe, and was recognised as the most powerful ruler which the civilised world had known since the days of Constantine.

The Isaurian dynasty in Constantinople had fallen meanwhile on evil days. In A.D. 780 Leo IV. died, leaving as joint sovereigns his widow Irene and her boy Constantine VI. When Constantine reached the age of twenty his mother, unwilling to share the power she had wielded alone during his boyhood, threw him into prison, put out his eyes, and reigned as Empress in Constantinople. This behaviour of a woman on the throne of the Caesars quenched any feeling of loyalty to Byzantium which was still flickering in the west.

Until Pepin was crowned, in A.D. 750, the Popes had recognised the Byzantine Emperor as in theory the supreme ruler of Christendom. Zacharias, who died in A.D. 752, was the last Pope who applied to him to confirm his election. What projects were now simmering in clerical brains can be gathered from a document which probably found its way into the papal archives during the pontificate of Stephen II. This document purports to record an imperial decree in terms of which Constantine on his conversion to Christianity recognised that

> St. Peter is on earth the appointed Vicar of God, so also the Pontiffs his vicegerents should receive from us and from our empire power and principality greater than belongs to our earthly empire. For we choose the same Prince of the Apostles and his vicars to be our patrons before God, and we decree that even like unto our own earthly imperial power so shall the sacro-sanct Church of Rome be honoured and venerated, and that higher than our terrestrial throne shall the most sacred seat of St. Peter be gloriously exalted.

This forged decretal goes on to recognise the power of the Pope to control the whole Christian priesthood and to regulate all matters appertaining to worship or faith. It details the gifts and properties purported to be conferred by Constantine on the Church, the dignities to be enjoyed by its subordinate officers, and especially confers on the Pope himself

> the imperial sceptre, with all standards and banners and similar imperial ornaments, and in short the whole array of our imperial dignity and the glory of our power. . . .
>
> Wherefore, that the pontifical crown may not grow too cheap, but may be adorned with glory and influence even

beyond the dignity of the earthly empire, lo! we hand over and relinquish our palace, the city of Rome, and all the provinces, places and cities of Italy and [or] the western regions, to the most blessed Pontiff and universal Pope, Silvester; and we ordain by our pragmatic constitution that they shall be governed by him and his successors, and we grant that they shall remain under the authority of the holy Roman Church.

Wherefore we have thought it fitting that our empire and our royal power be transferred to the Eastern regions, and that a city bearing our name be built in an excellent place in the province of Byzantia, and that there our empire be founded, since where the sovereign of priests and the head of the Christian religion has been placed by the Heavenly Emperor, it is not fitting that there the earthly Emperor should also bear sway.

The document [says Hodgkin] ends with solemn injunctions to all future Emperors, to all nobles, 'satraps', and senators, to keep this grant for ever inviolate. Anathemas are uttered on anyone who shall dare to infringe it; and hell fire is invoked for his destruction.[2]

Writing to Charles in A.D. 778, Pope Hadrian refers to this fabulous grant of Constantine in the following words:

And as in the time of St. Silvester the Holy Catholic and Apostolic Church of Rome was exalted by the generosity of the most pious Constantine, the great Emperor, of holy memory, and he deigned to bestow on it power in these regions of Hesperia, so in these times, which are so prosperous for you and for us, may the Holy Church of God, that is of the blessed Apostle Peter, grow and flourish and be more than more exalted, that all the nations when they hear of it may shout, "O Lord, save the King, and hear us in the day when we call upon Thee, for, lo, a new and most Christian Emperor Constantine has arisen in our day, through whom God has been pleased to bestow all gifts on His Holy Church."[3]

Thus was the authority of Constantine invoked for reversing his policy, for restoring to the banks of the Tiber the capital of the world transferred by him to the shores of the Bosphorus.

That wellnigh impregnable fortress had long guarded and was still longer to guard a title too large for the narrowing territories governed from its walls. But the Frankish nobles felt with the Roman priests that the imperial title usurped by an infamous woman more properly belonged to the real champion of Christendom, the greatest potentate in Europe, who in every sense was a king of men. Charles himself evidently thought that a time was approaching when forms must be reconciled with facts, as when his father had sent Childeric to a monastery and mounted the throne. But his long experience of priestcraft made him hesitate to accept the imperial title as his father had accepted the royal title at the hands of the Papacy. For years the popes had pestered him with appeals to enlarge their temporal powers and possessions supported by blasphemous promises and threats. We know the effect which these letters left on his mind from his own words:

We wish to ask the chief ecclesiastics and all those who are engaged in teaching from the Holy Scriptures, who are those to whom the Apostle saith, "Be ye imitators of me"? or what he meant when he said, "No one who is a soldier of God entangleth himself with the things of this world"? How is the Apostle to be imitated? How is anyone to be a soldier of God? Pray let them show us truly what is meant by that "renouncing the world" of which they so often speak, and explain how we are to distinguish between those who renounce and those who follow the world. Is the difference only in this, that the former do not bear arms and are not publicly married? I would enquire also if that man can be said to have renounced the world who is unceasingly striving to augment his possessions by drawing persuasive pictures of the blessedness of heaven, and by threatening men with the everlasting punishments of hell? or that man who, in the name of God or of some saint, is for ever stripping simpler people, rich or poor, of their possessions, disinheriting the lawful heirs, and driving men thus unjustly deprived of their paternal estates to robbery and all sorts of crimes? [4]

In A.D. 795 Hadrian died. On April 25 Leo III. was attacked on his way to St. Peter's by two clerics of his own household who attempted to blind him and cut out his tongue. Though badly injured in the eyes and mouth, he escaped and sought refuge at the court of Charles, which he reached in July. Charles' most trusted adviser was an Englishman, Alcuin of York, who had now retired as Abbot of Tours. On hearing of the outrage he wrote to Charles urging that he "as more excellent in power" than Pope or Emperor, "more illustrious in wisdom, more sublime in the dignity of your kingdom", was now called upon to deal with the growing corruption of both papal and imperial courts.

In the autumn of A.D. 799 Charles sent Leo III. back to Rome under an escort strong enough to protect him, intending to follow him presently. As Alcuin, who frankly described the atmosphere of Rome as poisonous, was unwilling to go there with him, Charles paid him a visit at Tours in the spring of A.D. 800. His queen, Liutgarda, died and was buried there during the visit.

We know that Charles and Alcuin were equally alive to the danger of accepting the imperial title, as Pepin had accepted his crown, at the hands of the Pope. They agreed in regarding the disorders at Rome and Constantinople as intolerable. The question before their minds was how Charles could acquire the authority to cleanse both these Augean stables.

On November 24 the Frankish king reached Rome, and on Christmas Day went in state to pay his devotions at the Basilica of St. Peter. He knelt on the spot where the body of the Apostle was supposed to rest, and, as he rose, the Pope placed on his head a golden crown, while the vast congregation burst into a cry: "To Carolus Augustus, crowned of God, mighty and pacific Emperor, be life and victory".

Charles accepted the *fait accompli*; but, according to Einhard, his biographer, he much disliked the title, and afterwards "declared that he would never have entered the church on that day, though it was a high festival, if he could have foreknown the pontiff's design". Apart from his disinclination to accept the position of Emperor at the hands of the Pope, Charles was anxious to avoid a rupture with Constantinople, and even entertained the repulsive idea of a matrimonial union with the infamous Irene. The manœuvre of the Pope had this far-reaching result—that Charles and his successors were never accepted at Constantinople. In his eagerness to restore the Empire to Rome under papal authority Leo finally frustrated the ideal of uniting Christendom under one emperor.

If Charles had acquired the imperial crown in succession to the emperors who had reigned in Constantinople, the popes could scarcely have claimed, as they afterwards did, to exercise the sovereignty of God upon earth. The dexterity of Leo in placing the crown on his head enabled the successors of Leo centuries later to advance that claim.

Charles the Great was a constant student of the *De Civitate Dei*; but he certainly did not view the Empire restored under his authority as in any respect the kingdom of Satan. When Augustine began his treatise, in A.D. 410, the persecution of the Church by the pagan emperors was still fresh in the memory of the Christians. In the centuries which divided Augustine from Charles, Church and Empire had become so closely identified as to be regarded merely as different aspects of the same institution. To Charles the Empire was the Kingdom of God as conceived by Augustine; but the successful and experienced statesman perhaps valued peace and order in this world at a higher rate than the Bishop of Hippo, and felt also that he knew how to achieve it. Nor did he ever allow his position as supreme head of the divine polity to be questioned. His right to rule the Church no less than the state was vigorously asserted.

What a pope had done on that eight-hundredth Christmas morning other popes might do again. In the centuries to come aspirants to the imperial throne were constantly suitors for the crown which Leo had assumed the right to bestow. It is true that for more than two centuries the popes applied to the emperors to confirm their elections. By the eleventh century the Papacy had fallen into such discredit that the emperors sought to reform it by themselves appointing vigorous bishops from Germany. The reform recoiled on the Empire by its very success. At the council of A.D. 1059 it was finally decreed that in future the elections of popes should rest with the cardinals, priests of the parishes of the city of Rome which lie at the cardinal points of the compass.

This reform was really the work of the great Hildebrand, who in A.D. 1073 became Pope under the name of Gregory VII. By the thirteenth century Innocent III. was claiming the right of the Pope to appoint the Emperor on the strength of the fact that Leo III. had placed the crown on the head of Charles the Great.

The messianic idea as formulated in the pages of Augustine thus dominated the history of Europe. In the Middle Ages human society was conceived as organised in one polity in preparation for that time when Christ would return to judge the quick and dead, to decide the future of each individual soul, to separate the wheat from the tares and the sheep from the goats, to condemn the wicked to eternal torment and gather the righteous to enjoy for ever the blessings of the heavenly kingdom.

In the eastern Empire where, since Constantine, emperors had reigned in unbroken succession, there was no doubt that the Emperor alone was the supreme representative of God upon earth. He appointed the Patriarch of Constantinople, and used him at his pleasure. And so the Byzantine Empire became indistinguishable from a typical eastern despotism.

With the Holy Roman Empire as reconstituted by Charles and Leo it was otherwise. The conditions under which it was instituted implied the coexistence of two powers, both claiming an authority which was sovereign in nature. The theories by which it was argued that Emperor and Pope were sovereign in different spheres could only mask the essential antagonism, for in practice their spheres were widely overlapping. There is in principle no room in one theocracy for two vicegerents of God. When their spheres conflict, each will claim that the other has received his power through himself, and the conflict between these claims can never be finally reconciled. The divine polity of the Middle Ages was delivered to the world unblemished by any conspicuous birthmark. And yet from the manner in which that delivery was handled it contracted a radical weakness which proved fatal to its normal development as a system of government based on authority. It carried that weakness to the grave. It brought not peace but the sword. From the ninth century to the nineteenth it frustrated the very blessings it was meant to provide, the unity and order of a Christian world.

In the eleventh century Hildebrand had asserted the principle that the pope's appointment should lie with the Church itself and in no way depend on the Emperor's sanction. Thenceforward the popes began to claim an authority as unlimited in the civil as in the spiritual sphere. In A.D. 1139 Innocent II. was addressing the Lateran Council as though he were the absolute master of Christendom:

> Ye know that Rome is the capital of the world, that ye hold your dignities by the Roman pontiff as a vassal holds

his fiefs of his sovereign, and that ye cannot retain them without his assent.

A Byzantine ambassador was heard to exclaim, "Your Pope Innocent is not a bishop, but an Emperor". Sixty years later Innocent III. had travelled further along this road, and was claiming sovereignty over all the kingdoms of Europe. In the case of England the claim was enforced by closing the churches to public worship, till in A.D. 1213 John surrendered his kingdom to be held from the Pope subject to a quit-rent of 1000 marks.[5] And till 1333 the tribute was paid. In A.D. 1299 Boniface VIII. received the envoys of the Emperor, Albert I., seated on a throne, crowned with the diadem of Constantine, holding a sceptre and girt with a sword. "Am not I", he said to them, "the supreme pontiff? Is not this the throne of Peter? Is it not mine to guard the laws of the Empire? I, I am the Emperor."

NOTES

[1] *Annales Laurissenses*, quoted by Hodgkin, vol. vii. p. 128.
[2] Hodgkin, vol. vii. pp. 145-50.
[3] *Codex Carolinus*, 61, quoted by Hodgkin, vol. viii. pp. 43-4.
[4] *Cap. Duplex Aquisgranense* (811), ap. Migne 330, quoted by Hodgkin, vol. viii. p. 132.
[5] H. W. C. Davis, *England under the Normans and Anjevins*, p. 368.

CHAPTER XXIX

THE PRINCIPLE OF AUTHORITY IN APPLICATION

THE claims of the Papacy could go no further. The authority of the Popes over temporal rulers was used to enforce obedience in spiritual matters. Since the time of Theodosius the powers of the state had been used to punish deviations from belief as prescribed by the Church. The infliction of torture and death as a punishment for heresy had indeed been condemned by the fathers, including Augustine. But the principle of authority overrode the sentiment of the early Christians with ruthless logic. Through the dark ages heretics were executed from time to time in various localities.

The first stirrings of the intellectual revival which eventually led to the Reformation were felt just at the moment when the Papacy was asserting its claim to unlimited sovereignty, and was imitating the Empire of Justinian's time by producing a jurisprudence of its own. At the close of the twelfth century there developed in Provence a formidable movement against sacerdotalism. In order to meet it, Innocent III. declared that treason against God was at least as heinous a crime as treason against temporal rulers, and admitted the logical consequence of this doctrine. Its practical expression was an organisation centralised in Rome for the suppression of heresy throughout Christendom. In every country of western Europe ecclesiastical courts were created for the purpose under the direction of the Grand Inquisitor in Rome. The inquisitors were authorised by papal decree to use torture in obtaining evidence or confession of guilt. They devised a procedure which deprived their victims of all ordinary means of defence, and left them at the mercy of their accusers. The ecclesiastical court, having sentenced the heretic, handed him over to the secular authorities to be burned alive, with a formal recommendation to mercy which was never observed in practice, and was in fact a conventional relic of the earlier Christian feeling against the infliction of capital punishment.

In most countries these ecclesiastical courts were viewed with some jealousy by the secular authorities. In Spain they were largely directed against Moors and Jews, who had falsely adopted the Christian religion, or were thought to have done so, and they worked in the closest alliance with the state. It is estimated that in Spain alone more than 31,000 persons were burned alive, while 290,000 were condemned to lesser punishments at the instance of the Inquisition. No less than 50,000 perished for their religion in the Netherlands under the reign of Charles V. These holocausts of victims became a public spectacle as popular as the gladiatorial games had been in Rome. They were used to celebrate the marriages of princes. This mighty engine for the suppression of thought financed itself by confiscating the property of its victims and even by selling licences to those able to pay for the privilege of holding beliefs contrary to the Catholic faith.

The Papacy, which had acquired the functions of a state without its normal resources, learned to replenish its treasury by similar methods. It began by remitting penalties imposed for infractions of Church law for a money payment. The penance imposed on a sinner by the Church operated to relieve him of so many ages of purgatory.

Historically speaking it is indisputable that the practice of Indulgences in the medieval Church arose out of the authoritative remission, in exceptional cases, of a certain proportion of this canonical penalty. At the same time, according to Catholic teaching, such Indulgence was not a mere permission to omit or postpone payment, but was, in fact, a *discharge* from the debt of temporal punishment which the sinner owed. The authority to grant such discharge was conceived to be included in the power of binding and loosing committed by Christ to His Church, and when in the course of time the vaguer theological conceptions of the first ages of Christianity assumed scientific form and shape at the hands of the Schoolmen, the doctrine came to prevail that this discharge of the sinner's debt was made through an application to the offender of what was called the "Treasure" of the Church. The infinite merits of Christ our Redeemer and the superabundant penance of the Saints, who offered to God a greater atonement than was required for the expiation of their own sins, were conceived of as creating a fund of satisfactions which the Church dispenses at will, and which she applies to those offenders who seem specially to deserve her favour.[1]

By the Middle Ages the Church had learnt to bestow her favours for cash and replenish her treasury by professing to relieve sinners from the penalties of their sins. Pardoners hawked indulgences through Europe like modern travellers in silks or soap.

A few words attributed to Jesus by one of his biographers, and pressed to their logical conclusion by the Church, had yielded an enormous and poisonous growth:

> Verily I say unto you, What things soever ye shall bind on earth shall be bound in heaven: and what things soever ye shall loose on earth shall be loosed in heaven.[2]

The Church has dwelt on these words with eager insistence and applied them in a literal and even mechanical sense. The doctrine that Jesus intended to create a machine for controlling the minds and consciences of men is at variance with that part of his teaching which bears the stamp of original thought, and also with the line of action which brought him into conflict with the Jewish hierarchy. He cannot have used these words with this meaning unless he had two minds, and on different occasions preached contrary principles. It is easier to suppose that his hearers had missed the profounder significance of some such phrase as that which he used in his last interview with Peter, and had all unconsciously twisted it into something which expressed their own ideas. His biographers, writing a whole generation after his death, believed him to have vindicated the truth of his teaching by working miracles. It was just as inevitable that they should make him propound the principle of authority against which his genuine doctrine and conduct are both directed.

In the long run principles issue in practice and are tested by results. The tares and the wheat may be hard to distinguish while still in the blade; but once they have ripened to seed the difference between them is plain to all who have eyes to see. It needed a mind powerful as Paul's to realise that Jesus had meant utterly to abolish the Mosaic law, and a courage and force no less than his to convince the world that this was so. But it never dawned on that mind that the teaching of Jesus could rest on any authority other than that upon which the law of Moses was presumed to rest. In Paul's view the truth about life could only be known through a supernatural revelation. His belief that Jesus had wrought miracles, had been raised from the dead and years later had commissioned Paul himself to preach the gospel to the Gentiles, was to him proof that God had chosen to reveal his truth to man through Christ, and also through successors divinely appointed by Christ. In controversy it was vital to Paul to establish his own apostolic commission. The principle of authority in human affairs was a postulate he never thought of examining. He failed to perceive that the system attacked by Jesus with fatal results to himself was the necessary outcome of that principle. Nor could he foresee how the principle inspiring the Mosaic system, renewed in the name of Christ, would reproduce a like system on a vastly extended scale; how the mockery of his trial by ecclesiastics and his execution by the secular arm would be multiplied through centuries, how the Church would derive its revenues from a traffic more flagitious than that which Jesus himself had expelled from the courts of the Temple.

Do men gather grapes of thorns, or figs of thistles? Even so every good tree bringeth forth good fruit; but the corrupt tree bringeth forth evil fruit. A good tree cannot bring forth evil fruit, neither can a corrupt tree bring forth good fruit. Every tree that bringeth not forth good fruit is hewn down, and cast into the fire. Therefore by their fruits ye shall know them.[3]

The ultimate goal of our quest is not to discover what Jesus said or did not say, but that pearl beyond price for which his career was a tireless search, the truth about life, the principles upon which men ought to live. The words just quoted impress our minds with a sense of profound intuition and impel us to believe that they fell from the lips of a master. They point to the test whereby principles based on the truth are in process of time separated and distinguished from those which are false. They afford no hope to our childlike yearning to be shown what is true by the supernatural light of direct revelation. They call on men to trust like Job only to the light that is in them, to the natural resources of their own minds. In the long run the validity of principles is proved in their application, and therefore only in the course of ages. It is this which vests history with its special importance, because it enables abstract principles to be studied in their application to life. With the light of eighteen centuries to guide us we are better able than the early Christians to discern what is really valuable in the gospel records. Over long periods of time the principle of authority and that of the commonwealth have found expression in institutions. In the past and present their effect on society can be closely studied. It is now possible for ordinary minds to discern, as it was not in the dawn of the Christian era, which of them is based on the verities of life.

Revolutions are often disguised by keeping old names, and reactions by changing them. The principle of authority challenged by Jesus in the guise of Judaism was all unconsciously re-established by his followers under the name of Christianity. Seed from the old tree reverently planted on his grave yielded fruit after its kind. In the course of ages the new system of authority exceeded Judaism by the measure that Europe exceeded Judea. Beyond question the Church has conferred on those who came under its influence benefits without number of immeasurable value. Its genuine achievements are fully admitted by competent historians outside the ranks of its own followers who are far from admitting its spiritual claims.[4] To the Church, as to its parents, Judaism and the Roman Empire, the structure of society owes an incalculable debt. Yet the fullest acknowledgment of its merits cannot alter the fact that Christendom, as organised in the Middle Ages, was, in principle and therefore in its ultimate effect, the direct antithesis of the polity which Jesus had conceived as essential to the ever continuous growth of virtue in men.

NOTES

[1] Father Thurston, S.J., *The Holy Year of Jubilee*, pp. 315-16.
[2] Matthew xviii. 18.
[3] Matthew vii. 16-20.
[4] See for instance A. L. Smith's *Church and State in the Middle Ages*.

CHAPTER XXX

SAXONS AND NORSEMEN

THE instinct of men to serve one another has been seen in the mind of Jesus as the element of absolute value in life. In a social system based on its exercise this instinct was capable of infinite growth. But the world in which he uttered these truths was rapidly moving in the opposite direction. The Roman Empire had failed to devise any system whereby the control of society could be based on the duty of men to each other. Even Roman citizens were learning to obey a divine authority backed by force. The mechanism of a commonwealth and some of its spirit still lingered in towns like those of Decapolis. But the Roman Empire had closely integrated the lives of all the communities surrounding the Mediterranean. The direct government of men by themselves was applicable only to the local interests of communities so small that their members could meet to discuss and settle them. It was narrowed to municipal limits. The various cities and races surrounding the Mediterranean were now integral parts of a great society with a common civilisation. Its existence depended on its general security. The Graeco-Roman world had developed no mechanism through which a community too large or too scattered to meet in one spot could govern its own affairs. To maintain a civilisation which had sprung from the principle of the commonwealth it was forced to accept the principle of autocracy, by virtue of which not cities only, but nations widely varying in race, language and thought, could be held together. The sense of permanence, which the Empire gave to its civilisation, was highly deceptive; for the spirit from which it had drawn its vitality languished and died for want of exercise.

In the barbarous tribes which burst through the northern frontiers and submerged the decadent Empire was the crude but vigorous germ of political life. The relation of chiefs to the peoples they led was not that of a Byzantine emperor to his cringing subjects. Charles the Great, at the zenith of his power, had constantly to pause on his tireless journeys to hold a *placitum* or diet. The warriors who followed a northern king expected to know what he meant to do and why he was doing it, as something which closely affected themselves. He must always be thinking how to retain or secure their approval. Here was the instinct which, centuries before, had developed commonwealths in Greece and the sense of a public interest in Rome. In the village communes of the Alps this instinct survived the Roman autocracy and was destined in course of time to produce the Helvetian republic. It burst into sudden and transitory life in the Lombard cities of northern Italy. It found expression in Sweden and Hungary, in the French estates, in those of the Netherlands and also in the diets of central Europe. In various directions and in different degrees the principle of the commonwealth was reduced to practice in institutions. But none of them ripened sufficiently to spread their seed into wider fields. Europe as a whole was in chaos. The Papacy, strong enough to emasculate the Empire, was unequal to the task of creating a genuine government for Christendom. Anarchy prevailed, especially in Italy and central Europe, the home of the Holy Roman Empire.

In conditions like these the people of every locality were accustomed to obey the military leader who was best able to afford them protection. The feudal system developed and in time the strongest leaders welded localities into organised kingdoms. Such rulers claimed to base their title on divine authority, some through the Emperor, some through the Pope and others direct from God, as best suited their immediate interests. The principle of autocracy was never at issue; but only the medium through which it was claimed. Popes, emperors and kings alike viewed with suspicion attempts on the part of ordinary men to manage their own affairs for themselves. The imperial tradition of Rome, though never expressed in a genuine system of government, pervaded the atmosphere and stifled the instinct for freedom in the northern regions of Europe, its natural home.

The revival of the commonwealth, its new development on a national scale, like its first appearance in the cities of Greece, was destined to occur where physical conditions had provided the degree of security needed for the purpose. Rome, saturated and transformed by Jewish tradition, had silently mastered its northern invaders, a reconquest that might have endured, but for a fact of physical geography. As the polar ice-caps melted at the close of the last glacial age, the sea had risen, submerging the estuary of the Rhine, till a group of territories was isolated from the continent of Europe by turbulent waters.

Before this age, when men have learned to fly, the British Isles were a fortress—inviolable whenever their inhabitants could unite to defend them. When Roman legions invaded them the Celtic tribes had acquired no semblance of national union. They were easily conquered and by the end of the fourth century had adopted the civilisation and language of Rome and also the Christian religion.

St. Augustine had scarcely finished his *De Civitate Dei* when in A.D. 430 Rome was withdrawing her legions and abandoning Britain to the rising tide of savage invaders. It may even be that the general disturbance caused by the Hunnish invasion of Europe may have set in motion this westward thrust. To pass from guess-work to fact, we know that Anglo-Saxons from Schleswig-Holstein swarmed to these shores and conquered the island so far as Devon and the mountainous regions of Scotland and Wales. Wherever they conquered and settled the Christian religion was extinguished. The culture and language of Rome was submerged. No contemporary records exist from which the history of this period can be framed because these barbarians were unable to write them. From evidence which the spade is constantly yielding we know that they everywhere burned the houses of the Romanised Britains and put their inhabitants to the sword. They had no desire to use for themselves the solid and comfortable dwellings of civilised men. They simply destroyed the traces of civilisation wherever they found them. As they reached these shores, our Saxon fathers were savages in the ordinary sense of that word.

We all know from our school-books how some English captives, exposed for sale in the Roman slave-market, attracted the notice of Gregory, Abbot of St. Andrews. Touched by their youth and their beauty, the Abbot was led to conceive the idea of converting England from heathenism. He had actually started on his mission when he was recalled and raised to the Chair of St. Peter. In A.D. 596 he commanded Augustine, his successor to the abbacy, to fulfil his still unaccomplished purpose. The mission was successful and in A.D. 601 Augustine was consecrated Archbishop of Canterbury. The Church in the south of England thus owed its foundation to the Papacy more directly than most in that age and the early English churchmen were eager champions of the papal claims. Geography was in time to prove stronger than history.

In Wales Christianity had survived the Saxon invasion. St. Patrick, a Welsh missionary, had carried it to Ireland in the fifth century. In A.D. 563 St. Columba carried it from Ireland to Scotland, whence it spread to Northumbria about A.D. 635. These Celtic churches and their English converts were less ready to acknowledge the authority of Rome than the church founded in the province of Canterbury.

The seeds of civilisation were thus replanted by Christianity. Churchmen were able to write. To them we owe it that once again we begin to know what was happening in England.

The Saxon settlers had lost their taste for the sea and were mainly devoted to farming. The lands they had left vacant in Denmark had been occupied by settlers of a kindred race from further north. In the course of ages the character of these Norsemen had been moulded in the fiords of Scandinavia, valleys of a mountainous country partly submerged at the close of the glacial age. On the edge of these fiords the Norsemen had settled wherever ground could be ploughed and cattle could be grazed on the slopes above. They could hunt in the forests and fish in the sea. As a rule the fishermen's boats were the only means of communication between the villages. In these stormy latitudes the primitive Norsemen became the most skilful and daring of mariners. At the period with which we are now dealing they were learning to build vessels which could traverse the open seas and thus to embark on distant adventures. They crossed the Baltic, founded the Russian Empire at Novgorod, descended the Dnieper and occupied Constantinople. They planted colonies in Iceland, Scotland, England and Ireland, in Normandy, Sicily and Calabria. They visited Greenland and Labrador.

Their amphibious life made them of all men the most resourceful and raised their energy to the highest voltage. But the discipline of the sea also developed an instinct for method and exactness. These opposite qualities naturally led to contrasts in the various colonies they founded. In Iceland these sea lawyers established

> a government developed only upon its judicial and (to a much smaller extent) upon its legislative side omitting altogether the executive and international sides.[1]

In Sicily they ruled a medley of races, languages and creeds, much as England ruled India in the nineteenth century. The despotism they founded in England was the crucible in which its refractory races were fused.

In the eighth century the heathen Norsemen began to plunder, conquer and occupy Christianised England from Denmark, much as the Anglo-Saxons had done three centuries earlier. At the close of this century the Saxon Alfred stopped their advance and drove them into the north-east. To the south of this 'Danelaw' Alfred established his power as king. The Danes were converted to Christianity and rapidly fused with the kindred Saxons. They had brought with them the word 'law' and some of the ideas which that word connotes. They had also established fortified towns on the rivers, often repairing old Roman walls. The English began to copy this practice in Wessex and, as they reconquered the Danelaw, parcelled it out into shires—military areas surrounding fortified towns.

For a brief period at the opening years of the tenth century a great part of the Viking world, Denmark, Norway, the Hebrides and England, was organised as an empire by the Danish king Canute. He conquered England and was elected as its king in A.D. 1017. Thereafter he ruled Saxons and Danes alike on a footing of equality. It is idle to speculate what might have happened if this great Norsemen had lived longer and left competent successors. When he died at the age of forty in A.D. 1035 his Empire dissolved and Edward the Confessor, of the House of Alfred, was elected by the English as king.

In the ninth century the Norsemen had preyed on both sides of the English Channel. They had pushed up the Seine as far as Rouen and had ravaged the country surrounding it. In the early years of the tenth century one of them, Rollo by name, had decided to settle there with his followers. By a treaty with Charles the Simple, king of France, he acquired a considerable area surrounding Rouen as duke of Normandy. He himself was baptized and ere long the Normans had adopted the French language, the feudal system as developed in France and the art of fighting on horseback. In his youth Edward the Confessor was trained in a Norman monastery and as king of England depended largely on Norman advisers. The Saxon earl Godwin had expelled these advisers and, when Edward died, Godwin's son Harold was elected to succeed him.

In A.D. 1035, the year of Canute's death, Robert the Devil, duke of Normandy, had also died on a pilgrimage to Jerusalem, bequeathing his dukedom to William, a bastard born to him by the daughter of a tanner. In A.D. 1064 Harold was wrecked on the Norman coast and fell into the power of William, who made him swear to support his claim to the throne of England on the death of Edward the Confessor. When Harold, ignoring his oath, was elected to the throne, William prepared to assert his claim. Through the influence of Hildebrand he secured the approval of the Pope for his enterprise. This was strictly in accordance with the theory of world sovereignty, which Hildebrand claimed for the Papacy. He was thus helping to temper the axe which, centuries later, would be laid to its root.

The death of Edward had fired the king of Norway, Harald Hardrada, with the hope of reviving the Empire of Canute. He landed in Yorkshire, where he and his host were destroyed by Harold at Stamford Bridge on September 28, A.D. 1066. Harold marched rapidly to the south to meet William, who had landed at Hastings. On October 14 their armies met; but the Saxon infantry were no match for the Norman cavalry and Harold was defeated and slain.

Within five years William had mastered the country up to the Cheviots and Wales. For the first time an effective political unity was forced on the English and was afterwards maintained, until it had become to them a habit of mind. This unity made the island impregnable and the conquest which created it was therefore the last to which it submitted. Henceforward English society acquired the character of a lake which is troubled only by the winds that reach it. In the atmosphere of Europe any local disturbance could raise a swell which spread through society to its furthest limits.

William brought to the task of government the superlative energy of his race and also their genius for organisation. While the feudal system as developed in France was imposed in its leading features, William made it clear that holders of land owed a duty to himself prior to the duty they owed to their lords. The duties imposed by the feudal system as well as the rights were accurately specified in a vast cadastral survey which bears comparison with the land settlement applied to India centuries later under William's successors. By making it clear that the king was paramount in the feudal system he prepared the way for its supersession.

The word 'feudalism' coined in the eighteenth century was unknown to the people who lived under that system. It developed, when the government provided by the Roman Empire had collapsed, as a means whereby the people in each locality could obtain some kind of security for life and property. A barbarian chief, who had seized the land, parcelled it out amongst his followers, to be held by them in return for military service and certain dues. He was thus provided with a force with which to resist the encroachments of neighbouring chiefs. His tenants allowed the people who lived on their land specified rights, again in return for military service, and also dues to be paid in cash, in kind or in actual labour. The labourers at the base of the system were serfs attached like chattels to the land. One chief, more powerful than the rest, would claim their allegiance and assert his title to be recognised as king. His nobles, tenants in chief, would then try to assert the principle that the royal authority could only be exercised through themselves. When justice had to be done between their henchmen it was they who must do it in courts of their own. The king could only do justice as between the tenants in chief. A strong king, on the other hand, was always seeking to extend his direct authority over the henchmen of his tenants in chief, to assert his right to decide their disputes in courts of his own, to make laws which applied to them all and commanded their obedience as against a lord in rebellion against him. In course of time he would claim that everyone in his dominions was liable to pay taxes to him direct and not to his lord only. It was only in so far as kings succeeded in establishing these rights that states in the real sense of the word were brought into being. Feudalism, based on the principle of contract, was incompatible with the principle of sovereignty, which is founded on dedication; and sovereignty is the essence of the state. As contrasted with systems like caste or feudalism the state is a vertebrate structure. The Norman and Plantagenet kings provided England with the backbone of a genuine government, a paramount authority which all their subjects had, in the last resort, to obey, even as against their local lords.

In parcelling out the land he had conquered to his barons or tenants in chief William the Conqueror was careful to see that he put no one of them in the kind of position which his ancestor Rollo had established for himself as duke of Normandy. To each of his barons he allotted a number of manors, but in different parts of the country. Great earldoms like Wessex, Mercia and Northumbria vanished under his system. He adopted the shires, which were relatively small, as administrative units.

NOTE

[1] Bryce, *Studies in History and Jurisprudence*, vol. i. p. 333.

CHAPTER XXXI

THE COMMONWEALTH RAISED TO THE NATIONAL SCALE

NORMAN and early Plantagenet kings would scarcely have understood the distinctions we draw between the judicial, executive and legislative branches of government. Conflicting claims to a piece of land, the penalties which were to be inflicted for crimes or the measures for suppressing a rising were all matters which the king must decide. His decision was expressed by a seal on a document prepared by a clerk who could read and write. His seal was, therefore, entrusted to a highly responsible officer, called a chancellor, who was usually a churchman. Yet, before making a decision and ordering his chancellor to impress the seal, the Nordic king felt it wise to secure the approval and support of his leading men. He therefore instructed the chancellor to summon the barons, bishops and some abbots to his court. This summons, issued in writing, was known as a writ.

In the great council, more often held in the camp than the palace, like the durbars held by an Indian prince, the king listened to rival claimants, discussed appropriate punishments for misconduct or the measures to be taken for suppressing a rebellion, and made his decisions after hearing what his councillors had to say. Judicial, executive and legislative action might all be involved in a single decision. In the king's absence his chancellor would preside over the council.

Throughout the kingdom there existed a great variety of Saxon, Danish and Norman customs. The practice adopted by the Norman kings in settling the disputes brought to their courts led to the development of a law common to the realm. Bishops and barons with a taste for judicial work became expert in the law that the court was developing.

In a country so large as England it was clearly impossible that all matters at issue could be brought for settlement to the king in his court. The Norman and Angevin kings realised the danger of leaving the local cases, which they could not deal with themselves, to be settled by feudal barons. They, therefore, instructed the sheriffs, who acted as their officers in the shires, to hold courts like their own, in which the business of the shire could be done. These county courts were the king's courts, no less than the court that he held in person.

The county courts naturally tended to settle cases in accordance with local custom. A notable step was taken when Henry II. commissioned members of his great council, barons skilled in the law there administered for the realm, to tour through the land and hold assizes in the county courts. In the composition of these courts the principle of representation begins to appear.

> By the terms of the royal writs ordering the sheriff to summon the county court for the visit of the itinerant justices, each *villa* had on that occasion to be represented by the reeve and four lawful men, each borough by twelve lawful burgesses.[1]

At these county assizes civil and criminal cases were adjudged in accordance with the law common to England, the law developed by the king in council. Henceforward the English were accustomed to obey a law common to all of them and came to regard it as binding, not only on themselves, but also on their rulers. The rule of law was thus established for a whole nation, as centuries before in the cities of Greece.

This increase of power, asserted by Henry II. on

behalf of the crown, was so abused by his son John that he drove into armed opposition not only the barons, but also the lesser gentry and merchants, the classes on whom his father had leaned for support. At Runnymede he was forced by the barons to sign a charter defining their privileges. Magna Carta went further than, perhaps, its authors had meant towards defining the rights of the subject irrespective of rank.

These troubles recurred when John's infant successor, Henry III., reached his majority and assumed his powers. Once more the barons rebelled under the leadership of Simon de Montfort. In A.D. 1264 the king and his son Edward were defeated at the battle of Lewes and imprisoned. As Simon de Montfort had now to govern the country himself he sought to strengthen his position by widening the basis of the great council. Even Henry III. had gone so far as to summon to his council knights from the shires. The towns had resented the taxes which the king had levied on their trade; so Simon now went a step further and summoned to the great council burgesses from the towns as well as knights from the shires. His period of authority was brief. In A.D. 1265 Prince Edward, who had cleverly escaped from his prison, defeated and slew him at the battle of Evesham.

Under Edward I., who came to the throne in A.D. 1272, experienced judges were appointed to sit in Westminster Hall and deal with most of the cases; though the right of appeal to the king in council was preserved. It was Edward I. who started the practice of declaring important aspects of law in the form of statutes framed by the judges and carefully discussed in the great council, the high court of parliament, which was thus becoming less of a court and more of a legislature.

The struggles of John and Henry III. with their

barons largely arose out of questions of money. In the feudal theory of that age the king was supposed to "live of his own" on the rents and dues paid by his vassals, just as they in turn were expected to live on the dues paid by their tenants. The king, conceived as a baron-in-chief, was less than a sovereign and until the principle of sovereignty was established no state in the real sense of the word could be founded. The kings could not in fact meet the costs of a genuine government from customary dues which were fixed in amount. They were constantly bargaining with barons, bishops, abbots and towns to increase or to supplement the customary dues. At times the relations of the king to his subjects were strained to the breaking-point. The results were Runnymede or the battle of Lewes.

Edward I. realised the mistake which his father and grandfather had both made in alienating the gentry and merchants and driving them to support the barons and bishops against the crown. He decided, therefore, to get into touch with them and bring them to his council. But thousands of writs could not be issued to knights and merchants as writs could be issued to the few hundred barons and bishops. His fallen enemy, Simon de Montfort, had shown him the way out of this difficulty and Edward I. followed his example in issuing writs ordering the county courts each to select a couple of knights and provide the money for sending them to attend the meetings of his council. Similar writs were issued to the boroughs. These knights and merchants were to settle with the king the revenue to be paid him from the shires and towns. The king, in the writs he issued from chancery, was careful to specify that the settlements made with him in council by these knights and merchants were to be final and not to be subject to further confirmation by the county courts and the borough councils which had sent them to bargain on their behalf. The settlements they made were to bind their constituents.

The said knights are to have full and sufficient power for themselves and for the community of the aforesaid county, and the said citizens and burgesses for themselves and the communities of the aforesaid cities and boroughs separately, there and then, for doing what shall then be ordained according to the Common Council in the premises, so that the aforesaid business shall not remain unfinished in any way for defect of this power.[2]

It is needless here to discuss whether the Plantagenet king had copied this provision from church assemblies. This at least is clear that when issuing these writs he had all-unconsciously supplied the link which Aristeides had missed when he planned the synod of Delos. The members of the synod might agree that so much money from each state was necessary to ensure the safety of Greece from Persian aggression; but the money was not payable until it was voted by every city which sent them to Delos. The estimates framed by the league were thus rendered abortive by the failure of constituent members to vote their quotas. The synod became a farce and, to save Greece from Persia, Athens, the dominant member of the league, forcibly collected the quotas due from members in default. The league ceased to be a league and became an empire, ruled by force in the hands of its strongest member, and Athens went down the primrose path to the bonfire prepared for those who deny all sanctions but physical force. If Edward I. had allowed the principle to develop that the knights and burgesses could only arrive at settlements with him, subject to approval by the counties and boroughs which sent them to his court, the whole arrangement would have broken down. The English kings must either have established an absolute monarchy, as in France, or else have drifted into the position which the Holy

Roman Emperors accepted as heads of a polity which was always futile because it was feudal.

On an earlier page we have seen how practical effect was first given to the principle of the commonwealth by nameless statesmen who taught village assemblies in Greece and Italy to end their discussions by taking a vote and allowing the majority to decide the issue. The statesman who made self-government possible for areas wider than city-states was Edward I. when he issued his writs to the counties and boroughs. The idea that spokesmen could voice the views of electorates had slowly developed in county courts. But the principle, at once more difficult and vital, that a majority of the spokesmen could commit not merely their own electors, but also the total electorate and pledge the wealth of the taxpayers as a whole, was finally established by Edward I. It was this that enabled Burke to tell his angry constituents at Bristol that he was elected by them as a pillar of the British constitution and not as a weather-cock on the top of the edifice. In creating a parliament which could bind its constituents, Edward I. had unknowingly created a body which could bind his successors by law. In the history of the commonwealth the principle that majorities can bind minorities is not more important than the principle that electors can be bound by those they elect.

The knights and burgesses called to parliament were expected to do more than agree to aids which the shires and boroughs were to make to the king. They were also to assess and collect the amounts due from the local taxpayers. So onerous were the duties that owners whose holdings were worth less than forty shillings a year had to be relieved from the burden of taking part in elections. Boroughs often petitioned to be freed from the burden of sending members to parliament. These ungrateful tasks, however, were faced by knights and merchants in sufficient numbers to establish the system. The shires and towns which sent them to parliament were broadly described as the 'communes'. So the body of men who represented these communes came to be known as the 'commons'.

It was clearly felt that even this limited number of people might make the council too large for practical purposes. The commons were also shy of raising their voices in the presence of the king and the lords of nobility. Arrangements were therefore made for the commons to appoint from amongst themselves a speaker who would say to the king in council whatever there was to be said for them all. They met behind closed doors in the chapter-house of Westminster to select their speaker and discuss what he should say.

Finance was only one part of their business. The commons were to bring to the king in council matters which aggrieved the people at large; for the king was thus to secure their support as against the feudal power of the nobles. So knights and burgesses came to parliament loaded with petitions from the shires and towns. When they came to compare them in the chapter-house of the Abbey they naturally found that some of the troubles complained of in different counties and towns arose from a general defect in the law. The king in council would then be petitioned by the speaker to make the necessary change in the law. The king was presently to find that the aids which the knights and burgesses were asked to approve were not forthcoming until he himself had promised to grant the petitions made by the commons. He was thus constrained to promise the enactment of statutes to redress their grievances. When the commons had adjourned, he would then promulgate statutes drafted by the judges which purported to give effect to the petitions. But when parliament met once more it was often complained that these laws were not in accord with that which the commons had asked for and the king had said should be done. So the commons began to prepare for themselves drafts of the statutes they wished the king to enact; and in this they were helped by lawyers practising in Westminster Hall on the other side of the road. The king in council was then petitioned by the commons to enact these drafts, which were called 'bills', and to give them the force of law as statutes. In A.D. 1414 a pledge was exacted from Henry V.

> that fro hens forth nothyng be enacted to the Petitions of his Commune that be contrarie of his askyng, wharby they should be bounde withoute their assent.[3]

In the course of centuries the principle was established that the king of himself could enact nothing except in the form of a statute which parliament had approved; and, finally, that bills which parliament had approved must be enacted. By then the position was also established that the title of the king himself to his throne was settled by an act of parliament.

The exact terms of the bills which the commons presented to the king in council had first to be settled by themselves in the chapter-house. Like the Greek and Roman assemblies they had learned the art of translating talk into action by dividing the house and allowing the majority to decide. But even so the decision could only be 'aye' or 'no' and, as everyone sees who has sat on the smallest committee, the task of settling the terms of a document in a large assembly is laborious and difficult. A way in which this can be done was developed little by little in the course of centuries and is now embodied in the procedure of the house of commons. The methods followed by legislative bodies throughout the world are largely based on it. As to how this procedure developed in the Middle Ages we have little information; for the commons, jealous of royal interference, met behind closed doors and kept no journals till the sixteenth century. This much we know, that a bill had in the first instance to be submitted to the house by an individual member. He would then describe his proposal and move that the bill be read out from the manuscript which he handed to the clerk of the house. Until bills could be printed, few of the members would have before them the text of the measures they were asked to discuss. They must have been largely limited to the question whether to accept or reject the draft as read out by the clerk. The amendment of bills had for the most part to be dealt with in committees small enough to handle a draft in writing.

The commonwealth is a system which enables the structure of society to be moulded by its own members in the light of experience. The invention of writing was a necessary step in its evolution, because no body of citizens could express their experience in laws until their decisions could be placed on record. Yet the power of popular assemblies to found laws on the general experience must have reached a certain point and stopped there, so long as the measures under discussion were presented only in handwriting. How greatly this power must have increased when each member could be furnished with a printed copy of a bill and also of amendments proposed, and still further when, by movable types, members could be given revised copies showing the amendments carried on previous days, will be best understood by anyone who has sat in a legislative body.

Acts of parliament were published in print as early as the reign of Henry VII. not many years after the time of Caxton. Yet so fearful were the commons of royal interference, and so jealous of the secrecy of their proceedings, that up to the eighteenth century, bills continued to be handled in manuscript only, until they had received the royal assent.

The first bill which the House directed to be printed and circulated amongst members before it was discussed was a bill of 1708, concerning large sums of public money which had passed through the hands of one Edward Whitaker, and about which discussion had been going on intermittently since 1702. It was an elaborate financial bill, giving acquittance to Edward Whitaker for all sums which he had handled since the death of William III.[4]

The use of printing to give members notice of proposed amendments and to show the amendments made in previous sittings was not introduced till the nineteenth century. The power of the house to deal with amendments was greatly increased by these expedients. In time the work became so technical that parliament called to its aid a staff of experts. The appointment of professional draftsmen in the middle of the nineteenth century is another landmark in parliamentary procedure.

Thus, with the aid of printing, representative bodies have acquired an unlimited power of moulding law in the light of common experience. Acts of parliament are no longer confined to brief declarations of general principles for judges to interpret. A modern statute is sometimes a volume in itself. Its chapters and sections are a complicated mechanism which reflects the intricate delicacy of the human relations to which it is applied. A parliament to-day is a mechanism which differs from that of Edward I. as a modern railway differs from a wheel-barrow. The difference is largely due to the invention of printing with movable types.

So far we have dealt with the commons rather than parliament. We must now go back to the early stages when the commons had framed a bill behind closed doors in the chapter-house of Westminster for their speaker to present to the king in council. When this happened the peers summoned to the council in their own right naturally wished to discuss in private what attitude to adopt towards the measure proposed by the commons. They also developed the habit of meeting without the king under the presidency of the lord chancellor. They often differed from the commons as to the principle of the measure or as to its details. If they could not agree as to the principle it was not presented to the king for his approval. If they differed only on details the lords and commons had then to agree on the terms of amendments. The procedure whereby this is done by the two houses sitting apart was developed. When both were agreed on principle and detail the bill was submitted to the king and enacted as law. The formula was as follows:

> Be it therefore enacted by the King's most Excellent Majesty, by and with the advice and consent of the Lords Spiritual and Temporal, and Commons, in this present Parliament assembled, and by the authority of the same as follows. . . .

The commons, however, asserted their exclusive right to settle the details of supply.

The high court of parliament had thus developed from the great council of the Norman kings and was destined in course of centuries to become a legislature with complete control of supply. Its judicial work, except for ultimate appeals, was devolved on separate courts, which also asserted their independence of royal interference. Executive matters remained in the hands of the king, and were dealt with by him and his privy council, a body which peers claimed a technical right to attend.

Legislative, judicial and executive functions were thus to a great extent distributed into three separate organs. Montesquieu, with his logical French mind, announced that this separation of powers was the essence of the British constitution, and indeed the secret of freedom itself, obscuring thereby the fact that the making, interpretation and enforcement of law are merely three aspects of sovereignty which can never be wholly divorced one from the other. Lord Haldane once opened an official interview with a government servant by saying, "I need hardly tell you that the judges have nothing to do with making or altering the law. They have only to interpret the law." "We are all familiar with that legal fiction", the government servant replied. "You, lord chancellor, know better than I do that where there are no precedents to follow the judges decide and in deciding they make the law." The official expression on Lord Haldane's face relaxed in a smile. "Within the four walls of this room I had better admit then that we judges are constantly making the law, and in fact legislate. So now let us talk of this matter on the basis of realities."

Of greater importance is the intimate connection between legislative and executive functions. The man or men responsible for administering the law will, as a rule, know better than any body of elected legislators what changes in the law are necessary to secure the safety of the realm. This applies especially to those laws which decide from year to year the contributions which each citizen must make to meet the expenses of government. In seeking to levy the ship-money from the inland counties Charles I. was right in believing that the cost of naval defence could not be left to counties washed by the sea. The soundness and equity of his claim was obscured by the fact that Charles I. was also set on asserting his claim to rule by divine authority, a claim which cost him his head. By the revolution, in which James II. lost his throne, it was settled once for all that whoever sat on that throne thereafter would sit there by virtue of an act of parliament and not by divine right.

The essential problem was still unsolved. The king and his ministers and parliament, the executive and legislature, might still be at odds as to what changes in the law, especially in the law of supply, were necessary for the safety of the realm. The king, though he could not legislate without parliament, could stop legislation and could, therefore, be removed only by another revolution. The cause of most revolutions is a deadlock in government, not oppression. In England the problem was solved, almost unconsciously, by transferring the executive power from the king to the minister able for the time being to command a majority in the house of commons. Such a minister could ask the house to frame the laws and vote the supplies which he deemed necessary for the safety of the realm. If they refused to support him, his place would be taken by a leader whom parliament was prepared to support; or else the defeated minister could dissolve parliament and ask the country to return one prepared to support him and abide the result. In the British constitution of to-day the real heir to the sovereignty of the Norman and Plantagenet kings is the prime minister, who is brought to office or can be removed from it by the will of parliament or else of the electorate. But, so long as he holds office, parliament must in the last instance do what he says or else remove him. Under British institutions the executive thus controls the legislature, so long as it is the executive.

By this process the lineal descendants of the Norman and Plantagenet kings have become the hereditary presidents of a republic. Just when the change had been made in England the founders of the American constitution, misled by the theories of Montesquieu, established an elective monarchy in the United States. The king who sits on the throne of Washington can only be changed every four years. In the interval the safety of the state may be jeopardised by a deadlock between the executive and legislature.

The first question to be asked about any system of government is not whether it represents the will of the people governed, but whether it is competent to meet their essential needs. History shows that good government cannot continue unless it is moving towards self-government. But it also shows that self-government cannot begin, or continue to exist, unless there is government in the real sense of the word. The instinct for realities that guided the English from Norman times was expressed in the Duke of Wellington's favourite phrase, "The king's government must be carried on". If the king was bound to consult the people through their representatives before taxing them, the people themselves were held to be bound by the settlements made by their representatives with the king. And if parliament could not be pledged to obey an hereditary king, they must then learn to obey the ruler whom they and the people had clothed for the time being with kingly power. The factor which enabled the English to construct a commonwealth on the national scale was this instinct that government must not be popularised beyond a point at which the system loses the quality of government.

NOTES

1 Pasquet, *An Essay on the Origins of the House of Commons*, p. 15.

2 Stubbs, *Select Charters*, pp. 476-77.

3 Redlich, *The Procedure of the House of Commons*, vol. i. p. 15.

4 Letter to the author from Sir C. Oman, who used the facilities he enjoyed as a member of parliament to examine its records.

CHAPTER XXXII

REACTIONS ON CHARACTER

THE great service which parliaments rendered in the middle ages was not, in fact, to make England a constitutional state, but to foster its growth into a national state based on something broader and deeper than monarchical centralisation, to make national unity a thing of the spirit rather than a territorial expression or a mechanical matter of administration, to evoke a common political consciousness at Westminster and then to propagate it in the constituencies. The value of parliaments consisted not so much in what members brought with them as in what they took away. Nationalism in the middle ages came nearer to Napoleon III.'s *la volonté de chacun* than to Rousseau's *la volonté générale*, and it was in and through parliaments that local and social prejudice was merged in a common sense. Every Englishman of to-day feels and realises his nationality to some extent; the degree is a matter of individual imagination, education, and interest. Generally speaking, his attachment to his country overrides every other affection except, perhaps, his devotion to himself and his family and in some cases his addiction to his religious or moral faith. But in the middle ages we are dealing with men whose nationalism came comparatively low in the scale of their affections. Men of the highest mind and character agreed with Archbishop Winchelsey that the loyalty they owed the pope came before the loyalty they owed the king. Barons were, as a rule, more devoted to their class than to either pope or king; the ordinary burgess or squire valued his local affinities more than his national bonds, and to the villager the parish was his world. When he threw himself upon his country—*posuit se super patriam*—his country consisted of his neighbours, and everyone else was a foreigner.

* * * * * *

The difference between modern and medieval Englishmen's patriotism is one of degree; in the middle ages locality preceded the nation, and it was through parliaments that the order was reversed.[1]

Trevelyan is expressing the same thought when he says that it was not England that made parliament but parliament which made England. Like Herodotus and Thucydides these historians see the character of their countrymen as shaped in the mould of their own institutions. There is also a darker side to the picture, as in Thucydides.

Perhaps the first European war that can be called national was the Hundred Years' War as waged by England. The armies she sent year after year to lay waste and plunder France were indeed very small, but their efficiency was the outcome of a national organization and a national spirit. England, on account of her insular and remote position, and her strong kings, had since the Norman Conquest outstripped the rest of Europe in obtaining a certain measure of internal peace, and was passing from feudalism to nationhood. As soon as King and Parliament had endowed her with administrative machinery and national self-consciousness, she exercised these new powers at the expense of that clumsy giant, the French feudal Kingdom. She became for a while the plunderer and bully of her continental neighbours, not because she had less conscience than they, but because she had more power.[2]

The victories of Crécy, Poitiers and Agincourt were due, so Trevelyan believes, to the structure of English society. It was this which enabled the English to wrest the control of the seas from Spain, to hold it against the French monarchy, to colonise or control a great part of the continents opened by Columbus and Vasco da Gama and to plant where they conquered the seed of their institutions. It was these institutions that led them to master the forces of nature and so to dominate the industry, commerce and finance of the world in the nineteenth century.

The air of superiority we too often betray in our dealings with foreigners is a remnant of the spirit which led the English to bully the French in the Middle Ages. This arrogance, whether in Athens or England, was not the product of free institutions, but sprang from the sense of superior strength which those institutions had given. It was due, not to the principle of the commonwealth, but rather to the fact that the principle was limited, in one case to a city, in the other to a nation. The principle can never be free from dangerous reactions on character until it is applied to society as a whole. We persist in thinking and acting as though the national commonwealth is the last word in human development. So Aristotle thought in his day that no commonwealth could ever exist on a scale larger than the Athens he knew. To have brought into being a commonwealth on the national scale is the greatest achievement in history and one, therefore, which points to a further and far more difficult task. When a real commonwealth of nations is created on a scale, however restricted, the most difficult stage will have been passed on the road to the ultimate goal, which can be no other than the organisation of all human society in one state based on the principle of the commonwealth.

On the continent of Europe the achievements of England were seen as results of her institutions, which were widely copied; though with very unequal success. In many directions attempts to apply the principle of the commonwealth have failed so completely that, as in the cities of ancient Greece, tyrannies have arisen to restore order and call into being governments which are really effective. More conspicuous still was the failure of China to establish republican government on the ruins of her ancient autocracy. Since the revolution of 1911 one-fifth part of humanity, and by no means the least cultured or intelligent part, has been plunged into anarchy.

In the light of these failures, it is often said that self-governing institutions can only be worked by peoples derived from the Anglo-Saxon stock which produced them. I myself have heard that view expressed by one who in former years had held offices of major importance in Liberal cabinets. One generally finds that the people who take this point of view believe that the qualities which enable Anglo-Saxon communities to govern themselves are derived from obscure biological causes, too complex to analyse and, therefore, not subject to human control. If the opposite view, that taken by Pollard and Trevelyan, is correct there is reason to hope that a like experience may in time develop these same qualities in all kinds of people. How far such qualities can be fostered by a conscious policy in domestic, imperial and foreign affairs is clearly a question of cardinal importance.

In order to form an opinion on this question one must have in one's mind some definite conception of the qualities which a people must develop in order to work a self-governing system. There must, to begin with, be a certain willingness on the part of minorities to accept the decisions of majorities. Such willingness can develop only in so far as majorities are felt to use their power of decision in the general interest rather than in their own. Minorities accustomed to think that the power of majorities is used in the interest of majorities alone lose their sense of membership in the state, develop the minds of aliens and resort to organised force for their own protection. If a state is to govern itself there must be a certain sense in a certain number of its members that the general interest is higher than their own. Where self-government can be made to operate at all this sense of the general interest will grow with exercise. As Trevelyan and Pollard have shown, the growth of this sense in the Middle Ages united the English and made them the first nation in Europe.

Enough citizens must also be found to devote their time to the public interest. The reluctance in Plantagenet times of knights and burgesses to attend parliament and of counties and towns to find their expenses was, perhaps, the most critical juncture in the history of the English commonwealth. To begin with they attended only because the king ordered them to attend. "The function of force in human affairs is", as Mahan has said, "to give moral ideas time to take root." By the close of the Middle Ages election to parliament was felt as a privilege and so too was the right to elect. The system also had this effect that it brought an ever-increasing number of Englishmen into contact with facts and obliged them to pass judgement on the facts. It was this, I suggest, which developed in England a somewhat higher sense of realities and also a somewhat deeper instinct for truth than is commonly found elsewhere.

In a word, my contention is that the quality which enables a people to govern themselves is not the instinct of men to insist on their own interests, but the instinct, weaker in some, but stronger in others, which enables them to put the public interest before their own. It is in fact the moral sense which alone differentiates men from animals; the faculty without which, as Aristotle said, men, equipped with the power of their intellect, would be only the most dangerous of the beasts. As remarked in an earlier chapter, a community of people clever and selfish as Iago could only be governed like a convict settlement. A community of people as simple and selfless as Humphry Clinker could, from the outset, govern themselves, and in doing so would acquire a wisdom and knowledge sufficient for the task.

The reader whose patience has lasted to this point

may well ask why he should be wearied with chapters on constitutional history which is or should be familiar to every child who has passed through a high school. The answer is that I see in these threadbare and commonplace details the first beginnings in the Christian era of the process whereby that creative and potent idea, the Kingdom of God, as viewed and expounded by Jesus of Nazareth, is destined to be realised. I believe that the process here begun will still be continued, till the rule of law produced from the mind and conscience of those who obey it will not be confined to national frontiers. I look forward to a time when the commonwealth will no longer be limited to the national state, when nations, conscious of their own distinctive histories and structures, will have learned to function as organs of one international commonwealth. I do not believe that the still small voice which was first overheard in the cities of Greece and was raised to the sound of a trumpet in England will be silenced till all men have heard it and learned to obey one paramount law, based on the mind and conscience of all.

Such ideas, it is safe to guess, never crossed the minds of those nameless knights and merchants through whose struggles and labours the English commonwealth was brought into being. As foretold by the Master who first projected an order of society based on realities, the Kingdom of Heaven was destined to come without observation.

NOTES

[1] Pollard, *The Evolution of Parliament*, pp. 133-4.
[2] Trevelyan, *History of England*, pp. 222-3.

CHAPTER XXXIII

RECAPITULATION

The Christian era began in a country where civilisations in conflict were preparing the stage for a great catastrophe. "The Kingdom of God is at hand" was the watchword of Judaism. To Zealots this meant that the God of Israel was about to destroy the Roman Empire and to put in its place a kingdom ruled by a scion of David. They looked on themselves as the instruments of a purpose to be gained by force. In the schools of the prophets the Kingdom of God had come to mean a supernatural transformation, a new heaven and a new earth, from which sorrow and sin would be banished for ever.

The founder of Christianity was trying to divert the attention of his countrymen from violent or visionary projects to realities as he saw them. To him the final reality was the spirit of goodness personified—God, conceived as a Father possessed with desire to perfect the children he had made in his likeness and not as a despot absorbed in the thought of his own glory and power. Goodness cannot exist without doing good and desiring to do it. It is, from its nature, creative. Some faint expression of this spirit, this essential reality, was immanent and incarnate in men. He saw it as the bond which unites society, as the principle of life, and something, therefore, capable of growth. God, who had made men in his likeness, had given them the power to distinguish evil from good. He taught that the ultimate good for men is to serve each other and not themselves. To become like their Father they must exercise his supreme faculty of creation.

But this they could only do in so far as they perfected the likeness for themselves. The means to this end was an order of society which would exercise and develop the instinct in men to serve one another. To develop the best in themselves they must strive to create a system based on realities, a divine polity, as the work of their own hands. His view of life was the outcome of faith that the ultimate reality was mind, not matter; that mind was eternal. So also was its work of creation in which men could share in communion with God.

His life was cut short by his enemies; but not before his ideas had been stated in sayings and parables that his followers remembered and placed on record, together with much else that in course of time they had come to believe that he had said and done. They lived in an empire from which its rulers were rapidly removing all traces of the parent commonwealth. Imperial Rome, no less than Judaism, was based on obedience to a supernatural authority. It is not to be wondered that disciples, so soon deprived of their Master, should have failed to see that the principles embodied in the church and state under which they lived were the very negation of those he had sought to expound. From the fury of the Zealots he had made them immune; but they viewed his teaching through the medium of those transcendental ideas which had found expression in the book of Enoch.[1] They saw in Jesus the Messiah of prophecy. He himself would return clothed with the power of God to establish his kingdom. Their task was to warn men of this and prepare them for it. From the writings of Paul we know how completely this outlook possessed their minds. Till a few generations ago it possessed all Christendom and still possesses a great part of it.

A belief rooted in unreality has produced in the course of ages a pantheon of idols which dominate civilisation. No single volume could attempt to analyse the trends of thought which have issued from this mixture and conflict of Greek and Roman with Jewish ideas. The notion of church and state, of two authorities competing for sovereignty, is among them and has led us to seclude religion and politics in separate compartments of our minds. In the teaching of Jesus there is no such distinction. To his mind religion and politics were merely two aspects of life, a sphere viewed from two different angles. He believed that men could grow to perfection in so far as they based their relations on the infinite duty of each to all. This supreme conception could only be realised by gradual developments such as we, in our language, would describe as political. Their fixed belief in supernatural events not destined to happen blinded his followers to these implications. Christianity became from the outset a matter of personal piety, a syncretic religion, heavily charged with older paganisms.

The fact must be squarely faced that for more than eighteen centuries Christendom held the belief, crystallised in the writings of St. Augustine, that the life men live on this earth is destined to end in a sudden cataclysm which may be expected at any moment. A belief held for a period like this creates unconscious habits of mind which determine the conduct of generations which no longer accept it. To this can be traced a political outlook which is short in its range and narrow in scope, which envisages little beyond the immediate interests of national groups. It explains why Christendom has failed to realise its supernational aspirations. No society can learn to think of itself as a whole which does not believe in its own future. Still less can it realise its own capacity for improvement and the structure it ought to attain, and so work on a plan. The growing confusion of the world is due to this failure, and will only be ended by those who face the question where it is going or ought to go. We talk of planning as the great panacea; but intelligent planning can only begin when men have asked and answered the question, what is the ultimate structure they mean to attain for human society? It is only by reference to such a conception that the steps which practical statesmen are taking from day to day can be judged. No political science can guide men far on their journey through life until it can say what is the goal to which the journey should lead.

As noticed in the opening chapter, science has developed an outlook different from that which Christianity adopted from Judaism. We now have reason to expect that society will continue to exist for a period enormously longer than that which has passed since men were first able to distinguish themselves from animals. The reactions on political thought may prove to be greater even than those produced by the speculations of Copernicus or Darwin. All but incurable pessimists would allow that men have attained to a level higher than that reached by their ancestors who lived as carnivorous animals in caves. If this can be done in thousands of years what achievements are possible in the millions which science is leading mankind to expect? This change in our outlook is an undeniable call to harvest the fields which "a greater than Aristotle" scattered with truths and enriched with his life. That the wheat and the tares could not be distinguished till both had grown up and yielded their fruit was itself a profound intuition. For us in our time it is possible to see what his teaching involves as applied to a world still in its infancy, with vistas of experience before it a thousandfold longer than those behind it. Now, at last, it is reasonable to consider the structure which human society as a whole should seek to attain, and to use that conception as a test for deciding what steps can be taken to approach it from day to day and from year to year. If once we allow ourselves to think of a world commonwealth as the goal of human endeavour we shall find that our minds are equipped with a standard which helps us to judge what ought to be done in the politics of a village no less than in those of the greater world. We have then a criterion to the test of which all measures proposed can be brought—how far will the measure in question tend to increase in those to whom it applies their sense of duty one to another? In so far as that test is satisfied, economic and political problems will begin to find unexpected solutions.

A government for the world can never be established merely by the knowledge and skill of technicians. We have knowledge sufficient to create it to-day, if the indispensable factor which binds men together in one society and makes it organic had now been developed enough for the purpose. To strengthen this factor in every part of the social tissue is the necessary process which will move faster as we learn to conceive this as the true purpose of politics, the essential task entrusted to statesmen. We in this age have an experience which those who recorded the gospels had not. We can see in the light of history the kind of society which in course of time slowly but surely increases the sense of duty in men to each other. We can ask how a policy or measure proposed will help to call this sense into play, whether we are ordering the affairs of nations or those of a parish. We can watch what we do to see how far it is having this effect, and revise our policies in the light of experience. All this will be possible as we learn to accept the government of men by themselves as the guiding principle in public affairs.

In the counsel of nations the policy of statesmen

is, indeed, guided by a principle, the avoidance of war. They are ever proclaiming that peace is their aim and are, I believe, more sincere in pursuing it than the cynics, who have not to deal with their practical difficulties, suspect. The reason why peace, accepted as a goal, fails as a principle of direction in policy is inherent in its negative character. A policy which treats the avoidance of war as its final criterion is merely an attempt to apply in the highest sphere of human relations the principle of the decalogue, which the greatest thinker of all time regarded as obsolete. Instead of a code mainly prohibitive he propounded a positive and constructive injunction, that men should seek the good of others as though it were their own. If he was right in believing that no other commandment is greater than this, it will not suffice for nations to abstain from coercing each other by force. They must learn to think how by steps, slow but patient and persistent, they can bring into being an order of society based on the duty of each to all, irrespective of national limits. International conferences will repeat their record of failures so long as the minds of governments are set on the task of avoiding collisions with each other. The manœuvres they execute are fraught with danger, and can end at best by leading nowhere, until they have recognised an ultimate goal, however remote, in front of them all and are thinking how they can reach it together. It will then be seen that the rule prescribed in the sermon on the mount as superseding the Ten Commandments applies to the whole sphere of conduct—to public no less than private affairs.

Man can attain peace, but only by learning to aim at an end which is greater than peace. Isaiah had seen this truth and expressed it in words that foreshadow the age in which we are living.

> Upon the land of my people shall come up thorns and briers: yea, upon all the houses of joy in the joyous city:

. . . until the spirit be poured upon us from on high, and the wilderness become a fruitful field. Then judgement shall dwell in the wilderness, and righteousness shall abide in the fruitful field. And the world of righteousness shall be peace: and the effect of righteousness quietness and confidence for ever. And my people shall abide in a peaceful habitation, and in sure dwellings, and in quiet resting places.[2]

That brief but pregnant aphorism "Seek ye first the Kingdom of God, and all things else shall be added unto you", was the greatest of all contributions to constructive thought: but its practical meaning was lost when transcendental ideas obscured from our minds the Kingdom of God as an order of society based on realities—as the goal of men's endeavour on earth.

No political science will furnish guidance in practical politics unless it proceeds from a definite conception of ultimate values. The system propounded by Jesus proceeds from the faith that right and wrong are valid distinctions of infinite importance. It therefore regards mind as the ultimate reality in the universe and as indestructible. Death is conceived as no more than a physical incident in the endless life of the spirit. It opens to man a prospect of achievement for which much time in space is required, time for which we have reason to hope. Yet, while science can tell us that, in all probability, we have ages before us in which to accomplish our work, it also assures us that a time must come when life on this earth and the earth itself will have ceased to exist. Belief in the infinite value of goodness is vain, unless we are justified in the faith that God is the God of the living and not of the dead, which, could it be proved, would cease to be faith. In this twentieth century the inexorable question must be faced, whether this view of reality can be proved by miracles and based on authority.

That spiritual values are the ultimate reality and

indestructible cannot be proved. No more can the opposite be proved; though a certain order of scientists would seem to think otherwise.[3] In the search for truth the limits of human knowledge must be recognised. Belief, in the true sense of the word, is not the assertion of knowledge, or dogma, but courage to act on the best hypothesis we are able to conceive. Unbelievers are those too timid or idle to guess at the truth and act on the guess. "The deepest, nay, the unique theme of the history of the world", says Goethe, "to which all other themes are subordinate, is the conflict of faith and unbelief. All epochs in which faith prevails—whatever its form may be—are noble, soul-elevating and fruitful for the present and for after times. All epochs in which unbelief, be it under what form it may, wins an unhappy victory, even though for the moment they are invested with a deceptive halo of glory, vanish and are forgotten by posterity; because no one willingly wastes his pains on what is barren and unfruitful."[4]

NOTES

[1] *Vide supra*, p. 108.

[2] Isaiah xxxii. 13-18.

[3] B. Russell, *Mysticism and Logic*, pp. 47, 48: "That Man is the product of causes which had no prevision of the end they were achieving; that his origin, his growth, his hopes and fears, his loves and beliefs, are but the outcome of accidental collocations of atoms; that no fire, no heroism, no intensity of thought and feeling, can preserve an individual life beyond the grave; that all the labours of the ages, all the devotion, all the inspiration, all the noonday brightness of human genius, are destined to extinction in the vast death of the solar system, and that the whole temple of Man's achievement must inevitably be buried beneath the débris of a universe in ruins—all these things, if not quite beyond dispute, are yet so nearly certain, that no philosophy which rejects them can hope to stand. Only within the scaffolding of these truths, only on the firm foundation of unyielding despair, can the soul's habitation henceforth be safely built."

[4] Quoted by Caird, *Lay Sermons and Addresses*, p. 85.

BOOK II

AN ATTEMPT TO SHOW HOW THE PAST HAS LED TO THE PRESENT POSITION IN WORLD AFFAIRS (DECEMBER 31, 1936)

CHAPTER I

THE MONGOL EMPIRE

THE process by which two aspects of truth were brought together in the teaching of Jesus has been traced in the previous book. The Hebrews and Greeks, each in their small communities, had felt, as no other peoples had felt as yet, the infinite difference which separates right from wrong. Hebrew prophets had reached the conclusion that behind the visible universe the ultimate reality must be something of the nature of personality, divested of all evil, a spirit of goodness and therefore creative—Jehovah—God. The Greek was more concerned with the question how this sense of morality affected the relations of men to each other. When Hebrew and Greek society had mingled in Palestine, these two conceptions were seen in the mind of Jesus as inseparable aspects of one indivisible truth. To serve God men must serve one another. Such service could only be rendered to the full by constant communion with ultimate reality, with the Father of all men in whom the children of God lived and moved and had their being.

Some glimmerings of this conception survived in all but the most paganised churches. The Christian religion took root in Europe where the order and culture of the Graeco-Roman Empire had prepared a soil in which it could grow. Its intrinsic ideas could there be revived, and find expression in a system of society based on the duty of men to each other.

In Asia no soil was ready for that aspect of the Christian idea which sprang from the cities of Greece. The idea of one God conceived by the Hebrew prophets was crystallised and hardened by Mahomet in regions untouched by the Graeco-Roman Empire. A creed which could yield nothing but despotisms was destined to dominate central Asia. It was carried by conquest from the desert to the steppes. The Turkish peoples on whom it was imposed were destined in turn to become the dominant powers in Islam, and even to rule in Arabia itself.

The mountain system of central Asia is roughly shaped like a pair of pincers, hinged at the massive north of India which is called the Pamirs and is known in Asia as the roof of the world. The lower claw is the Himalayan range, which, curving to the south-east, creates a natural frontier for India. The upper claw stretches in a series of ranges from the Pamirs to the south of Lake Baikal and thence through northern Manchuria to the sea. The Gobi desert to the south of this claw forms a barrier harder to cross than the mountains themselves. South-west of the Gobi desert and north of the Himalayas, Tibet, with an altitude of more than 10,000 feet, is a plateau difficult to traverse. The fertile regions south-east of those physical barriers, known to us as China, were colonised in early times from the steppes by Mongols who had taken to agriculture and abandoned the life of shepherds. They developed a civilisation older and more elaborate than that of the Roman Empire itself. Their skill as farmers and craftsmen had made them the largest section of the human race united by one civilisation.

The Turks were in race mainly Caucasians who had somehow adopted a Mongol language. In the sixth century A.D. they spread from the Pamirs down the Oxus and Jaxartes, rivers which carry their melting snows to the Sea of Aral. In the valleys of their mountainous country they learned to combine agriculture with pastoral life, and to live in cities which were centres of trade.

Before the close of the seventh century the Arabs had conquered Persia and converted the Persians to Islam. In the eighth century the Moslem rulers of Persia extended their conquests and religion to Turkestan. The creed of Mahomet had the same effect on the tribal society of Turkestan as it had on that of Arabia, though not so quickly. It enabled Turkish leaders to create organised states and, so organised, the Turks became more powerful than Arabs or Persians. Before the twelfth century the Turkish Seljuks had conquered Persia, had established their power in Asia Minor and were ruling Palestine. Thenceforward Turks superseded Arabs as the dominant factor in the world of Islam.

In the course of the twelfth century the power of the Seljukian Empire declined. At the close of that century the most powerful successor-state of the caliphate centred in Khiva, just south of Lake Aral. From that city a Turkish potentate Mohammed Shah ruled over regions which lay between India and the Caspian Sea.

East of this empire the further conquests of Islam had been brought to a standstill by the Gobi desert, and the Altai Mountains to the north, which geographers describe as a region similar in character to Switzerland but covering an area five times as large. North-east of this region lay the steppes of Mongolia, the nursery in which the Mongol race had acquired its physical characteristics. In these regions nomadic society had never changed its pastoral and warlike habits since the days of Attila. The tracks which connected these nomads with Turkestan were known only to traders, whose hereditary knowledge and skill enabled them to lead their camels for more than a thousand miles, either through waterless deserts or else through the snows and glaciers of mountain passes. From China they came loaded with silk. Returning they carried weapons and coats of mail. In the Middle Ages the Moslem smiths had learned the secret of hardening iron into steel. On the steppes of Mongolia their products were as eagerly sought as are modern rifles in Afghanistan.

Nestorian Christians had reached China,[1] in the caravans which conducted this trade, and certain Mongolian hordes had adhered to their faith.

Wang-Khan, the chief of one of these hordes in the twelfth century, was perhaps the historic original of the legendary Prester John.[2] Yesukai the paramount chief in Mongolia was a pagan. When he died in 1175 the Nestorian hordes refused to obey his son Temuchin, a boy of thirteen. In the thirty years' struggle which followed Temuchin acquired the title of Cheng-sze, Inflexible Warrior. He is known to history as Genghis-Khan, the greatest leader ever produced by nomadic society. In 1203 he finally defeated Wang-Khan. In 1206, as undisputed master of the steppes, he assembled his hosts on the banks of the Onon, a tributary of the Amur, in those regions where Russian and Japanese armies are now watching each other with anxious eyes, and set them in motion to the south. After conquering China from the Great Wall to the Yangtze river he returned to Mongolia and established his camp at Karakorum, to the south of Lake Baikal, where the foothills begin to merge in the deserts of Gobi.

This campaign in China was the prelude of achievements which have since made themselves felt to the furthest limits of the world. It had made him conscious of his own genius as a military leader, and whetted his passion for great adventures. Ten years in the field had enabled him to reduce his Tartar[3] hordes to an organised and disciplined army. It still consisted of herdsmen and horses enured on the steppes to the greatest hardships which animal life can sustain. His warriors could live on the milk and flesh of their herds, a commissariat nearly as mobile as the horses they rode. In the last extremity they could open the veins of their steeds and subsist on their blood.

In conquering China Genghis had realised the military value of various machines devised by its engineers for breaking the walls of fortified cities. These machines, with Chinese artificers who knew how to work them, were now a regular part of his army. In packing and carting gear on their wagons, the Mongol nomads were as clever as a travelling circus.

There is also reason to suppose that the Mongols had learned from the Chinese that sulphur, saltpetre and charcoal mixed in certain proportions produce an explosive, and used it to terrify their enemies in the form of bombs or grenades.

The ferocious vigour of nomad society was thus combined with the arts of an ancient civilisation to produce in the hands of a born leader an army which could travel thousands of miles and still be strong enough to destroy superior forces in the field and reduce fortified cities to ruins.

At Karakorum, Genghis was careful to glean from the traders who came there what knowledge he could of the countries beyond the deserts and mountains. He thus came to know of Mohammed Shah as their paramount ruler, and sent him an embassy, which obtained a rather unwilling agreement to protect the traffic between Mongolia and Turkestan. Mohammed Shah does not seem to have realised that, since the conquest of China, Genghis was no longer a tribal chief, but a monarch with all the resources of a civilised empire behind him. No Moslem army had tried to cross the Altai Mountains, and it never occurred to Mohammed Shah that hordes from the distant steppes of Mongolia could attack him in Turkestan. Suspecting that Genghis was using the traders as spies, he butchered a whole caravan which had come through the mountains from Karakorum. When Genghis despatched an embassy to protest, he singed their beards and murdered their leader.

Mohammed Shah had thus offered the occasion for which Genghis was looking. In the spring of 1219 the Mongol hordes began to move on their westward march. As the crow flies the distance between the Mongol capital at Karakorum and Khiva, the Turkish capital, is more than two thousand miles. The tracks followed by traders ran through deserts and over mountains where snow lay deep in the height of summer. The movement of siege-trains as well as of mounted troops across such country may rank as the greatest feat in military transport, an achievement possible only to horsemen hardened from birth on the northern steppes and directed by a leader who left nothing to chance. When the Mongol cavalry reached the Jaxartes they cut through the first lines of the Turkish defence by the sheer ferocity of their onset. The armies which blocked the valleys beyond were presently demoralised by finding their retreat cut off by hordes which had crossed lateral ranges that by all the rules of war were impassable.

Outmatched by the Mongol tactics and strategy, Mohammed Shah withdrew what remained of his armies into walled cities, and thought to wait till the storm had passed. He had not reckoned with the foresight of Genghis in providing equipment for taking strongholds after he had driven his enemy from the field. The walls of Otrar, Tashkent, Bokhara and Samarkand were breached and stormed. Mohammed Shah, with a dwindling following, was chased till he perished on an island in the Caspian. By the autumn of 1221 Genghis was master of central Asia to the Indus.

With a prudence rare in such conquerors, he there realised that the climate of India was a death-trap for warriors bred on the steppes; so he turned his hordes to the north-west. His sons and generals carried their conquests into Asia Minor and north of the Black Sea, through Russia and into Hungary.

The greatness of Genghis is shown by the fact that he left these further conquests to subordinates in order to devote his personal attention to the more important, though less sensational, task of converting the tracks which traders had followed through the deserts and mountains into military routes. Along these routes he erected buildings with ample stabling at convenient stages, large enough to shelter his troops as they passed between eastern and western Asia. At these posts were established ranches stocked with enormous herds of transport animals, so that each detachment after a night's rest and refreshment could exchange their weary cattle and resume their journey with animals that were fresh. Along this chain of posts his orders travelled as fast as horses could gallop and riders could hand their despatches to couriers waiting to bear them a further stage.

Having thus ensured his communications with the Mongol forces engaged on western conquests, he himself resumed the task of conquering China south of the Yangtze, but died in 1227 before he could finish it.

NOTES

[1] Toynbee, *A Study of History*, vol. ii. p. 375.

[2] *Ibid.* p. 237.

[3] For my reason for retaining the traditional spelling of this word, see *The Capital Question of China*, chap. ii.

CHAPTER II

GERMANY AND ITALY IN THE MIDDLE AGES

In Europe the Mongol storms, as they rolled and flashed on the eastern horizon, were watched with a terror not unmingled with hope. The tempest had dealt a formidable blow to the world of Islam which stood in its path. The Church, which had mastered heathen invaders centuries before, might repeat her achievements and enlist the Mongols in the task of extinguishing Islam from the face of the earth. In 1245 Innocent IV. sent a Franciscan, John of Pian de Carpini, across the Tartar routes to convert Kuyuk-Khan, the successor of Genghis at Karakorum. He was followed in 1251 by another Friar, William of Rubruck. They both failed; but, had they succeeded, the conversion of the paramount Khan in Mongolia would scarcely have counteracted the pervading influence of the creed which the Mongol generals were breathing in Turkestan. The conquered Turks were themselves largely Mongol in blood, and their kindred rulers rapidly merged in their civilisation.

In any case Christendom was too divided in counsel and sympathy to compete with Islam in Asia. In the Graeco-Roman Empire Latin and Greek had been used with equal fluency by the ruling classes. After the Greek Empire and Church had been severed from Rome, the Greek language was totally forgotten in the west. In these two great divisions of Christendom the educated classes, no longer able to exchange ideas, had drifted so far apart in sympathy, that in time they began to hate each other at least as bitterly as they hated Islam.

Since Charles the Great had re-established the Roman Empire in name, western Europe had been torn by the conflict of two authorities, the one derived from the Roman Empire, the other through the Church from Jewish theocracy. The Papacy centred in Italy, the Empire in Germany, and these two countries were the primary sufferers.

The successors of Charles, lured by the glamour of this adopted title, exhausted their energies in endeavouring to realize their position as Emperors of Rome by the conquest of Italy. In Germany itself a condition of disorder was allowed to continue, until the weak were driven to barter their freedom to the strong in exchange for protection. The feudal system which Germany now developed was nothing more nor less than the attempt of a society which had failed to organize itself as a state to make contract do the work of patriotism. The Emperors themselves accepted the principle, distributing their sovereignty amongst their princes and nobles in exchange for support in their Italian wars. The result was that the rank and file served as the retainers of the feudal potentate, not as the subjects of the Emperor. While the attention of the Emperor was absorbed in Italy, the feudal lords were the *de facto* governments of their respective principalities in Germany, and the Emperor never established a direct relation of sovereignty with the German people themselves. As Emperor he never attained the right to tax the people direct. It was to the local prince that they paid their taxes and looked for orders. It was him they followed when he chose to disobey the orders of the Emperor. Against the disobedience of a prince the only remedy of the Emperor was war. In taking sides for or against the Emperor the other princes were guided by their own interests, and not by those of the Empire, still less by the interests of Christendom or mankind. The German monarchs, in masquerading as the Emperors of humanity, were diverted from establishing a government for the German people. The Holy Roman Empire was not even a fiction. It was a sham which actually deceived men and hid from their eyes the less pretentious but more valuable reality which might have been achieved. In theory, the Emperor was the temporal Vicegerent of God, the King of Kings, from whose authority the princes of Europe derived their own. In practice, many of these princes, like those of England (Richard I. was an unwilling exception), repudiated his authority. Those who acknowledged it persistently disregarded it whenever they saw a chance of aggrandizing themselves at the expense of their neighbours; and the Emperor had no means of enforcing it, except those he controlled by virtue of his own inherited possessions. His election as Emperor added nothing to the actual power he already possessed as an hereditary prince. His authority, therefore, was similar to that of a foreman who secures obedience from the members of his gang only so far as he is able to coerce them with his own fists, a system which makes for peace only when the foreman is a person of gigantic strength. When the practice was established amongst the German princes of electing the Emperor, the electors were careful to avoid the choice of a sovereign strong enough to coerce them. Society was supposed to be constructed in accordance with a lofty conception which had grown from the habit of idealizing the Roman Empire. The Emperors of the Middle Ages accepted the style and functions of Empire without the Imperium. They were given the right to command all men without the actual power to enforce obedience. In practice they did little to cure the intestine disorders of Europe and nothing to defend it from the encroachments of Asia. That all-important task was left to the Eastern remnant of the real Roman Empire, which guarded the Bosphorus till the close of the Middle Ages. German sovereigns who claimed to be the champions of European civilization were unable to marshal one soldier to save from the Turk the very countries in which it had been cradled. In the Balkan Peninsula centuries of misery have commemorated the failure of the Holy Roman Empire to justify the title and traditions it assumed.

After the fall of the Roman Empire the Teutonic races who had destroyed it were the strongest element of European society. If Charles and his successors had confined themselves to the task of consolidating their own people into a state, the Germans would have been the first people to realize nationality in the modern sense of the term. As it was, they were the last, and the penalty they paid for this failure was a thousand years of fratricidal strife in which

Europe at large was repeatedly involved. Till the time of Luther it would be difficult to point to any period in which German armies were not fighting each other on German soil. In the seventeenth century Germany was devastated by the Thirty Years' War. In the eighteenth century the German States were involved in the quarrels of Austria and Prussia. At the beginning of the nineteenth century Germany was trampled underfoot by Napoleonic armies largely reinforced by German troops. In the struggle between Austria and Prussia of 1866 the States of Northern Germany were at war with those of the South. Had Charles the Great and his successors united Germany as the Norman and Plantagenet kings united England, it is not too much to say that most of the wars which have since distracted not only Germany but Europe itself might never have been fought. Up to the year 1870, the Germans might still have been described in the words applied by Stubbs to their primitive ancestors as being "singularly capable of entering into new combinations: singularly liable to be united and dissolved in short-lived confederations".[1] And the process was one of incessant violence, which was constantly spreading to the whole continent of Europe.

In the course of ages of violence the rudimentary institutions of freedom, to which Tacitus bears evidence, were for the most part extinguished by the necessities of military rule. "The Diet, originally an assembly of the whole people, and thereafter of the feudal tenants-in-chief, meeting from time to time like our early English Parliaments, became in A.D. 1654 a permanent body, at which the electors, princes, and cities were represented by their envoys. In other words, it was not so much a national Parliament as an international congress of diplomatists. Where the sacrifice of imperial, or rather federal, rights to state rights was so complete, we may wonder that the farce of an Empire should have been retained at all. A mere German Empire would probably have perished; but the Teutonic people could not bring itself to abandon the venerable heritage of Rome."[2] Except in some isolated cities personal authority backed by force was the only kind of government which counted. . . . Belief in force as the ultimate basis of government is the natural consequence of the protracted violence into which Europe was plunged by the failure of Germany till 1870 to realize for herself the unity of a state. Throughout the continent of Europe from the downfall of the Roman Empire there was no period during which order was maintained long enough to create the tradition that the law is above the visible ruler and more entitled than him to the ultimate obedience of the citizen. The upshot has been that, with the partial exception of Switzerland and Holland, the principle of the commonwealth failed to re-establish itself on the continent of Europe with sufficient strength to counteract the theocratic and despotic tradition of government which the Roman Empire left behind it. The ideas of government which prevailed in Germany to the first decades of the nineteenth century were, no less than those of the Latin peoples, inherited from Rome. The shade of that vanished Empire rose from its grave to haunt its destroyers. Hovering before their eyes, this phantom beguiled them into the morass of Italian politics at the outset of their march towards German union and freedom. From the one sure path their footsteps strayed, never to refind it for a thousand years.[3]

Germany and Italy each left to themselves might have attained national unity as readily as France or Spain; for a country in which all the people can exchange their ideas in one language is the natural home of a national state. In both cases the achievement of national unity was arrested, with results that the world is feeling to-day. While vainly trying to assert their claim to Imperial power in Italy, the emperors failed to establish their power to rule in Germany. They bartered their sovereignty to feudal princes in return for military aid. The peoples who spoke the German language continued to obey these princes rather than the emperor, and the princes were always at war with each other and the emperor himself. Till 1866 Germans were constantly fighting Germans under German princes on German soil. Till 1861 the Italians were never united as a people. If Germans and Italians now act as though nothing but force counts in this world, that terrible fact can be traced to the rival ambitions of emperors and popes.

NOTES

[1] Stubbs, *Constitutional History*, p. 36.
[2] Bryce, *The Holy Roman Empire*, chap. xx. pp. 391, 392.
[3] *The Commonwealth of Nations*, pp. 73-7.

CHAPTER III

IMPACT OF CHINA ON EUROPE

In Italy merchants and craftsmen had sought to protect themselves from the endless rivalries of popes and emperors in walled communities which they themselves could control and defend. Italian cities began to develop a way of life closely comparable to that of the ancient commonwealths of Greece. In towns like Venice, Genoa, Milan, Florence and Padua the trade and culture of Athens, Corinth, Ephesus or Smyrna was reproduced. As in Greece, these cities were frequently at war with each other. Those on the coast, like Venice and Genoa, had fleets which constantly fought for the trade upon which their merchants grew rich. This trade consisted for the most part in articles of luxury which would bear transport from the East on the backs of camels to the shores of the Levant and the Black Sea. Of these the most important were gems and spices from the Indies. In the Middle Ages there was little exchange of staple foods. Every locality lived on the foodstuffs produced for itself, which, even in summer, were few in kind. Spices to flavour a monotonous diet were eagerly sought by the wealthier classes. The trade of Genoa and Venice was thus largely concerned with pepper, cloves, cinnamon, nutmeg and mace, which were carried through Asia to Mediterranean and Black Sea ports on the backs of camels. These spices were brought by sea to Genoa and Venice and then sold for enormous prices throughout Europe. The crest used by the Grocers' Company in London records the part which the camel played in this trade.

One of the routes across Asia led to the northern shores of the Black Sea where Venice and Genoa controlled the ports. When the Mongol hordes swept down these routes into Russia they came into touch with Italian merchants in and about the Crimea. Their common hostility to Islam led to friendly relations. Under Mongol protection the Italians began to use these routes and to carry their trade into central Asia.

The Khans visited by Pian de Carpini and William of Rubruck were succeeded by Kublai, a grandson of Genghis who inherited his genius for civil and military organisation. He completed the work of Genghis by conquering China south of the Yangtze. From "the city of the great king", Khan-baligh or Cambaluc, which he built on the site of Peking (the modern Peiping), he ruled the whole of China and levied tribute as far as Russia.

In 1260 two merchants of Venice, the brothers Nicolo and Maffeo Polo, went from the Crimea to the camp of the Golden Horde on the Volga. After selling their jewels for a large profit they journeyed to Bokhara and there established themselves as traders. Their presence was reported to Kublai-Khan, who invited them to visit his court at Cambaluc. Having learned from them all they could tell him of Christendom, he sent them with a letter asking the Pope to send him a hundred missionaries. While seeking some influence to counterbalance the native philosophy of Confucius he may well have dreaded an eastward extension of Islam. Unwilling to be wholly dependent on a Chinese bureaucracy for administrative work, he probably hoped to employ the western clerics as officers of state.

When the Polos reached Acre in 1269 the Pope, Clement V., had died. His successor, Gregory X., who was not elected till 1271, was either unable to find, or unwilling to spare, men of the courage and capacity needed to satisfy Kublai's request. He commissioned two Dominican Friars to accompany the Polos with a letter to Kublai. In Armenia the Friars took fright and returned to the coast. Augustine and Gregory the Great must have turned in their graves.[1] Three centuries later St. Francis Xavier must have wrung his hands if he knew of the chance which the Church had missed.

The Polos resumed their journey accompanied by Nicolo's son Marco. In the summer of 1275 they were welcomed by Kublai-Khan in his "lordly pleasure house" at Shandu in Manchuria (the Xanadu of Coleridge's dream). Marco was taken into his service, employed on important missions, and at one time governed Yang-Chow. In 1292 he allowed the Polos to return as escort to a princess, whose hand the Mongol Khan of Persia had asked in marriage. The party journeyed by sea through the Straits of Malacca. They visited Sumatra and India on their way to Persia. The Polos reached Venice in 1295, a year after the death of Kublai.

In 1298 Marco was taken prisoner in a fight with the Genoese, and beguiled his enforced leisure by dictating to a fellow prisoner an account of his travels. His book was destined to shape western ideas of the Far East, but had little effect until it was printed two centuries later.

The Polos must have been passed on their homeward voyage by an emissary of the Pope, who reached Cambaluc in 1294. In 1289 the Pope had despatched a Franciscan, John of Monte-Corvino, on a mission to the great Khan. After visiting India he travelled to China with a merchant, Peter of Lucolongo, who had joined him at Tabriz. At Cambaluc he built a church with money supplied by Peter. In 1307 the Pope created him archbishop of Cambaluc and several bishops were sent to assist him. A mission to southern China was established at Amoy. A chain of Franciscan missions was established across central Asia to the ports of the Black Sea. But in semi-nomadic society the Christian missionaries were no rivals for the simple and militant creed of Islam. By the middle of the fourteenth century the Mongol rulers had become Mohammedans, and the trade routes were closed once more alike to merchants and missionaries of Christendom. In 1368 a native rising in China under the Mings expelled the Mongol emperors there and also the Christian missions which had flourished under their rule. The routes which Genghis had opened with Europe across Asia were thus destroyed from end to end. The western and eastern hemispheres once more lost touch with each other. Yet this slight contact of western society with the ancient civilisation of China was destined to generate in Europe and yield an incredible progeny. It created the main factor which led the families of men to a knowledge of each other, and brought into being that need for organic unity which is the key to their problems to-day.

In A.D. 105 a eunuch, Ts'ai Lun, had discovered that the fibres of cotton, bark or bamboo could be pounded with water to a pulp and then dried into thin sheets which easily received the marks of paint or ink from a brush. In the Dark Ages this useful art of making paper travelled slowly across Asia through the furthest limits of the Moslem world till it reached Spain. In the Middle Ages it spread through France to the Netherlands and Germany.

While Europe was still in the Dark Ages, Chinese scholars and artists had learned to paste the paper on which they had worked face down upon blocks of wood, so that the marks traced on the paper could be seen in reverse. The paper and wood was then chiselled away till the marks were left in relief. By brushing ink on the raised surface any number of accurate copies could be taken on sheets of paper.

This means of publishing books and pictures was general in the age of the Mongol dynasty.

We know that John of Monte-Corvino translated the Psalms and the New Testament into Chinese. For the "benefit of the ignorant" who could not read he prepared religious pictures. It is safe to conjecture that both the translations and the pictures would be published in China by means of printing. Within fifty years religious pictures "for the ignorant" were printed on blocks in Europe. That Friars had brought the idea from China is a guess which almost amounts to certainty.

The Chinese had further developed the idea of making moulds of single characters from which any number of casts could be taken in pottery or lead. These movable types could then be arranged and blocked together in the right order. This invention was largely developed in Korea. As Chinese characters each stand for a whole word or idea and are numbered by thousands, it was almost as easy to cut every page of a Chinese book on a separate block. With the alphabets of Europe it was otherwise. When some twenty-six moulds had been cut, movable types in unlimited numbers could be cast from each mould. About 1440 Coster at Haarlem and Gutenberg at Mainz were casting movable types and printing books from them. The art of making paper had just reached the Germanic world through France and Spain. Methods invented in China were thus developed in Europe on lines which quickly began to affect the whole structure of human society.[2]

The invention of gunpowder seems to have passed through similar stages. Fireworks had long been made in China, and the Mongols appear to have used them in battle to frighten their enemies. The secret of making explosives in Europe was probably learned from Mongol invaders. The idea of using the explosive to drive projectiles from a tube was conceived in Europe. Guns were among the physical instruments destined to merge all nations and kindreds in one society. Printing was destined to ensure that the unity it needed and needs must be based on the principle of the commonwealth, and not on the principle of authority.

NOTES

[1] See p. 254.

[2] Carter, *The Invention of Printing in China.* New York, Columbia University Press, 1925.

CHAPTER IV

THE OSMANLI EMPIRE

IN 1219 the hordes of Genghis had driven some fifty thousand Turkish families across the Euphrates into the Seljukian Empire known as Rum (Rome). In 1224 their leader, Suleiman Shah, was drowned when trying to recross the Euphrates. The mass of his followers crossed and went eastward; but one of his sons, Ertogrul, seeing in the fate of his father a warning, retreated to the west with four hundred families. This small party of Turks chanced on a battle in which the Seljukian Sultan Alaeddin was fighting for his life with a Mongol horde. By his sudden intervention Ertogrul put the Mongols to flight. He was given in reward a small fief in country which lies south of the Sea of Marmora, where he lived with his Turkish followers till his death in 1288.[1]

His son Osman is marked as the founder of the Osmanli people and Empire by the fact that he gave them his name. By a Moslem friend he was led to study the Koran and became an enthusiast for the creed as preached by its founder. He absorbed the idea of conquering the world for Islam. To him, Constantinople was the axis of the world.

The Moslem creed, adopted by Osman in its pure and original form, imposed on his tribe the structure of an organised and militant state. It began to encroach on the regions in Asia Minor which were still ruled from Constantinople. A great part of the peoples it conquered were absorbed into its structure and quickly adopted its religion and language. The rapid conversion of so-called Christians to the faith of Islam had been made possible by the state of religious, moral and political demoralisation to which Byzantine society had fallen. The militant and organised faith of Islam appeared by contrast as a social and religious reform. The Osmanli Empire in Europe was scarcely Turkish except in respect of its language. The so-called Turkish nation is, in fact, made up of heterogeneous peoples which the emperors at Constantinople had ruled, converted to the creed of Mahomet. In effect the Byzantine Empire which had held the eastern gate of Christendom began in the fourteenth century to go over to Islam. The process was merely completed when Constantinople itself was taken by the Turks in 1453.

When Osman died in 1326 his son Orkhan succeeded to the rule of a small but powerful state in Asia Minor. Cantacuzenos, the chancellor in Constantinople, was scheming to usurp the Imperial throne, and in 1345 induced Orkhan to support him. In 1353 he allowed his Moslem ally to occupy a fort in Gallipoli, and from that moment onwards the Osmanlis controlled the crossing from Asia to Europe. In 1354 Orkhan quarrelled with Cantacuzenos and began to conquer his dominions in Europe for himself. His son Murad extended these conquests and in 1366 established the capital of his empire at Adrianople. From that date the Byzantine emperors ruled little beyond the walls of Constantinople. Murad completed the conquest of Bulgaria, Serbia and Macedonia. His son Bayezid extended these conquests to include Albania and most of Greece. In 1391 he began the siege of Constantinople. He also extended his conquests eastwards.

His progress to the east brought Bayezid into sudden and disastrous collision with a Moslem ruler, the range of whose conquests was surpassed only by those of Genghis. Jagatai, who succeeded to the power of his father Genghis in Turkestan, had a minister and commander-in-chief called Karachar Nevian, the first of the Mongol generals to adopt the religion of Mahomet. His great-grandson, who was also a fanatical Moslem, developed gifts as a leader of hordes comparable to those of Genghis himself, a fact recorded in his name Timur, which means in the Mongol language a man of iron. In 1369 he established his throne at Samarkand. From there he conquered and ravaged as far south as Delhi, and as far west as Damascus, Smyrna and the Volga river. About 1400 these two Mohammedan war-lords were facing each other on the Euphrates. The arrogance of Bayezid provoked Timur to invade his territories. When they met at Angora in 1402 the Osmanlis were utterly defeated. Bayezid was captured and the conquests of Timur were extended to Damascus and Smyrna. Timur then returned with his booty to Turkestan to fulfil his purpose of reviving the empire of Genghis by reconquering China from the Mings; but he died in 1403 before he could pass the mountain ranges.

Bayezid died in captivity and for ten years his sons fought for the throne of Adrianople. By 1413 Mohammed I. was established at Adrianople as ruler of the Osmanli Empire. The blow delivered at Angora had merely shown how firmly Osman had laid the foundations of the Ottoman Empire. It was destined to become the spear-head of Islam in its secular struggle with Christendom.

The ancient fortress of Constantinople was again surrounded by Ottoman armies. The Emperor, John VI., agreed to unite Christendom under the authority of the Pope in the vain hope that Europe would come to his rescue (1439). But the eastern clergy refused to endorse the agreement, and in 1443 the Patriarchs of Jerusalem, Antioch and Alexandria openly denounced it. When John VI. died in 1448 the end was near. In 1453 Mohammed II. stormed Constantinople and the last of its emperors, Constantine, perished in the slaughter.

In the tenth century the chivalry of Europe had flocked at the call of the Pope to wrest Palestine from the infidel. The complete failure of popes in the fifteenth century to raise forces strong enough to recover from Islam the eastern citadel of Europe shows how far the Papacy had lost the authority it was once able to exercise. The sceptre of Europe was passing from the great theocracy raised by the Jewish idea on the ruined foundations of the Roman Empire. The Turk threatened and mocked it from the walls which Constantine the Great had once raised as its bulwark.

NOTE

[1] Gibbons, *The Foundation of the Ottoman Empire*, p. 19, from which is derived the information in the following pages.

CHAPTER V

RUSSIA

THE Greek part of the Empire which sprang from the conquests of the Roman republic had completely assumed the form of an eastern despotism. Its spirit was destined to find a new incarnation in the vast and monotonous regions north of the Black Sea and to bring them into the pages of history.[1]

In the Dark Ages "men of Rus", Norsemen from Sweden, in search of plunder and trade, had made their way by lakes and rivers to the Black Sea. One of their leaders, Rurik, had established his capital at Novgorod. By the tenth century they were firmly established at Kiev on the Dnieper and were threatening Constantinople. The threat was averted by the Emperor who gave his sister in marriage to the Norse leader Vladimir I., who agreed to adopt the Christian religion. Christianity was thus introduced to Russia in a form which accustomed its people to regard the autocrats who ruled them as head of the church as well as of the state.

The senior descendants of Rurik at Kiev never established a real authority over his kinsmen, who were busy conquering and ruling principalities for themselves and fighting each other.

In Book II., Chapter I., we have seen how Genghis in 1221 wisely turned from the conquest of India and despatched his hordes westwards to regions north of the Black Sea, suitable to the pastoral life of his Mongols. The Russian princes, descendants of Rurik, were utterly defeated by the Mongols in 1224 on the banks of the Kulka. After further wanderings the invaders returned and established a permanent camp at Sarai on the lower Volga. Here the Khan of "the Golden Horde", as this western arm of the Mongol Empire was called, fixed his headquarters. The country was suitable for a tribe in the pastoral stage of society and enabled them to follow the precepts of Genghis, who warned his people not to abandon that mode of life.

The Golden Horde was thus able to maintain its capacity for movement and military prowess, and for nearly two centuries exacted tribute from the princes of Russia. In course of time one of these princes, Ivan the Money Bag, who ruled in Moscow from 1328 to 1341, acquired the position of general tax-gatherer for the Golden Horde. The riches and influence thus created for his dynasty at Moscow enabled one of his successors, Dimitri of the Don, to revolt and defeat the Golden Horde in 1380 at Koulikovo. The remnants of their power were destroyed from the opposite side in 1394 by the armies of Timur.

The Grand Dukes of Moscow thus acquired the spiritual heritage of the Caesars who had ruled at Constantinople, coupled with the power of the Tartar Khans which the genius of Genghis had launched from the steppes of Mongolia. When Constantinople had fallen to the Turk, Ivan the Great (1462–1505) married a Byzantine princess, adopted the eagle as the arms of his dynasty and assumed the title of Caesar or Tzar. In the next four centuries this reincarnation of Byzantine despotism was destined to spread its authority from the frontiers of Germany to the shores of Manchuria, over most of those vast regions which the nomad armies of Genghis had trampled. Their peasant and pastoral inhabitants learned to obey the Emperor in Moscow as one vested with power from on high.

The Tartar hordes on the steppes never recovered the defeats inflicted from opposite directions, by the

Russians from the west and by Timur from the east. In the days of our Queen Elizabeth hunters from Russia crossed the Urals and began to penetrate into Siberia, in search of the costly furs which readily found a market in Europe. This movement closely resembled that which began in America a century later, in regions along the Arctic circle, when Prince Rupert had founded the Hudson's Bay Company. The Russian trappers, as they advanced, established forts under military officers at convenient centres, and peasants were settled to raise the food they required. The dominions claimed by the Tzar were thus carried steadily eastwards. In 1628 the Russians had reached the Lena, and in 1637 founded the fort of Yakutsk on its upper waters. In 1639 they had reached the Pacific coast and had founded Oklotsk on the shores of the northern sea which bears its name. Having reached the ocean they began to turn south. In 1648 they established a post in the region where four centuries earlier Genghis had camped at Karakorum. By 1650 they had occupied the banks of the Amur; but their further progress was here checked by the Chinese Empire. By the Treaty of Nerchinsk in 1689 Russia agreed to abandon the Amur. The Tzar's dominion was thus carried in the seventeenth century by traders in quest of ermine and sable, till it stretched from the Baltic to the shores of the northern Pacific. These obscure movements were destined to yield prodigious results in our own time.

NOTE

[1] For the facts in this chapter see Fisher, *A History of Europe*, vol. i. chap. xxxii.

CHAPTER VI

PRINTING AND REVIVAL OF LEARNING

In a previous chapter we have seen that in Italy city commonwealths, closely resembling those of Greece, had sprung into being despite, or rather because of, the general disorder maintained by the conflict of popes with emperors. The commerce of these cities with each other and the world overseas had led, as in ancient Greece, to a great outburst of mental activity. Though Italian now differed from Latin as one language from another, the liturgies of the Roman Church had preserved a widespread knowledge of Latin. In the fourteenth century the poets and historians of classical Rome began to be studied by Petrarch and other Italian scholars. These studies aroused in their minds an insatiable desire to read the older works of the Greeks to whom the writers of classical Rome refer as their masters.

Since the Greek Church had been finally separated from the Latin in the fifth century, all knowledge of classical Greek had practically vanished from the west. "Even at Constantinople such knowledge was then possessed only by a few persons of superior education, including those who were professional students or men of letters." [1]

The doom which was now written on its walls for everyone to read enabled the scholars of Italy to satisfy their thirst. When the siege of Constantinople had begun the Emperor had sent to Italy one of its leading scholars, Manuel Chrysoloras, in a vain attempt to obtain succour from western Christendom. Some Florentine scholars who had met him induced the senate of Florence to secure his services as a teacher of classical Greek. He accepted the offer and lectured in Florence from 1397 to 1400. To the cultivated scholar this lovely city must have seemed an Elysium in contrast with a fortress battered by Moslems. His example was quickly and freely followed by others like himself. Till the fall of Constantinople in 1453 the sea route to Constantinople was open and constantly traversed by the ships of Venice and Genoa. In the course of this half-century numbers of scholars were carried in Italian ships with Greek manuscripts from the libraries of the doomed city. The blow which Timur dealt to the Ottoman Empire in 1402 had saved the heritage of classical Greece for the world.

The passion for learning aroused by the study of Greek classics crossed the Alps and created a thirst for reading in northern Europe. In the Roman Empire of classical times the demand for books had been met by employing as copyists large numbers of cultivated Greeks captured in war and enslaved by the captors. In the fifteenth century no such slaves were available. The growing demand for books at a reasonable price was met by the invention of printing on paper with movable types.

Coster at Haarlem and Gutenberg at Mainz began to print with movable types about 1440. The art spread with incredible rapidity. In 1467 two German printers, Schweinheim and Pannartz, began to issue editions of Caesar, Livy, Virgil, Lucan and Ovid. In 1476 Greek grammars and texts were published in Milan. Aldo (1450–1515), an Italian scholar who had mastered Greek, conceived the design of printing all the masterpieces of Greek literature in volumes small enough for the reader to carry in his pocket. He started his press at Venice in 1490, and in 1500 founded a society called the Neacademia, of which the Dutchman Erasmus and the Englishman Linacre, a fellow of All Souls

College at Oxford, became honorary members. Aldo's ambition was almost realised when he died in 1515. The printing of Aeschylus on his press in 1518 completed it.

In northern Europe the interest in printing was religious rather than literary. The first book finished by Gutenberg in 1456 was the Latin Bible. Before the end of that century ninety-seven other editions were issued in Europe, which was thus flooded with Hebrew as well as with Greek literature. "The clergy—to quote the words of Archbishop Berthold of Mainz, hailed printing as a divine art. They endowed printing-presses."[2] This clerical interest in printing is recorded by the curious fact that, in our own country, members of trade-unions in printing-shops call themselves 'chapels'. The Church was at first slow to realise what would happen to its claims when large numbers of thinking laymen were able to read and interpret the scripture for themselves.

That *The Travels of Marco Polo* was one of the earliest books to be printed may be counted a tribute to the fitness of things. It illustrates, too, the quickening power which the art of printing gave to recorded knowledge in Europe.

NOTES

[1] Jebb, *The Cambridge Modern History*, vol. i. p. 540.
[2] Barry, *The Cambridge Modern History*, vol. i. p. 633.

CHAPTER VII

HENRY THE NAVIGATOR

IN 1385 John, Grand Master of the Knights of Aviz, was elected king of Portugal and in the same year asserted its independence of Castile at the battle of Aljubarota, which he won with the aid of 500 English archers. Next year he was joined by 5000 English under John of Gaunt. The Treaty of Windsor, 1387, and his marriage with Philippa, daughter of John of Gaunt, laid the foundation of the close connection which has since governed the relations of England and Portugal. Three sons of this marriage, Edward, Pedro and Henry, in the spirit of crusaders, desired to win knighthood by service against the Moors, the historic enemies of their country and creed. In 1415 they set sail with a reinforcement of English sent by Henry V. and took Ceuta from the Moors. The youngest of the brothers, Prince Henry, was especially distinguished by his valour.

Since the Moors had been driven from the Spanish peninsula they had long continued to dominate the western Mediterranean by their sea power. Their wealth was also partly derived through their land connections across the Sahara with the fertile banks of the Senegal river, which supplied them with gold, ivory and negro slaves. This region they called Bilad Ghana, the land of wealth, known to Europe as Guinea. Henry conceived the strategic idea of reaching Guinea by sea. He thought not only to tap its wealth but to navigate the Senegal river up to a mythical lake, from which both this river and the Nile were supposed to derive their waters. He thus hoped to turn the flank of Islam from its rear, join hands with the Christian Empire in Abyssinia, and deliver the holy sepulchre at Jerusalem from the infidel. But Henry, like Cecil Rhodes, had dreams which far exceeded his African projects. In 1428 his brother Pedro had found in Venice and brought to Portugal a copy of Marco Polo's book and a map "with all the parts of the earth described, whereby Prince Henry was much furthered".[1]

In order to realise his aims this mediaeval crusader set to work with the patience and exactitude of a modern researcher, and his methods led to practical results more grand than his dreams. The problem he set himself was how to construct ships which, instead of hugging the shore, could maintain their course for weeks and months out of sight of land, face the Atlantic storms and still be able to fight their enemies. To effect these objects it was clearly necessary to dispense with the oars that had always been used to propel warships in the Mediterranean. His ships must depend for their movement on wind alone. Their captains must be given the means of directing their course when no land was in sight. They must also be trained to record on charts geographical data acquired on their voyages. In order to solve these problems Prince Henry retired in 1418 to the promontory of Sagres and there established an observatory, a naval arsenal and a school for the study of navigation and chart making. The cost was met from the revenues of the crusading Order of Christ, of which Prince Henry was Grand Master.

In 1420 his captains rediscovered the island of Madeira. It was then uninhabited and his manner of planting it shows that Henry was something more than a mere crusader. In the course of the Middle Ages Europe had learned the use of sugar. The tropical reed from which it was pressed had been brought by the Arabs from India to Egypt and thence to Cyprus, Sicily and Spain. But it never flourished in Europe, and Henry thought of planting a colony to grow it in Madeira, where it found at last a congenial home.

Meanwhile the captains were feeling their way down the African coast. Point after point was annexed to the Portuguese crown, and a series of bulls were issued from Rome to confirm the titles.

In 1445 the Senegal river was at last reached and the ships returned with some negro slaves. The maritime enterprise of Portugal was already creating a scarcity of labour in the little community, and the negro slaves were imported to cultivate the soil, a practice which rapidly spread to Spain.

Prince Henry died in 1460. In 1469 Affonso V. granted a monopoly of the Guinea trade to Fernam Gomes. His captains rounded Cape Palmas and, as the coast now pointed in a north-easterly direction, probably thought that the way to the Indian Ocean had been found. If so, they presently learned their mistake.

The crusading motive which had first inspired Prince Henry was in the course of the fifteenth century reinforced by purely commercial aims. The fall of Constantinople and Turkish conquests in the Levant enabled the Osmanlis to levy enormous tolls on the camel-borne trade with the East. Spices were almost as costly as jewels and, if the story, old as Herodotus, were true that Phoenician mariners had rounded the western coast of Africa and sailed in the Indian Ocean, then a fortune awaited the mariners who could first reach India and return to Europe with a ship-load of spices.

It was now in the hope of finding this route that the Portuguese captains extended their voyages round the Gulf of Guinea till the coast once more trended due south. In 1484 Diego Cam discovered the mouth of the Congo. In 1486 Bartholomew Diaz rounded the Cape of Good Hope and, before he returned, followed the coast as far as the Great Fish river, far enough to see that it here finally trended to the north-east. The effect of this news in Portugal is shown by the fact that the King changed the name which Diaz had noted on his chart from the Cape of Storms to the Cape of Good Hope.

NOTE

[1] Hudson, *Europe and China*, p. 164.

CHAPTER VIII

COLUMBUS

When Diaz returned in 1486, John II. had rejected a rival scheme for opening a route by the sea to Asia. Christopher Columbus, a Genoese captain, had in 1478 married Felipa Perestrello, daughter of one of Prince Henry's captains, and was thus led to study the logs and charts left by his father-in-law. He also began to read *The Travels of Marco Polo*. The interest which Henry the Navigator had taken in the copy discovered in 1428 by his brother Pedro would certainly have spread to his captains and pupils, and this probably explains why a Latin translation was one of the earliest books to be printed. The copy which Christopher Columbus used is still in existence, and the notes which he made with his own hand on seventy pages show that it largely formed his ideas. Another book, *Imago Mundi* by Pierre d'Ailly, gave him the notion, old as the Greeks, that the world was a sphere. He thus conceived the correct idea that a journey pushed to the west from Europe would eventually bring the traveller to Asia. He could not know, and indeed never realised, that a whole continent was blocking this western route, which would have to be rounded like Africa at its southern extremity.

Columbus entered the Portuguese service, and after returning from a voyage to the Gold Coast in 1482 submitted his scheme to John II. The scheme was rejected by his Council; but to satisfy his own curiosity John commissioned a ship to explore the western route behind the back of Columbus. When the ship returned, having done nothing, Columbus, enraged at this breach of faith, left Portugal to try his fortunes elsewhere.

The Council of State in Lisbon had rejected the scheme of Columbus for the very good reason that if a western route were discovered they could not control it as they now controlled the route down the African coast under papal authority. Columbus next applied in vain to his own city, Genoa, and then to Venice, but neither were interested in a scheme which, if it succeeded, would ruin their established trade with Levantine ports. Columbus then saw that his only chance lay with one of the western sea powers. So he carried his plan to Ferdinand and Isabella of Spain and commissioned his brother to submit it to Henry VII. in England, or, failing there, to approach the court of France. The negotiations in all three countries were protracted for years, and when in 1492 a message from Henry VII. arrived inviting Columbus to a conference in England, he had come to terms with the court in Spain.

On August 3, 1492, Christopher Columbus set sail from Spain and held on his western course till he sighted land and supposed that he had reached the islands off the coast of China which Marco Polo had described. On October 12 he landed on one of the Bahamas and claimed it for the crown of Castile. After visiting Cuba and Haiti and acquiring a general idea of the West Indies, he returned.

In 1493, 1498 and 1502 Columbus made three further voyages in the course of which he discovered the coast of the mainland and founded colonies. He died in 1505, in the full belief that he had reached the coast of Asia; a fact which explains why America now bears the name of a Florentine impostor. While Columbus was on his last voyage, Amerigo Vespucci, a former clerk in the trading firm of the Medici and probably their agent in Spain, was writing to Florence accounts of voyages in which he claimed to have discovered a new continent. His letters were widely published, and also believed, until further discoveries had shown that the voyages he described were not consistent with the facts of geography. Before this happened the world had realised that not Asia, but a new continent had been found, and in 1507 Martin Waldsemüller, professor of cosmography in St. Die University in Lorraine, suggested that the fourth continent should be called "America because Americus discovered it". And the name has stood, a monument to the power of publicity more enduring than brass.

Mindful of the precedent set by Portugal, the Spanish crown lost no time in securing from Rome a title-deed to the countries discovered by Columbus. By a bull dated May 14, 1493, Pope Alexander VI. assigned to the Kings of Castile and Leon—

> All the main lands and islands found or to be found, discovered or to be discovered, toward the west and south, drawing a line from the Arctic pole to the Antarctic pole, that is, from the north to the south, Containing in this donation, whatsoever main lands or islands are found or to be found toward India, or toward any other part whatsoever it be, being distant from, or without the aforesaid line drawn a hundred leagues toward the west and south from any of the islands which are commonly called De los Azores or Cape Verde.[1]

In the following year Spain and Portugal, by the Treaty of Tordesillas, ratified by the Pope, agreed that the line dividing their empires should be drawn about half-way between Lisbon and Florida. When the trend of the South American coast afterwards came to be known it was found that Brazil was east of this line and so in the sphere of Portugal.

NOTE

[1] Weare, *Cabot's Discovery of North America*, pp. 67, 68.

CHAPTER IX

VASCO DA GAMA

THE right to use the western route to Asia was limited to Spain by the papal bulls. To discover an eastern route was, therefore, vital to Portugal, and Vasco da Gama was commissioned by Manoel the Fortunate to exploit the achievement of Bartholomew Diaz. In January 1497 he sailed from Lisbon with four vessels to the Cape Verde Islands. Instead of hugging the African coast, like Diaz, he attempted to steer straight for the Cape of Good Hope, as he judged its position from the data collected by Diaz in 1486. After crossing the equator he encountered the contrary trade wind, which obliged him to steer to the south-west. He was almost in sight of the South American coast when he got a new wind. Changing his course he ran to the south-east and at last sighted the African coast a few days' sail north of the Cape. In December he rounded the Cape. In March 1498 the Arabs at Mozambique saw with amazement four strangely rigged vessels coming towards them from the mysterious south. Vasco da Gama found himself entering a port which was known in Europe. He was here able to converse with the local inhabitants through Arab interpreters and obtain pilots who could guide him to India. In April he reached Malindi north of Mombasa, and found in these ports Indian traders, whom he called Christians because they were not Mohammedans. The monsoon was just beginning to blow from the south-west and, guided by Hindu pilots, he crossed the Indian Ocean on this favourable breeze. On May 20, 1498, he dropped anchor in Calicut harbour.

This port on the western coast of India was the great emporium at which goods passing from China and the Indies to Europe were collected. The seaborne trade from Calicut to the Persian Gulf and the Red Sea was entirely controlled by the Arabs, to whom the appearance of Europeans in ships at an Indian port came like a bolt from the blue.

> "What in the name of Shaitan are *you* doing here?" shouted a voice in Arabic from the dense and interested crowd surrounding da Gama and his officers as they passed through the streets.[1]

Under pressure from the merchants of Mecca, the Hindu Zamorin imprisoned da Gama and his officers. They were presently released; but the insult was never forgotten and twice revenged. Vasco da Gama returned to Portugal in triumph and in 1500 a second and stronger expedition started from Lisbon under Cabral. Following the same course as the first expedition, Cabral discovered the coast of Brazil before he turned to the south-east. He reached Calicut at the close of the year and established a factory by the leave of the Zamorin. The Arab merchants attacked the factory and butchered the staff. But they had not reckoned with the Portuguese guns which Cabral turned on their ships and sank every one of them. He then bombarded the Hindu town and left it in ruins.

In 1502 a third expedition was sent under Vasco da Gama, who met the combined Arab fleets off the coast of Malabar and almost destroyed them. The dhows, which were armed with mortars, were no match for the ships, seamanship and guns of the Portuguese. The event proved how well Henry the Navigator had laid the foundation of their maritime power.

The task of developing these achievements fell to the great Albuquerque, who proceeded to survey the maritime problem of the eastern trade. At this period the island of Ormuz in the mouth of the Persian Gulf was the focus of sea-borne trade west of India. From Mesopotamia to Malabar articles of commerce were shipped to that point. To the east of India the trade was collected at Malacca on the straits between the Malay peninsula and Sumatra, the maritime road which connects the Bay of Bengal and the China seas. Goods destined for Europe were shipped from Malacca and Ormuz to Egypt by the Arabs, who controlled the whole of these seas.

In a series of desperate engagements Albuquerque seized and occupied the island of Socotra at the mouth of the Red Sea, Ormuz at the mouth of the Persian Gulf, and then Goa on the coast of India, which he made the capital of the Portuguese Empire in the East. From this base he was able to capture Malacca, which then acknowledged the suzerainty of China. The Arabs were swept from the seas. Till the close of the sixteenth century the whole trade from the East to Europe was controlled by the Portuguese. The spices and silks for her markets were carried by sea to Lisbon and thence distributed to the ports of Europe by Dutch traders. So much was accomplished when Albuquerque died at Goa in 1515.

When Albuquerque stormed Malacca in 1511 the eastern limit of the Portuguese Empire was carried to that point. The king of Portugal had styled himself 'Emperor of India'; but his great servants in the East had realised better than their master the relative weakness of the kingdom behind them. Almeida had strongly opposed Albuquerque's schemes for occupying ports like Ormuz, Goa and Malacca. But even the forceful Albuquerque realised that so small a power as Portugal must rest content with the empire of the sea.

About 1517 Portuguese ships reached Canton. In

the next few years there were several violent collisions between Portuguese and Chinese forces. An envoy, Thomé Pires, sent to visit the court of Peking in 1521, was arrested and probably died in prison. Requests for permission to trade were rebuffed. It was not till 1557 that the Portuguese, by bribing the local officials, were able to open a trading station on Macao, a peninsula at the mouth of the Canton river.

In 1517 the Portuguese had thus reached by sea the fabled Empire of Cathay which Marco Polo had explored by land. In the next few years Spain was approaching these distant regions from the opposite direction. Magalhães, a Portuguese mariner, incensed by failure to secure an increase of pay, deserted the service of Manoel and offered to prove by a westward voyage that the Spice Islands belonged to the Empire of Charles V. in terms of the bull issued in 1494. The offer was accepted, and in 1520 he passed the straits which bear his name (Magellan) and reached the Philippine Islands, where he perished in 1521. But one of his ships, the *Victoria*, returned to Spain by the Cape of Good Hope in 1522, thus proving beyond dispute that the human race lived on a ball suspended in space.

The settlement of a line down the Pacific to divide the two Empires was at once demanded by Spain. After long negotiations this line was fixed in 1529 by the Treaty of Saragossa at 17° east of the Moluccas. In the light of the facts then known it was not realised by either party that this line would assign the Philippines to the Portuguese. When in later years the Spaniards annexed the islands they simply ignored the letter of the treaty, and the Portuguese were unable to assert their technical claim.[2]

In America Spain, with greater resources, was confronted by races weaker than those of Asia, to whom horses as well as guns were unknown. Columbus, bred in the Portuguese school which had conquered Guinea, thought of gold and slaves as the proper rewards of discovery. His colonies were founded to export those commodities to Spain. By 1521, seven hundred Spaniards commanded by Cortes had conquered the Mexican Empire. By 1532 one hundred and eighty-three Spaniards led by Pizarro had mastered Peru. Gold which the natives had hoarded for centuries began to pour into the coffers of Spain. The forcible conversion of the natives to the Catholic religion went hand in hand with these conquests. In 1543 the Philippine Islands were conquered and Christianised and Manila was founded as the seat of its government. The task of converting natives was entrusted to the Orders of St. Augustine, St. Dominic and St. Francis.

In 1557, when the Portuguese had secured their station at Macao, the western and eastern outposts of the Spanish and Portuguese Empires were facing each other in the Pacific. To the natives of those regions it had also become clear that conquest and conversion to the Catholic faith were parts of the same process. Behind the conventional terms in which popes issued their mandates to kings was a stern reality.

NOTES

[1] Ballard, *Rulers of the Indian Ocean*, p. 33.
[2] Abbott, *The Expansion of Europe*, vol. i. chap. iv.

CHAPTER X

WYCLIFFE AND HUS

THE discoveries of Christopher Columbus had given occasion for the Papacy to state in final and absolute terms its claim to unlimited sovereignty on earth.

> We by the authority of Almighty God granted unto us in Saint Peter, and by the office which we bear on the earth in the stead of Jesus Christ, do for ever by the tenour of these presents, give, grant, and assign unto you, your heirs and successors (the Kings of Castile and Leon), all these lands and islands, with their dominions, territories, cities, castles, towers, places, and villages, with all the right and jurisdiction thereunto pertaining: constituting, assigning, and deputing you, your heirs and successors, the lords thereof, with full and free power, authority, and jurisdiction. . . . We furthermore inhibit all manner of persons, of what state, degree, order, or condition soever they be, although of Imperial and regal dignity, under the pain of the sentence of excommunication which they shall incur if they do to the contrary, that they in no case presume, without special licence of you, your heirs and successors, to travel for merchandise or for any other cause, to the said lands or islands, found or to be found, discovered or to be discovered, towards the west and south.[1]

The opening of routes by the high seas to the distant continents had shifted the economic balance of Europe from Mediterranean to Atlantic shores. The northern nations on those shores were threatened with excommunication if they ventured to challenge the vast monopolies which the Pope had assigned to the crowns of Portugal and Spain. But in northern Europe forces had long been at work which were now beginning to rob this threat of its terrors in the minds of whole nations. In order to explain the growth of these forces, our narrative must return to events which had happened in England centuries before.

From the reign of King John, England in theory was a fief of the Papal Empire, and its status as such was acknowledged by the payment of tribute. Much as the king resented this position, his subjects (not excluding the clergy) resented it more. The creation of parliament as an organ of public opinion immediately strengthened his hands in disputing the Pope's right to be recognised as the suzerain power. In 1299 Boniface VIII. was pressing his claim to universal empire to its logical conclusion. In 1296 he forbade the kings to levy taxation on the clergy. In 1299 he declared that Scotland was a fief, not of England, but of Rome, and ordered Edward to desist from its conquest. In 1301 the parliament of Lincoln opposed these claims with a declaration that

> The kings of England neither have been wont to answer nor ought to answer, touching their rights in the said kingdom, or any other temporal rights, before any judge ecclesiastical or secular.[2]

In France, Philip the Fair was meeting the claims of Boniface VIII. with a curse pronounced on his own sons should they ever admit that the French crown could be held from anyone but God himself. When the Pope could no longer secure the obedience of kings, a king might secure the obedience of popes. In 1305 the reigning Pope died, and Philip secured the election of a French archbishop as Clement V. In 1309 the Pope moved his court from Rome to Avignon. For seventy years the vicars of Christ were obedient tools of the French monarchy.

It was during the period when the papal court was removed from Italy to France that two scholars, one an Italian, the other an Englishman, launched an indictment of papal authority which in time destroyed its very foundations. Marsiglio, born of a burgher family in Padua, brought to the study of Aristotle's *Politics* an insight possible in that age only to a thinker bred in surroundings so like those of the city-states in which the Greek had lived and reasoned. In Marsiglio's view the basis of human authority was

> the people or community of the citizens, or the majority of them, determining by their choice or will, expressed by word in a general assembly, that anything should be done or omitted regarding man's civil acts under pain of temporal punishment.[3]

The authority of princes to enforce the law is derived from the people, who may cancel the authority if princes themselves break the law. The practical working of a system of government based on this principle was deranged by the Pope's claim to enforce the authority of Christ on earth. Marsiglio challenged that claim. He exhibited the Papacy to his readers as the great disturbing cause in human society. This tremendous conclusion was implied in the title of his treatise, *Defensor Pacis,* produced at Paris in 1324. Clement VI. exclaimed that he had never read a more pestilent heretic.

The great English schoolman, William of Ockham (the Surrey village in which he was born), went from Oxford to the university of Paris. He there fell in with Marsiglio and absorbed his political ideas which were spread through Europe by Ockham's books rather than by his own.

Englishmen, after their manner, acted before they reasoned. In 1333 parliament refused to vote money for paying the papal tribute. Some five years later began the struggle with France which lasted for over a century. The French popes at Avignon were regarded in England with growing distrust, and in 1366 the legal obligation to pay the tribute was expressly denounced by Lords and Commons. When a monk protested, Wycliffe, an Oxford scholar, was employed by parliament to frame a reply, and he did so in a formidable paper asserting the right of the government to deprive the Church of its possessions in case of need. Wycliffe was familiar with the doctrines of Marsiglio, at least in so far as they found expression in the writings of Ockham.

In the axis of systems which claim to depend on divine authority as their actuating principle is a flaw which will sooner or later be exposed by the working of their mechanism. The Pope claimed to be the final human authority through whose lips God had chosen to declare his will to mankind. But by what means did God at any particular moment specify the person to act as the mouthpiece of his wisdom and the agent of his will? Custom developed through centuries had long supplied an answer to this question. When a pope died the cardinals assembled in conclave, and the Holy Spirit was believed to reveal to them the man chosen by God to act as his vicar on earth. It was clearly necessary to this theory that every member of the conclave should agree in naming the same person. The process of reaching agreement was very much that which is now followed by American parties in selecting a candidate for the presidency, with this difference, that it was and is not exposed at any point to the public gaze. Inside locked doors the conclave was a focus of intrigue where influences of a strictly human order, personal and political, strove for the mastery. At intervals votes were taken until it became clear that one of the candidates could count on a two-thirds majority. When this point was reached the voting papers were burned, the successful candidate was elected by unanimous vote, and presented to the world as pope. A failure of this mechanism to determine which of two or more persons God had revealed to the cardinals as his vicar was bound to provoke the question whether God really moved them at all—whether indeed any one person was chosen by God as the mouthpiece of his purpose and will.

In 1378 such a failure occurred when Gregory XI. died on a visit to Rome. For the first time for over seventy years a papal election took place in Rome, and the cardinals, yielding to the violence of the mob, elected an Italian, Bartolommeo Prignano, who ascended the throne as Urban VI. He at once reinforced his position by creating twenty-eight new cardinals, enough to swamp the French majority in the college. The French cardinals seceded and elected Robert of Geneva as Clement VII., who established his court at Avignon. The schism lasted till 1417, and during the interval there were two, and at one time three, rival popes. The figment that God chooses one man as his vicar and reveals his choice to the world was thus exposed by unanswerable facts.

On Wycliffe's mind the effect of this schism was decisive. In a series of writings he challenged the spiritual as well as the temporal claims of the Pope, and appealed from the authority of the Church to the authority of scripture. In one respect he went further than Marsiglio or Ockham. Wycliffe had seen that the great power of the clergy was founded in the popular belief that priests could change bread and wine into the body and blood of Christ, by virtue of which alone men can be saved from eternal damnation. The doctrine of transubstantiation is liable to misunderstanding because in the language of the schoolmen 'substance' implies 'essence', an idea the opposite of that which the word 'substance' connotes to ordinary minds. But this does not alter the fact that the great mass of clergy and laity interpreted the doctrine in its material sense. In the orthodox phrase of the time priests had the power of "making the body of Christ", and their right of giving or withholding it determined the whole future of laymen for weal or woe. That matter and sense are themselves evil is the great obsession which has spread from India to China and from Persia to Europe. An ordinance instituted as a protest against this idea had in course of ages been degraded to the level of paganism. Wycliffe denied that these claims to magical powers had any authority in scripture. He went on to declare that the scriptures must be given to the laity in their mother tongue. The closing years of his life were spent in translating the Bible and in training itinerant teachers to expound its pages to the people at large. His immense popularity alone saved him from the fury of the Church. He died in his bed in 1384.

The doctrines of Wycliffe, as spread by his followers the Lollards, made great headway in England for several years. In 1399 the movement was checked when Henry IV. was raised to the throne with the support of the Archbishop of Canterbury. By conviction, as well as in gratitude to the Church, the Lancastrian dynasty repressed the Lollards; but the movement, never extinguished, smouldered on till the storm raised by Luther in Germany blew it into flame in the sixteenth century. That storm was itself an after-result of a previous revolution in Bohemia directly stimulated by the writings of Wycliffe.

In 1388 Adalbert Rauconis, a teacher at Prague, founded some travelling scholarships to enable Bohemians to study at Paris and Oxford. These Czech scholars seized on the writings of Wycliffe, eagerly copied them, and brought the copies to Prague. From that great University they spread rapidly throughout Bohemia and central Europe. They were studied by John Hus, a leading teacher at Prague and a popular preacher in the Czech tongue.

In 1405 Hus was commissioned with two others

by Zbynek, Archbishop of Prague, to enquire into certain reputed miracles which were drawing pilgrims from all Europe to a church near Wittenberg. The report on the miracles was such that the Archbishop prohibited further pilgrimage from Bohemia to this church. Hus followed this up with a book denouncing false miracles and ecclesiastical greed. He condemned the habit of seeking for visible signs of Christ's presence, and directed Christians to look for their Master in scripture. From the pulpit of the Bethlehem Chapel he attacked the corruption of the clergy and preached the doctrines of Wycliffe in the vulgar tongue.

The Papacy had been quick to realise how fatal to its claims were those doctrines, and Innocent VII. now called on the Archbishop to stamp them out of Bohemia. Zbynek complied by removing Hus from his office as preacher.

In 1409 a general council of bishops at Pisa sought to heal the great schism by deposing both the two rival popes, Gregory XII. and Benedict XIII., and electing a new pope, Alexander V. Zbynek adhered to Alexander V., and, in obedience to his orders, excommunicated Hus and burned over two hundred copies of Wycliffe's writings. In doing so he made the doctrines they contained the popular religion of Bohemia and Hus its national hero.

In 1410 Alexander V. died, and the Italian cardinals elected to succeed him a soldier of fortune and notorious evil-liver. Baldassare Cossa ascended the papal throne as John XXIII. The Emperor Sigismund persuaded John to summon a general council to meet at Constance in 1414 for the purpose of restoring unity to the Church. The Bohemian movement led by Hus was rightly regarded as a natural consequence of the schism. So one of the first acts of the Council was to summon Hus to appear before it. Hus came to Constance under a safe-conduct from

Sigismund. In a few weeks the Pope and cardinals had him in prison. Commissions were appointed to examine the opinions of Wycliffe and Hus. The Council condemned the writings of Wycliffe to be burned and his corpse to be torn from the grave at Lutterworth and given to the flames, an order faithfully executed in 1428 by Fleming, Bishop of Lincoln, the founder of Lincoln College at Oxford.

Meanwhile the Italian profligate John XXIII. was at daggers-drawn with the Council he had summoned to Constance. He deemed it prudent to leave that city; but, according to Gibbon,

> was brought back a prisoner: the most scandalous charges were suppressed; the vicar of Christ was only accused of piracy, murder, rape, sodomy, and incest; and after subscribing his own condemnation, he expiated in prison the imprudence of trusting his person to a free city beyond the Alps.[4]

The way was thus opened to the eventual election of a pope recognised as such by the whole Catholic world.

These events naturally led to a revival in orthodox circles of the doctrine that ultimate authority rested not with the pope but in general councils. This increased the anxiety of the Council at Constance to suppress those in England and Bohemia who were denying the final authority of the Church and appealing to scripture as interpreted by each for himself. The Council was thus resolved that Hus should acknowledge their authority as higher than that of his own conscience, or else perish at the stake.

Few chapters in history have repeated themselves so nearly as the trial of Christ by the Sanhedrin and his crucifixion by a Roman procurator was repeated in the trial of Hus by the Council of Constance, and his burning at the stake by the "King of the Romans". The vacillations of Pilate compare favourably with the cold treachery of the Emperor Sigismund.

The long controversy of Hus with the Council led to an issue so real that it could only be compromised by fear. The Council was confronted by one who was fearless. Calmly but steadfastly Hus refused to accept its dictates as against those of his own conscience. Like Socrates and Jesus, he died in that faith.

Hus was burnt at the stake on July 6, 1415. Two days before this tragedy was enacted Gregory XII. had formally abdicated. The remaining Pope, Benedict XIII., persistently refused to resign, and on July 26, 1417, was deposed by the Council. The papal throne was now vacant, and the Germans, led by the Emperor Sigismund, urged that before a new pope was elected definite reforms should be made in his powers of exacting money. By skilfully playing one nation against another, the cardinals outwitted the Emperor. In October 1417 the Council agreed to the election of a pope by a conclave consisting of the cardinals together with six deputies elected by each of the nations recognised in the Council. These nations, the French contended, were the Italian, German, Spanish and themselves. The English claimed to rank as a fifth. The victory which Henry V. had won at the battle of Agincourt could not be ignored, and the English carried their point in the Council. The status of England as one of the great powers of Christendom was thus officially established at the Council of Constance.

This point having been settled, the conclave met in November and elected Cardinal Colonna, who was crowned Pope as Martin V. On the following day he exercised his power to confirm the rights of the papal vice-chancellor and the regulations of the curia under which he acted. The despotic authority of the Pope was thus used to re-establish the principal abuses which the Council of Constance had sought to reform. The Council had ended the schism, but only on terms which a century later drove half Europe to repudiate the claims of the great theocracy.

When the schism in the Papacy was at last healed a strong party in the Church wished to maintain General Councils as a check on the pope. Such a council was actually in session at Basel from 1431 to 1448. In the end the popes succeeded in dissolving it, and suppressed the conciliar movement. Thus at the close of the fifteenth century the Papal Autocracy appeared to the world as more firmly established than ever in its previous history. Alexander VI. and Julius II. asserted their right to be recognised as political rulers of the vast papal estates.

The result was that in northern Europe they came to be thought of as temporal princes in Italy, rather than as spiritual heads of Christendom. While Christopher Columbus and Vasco da Gama were revealing continents to the eyes of Europe, the revival of classical learning had risen to its zenith in Italy. Rome was itself the centre of the movement which was there finding expression in buildings designed and adorned by masters of sculpture and painting. The cost of these buildings and the gorgeous luxury of the papal court was largely met by the sale of indulgences throughout Europe.[5]

NOTES

[1] Weare, *Cabot's Discovery of North America*, pp. 67, 68.
[2] Poole, *Wycliffe and Movements for Reform*, p. 4.
[3] Creighton, *A History of the Papacy*, vol. i. p. 43 (1919 edition).
[4] Gibbon, *Decline and Fall of the Roman Empire*, chap. lxx.
[5] In this chapter Creighton's *A History of the Papacy* has been followed.

CHAPTER XI

LUTHER

In the early years of the sixteenth century, the Elector Frederick of Saxony, known as the Wise, had founded a University in Wittenberg. In 1508 Martin Luther, a young monk in the Order of the Augustinian Eremites, was brought to Wittenberg as professor of theology. In 1512 he was sent to Rome on the business of his Order.

When he first caught sight of the city Luther raised his hands in an ecstasy, exclaiming, "I greet thee, thou Holy Rome, thrice holy from the blood of the Martyrs" . . . The city he had greeted as holy, he found to be a sink of iniquity; its very priests were infidel, and openly scoffed at the sacred services they performed ; the papal courtiers were men of depraved lives; the Cardinals of the Church lived in open sin.[1]

On returning to Wittenberg Luther began to attack the sale of indulgences by the Pope, which were in fact licences to sin relieved of all penalties here and hereafter. In 1517 he nailed to the door of the church in Wittenberg ninety-five theses, heads of propositions, which he offered to sustain in dispute against all comers.

This academic proceeding led to a greater publicity than Luther himself had perhaps expected. In spite of the efforts of the Church to suppress the writings of Wycliffe and Hus, the atmosphere of northern Europe had been saturated with their teaching, which had influenced the mind of Luther himself. Copies of the ninety-five theses were sent to the University printers, who could not publish them fast enough to meet the public demand. From that moment Luther became the most popular and powerful figure in Germany. Luther's challenge was taken up by a former friend, John Eck of Ingolstadt, who in public disputation at Wittenberg drove Luther to declare his sympathy with some of the teachings of Wycliffe and Hus. For Luther had now studied the forged decretals and had realised the fraud which underlay them. In 1520 he issued a manifesto in which, like Wycliffe, he questioned the power of priests to save souls by administering sacraments. He denied the claim of the Pope to decide what the Scriptures meant, asserting the right of all men to read and interpret the Scriptures for themselves. He advised that the clergy should marry, attacked the extravagance and vices of the papal court, and urged the creation of a national church in Germany.

The Pope's reply to this manifesto was a bull excommunicating Luther, who burnt it in public. The Pope then called on the Emperor to execute Luther.

At this juncture Charles V., the youthful grandson of Ferdinand and Isabella who had sent Columbus on his voyages, had just been elected as Emperor. By inheritance, he ruled over widely scattered dominions, the Netherlands, Burgundy, Naples, Sardinia and Sicily. As King of Spain he ruled the Americas. In Germany he now wielded the dubious authority of the Holy Roman Empire, and before he could execute the papal bull on the person of Luther he had first to secure the approval of the Diet of Princes. In 1521 the Diet was convened at Worms and Luther, when granted a safe-conduct, appeared before it. Summoned by Charles to retract his doctrine that all men were entitled to interpret the Scriptures for themselves, he stoutly refused. The ban of the Diet was passed against him; but Frederick of Saxony saw to it that the safe-conduct was observed. He himself arrested Luther and interned him in the castle of Wartburg where he kept him safe. A time had come when princes as well as peoples were ceasing to believe in and fear the power of the Church to condemn men to punishment here or hereafter, or to loose them from it. Germany was divided between states which recognised and those which denied the claims of the Church. Generations of internecine wars arrested her civilisation and her progress to national unity, which is not completed even to-day. Neither she nor Italy could take any part in the great contest of nations bordering the Atlantic for controlling the continents opened by Christopher Columbus and Vasco da Gama.

The influence of Luther was quickly spread by the agency of printing. In France his works were read by John Calvin, a young lawyer who had also studied the New Testament as edited by Erasmus. From the fierce persecution of the French King, Francis II., he found safety in Geneva, which secured its religious freedom from Rome by joining the Swiss Federation. He also escaped the fate which had overtaken John Hus. His writings continued to inspire the Huguenot movement in France. But the French monarchy, which wielded powers denied to the Emperor in Germany, was eventually able to crush it.

NOTE

[1] Lindsay, *The Cambridge Modern History*, vol. ii. pp. 117, 118.

CHAPTER XII

THE REFORMATION IN ENGLAND AND THE NETHERLANDS

In England the flame kindled by Wycliffe had never been quenched, even by the terrible laws which Lancastrian kings had enacted against the Lollards. Luther's appeal from the Church to Scripture quickly revived it. In 1524 Tyndale visited Luther at Wittenberg and started to print in Germany his English translation of the New Testament. The Church was now alive to the danger of encouraging laymen to read the Scriptures. When Warham, Archbishop of Canterbury, found that he could not prevent copies of Tyndale's Bible from reaching England, he commissioned agents to buy up the whole issue in Germany. Henry VIII. himself published a book against Luther, earning thereby from the Pope the title of Fidei Defensor, which the crown to this day quaintly preserves. But the Roman claim to supremacy had long been sapped by the growth of self-government, and the sense of nationalism bred thereby. The belief, so potent in the time of King John, that the pope could assign a whole nation to eternal perdition, had lost its hold on the mind of the English. They began to ask why such huge estates and revenues drawn from the land should support in ease large numbers of priests and monks. The King and his courtiers were casting covetous eyes on these lands and revenues.

The spirit of revolt from Rome was brought to a head by the strong passions of Henry VIII. He had tired of his queen, Catherine of Aragon, the near kinswoman of the Emperor Charles V., and wished to replace her by Anne Boleyn. The Pope refused to sanction Catherine's divorce. In 1535 parliament, at the instance of Henry VIII., passed the Act of Supremacy by which church and state were severed from all obedience to Rome. The monasteries were abolished and their lands seized by the King and his courtiers.

This formal defection of a Christian country, which ranked almost with Spain and France, was felt in Rome as a threat even more serious than the advancing power of the Turkish Empire in the east. The Pope called on Christendom to reassert his authority in England. His appeal was frustrated by the skill with which Henry VIII. played on the rival ambitions of Spain and France.

In 1547 Henry VIII. was succeeded by Edward VI. at the age of ten. The death of the boy king in 1553 brought to the throne Mary, the daughter of Catherine of Aragon, a devout Catholic. In 1554 she married Philip, son of the Emperor Charles V., who, wearied of life, in 1555 retired into monastic seclusion, conferring on Philip the sovereignty of the Netherlands, Spain and his widely scattered dominions. To these Philip had now added the throne of England in consort with Mary. They induced parliament to restore the obedience of England to Rome, and strove to extinguish heresy by force. In result they destroyed all future hope of obedience to Rome by the fires in which some hundreds of Protestants were burned. When Mary died, leaving no issue, in 1558 the right of her husband to rule in England came to an end. Elizabeth, daughter of Anne Boleyn, came to the throne and obedience to Rome was finally ended by the Act of Supremacy which the English parliament passed in 1559.

Meanwhile the teaching of Luther and Calvin had spread to the Netherlands, and here Philip was preparing measures to assert the authority of Rome.

He could no more doubt of the final triumph than he could doubt the sacredness of the cause he had inherited. His slow, laborious mind was incapable of change or adaptations; a conviction once assimilated by him could only with great difficulty be eradicated. He had been taught that his royal House and his Spanish people were divinely appointed to champion the system which was to bring about God's kingdom upon earth. Suffering, hardship, oppression, cruelty, might be necessary for the attainment of the glorious object, of which he and Spain were to be the instrumental factors.[1]

In England under Philip and Mary a few hundreds had died by fire. In the Netherlands, tens of thousands were burned at the stake and put to the sword by the Spanish soldiers. The Protestants, driven into open revolt, found a consummate leader in William the Silent, Prince of Orange. William realised that his raw Protestant levies were always out-matched by the Spanish armies led by the able and pitiless Alva. So he issued letters of marque to Dutch privateers, who were known as the Beggars of the Sea. Between Spain and the Netherlands lay the always hostile kingdom of France. The Dutch privateers, incomparably better as sailors than Spaniards, made it almost impossible for Philip to support Alva in Holland. In their utmost extremity the Dutch were induced by William to cut their dykes and submerge the country. Their ships were carried by the floods to relieve towns besieged by the Spaniards. The struggle continued till Philip put a price on the head of William, who was killed in his own house by a Catholic fanatic in 1584. But his work survived him in the Dutch Republic, a sea power whose navy henceforth disputed with England the ocean supremacy of Spain.

In 1569 ships carrying 450,000 ducats to Alva were driven by privateers to take refuge in Plymouth harbour, where the money was seized by Queen Elizabeth. The results in the Netherlands were far-reaching. Alva, in desperate need of money, was driven to impose taxes which drove the Catholics as well as the Protestants into rebellion. The Spanish troops, who went unpaid, mutinied, pillaged and massacred Catholics and Protestants alike.

NOTE

[1] Martin Hume, *The Cambridge Modern History*, vol. iii. p. 508.

CHAPTER XIII

THE ARMADA

WHEN Elizabeth came to the throne and parliament had renounced all obedience to Rome, the papal bulls which had granted to Spain and Portugal an exclusive right to the world beyond Europe had become waste paper in the eyes of Englishmen. As Elizabeth said,

> Prescription without possession availeth nothing. The use of the sea and air is common to all . . . as neither nature, nor public use and custom permitteth any possession thereof.[1]

For centuries the Catholic Church had claimed that its head was vicegerent of God upon earth. In the closing years of the fifteenth century Rome had been able to exercise that claim to its logical extreme, only to find in a few decades that the claim itself was flatly denied by half Europe. The principle of authority, swelled like a bubble to its utmost capacity, had burst. That the Reformation had followed so quickly on the opening of the world to Christendom was more than an accident. From that time onwards the organisation of human society under one paramount law was its greatest need. In the theory of that age such a paramount law already existed, and indeed received an immediate expression in the bull issued by Pope Alexander VI. But the principle of authority in which that theory was founded was a sandbank of falsities, and the structure of world government built on it collapsed by its own weight. Henceforward the problem of politics was, and is, to find a foundation of rock, which can be no other than the principle of the commonwealth, the infinite duty of each to all.

In the opening years of her reign Elizabeth owed the security of her throne to the troubles in Holland, which the bigotry of Philip had brought on his own head. She was not as yet prepared for an open conflict with Spain, but allowed adventurous seamen like Hawkins and Drake to challenge the Spanish monopoly of America, and shared in the profits of their trade and piracy. In 1578 Drake rounded the Horn, and gathered an enormous booty by pillaging Spanish ships off the coasts of Chili and Peru. Crossing the Pacific he then returned by the Cape of Good Hope, and reaching England in 1580, was knighted on board his ship by Elizabeth.

Philip was now beginning to realise that the empire conferred by Rome on his House was a mere figment unless he controlled England as well as the Netherlands.

As a first step to that end he entrusted the conquest of Portugal to Alva. By seizing the crown of Portugal and annexing that country to Spain in 1580 two objects were achieved. In the first place, he acquired a titular right to the whole empire of the world opened by Vasco da Gama as well as by Christopher Columbus. In the second, he was now able to use Lisbon and the ports on the Portuguese coasts as a naval base for his struggle with England.

In 1584 Philip laid an embargo on English ships in the ports of Spain. Next year Elizabeth replied by commissioning Drake to pillage the West Indies. The Spanish settlements were laid waste and in 1586 the English raiders returned with their booty.

Philip, stung by this insult, resolved to concentrate all his forces on the conquest of England. The Pope promised 1,000,000 crowns — when the Spanish armies had landed in England. The work of constructing the great Armada in the harbours of Spain and Portugal began in real earnest. The work was delayed and embarrassed by the action of Drake, who in 1587 descended on Cadiz and destroyed most of the shipping in the harbour. He then seized upon Sagres, the historic basis of Henry the Navigator. From this stronghold his ships operated to paralyse the coast trade of the peninsula. He captured and destroyed so many vessels laden with wine, that the great Armada was furnished with barrels built from wood so green that they leaked. In the final battle the Spanish crews were largely disabled by thirst.

In May 1588 the Armada set out from its basis at Lisbon. Its orders were to sail up the English Channel and enable the Duke of Parma in the Netherlands to land his army on the English coast. Drake lay ready to meet it at Plymouth and a Dutch flotilla was also watching to embarrass Parma in shipping his troops. On July 21 the Armada had passed the Lizard and was under fire from the English fleet. The Spanish ships, which carried more soldiers than sailors, were constructed and manned in the Mediterranean tradition. They were meant to grapple with the enemy's ships, and then overwhelm their crews by the number of soldiers they carried. The English ships were constructed and rigged and their crews trained for sailing the Atlantic waters in which they were fighting. Drake had long realised that the power of a ship lay in its use as a platform for guns and not as a transport for troops. The lumbering Spanish galleons, crowded with soldiers and manned by inadequate crews who were wracked by thirst, lay at the mercy of the English ships as soon as they came within reach of their guns. Such as escaped the first onset fled for safety to the roads of Calais, from which they were smoked by the English fire-ships. Continuing their flight to the north, the Spanish ships made their way through the Orkney and Shetland Islands. They here began to encounter

Atlantic storms which scattered the coasts of the Hebrides, of Ireland and even Cornwall with wrecks. Scarcely half the vessels which had left the Spanish peninsula returned to its ports to tell the tale of disaster.

The resources of Spain had been strained to the utmost to build and equip the Armada. Its destruction finally ended the power of Spain on the sea, though the English were slow to realise the fact for a whole generation. With the fall of Spanish sea power was stultified once for all the claim of the Pope as vicegerent of God, to delegate to this sovereign or that the government of the earth. Henceforward Catholic as well as Protestant kings ceased to regard their authority as derived from the Catholic Church, and claimed to derive it from God himself. Divine right was based, in theory on heredity, in reality on physical power. The fact was typified when Napoleon, having summoned the Pope to crown him, at the critical moment seized the symbol of sovereignty from his hands and crowned himself with it.

The fall of the Spanish Armada decided the long rivalry between Spain and France in the interests of France. For the next two centuries England and France appear on the stage of the world as protagonists. In the French monarchy was embodied the principle of authority based on divine right. In British civilisation the principle of the commonwealth was finding expression.

NOTE

[1] Camden, *History of Elizabeth*, p. 255 (ed. 1675). Quoted by Hunter in *A History of British India*, vol. i. p. 207.

CHAPTER XIV

THE FAR EAST

THE revolt in Germany had quickly reacted on the latinised world to revive its loyalty to the Catholic faith. A Spanish soldier, Ignatius Loyola, conceived the idea of founding the Jesuit Order on military rather than collegiate principles, to fight the battles of the Catholic church. In 1540 the King of Portugal applied to Rome for missionaries to convert his Indian empire. The task was entrusted to Francis Xavier, the first secretary of the new Order. He landed at Goa in 1542 and went on to Malacca. A Japanese exile Yaziro, whom he met there, moved him to attempt the conversion of Japan. No European had visited that empire; but about this time three Portuguese on their way to China were carried by a storm to the island of Tanegashima. They taught the inhabitants the use of firearms, which quickly spread through the whole of Japan. The Portuguese traders were encouraged to bring more of these weapons, and in 1549 Xavier was able to reach Japan in one of their ships.

The Japanese islands were in theory ruled by the Emperor at Kyoto. But the real authority lay with the Daimyo, feudal chiefs, who were always at war one with another. The firearms brought by the Portuguese enabled one of them, Nobunaga, to establish his power in western Japan. He allowed the traders to introduce Jesuit missionaries who founded a station at Nagasaki, in the island of Kiushiu. By 1581 their converts numbered 150,000.

To convert the natives, Spain employed Augustinians, Franciscans and Dominicans, in whose eyes the Jesuits were impertinent upstarts. In 1585 the Pope tried to avert a conflict by reserving China and Japan to the Jesuits, and the Philippine islands to the older Orders. But the Friars were always looking for a chance to evade a settlement which reserved for their rivals so vast a sphere of activity.

In 1582 Nobunaga was murdered; but his work was completed by one of his generals, Hideyoshi, a man raised by transcendent abilities from the lowest rank of society. By 1591 he was ruling the whole of Japan as dictator.

By seizing the throne of Portugal in 1580 Philip II. was now entitled to claim for himself the whole empire of the Eastern Hemisphere, which papal bulls had divided between Portugal and Spain. Hideyoshi began to see that the Japanese converted to the Catholic faith might end by obeying the head of their Church in Rome, and support the claim of Philip conferred by the Pope to rule in Japan. To bring matters to a test he called on Don Gomez de Marinas, the Governor of the Philippines, to acknowledge Japan as his suzerain power. Don Gomez, powerless to resist, decided to temporise, and in 1573 he sent an embassage to Japan. The Franciscans managed to secure that four of their number should go as envoys. They thus got access to Hideyoshi, and Father Baptiste, their leader, swore to him that the Governor would accept his demands and thus secured his permission to remain in Japan.

Hideyoshi now felt himself free to embark on a project of world empire, to begin with the conquest of China. Instead of expelling the Spaniards from the Philippine islands, which he might have done with the greatest ease, he invaded and conquered Korea.

The four Franciscans meanwhile started to preach and build churches in Japan, blind to the danger which threatened the missionary movement and ignoring the advice offered by the Jesuits with their greater local experience. The disturbance they caused attracted the notice of the Japanese ruler. In 1596 a Spanish captain, whose ship had been wrecked on the coast of Japan, foolishly boasted that missionaries rendered the subsequent work of conquest easy by converting the loyalty of the people to the Catholic conquerors. On learning this, Hideyoshi realised that the Franciscans had used their position as envoys to conduct propaganda. He ordered the execution of a number of missionaries and a general expulsion of all of them. Some Jesuits, however, were able to evade the decree through the loyalty of their Japanese converts.

In 1598 Hideyoshi and Philip II. died within three days of each other. Iyeyasu, the ablest of the Daimyo and head of the Tokugawa clan, immediately grasped the reins of power. Of noble birth, he was able to obtain from the Emperor of Kyoto the office of shogun (Barbarian-subduing generalissimo), an office capable of transmission to his son. His mind was set on founding a dynasty of shoguns and on building up a corps of officials strong enough to support it, a project in which he succeeded so well that after his time the permanent officials were the real government of Japan.

The conflicts aroused by the Protestant revolt in Europe were already beginning to trouble the opposite side of the globe. In 1594 Philip II., by closing Lisbon to the Dutch, had driven them to challenge the monopoly of trade which Portugal claimed with the Far East. In 1600 a Dutch vessel, the *Liefde*, reached Japan. The Jesuits hastened to denounce her as a pirate. Iyeyasu, however, sent for her English pilot, Will Adams, and appointed him master shipbuilder in his own service. Adams obtained for the Dutch a trading station at Hirado in the western island of Kiushiu, and the Japanese learned from him all that the West could teach as to the building and sailing of ships. He explained to Iyeyasu that Protestants were also Christians who resisted the attempt of Spain to convert them by conquest to the Catholic religion.

Iyeyasu was also warned by his spies in Europe that Spain was looking to the Catholic missionaries to facilitate the conquest of Japan. He therefore resolved on a ruthless persecution to root Christianity out of the country. After his death the persecution was continued and intensified by officials who governed Japan in the name of his son. The Christian peasantry of Kiushiu were at length driven to revolt and in 1637 made their last stand in the fortress of Shimabara. Its walls were breached with the aid of Dutch artillery, but 13,000 Japanese soldiers fell before they were finally taken. The Christian defenders, who used as their war-cries the words 'Jesus', 'Marie' and 'St. Iago', the battle-cry of Spain, were slaughtered to the number of 37,000.

So great were the fears aroused by this struggle that the government of Japan then decided to forbid any further contact of the Japanese people with the outer world. All foreigners were excluded, while the Japanese people were forbidden to build any boat large enough to sail further than their own territorial waters. One yearly visit of a ship from Holland was allowed, in order that the government might learn from its captain what was happening in the world at large. From this almost complete seclusion Japan emerged more than two centuries later to find Europeans firmly established around the Pacific and on most of the islands. Her belated effort to regain the ground lost in those centuries is profoundly affecting the whole structure of human society to-day.

In China, as well as in Japan, ruin was brought to the Catholic cause by the mutual jealousies of the Friars and Jesuits. The Chinese Emperor with Jesuits at his court found that his edicts were contradicted by papal bulls issued to China under the influence of Franciscans and Dominicans. In 1724 the Emperor Yung Cheng forbade the teaching of Christianity and confiscated the property of the Church.

The claim of the Pope to order human affairs as the vicegerent of God upon earth was thus defeated by domestic quarrels of his own emissaries, in lands too remote for Rome to control them. These quarrels were symptoms only of the wider causes at work. The idea of the Catholic church as the kingdom of God upon earth might be recognised in Europe, so long as Europe could think of itself as the world. The claim of the Church to order mankind in the name of God was bound to collapse when applied to mankind as it really is. The facts were too large for the claim and defeated it. The real destroyers were three men who had opened the world to Europe in the name of the Catholic religion, Henry the Navigator, Christopher Columbus and Vasco da Gama.

CHAPTER XV

EFFECTS OF THE REFORMATION ON THOUGHT

TILL the Reformation the Papacy had endeavoured to solve the problem of church and state by establishing the position of the Church as a world empire in which the nations were subordinate provinces. The Reformation consigned that idea to the land of dreams, and the question of church and state was now to enter on a new phase. In the lives of the ancient Greeks and Romans that question had no real counterpart. The Church as an institution in antithesis to the state was produced by the contact and conflict of Semitic with Graeco-Roman ideas.

Wherein did the difference in outlook of Hebrew and Greek consist? They were both pioneers in the realm of thought. Even more, perhaps, than the Greek, the Hebrew was trying to know what is right, what is good. But, unlike the Greeks, the Hebrews failed to grasp the importance of answering the further questions "What is truth?" "Of what nature is knowledge itself?" "By what means do we know?" When, after earnest seeking, the mind of the Hebrew prophet attained to a new aspect of truth, he regarded it as a supernatural message disclosed to him by God for transmission to his people. "Thus saith the Lord" was the accepted form of the announcement, uttered with perfect sincerity, alike when the message conveyed profound intuitions or a mere repetition of traditional folk-lore. It never occurred to the Hebrew as it did to the Greek, that the essential idea of God was an hypothesis as to the nature of reality framed to account for his own intuitive sense of right and wrong, and for all that the difference between them, if valid, implies. In its quest for truth Semitic thought never got free from the presupposition of supernatural authority, the ultimate issue of which is fanaticism. It leaves no room for the arduous faith which nerves men to stake their all on a splendid guess that reality consists in that which they feel in their hearts to be highest and best.

Their uncritical theory of knowledge led the Jews to regard certain writings as the source of revealed truth, and presently as the only source. When they came into contact with the Greek world and its more intrepid methods of thought, they began to close the canon in self-defence. The Old Testament was the result. This idea imposed itself on the Christian world, which added a New Testament of its own and then, once for all, closed the canon. Till recent years Europe accepted the view, almost without question, that the Hebrew and Christian Scriptures stand in a different category from anything else which the mind of man has produced. They were in fact the Word of God. All other writings were mere speculations of human intelligence.

Jesus saw in human conscience the foundation of all things, and saw no bounds to its capacity for growth. With the prophets he could only explain the validity of conscience by conceiving ultimate reality in terms of all that was best in human nature, personality charged with creative desire for goodness. With this ultimate reality, God, he believed that men could hold spiritual intercourse, and draw therefrom in infinite measure the kind of strength they derive from communion with the best of their fellows. To him the secret of life was to order society in harmony with ultimate reality rightly conceived. The minds of his Jewish hearers were filled with nationalist dreams of the Kingdom of God. He endeavoured to teach them wherein the Kingdom of God lay, and to convince them that the true Kingdom of the real

God could only be based on the instinct in men to do good to each other. This instinct, he urged, would respond to exercise and was capable of infinite growth in a polity so organised as to call it into play. These ideas are implicit in sayings and parables remembered and recorded by followers who failed to grasp their profound significance. They interpreted his idea of the Kingdom of God in terms of Jewish apocalypse. Some figurative words he had used, coupled, perhaps, with some circumstance connected with his death, created a fanatical belief in their minds that Jesus would shortly return, clothed with miraculous power to dismiss the wicked to punishment, to eliminate evil and inaugurate a new and perfected world for those who believed in and practised his precepts.

These ideas inspired the early Christian communities to order their lives in accordance with the example of Christ. In doing so they lifted life to a higher plane and gave Christianity an impetus it has never entirely lost and has always regained wherever Christians have attempted in earnest to follow that example. But the principle of authority was imposed on their organisation, partly by Jewish habits of mind, and partly by the institutions of the Roman Empire in which they grew up. The authority of Christ, as interpreted by those who had known him, was accepted as paramount. As they passed away, the authority they derived from Christ was regarded as resting in the officers of the churches on whom they had laid their hands. The churches thus developed a hierarchy. In course of years the remembered teachings of Christ had been written down mixed with a mass of Jewish tradition and ideas which possessed the minds of the writers, together with legends which had gathered like weeds round the Master's career. These writings, together with letters written or believed to be written by Apostles, with a new and Christianised chapter of Apocalypse, were recognised as a New Testament, as a higher, because fuller, source of revealed truth even than the old Jewish canon.

These sacred writings, however, admitted of a wide variety of interpretation. The hierarchy, more concerned with the strength of their organisation than with the principles which ought to inspire it, claimed the sole right of interpretation. The passages upon which they chose to dwell were less those fraught with spiritual insight than those which made for the strength of their organisation and promoted its growth. In the presence of schism the Church emphasised the power given to Peter to bind and loose. When oppressed by the Empire it dwelt on the physical horrors of future punishment, and the joys of heaven as figured in the visions of Jewish apocalypse. Particular prominence was given to words in the Gospels which seemed to support these theories.

Meanwhile the principle of authority as embodied in the Church had collided with the principle of authority as embodied in the Empire. An emperor who himself claimed divinity could scarcely be expected to tolerate a creed which taught its converts to regard Jesus the Son of God as their ultimate authority. In vain some emperors strove to extinguish the rising sect, and the conflict was not composed till the emperors accepted Christianity as the state religion, and, for themselves, the position of Christ's vicegerent on earth.

When Augustine wrote his *City of God* Christianity was the state religion of the Empire. But the habit of regarding the Empire as the city of this world, or indeed of the devil, had been burned into Christian thought for centuries by the hot irons of persecution. The state was at best something which had to be accepted as a temporary necessity till Christ returned to supersede it. The real question for each individual which overshadowed all others was whether he was qualified for admission to the City of God; for on this depended the most fearful issue, endless torment or endless bliss. Concern for the individual, a belief in their own exclusive power to offer him salvation, coupled with indifference to the fate of the Empire, enabled churchmen to convert the barbarian invaders and exercise a powerful influence over their conduct.

Augustine, who naturally regarded the collapse of civil society as a prelude to the end of the world, can scarcely have realised how the awful power which the Church exercised over its converts would react on itself. The penalties which a mere priest could threaten were more far-reaching than any which the Emperor could inflict from his throne.

On the disappearance of the Emperor from Rome, its bishop stood out as the foremost figure in western Christendom. He there came to be recognised as the vicegerent in whose hands were gathered and exercised the immeasurable powers which Christ had committed to his Church. Popes, by a word, could relegate to eternal perdition a king no less than his meanest subject. Clothed with such power as no monarch has ever wielded over men, in the Middle Ages the popes claimed the position, and at times almost the name, of emperor. But in fact they were never able to govern Europe as the Antonines had governed the Empire of Caesar. They never succeeded in giving to the polity they created the essential attributes of a state.

To what was this failure due? A whole book might be written in answer to that question; yet most if not all of the reasons adduced might be found traceable to one outstanding idea. Through Christianity, the transcendentalism, essentially Jewish, which found expression in every page of Augustine, had mastered Europe. The structure of human society was no longer a matter of primary importance, for the Kingdom of Heaven was not to be realised in this world. Pending the hour when Christ would return to reconstitute creation, the Church was the nucleus of that Kingdom. Exclusion from its ranks meant unutterable and unending woe. The Church was vested with absolute power to settle the issue for each individual. The perfection of human character which Christ himself had seen as the end and object of life fell into the background. The thoughts of each man were centred on his own future, in comparison with which the state of society in which he lived became a matter of secondary importance.

The primary concern of the Church was not in the maintenance of order amongst men, or in the tasks inseparable therefrom, of which public finance is the most essential. It left such matters to princes, relying on the vast authority it wielded over the princes as well as their subjects. The feudal system, as it developed, exactly suited this attitude, and the papal conception of a world polity never emerged from the stage of feudalism. To maintain its position, and still more to assert its pretensions, the Papacy needed the revenues of an empire, but developed no organised system of police or of public finance.

Its attempt to solve these difficulties by reviving the Empire in the person of Charles and his successors merely enhanced them. The emperors refused to accept the position of adjutants, and papal finances were constantly embarrassed in the task of reducing emperors to submission. The popes triumphed in the long struggle with their own creature; but, failing to develop normal powers of taxation, reverted to the sale of benefits which flowed from their vast spiritual claims—lucrative offices, pardons for sin and indeed salvation in the future world.

This traffic in holy things in time led the descendants of the northern barbarians to question the spiritual claims upon which it was based, and also the temporal claims to sovereignty which followed as a logical consequence. The right claimed by the Pope to reserve three continents to two princes of southern Europe ranged economic as well as political forces behind the revolt.

At the Reformation the northern peoples denied the authority of the Catholic Church to decide either the future of souls or the rights of nations. But, none the less, the Protestants took with them the outlook on life which the Church had derived from Jewish apocalypse. They continued to think that weal or woe in the future life of the individual depended mainly upon what he believed, especially at the moment of death, and only in a minor degree upon what he had done and upon what he had been. To hold the right doctrine was still of cardinal importance. The assumption that truth in such matters could only be known through supernatural means was unquestioned. They agreed with the Catholic Church that the final revelation was on record in Scripture, while denying its claim to decide what the Scriptures meant. The right of each individual to interpret Scripture for himself had still to achieve recognition after long struggles. The Protestant peoples organised Churches of their own, which, after the manner of their prototype, sometimes tried to control the State. But the fear of ecclesiastical authority in civil matters, which the Catholic Church had engendered in Protestant minds, was so deeply ingrained that sooner or later the State asserted its right to control the Church. The Church was the organisation through which men might secure their future salvation. The State was the mechanism through which to develop the structure of human society. Religion and politics were studiously separated.

In the long run the Reformation produced similar

results in the Catholic world, though by different means. It dismissed to the land of dreams the idea of Christendom organised as one state with the Vicar of Christ at its head dispensing divine authority to temporal sovereigns. Henceforward the dynasts, Catholic and Protestant alike, claimed to derive their authority direct from God. On the other hand the energies of the Catholic Church were directed, as they had not been since its first era, to the saving of souls. Ignatius Loyola and Francis Xavier were the greatest organisers of missionary enterprise that the Church had produced since the days of Gregory. Through the Middle Ages the power of closing the doors of heaven was used by the Church with terrible effect. From the Reformation she preferred to emphasise her power to open them. While maintaining her claims intact, she grew more cautious of pressing them to logical results in political matters, and tacitly accepted her position as an institution distinct from the State. Catholics and Protestants alike reverted to the dualism which runs through every page of Augustine. In this dualism the twin truths which inspired the teaching of Christ were ignored, the truth that the structure of society will reflect men's view of ultimate reality, and the truth that what men can become is profoundly affected by the structure of the society in which they grow up. With the Protestant as with the Catholic Churches the teaching of Christ was to guide men's conduct and faith with a view to their future salvation. It had little or no bearing on the relations of men to each other in the state and still less on the future relations of states to each other. In the eighteenth century Rousseau was exactly expressing this view when he wrote:

Christianity is an entirely spiritual religion concerned solely with heavenly things; the Christian's country is not of this world. He does his duty, it is true; but he does it with a profound indifference as to the good or ill success of his endeavours. Provided that he has nothing to reproach himself with, it matters little to him whether all goes well or ill here below. If the State flourishes, he scarcely dares to enjoy the public felicity. If the State declines, he blesses the hand of God which lies heavy on his people.[1]

NOTE

[1] Rousseau, *The Social Contract*, Book IV. chap. viii.

CHAPTER XVI

POLITICAL AND ECONOMIC EFFECTS OF THE REFORMATION

THE revolt against Roman authority, which Luther had started, could not in Germany reach its ultimate conclusions. For Germany was no more than a racial or even a linguistic expression. In seeking the empire of Christendom the German emperors had failed to secure for themselves the active allegiance of their own people. Germany was a medley of minor states whose subjects followed their dynastic prince whenever he challenged the Imperial authority. The futile attempts of the emperor to establish his position maintained a state of intestine war in which military despotisms alone counted. City republics like Hamburg or Frankfort remained cities and nothing more. In the seventeenth century Germany was involved in a prolonged and murderous struggle of Protestant with Catholic princes. The emperors cast in their lot with the Catholic cause. The Protestant princes founded their claim on divine right. So far as the German people were concerned the Reformation did little to disturb the principle of authority as the basis of government.

In the mountains of Switzerland and the marshes flooded by the mouths of the Rhine, national commonwealths had begun to appear. The Netherlands had access to the sea, but with land frontiers to defend the Dutch were too hard pressed to become in a wider field protagonists of a principle which lay at the root of their institutions. The English alone were free to concentrate their energies on the sea, and no power in Europe could touch them unless it could first wrest from them control of the element on which they were masters. In England alone could the principles of the great revolt find their fullest expression in the sphere of politics as well as of religion.

It is here necessary to recall the fact that from the first moment when the five continents were brought into touch with each other the people of Europe appear as an active factor, and those of the other continents as relatively passive. The fact can be illustrated in a simple way. The communications first opened by Columbus and Vasco da Gama have since been maintained by Europeans up till the present generation, when Japanese ships began to ply between the continents. From the sixteenth century onwards the ships of Europe and of colonies peopled from Europe visit every coast of the world. The idea of African, Indian or Chinese shipping in Atlantic ports never crosses our mind. Throughout modern history the currents of energy radiate from the peoples of Europe. They excite profound revolutions in all other parts of the world, and these in turn react on Europe.

In Europe two different and conflicting systems of life had developed, which came to an issue at the very moment when the rest of the world was exposed to her influence—by no mere coincidence, but because of that fact. From the Reformation onwards the principle of authority which had previously found expression in the Papacy and Empire was entrenched in the national monarchies of Europe. But the Reformation had also made the rulers of Europe aware of the different and conflicting principle of life which had found political expression in England. They rightly thought that this system, left to develop in England, must, in time, spread to Europe and destroy their own. They were always seeking to derive material power to destroy it from the wealth of the newly opened world. From the same source England was seeking to derive power to maintain herself and her institutions. The long struggle for dominion in America, Asia and Africa was at root a struggle for survival between two systems in Europe. A crude desire to exploit and enjoy the wealth of the newly opened continents was doubtless the conscious motive of adventurers, whether English, Spanish or French. But the struggles between them had also to determine whether the principle of the commonwealth or the principle of authority was to dominate the world.

The discoveries of Columbus and Vasco da Gama thus definitely closed the Middle Ages at the end of the fifteenth century and opened the epoch of modern history: thenceforward national monarchies like France and Spain, backed by Rome, appeared as the champions of authority. Spain relied on the precious metals found in the mines of America to enforce the monopoly she claimed, and so embarked on the fatal policy of taking from countries beyond the seas without giving in return. The English and Dutch had goods to exchange and were eager for trade. Release from Catholic authority gave a definite impetus to their industry and commerce. Strange as it may seem, the practice of usury, in which Jews are regarded as adepts, is contrary to the law of Moses. The Church, on the other hand, had always been studious to enforce these particular prescriptions of Jewish morality. Throughout the Middle Ages the growth of industry and commerce was hampered by the feeling that it was contrary to religion to charge interest for the use of money. Charitable foundations were created, called 'Mounts of Piety', for the purpose of lending money on pledged securities to pious debtors in need of help. These institutions were faced by the question whether the cost of administration could also be charged to the debtor. Such was the feeling against usury on the very eve of the Reformation that this question was referred to the Lateran Council, in 1512. With great hesitation the Council sanctioned the practice; but added that it was better for pious benefactors to provide 'Mounts of Piety', not merely with capital to be loaned, but also with endowments to meet the cost of administration without imposing on debtors a charge which looked like usury.

In countries which renounced their allegiance to Rome these ancient prescriptions rapidly lost their force. Traders, who necessarily charged and paid interest on capital, were relieved from the stigma of earning their living by practices contrary to religion. This relief from a moral dogma gave a new incentive to the habit of saving. Trade and industry came to be regarded as callings appropriate to Protestant Christians. In production and trade the Protestant countries rapidly outdistanced the Catholic states. The spirit of revolt which pervaded the northern nations had already produced this change before the actual break with Rome in the sixteenth century.

The Reformation was also helping to give England a commanding position in the textile industry. From time immemorial Saxon villagers had known how to twist their wool into thread and to weave rough cloth on rudely constructed looms. When England and Flanders were fighting France, Edward III. had allowed Flemish weavers to find an asylum across the Channel. In spite of royal protection, they were viewed with jealousy by the English weavers and massacred in 1381. After the Reformation French Huguenots as well as Flemish Protestants found safety in England, where, as fellow Protestants, they were welcomed in spite of their foreign blood. The English weavers acquired their technique. In the sixteenth century their looms were producing fabrics which could readily be sold in foreign markets. England had thus a surplus of goods to exchange for the products she sought from the distant continents.

In previous chapters we have seen how the coasts of the African, Asian and American continents were unfolded to Europe within one generation, and connected by facilities for commerce in their heavier products. The end to which all this pointed began to dawn on political thinkers. So early as 1577 a Frenchman wrote :

> We can affirm that the whole world is now known, and all the races of men; they can interchange all their commodities and mutually supply their needs, *as inhabitants of the same city or world-state.*[1]

NOTE

[1] Louis Le Roy, *On the Vicissitude or Variety of the Things in the Universe*. Quoted by Bury in *The Idea of Progress*, p. 45.

CHAPTER XVII

MUTUAL REACTIONS OF FOUR CONTINENTS

For reasons sketched in Book I., Chapter XIV., life in the Far East continued to flow apart from the channel where streams from the rest of the world were meeting. We have now to consider how these currents were affecting each other.

After the loss of her Armada, Spain was unable to assert her papal title to the American continent north of Mexico. As the dominant power in Europe she was rapidly supplanted by France. In 1603 de Champlain sailed up the St. Lawrence and in 1608 planted the fleur-de-lis on the heights of Quebec, and there established a French colony.

In 1607 the London Company, with Sir Thomas Smythe at its head, succeeded, where Raleigh had previously failed, in planting a colony in Virginia. It was soon to produce tobacco, grown on plantations by convicts or slaves, which the colonists could exchange for goods manufactured in England. In 1620 a small body of English Puritans, who refused to obey the discipline of the Anglican Church, landed at Cape Cod in the region now known as New England. The climate was temperate and the country heavily timbered, but suitable when cleared for farming as practised in England. In 1621 the settlers obtained a patent from the King to found a colony at New Plymouth. In the course of the next hundred and fifty years thirteen colonies, on these two models, were planted south of the territory annexed to France under charters from the crown.

The opening of western America was greatly accelerated by the silver-birch, a tree with rind which resembles oilcloth. From this rind the Indians had learned to fashion canoes light enough for one man to carry past rapids and watersheds. By means of these birch-bark canoes European explorers could pass from one riverine system to another. The French were thus able to make their way from the St. Lawrence through the great lakes to the upper waters of the Mississippi. They travelled down the 'father of waters' to its mouth in the sub-tropical region, and there founded Louisiana, a colony of the planter type. The English colonies were thus cut off from the interior by a vast French dominion shaped like a crescent with its horns resting on the mouths of the St. Lawrence and Mississippi. It was ruled by a governor who wielded viceregal powers.

In the English colonies the governing bodies were modelled on the guild-courts through which merchants and craftsmen in the Middle Ages managed their business. But the business of the colonists involved the management of the territories in which they lived, and the bodies they elected soon lost the character of guild-courts and grew into state legislatures. They became, in fact, miniature parliaments. But their business was not transacted in the King's palace at Westminster, or under the guidance of a powerful nobility. They had not, as in England, centuries of local tradition behind them. Gentlemen, farmers, craftsmen and traders found that they could handle affairs of state and make laws for themselves without the guidance of bishops and nobles.

In the south the colonists planted tobacco, cotton and sugar. The habit of smoking, confined to America before the discovery of that continent, was carried to Europe, and by the Spanish through the Philippines to Asia. Sugar which had been grown in Madeira by Henry the Navigator and then in the Canaries was transplanted thence to the West Indies. A few years after the discovery of these islands their native inhabitants were threatened with extinction. In the gold mines the Arawaks perished by thousands, and when sugar was introduced some other supply of labour had to be found. The cause of the natives was nobly championed by Las Casas, the bishop sent to the West Indies to regulate the affairs of the Church. To save them he advised the introduction of negroes from Spain, and lived to regret that his advice was taken. The plantation of sugar grew so rapidly that the planters were soon importing their slaves direct from Africa. Gangs were collected at stations on the coast and shipped thence to the West Indies.

In Virginia and English territories to the south of it colonists began planting tobacco, cotton and sugar with convict labour. The supply from England proved inadequate. On the mainland and also in the islands which the English took from the Spaniards, the English planters adopted the practice of purchasing cargoes of negro slaves, as did all the nations which found a footing in the new world. When English colonies were found to be suitable for cotton the demand for slaves was greatly increased. As the ships of Holland and England outgrew others in number, the lion's share of the trade passed to the merchants of these countries. Bristol and Liverpool were especially active. Stations on the coast to which slaves were brought from the whole of tropical Africa for sale were seized from the Portuguese.

The slaves were collected by traders of mixed Arab and African blood. In armed parties they ranged over Africa for their quarry. Powerful tribes were encouraged to attack their weaker neighbours, and capture their men, women and children for sale. In primitive Africa continuous war was promoted to meet the demand for tobacco, sugar and cotton in Europe, and for slaves to grow these products in America. The country became impenetrable to travellers from Europe, and the contact of civilisation with barbarism was restricted to the intercourse of European with African slave dealers on the coast. Beyond, no civilised man could live to record the wrongs which were done. Till long after the trade was abolished the interior remained unknown and unmapped, and had earned the name of 'the dark continent'. It can safely be said that so vast a country and so helpless a race have never endured such evils so long. Had the trade continued, tropical Africa would by now be one vast solitude, unless re-peopled from Asia and Europe.

When negro slavery was abolished, the mischief done to the structure of society in America was beyond repair. In Book I., Chapter III., we have seen how the institution of caste was produced in India through the conquest of a tropical people by a white race from the temperate zone. The same result has followed, and is still following, the introduction of a tropical race to North America. The instinctive repulsion of the white colonists has had the effect of establishing caste as one of the recognised principles of society in the United States. In many of the states intermarriage of white with coloured people is forbidden by law. The white American still regards his coloured fellow-citizens as a social element separate from his own. This does not prevent an illicit mixture of blood, for in sexual relations abnormal attraction shadows repulsion. The two are related and pass to each other as readily as the negative to the positive in photography. At no distant date every descendant of the African slaves will have in his veins the blood of some European. But the human being with a coloured ancestor, however remote, is regarded by the pure white as relegated to a caste eternally distinct from his own.

The mixed castes, on the other hand, take pride in their white blood and like to avoid mixing it with strains darker than their own. The result, as in India, is seen in the gradual development of social layers, each lighter than the one below it and tending to hold itself aloof. The same results can be seen in South Africa, where also the climate is such that whites and negroes can both live and propagate their kind.

Had sheer power been the final and dominating quality of Western civilisation, it would in the end have destroyed negro society in the continent which produced it. There were no states to resist its impact. Conquerors there had been in plenty, but the village communities of Africa crumbled in their hands. They were too primitive to serve even as material for a crude autocracy.

With the peoples of Asia it was otherwise. Both in India and China society had reached a certain level of civilisation ages before the peoples of Europe had emerged from tribal conditions. For centuries China had been organised as an empire. In her arts and literature she had reached a stage comparable to that of ancient Egypt. India with a greater diversity of races and a more enervating climate was unable to achieve political unity, until it was imposed from without. Caste was a further impediment, though it gave a certain stability to the social structure.

In the century which followed the landing of Vasco da Gama at Calicut, most of India was united in one empire by Mohammedan conquerors from the north. In Samarkand a direct descendant of Timur, Zahir ud-din-Mahomet, nicknamed Babar, or The Tiger, inherited the gifts of his terrible ancestor and established his power by similar means. In 1526 he invaded India and laid the foundations of the so-called Mogul Empire. In India northern invaders were described as Mongols in much the same way as in 1914 Germans were branded with the name of Huns. In contemporary portraits of themselves which these

Turki conquerors have left there is little resembling the Mongolian physique, and much to suggest a kinship with the first Caucasian invaders who descended on India thousands of years before. Babar, in his memoirs, always refers with contempt to the Mongols. The word Mogul as applied to the dynasty he founded must therefore be used as a convenient nickname and not as proof of its racial character.

Babar's Indian conquests were lost and recovered by his son and extended by his grandson, Akbar, whose reign coincided with that of our Queen Elizabeth. His nominal empire extended from Persia to the Bay of Bengal, and where his rule was effective the people enjoyed a higher standard of justice and order than India had known before.

Goa and some other fortified ports, which the Portuguese had held, remained under their rule. Till 1580 they controlled the entire trade from India to Europe, but left to the Dutch the business of distributing the goods brought to Lisbon. The absorption of Portugal in 1580 by their enemy Spain forced the Dutch to embark on the Eastern trade, and to drive the Portuguese from the Spice Islands. The prices they charged provoked the growing resentment of English consumers, and in 1599 an unwarranted rise in the price of pepper moved some London merchants to apply to the Queen for power to incorporate themselves as a guild for trading direct with the East Indies. The advent of the Protestant traders was not unwelcome to Moguls, who regarded the Portuguese as idolaters and, having no navy, were unable to control them. So the English East India Company left the islands to the formidable Dutch, and built up their trade in India, where they proved to be more than a match for the Portuguese.

In the time of Akbar and his successors there was

ample security for the English factories. In the course of the seventeenth century the Mogul Empire began to go the way of dynasties. The satraps who ruled the provinces ignored the Emperor's declining authority and made war on each other. The Hindus revolted against their Mohammedan conquerors, and life and property were no longer safe as in Akbar's time. Towards the close of the seventeenth century the English company was driven to acquire and hold for itself defensible ports where merchandise collected for shipment could be fenced by ramparts and moats, and vessels could lie under cover of guns. Madras was occupied in 1640. Bombay was acquired in the reign of Charles II. in the dowry of his queen, Catharine of Braganza. Calcutta was founded in 1690.

From these strongholds protection was presently extended beyond the walls of the warehouses and offices to Indians who came to trade with their goods or to set up their looms for weaving the calico they sold to the company. The English settlements were thus rapidly surrounded by mushroom Indian cities. It was soon found necessary to extend the fortifications so as to include and defend these cities. Naval bases were thus established large and strong enough to enable the British to maintain their control of the sea.

For our present purpose it is enough to add that the French East India Company had acquired a similar position. It held fortified ports at Mahé on the west coast, and at Karikal, Pondicherry and Chandernagore on the east.

CHAPTER XVIII

THE STRUGGLE FOR SUPREMACY IN EUROPE AND THE WORLD

In Book II., Chapter XV., we saw how the Reformation combined with the opening of the world to efface the idea that the right of rulers to rule was derived through the head of the Church entitled to dispense authority as God's vicegerent on earth. Even monarchs who adhered to the Catholic Church, like the kings of France and the emperors in Austria, thought of themselves as commissioned to rule by Heaven direct. The conception of Christendom as one great polity vanished to the limbo of forgotten things. Church and state were regarded as separate and collateral authorities.

Even a king, who is thought to hold his commission from God, is mortal, and knows it. Natural affection leads him to hope that his title to rule will pass to his son. The divine right is thus regarded as attached to a dynasty and vested in its head. Belief in a supernatural authority clothes with a moral sanction the human instinct of rulers to regard power as an end in itself. The motive for extending the power of his dynasty over more lands and more subjects can seldom be far from the mind of a monarch who thinks that his title to rule is divine. The dynasts were always scheming to acquire lands and peoples to rule, the more powerful hoping thereby to dominate Europe as a whole. The means they employed to these ends were treaties, marriages, bequests and wars. In result whole countries like Italy and Poland, whose peoples professed one religion, spoke the same language and belonged to one race, were parcelled out by their rulers as if they were private estates. In actual practice government based on the principle of authority meant that the interests of subjects was as nothing compared with those of the ruling families.

To our modern and very recent ideas there is something amiss when one part of a national state is cut off from another. We find it hard to believe that the separation of one part of Germany from another by a strip of Polish territory can endure. The reader who turns the pages of an historical atlas will see how, till the nineteenth century, isolated fragments of Europe were included in one monarchy, and were constantly changing hands like private estates. The territories ruled by the Emperor Charles V. in the sixteenth century are a case in point. Amongst them were included Spain, the Netherlands, Luxemburg, an isolated territory round Besançon, to the west of it a tiny enclave in France called Charolais, to the east of it Freiburg and Augsburg. To the east again was a territory of about the same size as Spain, extending from the Tyrol to Transylvania, and from south of Berlin to south of Trieste with Austria as its centre. South of the Alps, Charles ruled the Duchy of Milan, Italy south of the papal states, Sicily and Sardinia. Over several hundred German states he exercised the dubious power of the Emperor.

When in 1555 Charles abdicated the crown of Spain and the Netherlands to his son Philip, he passed the title of Emperor to his brother Ferdinand together with the sovereignty of his eastern dominions. The appearance of Austria as one of the great powers and her rivalry with France for the mastery of Europe dates from this act. Except for the years 1740 to 1745, when France was able to secure the election of Charles VII. of Bavaria as Emperor, the Imperial Crown was held by the Austrian Habsburgs, till Napoleon abolished the shadowy title in 1806.

Towards the close of the seventeenth century, two other dynasties were developing strength to contest the hegemony of Europe with the Habsburgs of Austria and the Bourbons of France.

In the north of Germany the Brandenburg Mark was ruled by the House of Hohenzollern with the title of Elector. The Hohenzollerns also ruled East Prussia, a region divided from Brandenburg by a wide strip of Polish territory, and in the west three isolated Duchies of Cleves, Mark and Regensburg. From 1640 to 1685 the Great Elector Frederick William devoted his life to the task of organising his subjects to defend these five patches of territory which were unprotected by any physical frontiers. To this end he created a system of government and an army more efficient than any which Europe had yet seen.

In 1701 his successor Frederick I. secured from the Emperor the right to be crowned King of Prussia. At his coronation he crowned himself with his own hands, to the indignation of Catholic Europe, a significant act which was afterwards copied by Napoleon.

His son Frederick William I. perfected the work begun by his grandfather. His industrious, docile, hardy, frugal and warlike people, were organised in every department of life to enhance the military power of the state. He married Sophia, a daughter of George I. Their son Frederick, who succeeded his father in 1740, was one of the great generals of history. Like Alexander of Macedon, Frederick the Great inherited a military weapon organised to perfection. He used it to raise Prussia to the place she has since filled as one of the great powers of Europe.

Russia had also produced a ruler who had seen that his dynasty might join in the struggle for power in Europe, if the vast though primitive resources of his country were modernised for the purpose. In Book II., Chapter V., we saw how, when Constantinople fell to the forces of Islam, the Byzantine Empire passed to a new incarnation in the Tzardom of Ivan the Great at Moscow. In 1598 the dynasty founded by the Norseman, Rurik, came to an end. Confusion followed and Russia was overrun by the Poles, who occupied Moscow. In 1612 the King of Poland, Sigismund III., aspired to the throne of the Tzars. The thought of a Polish and Roman Catholic dynasty in Moscow nerved the Russians to unite and expel the invaders. In 1613 a Grand National Assembly elected as Tzar Michael Romanov, the youthful son of the metropolitan Philaret, connected by marriage with the House of Rurik.

Till the close of the seventeenth century the Russians had little in common with western Europe but a highly paganised form of the Christian religion. Their manner of life and habits of mind were those of Asia. In the reign of Alexius, who succeeded his father Michael Romanov in 1645, numerous foreigners from the west were allowed to settle in Moscow, and western books began to be read in the capital and court. A shock was given to traditional feelings when Alexius discarded the flowing robes of the east, adopted the garb of western civilisation and allowed his consort to pass through the streets with her face unveiled.

In 1682 his son, Peter the Great, ascended the throne. This forceful genius perceived the immense power in Europe which his dynasty could wield, if the vast weight of Russian resources and numbers were tipped with a spear-head of western efficiency. He created an administrative and military system copied from western models, and sought to open an outlet to the sea for his land-locked empire. When his army had reached the requisite state of efficiency, he conquered the territories which barred his way to the Baltic and founded St. Petersburg at the mouth of the Neva, as "a window through which his people might look into Europe". With the fleet which he here proceeded to build, he established Russia as a maritime power. Defying the national sentiment, he moved his capital from Moscow to St. Petersburg. In 1711 he assumed the title of Emperor of the Russians, to the indignation of western powers, more especially of Austria, which deeply resented the claim of a barbarous monarch to rank with the Holy Roman Emperor. But facts were too strong for the western dynasts. Since the time of Peter the Great Russia has been recognised as one of the leading powers of the world.

Thus in the eighteenth century Europe became a battlefield for the rival ambitions of four powerful dynasties, of the Bourbons in France, of the Habsburgs in Austria, of the Hohenzollerns in Prussia and the Romanovs in Russia. In their struggles the kingdom of Poland, which produced no ruler of outstanding ability, was torn to pieces and vanished from the map. Germans with their instinct for thoroughness, whether Protestant or Catholic, regarded the vague imaginative Poles as racial inferiors. As Catholics they were hated by their kindred in Russia.

Though England was constantly drawn into the struggles of the great dynasties it was not through any desire to share in the prizes they sought in Europe. Since the opening of the seas, her interests had increasingly lain in exploiting the resources of America and Asia, of the slave-trade from Africa, in selling the products of her industry to Europe, and also in securing the supply of materials for building ships which she drew from the shores of the Baltic. In this enterprise her principal rival was France. The greatest issue at stake in the eighteenth century was whether the French monarchy or the British Commonwealth should control the high seas and the future development of America, Africa, Asia and Australia.

In this long-drawn struggle for world power between France and England the strategic point was Belgium, because from its harbours England could be threatened with invasion, and her commerce through the English Channel and North Sea harried and destroyed. It was, therefore, the aim of the French monarchy to wrest Belgium from the moribund hands of Spain.

When in 1700 Charles II. of Spain died without issue, he left a will bequeathing all his dominions, including Belgium, to Philip of Anjou, grandson of Louis XIV. The will provided, however, that if the bequest was not accepted in its entirety, it should pass to Charles, the second son of Leopold II. of Austria.

The decision of Louis XIV. to claim this bequest on behalf of his grandson, brought England and Holland into the field against France on the side of Austria. The war of the Spanish Succession (1701–1713) was mainly decided by the victories of Marlborough. It was closed by the Treaty of Utrecht, which placed the grandson of Louis XIV. on the throne of Spain, but transferred to Austria the Spanish possessions in the low countries and Italy, whilst England acquired Gibraltar and Minorca.

In the struggles for mastery in Europe which followed the Treaty of Utrecht, the power of England was always thrown into the scale against France, with the primary object of securing for herself the control of the high seas, and of trade with the countries which lay beyond them. She largely financed the enemies of France, and at times landed small armies in Europe. Her losses in man-power were slight, and with trifling exceptions the struggle was never waged on her own soil. Her industries, fed by overseas trade, grew and flourished, while armies were trampling Europe.

Had France devoted all her resources to wresting naval supremacy from England she might well have succeeded in winning control of America, Africa and India. With the trade of the world in her hands the power to dominate all Europe would then have been hers. But struggles for supremacy in Europe were always more to the taste of the Bourbon dynasty and court than struggles for supremacy at sea. The best of her human and material resources were spent on her armies and the interests of her navy came second. In seeking to achieve supremacy by land as well as by sea she ended by losing both. The prize of naval supremacy fell to England because she was able to devote all her resources to winning it.

CHAPTER XIX

THE UNION OF ENGLAND AND SCOTLAND

In the seventeenth century the English and French were thus confronting each other in America and Asia. In their struggles with France before that century England had always been weakened by the danger of attack in her rear from the kingdom of Scotland north of the Tweed. This danger was largely relieved when James VI. of Scotland succeeded to the English throne as James I.

The Scottish parliament, faintly copied from that of England, had failed to acquire the power or influence of its model. In trying to reduce the authority of the English parliament to the same level as the Scottish parliament the Stuart kings accomplished the downfall of their own dynasty. In result they established the power of the English parliament, which, in turn, reacted to establish a collateral authority in the Scottish parliament.

As in the course of the seventeenth century the effective authority passed from the crown to the two parliaments, so the effect which the crown had had in uniting the two kingdoms was undermined. By the reign of Queen Anne the two parliaments were expressing interests the one English, the other Scottish, which were separate and often opposed, more especially in the field of external affairs.

These difficulties were brought to a head by the growing trade with the Far East, which the English East India Company aspired to monopolise. A Scotsman of genius, William Paterson, devised a scheme for breaking this monopoly in favour of Scotland. His plan was for Scotland to found a colony at

Darien, which could control the short land route across the narrow isthmus which there divides the Atlantic from the Pacific ocean, a route first opened by the Spanish discoverer Balboa in 1513. The trade from India and China was thus to be drawn across the Pacific, to be carried by land across the isthmus of Darien, and thence reshipped across the Atlantic to Scotland. In 1693 the Scottish parliament passed an Act establishing a company for the purpose, and half the total savings of the Scottish people were invested in the project.

In 1698 the Scottish company founded a town which they called New Edinburgh on the isthmus of Darien. The fact that this isthmus belonged to Spain by right of discovery was simply ignored by the Scottish adventurers, who were presently arrested by the Spanish authorities. They were thrown into prison and threatened with execution as pirates, but were finally released on the intervention of the English ambassador.

The Scottish parliament then appealed to the King to assert their right to colonise Darien against Spain. The English parliament opposed the appeal on the ground that the English fleet ought not to be used to support a scheme which aimed at destroying the English monopoly of the Eastern trade in the interests of Scotland. Meanwhile the failure of the Scottish company had reduced Scotland to the depths of poverty.

In 1701 the Scottish parliament passed an Act providing that on the death of Queen Anne the crown of Scotland should be separated from the crown of England. They also took measures to support separation by force of arms. The English parliament replied with an Act providing that unless the question of succession was settled by Christmas Day 1705, Scots should thereafter be treated as aliens in England, and their goods excluded from all its markets. But the Act also empowered the Queen to appoint commissioners to negotiate a union of England with Scotland. The Scottish parliament agreed to negotiate and appointed commissioners. The joint commission produced a scheme which was ratified by both parliaments. The result as described by Professor Dicey was that "the Parliaments both of England and of Scotland did, at the time of the Union, each transfer sovereign power to a new sovereign body, namely, the Parliament of Great Britain".[1] The motives which induced the Scottish parliament to accord its legal sanction to the project were threefold. In the background was fear of a war with England. In the foreground was fear of the ruin which Scotland must face by exclusion from English markets. In addition to both these public motives were the personal inducements to individual members promised and given by the crown which secured the decisive majority.

It is safe to assume that the people of Scotland would have refused to ratify the Union by an overwhelming majority if the question had been submitted to a popular plebiscite. And yet in a few generations the maintenance of the Union might have been submitted with safety to a popular vote. To watch the crowds who daily visit the memorial to Scots who gave their lives in the Great War which crowns the castle of Edinburgh, is to realise how completely and finally this people feel themselves part of the British Commonwealth.

The governing factor which brought together on a footing of equality in one commonwealth two peoples so unequal in size and different in character, was geographic. They had dwelt in the same island as separate states divided only by moorlands, in equal contact and separation from western Europe. The opening of the world to Europe and the great revolt from Rome had affected them both alike. A short experience of Union was enough to convince the enterprising Scots of its overwhelming advantage to their industry and trade. They shared to the full in the enterprise which Britain had developed in distant continents. As Protestants they were able to take their part in all the activities of the government at home. They approved no less than the English of the laws excluding the papists from public life. The essential factor which brought these two very different peoples together was their common attitude to religious questions, a result of living in one territory ringed by the sea.

NOTE

[1] Dicey, *The Law of the Constitution*, pp. 66, 67.

CHAPTER XX

IRELAND

In 1703, four years before the Scotch Union was completed, both Houses of Parliament in Ireland concurred in a representation to the Queen in favour of a legislative Union between England and Ireland, and in 1707 the Irish House of Commons, while congratulating the Queen on the consummation of the Scotch measure, expressed a hope that God might put it into her heart to add greater strength and lustre to her crown by a yet more comprehensive union. . . . In the pliant, plastic condition to which Ireland was then reduced, a slight touch of sagacious statesmanship might have changed the whole course of its future development. But in this as in so many other periods of Irish history, the favourable moment was suffered to pass. The spirit of commercial monopoly triumphed. The petition of the Irish Parliament was treated with contempt, and a long period of commercial restrictions, and penal laws, and complete parliamentary servitude, ensued.[1]

The success which attended the Union of England and Scotland is in startling contrast with the ever-recurring failure to bring the inhabitants of Great Britain and Ireland into permanent and stable relations. At the root of this failure was a physical cause the opposite of that which had led to the Union of England and Scotland. Great Britain and Ireland were separate islands, divided by seas wider and rougher than those which divide the larger island from Europe. The Roman armies which brought to Britain the idea of the state and the rule of law, never crossed the wider straits to Ireland. Missionaries crossed in the Dark Ages and founded monasteries, oases of culture and learning from which the message of the Church was carried to the pagans of England and Germany. They converted the Irish to the Christian religion but laid no foundations for political life.

In the reign of Henry II. the paramount chief of Leinster, Diarmait Machmaida, was worsted in some tribal affray. He secured from England the aid of Richard de Claire, Earl of Pembroke (known to history as Strongbow), in return for which he granted him and his followers large areas of tribal land in Wexford. Henry II. quickly followed, exacted homage from the Norman adventurers and appointed a viceroy at Dublin, whose jurisdiction was limited to a narrow circle surrounded by a ditch and stockade, known as the Pale. In the country beyond, Norman adventurers conquered fiefs for themselves, were then rapidly absorbed into the tribal society about them and assumed the position of tribal chiefs.

In 1295, when Edward I. summoned representatives from English counties and towns to discuss the provision of money required to meet the needs of government, he instructed his viceroy at Dublin to follow the same procedure in Ireland. There was thus created a parliament in Dublin which rapidly acquired the power of making laws, subject to the viceroy's assent. This was often granted with little or no reference to the king. During the Wars of the Roses the Irish parliament denied that Ireland was subject to the laws of England. The English colony in Ireland, siding with the House of York, was a menace to Lancastrian kings. The rebellions of Lambert Simnel and Perkin Warbeck, fostered in Ireland, convinced Henry VII. that no king could secure his position in England unless he established his authority in Dublin. So he sent there Sir Edward Poyning, a resolute man, as his Lord Deputy, who summoned a parliament, and made it declare that no future parliament should be summoned except by the king, and should then consider only such matters as the king had already approved in Council. The existing Statutes of England were also applied to Ireland. These enactments were known as Poyning's law.

Whilst these matters were in process Columbus was disclosing America to Europe, and Vasco da Gama was preparing to open the route to India round the Cape of Good Hope. Their discoveries revived the impulse which centuries before had led Saxons and Norsemen to seek their fortunes in England. Their English descendants were moved by a spirit of adventure to win for themselves lands and wealth in the newly opened continents. The passion for exploitation grew with its own momentum; till presently adventurers, less bold than the Drakes and Frobishers of that time, began to realise that in primitive Ireland beyond the Pale was a prey within easier reach, that the proceeds of Irish land once seized could be largely drawn to and enjoyed in their English homes. These hordes of adventurers were encouraged by Tudor sovereigns to dispossess, and indeed exterminate, the Irish tribes whose chiefs were now largely of Norman descent. To English eyes the native Irish appeared as savages no more entitled to pity than African negroes or North American Indians.

The ruthless temper of the English conquerors was further inflamed by the passions let loose by the Reformation, which had left the primitive Irish untouched. In slaughtering the Papists and seizing their land the Protestant conquerors felt they were following the example set when the children of Israel invaded Canaan.

What number of Irish perished by sword and famine in the time of the Tudors can never be known. A number found refuge in the western bogs of Connaught, in lands too barren for the English adventurers to covet. The better lands of Leinster, Munster and Ulster fell into the hands of English landlords, who quickly found that it paid them to spare the native survivors of conquest. These estates were leased in small holdings to Irish peasants at exorbitant rents, which were partly drawn to and spent in England. The Protestant Episcopal Church of the landlords was established in Ireland and the cost of its maintenance was charged on the land. The wrongs endured at the hands of alien and Protestant conquerors confirmed the devotion of the native Irish to the Catholic faith. As Catholics they were barred from all share in the government of their country.

When the Tudor dynasty came to an end with Queen Elizabeth and James VI. of Scotland had inherited the throne of England, he thought to unite both nations in common obedience to the Episcopal Church, which recognised the king instead of the pope as its spiritual head. This ecclesiastical policy was resented by his own Presbyterian subjects in Scotland. In the early years of his reign the King's Bench had declared invalid the tribal law under which the title to Irish land vested in the tribe. By this decision the six counties in northern Ireland nearest to Scotland were placed at the disposal of the crown. As a number of Scottish immigrants had already settled there, James decided to open the north of Ireland as a field to which Presbyterians from Great Britain might be drawn. In his reign numbers of Presbyterians, largely Scottish, were settled in northern Ireland. They were mostly farmers and tradesmen and especially weavers.

In his struggle with the English parliament Charles I. relied on support from the Irish. When Cromwell had beaten and beheaded the King he conquered Ireland with methods so ruthless that by 1652 nearly half its inhabitants had perished in the struggle. The greed of English adventurers for Irish lands was revived. His soldiers were settled in large numbers on estates forfeited by Protestant royalists as well as by Catholics. Cromwell abolished the Irish parliament, and provided that thirty members from Ireland should sit in the parliament of Westminster.

When Charles II. was restored to the English throne he re-established the Irish parliament, but left the Cromwellian settlers in possession of the lands they had conquered. Unlike the Scottish settlers massed in northern Ireland, the Cromwellian settlers in the south merged in a few generations into Irish society, as the Norman conquerors had merged in the Middle Ages.

When the aims of James II. to re-establish Catholicism in England led to his downfall, he took refuge in Ireland and was there defeated in 1690 at the battle of the Boyne, by William of Orange, who thereafter figured as the symbol of Protestant ascendency in Ireland. Not more than a quarter of the people in Ireland were Protestants, members of the Episcopal Church, Presbyterians and other dissenters. But of this quarter, political power and representation in the Irish parliament was confined to members of the Church of Ireland. The remaining three-quarters of the people were Catholics, including some gentry, descendants of the English who had seized Irish estates in the Middle Ages.

In the second half of the seventeenth century the Scottish and Cromwellian settlers began to produce from their farms and looms goods which competed with those of the English farmers and industrialists in the English markets. The moment this competition was felt the English parliament passed laws excluding the products of Ireland from England. So desperate did the case of Ireland become, that when the Union of Scotland with England was under discussion the Irish parliament prayed that Ireland also might be included in a similar Union. That the plea was ignored at the very time when the English government were forcing the Union on Scotland was due to the facts of geography noted at the opening of this chapter. The English fleet was now paramount on the sea. The soil of England was not threatened by invasion of Irish forces in alliance with foreign powers, such as those which were yet to march into England even after the Union. The sea ordained that in Ireland there was destined to grow a national feeling acutely separate from that of Great Britain. But its growth was not sufficiently rapid seriously to embarrass Great Britain in her struggle with France to control the distant continents in the eighteenth century.

NOTE

[1] Lecky, *History of Ireland*, vol. v. pp. 124, 125.

CHAPTER XXI

THE SEVEN YEARS' WAR

THE opening of the world to Europe and the Reformation had thus in two centuries the effect of uniting the people of Great Britain as one commonwealth. In view of the great struggle with France for control in the eastern and western hemispheres, to be settled in the eighteenth century, the fact that the Union of England and Scotland was effected before that struggle is of primary importance.

Till the middle of the eighteenth century the British and French were still confronting each other in America and Asia. In either hemisphere the decisive factor was the more effective support which Great Britain was able to render her land forces, by reason of her superior power at sea. In both continents the decision was reached in the war which began in 1756 and was ended in 1763 by the Peace of Paris. The day of France in North America came to an end when Wolfe defeated Montcalm on the heights of Abraham and captured Quebec in 1759.

In India the French power was broken in the following year. Since the end of the seventeenth century the Mogul Empire had continued in name only, and no longer controlled the great hereditary satraps who ruled the provinces. There were constant struggles between rival claimants to their thrones, and the state of India was comparable to that which exists in China to-day. Dupleix, the French leader in India, realised how much more formidable a given body of oriental soldiers becomes when organised and led by Europeans. He contracted relations with Indian princes, and organised their troops with a view to the expulsion of the English. The rivals of these princes formed similar relations with the British under Clive, who had joined the East India Company as a clerk, and Dupleix was beaten by Clive at his own game. In 1757 he defeated the Nawab of Bengal and his French allies at Plassey. In 1760 the downfall of the French power in India was completed at Wandewash, by a victory which secured Madras for the British.

In the light of after events it is manifest that European ideas were certain to become a dominating factor in all the continents, when once her mariners had opened paths to their shores. At this juncture European ideas had already diverged into two main channels. Continental Europe was dominated by the principle of authority which found its religious expression in the Catholic Church and its political expression in powerful autocracies. In Britain the principle of the commonwealth had taken root. It had found its expression in a system which made questions of government subject to discussion and referred ultimate decisions to a popular electorate. In the Indies and Americas England was fighting for power to preserve her own institutions at home. But much more than this was settled by her victories on opposite sides of the world and by her power to control the seas which made them possible. The crowning achievements of Clive at Plassey and of Wolfe at Quebec, in their ultimate result, meant that Europe would extend to the whole world the finest product of her civilisation, a system of life based on the principle of the commonwealth. Had France prevailed, the French Revolution would not have happened when it did. In India an empire would have been founded, distinguished only from that of the Moguls by its higher efficiency; and even this under eastern conditions it would presently have lost. In America the new and vigorous growth of popular government would have been stifled, and could never have exercised the vast influence it has had on the rest of the world. The influence of England herself would have been no greater than that of Holland or the Swiss Republic has been. The position won in the eighteenth century had still to be defended in the long struggle with Napoleon, and again a century later with the empires of central Europe. But the issue of the Seven Years' War was none the less the great decision of modern history.

CHAPTER XXII

THE AMERICAN REVOLUTION

GREEKS, when they founded a colony, made it a sovereign state from the outset, a city in no organic relation to the state from which its founders came. The English colonies, like those of Spain and France, were assumed to be part of the parent state; for the process by which England became a commonwealth was achieved without discarding the forms of monarchy. The radical nature of the change was masked by these forms. While Englishmen boasted rights denied to the subjects of sovereigns other than their own, they failed to realise that the principles of their polity differed in kind and not in degree only from those of Spain and France, or to foresee the practical conclusions in which those principles would issue. To a great extent this was true of the colonists themselves. A more than human intelligence would have been needed in that generation to grasp truths which to us seem evident—in the light of after events.

As Mexico was assumed to belong to the realm of Spain, and Quebec to the realm of France, so Virginia and New England were assumed to belong to the British realm. They had indeed local rights of self-government as the privileges of English subjects required. The British government, the King in Council, was none the less responsible for all their external relations. To that authority the colonies looked to defend them from Spanish or French aggression. The task was assumed by British ministers as a matter of course, and with it the correlative powers. The King in Council and, if necessary, the King in Parliament must be competent to order whatever was needful. The trade and taxation of the colonists must on occasion be subject to Orders in Council and Acts of Parliament.

A theoretical compact was presumed to govern the situation. In return for defence, especially by sea, the trade of the colonies was reserved for the mother country and was deemed to be subject to its control. Some colonial products, like tobacco, enjoyed a monopoly in the English market. But under the free colonial system the British Government had no effective power of preventing colonial traders from dealing with foreign countries direct. The habit of trading with French and Spanish territories developed largely, and vested interests grew on the strength of it. When England was fighting France and Spain, colonial traders in English colonies were unwilling to forgo the profits to which they were used. The supplies they furnished to the enemy prolonged the war. They largely controlled the colonial governments which, in any case, were too numerous to concert the action necessary to restrain the trade. This state of affairs enabled the colonists to do what they liked without concern for the consequences. It divorced power from responsibility.

So long as the military power of France on American soil remained unbroken colonial forces played a substantial part in the struggle. When that menace had been banished and peace had been made, the unsettled state of the Indian tribes imposed the maintenance of defensive forces. The burden of debt left by the war on British taxpayers was heavy, and the thirteen colonies were called upon to share in the cost of their own defence. To have left the colonial legislatures, when they failed to respond, to concert all measures for themselves, and to pay for them, would have been a wise and practical policy. They would thus have been brought, as they were brought later, to realise that their whole system of government in America needed revision. But, again, all this is clear to us only in the light of experience. As it was, the British government lost patience and imposed the necessary taxes by Act of Parliament. Had the colonies submitted to these measures, they would only have saved the unity of the commonwealth at the cost of its principle. They resisted, and unhappily the British government sought to override their resistance, until it was too late. To analyse further the causes of the great schism in the commonwealth is beside our purpose, which is rather to follow its subsequent effect on the structure of human society.

In the struggle with France for world power, the Union of England and Scotland had been an important factor in favour of the British. In the struggle which followed the Seven Years' War of Great Britain with her own colonies, failure to include Ireland in the Union was one of the factors which led to the British defeat in America. The policy was adopted of ruling Ireland through a parliament mainly composed of landlords of English descent who followed the Episcopal faith. The measures adopted by this parliament were so oppressive to tenants that numbers of Presbyterian farmers, more independent than the Catholic Irish, were driven to seek the freer air of America. The British parliament also controlled the trade relations of Ireland so harshly in favour of the trade relations of England, that numbers of Presbyterian weavers were also driven to emigrate. In the course of the eighteenth century Presbyterian farmers and mechanics were thus streaming from Ireland to America with a bitter hatred of British rule in their hearts. It was these Protestant Irish who furnished the most formidable element in the armies that Washington raised and led.

In this long struggle with her own kindred

England was able to produce no general to counter that supreme capacity of leadership, which enabled Washington to defeat her immensely superior resources. The inferior quality of her statesmen and generals in these years, and the blunders they made, were results of a definite cause. George I. and George II. were more interested in the government of Hanover than of England, and neither was at home in the English language. The direction of policy had passed to ministers able to control parliament and the British electorate. In their reigns the destinies of England had been guided by men of the stature of Walpole and Chatham. George III. came to the throne in 1760 resolved to reverse this process, and to take the direction of policy into his own hands. He sought to control parliament by corrupting its members. As ministers he chose men of inferior capacity like Bute, Grafton and North who were willing to waive their own opinions, to accept the royal decisions and remain in office. The surrender of General Burgoyne at Saratoga in October 1777 was directly caused by their indolence and errors.

This resounding catastrophe changed the whole aspect of affairs. France threw her naval and military power into the scale on the side of the colonists. Spain followed suit in 1779, Holland in 1780 and a league of northern powers was organised by Russia to resist the claims of the British to search their ships for contraband of war. A struggle to repress the rebellion of colonists was thus raised to the scale of a world war in which England was facing not only her own kindred in America, but also the leading powers of Europe. Her navy lost control of the sea, and in 1782 Cornwallis was forced to surrender his army to Washington at Yorktown. In the Peace of Versailles which was signed in January 1783 England recognised the independence of the United States. In the course of the struggle she had lost eight of her islands in the West Indies, Florida and Minorca. Her hold on India was saved only by Warren Hastings. The corruption and incompetence of the ministers in England was there unable to ruin the work of that much-enduring man.

The refusal to include Ireland in the measure of 1707 which united England and Scotland under one parliament had also come home to roost. Ireland had continued to suffer from those restrictions on trade against which the American colonists had revolted. The Presbyterians of Northern Ireland, disfranchised by the Test Acts, were the principal sufferers. When the colonists revolted, "the North of Ireland" as Chatham said, "was American to a man". They began to demand the removal of all restrictions on Irish trade and the right to vote. When France entered the war and England had lost control of the sea, and Ireland, denuded of troops, was threatened with invasion, the situation was changed for the moment; for the Irish Protestants formed a volunteer army to resist the landing of Catholic troops by France. With arms in their hands the volunteers were now masters of Ireland, and the Irish parliament led by Grattan became their tool. The commercial restrictions and the Test Acts were swept away.

The Irish Parliament, in which the dissenters were now represented, proceeded to demand that the British Parliament should renounce all future right to legislate for Ireland. They were backed by 100,000 men under arms. In 1782 the British Parliament, which was now preparing to accept defeat in America, renounced its jurisdiction over Ireland in every shape and form. For the rest of the century Ireland was linked to Great Britain only by such authority as the crown retained.

It remains to trace the after effects of this struggle on the three principal countries concerned, and through them on the rest of the world Few wars in history have led to results so widely different from those that contemporaries thought would follow its close. The successful revolt of the American colonists had started the great revolution which was destined to end the rule of dynasties and call into being the national states of the modern world.

CHAPTER XXIII

EFFECT OF THE AMERICAN REVOLUTION ON THE BRITISH COMMONWEALTH

In England public opinion was quick to recognise and deal with the cause which had brought the commonwealth to the verge of destruction. In 1782 Lord North resigned, and measures were passed which deprived the king of his power to control votes in the House of Commons by bestowing offices, pensions and contracts on its members. A rapid succession of ministries was ended when, on December 23, 1784, Chatham's son, William Pitt, became Prime Minister at the age of 24.

He was too strong a minister to pursue a dictated policy or to tolerate cabals against his power, and the old system of a divided Cabinet, of 'King's friends' maintained in office for the purpose of controlling, and, if commanded, overthrowing their chief, now came finally and decisively to an end.[1]

He remained in office till the year 1801 and then resigned, because George III. held that the bill removing Catholic disabilities, to which Pitt was pledged when he united Ireland to England, was contrary to the oath which the king took at his coronation. None the less, in the seventeen years the principle was finally established that in the British Commonwealth the ruler is the minister who for the time being can command a majority in parliament or the electorate. With the crown has remained responsibility for seeing that ministers and parliaments do not usurp the sovereignty which rests with the electorate. If ministers supported by parliament ever persisted in office long after it appeared that their popular mandate was exhausted, it would then be the duty of the monarch to dismiss them and call to office a ministry pledged to hold a general election. As Professor Seeley has said, the prime minister is the real successor of Plantagenet kings. Their descendants on the throne are hereditary presidents of a commonwealth, who hold for the sovereign electorate their final power of attorney.

The crisis which split from the parent commonwealth the communities it had brought into being in the new world, was withal the most dangerous through which it had passed. When England acknowledged the independence of the United States it was commonly supposed at home and abroad that her sun had set never to rise. For the moment it seemed she had lost her position as one of the great powers in Europe and the world. Her amazing and unlooked-for recovery in the course of one decade was due to causes which all had their roots in her institutions. Her craftsmen were learning to master the forces of nature; but of this we must treat in a separate chapter. In contrast with those of France, British institutions were designed to expose the defects of their own working. The appalling state of corruption in political circles and also in India was the subject of constant discussion in parliament which no one could muzzle, and these discussions created a public opinion which led to reform. The revival of the system, under which the ruling power was held by a minister responsible to parliament, secured for the public service statesmen far abler than the creatures who had served the ambitions of George III., or the ministers who served the Bourbons in France. Under the parliamentary system, even as then developed, the perilous state of the national finances could not be concealed, as it was in France, and is in countries to-day under modern dictatorships. At this critical juncture the British electorate placed in power and kept there a young statesman highly qualified to deal with the evils from which it had suffered. The writings of Adam Smith, which Pitt had studied, had also prepared the public mind for the drastic reforms required to ensure that as much as possible of the money paid by the tax-payer should reach the coffers of the state. In obedience to the teaching of his great master he freed the industries of the country from many of its ancient shackles and enabled them to take advantage of the new mechanical inventions. The natural growth of business which resulted more than made up for the futile attempts to monopolise American and Irish trade. But William Pitt knew how to spend the public revenues wisely, as well as to save them. In a few years he restored to the British navy the state of efficiency it had reached under his father in the Seven Years' War.

When the peace was signed at Versailles in 1783 the British government had, without knowing it, retained under its jurisdiction in North America territories wider than those conceded to the United States. To begin with the French inhabitants of Quebec, so recently conquered by the English from France, had abstained from all part in the struggles of the colonies to the south of them to renounce their allegiance to England. In this simple community the Catholic priests were the dominant power, and they had nothing in sympathy with the Protestant colonies to the south. The British government, moreover, had left them to enjoy their own language and laws as well as their religion. The Breton peasants had deeply resented the enforcement of military service upon them by the French monarchy in the Seven Years' War. The British government had made no attempt to impose such obligations; so that even when France entered the struggle on the side of the colonists they still refused to come to her aid. By the irony of events French Canada remained under the British crown when the independence of the English colonies was established by the Peace of Versailles.

Like all revolutions the secession of these colonies was the work of a small but active minority. According to American historians, not five per cent of the colonists would have voted for the Declaration of Independence had a plebiscite been taken when it was published. Till the end of this long-drawn struggle there was still a large though dwindling minority strongly opposed to political severance from England. As must always happen in revolutions, this minority was the object of persecution when British protection was finally withdrawn. Some 40,000 of these Loyalists fled to the north and settled in the wilderness to the east and west of the province of Quebec. The British government expended some £4,000,000 in helping them to settle in the provinces now known as New Brunswick, Nova Scotia and Ontario. To the north and west of these British territories were the vast and desolate hunting grounds of the Hudson's Bay Company, formed in the reign of Charles II. While the struggle in eastern America was in actual progress British ships, under Captain Cook, had reached and surveyed the Pacific coast of these western regions. The train of events which had led to this expedition is so relevant to our theme, that it calls for treatment in a separate chapter.

NOTE

[1] Lecky, *History of England in the Eighteenth Century*, vol. v. p. 284.

CHAPTER XXIV

THE ROYAL SOCIETY AND CAPTAIN COOK

In the Middle Ages the Church was conceived in Europe as the Kingdom of God upon earth. As the distant continents were revealed by Columbus and Vasco da Gama, the Church had assigned America to Spain and Asia to Portugal. This opening of the world had led whole nations in northern Europe, and especially the English, to deny that claim to universal authority which the Church was trying to assert.

Three hundred years from the day when Vasco da Gama had landed at Calicut, Great Britain was the ruling power in India, and was all unconsciously laying foundations in that sub-continent which would carry a structure of government based on the principle of the commonwealth. In America a commonwealth was in being which, though severed from that of Great Britain, was inspired by English ideas.

When the Seven Years' War had decided these issues there were still considerable gaps to be filled by discoverers. As yet little was known of two regions, one covered by sea but dotted with islands great and small, the other by land. Sailors had crossed but had not explored the Pacific. They could visit the shores of the African continent, but its vast interior was closed to civilised man by the horrors of the slave trade.

The work begun by explorers trained in the school of Henry the Navigator was from its nature destined to be brought to completion. That work, now almost completed, has shown mankind the limits of his home. It has made all the families of men aware of each other, and has linked them together in one society. All this was achieved by the mariners who brought to our ken the visible face of the globe upon which we live. But in various ways their achievements opened a field for exploration which was not limited like the visible face of the planet, a realm of knowledge which brought to men as they entered it a mastery of nature that already goes further and deeper than any mere knowledge of geography can bestow. The discovery of the visible world as a whole which broke on mankind in the sixteenth century, was to bring to our knowledge invisible forces incarnate in the palpable world about us.

The idea that God had revealed to man all that was needful for man to know was implicit in the doctrine of authority. At the close of the Middle Ages physical science had advanced but little beyond the point reached by the Greeks. Their thinkers had opened the springs of knowledge, but the Church had turned their books into lids which shut up the wells sunk by their authors. In philosophy and science Aristotle was invested with the same deadening authority as the Hebrew and Greek scriptures in the field of religion. The theory propounded by Copernicus that the sun, not the earth, is the centre of the planetary system, was formally denounced by the Church, not merely as contrary to scripture, but also as absurd in philosophy. The work of explorers convinced the world that the Church was wrong and Copernicus right. Men awoke to the fact of their own ignorance, recognition of which is the key to learning.

The opening of the world had brought to a head the revolt from Rome in northern Europe. In Protestant countries authorities approved by the Church could be questioned without fear of the Inquisition. The idea of a knowledge, deeper than any to be found in existing books, to be sought by studying facts of nature, had found expression in the writings of Francis Bacon. His empirical methods of research were the natural outcome of a polity based on experience rather than authority. Even in his time the guesses at truth made by Ptolemy could only be questioned in Catholic Europe at the risk of liberty and life. In 1633 Galileo was forced, under fear of torture, to deny that he held views like those of Copernicus.

Some twelve years later there began to be held weekly meetings at Dr. Goddard's lodgings in Wood Street or the Bull-head tavern in Cheapside, of "divers worthy persons, inquisitive into natural philosophy and other parts of human learning, and particularly of what had been called the *New Philosophy or Experimental Philosophy*". In 1648 some of them, resident in Oxford, formed the Philosophical Society which met at Wadham College in the rooms of the warden, Dr. Wilkins. The activities of the two meetings were presently concentrated at Gresham College in London. The first report of proceedings opens as follows:

Memorandum that Novemb. 28, 1660, These persons following according to the usual custom of most of them, mett together at Gresham College to heare Mr. Wren's lecture, viz., The Lord Brouncher, Mr. Boyle, Mr. Bruce, Sir Rober Moray, Sir Paul Neile, Dr. Wilkins, Dr. Goddard, Dr. Petty, Mr. Ball, Mr. Hooke, Mr. Wren, Mr. Hill. And after the lecture was ended, they did, according to the usuall manner, withdrawe for mutuall converse, where amongst other matters that were discoursed of, something was offered about a designe of founding a Colledge for the promoting of Physico-Mathematicall Experimentall Learning.

Mr. Wren, a fellow of All Souls College, was the future architect of St. Paul's Cathedral. In 1661 King Charles II. became a member, and in 1662 incorporated the body as 'The Royal Society'.

Thereafter its advice was constantly sought or accepted by the government in such matters as the Royal Observatory, the calendar, prison ventilation and questions affecting navigation.

In 1768 the Society persuaded the government of Lord North that an expedition should be sent to observe the impending transit of Venus from the southern Pacific, and further to explore those regions. Cook was appointed to lead it and took with him Banks the botanist and others eminent in the field of science. They rounded Cape Horn and reached Tahiti in time to observe the transit on June 3, 1769. In honour of the Royal Society the group to which Tahiti belongs was named 'The Society Islands'. Cook then proceeded to chart the coasts of New Zealand and eastern Australia where the name of Botany Bay commemorates the landing of Banks. He then sailed through the straits south of New Guinea to Java and thence to the Cape of Good Hope, returning to England on June 12, 1770.

In 1772 he again set sail for New Zealand by the Cape of Good Hope and, in a voyage which covered more than 60,000 miles, disproved the existence of a habitable continent south of those islands. He visited the Marquesas, the Friendly Islands and the New Hebrides which he named, and discovered New Caledonia, Norfolk Island and the Isle of Pines. He then made for the Horn, surveyed Tierra del Fuego and got back to England in 1775 after visiting the Cape of Good Hope.

In 1776 he was commissioned to settle the question whether America could be rounded by the north from the Pacific. He made his way to Tasmania by the Cape of Good Hope and thence to New Zealand, Tonga and The Society Islands, discovering on the way the larger members of the Cook Archipelago. On his voyage north he rediscovered Hawaii (which the Spaniards had found and afterwards lost) and named the group The Sandwich Islands after the First Lord of the Admiralty. He then struck the coast of America where the state of Oregon now is, and charted the coast up to Behring Straits till a wall of ice blocked his further advance. On his way home he revisited Hawaii, and there perished in a quarrel with the natives on February 14, 1779.

Ships engaged in the Far Eastern trade were attracted to these regions by Cook's discoveries. In trading with China the main problem at this period was to find commodities which the Chinese were prepared to accept in exchange for the tea, silk and porcelain which Europe was anxious to obtain. An illicit trade in opium was the main solution of this problem; but furs were also in demand in the colder regions of northern China. There was also ginseng, a valuable root, from which wealthy Chinese prepare a kind of tea for the entertainment of distinguished guests. A Jesuit priest, who had served as a missionary in China and was afterwards sent to America, recognised the plant growing wild on the mountain slopes of New England. He collected some of the root and sent it as a gift to the Emperor of China, who pronounced it as equal in flavour to the best Mongolian ginseng. A trade was thus established in ginseng from the British colonies in America to China. The root is still sought for the Chinese market on the slopes of Mount Greylock above Williamstown. It is also grown in Canada for export to China; but the wild variety always commands a higher price.

When the tea was thrown into Boston harbour and the colonies were at war with their mother country, the supply of this valuable root to the Chinese market was cut off. In the light of Cook's discoveries, some merchants, trading under the auspices of the British East India Company in China, conceived the idea of crossing the Pacific from China in the hope of obtaining furs and ginseng on the western coast of America. In 1788 they established a settlement in the sound between Vancouver Island and the smaller island of Nootka.

On hearing of these doings, the Spaniards resolved to assert the rights which they held to be theirs by virtue of the bull issued by Pope Alexander VI. in 1493. So in 1789 Flores, Viceroy of Mexico, sent two ships to occupy Nootka. There they found at anchor two English ships, the *Iphegenia* and *Argonaut*, which they seized, imprisoning the crews.

When the news reached England in 1790, the younger Pitt instantly threatened war unless the crews were released and the British flag rehoisted at Nootka. This dispute over a region scarcely inhabited even to-day had important reactions on the history of Ireland and the French Revolution.[1] The Jacobins were opposed to a war in alliance with Spain which might lead to a royalist reaction. Spain had therefore to submit to a settlement with England, in which she at last abandoned the right she had long claimed under papal authority to the western hemisphere. England agreed to recognise the exclusive rights of Spain to the coast south of San Francisco. North of that point both nations were to enjoy equal rights in the matter of trade and settlement. Captain Vancouver, who had served under Cook, was then sent to restore the British settlement at Nootka Sound, and gave his name to the larger island.

In course of time the United States forced Spain to surrender all claims to this coast north of the frontier which now divides the American Commonwealth from the Republic of Mexico. The coast-line up to Alaska would then have fallen to the United States, but for the resolute action which Pitt had taken in 1790 to assert the British claim created by Cook and the China merchants who founded the settlement at Nootka Sound. The fact that Canada now fronts the Pacific as well as the Atlantic is due to that incident.

The British government had shipped convicts to work on cotton and tobacco plantations of American colonists. This convenient dumping-ground for the criminal classes was closed when the colonies revolted, and the British government then established a convict station at Botany Bay, which Cook had discovered in Australia. A nucleus of government was thus established in the antipodes. In the following century the country was opened to colonisation and New Zealand as well as Australia was settled with emigrants from the British Isles.

The British and American Commonwealths were thus firmly established on the western shores of the ocean which divides the continent opened to Europe by Columbus, from the continent opened by Vasco da Gama. Australia, New Zealand and a number of islands which dot the Pacific were also annexed to the British Commonwealth. Self-imprisoned in their own islands and their own past, the Japanese people were unconscious of the fact that their natural heritage was passing to the Anglo-Saxon commonwealths.

NOTE

[1] *The Commonwealth of Nations*, p. 498.

CHAPTER XXV

THE AMERICAN COMMONWEALTH

In the peace which was signed at Versailles in 1783 the leading powers of the world had recognised thirteen states as separate sovereignties independent of Great Britain. They were also independent one of another. In the struggle with England these thirteen states had been forced to establish a joint body or congress, composed of delegates sent from their several legislatures. This Congress was given no power to tax or otherwise control the citizens of the separate states, except by virtue of laws passed at its instance by the state legislatures. Their failure to pass such laws when requested by Congress to do so, had greatly delayed the American victory, which was in the upshot mainly due to the genius of Washington aided by the French, and to the hatred of British rule, which led numbers of Irish to join Washington's forces.

The funds needed to meet the costs of the war had largely been raised by loans. When the peace was signed at Paris, Congress was owing $42,000,000 to France, to sympathisers in Holland and to American citizens who had risked their property in the national cause. In addition to this were arrears of pay and the pensions due to the army whose valour had won the war.

Congress applied to the legislatures of the thirteen states for the funds necessary to meet these debts. By 1786 four requisitions had been made to the total amount of $15,870,987. In response to these requisitions no more than $2,450,803 were remitted to Congress by the state legislatures. By 1786 Congress was in open and acknowledged default to its creditors. But this was not all. By the Treaty of Paris the Americans were bound to remove every impediment to the recovery of private debts owed by Americans to British subjects. Some of the state legislatures passed laws which made this impossible; so the British government refused to evacuate posts which they still held in American territory when the peace was signed. But the trouble was not confined to Great Britain. The American government had agreed with Spain that the lower waters of the Mississippi should be closed to American shipping and the southern states were threatening to secede and return to their British allegiance.

In New England the stability of the state governments themselves began to be threatened. Captain Shay, an officer who had served in the war, raised a rebellion and attempted to prevent the courts of Massachusetts from enforcing the collection of taxes and debts. The danger of general anarchy was so great that Washington was implored to come to New England and use his influence to restore order. Washington replied with the memorable phrase that "Influence is not government".

Events had forced Washington and his friends to grasp what government means and to see why it is necessary to freedom. They had realised that no commonwealth in the genuine sense of that word can be founded by virtue of contract between separate and sovereign states, nor indeed by virtue of contract at all. 'The state' and 'government' are correlative terms, and this is equally true when the state is a commonwealth founded on reason, and not an autocracy based on authority. A commonwealth, rightly so-called, must be based on the dedication of each to all. It must rest on the principle that each of its members owes an unlimited duty to the members as a whole. One all-important expression of this principle was a right vested in the government to collect from each citizen such part of his property as it needs to ensure the safety, welfare and honour of the commonwealth as a whole.

Such a right was established by the constitution which was framed by the Philadelphia Convention of 1787, and thereafter ratified, not by the state legislatures, but by special conventions which represented the people of the states.

Whilst this draft constitution was before the American people, its principles were expounded by the young followers of Washington in a series of pamphlets, afterwards gathered in one volume entitled *The Federalist*. As a contribution to constructive political thought, these papers deserve to rank with the funeral speech of Pericles and *The Crito*. They expound in detail the truths summarised in the four words of Washington's aphorism, "Influence is not government". Their reasoning is largely ignored by political thinkers who cannot digest that hard but indestructible truth.

The value of this constitution to the world at large, as well as to the people of the states it united, was greatly enhanced by the practical sense which confined the principles it embodied to the actual necessities of the commonwealth it created. The power of the federal government to tax the citizen was limited to federal functions. The federal government was only given those powers which the state governments could not in fact exercise. All powers which the states could exercise with effect were still reserved to the state legislatures. The word 'state' though preserved was, in fact, a misnomer. The former states with their legislatures were preserved to function as provinces, with local governments of their own.

The maintenance of the states as provincial governments was a vital step in the history of the commonwealth. Without it, the growth of the commonwealth would have been limited to countries no larger than Great Britain. The idea that a national government is strengthened by concentrating all powers in one assembly at one centre is a dangerous fallacy which constantly impedes the growth of the commonwealth. The reasons why one organ of government cannot control all the affairs of a great country are many. It suffices to mention one which, like other facts that are obvious, is constantly overlooked. In an hour there are 60 minutes, in a day 24 hours, in a year 365 days. The amount of business which any human being can transact is inexorably limited by these facts. An autocrat, who makes his decisions without any public discussion, can transact business far more rapidly than a government which has to show in a public assembly reasons for what it proposes. This explains why autocrats are able to govern vast empires. The government of a commonwealth can only control a large territory by devolving on local governments every function which can be localised, thus freeing its hands for, and confining its time to, those matters which a central government alone can control. The enlargement of commonwealths depends upon how far the central government can be relieved of all functions which can be discharged, at least as well (and often not quite so well), by localised authorities.

It was this principle which the federal government of America, which came into force in 1789, exemplified. It made possible the incorporation not only of the thirteen states in one commonwealth, but the subsequent inclusion of thirty-five other states carved out, in course of years, from the vast territory which lay between the colonies settled from England and the Pacific coast. To-day the United States include a country larger than Europe west of Russia, with a population of 140,000,000 souls.

The system by which the powers of government were apportioned between the federal authority and the states was of course imperfect. Its defects are the source of serious troubles which are calling for remedy to-day. But they cannot obscure the success achieved by recognition in 1787 that the whole of this vast territory could not be governed by a single executive and legislature. The American constitution brought into being a commonwealth so great that it now affects the movement of all nations, not merely by the track which it follows, but even by the manner in which it revolves on its own axis. The statesmen who effected the Union of England with Scotland had no such example before them to suggest that the government of Great Britain might in the end have been strengthened, if England and Scotland had each retained provincial assemblies and parliaments of their own.

CHAPTER XXVI

MUNRO AND ELPHINSTONE IN INDIA

FROM 1772 to 1784 the authority which England was losing in the west was tenaciously upheld by Hastings in India. Before the outbreak of the Seven Years' War the British East India Company had drawn its dividends only from trade, and had occupied and garrisoned ports like Bombay, Madras and Calcutta to protect their stocks and the textile industries which supplied them. After the war the Company's dividends were swelled by the revenues of whole provinces which it owned and ruled. But now as formerly the conspicuous fortunes were made not by the shareholders but rather by the servants of the Company, who grew richer by oppressing the natives than they had formerly by trading for themselves. By the purchase of rotten boroughs they were able to acquire a formidable influence in the House of Commons. The British Commonwealth was thus menaced with the very danger which had undermined the city republics of Greece and Rome. An empire gained through the vigour inherent in its system of government was threatening to destroy that system. The sequel proved that a commonwealth on the national scale is better able to survive such dangers than one based on the narrow foundations of a city community.

In demanding reforms in India, the British were prompted by motives other than fear for their own liberties. The long enjoyment of these liberties had developed a sense of right and wrong in public affairs. There were Englishmen who hated the thought of injustice inflicted by countrymen of their own on a helpless people—a handful of salt perhaps, but of virtue enough to savour the commonwealth. The facilities for public enquiry and discussion provided by parliament enabled them to appeal to and arouse the national conscience. By the irony of fate this movement was to reach its classic expression in the trial of Warren Hastings, who was, in fact, the most active agent of reform.

In the days of Clive the servants of the Company were paid salaries upon which it was scarcely possible for Europeans to live. Yet many of them were able to retire with considerable fortunes. In this the Company was merely following a practice not uncommon in Europe and universal in Asia. In the East functionaries had always expected to derive their principal reward from the pickings of office. The prevalence of this habit amongst the Chinese more than anything else explains why they are finding it so difficult to lay the foundations of a government for themselves.

In this practice the reformers rightly saw the evil which was certain to discredit British rule in India and, left to take its course, to taint the commonwealth at its fountain-head. The administrative officers of the Company were secured in the enjoyment of liberal salaries and retiring allowances, and forbidden by stringent enactments to accept payments even as gifts from those they ruled. A career was thus opened to men of honour and education in which they could rise to distinction only by devotion to the welfare of the people entrusted to their care. It was officers of this quality, and with this point of view, whose studious industry built up an administrative system upon which the people of India are to-day founding the structure of self-government.

The administration of those provinces which came under British control from the time of Hastings onwards was thus organised by men of the highest character and ability that the British Commonwealth could produce. Their aim was to endow India with the best fruits of Western civilisation so far as her people were able to receive them. Of these the most comprehensive and fundamental was a greater measure of justice than any people of Asia had yet enjoyed. But justice demands more of rulers than a disposition to judge fairly between rival claimants. It involves a continuous and constructive attention to an infinite mass of tedious detail. It consists in providing effective remedies for the grievances from which men find they suffer, and for this reason the Romans and British have earned distinction as exponents of justice.

In reforming the courts the English experience of centuries was comparatively easy to apply. The most fundamental and original reform made by the British administrators was in the sphere of revenue. In the theory of the East the position of ruler and landowner was scarcely distinguished. The ruler was legally entitled to all he could get from the land. A good ruler was one who left the cultivators a fair subsistence by husbanding expenditure on his own establishment. The exactions of a bad and extravagant ruler were only limited by the fear lest the peasants in despair should leave their holdings untilled and take to brigandage, as happens in China to-day. In an empire so great as that of the Moguls the revenue collected from the peasants had to pass through a great number of hands, and vastly more was retained by the intermediate officers than ever reached the Imperial treasury. Such a system must always tend to concentrate the wealth of the country in the hands of a powerful minority, to bankrupt the state and impoverish the great mass of producers. These results can only be prevented by methods foreign to Eastern ideas. It needed the kind of thoroughness and exactitude in public finance which the constant scrutiny of parliament required and the younger Pitt had reduced to practice.

A revenue system based on the rent of land involves a government at every point in questions of tenure. It has to determine what are the rights of each individual in the land, as well as the amounts which he is to pay for enjoying those rights. In assessing and collecting the revenues from lands under their control the British officers used the higher exactitude which business or government, as conducted in Europe, require. The amount due from each particular field and the periods for which that amount would be due were reduced to accurate record. The periods during which the amount due to the governments remained unchanged were steadily lengthened. An army of Indian officials were trained to these methods, and were narrowly watched by the handful of British administrators to ensure that so far as possible no more was wrung from the peasants than was rightly due.

Of those who created the revenue system the greatest perhaps was Thomas Munro, who began life in India as a military officer in the time of Hastings and died as Governor of Madras in 1827. The nature of the problem as he viewed it is best described in his own words:

> The peculiar character and condition of the ryots require that some laws should be made specially for their protection. The non-resistance of the ryots in general to oppression has been too little attended to in our Regulations. We make laws for them as though they were Englishmen, and are surprised that they should have no operation. A law might be a very good one in England and useless here. This arises from the different characters of the people. In England the people resist oppression and it is their spirit which gives efficacy to the law: in India the people rarely resist oppression, and the law intended to secure them from it can therefore derive no aid from themselves. Though the ryots frequently complain of illegal exactions, they very seldom

resist them: they more commonly submit without complaining, and they often abscond when they have no longer the means of paying for them. . . . As, therefore, they will not protect themselves by resisting injustice, we must endeavour to protect them by laws which would be unnecessary in England, or in almost any other country not under foreign dominion; and we must, for this salutary purpose, invest the Collector and Magistrate, the person most interested in their welfare, with power to secure them from exaction, by authorizing him to make summary inquiry into all illegal exactions, to recover the amount, to restore whatever is recovered to the ryots, and to punish the offenders.[1]

These exacting methods applied to the slipshod conditions of India naturally led to new difficulties, and the balance of profit and loss is accurately stated in the words of Munro's contemporary, Elphinstone:

To sum up the effects of our revenue, policy, and judicial systems, we have, lighter, and more equal and more certain assessment, less peculation, and consequently less profit to the agents of Government. In police more attention and more vigour, but less violence, and so far less efficiency. In civil justice, the great change is that Government has taken on itself the whole responsibility of protecting people's rights, but there is more form, more purity, more delay in some cases and less in others. In criminal justice, more system, more scruples, more trials, more acquittals, more certain punishment for all crimes except robbery, and for that both less certain and less severe.[2]

Since the loss of the American colonies men of this stamp had come to regard a permanent connection even with India as undesirable. In 1819 Elphinstone wrote:

If we can manage our native army, and keep out the Russians, I see nothing to threaten the safety of our Empire —until the natives become enlightened under our tuition, and a separation becomes desirable to both parties.

In 1824 Munro wrote in a similar strain:

We should look upon India, not as a temporary possession, but as one which is to be maintained permanently, until the natives shall in some future age have abandoned most of their superstitions and prejudices, and become sufficiently enlightened, to frame a regular government for themselves, and to conduct and preserve it. Whenever such a time shall arrive, it will probably be best for both countries that the British control over India should be gradually withdrawn. That the desirable change contemplated may in some after age be effected in India, there is no cause to despair. Such a change was at one time in Britain itself at least as hopeless as it is here. *When we reflect how much the character of nations has always been influenced by that of governments, and that some, once the most cultivated, have sunk into barbarism, while others, formerly the rudest, have attained the highest point of civilisation, we shall see no reason to doubt that if we pursue steadily the proper measures, we shall in time so far improve the character of our Indian subjects as to enable them to govern and protect themselves.*[3]

The traditions which have made British rule in India, with all its mistakes and defects, the noblest chapter in the long history of Europe's relations with Asia, were largely created by professional officers like Elphinstone and Munro. The word 'created' is used advisedly. The idea that a subject people should be trained by their foreign rulers to govern themselves, and be so prepared to dispense with those rulers, was without parallel in previous history. As Munro saw, a definite change in their attitude to life was a necessary means to that end. He had also grasped the truth that the system of society under which men live is the principal factor in shaping their characters.

In Book I., Chapter III., we saw how, before the dawn of recorded history, there descended on India parties of tall, fair, active and highly intelligent conquerors. The gloom of the jungle and the scorching heat of the Indian plain had yet to cast its shadow across their minds; but in tropical surroundings they began to acquire the same sense of fear as inspired the

Dravidian people in whom they were merged, and with it the ritual developed as an antidote to fear. They adopted the practices of the people in whom they were merged, in much the same way as the Hebrew invaders with their puritan outlook came to adopt the elaborate ritual of sacrifice practised by the conquered people of Canaan.

In India the purer descendants of the conquering races were accepted as the masters of this ritual. We have seen how the instinct of the light northern race to hold themselves apart from the dark tropical people led to the institution of castes which continued to multiply, till they are now thousands in number. This elaborate social structure was closely connected with religious ideas. The Indian regarded his life as but one of innumerable lives past and to come. In his present life nothing could change the caste into which he was born, but he might be reborn in a future existence to a higher or lower caste, and the best he could hope for in the end was to rise beyond separate conscious existence and be lost in the infinite. On right or wrong conduct in this life depended his rise or fall in the next. By conduct he thought in the main of ritual, the full knowledge of which was possessed by the highest or Brahmin caste, that which retained the purest admixture of Aryan blood. The supposed possession of this knowledge gave to the Brahmins the greatest power which any hereditary class has ever exercised in a social system.

In this view of existence, human relations and the pleasures and pains of this present life were of little account, when weighed in the balance with the infinite results which would follow a right or wrong observance of ritual; for that in the main would determine the weal or woe of the human soul through countless ages to come. This explains why an Indian in Munro's day would take no steps to resist injustice nor even complain of it. In his view the exactions of a landlord or money-lender affected so small a part of his existence as not to be worth considering in comparison with the right or wrong performance of duties which affected his future happiness through indefinite ages.

Munro believed that a habit of mind so deeply engrained in a whole people could only be altered, and that slowly, by a change in their habit of life. By a long experience of pure and effective justice the people of India would come to realise how the right conduct of men to each other alone determines the future of the soul, which cannot in fact be redeemed by ritual performance. And when that change of outlook was effected he believed that India would support a sufficient system of justice for herself.

NOTES

[1] Arbuthnot, *Minutes of Sir T. Munro*, 258, R.M. pp. 285, 286.
[2] Forrest, *Select Writings of Elphinstone*, 310, R.M. pp. 292, 293.
[3] Arbuthnot, *Minutes of Sir T. Munro*, 573, R.M. pp. 284, 285.

CHAPTER XXVII

THE CONQUEST OF NATURE

As the British Commonwealth established its rule in India, seeds from its institutions began to take root in that uncongenial soil. Their subsequent growth was destined in course of time to change the whole outlook of India and indeed of Asia on life. But closer contact with Asia had already started a train of events which changed the whole structure of life in England, and was destined to change the structure of human society in a few generations.

This train of events was mainly started in that department of civilised life concerned with the making of clothes. In the Stone Ages primitive man wrapped his body in the skins of the larger beasts which he killed for food. The art of twisting wool into threads and of weaving the thread into cloth can scarcely have been developed until men had learned to domesticate sheep, and also to forge instruments sharp enough to shear the wool from their backs. The lake-dwellers had found how to twist flax into cords. In course of time a finer thread was produced from this vegetable fibre and woven into linen, a fabric pleasant to wear next the skin. But the labour of separating the fibre from flax is such that linen has always remained something of a luxury. In the eighteenth century the people of Europe were mainly dependent for their clothing upon wool, the product of pastoral industry which must always require much larger areas of land than fibre produced from a cultivated plant.

The people of India, from times beyond record, were dressed in cotton, a vegetable wool more easily separated from the plant which yields it than fibre from flax. They could therefore devote a larger proportion of their land to producing their food. In their tropical climate less food and clothing were needed than in Europe. So long as each civilised continent was dependent on its own soil for subsistence Europe could support but a small population as compared with the warmer regions of Asia. The habit of using vegetable as well as animal wool acquired from India, released an important check on the multiplication of people in Europe. It largely accounts for the fact that the population of Europe has increased by more than 350,000,000 since the eighteenth century.

Towards the close of the seventeenth century the East India Company was finding in England a ready market for cotton fabrics woven in India. The material, though not so warm as wool, was smoother, less liable to shrink when washed, easier than silk to produce in ever-increasing quantities, and specially suitable for underclothing and female attire. The taste for these Indian fabrics grew so quickly that wool-spinning and weaving, the staple manufactures of England, were seriously threatened. In 1700 and again in 1721 parliament forbade the use of cotton. But the spinners and weavers made such protection unnecessary by obtaining the raw cotton for themselves and learning how to produce from it cloth cheaper and better than the Indian fabrics. The moist climate of Lancashire was peculiarly suitable for the industry, which began to find its centre in Manchester. In 1736 the manufacture was legalised. Cotton fabrics were now in demand for export. Throughout Europe tillage began to encroach on pasture, grain on wool, and the population to expand accordingly, especially in England. In the course of the eighteenth century clothing woven from cotton ceased to rank as a luxury, and came to be thought of as one of the leading necessities of life.

The results of this change were so stupendous that it is here necessary to trace its development to the present day, because that development is the basis and background of much which has followed.

"Commerce, like war, is an affair of positions to start with."[1] The initial advantage of Great Britain in this respect can be grasped by anyone who takes an ordinary school globe and turns it about until it presents to his eye the largest possible amount of land to be seen on its surface. This aspect of the globe is technically known as 'the land hemisphere'. England is almost at the centre of this hemisphere. In no other place can raw materials be gathered from all parts of the world so easily as in this country. Its insular safety, moreover, conferred on its people an initial advantage in preparing these raw materials for use by consumers. Not forced to maintain large standing armies, a larger proportion of its people than in Europe was available for industry; and the instruments and system of industry they developed were not destroyed by the ravages of war.

In Book II., Chapter XVI., we saw how Flemish and French weavers found sanctuary in England and taught the English their higher technique. It was not, however, till well into the eighteenth century that the natural advantages of England as a centre of industry began to be felt. In 1730 there was scarcely an industry of importance in which England was not excelled in some continental country. By the end of the century British producers had a dominant position in most of them.

Of the three fundamental necessaries of life, food, clothing and shelter, clothing lends itself most readily to industrial organisation; for its raw materials are more durable than food and more portable than those of building. Nearly every dwelling has its own kitchen, but before the end of the seventeenth century the English were fast ceasing to dress in cloth spun and woven in their own houses. Though women long continued to employ their leisure at spinning, as they still employ it by knitting, the making of yarn was mainly in the hands of wage-earners working at home. When parliament had legalised the weaving of cotton, the demand for calico became so great that weavers soon experienced a difficulty in obtaining yarn for their looms. The price of yarn and the wages of spinners increased so fast that a fortune awaited any contrivance for economising labour. A machine patented by Paul of Birmingham in 1738 was not a commercial success. Between 1764 and 1767 Hargreaves invented a machine on a different principle which enabled at least sixteen threads to be spun by a single person. In 1769 and 1775 Arkwright, a Lancashire barber, patented a machine in which he successfully applied the principle used in Paul's abortive invention. By 1779 Crompton had hybridised the principles of Hargreaves' and Arkwright's inventions in a frame which was, therefore, known as 'the mule'.

By these machines yarn was twisted more quickly than weavers could use it, and inventors now turned to the loom. The results were Kay's flying-shuttle and the loom worked by mechanical power which Cartwright brought to the stage of practical production in 1787.

These inventors had seen that some of the energy used to operate machines might be supplied from sources other than the muscles of the workman. Horses were used, but the manufacturers were quick to note that millers had long ago found that water could be made to turn a wheel and roll the stones which ground their grain better than horses. So factories were erected wherever a fall in a stream could be found to drive them. They thus came to be known as 'cotton mills' and Arkwright's machines were described as 'water-frames'. The volume of streams is intermittent, and the spots where an adequate fall can be found limited in number. A demand arose for some constant power greater than the horse could supply, and not tied like the water-wheel to the beds of streams. Before the end of the eighteenth century the inventions of a Scottish mechanic, Watt, supplemented those of Arkwright, Crompton and Cartwright.

Till the first years of that century charcoal was used to extract iron from ore. When charcoal burners had exhausted the English forests the smelting industry was moved for a time to Ireland. In the early years of the eighteenth century it was brought back to England by Abraham Darby, who discovered that iron could be smelted with coke produced from fossilised vegetation which the shrinking crust of this planet had buried and compressed into coal, ages before the existence of man. England was richly stored with this subterranean fuel. Darby's invention cheapened iron, and also increased the importance of mining as a national industry.

As mines deepen the problem of freeing the workings from water increases. Newcomen (1663–1729) devised a machine in which the pressure of the air was used for pumping. At the bottom of the mine was a pump, connected with the surface by a shaft. Some power was needed to lift this shaft which, when raised and released, was heavy enough to drive the water in the pump to the surface. Newcomen conceived the idea of lifting the shaft by suction. At its upper end was a piston in a cylinder. The air was expelled from the cylinder by steam, which was then condensed by injecting cold water into the cylinder. A vacuum was thus created and the pressure of the air on the other side of the piston was sufficient to lift the shaft of the pump. When the air was again admitted to the cylinder the shaft fell and drove the water in the pump to the surface by its weight. The contrivance moved with a series of pauses and jerks, as anyone may see who watches the working model, now at South Kensington Museum.

In the copper and tin mines of Cornwall, remote from the coal fields, the cost of the fuel consumed by the Newcomen engine was a serious matter. The problem of how to reduce the amount of fuel required to drive the engine was attacked by Watt. He saw that the walls of the cylinder were cooled by the water used to condense the steam. He therefore allowed the steam to escape into a separate condenser, and cooled it there, thus leaving the cylinder hot.

In Newcomen's engine all but ·5 per cent of the potential energy in the coal was wasted. With the separate condenser the energy developed was at least twenty times greater. In Watt's engine one ton of coal would do the work which had needed no less than twenty tons in Newcomen's engine. The economy in fuel was enormous, greater perhaps than has since been achieved by any one subsequent invention.

Watt then went on to create a vacuum on the other side of the piston, thus increasing the force of the stroke by adding the weight of the atmosphere to the weight of the shaft which drove the pump.

This double use of the cylinder, together with the separate condenser, greatly reduced the pauses and jerks in the action of the Newcomen engine. The almost continuous action of the piston could thus be used for turning a fly-wheel, and so for producing motion in one direction only.

The incentive to make this further improvement was applied to Watt by his partner Boulton, who in 1781 wrote to him as follows—"The people in London, Manchester and Birmingham are *steam mill mad.* I don't mean to hurry you but I think in the course of a month or two, we should determine to take out a patent for certain methods of producing rotative motion from . . . the fire engine. . . . There is no other Cornwall to be found, and the most likely line for the consumption of our engines is the application of them to mills which is certainly an extensive field".[2]

Boulton and Watt were still clinging to Newcomen's notion of using the pressure of the air to move the piston. Steam was merely employed to create a vacuum behind the piston.

In this same year, 1781, Boulton and Watt heard with alarm that another inventor, Hornblower, was seeking to patent an engine in which the pressure of steam was used as the motive power. They set to work to forestall him and soon placed on the market an engine in which the pressure of steam on the piston began to replace the pressure of the air. It was also made to turn a wheel and could, therefore, be used to drive the spinning frames and looms of the cloth workers.

The pressure of the air can never exceed 14 lbs. to the square inch. By slow and hesitant steps Watt had come to discard this limited source of power, and had learned how to use in its place the pressure of steam which could be increased to almost any extent by increasing the size and strength of the boiler and cylinder.

We know from a letter written by Boulton to Watt's son in 1796 what the steam engine was capable of doing in the closing years of that century.

One bushel (84 lbs.) of Newcastle or Swansey coal

(1) Will raise 30 million lbs. of water 1 foot high.
(2) Will grind & dress 10, or 11, or 12 bushels of wheat, according to the state of it.
(3) Will turn 1000 or more cotton spinning spindles per hour.

(4) Will roll & slit 4 cwt. of bar iron into small nailor's rods.
(5) Will do as much work per hour as ten horses.[3]

These last words refer to the fact that manufacturers who could not obtain water power were driven to use horses to drive their machines. They explain why horse-power is now used as the standard unit in measuring the capacity of engines.

By 1790 the older and more conservative wool trade had adopted the mechanical methods of spinning and weaving employed by the cotton workers. By 1804 the use of steam power in the textile factories became general, and the rapid growth of these industries was raising new problems. In ever-increasing quantities the raw materials and coal had to be brought to the factories, and their finished products had to be delivered to the world at large. Rivers and streams were canalised; but heavy loads had still to be drawn by horses across the watersheds from one canal to another. It was found that a horse could draw a much heavier load in wagons with flanged wheels running on iron rails; and such railways were made to connect the canals. It was then seen that rails could be strengthened to carry the weight of an engine with flanged wheels driven by steam. Such an engine was built by George Stephenson. In 1825 a railroad from Stockton to Darlington was opened for wagons drawn in long trains by a steam locomotive which could move the loads of hundreds of horses at 15 miles an hour, the pace of the fastest mail coach.

Inventors began to devise vehicles driven by steam which could travel on ordinary roads. In the forties a fox-hunting parliament passed a law which required that in front of such vehicles a man must walk displaying a flag; thus restricting their pace to less than four miles an hour. But for this law England, instead of France and America, would have led the way in developing the motor car industry.

The tendency of industries using steam power to concentrate in factories was accelerated by railways which enabled an army of operatives housed near the factory to be fed. Cities, dependent on a network of railways for their daily subsistence, sprang into being and quickly outgrew the capacity of English soil to produce their food. The new power could be easily applied to transport by sea, and in 1838 a vessel crossed the Atlantic under its own steam. The substitution of iron for wood in the construction of ships, and of steam for sails, was soon to render carriage by sea cheaper than carriage by land and almost as safe. By 1850 trade was flowing more freely between English cities and the distant continents than a century before it had flowed between these cities and rural districts of England itself. In the land where this access of physical power was first achieved, its quantitative and qualitative reactions on society can be seen at a glance. Since 1801 the population has grown in the ratio of 1 to 5, while of this 5 the added 4 have been housed in cities, which depend for their daily subsistence on the punctual working of machinery.

The coke which Darby had shown could be used instead of charcoal for smelting iron was produced by baking coal in ovens. In the process inflammable gas was thrown off. In 1799 Murdock, a millwright, employed by Boulton and Watt at the Soho works where their engines were built, thought of using this gas in flares to light up the yards of the works. This presently led to the use of the gas for lighting the works inside. In 1808 certain London streets were lighted with gas. Its use for interiors soon became general in towns.

Occasional accidents showed that coal-gas when mixed with air is explosive. In course of time inventors contrived means of using this explosive mixture of gas and air to move pistons in cylinders, and impart a rotary motion to wheels. The internal combustion engine thus began to appear in its crudest form.

At the opening of the nineteenth century the growth of the commonwealth in England, aided by physical causes, had thus led to a sudden access of man's power over nature. The instruments of this power were in the first instance the inventions of craftsmen and mechanics. Had the change in methods continued to depend upon men of business who were primarily interested in profits it would presently have worked itself out and come to a standstill. But side by side with the process of mechanical invention was proceeding enquiry into physical nature by men working in laboratories whose ruling passion was a thirst for knowledge. It was studies of this kind which the Royal Society had been founded to promote in the seventeenth century. We have seen already how these studies were yielding practical fruit in the eighteenth century. The help of astronomers was used by the government to improve the art of navigating ships. It was also used to remove defects in the calendar, in the system of measuring time established by Julius Caesar. By the close of the eighteenth century the foundations of astronomy, anatomy, chemistry and physics had been firmly laid. They were yielding practical results, and were used to extend indefinitely the control of natural forces which was first achieved by mechanical inventors.

Six hundred years before the Christian era the philosopher, Thales, is said by Pliny to have noticed that amber (ἤλεκτρον) when rubbed with a cloth will attract light objects like feathers. The first scientific work on the subject was published 2200 years later in A.D. 1600 by William Gilbert, physician to Queen Elizabeth. In the following century Otto von Guericke constructed the first machine for generating electric current, which was much improved by Sir Isaac Newton. In 1752 Benjamin Franklin showed that lightning is produced by electric energy, and invented the lightning conductor. Further advances were made in these studies by Cavendish in England, by Coulomb and Ampère in France, by Ohm in Germany and by Volta in Italy. Volta showed that electric current could be produced by placing wet cloth between plates of copper and zinc. The 'Voltaic pile', with various improvements, led to the invention of the primary battery.

The idea, which had first occurred to Ampère, that electric current might be used to transmit signals through wires, solved a practical problem, raised by the growth of railways—the problem of controlling the movement of trains on the lines. Current supplied by Voltaic batteries was strong enough to move the needles of a telegraph, and in 1837 the first electric telegraph was installed on the London and Birmingham railway (afterwards merged in the London and North Western and then in the London Midland and Scottish).

Meanwhile the problem of how to produce electric currents of unlimited strength was approaching solution. In 1825 William Sturgeon of London had discovered that a bar of soft iron shaped like a horseshoe and wrapped with an insulated wire becomes a powerful magnet, so long as electric current is passed through the wire. He had thus shown that magnetism can be produced by electricity. The discovery that electricity can be produced by magnetism was made by Faraday in 1831. By a series of brilliant experiments he found that a copper disc, rotating between the poles of an ordinary magnet, will generate current. This invention is called the magneto. It was afterwards found that current of any strength could be generated by using electro-magnets. To these more powerful generators the name of dynamo was given by Henry Wilde of Manchester in 1867. The magneto and dynamo are both from their nature reversible; that is to say, when a current is passed through them, the armature revolves. In a word, they can also be used as motors. It was thus made possible to convert the power developed by engines or falling water into electric current which could then be distributed over large areas through wires, and again be produced at any point in the area in the form of light and heat as well as of power. This immense control of natural energy is the practical fruit of work done in a laboratory by a scientist seeking to unravel the secrets of nature.

In the course of these brilliant experiments Faraday had found that if a current flowing in a conductor varies, and only if it varies, currents are induced in a neighbouring circuit. This discovery led to the idea of electro-magnetic waves, an idea which Faraday tried to explain by the words 'lines of force'. His explanation was ridiculed by contemporaries, including that brilliant errorist Whewell. Clerk Maxwell presently saw that Faraday had really 'smelt the truth' which his critics had missed. The whole of modern electro-magnetic theory, including 'wireless', is based on Maxwell's translation of Faraday's ideas into mathematical form. In Germany Hertz was to prove that electro-magnetic waves (of the sort now used in wireless) can in fact be refracted and reflected as Maxwell predicted, like waves of light from which they differ only in length. The wireless transmission of signals and sound, perhaps the most potent invention since printing, is one of the fruits of Faraday's work.

The wireless transmission of power strong enough to be used, not only for signals, but also for turning the wheels of industry and for reconversion into light or heat is a problem still to be solved. Its solution will mean a further change in the structure of human society, the extent of which will scarcely be realised till it is reached.

Faraday was a chemist as well as a physicist. When gas was first manufactured for lighting, the tar produced in the process polluted rivers and even springs when they tried to bury it. The discovery that tar contains innumerable free chemicals, including sulphate of ammonia for manuring and the aniline dyes now used in the textile industries, was based on Faraday's amazing grasp of chemical manipulation. The actual discovery of the aniline dyes was made by an Englishman, Perkin. Its commercial development was the work of the Germans. Chemists were also making a wide range of natural products available for use in new directions. Rubber, the sap of certain trees, which now plays an essential part in the structure of machines, is a case in point. Wood is another. Through the work of chemists as well as of mechanists it yields the paper which has given the press the power it wields in human affairs. The cheap production from wood-pulp of thread with the qualities of silk, and in certain respects superior to silk, is already a fact. The synthetic production of cotton and wool will, when it comes, be a further addition to human comfort; but may also reduce to poverty the producers of natural cotton and wool, as rayon has impoverished silk growers in Italy, China and Japan.

Most important of all the materials which chemists have brought into use is oil exuded from rocks. In 1850 James Young patented a process for distilling from the shales of Derbyshire an oil which would burn in lamps, which he called paraffin. His invention at once gave commercial value to the floods of petroleum which poured from springs in America when opened by boring. In 1859 the petroleum industry was started at Oil Creek in Pennsylvania. Within fifty years America alone was producing 50,000,000 barrels a year.

A vastly greater expansion of the oil industry in various parts of the world was due to the work of chemists in improving the process of refinement.

On a previous page we have seen how the use of coal-gas for lighting led to the invention of the internal combustion engine. An engine fed from a gas-main must in the nature of things be stationary. In the latter half of the nineteenth century chemists learned to produce from petroleum a spirit which turned into gas when exposed to a moderate heat. This meant that internal combustion engines could carry the gas required to drive them in liquid form. The internal combustion engine could thus be freed from connection with gas-mains, and be used as a locomotive. Unlike an engine fuelled with coal, it could drive vehicles light enough to run at high speed on ordinary roads. Electric ignition of the gas increased its efficiency. Indiarubber tyres cushioned with air reduced the vibration. The law which forbade such vehicles to be used on English roads was not repealed till the very end of the nineteenth century. The initiative in applying mechanical power to traction on ordinary roads was left meanwhile to French and American inventors.

The internal combustion engine has made it possible to construct vessels which can move like fish in the depths of the sea. No important use has, as yet, been found for these submarine vessels, except to destroy vessels which float on the surface; but that use has radically altered the condition of naval warfare.

In the opening years of the twentieth century internal combustion engines were built which would drive inclined planes through the air with a force great enough to lift the machine and its driver from the ground. This power of flight acquired in our own generation is affecting human society in opposite ways. It is fast creating between all nations that inhabit the earth an intercourse closer than was possible a century ago for the counties of England. It also means that the horrors of war will be felt first not by armies and fleets, but by civil populations massed in industrial cities.

Meanwhile, innumerable inventors were devising machines or processes for producing with a smaller expenditure of human labour goods which mechanical transport could distribute through all the continents. Such inventions proceeded far more rapidly than men could change their habits of life and mind. Two examples will suffice to illustrate the reaction of invention on the structure of human society. The increasing use of oil as fuel has destroyed the livelihood of thousands of miners, and has greatly reduced employment in ships. In recent years the invention of the combine is producing the greatest revolution ever achieved in agriculture. This machine, driven over prairie land by the internal combustion engine, enables wheat to be harvested with no more labour than it takes to plant it. Wheat harvested with the combine on the plains of America and Australia is now being sold in China and India more cheaply than rice can be grown in those countries. The production of rice grown under water cannot be mechanised like the production of wheat. A single American invention is threatening to dislocate an industry which for ages has supported hundreds of millions of peasants in Asia.

Man's increasing mastery of natural forces has not, of course, been confined to machines for producing and distributing wealth. National governments have used this knowledge to devise machines whereby one man can destroy the largest number of their enemies and their enemies' property. With this object in view, the work of chemists in producing high explosives and poison gases has been one important factor. But mechanised transport has reversed the logical result that mechanised war would need fewer soldiers, just as mechanised industry needs fewer hands. The danger of mechanised war when it breaks out is so great that every government involved must employ the whole of its human as well as its material resources. Mechanised transport enables a government to mobilise the whole population of military age and sex in a few months and also to feed them when mobilised. Napoleon took twenty years to drain the manhood of France and put them into the field.

In the early days of the war the highly mechanised armies of Germany were advancing through Belgium with a force which seemed irresistible. Writing in *The Times*, Clutton Brock exclaimed in words pregnant with meaning that this was "freedom betrayed by science". The empires of central Europe were using that mastery of physical forces, which men could never have reached under governments based on authority, to uproot from the world the system of society which had opened to man this knowledge of nature.

The principle of the commonwealth operates to extend the control of human relations to ever-widening circles of men. It tends to the rule of majorities. The control of physical forces to which it has led seems to tend in the opposite direction. Our control of nature reacts on society to render it highly organic. The life of the whole comes to depend on the accurate and continuous working of all its organs. In certain industries like mining, a minority can coerce a whole nation of consumers by refusing to work. A great community which depends for its power on one electrical system, can be paralysed in a moment by the handful of men who control the generating stations. The rulers of one nation which achieves pre-eminence in the knowledge and arts of mechanisation can dream of controlling the world by force.

In the history of the last two hundred years our growing control of natural forces, based on increasing knowledge of what those forces are, is the most significant aspect. We have always to hold in mind the extent to which that control of natural forces has changed, is changing and will always continue to change the volume and structure of human society. The opening of the world in the sixteenth century had brought all the families of mankind to a knowledge of each other. The mutual commerce established thereby made the welfare of each depend on the welfare of all. Humanity was becoming a single society, and was likewise aware of itself as such. The effect of all this was immensely increased by mechanical inventions, and the growing knowledge of natural forces which vastly increased the range and power of mechanical invention. The resources of nature were rendered available to human society as a whole. This greatly increased its size and made every part of it interdependent. It developed a structure which was highly organic so far as material needs were concerned.

How human intelligence can be made to control this highly organic structure is a problem yet to be solved. The power of men to control natural forces has greatly outrun the power of men to control themselves, and thus to control society as a whole. We are now beginning to realise how much more easy it is to change the physical conditions under which we live than to adjust our own habits of mind to the change.

Why are all the proffered solutions so unsatisfactory? What stands in the way of assured, effective solutions and efforts to meet the world's great problem?

The answer is to be found not in any material difficulties but in the natural disingenuousness of everyone in the matter of the common welfare. Let us face this elementary fact of human nature.

Each one of us, long before he begins to take up the large questions of social and political and economic life, has gone far to develop a "way of living" of his own, has built up a complexity of affections, ambitions and submissions, and accepted a thousand uncriticized assumptions. It is in our human nature, as it is in the nature of every living thing, for each individual to defend the "way of living" into which it has fitted itself from the cradle onward. We parody Commodore Decatur in effect and say, "my way of living, right or wrong". We resist changes that invade our developing personalities. We dread foreign and unfamiliar things. Our family, our schoolmates, our personal rivals, loom larger than mankind, our home-town hides the world from us, family pride, patriotism, race prides, defend the precious self at the core of things. We insist we must work, reckon, talk as we are "used" to do. We are all like that. In our hearts all of us, the whole two thousand millions of us, are instinctively on the defensive against the cold great challenge of these new conditions, against this new commandment to change.[4]

There are those who seem to think that men can be brought to change their characters simply by telling them to change. There are others who hold that human nature in the mass is unchangeable. From these counsels of despair it is time to turn, and to face the inexorable question, what are the influences which really change the minds of masses of men. An answer to that question is now more important to the world than further answers to physical problems.

NOTES

[1] Grant Robertson, *England under the Hanoverians*, p. 344.
[2] Dickinson, *James Watt, Craftsman and Engineer*, p. 124.
[3] *Ibid.* p. 181.
[4] Wells, *The New America: The New World*, pp. 14-16.

CHAPTER XXVIII

THE FRENCH REVOLUTION

THROUGHOUT the remaining chapters the reader must hold in mind that when Cornwallis surrendered at Yorktown in 1782, Watt in England, by harnessing the physical energy latent in coal, had set in motion a revolution more subtle, profound and far-reaching even than that which began when the English colonists in America broke from the mother country.

In revenge for the loss of Canada the French monarchy had joined in that struggle. Its sea-power had decided the issue and the pride of England was humbled to the dust. But the fruits of victory, as they touched the lips of the Bourbon dynasty, were turned into ashes. The subsequent cost of the war, which Watt's invention enabled the vanquished country to bear, ruined the French exchequer and destroyed the monarchy. The revolution in which it perished was largely inspired by the history and example of its ancient foe.

In England a long series of steps had converted a kingdom into a commonwealth, with no conspicuous change in its outward appearance. The time-honoured face of the monarchy in front of the altered mechanism registered its movement, but masked its novelty. At the close of the eighteenth century the French still regarded the English as a people ruled by kings from whom they had wrested certain liberties. But after the Declaration of Independence no one could mistake the American colonies for anything but commonwealths. The House of Bourbon was sapping its own foundations when it sent

Frenchmen to fraternise with a people who governed their country so much better than kings had ever governed in France.

The revolution, begun by scattering tea on Boston harbour, was ended when England acknowledged her defeat in 1783. The Peace of Versailles was the Brest-Litovsk[1] of the French monarchy. The constitution, under which the Americans still live, came into force in 1789. In that same year the people of Paris stormed the Bastille and started the French Revolution. But a hundred years were to pass before it could be said that republican institutions were firmly established in France.

The difference was a matter of previous history. The English colonies had developed from the outset on the principle of the commonwealth, and their institutions had reproduced in the colonists the qualities needed for their operation. These institutions were not impaired by the revolution, and were afterwards used as component parts in the framework of a larger national life. But of all this the French, who had no experience in governing themselves, knew little. To them it seemed that the mere abolition of monarchy was the golden road to the freedom and equality that Americans enjoyed. The prophecy of Louis XV., *après moi le déluge*, was the natural sequel to his great-grandfather's premise, *l'état, c'est moi*. In destroying their monarchy the French destroyed the entire mechanism of their national life. To do all this was easier than to copy methods of government which Anglo-Saxons had practised for centuries.

For ten long years France was condemned to endure all the horrors of hunger and anarchy. In Paris power was seized by a rapid succession of groups, who each sought to maintain their authority, first by destroying others who might try to supplant them, and then by enlisting the starving masses into armies which preyed upon neighbouring countries.

As we look back on the state of confusion which existed in France, the efficiency with which her armies were organised and led seems little short of a miracle. We can only explain it by remembering how narrow was the circle from which the French monarchy was able to draw the men who directed public affairs. The great mass of the French people were called upon to supply the rank and file of her armies, and taxes to meet the expenses of the state. The ministers, generals and superior officers, who organised and directed the national resources were, with few exceptions, drawn from a small privileged class who were largely exempt from public burdens. The political system which in England brought men like the Pitts, Wolfe, Hastings or Nelson to positions of command, was wanting in France and indeed in the monarchies of Europe.

The French Revolution destroyed or banished the privileged class, but opened to the vast majority of the people the path to power for all with the natural gift to command. When the privileged class had fled or been slaughtered, every man in France began to feel that he counted for that which he himself was, and not for what his fathers had been. France was the whole of the people who lived in it. They were seized with the sense of nationalism which two centuries earlier had stirred the English in Shakespeare's plays. It spread from France and began to infect Europe at large. Monarchs and the privileged classes about them everywhere trembled. The danger that the bulk of their subjects might join forces with French democracy and hurl them from power was imminent and real.

No group in Paris could hope to control that seething chaos except by virtue of the passions which war provokes. The threat of invasion was needed to distract public attention, while committees of public safety plundered a starving nation. It allowed them to denounce possible rivals as traitors and send them to the scaffold. It helped them to bring masses of starving and dangerous men under military discipline. It enabled them to send them out as crusaders to free men like themselves from bondage throughout Europe. In the early years of the Revolution the rank and file of the French armies were inspired by a genuine and fervent ideal.

The first and most obvious enemy was the Austrian monarchy which was set on saving or avenging the hated queen it had sent to France. The French nobles were preparing for revenge in Austrian territory. The Austrian Netherlands, largely inhabited by a French-speaking people, was the nearest prey. They were easily moved to a revolution supported by French troops. The republic rapidly seized and held the countries which controlled the mouths of the Scheldt, the countries which kings of France had coveted in vain.

Since England had acknowledged her defeat in 1783, Pitt had devoted his mind to the fiscal and social reforms needed to restore the national fortunes, economy of public expenditure, the promotion of trade and industry which was feeling the impulse of mechanisation. He had even encouraged such movements as those for electoral reform and the abolition of slavery in the colonies. For all these projects the paramount need was peace. His heart was set on keeping England out of the wars with which the collapse of the French monarchy was threatening Europe. He was even prepared to ignore the intrigues of the French to provoke a rebellion in Ireland. But the virtual absorption of the Netherlands by France realised the dangers which the battles of Marlborough had been fought to avert. By declaring war on France in 1793 the British Commonwealth threw in its lot with the emperors and kings who were destined to struggle for long years to preserve their thrones from the oncoming tide of the French Revolution. The conflict was thus extended from the continent of Europe to the world at large. Before it closed the United States was again at war with the parent commonwealth from which it had sprung.

While Frenchmen at home were slaughtering each other, Frenchmen on the frontiers faced by the enemies of France were learning to obey their officers, and discovering those who were worth obeying. In 1793, whilst Robespierre was drenching the streets of Paris in blood, an artillery officer, Bonaparte, was breaching the walls of Toulon where the British fleet was supporting a royalist garrison. In 1794 Robespierre was overpowered and sent to the guillotine by Barras, who now became the dominant figure. Though the daily butcheries ceased, the terrorists strengthened their hold on office by a change in the constitution. Moderates began to support the surviving royalists. In October 1795 Barras and his fellow-directors, threatened by a formidable rising, entrusted their defence to Napoleon, who quickly sent for the guns and cleared the streets of Paris with grapeshot. In 1796 he was given command of the armies sent to 'liberate' Italy from Austrian, Papal and Bourbon rule.

By April 1797 Napoleon was master of northern Italy and had forced Austria to sign the preliminaries of peace at Leoben. The wealth and treasures of Italy were drained into France and used to support her armies in comfort. The victorious general was the idol of his troops. As in Rome in the days of Marius, Sulla and Caesar, the real authority had passed from a so-called republic to the general at the head of the armies wherever he was. Henceforth Napoleon, himself an Italian, felt himself destined to realise the aims of Caesar on a grandiose scale. From the outset he dreamed of mastering not Europe only, but a world wider than Caesar had known. In the power of England he saw the obstacle which lay in that path. But with all his greatness he failed to realise how much more difficult it is to create victorious fleets than armies. The privileged class had supplied the officers who held the responsible posts in the French navy. They had most of them fled or been killed in the terror. More time and experience was needed to fill their posts than to officer the army from subordinate ranks.

In the light of after-events Napoleon might have made himself master of Europe in a very short time, had he applied himself to that task in 1797 fresh from the conquest of northern Italy. With its vast resources behind him he might then have developed a naval power strong enough to strangle British trade and at length acquire control of the sea. The British Commonwealth would then have been doomed. After his victories in Italy the Directory urged him to invade England; but when Admirals Jervis and Nelson had defeated the Spanish fleet off Cape St. Vincent and Duncan had beaten the Dutch at Camperdown in 1797, Napoleon saw clearly enough the folly of such projects. He conceived, however, the idea of countering the naval power of England by raising the Eastern world against her. The nature of these far-reaching plans is clearly expressed in the secret decree signed by the Directory on April 12, 1798, which Napoleon had drawn with his own hand:

> The army of the East shall take possession of Egypt; the Commander-in-chief shall chase the English from all their possessions in the East which he can reach. . . . He shall have the Isthmus of Suez cut through; and he shall take all the steps necessary to assure the free and exclusive possession of the Red Sea to the French Republic.[2]

In the summer of 1798 Napoleon set sail from

Toulon, evaded the British fleet, seized Malta, landed his army at Alexandria and mastered Egypt at the battle of the Pyramids.

In August Nelson destroyed his fleet off the mouths of the Nile, and with it all hope of returning to France with his army by sea. Napoleon now entertained the idea of marching back to Europe by land and of taking Constantinople *en route*. He turned his armies to the north, and the news of his conquest of Palestine more than obscured in France the strategic failure of the eastern campaign. The defence of Acre by Sir Sidney Smith, on the coast opposite the Lake of Galilee, checked his advance into Syria and saved him from the blunder he afterwards made in marching on Moscow. He returned to Egypt and in July 1799 utterly destroyed the army which the Turks had landed at Aboukir Bay to bar his retreat.

The battle of the Nile had enabled Pitt to unite Austria and Russia in an effort, supported by British gold, to force back the armies of France to her own frontiers. While Napoleon was winning his last battle in Egypt, the Russian General Suvaroff was defeating the French in Italy. Their armies were only saved from destruction by the Austrian failure to support Suvaroff. The Tzar, in disgust, broke with Austria, while Napoleon escaped from Egypt and landed in France on October 9.

NOTES

[1] See below, p. 660.

[2] *The Cambridge Modern History*, vol. viii. p. 597.

CHAPTER XXIX

UNION OF GREAT BRITAIN AND IRELAND

ON what do the destinies of empires hang? . . . If instead of the expedition of Egypt,—I had made that of Ireland . . what would England have been to-day? And the Continent? And the political world? [1]

Such were the thoughts of Napoleon in the closing years of his life, and to grasp their full significance it is necessary to recall that in 1782 the British parliament had solemnly renounced all jurisdiction over Ireland. An exclusive right to make laws for Ireland was thereafter vested in the Irish parliament. But none the less the king appointed the viceroy and the viceroy appointed the chancellor and his ministers. His disastrous attempt to coerce the American colonies had now compelled George III. to accept the principle that he must act on the advice of the ministers who commanded support for the time being in the House of Commons. The result was that the viceroy in Ireland was in fact appointed by the ministry responsible to the British parliament. The Irish parliament could not control the Irish executive; but could only paralyse its action. The American revolution had recreated in Ireland the system which had led in America to that revolution. Fitzgibbon, the chancellor, a strong reactionary, was always in conflict with Grattan, who led the Irish parliament.

The dangers involved in this system were shown when Pitt was threatening war over Nootka Sound. A pamphlet was published over the signature 'Hibernicus' which called on the Irish parliament to declare that Ireland was neutral if England went to war with Spain. The writer was Wolfe Tone. In 1791 he founded a society by which he proposed to unite Catholics and Protestants in a movement to reform the Irish constitution. It was, therefore, called the United Irishmen. In 1795 it was reconstructed with the avowed object of establishing a republic in Ireland with the help of the French, who were now at war with Great Britain. Tone himself went to France to persuade the Directory to invade Ireland. In December 1796 Tone set out with General Hoche from Brest with 15,000 men and arms to equip 41,000 rebels in Ireland. There were close on 300,000 United Irishmen waiting for arms. A violent storm prevented this expedition from landing. The viceroy's government was paralysed by the Irish parliament led by Grattan. It was powerless to maintain order and would have been at the mercy of Hoche and Tone had they been able to land. The general confusion had defeated the plan of uniting Protestants with the Catholics in alliance with the French. Tone himself had adopted the Catholic religion. The old religious conflict was acutely revived, and in Ulster the Protestants formed the Orange societies to defend themselves against the United Irishmen. The Earl of Clare, as Fitzgibbon had now become, declared martial law and armed the loyalists to enforce it. Organised as yeomanry regiments, they inflicted frightful barbarities on the Catholic peasants. In May 1798 the peasants broke into open revolt, which was bloodily quelled by the Protestant yeomanry, and the rebels were shipped by thousands as convicts to Australia. Too late to help them Humbert, a French commander, succeeded in landing with rather more than 1000 men on August 6, 1798. After one initial success he surrendered with all his men on September 8; but the rebels who had joined him were ruthlessly slaughtered. Wolfe Tone with a larger French expedition was captured at sea on October 12 and died by his own hand.

For the moment the danger of a further invasion from France was averted by the victory of Nelson at the mouth of the Nile. But experience had now satisfied Pitt that a government in Dublin unable to control the Irish legislature was powerless to prevent Catholics and Protestants from slaughtering each other, or to deal with French attempts supported by Irish rebels to use Ireland as a basis from which to attack Great Britain.

The British parliament had no legal power to abolish the Irish parliament, which could only abolish itself. It largely consisted of members for 'rotten boroughs' which were bought and sold, and were worth in the market from £14,000 to £16,000 a piece. Pitt offered to buy them all out for a sum of £1,260,000 and to give them seats in the British parliament. A number of members were persuaded to vote for the union by giving them titles. The times were desperate and by such means a majority was obtained in the Irish parliament. It voted itself out of existence in 1800.

The Irish Catholics had been given the vote, but were not allowed to sit in their parliament. To conciliate Catholic opinion Pitt had promised to pass legislation allowing Catholics to sit in the parliament of the United Kingdom, and to remove other disabilities. The union came into effect on January 1, 1801, and Pitt at once proposed a measure for Catholic emancipation. Lord Clare, the Archbishop of Canterbury and the Primate of Ireland combined to persuade George III. that the measure proposed was contrary to the oath he had taken when crowned. In February 1801, for the last time, the king, encouraged by their support, resolved to reject the advice of his minister—and again with fatal results. Pitt sent in his resignation, and the promise made to the Catholics was only redeemed in 1829, long after his death, and too late to reconcile the Irish

Catholics to the union.

In 1803 Robert Emmet got into touch with Napoleon and raised a second rebellion in Ireland. It was easily suppressed and Emmet was hanged. But Tone and Emmet were enshrined as the martyrs of Irish nationalism. Their example remained to hallow future attempts to use the hour of England's weakness to throw off her yoke.

NOTE

[1] Las Cases, *Mémoires de Sainte-Hélène*, vol. ii. p. 335 (ed. 1823).

CHAPTER XXX

NAPOLEON

When Napoleon landed in France in October 1799, the country rang with the news of his recent victory at Aboukir. The fact that his army had been left to their fate in Egypt was overlooked. The soldiers in Paris rallied to his side. At his bidding they dissolved the Directory and Assembly within one month of his landing in France. By a plebiscite the nation endorsed their action, and elected Napoleon as 'First Consul'. By a second plebiscite in 1802 he was given the title for life. By a third he was given the style of monarchy without further disguise, and Napoleon became Emperor of the French with the right of transmitting it to his heirs. For fifteen years he remained the undisputed master of France, wielding authority to rule by virtue of inherent capacity and not by inherited right—the first of the modern dictators.

The Revolution had destroyed the monarchy, but had failed to create in its place any system deserving the name of a government. The conditions which prevailed in France from 1789 to 1799 can best be described as anarchy. Napoleon established a government more efficient than any which France had known in her history. Under the monarchy responsible posts were filled from the narrow circle of the titled nobility. After its fall they were seized by the demagogues who best knew how to exploit the public passions in their own interests. Napoleon filled them with men distinguished by real capacity for administration. Under the monarchy the law was a medley of local customs in which all kinds of privileges were entrenched. The Revolution which swept this away had failed to create anything in its place. As First Consul Napoleon created a simple and unified law, which henceforward prevailed not only in France but in many of the countries he conquered. The Code Napoléon was the greatest constructive achievement ever attained in the realm of law, in so short a time.

Napoleon knew what he wanted, and his mind worked with incredible speed. His power to do whatever he wanted was, in fact, based, not on plebiscites, but on the implicit obedience of the armies he led. But this source of power could only remain so long as his armies were refreshed by victories, and the plunder they brought. He could not afford to accept the reverses which the arms of France had sustained in his absence. Apart from the fact that he felt himself destined to master Europe and the world, war with Austria and England was to him a vital necessity. In 1800 he crossed the Alps and reconquered Italy. In December Moreau defeated the Austrians at Hohenlinden. In February 1801 the Austrian Emperor at Lunéville signed a peace which accepted the Rhine as the frontier of France, and recognised four republics, two in Italy, one in Switzerland, another in the Netherlands, outposts of France at either end of the Rhine frontier.

At this juncture Pitt resigned, because George III. had refused to allow him to introduce the bill to emancipate Catholics, which Pitt had promised to Ireland. In March 1802 his successor, Addington, signed the Peace of Amiens with France. To Napoleon the peace was no more than a truce which he needed to organise his final attack on the power which commanded the sea. In May 1803 the war was renewed, and Napoleon massed his armies at Boulogne where a great flotilla had long been prepared to convey them across the Channel. In 1805 Pitt, who had now returned to office, secured the alliance of Russia and Austria against Napoleon. In October Nelson destroyed the combined fleets of France and Spain at Trafalgar. Napoleon, seeing that all hope of invading England was gone, turned eastwards to deal with Austria and Russia and destroyed their armies at Austerlitz. In January 1806 a peace between Austria and France was signed at Pressburg. The Holy Roman Empire, which lay like a shadow across the path which Napoleon had traced for himself, was brought to an end, though Francis was suffered to retain the title of Emperor of Austria.

England, whose fleet stood between him and the world dominion to which he aspired, was to Napoleon the essential enemy. After Trafalgar his efforts were directed to destroying the foreign trade which enabled England to live and maintain her fleet. His paramount aim was to ruin her by excluding her merchants from all the markets of Europe. His immediate aim was, therefore, to acquire control of the continent. This in practice meant the inclusion of all Europe in one empire ruled by himself.

When Napoleon extinguished the Holy Roman Empire in 1806, Germany was divided into some 300 states, which were constantly fighting each other. In the course of these struggles the kingdom of Prussia had acquired a power which its German neighbours viewed with jealousy and alarm. In attacking Prussia Napoleon could count on the aid of forces sent by Bavaria, Würtemberg and German princes along the Rhine. In October 1806 the Prussian army was utterly defeated at Jena. Napoleon entered Berlin and from that city forbade all commerce with the British Isles. Spain, Naples, Holland and all his other allies were required to conform. "I have every reason to hope", he wrote, "that this measure will deal a deadly blow to England." In 1807 England replied by orders in council which made neutral ships trading with France and her allies subject to confiscation.

At this juncture, when Napoleon was preparing to wipe Prussia from the map of Europe, Alexander I., Emperor of Russia, decided to throw in his lot with him. In July 1807 the two Emperors met on a raft in the Niemen at Tilsit. Alexander agreed that Denmark, Sweden, Portugal and Austria should be forced to join in the continental blockade; but refused to countenance the utter destruction of Prussia. Napoleon agreed to allow Frederick William III. to retain about half his kingdom and lived to regret this concession to the feelings of his Russian ally.

Canning, who was now Foreign Minister, replied by seizing the Danish fleet and also Heligoland, an island in the North Sea which belonged to the Danes. Napoleon invaded Portugal, and in 1808 seized the throne of Spain for his brother Joseph in order to ensure that the whole peninsula should take its part in the continental blockade of Great Britain.

The events which followed mark the turn in the tide of Napoleon's fortunes. It now became clear that in order to enforce the blockade against England, Europe must submit to the empire of France, with members of the Bonaparte family or his favourite generals ruling subordinate kingdoms. Illiterate and caste-ridden peasants began to realise that the costs of this empire were to be met in terms of their own money and blood. The hope of liberty, which had spread through Europe from France, was quenched by the power which raised it. Patriots who had welcomed the French armies as friends sent to deliver them from the rule of the privileged classes began to find them the worst of oppressors, with a strong and pitiless tyrant at their head.

This revulsion began in Spain and Portugal, the most caste-ridden countries in Europe. When in 1808 Napoleon dethroned their worthless kings to make room for his general Murat and his brother Joseph, the whole population rose in rebellion. The British government came to their aid with an army led by Sir Arthur Wellesley. In July 18,000 French soldiers under Dupont surrendered at Baylen, 3000 more had already been killed in battle. In August the British defeated the French at Vimiero. Napoleon hastened to restore the position in Spain and occupied Madrid; but the British army was saved by the skilful retreat of Moore to Corunna.

The course of events in Spain and Portugal had shown clearly enough the fate which awaited the ancient dynasties at Napoleon's hands. His absence in Spain nerved Francis of Austria to renew the struggle with France. Napoleon was thus driven to leave the Peninsula war to subordinate generals. Hastening back to central Europe he won a series of victories in 1809 and entered Vienna. But these hard-fought battles, especially Wagram, showed that the peoples of Europe were finding the little finger of Napoleon's empire thicker than the thigh of their own dynasties. He was fast uniting the nations in support of their ancient rulers. But the victories which always attended his presence in the field increased his self-confidence, and his mind was set more firmly than ever on the conquest of India by way of Russia. There, as in western Europe, his measures to destroy trade with Great Britain were estranging the nobles and mercantile classes.

In 1810 Napoleon married the daughter of Francis of Austria. In 1811 she bore him the King of Rome, a title conferred on the infant before his birth.

The idea of Christendom with one emperor at its head was cherished in Vienna till the eighteenth century. The Habsburgs were deeply outraged when Peter the Great assumed the imperial title, and Peter's successor can have shed no tears when he heard that Napoleon had extinguished the Holy

Roman Empire. The Romanovs were now the only surviving heirs to the claims of the Caesars. Such dreams were rudely disturbed when Napoleon married a Habsburg princess, and proclaimed her son as 'the King of Rome'. From the ashes of the Holy Roman Empire was rising a Caesarism stronger than any which had come into being since Charles the Great.

Napoleon, who saw where matters were tending in Russia, determined to sweep his doubtful ally from his path as he had swept Austria and Prussia. With Russia at his feet, he would then be free to realise his youthful dream of conquering India. By this conquest he would finally destroy the power of England. In the spring of 1812 he collected an army of 680,000 men. Of these more than half were Italians, Illyrians, Poles, Austrians and Germans. In June he crossed the Niemen, and with ever-increasing losses fought his way through the heart of Russia. In September he entered and occupied Moscow. In the course of the next few days the city burst into flames. A month later Napoleon was forced to evacuate Moscow and begin his retreat. His Polish, Italian and German troops were becoming a rabble, and the stragglers were massacred in detail by the peasants. Guerilla bands everywhere rose to support the regular armies of the Tzar. As the Russian winter set in multitudes perished of hunger and cold. Not one-sixth part of Napoleon's army ever recrossed the Niemen. More than 500,000 were lost in Russia with 1000 guns and 150,000 horses. By this time Napoleon had abandoned his army. On December 5 he set out with a small escort and reached Paris in a fortnight.

In the years which had followed the battles of Austerlitz and Jena the peoples of central Europe had realised that the victories of Napoleon had brought them no freedom but only compulsion to serve in his armies and grinding taxation. For the first time in their history the German peoples began to unite in a common resolve to throw off the yoke of a foreign oppressor. The most active centres of the movement were the university classrooms. Leadership was provided by Stein in that remnant of Prussia which Napoleon had spared as the price of his Russian alliance in 1807. Austria and Prussia united with Russia and England to drive the French armies back to the frontiers of France.

Divided counsels, which always hamper the action of allies, delayed the effect of their overwhelming numbers. After several defeats they were still able to muster at Leipzig 300,000 men, while Napoleon's army had shrunk to 190,000. In the fighting which lasted four days 120,000 were killed and wounded. The Saxon troops who were still serving Napoleon changed sides in the course of the battle. His entire army might have been captured if a single commander had directed the allied forces. As it was, he escaped, and was able to cross the Rhine with 70,000 men. On French soil he beat his pursuers in several battles; but the odds were too heavy, even for him. The allies occupied Paris, and Wellington, who had driven the French from Spain and crossed the Pyrenees, was approaching from the south. In April 1814 Napoleon was compelled by his war-weary generals to agree to retire to the island of Elba. The Bourbons were restored to the throne of France in the person of Louis XVIII., while the allies met at Vienna to redistribute the map of Europe.

In March 1815 the Congress was interrupted by the sudden return of Napoleon from Elba. The soldiers of France rallied to his side. In June he led them to defeat at the battle of Waterloo. Napoleon was sent on a British ship to end his days on St. Helena, while the Congress of Vienna resumed its proceedings.

CHAPTER XXXI

THE CONGRESS OF VIENNA

As we have seen in the first part of this work, monarchy, in the original and absolute sense of that word, rests on a supernatural authority. The right of a monarch to rule is conferred by God from above, and not from below by the people he rules. A king who devoutly believes this theory must tend to think of himself as of greater importance than all his subjects taken together. In the mind of Louis XIV. it had led to the doctrine expressed in the words *l'état, c'est moi*—I myself am the state. The creation of kingdoms and empires in separate pieces scattered about Europe like private estates was an expression of this idea.

In England this idea of the state had been undermined by the fact that the people themselves slowly and half unconsciously developed a power of governing themselves. Because they did so they came to think of themselves as the state. The result was somewhat obscured by the fact that a limited monarchy was maintained. But when the American colonists had renounced their allegiance to the crown and governed themselves as a federal republic, the idea that the people themselves were the state was unmistakeably realised. Nationalism was a product of British institutions, carried to their logical expression in a country free from the forms and fetters of tradition. It spread like a fire to France and destroyed the monarchy and privileged classes. The French Revolution was in fact the negation of the doctrine of monarchy as carried to its ultimate conclusion by Bourbon kings. The example of France began to awake a sense of nationalism in all the peoples of Europe. Had France, like America, been able to show how a nation can govern itself, governments based on a supernatural authority would sooner have vanished from the continent of Europe.

Order was only restored in France by a soldier of genius, who used her armies to conquer and plunder Europe in the name of the French Revolution. In a few years he had ranged the rising sense of nationalism in the nations of Europe against the country from which it had spread to them. His exactions made them regard their dynastic governments as national institutions. He was beaten in the end by nations who rallied to defend their princes. When the final victory was won and the time came to create some order from the ruins left by two decades of warfare, it was princes, rather than peoples, who gathered at Vienna to settle the future map of Europe. At the end of a war won by the peoples, the settlement was mainly determined by dynastic tradition. The national feeling which the French Revolution had kindled and fanned was suppressed, and left to break out and find its expression in the next generation.

Truths which are plain beyond question in the light of after events are not often perceived by contemporaries. The dynastic governments which met at Vienna were blind to the fact that the peoples rather than their governments had defeated Napoleon's ambitions. The rising force of nationalism, which was destined to dominate the world in the coming generations, received no expression in the settlements they made—settlements conceived on the principle of restoring the ancient dynasties. In accordance with this principle, the monarchy in Piedmont was preserved, but the rest of northern Italy was restored to the Austrian Empire. To the south of these territories the daughter of the Austrian

Emperor, and wife of Napoleon, was given, for her maintenance, a duchy with her capital at Florence. The Papal States were restored to the Pope. The Bourbon dynasties were re-established in Naples, in Spain and in France. Poland, shorn of the regions annexed to Prussia and Austria, became an unwilling dependency of the Russian autocracy.

The assembled diplomats were set on creating a dynastic barrier to oppose any recurrence of revolutionary danger from France. At the north of her frontier Catholic and French-speaking Belgium was merged into Holland, under the rule of the House of Orange. South of the Netherlands an enlarged and strengthened Prussia under the Hohenzollerns was to act as guardian on the Rhine.

The Holy Roman Empire had vanished beyond recall. In its place was created a German Confederation, with a diet to control it and develop its constitution, in which Austria secured the presidency. This new combination was rendered more easy by the fact that the changes imposed by Napoleon had reduced the 300 German states which had claimed sovereignty to no more than 39, a change which the Congress of Vienna preserved. This German Confederation was no more than a league of sovereign German states, in which Austria secured the predominant voice. And Austria was set on thwarting the growing power of Prussia.

The dynastic principle led to a more statesmanlike treatment of France than republican Germany received in the hour of defeat a century later. It meant restoring to power a king whose brother and predecessor had perished in the French Revolution. The victors perceived the unwisdom of making the regime they imposed upon France the symbol of utter humiliation. The man who saw this most clearly was Wellington, the one soldier of genius who emerged in the struggle and won the battle which closed it. The victor of Waterloo was a statesman to whom emperors and kings had to listen when he spoke to them. Both before and after Waterloo the government imposed by the victors on France was admitted to their counsels at Vienna. The ablest of Napoleon's ministers, Talleyrand, had hastened to place at the service of Louis XVIII. those incomparable talents which secured for the vanquished country a real voice in the terms of settlement.

CHAPTER XXXII

THE OVERSEA SETTLEMENT LEFT TO ENGLAND

THE assertion of maritime power by England, especially of the right to search ships for contraband of war, had enabled Napoleon at one time to combine the leading powers of Europe for her destruction. In self-defence England had tightened her hold on the sea, till in 1812 she had blundered once more into a fratricidal war with her former colonists in America, at the moment when nations in Europe were at last combining to throw off the yoke of their common oppressor Napoleon. The inventions of mechanists like Arkwright, Crompton and Watt, for which the maritime power of England had secured free scope, enabled her to supply the sinews of war in which Europe, impoverished by Napoleon, was lacking. In his final downfall the maritime power of England was a factor second in importance to no other. The American Commonwealth was not represented at Vienna, and the rights of neutrals in war were not even discussed at the Congress. Every yard of territory that France and Holland had once acquired beyond the seas was in British hands, and England was left by the Congress to do what she chose with them.

The settlement she made was designed to remove any chance that the French might again challenge her position in India. Their original settlements at Mahé, Karikal, Pondicherry and Chandernagore were restored, and remain in their hands till this day, a concession designed to save the prestige of the French monarchy. But all the points which controlled the maritime route to India were retained by the British—the Cape Colony, and also Mauritius and the other French islands which lay on the route from the Cape to India. For the Cape £7,000,000 was paid to the Netherlands to be spent on constructing forts to protect their southern frontiers against the French. The Dutch possessions of Ceylon and Cochin on the mainland of India were retained by the British. Sumatra, Java and the other East Indian islands were returned to the Netherlands. The island of Singapore, which Sir Stamford Raffles had annexed to secure control of the Straits of Malacca and the route to China, was retained by Great Britain.

In the West Indies she retained Trinidad, St. Lucia and Tobago, returning to France the rest of the islands she had formerly occupied. In the Mediterranean she kept Malta, Corfu and the islands adjacent thereto.

In the North Sea the island of Heligoland, which the British had taken from the Danes in 1807, was formally ceded to Great Britain in 1814.

CHAPTER XXXIII

THE GRAND ALLIANCE

At Vienna the concert of Europe had come into being. When the Congress closed the dominant figure in its counsels was the Tzar, whose position in some ways resembled that which President Wilson afterwards filled at the Conference of Paris. Like Wilson he dreamed of creating a body to order the general affairs of mankind. In September 1815 he invited the governments of Europe to recognise that all human authority is derived from God, and to join in 'a Holy Alliance' to assert that principle. Great Britain declined to respond. The Pope stood aloof; but all other sovereigns in Christendom signed. In November, however, Alexander persuaded Great Britain to unite with Russia, Austria and Prussia in a Grand Alliance, the terms of which were less in the air. Its immediate object, with which Great Britain was in genuine accord, was to prevent any further outbreak in France which might threaten the peace of Europe. But the treaty went further than this. By Article 6 the allies agreed that in order

> to consolidate the connections which at the present moment so closely unite the four Sovereigns for the happiness of the world, the High Contracting Parties have agreed to renew their meetings at fixed periods, either under the immediate auspices of the Sovereigns themselves or by their respective Ministers, for the purpose of consulting upon their common interests, and for the consideration of the measures which at each of these periods shall be considered the most salutary for the repose and prosperity of nations and for the maintenance of the peace of Europe.[1]

Alexander hoped through this Article to realise the

dreams of a world-government foreshadowed in the Holy Alliance, and Castlereagh must have accepted it only to avoid giving him offence. England was prepared to co-operate with Russia, Austria and Prussia with regard to future relations between the states which emerged from the Congress of Vienna. She was also prepared to join them in repressing a fresh revolution in France. But, with this exception, she was not prepared to use the Alliance to interfere in the domestic affairs of nations other than France. To the courts of Russia, Austria and Prussia it was clear enough that revolutions in countries other than France might disturb international relations as established at Vienna. From their nature they were deeply concerned to repress popular movements before they came to a head and tried to use the power and authority of the Grand Alliance for that purpose. Castlereagh and Canning, who succeeded him, were firmly resolved not to commit the British government to a policy of general interference in the internal affairs of nations, which in practice meant a policy of repressing national movements. For the question how such national movements could be kept from disturbing the relations of states to each other and provoking wars, they had no solution to offer. They simply refused to co-operate in the various measures proposed by the monarchs for suppressing such popular movements as threatened to impair the authority of dynastic governments in Europe.

In a few years the monarchs were proposing to apply such measures to the new world as well as to the old, and Canning passed from refusal to co-operate to active opposition. When Napoleon reduced Spain to the status of a French dependency the Spanish colonies in America had established national governments of their own; Ferdinand, restored to his throne, thought to recover his oversea empire, and sent troops to America to force the colonists to acknowledge his sovereignty.

In 1818 the allies agreed to remove the forces which had occupied France, and Louis XVIII. was himself admitted to the Grand Alliance and pledged to the task of maintaining dynastic government in Europe. In 1820 Spain, impoverished by the effort to reconquer her American empire, was threatened with revolution. Louis XVIII. proposed that France should support the Spanish dynasty, as the instrument of the Grand Alliance, and Ferdinand of Spain invoked its aid. At the Conference of Verona, which met to consider the matter, England made it clear that she would have nothing to do with such projects and severed her connection with the Alliance. A French army, nevertheless, marched into Spain and restored the despotic power of Ferdinand. He was clearly unequal to the task of compelling the colonies to acknowledge his sovereignty. The question whether the Grand Alliance would send troops across the Atlantic to do this for him hung in the balance.

When these colonies had severed their connection with Spain, British merchants had found there an opening for the trade which Napoleon was then excluding from Europe. This promising market would be closed if the colonies were included once more in the empire of Spain. Apart from their natural sympathies the British had strong commercial motives for thwarting the schemes of the Grand Alliance for reconquering these colonies for the Spanish crown. The United States, for obvious political reasons, was deeply disturbed by the prospect of armies from Europe landing on American soil. So Canning proposed that the British and American Commonwealths should together issue a declaration that any attempt on the part of the Grand Alliance to reconquer the Spanish dominions in America would be jointly opposed by their maritime power. President Monroe was shy of a plan which amounted in fact to an Anglo-American alliance; but the end in view was achieved by the separate action of both governments. The allied powers were informed by Canning that England would refuse to countenance any action on their part to reconquer for Spain her American colonies. On December 2, 1823, in a message to Congress, President Monroe declared that the United States would "consider any attempt on their part to extend their system to any portion of this hemisphere as dangerous to our peace and safety".[2]

In 1825 London, following the example previously set by Washington, formally recognised the independence of the Spanish colonies on the mainland of America. The Grand Alliance was thus led to realise that its power to uphold dynastic interests against popular movements was limited to Europe by the maritime power of the British and American Commonwealths.

NOTES

[1] Webster, *Congress of Vienna*, p. 144.
[2] Henderson, *American Diplomatic Operations*, p. 337.

CHAPTER XXXIV

RUSSIA IN CENTRAL ASIA

THE schemes of the Grand Alliance for extending its influence from Europe to America were thus finally thwarted in 1825. In that year Alexander died. For the next thirty years his brother Nicholas I. ruled with an iron resolve to protect his dynasty from the fate which had overtaken the Bourbons in 1789. His fears as to what would happen in Russia, if ever the system of authority inherited from Byzantium should collapse, were verified a century later. Alexander had abolished the secret police. Nicholas revived it and, under his rule, it became the real power in the government of Russia, and has so remained to the present day. In 1828 a rigorous censorship was established. In 1831 the Poles were deprived of their constitution, and Poland became a province of Russia. In 1839 all sects which denied the authority of the national church were suppressed. Nearly half the people of Russia were serfs attached to the soil whose persons were liable to sale by their owners. Peasant revolts were the order of the day, but were easily and ruthlessly suppressed by the army, on the maintenance of which a large proportion of the public revenue was spent. The policy was adopted of sending the rebels to colonise Siberia. The peasants, indeed, came to regard its wastes as a field of comparative freedom, often committing offences in Russia in order to be sent there.

It was this movement of colonisation which led to the great extension of the Russian Empire over Turkestan, the country which Genghis-Khan and his Mongol hordes had seized from Mohammed Shah in 1220. In the seventeenth century the Russian hunters and traders who crossed the Urals had kept to the desolate regions near the Arctic Circle, where furs were obtained. But even if Turkestan had yielded the ermine and sable they sought, their numbers were far too small to attempt the conquest of the warm and populous regions to the south. It was otherwise with the parties of colonists sent by the government of Nicholas under strong military escort. Since the days of Peter the Great the Russian army had been organised and equipped on western lines. It was now in force in Siberia and its Cossack regiments were thoroughly competent to deal with the Turkish tribes wherever they came into contact with them. When Nicholas died in 1855 his army had added to his empire the region east of the Caspian, to the frontiers of Afghanistan, as far east as the watershed of the mountains through which Genghis had forced his way, in extent some 742,000 square miles.

For thirty years the reactionary policy of Nicholas, especially in Poland, had antagonised liberal opinion in France and England. As the Russian conquest of Turkestan brought Cossack regiments nearer to India, the British aversion to Russia was inflamed to a point which led to the outbreak of the Crimean war. Exhausted by the effort to fight the English, French, Turks and Italians in the Crimea, Russia was no longer able to exert that influence in Europe which Alexander I., and to a lesser degree his successor, had wielded.

CHAPTER XXXV

REVOLUTIONS OF 1830 AND 1848: THEIR EFFECT IN THE NETHERLANDS AND POLAND

FEARS that a further upheaval in France might disturb the settlements made at Vienna were justified by events. In 1824 Louis XVIII. was succeeded by his brother Charles X.

His sovereignty claimed to be a government by divine right, supporting and supported by the Church in an attempt to wean men's minds from the recollection of the Revolution and the Empire.[1]

In July 1830, Charles X. was driven from France by a sudden revolution in Paris. But the French people outside Paris were not prepared to risk the horrors which had followed the Revolution of 1789, and their views were voiced by the legislators whom Charles X. had dismissed. The revolution of 1830 was quickly closed by a compromise which brought to the throne the Duke of Orleans, Louis-Philippe, as a constitutional monarch, with a title based upon popular suffrage.

In February 1848 Louis-Philippe was driven from the throne by a third revolution in Paris. The second republic was established, in which Louis-Napoleon, the nephew of Bonaparte, was the dominating figure. In November 1852 Louis-Napoleon was created hereditary Emperor of the French by a plebiscite. Like Louis-Philippe, he reigned for some eighteen years.

These two revolutions in Paris in 1830 and 1848 are pivotal points in the history of Europe in the first half of the nineteenth century. They mark the successive stages whereby the rising sense of nationalism shattered the dynastic settlements made at the Congress of Vienna.

The Paris revolution of 1830 was immediately

followed by rebellions in Brussels, in Poland, in Rome and in various German states. A conflagration throughout Europe was only prevented by the prudence of Louis-Philippe in refusing to risk his throne in a war either with England, Russia or Austria.

The Congress of Vienna had sought to prevent the domination of Belgium by France by annexing Belgium to Holland. The intention had been to unite the Netherlands under the House of Orange as one of the great European powers, strong enough of itself to resist the ambitions of France to dominate the mouths of the Rhine and the ports of the North Sea. These intentions were defeated by the incapacity of the Protestant Dutch and their king to consider the national feelings of the Catholic Belgians, whose language was French. The maintenance of Dutch as the only official language excluded the Belgians from any important share in the public offices or in public life.

In August 1830 the population in Brussels, encouraged by the outbreak in Paris in July, rose in rebellion. King William's troops were expelled from the town, and the crown of Belgium was offered to the Duke of Nemours, a son of Louis-Philippe, who wisely declined the honour. It was then conferred on Prince Leopold of Saxe-Coburg. In 1832 the independence of Belgium was guaranteed by England, France, Austria, Prussia and Russia. It was thus hoped to secure Belgium once for all from absorption by any leading power in Europe. For centuries England had struggled against that danger. In the light of after events King William's failure to maintain the union of Belgium with Holland must be reckoned as one of the great disappointments of history. That the task imposed on him was not from its nature impossible is shown by the Swiss, who have wrought into one self-governing state Catholic and Protestant communities, which speak not two but three or more tongues. The united Netherlands with its oversea empire would have been a castle disposed to peace and strong enough to weight the scales against ambitions likely to disturb it. By their separation Holland and Belgium were reduced to the status of pawns on the chessboard of Europe.

From Paris and Brussels the revolutionary movement spread in a few months to Warsaw. Shorn of the territories restored to Prussia and Austria, Poland was established in 1815 as a constitutional monarchy under the Romanov dynasty, and Alexander I. had sworn to respect the constitution. When he died in 1825 his relations with the diet had already been strained. Under Nicholas I. the breach was rapidly widened, and a movement to throw off the rule of the Romanovs developed in Warsaw, a movement in which the Polish army was involved. In 1830 Nicholas called on the Polish army to assist him in restoring Charles to the throne of France. But the Poles were in sympathy with the French revolution and turned upon Russia. The struggle lasted till October 1831, when the Polish army was finally crushed. The constitution and all electoral institutions were abolished. The Polish army was incorporated in the army of Russia. All leading government posts were filled by Russians, and the Russian language was as far as possible made compulsory in administration. Poland was in fact reduced to a province of the great Russian autocracy. Her leading soldiers, musicians and men of letters fled to the capitals of Europe and especially to Paris, and did much to create feelings which led to the Crimean war. The rebellion which cost the Poles their last remnants of liberty had saved France from a Russian invasion to re-establish a reactionary government in Paris.

NOTE

[1] Émile Bourgeois in *The Cambridge Modern History*, vol. x. p. 85.

CHAPTER XXXVI

THE NATIONAL UNION OF ITALY

THE separation of Belgium from Holland increased the number of national states which fringe the Atlantic coast of Europe. Most of these states had acquired some footing in the continents opened by the labours of Henry the Navigator. The peoples east of these states had no such possessions, and had taken no part in the maritime struggle for trade with America, Asia and Africa. The Germans, says Mr. Fisher, "were cut off from the colonizing enterprises which in the seventeenth century enriched the life of the oceanic powers . . . by reason of their geographic position".[1] With the utmost deference to so great an authority, I submit that history and politics rather than geography are the true explanation. Till the second half of the nineteenth century the Germans had failed to achieve the structure of a national state. There was no Germany capable of playing a part on the high seas, in the world beyond Europe. The ghost of the Roman Empire had haunted the people who destroyed it. The successors of Charles the Great, whilst struggling to realise their claims in Italy as the heirs of the Caesars, had left Germany in feudal chaos. Instead of a national sovereignty they only created a counterfeit empire. The struggles of popes with emperors had fastened disunion on Italy. Till the close of the eighteenth century Germany and Italy were a medley of states, none of them able to play any serious part in the struggle for world dominion which for nearly three centuries engaged the navies of Portugal, Spain, of France and Great Britain, of Holland and even of Denmark.

The idea that a state consists of the people it contains, and not of a dynasty which rules, developed in England and rendered explicit in North America, had returned across the Atlantic to kindle the revolution in France. It had run like fire across Europe to be smothered for a time at the Congress of Vienna. The Empire of Austria was re-established by Metternich as a medley of races to be ruled by the Habsburg dynasty. Austria was German and its German dynasty was to rule Czechs in Bohemia, Magyars in Hungary, Slavs on the coast of the Adriatic, Italians in Lombardy and Venice. The rest of Italy was parcelled out into three duchies, Parma, Modena and Tuscany, the Papal States, and the two Sicilies under a Bourbon king, sovereignties in name but in fact satellites of Austria. The only government which could look through Italian rather than Austrian eyes was the House of Savoy, which ruled Piedmont and Sardinia in the north-west corner of Italy. North of the Alps was Germany, where Napoleon had reduced 300 sovereign states to less than 40. The Congress of Vienna preserved this reduction; but the gibe, uttered by Voltaire, that the Holy Roman Empire was neither holy, nor Roman, nor even an empire, was mordant enough to defeat any proposal to exhume the corpse which Napoleon had buried. A German confederation with a diet in which the dynastic governments of the German states were represented under the presidency of Austria, was perhaps a slight concession made by the Congress to the rising feeling for national unity. *Austriae est imperare orbi universo* (A.E.I.O.U.), Austria's prerogative is to rule the entire universe, was the boast of the Habsburg dynasty. The arrangements of Metternich were intended to secure that Austria should be paramount, at any rate throughout the German and Italian worlds, as well as over the medley of races she ruled as subjects. His policy was to maintain in all the German and Italian states governments which did not pretend to draw their authority or direction from the people they ruled. Such governments were from their nature disposed to support Austria in suppressing popular movements. A German or Italian government might show some sympathy for a national union, but when the movement began to threaten its own sovereignty its support would be given to the anti-national policy of Austria. The two leading exceptions to this rule were Prussia and Piedmont. The Prussian autocracy felt itself strong enough to unite and dominate Germany. As Piedmont renounced the doctrine of authority, and developed a constitutional monarchy, it ceased to support the policy of Austria in suppressing popular government. It aspired to unite Italy on the model of England, with a parliamentary government under the constitutional crown of Savoy.

In all the Italian states were movements to secure constitutions and personal liberties such as England enjoyed, which Austria was always trying to suppress. The French revolution of 1830 immediately led to risings in Rome, Parma and Modena, which were quickly suppressed with the aid of Austrian troops. The young Mazzini was arrested in Piedmont. In the leisure imposed by six months' imprisonment he reached the conclusion that Italians could only achieve the liberties they desired by uniting the country under one government responsible to themselves. He was destined to make national union the creed of his people. In 1831, an exile at Marseilles, he there founded 'young Italy'. In 1834 he was forced to take refuge in London; but his writings and influence were rapidly bringing the idea of political union to the forefront. He had made it the ruling passion throughout Italy and Sicily when in 1848 the established order was everywhere threatened by risings. Mazzini himself desired an Italian republic, an aim which he would not compromise. At the other extreme were those who sought to conciliate the existing governments by demanding a federal union for Italy, with, perhaps, the Pope at its head. Between these extremes were those who believed that national union could best be achieved by a constitutional monarchy under the House of Savoy. Events were to prove they were right.

In 1846, when Gregory XVI. died, Austria hoped to secure the election of another reactionary Pope. Before the Austrian cardinal could arrive the Italian cardinals had elected as Pius IX. an Italian bishop who favoured the idea of a national union for his country. This brought to the forefront the project of uniting the existing states in a federal union under the leadership of the Pope. Some liberal reforms which he granted enabled the people of Rome to express their feelings. A clamour was raised for a federal movement to drive the Austrians from Italy.

In January 1848 a rising which started in Sicily forced Ferdinand II., the King of Naples, to grant his subjects a constitution, which he would have refused had Pius IX. not forbidden Austrian troops to march through the Papal States into Naples. In Piedmont a movement led by Count Cavour induced Charles Albert, the king, to grant a constitution modelled on that of Great Britain, which was destined to become the constitution of Italy. Under the influence of Cavour he declared war upon Austria and called on the rest of Italy to support him. Venice revolted and threw in its lot with Piedmont. He was joined by troops from the duchies and Naples, though Ferdinand II. was in sympathy with the Austrians. The Pope now began to realise that his position as temporal ruler in the centre of Italy, and also as head of a world-theocracy, in which Austria was the strongest political element, was hard to reconcile with support for the movement for the union of

Italy. He began to temporise, refused to declare war on Austria, yet allowed his troops to take part in the struggle.

The Austrians were embarrassed by the revolution which broke out in Vienna, and drove Metternich into exile. Charles Albert, however, as a military leader, was no match for old Marshal Radetzky at the head of the Austrian army. After some initial successes the Italians were utterly defeated at Custozza and again at Novara in March 1849. Charles Albert relinquished his throne to his son Victor Emmanuel, who was forced to accept a humiliating peace. In the other Italian states the despotic governments were re-established under Austrian protection.

The Pope, meanwhile, had come to an open rupture with the people of Rome. In November 1848 he had fled to Gaeta on the Neapolitan coast. In February 1849 a constituent assembly in Rome voted the downfall of the temporal power, and proclaimed a republic. Mazzini conceived the idea that it might be extended to include Italy in one republic with Rome as its capital. So he hastened to Rome and at once became the leading member of a ruling triumvirate. In April 1849 Garibaldi with 500 followers came to support him.

Mazzini had made the mistake, which Cavour always avoided, of provoking Catholic feeling abroad, and throwing it into the scale against the national union of Italy. The revolution of 1848 had driven Louis-Philippe from his throne, and had brought Louis-Napoleon to power in France. His wife was a bigoted Catholic, and Napoleon, intent on securing the support of the Catholic party in France, sent an army by sea, which, in June 1849, occupied Rome, suppressed the republic and restored Pius IX. to the Vatican and power. Mazzini escaped. Garibaldi retreated with 4000 men, in the hope of assisting Venice. When his army melted away he was able to reach Piedmont in disguise. From Piedmont he fled to America. This disastrous failure of a premature enterprise had lasting effects. It established the idea that the union of Italy must centre in Rome, the eternal city. History combined with its place on the map in pointing to Rome as the destined capital.

The lesson of all these failures was read and applied by Cavour. He saw that the Austrians could never be driven from Italy unless she obtained the support of other powers in Europe. In 1854 war was declared on Russia by France and England. The factor which made such a war possible was the public feeling created by Nicholas. In western Europe he had come to be thought of as the arch-foe of all human liberties. Piedmont had no contacts with Russia or interest in the controversies which had led to the war. Yet in 1855 Cavour was able to use the feeling against the reactionary Tzar to bring Piedmont into alliance with England and France. In the Crimea a small army of Piedmontese fought with distinction. Henceforth Cavour was able to count on French and on English sympathies. He now set out to obtain the active alliance of France against Austria. In 1858 he was able to make a secret agreement with Napoleon III. that a French army should help Piedmont to drive the Austrians from Italy, in return for the cession by Piedmont to France of Nice and Savoy.

In January 1859 Napoleon threatened war and then drew back, but in April Austria saved the situation for Cavour by invading Piedmont, thus bringing France to the rescue. In May and June the Austrians were beaten in five battles. But again Napoleon drew back and in July arranged an armistice with Austria. Napoleon III. had no real desire for the national union of Italy. His object was to oust Austria from Italy and replace her there as the dominant power. Prussia, moreover, had placed her army on a war footing and was threatening France on the Rhine. On November 10, 1859, Victor Emmanuel was obliged to sign a peace which gave him nothing but Lombardy, leaving Venice in the hands of Austria. But Parma, Modena and Tuscany revolted, expelled their despots and insisted on joining the kingdom of Piedmont. So also did the people of Romagna, at the north of the Papal States. Napoleon was forced to agree. In result the House of Savoy acquired the whole of north Italy except Venetia. Their frontiers marched with those of the Pope, a belt across Italy dividing the kingdom of Sardinia from the kingdom of Naples. Napoleon III. was induced to accept these results by the cession to France of Nice, where Garibaldi was born, as well as Savoy. In April 1860 the parliament of Piedmont reluctantly ratified the cession, but Garibaldi was scarcely restrained from an armed expedition to resist the transfer of Nice to France.

His energies were presently diverted to the south. A revolt, led by Mazzini's agents, had already started in Sicily. In May Garibaldi with 1000 followers sailed from a place near Genoa and landed in Sicily at its western extremity. By the end of July he had driven the Neapolitan forces to its eastern extremity where they shut themselves up in the walls of Messina. Garibaldi proclaimed that he held the island in the name of Victor Emmanuel.

In August (1860) Garibaldi with over 3000 troops crossed in two ships to the southernmost point of Italy. The Bourbon troops fled before his advance and their king took refuge in Gaeta. On September 7 Garibaldi occupied Naples. In his ranks were many who had followed Mazzini, and hoped that Garibaldi would march on Rome and there proclaim an Italian republic. Cavour had realised that, in this event, Napoleon III., as in 1849, would come to the aid of the Pope. There were also risings in Umbria and the Marches which papal troops were sent to suppress. So Cavour felt that the moment had come when Victor Emmanuel must take the initiative. On September 11 (1860) he marched from Romagna into the Papal States, and a week later had crushed the papal army at Castelfidardo. On the 19th Garibaldi attacked the Neapolitan army which held the Volturno river to the north of Naples, but did not carry the position till October 2. Meanwhile the Piedmontese were marching south. On October 29 Victor Emmanuel and Garibaldi met. On November 7 they entered Naples together. Garibaldi, loyal to the cause of Italian unity, resigned his authority to the king, and retired to his home on the island of Caprera.

The Pope was left in possession of Rome and the districts surrounding it, known as the Patrimony of Peter. Umbria and the Marches, the rest of the papal dominions, were annexed by Victor Emmanuel, who defied the sentence of excommunication pronounced by the Pope. Venice remained under Austrian rule; but, with these two exceptions, the whole of Italy was in 1860 united under the House of Savoy. The capital was moved from Turin to Florence.

NOTE

[1] Fisher, *A History of Europe*, vol. ii. p. 611.

CHAPTER XXXVII

THE NATIONAL UNION OF GERMANY

In Germany, as in Italy, the dynastic governments of the German states, and the constant desire of Austria to control their relations one with another were the principal obstacles to national union. After the disastrous retreat from Moscow, Metternich had taken the lead in persuading the German princes along the Rhine to join the allies against Napoleon. Fearing the creation of a powerful German empire controlled by Prussia, he had no hesitation in guaranteeing the absolute sovereignty of the less powerful German princes. He hoped to establish a loose confederation of sovereign states in which Austria could exercise the dominant influence. His ideas prevailed in the Congress of Vienna. No attempt was made to go back to the states, 300 in number, which Napoleon reduced to 39. The sovereignty of these 39 states was confirmed. They were each to send delegates to a federal diet, an Austrian delegate presiding. A unanimous vote was necessary for changing "fundamental laws, organic institutions, individual rights, or in matters of religion". Austria was recognised by the princes as the special guardian of their sovereign rights, as against Prussia, and also as against popular movements from within. The guiding principle of Metternich was to maintain the *status quo* as established by the Congress of Vienna. In this he succeeded till the revolutions of 1830 began to disturb the political stagnation.

The Germans were now beginning to adopt the methods of mechanised industry developed in

England, and found themselves greatly impeded by the network of customs barriers which divided their sovereign states. In overcoming these difficulties the able and industrious officials of Prussia took the initiative. Little by little they established a customs union, which by the middle of the century had come to include nearly the whole of Germany. It was this union which enabled the Germans to develop their railways. Here, as elsewhere, railways were a primary factor in uniting the national states of the modern world. Austria remained outside this customs union, with Prussia at its head, and bitterly opposed it as tending to diminish the importance of the German diet in which she herself held the dominant power.

The political structure which Metternich tried so hard to uphold was violently shaken by the revolutions which swept Europe in 1848. In March Metternich was driven into exile by a revolution in the streets of Vienna. Bohemians and Hungarians as well as Italians rose in rebellion. But quickly the tide turned. While Radetzky was defeating Italian armies, Windischgrätz was suppressing the Czechs in Bohemia. In October Vienna was bombarded by Windischgrätz. The popular government there was suppressed. A strong reactionary, Schwarzenberg, was placed in power. In December 1848 he induced the Emperor Ferdinand to abdicate his throne in favour of his nephew Francis Joseph. The help of the Tzar Nicholas was then secured for the subjugation of Hungary. In the summer of 1849, 80,000 Russians marched into Hungary and suppressed the republic established by Kossuth.

The revolution had run, meanwhile, through the German states like a fire. Even the Prussian autocracy trembled. When in March 1848 a revolution had broken out in Berlin, Frederick William IV. withdrew his troops, and headed a procession through the streets wrapped in the German tricolour.

On March 30 the federal diet also hoisted the tricolour and authorised the assembly of a German national parliament. It came into being at Frankfort on May 18. This body, which represented electorates, was taken as superseding the diet composed of delegates from the governments, which was never dissolved, but simply dispersed.

Throughout the rest of that year the Frankfort parliament was trying to frame a constitution, under which the people of Germany might attain their national unity. They were faced at once by the problem of Austria, which to this day remains unsolved. In Austria were 8,000,000 Germans, the most cultured members of their race, Catholics with whom their co-religionists in Bavaria and other Catholic states were in closer sympathy than with Prussia, the champion of the Lutheran faith. This important section of the German people was the dominant part of an empire which included Hungary, Bohemia and a large variety of Slavonic peoples. A federal state which included the Austrian Empire with the 39 German states could never fulfil the aspirations of the Germans who yearned for a national union of the peoples who spoke their tongue. The problem could not be solved. After nearly a year of public discussion the Frankfort parliament was driven to resolve that the Austrian Germans must be left out of the union. It then went on to decide that the head of the German union should be given the title of Emperor. By a small majority they decided that the title should be offered to Frederick William IV. of Prussia.

Schwarzenberg and the young Francis Joseph, whom he had just placed on the throne of the Habsburgs, were resolved to defeat these proposals. From the outset their task was rendered easy by Frederick William IV. He had now been forced to grant a constitution to his own subjects in Prussia, and had come to realise what it meant to govern with a parliament which claimed to derive its authority from the people themselves. He declined the title of German Emperor until it was offered by the ruling princes of Germany. In his own words he refused "to pick up a crown out of the gutter". When a popular agitation was started to force the princes to accept the Frankfort constitution, he sent Prussian troops to suppress the risings which were threatening the governments in Würtemberg, Saxony, Baden and Rhenish Bavaria. In June 1849 the Frankfort parliament was finally dissolved. The attempt to unite Germany on a basis of popular government by constitutional means had signally failed. The Frankfort parliament of 1848 lacked the previous experience of constitutional methods which had made it possible for the convention which met at Philadelphia in 1787 to accomplish their task. Governments which denied them that kind of experience, and claimed to derive their authority from on high, had frustrated their efforts. Such union as Germany was to achieve was accomplished by methods which those governments understood.

In 1850 Austria persuaded some of the German states to reconstitute at Frankfort the diet created in 1815. Prussia persuaded some other states to enter a union, more on the lines of the constitution which the popular parliament of Frankfort had framed in 1848. War between the two groups was imminent. But Austria with Russian assistance had now stamped out the rising in Hungary, and the Prussian generals knew that their army was not at the moment sufficiently prepared for the struggle. Their foreign minister, Manteuffel, met Schwarzenberg at Olmütz in November 1850 and virtually yielded all his demands. In 1851 the old diet resumed its meetings at Frankfort as if nothing had happened. The envoy commissioned to represent Prussia was young Otto von Bismarck.

In 1852 an order was passed in the Prussian cabinet, which must here be noted for its effects on the constitution which Bismarck afterwards framed for Germany. The minister-president was made solely responsible to the king for the acts of all other ministers of state, who thus became his subordinates.[1]

In 1858 Frederick William IV. became insane. Till his death in 1861 his brother William acted as regent with Otto von Bismarck as his personal adviser. The union of Italy under the House of Savoy had reacted on Germany to encourage fresh efforts for national union. In 1862 the German states were invited by Austria to send delegates to Frankfort to discuss the problem. King William was persuaded by Bismarck, who was now his minister-president, to refuse to attend the meeting. He declined to consider any project of union in which Prussia did not stand on a footing of absolute equality with Austria. Prussia, he added, "will yield no tittle of her rights save to a parliament representing the whole German nation". For tactical reasons King William was committed by Bismarck to a position the reverse of that which his brother had adopted when refusing the imperial crown in 1849. Whilst defying the German dynasties he was making a bid to the democrats. Bismarck despised parliaments and their ways, but, like Napoleon, was always ready to appeal to popular votes when he thought the result would advance his ends. His real feelings were expressed when a few days after this message was sent he told the Prussian chamber that the problem of German union could not be solved 'by parliamentary decrees', but only 'by blood and iron'.

He was quick to seize on a question which had long been vexing the German world as a means of applying these methods. On the isthmus which joins Denmark to Germany were two duchies, Schleswig and

Holstein. They were claimed by the German diet, headed by Austria, as members of the German confederation. They were also claimed by the King of Denmark, who wished to include them in his kingdom. Bismarck resolved to take the duchies from Denmark by force, and then, instead of handing them over to the German diet, to annex them to Prussia. The control of Schleswig-Holstein would enable Prussia to cut a canal through the isthmus from Kiel to the North Sea, and thus become an Atlantic power, with an exit of her own from the Baltic which the Danes could not close against her. He also foresaw that the annexation of Schleswig-Holstein to Prussia would enable him to settle accounts with Austria, which would certainly fight to prevent it. If Austria were thoroughly beaten, Prussia could destroy the confederation which Austria controlled, and then unite the rest of Germany under Prussian control.

In these plans he was ably supported by von Roon, the minister of war, and von Moltke, the commander-in-chief. Austria was willing to join Prussia in attacking the Danes. In February 1864 the Austrian and Prussian troops crossed the Eider and easily defeated the Danish army. In August a treaty was signed by Denmark by which Schleswig and Holstein were ceded to Austria and Prussia jointly.

Roon, Moltke and Bismarck then turned to prepare for the struggle with Austria. They had seen that the factor of mechanisation was now decisive in war. Their troops were the first to be armed with breech-loading rifles. So equipped, they could fire four rounds while the enemy were charging their rifles with ramrods. They realised the importance of railways in strategy and their plans for mobilisation were developed with Prussian exactness. In the field of diplomacy Bismarck was tireless. He made an alliance with Italy with the promise of Venice as her reward when Austria was beaten. The neutrality of Louis-Napoleon was secured by a vague promise of compensation.

By the summer of 1866 Bismarck was ready for action. He then announced that Prussia would only allow the federal diet to settle the Schleswig-Holstein question when the diet itself had been reformed. By reform he meant the exclusion of Austria, a parliament elected by the rest of Germany on the basis of manhood suffrage, a joint command of the army by Prussia and Bavaria, and the creation of a German navy. Austria replied with a motion in the federal diet that the rest of Germany should make war on Prussia, and carried the motion by 9 votes to 6. Next day the Prussian army was marching through Saxony on Austria. On July 3, 1866, the Austrians were utterly defeated at Königgrätz (Sadowa). On July 26 a treaty was signed in which Austria conceded all the demands of Prussia and Venice to Italy, despite the fact that her army there had beaten the Italians.

Machiavelli has said that when you have conquered a people you must either destroy them or else make friends with them. When Austria had recognised that Bismarck was free to deal with the rest of Germany as he chose, he treated her as the future ally of the German union he meant to create. As he wished to consolidate Prussia in one continuous territory, he extinguished the states which divided her western and eastern dominions. On September 20 Hanover, Hesse-Cassel, Nassau and Frankfort were annexed to Prussia, which thereafter extended from the North Sea and the frontiers of Holland, Belgium, Luxemburg and France to the frontier of Russia. By annexing Hanover, Prussia acquired a number of ports on the Atlantic. In undisputed possession of Schleswig-Holstein she was now free to connect her Baltic and North Sea ports by cutting the Kiel canal.

With the other German states, many of which were surrounded by Prussian territory, he dealt as tenderly as he dealt with Austria. The states south of the Main, Darmstadt, Baden, Bavaria and Würtemberg, were left for the moment to lick their wounds. Those north of the Main were united with Prussia in the North German Confederation by a constitution which Bismarck dictated. On February 24, 1867, his draft was accepted, with unimportant amendments, by the representatives of the various states. It created two organs of government, the *Bundesrat* or Federal Council in which the governments of the states were represented, and the *Reichstag*, a parliament elected by all Germans embraced in the union.

The Bismarckian constitution was an illogical combination of the system inherited from the Holy Roman Empire, with the aspirations of liberal Germans. The Bundesrat was merely the old diet confined for the moment to the states north of the Main, and led by Prussia instead of by Austria. It consisted of delegates appointed by the princes who met in secret, and over it Bismarck presided in the name of the King of Prussia. It discussed all measures, whether bills, estimates or questions of policy before they became public. Bills and estimates, as settled by this council of state, were then submitted to the Reichstag for public discussion; but all initiative remained with the Bundesrat. The confederate army consisted of the armies of all the states; but in time of war the supreme command was held by the King of Prussia, whose army was greater than those of all the remaining states. The navy was entirely federal like that of the United States.

The key to this strange constitution, which to theorists seemed so unworkable, was the character of its author, a statesman of transcendent abilities, with all the prestige those abilities had brought him. By virtue of the system established in Prussia in 1852 the minister-president was supreme so long as he retained the confidence of his sovereign. He alone had access to the king and all other ministers were under his orders. In his constitution Bismarck secured that the minister-president of Prussia should always be chancellor of the North German Confederation, with the right to preside over the Bundesrat. In the Bundesrat he was able to establish the principle already established in the government of Prussia. All the ministers were to rank as the chancellor's subordinates. He alone was responsible to the King of Prussia as president of the North German Confederation. He relied on his own transcendent abilities to control the Reichstag as well as the Bundesrat. The dictatorial powers which Bismarck was destined to wield for the next thirty years were carefully masked by constitutional forms, which worked so long as behind them was a despot of superlative quality. How this constitution would work in the hands of successors who lacked his experienced sagacity remained to be seen. As Liebknecht afterwards said, the Reichstag was no more than the fig-leaf of an autocracy.

This union of German states which Bismarck created was essentially different from the Holy Roman Empire, the Germanic Confederations which Austria had fostered, or even the German Zollverein. The difference was carefully masked by the title of North German Confederation, with the King of Prussia as *ex-officio* president. Those previous unions were all inorganic, with the same defect as the League of Delos, the confederation of American States, or the League of Nations, in that sovereignty vested in the several states forming these unions. The North German Confederation, despite its name, had in fact transferred the sovereignty of the states which composed it to a central authority. Its quality as a genuine organ of government was mainly due to the quality of the ruler who was destined for thirty years to control the intricate machinery which he himself had devised. His work was done with amazing rapidity. It was finished before the French had time to realise that the whole balance of power was altered. Napoleon III. had been raised to his throne in the faith that a man of his name would secure to France the hegemony of Europe. His empire itself was threatened by the sudden creation of a genuine government competent to wield all the resources of Germany north of the Main. If this union went on to include Bavaria and the states south of the Main the future position of France would be gravely compromised.

The North German Confederation had been created at the cost of a war in which, as in previous centuries, Germans had slaughtered Germans. If the union could enlist the states south of the Main, which were still outside it, in a war with the foreign power which had once trampled all Germany under foot, their inclusion would then be easy. The dream of a German empire with Austria only excluded would then be realised. A war with France was exactly what Bismarck wanted.

The French were demanding compensations for the new annexations which Prussia had made. Belgium, Luxemburg and a slice of Germany south of the Main were mentioned by Louis-Napoleon. Bismarck took care that the countries concerned should know what Napoleon was asking. The demand for Belgium estranged the sympathies of England from France. The demand for a slice of south Germany threw Bavaria and the states south of the Main into the arms of Bismarck.

He intended that France should declare war upon Prussia and moulded events to that end. In 1868 the

Spanish navy and army had mutinied and expelled the Bourbon queen, Isabella. Europe was ransacked by the military leaders for a prince who was willing to fill her place. In secret Bismarck supported an offer which was made to a prince of the Hohenzollern family. This proposal to place a Prussian prince on the throne of Charles V. at once brought France to the verge of war. But the aged King William, averse to war, agreed to discourage the candidature, which was then refused by the Hohenzollern prince and his father. This diplomatic reverse was near to ending Bismarck's career, and he thought of retirement. But Gramont, the French minister, not content with his triumph, persuaded Napoleon III. to require guarantees that such a proposal would never again be considered. Benedetti, the French ambassador, was instructed accordingly. On July 12, 1870, King William was at Ems taking the waters, met Benedetti on the public promenade and showed him a copy of the *Cologne Gazette* which announced the prince's withdrawal. In obedience to Gramont's fatal instructions, Benedetti then asked him to promise that the question would never be opened again. King William stoutly refused, closed the interview and telegraphed the facts to Bismarck at Berlin, suggesting their publication.

Bismarck, Moltke and Roon were dining together when the telegram arrived. They were all deeply depressed by their master's unwillingness to engage in a war with France. Their mood rapidly changed on reading the telegram. Bismarck drafted a public announcement based on the actual words of the telegram, but phrased so cleverly as to give the impression that the French ambassador had failed in respect to the King of Prussia and been snubbed in return. As Moltke remarked, the note of retreat in the king's telegram was in Bismarck's announcement changed to a challenge. It was published that night in a special edition of the *North German Gazette*. The whole of Germany north of Austria blazed with a sense of national insult. The southern states were instantly swept into line with the North German Confederation. In France the sense of a national insult was no less decisive. On July 14 Napoleon agreed to declare war. On the 19th the French declaration of war was received in Berlin. It accomplished that union of Germany in arms for which Bismarck had laboured.

Events moved with startling rapidity; for Roon and Moltke had realised to the full the power which mechanisation brings to the organisation of physical force. By September the French armies were surrounded at Sedan, and Louis-Napoleon, who had come to negotiate, had remained in the German lines. On September 4 a revolution had established the third republic in Paris, and prepared to defend the capital. By September 19 the German armies had surrounded Paris with their headquarters in the great palace of Louis XIV. at Versailles. The southern princes were now eager to bring their states into the German union. The terms were arranged by Bismarck at Versailles, and on January 18, 1871, William I. was proclaimed Emperor of Germany in the Salle des Glaces by the assembled princes. A few days later the German armies marched into Paris. On May 10, 1871, the Treaty of Frankfort was signed, by which the republic ceded Alsace and Lorraine and agreed to pay an indemnity of £200,000,000.

The long train of causes which condemned Germans and Italians to centuries of chaos had at last worked themselves out. When declaring war on Germany Louis-Napoleon had been forced to withdraw from Rome the troops which alone sustained the temporal power. Victor Emmanuel at once invited the Pope to complete the national union of Italy by ceding his claims as a temporal ruler. When the Pope refused the walls of Rome were breached by Italian guns. At the end of September 1870 the Italian army occupied the city. A few months after the German Empire was proclaimed at Versailles, the Kingdom of Italy was completed with Rome as its capital.

NOTE

[1] Headlam (Morley), *Bismarck*, p. 454.

CHAPTER XXXVIII

THE BIRTH OF COMMUNISM

WHILE the sword was achieving the belated unity of the German people, two Prussians almost unnoticed had written a paper that scarcely affected the contemporary course of events during their lives. It was destined to leave its mark on history, as deeply as *The Social Contract* of Rousseau or the practical achievements of Bismarck and Cavour. Karl Marx was born in 1818 and Friedrich Engels in 1820, the one at Trèves, the other at Barmen. Marx, the son of a Jewish lawyer who embraced Christianity, read philosophy at Bonn and Berlin, where he took a doctor's degree in 1841. But his hopes of a career in a Prussian university were closed by the radical views he developed. In 1843 he went to Paris to study the socialist movement. Engels, the son of a pious manufacturer at Barmen, was led by the writings of Strauss to reject the religious and political views of his family. In 1842 his father sent him to England to learn his business at a factory which he owned in Manchester. In the course of a journey from England to Barmen in 1844 he visited Paris "hallowed by the memories of Babeuf, Marat and Robespierre".[1] On this brief visit was established his historic friendship with Marx. In 1845 Marx was expelled from Paris at the instance of Prussia, and took refuge in Brussels. Henceforward Marx was enabled to live and continue his work largely by funds supplied by Engels.

The 'hungry forties' were moving to the revolutions which shook the established order in 1848. A movement to combine extremist societies in one international movement was fostered by Marx and Engels. In November 1847 a congress of communist societies in London commissioned them to draft them a manifesto. The result of their labours was produced and adopted in January 1848. It was seen by a few hundred communists and had no influence on the revolutions which followed in the course of that year. Its ultimate effects may perhaps be greater than those of any pronouncement since Luther nailed his thesis to the door of the church in Wittenberg. In 1849 Marx was obliged to take refuge in London, where, befriended by Engels, he devoted the rest of his life to developing the thesis, brilliantly outlined in the Communist Manifesto, in a work called *Das Kapital*. From materials left at his death in 1883 Engels completed the last two volumes, a task for which he was equipped by his intellectual gifts and his intimate knowledge of Marx. He died in London in 1895.

The manifesto of 1848 was written in German. In a preface to an English translation published forty years later, and after the death of Marx, the following statement was made by Engels:

> The *Manifesto* being our joint production, I consider myself bound to state that the fundamental proposition which forms its nucleus, belongs to Marx. That proposition is: That in every historical epoch, the prevailing mode of economic production and exchange, and the social organisation necessarily following from it, form the basis upon which is built up, and from which alone can be explained, the political and intellectual history of that epoch; that consequently the whole history of mankind (since the dissolution of primitive tribal society, holding land in common ownership) has been a history of class struggles, contests between exploiting and exploited, ruling and oppressed classes; that the history of these class struggles form a series of evolutions in which, nowadays, a stage has been reached where the exploited and oppressed class—

the proletariat—cannot attain its emancipation from the sway of the exploiting and ruling class—the bourgeoisie—without, at the same time, and once and for all emancipating society at large from all exploitation, oppression, class distinctions and class struggles.

This proposition, which, in my opinion, is destined to do for history what Darwin's theory has done for biology, we, both of us, had been gradually approaching for some years before 1845. How far I had independently progressed towards it, is best shown by my *Condition of the Working Class in England*. But when I again met Marx at Brussels, in spring, 1845, he had it already worked out, and put it before me, in terms almost as clear as those in which I have stated it here.

The thesis set forth in the manifesto as developed by Marx and his followers in subsequent writings may be sketched as follows.

Since men emerged from tribal society and states were organised, the wealth produced by the great mass of workers has been engrossed for their own enjoyment by comparatively idle minorities or classes who owned the instruments of production, including the land. The struggle between the masses and classes for the wealth produced by the masses is the real explanation of all history. States, governments, customs, laws and religions were created and utilised to control the majority in the interest of minorities. The opening of the seas and of the continents beyond them to trade inspired the more vigorous elements in the masses, described as the bourgeoisie, to insist on individual rights, especially the right of the individual to hold and enjoy property in land, irrespective of the class in which he is born. The bourgeoisie were thus able to destroy the privileges of the feudal classes, and seize the control of religious and secular institutions. Freed from feudal restraints, they were able to devise costly labour-saving machines to supersede the hand tools formerly owned by the worker himself. Till Watt invented the steam-engine, the goods which civilised men require were mainly produced by craftsmen who owned the tools with which they worked. The spinner owned his spinning-wheel, and sold the yarn which he twisted to a weaver next door, who wove the yarn into cloth on a hand-loom built into the room of his cottage. The cloth was distributed to shops by carriers who usually owned the wagons they drove. The spinners, the weavers and carriers were as much their own masters as yeomen. And the same was true of the blacksmiths and joiners who made the spinning-wheels, looms and wagons.

The invention of the spinning jenny, the power-loom and the railway driven by steam had changed all this. The volume of goods produced by the same number of spinners, weavers and carriers was immensely increased and rendered so cheap that the craftsman who owned his spinning-wheel and hand-loom was put out of business. The machines were too costly for the workmen who used them as tools to acquire and possess. To begin with, the more enterprising and thrifty of the workmen had purchased machines from their savings and with money they were able to borrow from merchants and bankers. They had then ceased to be workmen and had hired workmen less fortunate than themselves to operate the machines. The more prosperous workmen had ceased to work with their hands and become capitalists and masters. The less prosperous majority had become their servants. The labour required to work the machines was the only commodity which the labourer had to sell. By improving the machines and reducing the number of hands required to produce a given volume of goods, the capitalist threw out of employment a number of workmen whose anxiety to earn wages helped to keep down the wage or price of labour payable to those in employment. The capitalist was thus able to secure for himself a great part of the value of the finished product. Marx argued that the whole value of the product was created by the workers and belonged to them by right. The surplus value or profit which capitalists stole from their workers was spent either on personal luxuries denied to the workers, or saved to increase their capital and thereby their power to control the capitalist system.

Thus the dominant motive of the employer was to earn a profit by selling the finished goods for more than they cost to produce when the wages of the workmen and the cost of the plant and the raw materials had been paid. Capitalist economists urged that this profit would be kept within reasonable limits by the competition of other employers in the same industry. But, as Marx foresaw, the depressing effect of competition on prices would tend to compel competing producers to merge their undertakings in larger units, controlled by fewer and abler capitalists. As subsequent experience has proved, capitalism, a system of production that is, in which the motive power is private profit, must tend to bring the control of the whole means of production into the hands of the owners of capital whose power would in fact be great enough to control the state itself even in democratic communities. These capitalists would need to use and control the forces of the national state in order to secure markets in the world beyond their own country. With this object in view each national state would seek to dominate subject peoples in distant continents, in order to exploit their labour and secure their markets. Capitalist states would thus be brought into collision with each other, and capitalism could only lead to devastating and world-wide wars which would end in its own ruin.

In result the bourgeoisie or capitalist class had merely displaced the old feudal classes, by asserting the legal right, assumed to be indefeasible, of the individual to own property. The masses, or proletariat, were more enslaved thereby than they had been under feudal privilege. But the old issue was now simplified by the division of all society into capitalists, a minority which owned and controlled the means of production and engrossed the products to their own enjoyment, and the proletariat, the majority who were left with the barest means of subsistence and denied the reality of freedom thereby. The relations of man to man were now reduced to naked self-interest and cash payment.

The feudal system depended on conserving existing methods of production. The capitalist system depended on constantly changing these methods, not only by improving machinery and the organisation of industry, but also by opening new markets in all parts of the globe. The capitalist system had thus transcended national limits, and was tending to impose itself as an international economic system on the world as a whole, on Asia and Africa as well as on Europe and America. It concentrated industry in towns and made the country districts dependent on them. It made the less civilised countries dependent on the more civilised. In one century it had called into being more productive forces than all previous history had done, and had greatly increased the world's population. The results are so great that capitalists are unable to control their own creation. The world is distracted by crises of increasing severity, in which masses of goods are produced which cannot be sold, while masses of workers are unemployed and cannot purchase these surplus goods. When capitalists try to remedy these evils by scrapping machinery, destroying the surplus products by forcing them on the old markets, and by conquering new ones, they are merely paving the way for greater and more destructive crises. By abstruse economic analysis, Marx and his followers have argued that the system of capitalism, left to itself, must result in a deadlock which will prove its destruction.[2]

Meanwhile the system is creating the force destined to destroy it, for it converts the proletariat it employs into an army increasing in numbers and organisation, and also in the sense of injustice it suffers. The capitalist system, by creating communications all over the world, is enabling the workers in the various countries to combine with each other as they could not in the Middle Ages. In England, France, America and Germany the workers are coming to see that the state, law, morality, religion and the family system are no more than expedients devised or used by the bourgeoisie, behind which to entrench the rights of property. The time will come when the proletariat in capitalist countries will combine and be strong enough to destroy the capitalists and their system.

The remedy is for the proletariat once for all to abolish the right of individuals to own property, that is to say, to own and control the means of production. It must seize and hold the means of production as communal property, to be operated not for the profit of individuals, but to serve the needs of the workers as a whole. No one man must be allowed to hire the labour of another for his own benefit. Each man must work for the common good, and be given such a share in the common product as will enable him to do his work with the greatest efficiency.

In order to gain control of the means of production the proletariat will have to abolish all existing institutions which are mere entrenchments for defending the rights of property. The capitalists deprived of their property must themselves be destroyed or become workers, with the result that classes will once for all cease to exist. If no one is allowed to own or control the means of production, to operate those means or hire the labour of another for his private profit, no privileged class can in future emerge, and mankind will become a classless society. This can only be done by creating a dictatorship of the proletariat, which in its own economic interest must destroy the classes, the states they control and the institution of private property. The proletariat must thus, to begin with, establish a government which, like all governments, is based upon force. When all opportunities of private gain have been closed once for all, and when every worker is secured his due share in the products of labour, the desire to serve the common welfare will become dominant in individuals and the actuating principle of the system as a whole. The need for government in the old sense of the word, that is, government based upon force, will vanish. Organs of administration will remain, but will not require force for their working.

To begin with, the proletariat in each country must deal with its own bourgeoisie. As these national revolutions are accomplished, the nations based on a communal system will live at peace with each other, because war has its real origin in the quest of capitalists for private gain. The communist nations will thus become organic parts of a world communist order.

The watchword of the movement was expressed in the words 'working men of all countries unite'.

In the Marxian view the desire of men to enjoy the goods which human labour produces from natural resources is the motive which prompts all human action. The loyalties which unite men in churches and states have their roots in figments, the clever inventions of the classes who have seized more than their due share of the world's goods—devices to blind the majority they exploit. As the eyes of the workers were opened they would realise that loyalty to country or state is a dangerous illusion. A grasp of their real interest would lead the workers in all countries to unite and destroy the states created by minorities to enslave them.

In the Marxian view the doctrine that material interests are the key to all human action applies to thought as well as to action, to philosophy no less than history. As consciously or unconsciously men always do what suits their material interests, so consciously or unconsciously they think what suits those interests. This doctrine pressed to its logical conclusion means that the minds of men can never really discover the truth about human affairs. Philosophies, in effect, are disguised propaganda. That his own philosophy was such, Marx would have frankly admitted. Nothing else could follow from his basic assumption that material interests are the key to all human action and thought. His philosophy was at points inconsistent with this; but so also was his life, throughout which he endured grinding poverty, in order to place his superlative gifts at the public service.

No serious student would question that all philosophies are largely shaped by the external conditions in which their authors have lived their lives, more especially in youth when their minds are plastic. The philosophy of Marx and Engels is a case in point. Their minds were both shaped in a Prussian environment, in an atmosphere charged with the doctrine of authority, in a state which relied on organised force. Had their youth been spent in England, as the greater part of their lives were spent, it is safe to assume that dogmatic assertion and physical force would have found a less prominent place in the creed they preached. Had Engels not been a rebel and had followed a military career, his genius might have raised him to a prominent place on the general staff of the Prussian army. The dogmatic temper, the emphasis placed upon force, which have characterised the Marxian school, are directly traceable to the character of the state in which its authors grew up. This explains why its influence and also its reactions have been so much greater in Europe and Asia than in Anglo-Saxon communities.

When Marx pointed out how historians and political thinkers had ignored bread-and-butter conditions, he rendered a notable service to the understanding of human affairs. But, like most other prophets, he was blinded by the brilliance of the truth he had seen to its limitations. As one of his ablest disciples has recently said:

> Men, even before they have got enough to eat and to clothe themselves against the weather, and to meet other needs upon the physical plane, begin to feel other desires as more insistent than the desire for more of these elementary goods. They make 'sacrifices' to their gods, even of food that they need for themselves; and they want some luxuries and adornments even before their bodily needs have been fully met. Man does not live by bread alone—even when he has not enough bread.[3]

The desire of a man who has made money to acquire a landed estate which will not yield him an income nearly so great as if its price were invested in shares cannot be ranked as a motive which is economic in the sense that Marx used that word. The passion for power and prestige in rulers like Louis XIV. or Napoleon was a motive of this sort and a real factor in history. But the passion is one which also inspires whole nations, which, indeed, inspires all nations. It is often more potent than the motive to secure the necessities of life. It develops most strongly under forms of government based on authority. It is better controlled in so far as a nation has realised the principle of the commonwealth in its system of government. That nations now try to explain their desire to hold or acquire subject territories on economic grounds is itself one of the results of Marxian teaching. To understand what has happened in Africa and Asia since 1871 we must, I submit, realise that human beings are governed by several motives, which vary in strength at different times, and under different conditions. Beyond question one of these motives is economic, the instinct to secure the material necessities of life. At the other extreme is the instinct of men to obey the dictates of conscience. Between these opposites is the passion for power or prestige which at times overrides them both, material interests no less than the sense of duty. In the view taken here any attempt to interpret human affairs which ignores any one of these motives is adrift of realities.

The further developments of the Marxian creed will be dealt with in subsequent chapters. For the moment it suffices for the reader to know what this creed was and to realise how, launched on the world in the middle of the nineteenth century, it began to germinate slowly till seventy years later it sprang to sudden and astonishing fruition. Attempts to apply and resist this creed are a major factor in the world situation to-day. Its potency is, I believe, due to the fact that in spite of inconsistencies, which always spring from dogmatic assumptions, and the violence of the methods it preached, it yet contains elements of truth, which in course of time the world will discover how to apply.

NOTES

[1] Gustav Mayer, *Friedrich Engels. A Biography*, p. 53. Published by Chapman and Hall, 1936.

[2] A lucid exposition of this analysis, which cannot be summarised in the space available here, will be found in *The Nature of the Capitalist Crisis*, by John Strachey. Published by Victor Gollancz, 1935.

[3] Cole, *A Guide to Modern Politics*, p. 458. Published by Gollancz, 1934.

CHAPTER XXXIX

THE AMERICAN COMMONWEALTH IN THE NINETEENTH CENTURY

When Germans and Italians had achieved the position of national states in 1871 the structure of Europe was fixed in outline for close upon fifty years. The convulsions which had broken in pieces the settlement of Europe made in 1815 had not disturbed the peace of the world at large, for the reason that after Trafalgar the fleets of Great Britain controlled the seas. We must now see what had been happening in America, Australia, New Zealand, Africa and Asia.

At the close of the Seven Years' War the French had lost the whole of their territories on the mainland of North America; Canada and the country east of the Mississippi was ceded to the British; New Orleans and the country west of the Mississippi, which retained the name of Louisiana, was ceded to Spain.

When the battle of the Nile had frustrated Napoleon's project of conquering an empire in the East, his thoughts were turned for a time to the western hemisphere. In 1800 he purchased Louisiana from Spain, but presently realised that his dream of ruling the world was futile so long as England controlled the seas. While the Peace of Amiens gave him a breathing space, he had made up his mind either to invade England across the Channel, or, failing that, to destroy the source of her power by excluding her trade from Europe. When war was renewed, New Orleans would fall an easy prey to the British fleet, and the rest of Louisiana north of it to the United States. Now, as always, his paramount need was cash; so he suddenly offered to sell these territories to the United States of America. The proposal was made in Paris to Livingston and James Monroe, who wisely exceeded their instructions, and on April 30, 1803, closed the bargain for a total payment of under £6,000,000. For this paltry sum they obtained territory, rich as any in the world, extending from the Gulf of Mexico to the present Canadian boundary, some 1,000,000 square miles in extent, five times as great as France, the region, in fact, which is now known as the Middle West. At a single stroke the United States had doubled its previous area. The American Commonwealth thus started the nineteenth century with enormous virgin territories in the centre of the continent ripe for development.

Climate and history had combined to impose on American colonists two systems of life so different that they could not be worked side by side. We have seen in an earlier chapter how the planting of tobacco, sugar and cotton led to the introduction of negro slavery to Virginia and the colonies in the South. The slave whose sole incentive is fear of punishment can be made to produce raw materials. But the process of turning such raw materials into goods to be used must, broadly speaking, be done by labourers who feel some interest in the work they are doing. A great manufacturing system cannot be based upon slave labour. It limits the capacity of the masters themselves, and unfits them to manage free workers whose incentive to industry is the wage they are paid and some interest in what they are doing.

The system also affects those Europeans who are not owners or masters of slaves. They come to regard labour as appropriate to a savage and servile race, and would sooner starve than earn their bread by

S

the sweat of their brow. And yet in a wide range of crafts the necessary skill can only be attained by youths prepared to face rough manual labour; for the school of skill is drudgery. In the southern States there were few openings for whites who did not inherit land or belong to professions, unless they could find positions as overseers. The 'mean whites', parasites devoid of all power to earn their own living or of pride in anything but their colour, were an ever-increasing class.

North of Virginia the soil and climate were unsuited to tobacco, sugar and cotton. These regions were developed by settlers accustomed to work with their hands, and slavery found no legal basis in the constitutions framed for the northern States by Quakers and Puritans. There was here no hindrance to a rapid development of small farming, and also of industries, except that such industries needed protection.

The planters in slave-States, with a rapidly increasing market in England for the raw material they produced, were opposed to protective tariffs. Until Watt had produced an engine which would drive spinning frames and looms, the British imports of raw cotton had never exceeded 4,000,000 lbs. By 1800 they had risen to 56,000,000 lbs., and by 1815 to close on 100,000,000 lbs., facts which explain why the British Commonwealth had survived a war lasting for twenty-two years with scarcely a break.

America was only producing 2,000,000 lbs. of cotton a year when Watt invented the steam engine. Production was checked by the difficulty, not of growing the plant, but of separating the seed from its clothing of vegetable wool. One slave could remove with his hands the seed from one pound of cotton in a day. In 1794 Eli Whitney invented the cotton gin and solved for cotton the problem which has never been solved for flax. With Whitney's machine a slave could clean 50 lbs. a day. Presently the machine, harnessed to steam, was cleaning 1000 lbs. a day to every man employed on its working. Every bale of cotton which the southern States could produce could be sold at a profit in Manchester. The wealth to be realised under the slave system was only limited by the territories to which it could be spread.

In 1820 the question was brought to a head by the proposal to create a new State in the Union called Missouri, carved out of the territory bought from Napoleon. Was slavery to be legalised or forbidden in this State? "This momentous question", wrote Jefferson, "like a fire-bell in the night awakened and filled me with terror. I considered it at once as the knell of the Union."

For the moment, however, the issues were compromised. In 1821 Missouri was admitted as a slave-State, but its southern boundary of 36° 30′ was henceforward to be taken as the frontier between freedom and slavery in the rest of Louisiana. This was the famous Dixon line.

The country south of parallel 42 which lay between Louisiana and the Pacific coast belonged to the Mexican Republic. The eastern part of this country between Louisiana and the Rio Grande river was known as Texas, which also contained large areas suited to the raising of cotton by slave labour. The Mexican government was presently alarmed by the fact that Mexican owners were selling these lands to planters from the United States who were pouring in to develop them. The money invested in these speculations in slave-raised cotton was coming from Europe as well as from America.

> By 1835 there were more than twenty thousand invaders in that flourishing province—hardy farmers, lordly planters, droves of slaves, hunters, adventurers, and outlaws.

. . . In 1829, a decree of the Mexican government abolished slavery; but a vigorous protest from the American settlers compelled it to exempt Texas from the operation of the order.[1]

In 1835 the settlers declared their independence, which they rendered effective in 1836 by destroying the Mexican forces sent to suppress them. They then proceeded to move Congress to annex Texas to the United States.

In the Senate this movement was opposed by senators from the States in which slavery was forbidden. They realised that, if Texas were annexed, this enormous region would be carved into several slave-States, each entitled to send two members to the Senate. The slave-States would thus ere long secure control of the Senate. The free States, which encouraged white settlement, could always count on controlling the lower house, where States were represented in proportion to population. But the slave-States could always defeat any future movement to abolish slavery, if once they secured a majority in the Senate.

Meanwhile American ships from New England had been making their way round Cape Horn to Mexican ports in search of furs which brought them fantastic profits in China. The government in Mexico city, two thousand miles to the south, was wholly unable to administer or colonise a country, equal to France and Germany, which lay between Texas and the Californian coast. The settlements in the Pacific ports were everywhere dominated by American traders. From Texas settlers were reaching California across the deserts and mountain ranges.

The financial interests in Texas became so widely spread that in 1845 a majority in Congress was at length secured for its annexation. This assertion of sovereignty led to a fight in Texas between American forces and those of Mexico. In the war which followed, American troops occupied the Mexican capital, while American ships seized two ports on the Californian coast. On February 2, 1848, the Mexican government was forced to sign a peace, ceding to the United States the country between Texas and the Pacific for a payment of £3,000,000. The war was bitterly denounced by opponents of slavery in the northern States. The speech which Abraham Lincoln made against it in Congress cost him his seat at the next election.

The party opposed to slavery had favoured the expansion of the U.S.A. to the north-west into regions suited to free labour, which were also too cold for development by slaves. The demand for the annexation of the region which is now British Columbia had come from this quarter, and had brought the British and American Commonwealths to the verge of war. Happily this was avoided by a treaty signed in June 1846 which fixed the boundary which now divides British Columbia from the United States.

By the middle of the nineteenth century the American Commonwealth had thus acquired the enormous territory which it now covers from ocean to ocean, in area greater than the whole of Europe west of Russia, the greatest field for colonisation which has ever been opened, and greater than can ever be opened again. Millions from Europe were eager to enter it.

To acquire the full rights of American citizens the settlers who poured into these territories had to form themselves into States suitable for inclusion in the federal commonwealth. Like the older States they produced their own constitutions. If a State constitution was framed on the model of the southern States, the future population would mainly consist of slaves, with room only for a small minority of white masters. If, on the other hand, a State constitution followed the model of States in the north, slavery was forbidden by its terms. It would then be peopled by a population mainly of whites willing to work with their own hands; but whites from the south bred to a system of slave economy could find no opening for their manner of life in a free State. A constitution admitting slavery thus closed the State to which it applied to settlement from the north. A constitution forbidding slavery closed the State to which it applied to settlement from the south.

This issue rapidly came to a head in those territories west of Missouri which are shown on the map as Kansas. In these territories settlers from the south drafted a constitution which legalised slavery in the State it was hoped to establish. Another constitution was prepared by settlers from the north which prohibited slavery. From 1850 to 1860 the armed conflicts between these parties earned for this region the name of 'bleeding Kansas'.

In the north a movement for the abolition of slavery as a thing evil in itself was in full swing. The southern States began to realise that the system on which their whole manner of life was founded could only be saved by their quitting the Union. In 1860 the election of Abraham Lincoln as President obliged them to face the issue. On the day following the election South Carolina seceded.

The assertion by one State of a right to secede from the Union at once raised for decision a conflict which had never been settled when the federal constitution was framed in 1788. In the minds of some the Union was no more than a contract between sovereign States, any one of which might, if it chose, cancel the contract and leave the Union. In the minds of others the whole body of people who entered the Union had created a new nation, a sovereign state, in the true sense of that word, from which the powers of the so-called States were derived. In their view the secession of one State, which implied refusal to obey the laws of the federal government, was an act of rebellion; and laws lost their validity unless the would-be rebels were forced to obey them. This was the view of President Lincoln who saw in the constitution, which his country had adopted in 1788, not a contract but a creed. To abstain from enforcing the federal law in South Carolina could only imply a tacit acceptance of the right of secession. Its example would quickly be followed by other slave-States, and not by them only. There were other issues than slavery. If the right of secession were once admitted, any State which remained in the Union would be tempted to use it when aggrieved by decisions of the federal electorate. The principle of government by majority in the commonwealth as a whole was at stake.

When Lincoln decided to enforce the federal law on South Carolina every State in the Union was obliged to decide whether to support him, or whether to support the claim which South Carolina was making of the right to secede from the Union. In the south, where the system was based on slavery, the States sided with South Carolina. In the north, where freedom prevailed, the States supported President Lincoln and the federal government. In the southern States every citizen was thus driven to decide for himself whether his allegiance was due to his State or to the United States as a whole, for loyalty to both was no longer possible. The command of the federal armies was offered to a soldier of genius, Robert E. Lee, who declined it on the ground that his final allegiance was due to the State of Virginia, and not to the American Commonwealth as a whole. He threw in his lot with the southern States and led their armies to a series of brilliant victories. For several years it seemed as though the issue would be decided by the gifts of a great military leader, as it had been when the colonies revolted from England.

In the end the factors which determined the issue were the strength inherent in the system of free labour, and the weakness inseparable from the system of slavery. For the reasons already explained the States in the north which were based on free labour had attracted more immigrants from Europe than the south. They had also been able to develop the new resources of a mechanised age. Their factories were producing the wealth, the munitions and supplies, which enabled them to equip their vastly superior numbers as armies in the field.

The greater resources of the northern States would have little availed them had Lincoln's appeals to their public spirit received no better response than those of Washington. Of the million Americans who perished in the war most of that number had given their lives to sustain the Union. When we think of the difficulties Washington faced in recruiting his miniature armies, which were often left by the States for which they were fighting to starve in the field, the contrast is as instructive as any in history. It proves the tremendous effect which institutions can have in the course of a few generations on the character and attitude to life of whole masses of people.[2] The issue was at length decided at Gettysburg at the cost of some 50,000 lives. The words that Lincoln spoke on that field are more widely known and better remembered than any which have fallen from the lips of a statesman since the days of Pericles. They read like a brief epitome of the speech uttered 2000 years before at the funeral pyre of the heroes who had given their lives for Athens, for similar occasions breed similar thoughts. Lincoln's claim that his fellow-citizens had died, as he himself was to die, "that government of the people, by the people, for the people, shall not perish from the earth" was destined to be justified by after events.

NOTES

[1] Beard, *The Rise of American Civilization*, vol. i. pp. 592, 593.

[2] For a fuller treatment of the subject dealt with in this chapter, see pp. 633-47 of *The Commonwealth of Nations*. After more than twenty years I see no reason for revising what I there wrote about 1912.

CHAPTER XL

FROM EMPIRE TO COMMONWEALTH: CANADA

In Book II., Chapter XXIII., we saw why Quebec and the country east and west of the French colony remained in the British Empire, when the colonies south of Quebec had severed their connection with the mother country. In Chapter XXIV. we have traced the curious course of events which in 1790 had led Great Britain to establish her claim to the coast facing the Pacific, thousands of miles to the west of Ontario.

Too late to change the issues of war with her own colonists, the British parliament had passed an act renouncing its claim to impose taxation on territories beyond the British Isles. It registered a lesson which no British government would again forget. But British statesmen were slow to grasp the main problem of which taxation was only one aspect. The Canadian executives were appointed from England, while the legislative power was vested in bodies responsible to local electorates. The inevitable deadlocks led to paralysis of government and friction, till, fifty years after Bunker Hill, the British government was again faced by rebellions in North America.

The American revolution had also led the British government to establish convict settlements in Australia. In 1803 Captain John Macarthur realised that the country was adapted for sheep-farming and free colonisation began to spread. Land was distributed to applicants in enormous tracts.

In 1827 Wakefield, an unscrupulous man of genius, was imprisoned for abducting and marrying a ward in Chancery. He probably thought of retiring to the colonies when released, and spent his enforced leisure in working out principles upon which the vacant territories of Australia and Canada might be developed. His conclusions, published while he was still in gaol, attracted the notice of men like James Mill, Torrens, Buller, Molesworth, Whately and also John George Lambton, first Earl of Durham. The Colonisation Society was founded shortly after his release in 1830.

This radical group, and especially Wakefield, had a gift, not often found in original thinkers, for translating their own ideas into action. They actually founded colonies in Australia and New Zealand. They induced the Colonial Office, instead of squandering the land, to issue it to purchasers at a fair price and use the proceeds for developing the colony. They forced the government to annex New Zealand. In the end they drove it to abandon the practice of sending convicts to Australia.

From economics they turned to politics, and in that field their constructive activities laid the foundations of the British Commonwealth as it now is. In 1837, the year in which Queen Victoria came to the throne, rebellions had broken out in Ontario and Quebec. In 1838 Durham was appointed governor-general, with instructions to report on the whole situation. He took Buller and Wakefield with him, but resigned after five months in Canada. On November 30 he landed at Plymouth. His report is dated January 31, 1839. He arranged, through Wakefield, for *The Times* to publish it at once, distrusting the government with whom he had quarrelled to produce it in full.

It was this report which first brought to light the structural defect which had vitiated the relations of England to her colonies since their first foundation. Their executives were appointed by and responsible to the government in London. Their legislatures were elected by and were answerable to local electorates. These legislatures could paralyse the executives by refusing them legislation and supplies they needed, but could not remove them. This resulted in paralysis of government which could only lead to revolution. As Durham saw, it was this which in England had for centuries brought the king into conflict with parliament, until the expedient was adopted of transferring the executive authority to the member of parliament who could for the time being command its obedience. Durham urged that colonial governors should be placed in the same position as the crown had accepted in England. He would have them appoint as their ministers the leaders who commanded a majority in the legislature, and give legal effect to whatever they advised. Thus only would colonial legislators and electorates acquire a sense of responsibility for their own government. This novel proposal to apply the system of responsible government to the colonies did much to bring home to the British the real nature of the system which they themselves had evolved.

Durham's plan was exposed to the objection that it would only establish harmony between colonial executives and legislatures at the cost of discord between Britain and her colonies, and would lead to a second rupture of the Empire. There was more truth in the first part of this criticism than in the second. Durham failed to see, or at least to admit, that the establishment of responsible government in the colonies would involve their growth into separate sovereignties. In the nature of things a government answerable to a colonial legislature and electorate must often desire changes unwelcome to ministers answerable to the British parliament and electorate: and, when matters of principle are at stake, the wishes of one electorate or other must prevail. On minor and formal issues colonial governments have often yielded. But whenever a large popular interest was at stake, the control of vacant lands, the protection of colonial industries against those of Great Britain herself, pardon, coinage, Dominion navies, right to control external relations and accredit envoys to foreign states, or the British veto on legislation, the wish of the younger community has finally prevailed against the conservative instincts of the old country, nowhere so strong as in its able and potent bureaucracy.

That this has been so is directly due to the war of American independence. In England the attempt to coerce the colonies was popular only with the minority who supported the reactionary efforts of George III. to recover the executive power for the crown. To the commons of England the long and ruinous war with their own kindred was a hateful memory. In handling controversies with the later colonies in the nineteenth century ministers were reminded by whips that the British electorate would never stand for a forcible settlement. If an issue could not be compromised by agreement, it must then be settled in accordance with the wishes of the younger community. Till the later years of the nineteenth century English statesmen commonly assumed that self-governing colonies must presently follow the example of the United States by severing their connection with the parent commonwealth. It was only the few who foresaw, and those imperfectly, what would happen when England had adopted a habit of yielding before a controversy had reached the flash-point. As their own historians have shown, the great majority of Americans were averse to secession until actual bloodshed had embittered the quarrel. The British feeling that never again must a difference with a self-governing colony be allowed to approach that point has meant that the younger communities have, step by step, acquired a sovereignty of their own and are in no way subject to that of Great Britain.

It has also meant that the colonies have never had any practical occasion for severing their connection with the older community. They have, therefore, remained members of a world-wide polity, with a central organisation which has gradually abandoned its claim to sovereignty. The right of secession, tacitly admitted, has never been forced.

In another direction the great achievement of the United States has influenced the growth of the colonies, and through them the structure of the whole British Commonwealth. Washington and Hamilton had divined that a so-called State was a unit too feeble to develop a genuine sovereignty of its own, and could only exist by inclusion in a larger national unit. In 1860 the southern States unconsciously recognised this fact by combining in a so-called 'confederation', which was in certain respects a closer form of union than the federation from which they were trying to secede.

Durham also had read this lesson, and in his report had urged that the provinces of Canada should apply it. When the victories of the north had finally preserved the American Union, Canadian statesmen had come to recognise that their own provinces were too weak to develop a genuine autonomy. Unless combined in some larger national unit they would sooner or later be absorbed by the great republic to the south, which was at that moment powerfully armed.

In 1864 a conference of delegates from the various colonies met at Quebec and agreed on a plan for uniting them all in a federal system. The plan was then carried to England and submitted to parliament in the form of a bill, which in 1867 passed into law as the British North America Act.

Like Washington, Canadian statesmen had realised the future importance of the uninhabited regions to the west. This vast area was the hunting-ground of the Hudson's Bay Company, which opposed colonisation because it interfered with their business of trapping wild animals for their skins. The discovery of gold on the Fraser river, however, had attracted settlers and led to the organisation of British Columbia as a Crown Colony. The Canadian statesmen conceived and executed the idea of connecting British Columbia with the Maritime Provinces by a line which was built by the Canadian Pacific Railway Company. The colonies and territories between the Atlantic and Pacific coasts were thus united in one federation greater in area than the United States. They adopted the model of its constitution, with improvements made in the light of the experience gained since it was framed. Powers not specifically assigned to provincial authorities were reserved to the national government. The method of harmonising the action of the legislatures and executives on the lines recommended by Durham was maintained. In this vital matter Canada, followed by the other Dominions, adhered to the British example and refused to follow that of the United States.

By creating a self-governing nation on the continental scale of the United States, without severing their connection with the United Kingdom, Canadian statesmen may be said to have launched the idea of a commonwealth of nations. Ideas are portable and indestructible. After one generation their example was followed on the other side of the world by the colonies of Australia, and ten years later by those of South Africa, each devising constitutions for themselves in the light of experience gained by their predecessors, adapted to suit their own conditions. Their right to decide issues for themselves is now no more in dispute than that of the United States. Their mutual relations give rise to many of the difficulties which beset separate and sovereign communities. In certain respects those difficulties are enhanced by membership in a larger polity, especially those arising from conflicts of race and colour. But the fact remains that in all disputes the idea of war is excluded. On none of their budgets appears one item of expenditure on armaments in view of a possible conflict with each other. Their voluntary union has stood the strain of a world war. Whether it would stand the strain of another such war is the subject of much discussion. But to guess at the future is idle when by looking at facts and reading their meaning we may help to shape it.

CHAPTER XLI

AUSTRALIA

After the Peace of Paris one of Cook's officers, Matra by name, proposed that the loyalists should be shipped from America, settled in New South Wales and encouraged to develop the land there with Chinese or Kanaka labour. Had this been done the Australian continent would have since been peopled by Chinese ruled by a handful of Europeans. Like the West Indies it would now be a group of Crown Colonies. The loyalists, however, were settled in Canada, and Lord Sydney, the Secretary of State, decided to use Australia for solving another of the problems raised when England lost her colonies. Her prisons were crowded with convicts who could no longer be sent to hoe tobacco and cotton on American plantations. In 1788 Governor Philip was sent to open the first convict settlement on the site where the city of Sydney now stands. In 1799 Irish rebels were transported in shiploads to Australia, a fact which explains why nearly one-fourth of its people are now Irish Catholics. In 1803, when the prisoners there had grown too many for discipline and safety, a branch penitentiary was established at Hobart. In 1824 another was founded at Brisbane.

On the ships which sailed to these settlements from England colonists who had not been convicted of crimes began to find their way to Australia, and to open up the interior. The more orderly convicts were allowed to serve them as labourers on ticket-of-leave. This explains why Australia was never developed like the southern colonies in America, or like South Africa by imported negroes or Asiatics.

An officer of the garrison in Sydney, Captain Macarthur, conceived the idea of producing wool to fill the empty holds of the ships sent to supply the convict settlements. He started his experiments with 29 merinos obtained from General Gordon's flocks in the Cape.[1] In 1803 he procured from King George himself some better sheep of the same breed. Others were quick to follow his lead, and, assisted by convict labour, the pastoral industry spread with amazing rapidity. In May 1835 Batman landed his flocks at Port Philip, and the city of Melbourne was founded in the following September.

In 1830 Sturt, an explorer, had made his way down the rivers which rise south of Sydney in the Blue Mountains to the Murray river, and had reached its mouth in the south of Australia. His report had attracted the attention of Gibbon Wakefield, Lord Durham and their associates in the Colonisation Society. Their scheme for the settlement of South Australia was embodied in an act of parliament. Adelaide was founded as its capital in 1836.

Ten years before this a station had been founded at King George's Sound, near the south-west corner of the continent, to forestall an attempt on the part of the French to annex this side of Australia. In 1829 colonists had been sent to occupy West Australia. Fremantle and Perth were founded at the mouth of the Swan river.

The foundation of convict settlements in Australia had established the fact that this continent was a suitable home for Europeans. Colonists reached it from the British Isles in ever-increasing numbers, and the stream was greatly increased when gold was discovered in the middle of the nineteenth century. In accordance with the habits and traditions of their race they demanded the right to manage their own affairs, those of the country in which they were making their homes. In colonies which centred round convict settlements like those at Sydney, Hobart and Brisbane, where the British government had to maintain regiments of soldiers to control the criminals, it was idle to talk of self-government. The British government must either resist the demand for it or close down its penal settlements. The movement started by Wakefield did much to convince the British government that Australians must be left to govern themselves. In 1842 an act of parliament 'for the government of New South Wales and Van Diemen's Land' established at Sydney a legislative council of 30 members. Of these 24 were elected by the settlers. It was found at once that members from Hobart and Melbourne could not in practice attend meetings of a council in Sydney.

In 1846 Earl Grey, who had been a member of Wakefield's group, became Secretary of State for the Colonies and War. In 1850 he submitted to parliament a bill to allow Victoria, Tasmania (Van Diemen's Land), South Australia and Queensland to be organised as colonies separate from New South Wales. The bill also included provisions for a federal government for all Australia, with a governor-general and a general assembly elected from all the colonies. In committee the federal provisions were dropped. The act as passed merely enabled the four younger colonies to be separated from New South Wales, and empowered the colonists to draft constitutions for themselves. In 1852 the transportation of criminals to Australia was finally brought to an end. In the course of the next few years responsible governments were established at Sydney, Melbourne, Adelaide, Hobart and Brisbane, under constitutions which the colonists had framed for themselves. In West Australia responsible government was established by an act of parliament in 1890.

In the meantime, the need for some organ of government to enable Australians to deal with interests which affected them as a whole began to be seen. The conflicting fiscal systems of New South Wales and Victoria gave rise to serious difficulties on their boundary. In Queensland the introduction of Kanaka labour threatened the future of a white Australia. The continental system of transportation was crippled by the fact that the colonies adopted three different gauges on their railways. The colonial governments were too much absorbed in their local affairs to face these issues, until in the closing years of the century annexations by foreign powers in the southern Pacific forced on the minds of Australians the need for national unity.

NOTE

[1] For this fact I am indebted to a lineal descendant of Captain Macarthur, Miss Macarthur Onslow, at whose home, Menangle in New South Wales, I have seen a flock which are the direct descendants of the sheep imported by Captain Macarthur from the Cape.

CHAPTER XLII

NEW ZEALAND

AUSTRALIA, physically the oldest of the continents, is a great plateau, upon which there are few bulges rising above 2000 feet from the sea. New Zealand is a range of mountains lifted in a late geological age by volcanic forces to points little lower than those of the Alps. It abounds in mountains and valleys and its coasts, unlike those of Australia, are broken by numerous bays and fiords. These islands are, therefore, divided into numerous small localities, separated by mountainous barriers, but easily approached by the sea. The facilities for inter-communication are greatly enhanced by the straits, named after Captain Cook, which divide the two larger islands. In area these islands are but one twenty-eighth that of Australia; but the ample and well-distributed rainfall of New Zealand may in time enable it to support a population equal to half that which the poorer climate of Australia will enable that continent to carry.[1]

The native inhabitants, whom Captain Cook found in Australia, are probably a remnant of a neolithic people, known as Aurignacians, because specimens of their skeletons were first discovered in 1860 at Aurignac in France. They were too primitive to offer any serious resistance to colonisation, or acquire the arts of civilised life. They retired in rapidly dwindling numbers into the arid and tropical regions where Europeans were unable to settle.

The Maoris, whom Cook found in New Zealand, were an off-shoot of the races who inhabit the tropical islands of the Pacific. Their ancestors must have crossed thousands of miles of ocean in open canoes with a seamanship daring and skilful as that of Columbus. They had been in New Zealand long enough to develop distinctive national characteristics, a language, a mythology and a decorative art of their own. They were none the less Stone Age cannibals, still in the stage of tribal society. Their clans, like those of the Scottish Highlands, rejoiced in raiding and fighting each other.

The establishment of a port at Sydney enabled whalers to visit the seas round New Zealand, who soon discovered that the Maoris produced a valuable flax from a plant called *phormium tenax* which grows in the marshes, and is now common in English gardens. From the whalers the Maoris quickly learned the value of fire-arms as weapons, and obtained them in exchange for bales of flax. It was soon realised that tribes with fire-arms could master and dominate their neighbours. Possession of muskets and ammunition became the condition of existence, and the Maoris left their *pas*, fortified villages, on promontories and mountain tops, to gather flax in the marshes, where they died by thousands of fever. Museums in Europe were eager to obtain specimens of Maori heads for the sake of the beautiful patterns tattooed on the skin, and were willing to pay as much as £500 for a head. The tribes were, therefore, encouraged to fight each other, for the sake of the heads they cut from their enemies killed in battle. The chiefs were also led to sell the tribal lands to Europeans for fire-arms. The Maori tribes were thus threatened with utter destruction by their first contact with civilisation.

In 1814 Samuel Marsden, the chaplain at Sydney, visited the islands and founded a missionary movement to befriend the Maoris. It was through the missionaries that the state of anarchy in New

Zealand with all its attendant horrors came to be realised in England. In 1833 the British government appointed James Busby as resident, but refused to annex the islands, unwilling to add to the troubles they were facing in Canada and the Cape. In 1837 Captain Hobson of the *Rattlesnake* who had helped in the founding of Melbourne, advised the establishment of settlements under British consuls at the principal harbours in New Zealand. As the government still refused to take action, Wakefield and Durham determined to force their hands. They formed a company for founding a colony in New Zealand on the lines of the scheme already projected in South Australia. When settlers had been despatched with Colonel Wakefield in command, Lord Durham informed the government what had been done.

At last the government decided to appoint Captain Hobson lieutenant-governor to annex the islands as part of the colony of New South Wales. At this very time a company was commissioned by Louis-Philippe to establish itself at Akaroa on the southern island and annex it to France.

Colonel Wakefield and his settlers were the first to arrive in New Zealand. He had made for Cook's Strait, where he claimed to have bought an enormous tract from the Maori chiefs and founded Wellington which was named in gratitude for the support which the Duke had given in the House of Lords to the company which had colonised South Australia. Hobson went to the Bay of Islands in the far north. In July 1840 the French frigate *L'Aube* with the agents and settlers of the Nanto-Bordelaise Company entered the Bay of Islands. Captain Hobson hastily despatched the British warship *Britomart* to Akaroa, and when *L'Aube* arrived there the French found the British flag flying over the promontory.

As soon as possible Hobson summoned the Maori chiefs to Waitangi, the place where Busby lived in the southern island. In the treaty which he there made with them, they yielded "all the rights and powers of sovereignty" to the Queen of England. The Maoris were guaranteed in "full and undisturbed possession of their lands". If they wished to sell any part of it they must offer it first to the government. They were given the full rights and privileges as British subjects. New Zealand was shortly afterwards recognised as a colony distinct from New South Wales.

The rights of the Maoris, as recognised at Waitangi, were hard to reconcile with the claims to land which Europeans professed to have bought from them. This was specially so in the case of Wakefield's company, which hastened to pour settlers into New Zealand. They were soon in conflict with the Maoris and Hobson, worn out by his efforts to keep the peace and to reconcile conflicting claims, died in 1842. Under Fitzroy, his successor, some Maori chiefs broke into open rebellion, till in 1845 a man strong enough to deal with the Wakefield company as well as with the Maori rebels appeared on the scene.

In 1837 a young officer, Captain George Grey, had been appointed resident magistrate at King George's Sound in West Australia. Lord John Russell, who was then Colonial Secretary, was impressed by the excellence of the work he had done for the settlement of the natives there. In 1841 he was sent as governor to unravel the tangled affairs of South Australia, which he did with such conspicuous success that in 1845 he was ordered to take over the government of New Zealand from Fitzroy. On reaching the Bay of Islands, Grey rapidly gained the confidence of the tribes who were still disposed to be friendly, and by their aid suppressed the rebellious chiefs. The claims of the Wakefield company and of other Europeans were reduced to reason and then enforced.

When George Grey was appointed governor, the Colonial Secretary, Earl Grey, had already devised a constitution for New Zealand, to suit the interests of the Wakefield company. George Grey, supported by Bishop Selwyn, successfully resisted the promulgation of this form of government. The company was forced into liquidation and its lands reverted to the government. Its experience, however, led the way to two better schemes. In 1848 a company was formed by members of the Free Kirk of Scotland, which founded a settlement for its followers in the south island at Dunedin (Gaelic for New Edinburgh). An Anglican company followed suit by founding a colony at Christchurch, which was largely supported by Oxford and Cambridge men.

Before leaving New Zealand in 1852 Grey had devised a constitution on a democratic basis, which carefully guarded Maori interests, under which the country was governed for the next 23 years. In 1854 he was sent to deal with native troubles in South Africa.

The manner in which the Maoris and colonists of New Zealand have lived together is the brightest page in the dark history of race relations. That this has been so is largely due to the loyalty and practical sense with which Grey applied the principles laid down in the Treaty of Waitangi.

NOTE

[1] Lord Bledisloe, letter to *The Times*, March 19, 1936.

CHAPTER XLIII

SOUTH AFRICA

Up to the eve of the French Revolution, the structure of society in Australasia had remained unaffected by events in the rest of the world. The problems with which Sir George Grey was called to deal in South Africa had their roots in the previous centuries. In 1594 Philip II., by closing the port of Lisbon, had driven the Dutch to seek for spices in the East Indies, where they were grown. Their fleets had quickly mastered the oceans opened by Vasco da Gama, and established a Batavian empire over Ceylon and the islands great and small to the north of Australia. The Cape of Good Hope was the half-way house to this empire, and in 1649 the Dutch East India Company sent van Riebeck to establish at Table Bay a settlement to furnish their ships with water and vegetables as an antidote to scurvy.

The Cape Peninsula was once an island, but the trade wind and the surf it raises have now blocked with silver sand the narrow strait which in prehistoric times had divided Table Mountain from the African continent. Across this sandy isthmus van Riebeck built a stockade to protect his settlement from natives on the mainland. As the settlers realised how few and feeble these natives were, they spread through the fertile belt on the coast of the mainland less than 100 miles in width, which the trade winds water with winter rains.

Beyond this fertile belt, the climate suddenly changes as the country rises 2000 feet to the great plateau which forms the south-eastern half of the African continent. A line drawn from the mouth of the Congo north-east to a point at the middle of the Red Sea will divide this mass from the north-western half of the continent which, except in Morocco and the Cameroons, is not greatly raised above sea level. The uplands visible from Table Mountain extend northwards across the equator to the ranges of Kenya and Abyssinia, where the waters which fertilise Egypt are gathered. In contrast with India this vast home of a tropical people has regions where altitude counteracts climate, and Europeans are able to make their homes.

The Cape Peninsula and the country north of it was sparsely inhabited by Hottentot tribes, neither dangerous as foes nor useful as labourers. The settlers from Holland or, to use their own language, 'the Boers' (the root is the same in our word 'neighbour'), had less difficulty in moving inland than American settlers who were constantly menaced by Red Indians. They imported slaves, Malays from the East, and negroes from western markets on the African coast north of the equator. Like the colonists in Virginia they learned to think of manual labour as appropriate only to a subject and inferior race.

The coastal belt between the isthmus and the slopes of the great plateau is watered by winter rains and suitable for tillage. As the slopes rise the climate changes as rapidly as the levels, and when Boers had climbed these slopes they found themselves in the vast and arid spaces of the Karroo. There flocks and herds could wander and live by nibbling the bushes; but cultivation was possible only in tiny oases. At once the Boers changed their habits, became pastoral and acquired the mobility of nomads whose wealth is in animals which breed for themselves, and also can move on their own feet. As their numerous sons came to manhood and married, they trekked with some of the family cattle further into the wilderness. This migratory habit was thoroughly established in the eighteenth century. Before its close this eastward tide of migration was approaching the watered and fertile belt between the Karroo and the Indian Ocean.

Down this eastern corridor were descending powerful and warlike Bantu tribes, set in motion, perhaps, by the ceaseless hunt for slaves in tropical Africa for American plantations. When the slave-owning and migratory Boers reached and desired these lands, they found that a host of formidable 'kaffirs' had largely forestalled them. In 1779 the Boers and Bantu were facing each other on the banks of the Fish river.

Holland had not been at war with England since 1674, and during that time had allowed the British East India Company to use Cape Town as a port of call. When in 1795 and in 1806 Holland was in the clutches of France, Cape Town was seized by the British to prevent its use by the French navy as a basis of operations. Experience had proved that the British could not maintain their position in India unless they controlled this half-way house on the sea road to the East. So Cape Town was one of the few conquests from Holland which England chose to retain when the map of the world was being revised after Waterloo. It never entered their heads that Cape Town was also the keyhole of a box as richly stored with troubles as the gift which Pandora received from the hands of Zeus. The British were unconsciously fingering the key which was destined to open this box of troubles and to bring them swarming about their ears.

When Wycliffe had first thought of translating the Gospels into a modern vernacular, he opened an epoch when men other than priests could reflect on the intuitions of Christ, and apply their meaning to conditions around them. The Gospels were an axe laid to the root of authority, and translations were hafts which ordinary men could wield in the place of the old ones which churchmen had kept to themselves and jealously guarded. The process was slow, but none the less sure. Escape from the spiritual and even physical torments, pictured in the images of Jewish apocalypse, was, until recent times, the aim of the Protestant Churches, no less than of those based on authority. The Reformation in its earliest form was a national revolt against the claims of a world-wide authority to decide such issues. The Puritan movement asserted the right and the duty of each individual to decide these issues apart from the state. One smaller movement had gone further. Quakers like John Woolman had seen that the institution of slavery was contrary to the teaching of Christ.

A typical exponent of the Puritan faith was John Wesley, approved by Cromwell's triers in 1658 as a minister in Dorset, and ejected from his living at the Restoration. The cinders of reaction buried but could not extinguish that fervent creed, which was kept alive, as by air from beneath, by the habit of reading the Gospels in English. It revived in the Evangelical movement started by Charles and John, grandsons of Wesley. As much as, or more than, previous religious reformers, the Wesleys were inspired with the sense of impending doom, which Jewish apocalypse had promised to unrepentant mankind at the hands of a vengeful God. But their master passion was love and reverence for the Christ whose pity had opened a way of escape to those who would take it. A constant study of his teaching led them, as it led the Quakers, to face its logical and practical conclusions. If desire for the good of all sentient creatures was the principle of life, that principle must apply to the natives of Africa. No vested, national or private interest could justify the essential iniquity of condemning a whole people to slavery.

John Wesley was a clergyman of the Anglican Church; but when he crossed the Atlantic his teaching revived the Puritan spirit. When bishops refused to support him he ordained ministers with his own hands, and thus separated the Methodists from the Episcopal Churches; but a large section of churchmen continued to follow his movement. It came to include men like Wilberforce who were powerful in social and political circles. It thus created a new community between men of religion in Episcopal and Nonconformist Churches in England and America. It brought the great body of earnest Protestants into the struggle against slavery and supplied the numerical support which the Quaker initiative had deserved, but lacked.

The first victory of the anti-slavery movement was an appeal to the principle of the commonwealth as embodied in the laws of England. In 1772 Lord Mansfield ruled that a slave was freed by landing in the British Isles.

The next stage in the movement was an agitation for an act of parliament forbidding the transport of slaves from Africa for sale in the colonies. Such an act was passed in 1807; but the trade could only be stopped by international agreements, which the Congress of Vienna did much to facilitate. At the very time when South Africa became subject to British rule, the Dutch colonists were cut off from further supplies of the only labour they knew how to use.

The immediate sufferers were the Hottentots, a primitive race thrust to this edge of the world, not worth enslaving so long as the colonists could purchase slaves from the East Indies or from tropical Africa. The stoppage of these supplies set up a demand which enabled even the Hottentots to bargain for wages. A free market for labour was utterly foreign to the minds of employers, who for five generations had learned to assume that the coloured races existed only for the sake of the white. They demanded laws to regulate the relations of master and servant. English governors, anxious to avoid trouble, gave them their way. Stoppage of the slave-trade thus deprived the Hottentots of such liberty as these landless nomads had before enjoyed.

The Evangelical movement had now entered on its missionary stage. In its earlier days the Catholic Church had eagerly obeyed the call of its master to carry his message of salvation throughout the world. In the sixteenth century the counter-reformation had led to a great revival of missionary enterprise on the part of the Catholic Church; but for two centuries Protestants were preoccupied in asserting the right and duty of each individual to save his soul for himself. At the close of the eighteenth century the Evangelical movement was largely responsible for reminding Christians of the call to spread the message which alone could save humanity from impending doom. In 1792 Carey, a Baptist cobbler, published his *Enquiry into the Obligations of Christians to use Means for the Conversion of the Heathens*, and next year departed for India. In 1795 the London Missionary Society was organised, to find in South Africa under British rule an appropriate sphere for its operations. The missionaries established stations in various parts of the country where the Hottentots could be gathered round churches and schools for instruction. These stations became asylums in which Hottentots could avoid the operation of laws directed to making them accept contracts of service under a farmer. The missionaries were regarded by the farmers as fanatics out of touch with realities, and as dangerous enemies of established order. Of significance for the future is the fact that this view was not confined to the Dutch. The same attitude was adopted by a group of colonists who in 1820 were brought from England and planted in the east of Cape Colony.

Complaints that their missionaries were making trouble reached the directors of the London Society. They decided, therefore, to send to Cape Town an able and responsible agent to supervise their various stations. For this delicate task they selected Dr. John Philip, a Scottish weaver who had left the loom for the work of a Congregational minister. He reached Cape Town in 1819 and became the dominant figure in South African politics till 1851.

Philip was the first to raise in explicit form the issue which has since distracted, and will long continue to distract, the African continent. He saw that the European regarded the African as existing for the sake of European society, from membership in which he was to be excluded by reason of race and, therefore, permanently. The laws regulating the relations of master to servant, and the policy which denied to the natives ownership in the soil were alike the expression of that view. Inspired by the Evangelical movement, Philip regarded the natives as potential members of civilised society, and set himself to secure the repeal of existing laws in conflict with that principle. With this end in view he secured the support of Wilberforce and his colleagues who in England were agitating for the abolition of slavery throughout the Commonwealth. They were now a power in the constituencies before which governments quailed. In 1828 South African opinion was overruled. Ordinance 50, enacted in that year, substantially embodied the views of Philip, and has since been regarded as the charter of the coloured people in the Cape.[1]

The abolition of slavery in the British colonies was still delayed by the strength of the vested interest involved, especially in the sugar plantations of the West Indies. In 1833 the first parliament after the Reform Act met, abolished slavery and voted £20,000,000 for the compensation of the slave owners. Wilberforce was cheered by the news on his death-bed.

Thus within five years British rule had imposed on the Boers two changes which destroyed the very foundations of their economic system, changes in conflict with their basic conception of social order. Naturally they regarded and still regard Philip as the principal author of all their troubles.

In January 1834 Sir Benjamin D'Urban was sent to the Cape as a governor in sympathy with native interests. In December some 20,000 Bantu warriors raided across the Fish river and ravaged large areas in the Cape Colony. The British troops and the Boer commandos, which D'Urban had summoned to support them, drove the invading kaffirs across the Fish river and beyond it as far as the Kei river. The country between these two rivers was then given by D'Urban to Boer farmers who had helped to conquer it from the kaffirs.

In April 1835 Lord Melbourne had come into power. The minister he placed in charge of colonial affairs was Lord Glenelg, whose father, Charles Grant, was one of the leaders of the anti-slavery movement. Glenelg wanted to protect the interests of the natives and also to restrict the area in which his government was responsible for the maintenance of order, and failed to realise how the second of these policies might defeat the first. In issuing his instructions to D'Urban he wrote that "the great evil of the Cape Colony consists in its magnitude". He then went on to remark that "the kaffirs had an ample justification for war; they had to resent, and endeavoured justly, though impotently, to avenge a series of encroachments". The governor was ordered to evacuate the territory beyond the Fish river, unless he could show good reason to the contrary. The dilatory D'Urban neglected to show such reason, until it was too late, and the Boers were withdrawn from the farms he had given them between the Fish and the Kei rivers. The loss of these farms brought to a head the feelings raised when the slaves were set free, for the compensation awarded to the masters had been slow in reaching them.

As already seen, the habit of moving into the wilderness had long been established amongst the Boers. The descent from the tropics of Bantu tribes, which had blocked their access to the fertile belt of the eastern coast, had reduced to solitudes the upland pastures covered with grass which lay to the north of Cape Colony. In Natal, Chaka, a leader of genius, had imposed military discipline on the Zulu tribes, whom he ruled with an iron hand. About 1824 Mosilikazi, one of his chiefs, had rebelled and fled with his tribe, who were called Matabele, through the uplands north of the Vaal, and had taken refuge north of the Limpopo, leaving behind him a desolation too hungry for the armies of Chaka to cross. Boers who could live on their herds and the game they shot could enter these regions all the more easily. The constant need of new fields for their growing families and flocks was sharpened by anger against an alien government which upset their method of life, and treated the interest of natives as paramount. A number of Boers conceived the idea of retreating beyond its jurisdiction, and founding republics of their own in the north. The movement began before Glenelg's orders were published. It became formidable when they were known. In 1837, the year when Victoria came to the throne, 2000 souls, "the flower of the frontiersmen", as D'Urban called them, were moving to the north on what is known as the Great Trek. They occupied the uplands north of the Orange river and across the Vaal to the Limpopo. Some of them then turned to the east, defeated the Zulus, reached Port Natal and opened negotiations with Holland. The British government, mindful of the reasons which had led to the occupation of Cape Town, ordered Sir Benjamin D'Urban to forestall the Dutch. The Boers were thrust back to the plateau, and in 1844 Natal was annexed by the British.

In the mountainous regions west of Natal, known as Basutoland, a chief, Moshesh, had collected fragments from a number of tribes, which under his statesmanlike rule were developing into a native state. The Boer commandos north of the Orange river were in constant conflict with Moshesh and other native chiefs. To end this state of anarchy the governor of the Cape, Sir Harry Smith, in 1848 annexed the territory north of the Orange river as far as the Vaal under the title of the Orange River Sovereignty.

North of the Vaal the Boers were drawing together to form a republic under Pretorius. Determined to recognise them as such, the British government in 1852 sent two commissioners to meet representatives of the Transvaal Republic at the Sand river. The independence of the Transvaal Republic was there recognised by Her Majesty's government. The Transvaalers promised to abstain from slavery, while the British government disclaimed "all alliances whatever and with whomsoever of the coloured nations north of the Vaal river".

The British government presently decided to carry this policy further. By the Bloemfontein Convention, signed in 1854, in the face of protests from some of the settlers, the British government renounced its sovereignty over territory north of the Orange river. The settlers between that river and the Vaal were left to establish a republic for themselves under the title of the Orange Free State.

North of the Orange river and west of Natal two Boer republics and the kaffir tribes were thus left to settle accounts with each other. The British government had done its best to apply the policy expressed by Lord Glenelg when he wrote that "the great evil of the colony consists in its magnitude". In result those elements in the Cape Colony who most bitterly resented the native policy of Lord Glenelg were enabled to form states on the borders of British territory, in which, short of slavery, they were free to establish a social system based on their own ideas. The relations of master and servant, abolished in the Cape by the ordinance of 1828, were revived in the Boer republics. That "in Church and State there is no equality between white and black" was laid down in their constitutions (*grondwets*).

Such was the situation which Sir George Grey found when he reached South Africa in 1854. In the Cape Colony he proceeded to develop the relations of the settlers and the natives on the lines he had thought out in Australia and New Zealand. In his view they were to be treated as inhabitants of one country, and he firmly laid the foundations of the policy which has since been stated by Rhodes as "equal rights for all civilised men". Before Grey's arrival the Colony had already been given an elected legislature. In the qualifications for voters there was no distinction between black and white. The Cape policy was, in fact, in direct antithesis to that expressed in the *grondwets* of the Boer republics.

The new Orange Free State and Moshesh were quickly at war with each other. In 1857 the Burghers attacked the Basutos, who invaded the republic with such effect that the president Boshoff appealed to the Transvaal and Grey for help. In 1858 Grey was able to patch up a peace between the combatants, and the Volksraad at Bloemfontein passed a resolution proposing a union, federal or otherwise, with the Cape Colony.

At this juncture the Colonial Secretary, Bulwer-Lytton, instructed Grey to report on the possibilities of a federal union between Cape Colony, Natal and the territories between them, with a view to releasing the bulk of the Imperial garrison. He was further asked what "the permanent line of policy" towards the republics should be.

As usual, Grey went beyond his instructions and wrote a despatch, which now reads like a prophecy. He urged that whatever boundaries and constitutions the various colonies and republics and native states might have, the relations of white and black throughout South Africa governed the whole situation. If these states could not come together in peace, they would surely meet one another in war. If the people of South Africa were united under one government of their own, they could then be trusted to work out for themselves the future relations in which the white and black races should live together. They would also be strong enough to do so without further expense to the British exchequer.

The wisdom of Grey's advice has been proved by after events; but the British government was committed to the policy of creating republics to bar any further extension of British dominion north of the Orange river. As Grey continued to press his own policy on the legislatures at Cape Town and Bloemfontein, Lytton recalled him in 1859. In 1860 Lytton's successor, Newcastle, allowed him to return to Cape Town, but only on condition that no attempt should be made to unite the Boer republics and British colonies. The history of South Africa, and perhaps of the world, might have been happier had Grey's advice been followed. In October 1893, on the eve of events which were destined to plunge

South Africa into war, Reitz, who was then president of the Free State, wrote to Sir George Grey:

> Had British ministers in times past been wise enough to follow your advice there would undoubtedly be to-day a British dominion extending from Table Bay to the Zambesi. . . . What the result would have been upon the welfare of the human race is a question I need not discuss; but there can be no doubt from an Englishman's point of view, the fact that your policy in this direction was so often rejected can only be regarded as a calamity.[2]

NOTES

[1] For this subject see Professor W. M. Macmillan's *The Cape Colour Question*, and *Bantu, Boer and Briton.*

[2] Henderson, *Sir George Grey*, pp. 172, 173.

CHAPTER XLIV

THE INDIAN MUTINY

THE peace, temporary as it was, between the Basutos and Free State was a greater achievement than appears on the surface. At the moment when Grey most needed the command of superior forces to support his authority as a peacemaker, he was asked by the British government to send to India every man, horse and all the cash he could spare to quell the mutiny which had broken out there. He discharged those instructions to the full and even exceeded them by diverting to Calcutta troops which were on the way to the war which had broken out in China. By rapid journeys on horseback in the summer of 1857 between the Free State and Port Elizabeth he managed to meet both calls on his energy. He supported Lord Canning (to use his own words) "just in the way and at the time help was required".[1]

We have now to examine the train of events which led to the great upheaval which shook the foundations of British rule in India and to trace the results which followed.

In Book II., Chapter XXVI., we saw the steps which officers like Munro and Elphinstone were taking to establish order in the provinces ruled by the British East India Company. The maintenance of this order was constantly threatened by the anarchy which persisted in the territories beyond their control. Indian princes, successors of the satraps who had governed provinces under the Moguls, continued to fight and intrigue to extend their power. Napoleon's attempts to foment these troubles were countered by the Wellesley brothers, whose victories led to vast extensions of British territories. The directors were always averse to wars which reduced their dividends, and in 1805 Lord Wellesley was recalled. But the need for one paramount authority in India was inexorable. As Elphinstone wrote in 1813:

> We have long since abandoned the policy which might perhaps have averted the jealousy of other Indian states: and we have stopped short in the midst of the only other line that was either safe or consistent—that of establishing our ascendancy over the whole of India. In consequence, we have still the odium without the energy of a conquering people, and all the responsibility of an extensive empire, without its resources or military advantages. There would be some reason in remaining in this dangerous position if we were strengthened by peace, but so far are we from that, that our provinces and the dominions of our allies are much more exposed to invasion and plunder than they would be in the time of war.

Wars could not in fact be avoided, and the process of conquest continued until about three-fifths of the Indian peninsula was annexed to the British Crown. But so strongly and consistently was the government in India pressed by directors to avoid war that it entered where possible into treaty relations with native chiefs. These rulers agreed to accept the suzerainty of the Company, and to maintain a certain standard of administration, in return for which the Company was to recognise and support their authority. Some of these chiefs ruled territories nearly as large as Great Britain, others were merely the owners of landed estates who retained certain political rights. The government of India has recognised some 675 such states which cover about two-fifths of the Indian peninsula and contain about one quarter of its population.[2] Their powers and position differ in every case according to the treaty or sannad they hold.

The qualities which enabled a few British soldiers

to conquer two-thirds of India with comparative ease were the same as those which the officers of the Company had brought to bear on administrative problems —qualities produced by a social system strange to the East. The people of India came to regard the British power as unconquerable, and the British fell into the old human mistake of regarding themselves as such.

The Company's charter, which was only granted for twenty years at a time, had come up for renewal in 1833. In preparation of this event parliament had in 1829 appointed a select committee which, after taking voluminous evidence, issued a report in 1832. The exclusive rights which the East India Company had enjoyed to the trade east of the Cape of Good Hope had long been the subject of attack. It was now decided to open this trade to all competitors. But as parliament was not as yet prepared to make itself wholly responsible for the government of India, it decided to retain for that purpose the machinery of the Company shorn of commercial functions. It became an agent performing its administrative duties, as the act renewing the charter declared "in trust for His Majesty, his heirs and successors, for the service of the Government of India". Its ships and other commercial assets were sold. The dividends due to the shareholders were fixed and secured on the revenues of India.

Lord Melbourne's return to office in 1835 led to the appointment of two men, whose policies were destined gravely to complicate the task of the Commonwealth in two continents. One was Glenelg, the results of whose policy in the Cape have been traced in the previous chapter. The other was Auckland, appointed in 1836 as governor-general of India for party reasons and contrary to the advice of the directors. Acting on wrong information he interfered in the affairs of Afghanistan. A British force was sent beyond the confines of India to occupy Kabul. Its position became untenable. In 1842 it endeavoured to retreat and was cut to pieces on the road. Of 4000 men but one returned to tell what had happened. The British power no longer appeared as unconquerable, and in fifteen years this first blow to its prestige was destined to bring it to the verge of destruction.

In Book II., Chapter XXVII., we saw how the importation of cotton from India to England had led through a series of mechanical inventions to an ever-increasing control of physical forces by men. This control reacted on human relations in various directions. When constructing the engine which was destined to change the course of human affairs, James Watt had to train his workmen to cast cylinders which were really cylindrical. Machinery imposed on those who made and handled it new standards of thoroughness and accuracy which reacted on business and administration. Enterprise was organised in larger units, each dependent for success on the punctual and accurate working of numerous departments, and demanding, therefore, a higher degree of exactitude from every person employed. A higher efficiency was also required in the sphere of government. The financial and administrative reforms of the younger Pitt, of Peel and of Gladstone were the outcome of an age when men had learned to harness physical power to their tools, and reserve their own to the task of guiding them.

Until this age of mechanisation, India had remained a typical example of the laws enunciated by Malthus. Indian methods of production and transport had continued unchanged for thousands of years, and the people were always increasing to numbers which these methods were unable to support. A serious shortage in the variable rainfall of summer resulted in famine, and pestilence usually followed in its train. From time to time millions perished by hunger and disease. In the Indian mind such catastrophes were regarded as the act of God; but British administrators, conscious of their new power over nature, were determined to reduce this destruction of life. In the snows of the Himalayas were frozen reservoirs drained by rivers whose waters, distributed by canals, would render whole districts immune from drought. Grain produced in these districts would in dry seasons save from starvation the people of areas dependent on rainfall, if the grain could be got to them in time. Railways would enable this to be done. So engineers were employed to devise schemes for distributing water and the food it produced. The construction of telegraphs was rapidly increasing the power by which a few British administrators were able to control one-sixth of the human race. More exacting standards were introduced in every branch of administration, especially in fixing and gathering the revenues due from land. Indians were trained by western officers to play their part in the intricate machinery of government control.

The novels of Charles Dickens, of Mrs. Gaskell or Charlotte Brontë show how impatient Englishmen were in their time of habits which stood in the way of mechanical progress. In the East custom has deeper roots than in England; but the sense of power in the Englishmen who governed the millions of India increased with exercise. In the early decades of the nineteenth century British administrators had hesitated to meddle with the practice of burning widows. They had feared that Christian missionaries might disturb the religious ideas of the natives, and opposed their entry. By the middle of the nineteenth century the Evangelical movement had caught the reforming energy of the time and the missionaries were firmly established in India, as intent upon saving the heathen from the fate in store for those who rejected their teaching, as were the administrators to save them from famine and disease. Their religious views were now shared by many of these officers.

The highly organic structure which England had developed for herself was thus rapidly imposed on India. Its vast society and its numerous parts began to react on each other as never before. In matters affecting her daily bread India was becoming an integral unit. But, as we have seen in a previous chapter, some two-fifths of the area was still subject to native rulers. Lines traced by the engineers for canals and railways had no relation to the boundaries settled by history. In such matters the native princes had to yield to administrative needs; but their independence often delayed beneficent schemes.

In January 1848 there landed in India a governor-general in whose character and outlook the daemonic spirit of that time was incarnate. Though only thirty-five years of age, Dalhousie had, as president of the Board of Trade, controlled the railway development of England then at its height. In India his energies were applied to pushing on schemes for covering India with a network of canals, railways and telegraphs. When he left the country in 1856 a large section of railroad was in actual working, and thousands of miles were under construction.

In India, as in England, the state must equip the railway builder with compulsory powers to purchase the land over which the track is to run. Even in the England of the 'forties the exercise of these powers was provoking widespread resentment. But here public discussion in parliament afforded a safety-valve. In India the disturbance of native feeling caused by wholesale expropriation, though less obvious, was more intense. It could find no vent in public discussion and served to increase the pressure which presently led to a violent explosion.

The driving power of the governor-general was by no means confined to works of construction, and was felt in every department of government. In 1854 Sir Charles Wood, president of the Board of Control, proposed a scheme for the institution of vernacular schools and universities, which Dalhousie pushed with such vigour that in 1857 universities were opened in Calcutta, Bombay and Madras. He completed the conquest of the Punjab and reduced it to the status of an orderly British province. He started the annexation of Burma. The native states with their lower standard of justice and efficiency offended his mind, and whenever a prince died without leaving an heir to his body his territory was annexed. As a penalty for maladministration the King of Oudh was dethroned, and his kingdom incorporated in the North-West Provinces.

Autocrat as he was, Dalhousie was none the less led by his parliamentary experience to lay the foundations upon which the constitutional developments of the twentieth century were destined to be based. He was shocked to find that measures framed by the government of India in its private deliberations were promulgated as laws without regular public discussion. He realised that a few legislators, however gifted, cannot foresee all the difficulties to which their proposals will lead. He therefore provided that bills should be submitted for public discussion to legislative councils consisting of the members of the executive council, to which additional members were added by appointment.

Dalhousie's motives have never been impugned even by his critics. Beyond question, his vigorous methods were intended to benefit the dumb millions of India, and attained their object. But, like other far-reaching reforms, they were slow in coming to fruition, while their first effect was a widespread disturbance of vested interests and the alienation of small but powerful classes. Princes were more alive to a fear of losing their wealth and position than their subjects to the prospect of milder rule and lighter taxation. The Brahmins saw in the educational scheme a threat to their ancient monopoly of learning, while inferior castes had yet to realise the advantage to themselves of western knowledge. They encouraged the idea that the British, like the Moguls before them, were preparing to destroy their religion and impose that of the conquering race. But a popular rising would certainly be nipped in the bud unless they could first undermine the loyalty of the native army to their British officers. It must start with a mutiny of the troops. In preparing for a general upheaval they adopted means which curiously recall the symbol used by the Jews to commemorate the revolt of Israel in Egypt. In 1856 cakes of unleavened bread began to pass from village to village and from regiment to regiment. But the meaning of all this was not realised till May 1857, more than a year after Canning had succeeded Dalhousie as governor-general.

The particular incident which fired the train shows how impatient the English rulers had grown of superstitions which seemed to hinder mechanical improvements. A new rifle had been introduced, in the loading of which soldiers were required to remove with their teeth the end of a cartridge sealed with beef-fat. Cartridges soaked in human blood would less have offended their lips. But one generation before the government of India had hesitated to forbid Hindu widows to be burned alive with the bodies of their husbands. This attempt to enforce an exercise which, as the sepoys thought, would involve their utter degradation in a future existence marks the change which had taken place. The rising which followed was suppressed with a ruthlessness which shows how easily a higher civilisation in conflict with a lower can borrow its methods of repression.

At the time of the Mutiny India was still governed by a joint stock company founded for purposes of trade in the reign of Elizabeth. This company was in turn controlled by the British government answerable to parliament. All this was a typical result of adapting machinery to the needs of the moment, the process by which the English Commonwealth has outgrown the island from which it sprang, till it ceased to be British, and assumed the figure of a world polity. The catastrophe of 1857 exposed this danger. Legal fictions are of service so long as they are not allowed to conceal realities from those who employ them, a danger which Englishmen are disposed to ignore. It was, therefore, decided to abolish the Company and to recognise Indians as subjects of the Crown entitled as such to the privileges which British subjects enjoy. The principle that India was to be governed for the benefit of its people and not for the profit of England was stated in terms. As for the Native States, the Crown adopted and promised to observe the treaties which the Company had made with their princes. Dalhousie's 'policy of lapse' was explicitly renounced.

At this period John Bright was alone in suggesting that the Indian subjects of the Queen should be taught to govern themselves. India was encouraged to believe that the British monarch would in future rule them as successor of the Mogul Emperors. In the document proclaiming the new system it was not found necessary to explain how all this was to be harmonised with a polity the antithesis of that which the great Mogul had ruled.

Scrupulous care was to be taken to maintain and further improve the quality of the British officers through whom India was governed. They were trained at the great universities and picked by tests which secured for the service from 1000 to 1200 of the most gifted and scholarly men that the British Isles could produce. No country has ever been governed by abler or more disinterested officers. Initiative and a faculty for decision are the natural product of the free institutions under which they were bred. These qualities were developed by the wide powers they exercised from the earliest years of their service in India over millions accustomed only to the obedience expected from the subjects of an eastern autocracy. The Mutiny had taught them the danger of ignoring habits and beliefs which to western minds were unreasonable or absurd. None the less, the engineering, educational and administrative projects initiated by Dalhousie were steadily advanced in their competent hands. Irrigation increased the supply of grain, and railways enabled that supply to be pooled. A local failure of rain no longer involved a wholesale destruction of life in the area affected. And, as in the West, factories were started, and began to compete with the industries which craftsmen practised at home.

Before the time of Dalhousie the territories now controlled by the government of India can scarcely have supported more than 200,000,000 souls. To-day they support upwards of 350,000,000. There are in India to-day at least 150,000,000 people who could not exist at all without the mechanisation which western science has provided. As in Europe and America, the power of men to control natural forces has integrated as well as enlarged the structure of Indian society. The continuous working of its delicate mechanism depends on a handful of officers whose fitness for the task is the product of the western society from which they spring.

The Indian Civil Service, which now includes an increasing proportion of Indians, was distributed into nine sections corresponding to the provinces into which British India was divided before 1936. Until 1919 the government of each province was mainly composed of officers trained in its district administration, and the government of India for the most part composed of officers drawn from the nine provincial governments, under the leadership of a viceroy appointed by the cabinet in London and responsible to that supreme authority. Though divided into sections according to provinces the Indian Civil Service is, none the less, a single administrative body, with a vivid sense of its corporate unity. Its knowledge of the complicated system it administers is unique. Its members, and they only, can prepare the information on which viceroys and governors appointed from England reach their decisions. Until 1919 it was, and to a great extent still is, the real government of India. The excellence of the books written by its members enables them to exercise a powerful influence over public opinion wherever English is spoken.

When in 1858 parliament sought to assume a direct responsibility for India, it failed to provide a substitute for the procedure which had kept it in touch with Indian affairs since the days of Burke. The Company's powers had lapsed every twenty years, and before renewing them parliament had always appointed a committee of its own members to examine witnesses and advise as to the terms upon which the charter should be renewed. The various interests affected had thus an opportunity of making their voice heard in London; and in parliament were members with first-hand sources of information who had thought on the problem of adjusting Indian policy to changing conditions. Any corps of professional officers, however able, is engrossed in the details of the policy it is charged to administer, and comes to regard the policy itself as part of the order of nature. It cannot be trusted to determine when or how that policy should be changed. For sixty years after the Mutiny parliament abandoned the practice of appointing its own committees to hear evidence on Indian affairs. Its members no longer realised when that policy demanded revision.

NOTES

[1] Henderson, *Sir George Grey*, p. 188.
[2] Lawrence, *The India We Served*, p. 179.

CHAPTER XLV

THE FAR EAST

TILL the earlier years of the nineteenth century the British East India Company had enjoyed an exclusive right to the British trade, not only with India but with all the countries east of the Cape of Good Hope. From the outset the Imperial government of China had tried to restrict trade with Europe to the narrowest limits. In 1557 the Portuguese had secured a grudging permission to establish a station at Macao. The Dutch East India Company, excluded thereby from the Canton river, in 1642 obtained a station of their own in the island of Formosa. In 1637 Captain John Weddell of the English East India Company, ignoring the Portuguese at Macao, had forced the Bogue, silenced the Chinese forts and, proceeding to Canton, had there disposed of his cargo, and had loaded his ship with sugar and ginger. In 1685 the English Company had secured the right to a factory at Canton, but did little with that trade for the next thirty years.

In the eighteenth century the traffic with China, slight though it was, had already created a demand in the West for Chinese products other than silk. Of these the most important was tea, which was fast becoming a popular drink in America. It was tea that fired the explosion that ruptured the British Commonwealth. In 1767 the American boycott created a glut in the British East India Company's warehouse of 17,000,000 lbs. By the end of the century 2 lbs. a head were consumed every year in Great Britain.

The traders were slow in finding commodities to

exchange for the luxuries which the West were eagerly demanding from China. It was this which had led them to cross the Pacific to Nootka Sound in search of ginseng and furs; but the problem of exchange was destined to find a more sinister solution. When the Spaniards had colonised the Philippines they introduced from America the habit of smoking tobacco. In treating malaria their surgeons adopted the practice of mixing opium and arsenic with the tobacco smoked by their patients. The Chinese who flocked to the Philippines copied this treatment and presently found that opium smoked by itself produced delicious sensations. It was thus through the use of tobacco that opium came to demoralise China. Opium smokers greatly preferred the kind of opium grown in India to that produced in their own country. In 1770 the British East India Company had assumed a monopoly of opium in Bengal, and 200 chests had been sent to China. By 1830 the export had grown to 4000 chests, by 1839 to 30,000 and by 1869 to 78,000, with a corresponding increase in Chinese production. These figures show the alarming hold which the drug obtained in the course of one century on an ancient and cultured people whose outlook on life is epicurean.

The court at Peking was opposed to trade with the western barbarians, but had no such control of its vast dominions as the government which guarded from all intrusion the coasts of Japan. Officials who throve on the trade at Canton represented the duties it paid as tribute due from barbarians who recognised the Emperor of China as Lord of the Universe. There was no intention of allowing them to enter the country. A location was provided on the foreshore at Canton where traders from various western countries were allowed to build their factories and lodgings. On specified days they were suffered to walk under superintendence in public gardens on an island opposite the location. Their treatment as inferiors was a constant offence, especially to the British whose ships were accustomed to dominate the seas. They resented the laws which forbade them leaving the factory, less as an injury to their health than to their dignity, and cherished the thought that the guns of an English frigate could silence the Chinese forts and sink their junks.

As the bulk of the trade passed through the hands of the British East India Company their superintendent was held responsible for order throughout the settlement at Canton. But when its monopoly was abolished by parliament in 1833, and the trade was opened to all British merchants, the British government appointed Lord Napier as superintendent of British trade. The viceroy refused to accept Lord Napier's letters except in the form of petitions as from a subject to a suzerain ruler. This attitude raised the question of status, an issue which affected all the nations now trading in Chinese waters.

The crisis, delayed by Napier's death, was brought to a head in 1838 by the question of opium. Originally started to correct the balance of exchange, the illicit import had now grown to a scale which was draining China of silver. The Emperor appointed a special commissioner, Lin Tse-hsü, to stop the import of opium at Canton. Lin demanded and obtained, through Captain Elliot, the British superintendent, a surrender of opium to the value of £1,000,000. He then went on to demand the surrender of certain Europeans for alleged crimes, and, when this was refused, closed the port of Canton to trade. Warships were sent to support Captain Elliot, and hostilities began in 1839. Chinese forts and junks were easily silenced and sunk by the British guns. By 1842 the British were controlling the Yangtze river and thus cut off the supplies of grain which Peking drew by the Grand Canal in the form of tribute from southern China. That the issue was something more than a local fracas with barbarians at Canton was at length realised by the Emperor and his court.

The Treaty of Nanking which closed this war was signed on board H.M.S. *Cornwallis* in the Yangtze river. Equality between the two nations was admitted in terms. The British obtained an island of their own near the mouth of the Canton river, where they could live under their own laws and flag to conduct their business unhampered by the manifold exactions of Chinese officials. The barren rock of Hongkong rapidly became the greatest emporium of the Far East. It also provided a residence for the representative of the British government in those regions. Amoy, Foochow, Ningpo and Shanghai, in addition to Canton, were opened to foreign trade. On the question of opium the treaty was silent. In despatches Palmerston admitted that the traffic was illegal, and the British negotiators urged the Chinese to legalise and regulate the trade. But the genuine believers in prohibition at Peking received sinister support from officials at Canton. For the southern mandarins stood to gain more from illicit than from legalised traffic. So in America ninety years later the temperance fanatics who wished to maintain prohibition were supported by bootleggers and public officials they had corrupted.

The British government, while admitting that the import of opium into China was illegal, did nothing to restrict its export from India. In the cultivation of opium the British East India Company had now discovered a lucrative source of revenue. The dangerous example was followed by Indian princes. When the Company was abolished the British government inherited a system under which the opium revenues had become an important item in budgets. A belief grew up in official minds that opium was essential to the health of Chinese.

We have seen in previous chapters how anxious the government in London was at this period to avoid annexations. The policy of demanding nothing from China but what seemed to be necessary for the purpose of trade was consciously adopted; and in trade they claimed no exclusive rights. By the Treaty of the Bogue in 1843 they secured that any privilege accorded to other nations should *ipso facto* be accorded to England. Henceforward the most-favoured-nation clause was included in treaties between China and foreign nations as a common form.

In other parts of the world the British government was often driven against its will to annex territory by the exigencies of traders, settlers or officials on the spot. There are various reasons why this did not happen in China after the Treaty of Nanking, but it probably would have happened but for the schism which had rent the Commonwealth in twain fifty years earlier. The creation in America of a world power independent of Great Britain profoundly affected the relations of Europe with the Far East in the nineteenth century.

When the Treaty of Nanking was signed, American trade with China was beginning to rival that of the British. The China merchants in Boston were now a factor in American politics. So Caleb Cushing was quickly sent by Daniel Webster, the Secretary of State, to negotiate a treaty with China. His instructions were to recognise as valid the laws of the Empire but also to "assert and maintain, on all occasions, the equality of independence of your own country". In 1844 he obtained the signature of the Treaty of Wanghia, in terms of which the U.S.A. secured the same privileges as the British had exacted in the Treaty of Nanking, but agreed to treat opium as contraband. The French followed suit in the Treaty of Whampoa. The powers of Europe and even some South American republics obtained similar privileges by insisting on the principle which England had first enunciated in the most-favoured-nation clause.

Under the Treaty of Nanking, the provisions of which were spread to all other nations in treaty with China, British subjects were allowed to reside in the Treaty Ports. They were not to be subject to Chinese laws, but only to those of their own country as administered by consuls appointed by the government in the Treaty Ports. Consuls thus came to acquire a position of exceptional importance in China. Those of Great Britain were organised as a corps separate from the rest of the consular service. Cadets were expected to master the language and also the technique of the intricate system established by the treaties. This service produced men like Sir Harry Parkes, Sir Robert Hart and Sir John Jordan, who have left their mark on the Far East.

Exemption of foreigners from Chinese law was the only arrangement possible at the time. In China justice was communal. A family, neighbourhood or guild was responsible for wrong done by its members. Justice could be satisfied by the punishment of any one member of the group involved, irrespective of individual guilt. In 1784 a salute fired from a British ship had caused the death of a Chinese. The supercargo, who happened to be on shore, was arrested and, in order to save his life, the Company's superintendent had to surrender the gunner who had fired the gun—to be strangled. When the Europeans had once asserted the power which lay in their warships such incidents could only lead to violent resistance. But the system led to dangerous abuse and was one of the factors which undermined the authority of government in China. It encouraged unscrupulous

Chinese to acquire the status of foreign subjects. Not all foreign consuls were incorruptible, and naturalisation was sold to Chinese who had motives for living beyond the reach of their own laws.

The right of foreigners to live at certain ports in reserves managed by themselves further enhanced the position of consuls and led to far-reaching results. Of these ports Shanghai was the most important. In the middle of the Chinese seaboard, and at the mouth of the Yangtze river, it was destined to attain in the Pacific the same kind of position that New York has attained in Atlantic trade.

Sea-going ships can traverse the Yangtze for over 1000 miles into the heart of China. The Whangpoo river runs into the mouth of the Yangtze from the south. On its left bank, about 12 miles from the Yangtze, stood the ancient walled city of Shanghai. Here Captain (afterwards Sir George) Balfour took up his residence as British consul in 1843. In 1845 he obtained from the Chinese authorities some land on the left bank of the Whangpoo, a little below the city, as a residence for British subjects. In 1849 the French consul secured the land between the city and the British settlement as a residence for his nationals. On the other side of the British area American missions and shipping interests began to acquire land. In 1854 the American consul took up his residence on the river-front just below the British settlement. This so-called American settlement was ultimately incorporated with the British area as the International Settlement.

The peculiar institutions of the International Settlement at Shanghai are the outcome of the American insistence on treaty rights. In 1848 Griswold, the American consul, had established his consulate in the British area, hoisted the stars and stripes, and had kept it flying in the face of British and Chinese protests, on the ground that England disclaimed all right to exclusive privilege.

In 1845 the British consul had agreed upon certain land regulations with the Chinese authorities. In 1854 these regulations, as revised by agreement between the British, French and American consuls, became the basis of municipal government in all three areas. By this agreement control of the International Settlement was practically vested in a small council elected by the foreign land-holders. In 1863 the French withdrew from this arrangement and promulgated regulations under which the French consul has since controlled the administration of the French Settlement. The British and American areas have remained as an International Settlement under the control of all the foreigners holding the land it covers. The regulations under which they exercise this power can be revised only by agreement between all the consuls concerned, some fourteen in number. If one refuses to agree, the matter must go to the foreign representatives at Peking and, failing agreement there, to the governments they represent. In the absence of any machinery like that of the League of Nations, a control which presumes agreement between numerous sovereign governments is purely fictitious. Thus there came into being on Chinese soil a powerful community of foreign traders exempt from Chinese law, administering their own local affairs, subject to no real control of their own governments, but largely controlling the principal gate of China.

In 1850 half the foreign trade of Shanghai was carried in American bottoms. But as in the next fifty years the enterprise of Americans was absorbed in developing the vast resources of their own continent, the British traders became the predominant element in Shanghai. This did not mean that the British government could control them. Such power of control as it exercised was derived from the fact that in the last resort the British community depended for protection on warships furnished by British taxpayers.

When the French negotiated the Treaty of Whampoa in 1844 Louis-Philippe was more interested in pushing the Catholic religion in China than trade, and instructed his envoy, de Lagrené, to recover for the Catholic missions the position they had lost in the previous century. In this he succeeded. The Catholic Church obtained the right to establish missions throughout China, and their properties confiscated in 1724 were restored.

Under the most-favoured-nation system these rights were extended to all countries in treaty with China. But the Protestant missions were not satisfied with the terms secured by the French, from which it might be inferred that the veneration of images was a feature of Christianity. A further declaration was secured at their instance from Peking, making it clear that Chinese subjects were free to adopt and practise Christianity in all its forms.

By virtue of these concessions China became the greatest field of missionary activity. American churches were especially active. Schools and colleges were established throughout China in which western ideas and science were taught. In course of time thousands of scholars passed from these schools to American universities, and some to Europe. Western teaching began to destroy the ideas which inspired the social and political system under which close on a quarter of the human race had been living for centuries. The art of printing was beginning to threaten the civilisation that had first produced it.

The ink was scarcely dry on these treaties before their disruptive effects began to appear. They had given a shattering blow to the prestige of the Manchu dynasty which ruled in Peking. The mandarins, powerless to cope with foreign governments, encouraged the populace in their hatred of foreigners. Secret societies flourished. War had filled the country with fire-arms, and officials made no effort to keep them out of the hands of the rabble.

In 1847 a native of Kwangtung, called Hung Siu-tsuen, received instruction from the Rev. Issachar J. Roberts, an American missionary. When refused baptism he formed an 'association for the worship of God', and announced himself a member of the Trinity under the title of Tien-Wang (Heavenly King). In 1850 he allied himself with the Triads, a secret society opposed to the Manchus, and chose as the title of his new dynasty 'Taiping' or 'Great Peace'. By 1853 he was master of all China south of the Yangtze, had stormed Nanking and had there proclaimed himself emperor.

Meanwhile the relations between Chinese and foreigners were going from bad to worse. In 1856 a dispute as to whether a vessel called the *Arrow* was subject to Chinese or British law led to an outbreak of war. The British admiral seized Canton and demanded that foreigners should be given their treaty rights to live in the city. The barrier forts fired on American ships, which replied and stormed them; but America refused to enter the war. The murder of a French missionary brought France into alliance with England.

The court at Peking was still trying to leave the relations of Chinese with foreign barbarians to be handled by the viceroys of provinces. France and England were now determined to handle such matters direct with Peking. To effect this it was necessary for their fleets to force the mouth of the Pei-ho river at Taku, to sail up the river to Tientsin and there land with forces strong enough to march on the capital and seize it. In 1857 and 1858 England was embarrassed by the Indian Mutiny. The forts at Taku were now equipped with modern artillery and in 1859 inflicted a serious reverse on the fleets. In 1860 Lord Elgin and Baron Gros returned with an overwhelming force. The foreign warships were now under steam power, and Chinese forts, as well as their war-junks, lay at the mercy of vessels which moved regardless of wind and tide. In October the allied armies entered Peking and the emperor was forced to receive ministers and legalise the trade in opium. The Russians and Americans also established legations at Peking, and the Tsung-li Yamen was established to deal with the foreign powers.

The Chinese had wrongly supposed that the allies would keep their troops at Peking after the treaty was signed. General Ignatieff, the Russian envoy, made skilful use of this misapprehension. In return for a promise to induce Lord Elgin and Baron Gros to withdraw their troops, he obtained from Prince Wang the Amur province north of Manchuria, a cession afterwards extended to include Vladivostok, opposite the coast of Japan.

The enormous and ancient empire of China was prostrate before the powers who wished to exploit its trade. It was now their policy to support the Manchu dynasty which would certainly have fallen without it. With the help of 'Chinese' Gordon the Taiping Rebellion was at length suppressed in 1864. Nanking was retaken and the Tien-Wang died by his own hand.

As noticed above, steam had begun to replace wind as the motive power of ships. The importance of stations where ships could count on supplies of coal was realised. In Hongkong the English had acquired such a station. American captains were eager to follow suit, and had actually hoisted the stars and stripes in the Bonin Islands and Formosa; but the Washington government had refused to confirm these annexations. New England merchants were just as anxious as their naval officers to emulate the British and French achievements in opening an eastern empire to the trade of the west. An excuse was provided by ill-use of American sailors wrecked on the Japanese coasts. In 1853 Commodore Perry, with four steamships, dropped anchor in the Bay of Yedo and demanded from the Shogun protection for shipwrecked Americans, and also the opening of ports to trade and the right to purchase supplies, especially coal. He departed, with a promise to return next year for the answer—with more steamships. In 1854 he returned. His demands were conceded in the Treaty of Kanagawa. The Shogun agreed to receive an American consul.

To this post was appointed Townshend Harris, a man great enough to feel that by seeing and studying the interests of this hermit people he could best serve those of his own. He was able to point to what was happening in China, as showing what Japan might expect at the hands of the European powers unless she made haste to meet the pacific views of his own government. He was thus able to secure in 1858, on the deck of the *Powhatan* in Yedo bay, a treaty which largely determined the future relations of Japan to the western powers.

For more than a century leaders of thought in Japan had been seeking to burst from within the seclusion imposed on their island empire by the Shoguns. The Tokugawa regime was viewed with increasing jealousy by the rival clans, who wished to restore the authority usurped by the Shoguns at Yedo to the ancient Imperial dynasty at Kyoto. The intellectuals were thus in sympathy with the feudal chiefs; but their joint aims were embarrassed by the Emperor Komei who still wished to exclude all foreigners. In 1864 the Chosiu clan, defying the Shogun, fired on Dutch, French and American ships in the straits of Shimonoseki. The British joined with these three countries in forcing the opening of the straits.

The Emperor Komei and the Shogun, Iemochi, both died in 1867. At the age of fourteen the Emperor Meiji, destined to prove himself a ruler of outstanding ability, succeeded to the throne of Kyoto. Iemochi's successor, Yoshinobu, resigned his authority into the emperor's hands on the ground that " the laws cannot be maintained in the face of the daily extension of our foreign relations, unless the government be conducted by one hand".

When, however, the clans which supported the Emperor assumed the right to guard his person at the ancient Imperial seat of Kyoto surrounded by mountains, Yoshinobu escaped to the vast fortress at Yedo which the Shoguns had built as the seat of their power near the coast. The Tokugawas rose to support him against the clans who had re-established the empire, but were finally overpowered in 1869. The Emperor then transferred his court to the Shogun fortress at Yedo and changed its name to Tokyo. Through the British envoy, Sir Harry Parkes, the foreign ministers were invited to a personal audience. The Emperor announced that his government would be guided by public opinion, as expressed through a parliament. "Knowledge should be sought for all over the world, and thus shall be strengthened the foundations of the imperial polity." In these words the seclusion imposed on Japan by the Tokugawa regime for over two centuries was officially ended. In the course of the next two years the revenues due to the heads of the clans were transferred to the Emperor, and the Daimyo accepted the position of Imperial officials. This change, formally consummated by the decree of August 29, 1871, dates the political union of Japan.

When forced to deal with western powers, Japan was able, as China was not, to 'greet the world arriving' and had known 'the day of her visitation'. The different results which the sudden shock had on two empires so closely connected by their race, culture and place on the map is as startling as anything in history.

In their island home the Japanese had, like the British, unconsciously developed an instinct for unity denied to the more numerous people distributed over the wider space of the neighbouring continent. The feudal system, preserved by their long seclusion, had created a spirit of devotion to the Daimyo, which readily passed to the emperor when the clans were dissolved and the Daimyo abolished. This capacity for a passionate loyalty to the state was undoubtedly fostered by the stoical outlook of a people enured to those sudden terrific convulsions of nature, earthquakes and cyclones. The Chinese outlook on life is profoundly epicurean, as anyone can see from the luminous pages of Lin Yutang.[1] In Japan may be seen the outlook of Zeno, in China the outlook of Epicurus, reduced to political terms.

NOTE

[1] Lin Yutang, *My Country and My People*. Published by Heinemann, 1936.

CHAPTER XLVI

AFRICA

THOUGH the shores of Africa can be seen from Europe, the continent which lay within those shores was the last to be opened to human knowledge and civilisation. This continent largely consists of a *massive* which falls rapidly as it nears a coast singularly destitute of harbours. In Asia and America the Ganges and Yangtze rivers, the St. Lawrence, the Mississippi and Amazon enabled explorers and commerce to reach the interior. In Africa the rivers, as they leave the plateau to reach the sea, break into rapids which close these natural arteries near their mouths. This lack of harbours and navigable rivers preserved Africa as the greatest stronghold of primitive barbarism and, therefore, of slavery, a trade which destroys all others. As seen in Book II., Chapter XVII., the demand for slaves in America to grow sugar, tobacco and cotton for Europe had closed the interior of Africa to civilised men. When the abolition of slavery and the doctrines preached by Dr. John Philip had driven the voortrekkers out of Cape Colony, the map of Africa was still, in the words of an expert geographer, 'virtually a blank' from the Transvaal to Timbuktu.[1]

Early in 1841 Philip received at his house at Cape Town a young man sent out to him by the London Missionary Society. David Livingstone had earned enough in a Lanarkshire cotton mill to get himself trained as a medical missionary at Glasgow. In the course of his month's sojourn with Philip he absorbed the ideas of his host. But he also developed the view that the missionary movement was clinging to regions which Europeans had colonised and was shirking its real task, which was, he conceived, to penetrate and civilise the vast mysterious regions of tropical Africa to the north. He was posted to Kuruman, the furthest missionary station which Moffat had established in Bechuanaland. There he spent several years exploring the country, and in 1844 established a mission station 200 miles north-east of Kuruman, on one of the sources of the Limpopo river, just west of the Transvaal. To this station he brought Mary, the heroic daughter of Moffat, as his wife. In 1846 they moved 40 miles further north to Chonuane, the centre of the Bakwains tribe, whose chief was Sechele. Threatened by the emigrant Boers in the Transvaal, in 1847 he moved the whole tribe 40 miles west to Kolobeng. In these years he travelled to the centre of the Transvaal through the region where Pretoria was afterwards founded. Believing that the Boers were trying to enslave the natives he was thinking how to protect their interests in accordance with Philip's ideas. In 1848 he met a commando moving to attack the Bakwains and with difficulty induced them to desist. Their hostile attitude finally resolved him to turn his attention from the Transvaal and to seek an asylum for the tribe in the north. The Boers, when they realised this, were determined to block his road to the north.

By 1851 Livingstone had reached the Zambesi at a point less than 50 miles above the Victoria Falls. Thence he returned with his wife and children to Cape Town, which he reached in April 1852. After sending his family home, he got back to the Moffats at Kuruman in August. Happily a broken wheel delayed his departure for Kolobeng, for at this juncture 400 Boers, with young Paul Kruger, who served as a field cornet, sacked Kolobeng. Had Livingstone been there he would probably have perished in the fight, as the Boers destroyed or seized everything he had there. As Livingstone wrote:

> the plundering only set me entirely free for my expedition to the north. . . . The Boers resolved to shut up the interior, and I determined to open the country; and we shall see who have been most successful in resolution—they or I.[2]

Keeping to the west to avoid the Boers, Livingstone moved north, and in December 1852 reached Linyanti, which is rather more than 100 miles west of the Victoria Falls, in what is now called the Caprivi Strip, between Bechuanaland and Northern Rhodesia. From this point he started in November 1853 northwards with twenty-seven natives up the Zambesi, till in February 1854 he reached lake Dilolo, which is close on 2000 miles as the crow flies from Cape Town. He now believed that if these regions were to be opened to civilisation it must be by some nearer route from the western or eastern coast. From Dilolo he turned west and made his way through a sodden country, racked by repeated attacks of fever, till in May 1854, almost a dying man, he reached Loanda on the Atlantic coast in Portuguese West Africa, 200 miles south of the Congo. He was nursed back to life in the house of the British consul. Some British warships entered the port and offered to take him to England. Livingstone, who felt himself bound to lead back his followers to Linyanti, declined this offer, but entrusted the records of his journey to the ships for delivery. Re-equipped by the sailors, in September 1854 he started back on his journey of 1500 miles to Linyanti, which he reached in September 1855. Resolved to discover a better route to central Africa from the Indian Ocean, he started in November to follow the Zambesi to its mouth, and a fortnight later discovered the Victoria Falls. In May 1856 he reached the mouth of the Zambesi at Quilimane, the first explorer to cross the continent. He was taken to Mauritius by a British man-of-war and reached England in December 1856 by the Red Sea, to find the world ringing with his fame. From the story of his travels, which were published in 1857, the horrors of the slave-trade which he had witnessed began to be realised, and moved the churches everywhere to send missions to the regions he had traversed.

In February 1858 he accepted the appointment of "Her Majesty's Consul at Quilimane for the eastern coast and the independent districts in the interior, and commander of an expedition for exploring eastern and central Africa". In May he reached the Zambesi with Dr. Kirk and his brother Charles. To his bitter disappointment he found that this river, like the Congo, is blocked by rapids in the lower part of its course. In 1859 he discovered lake Nyassa and spent five years exploring the lake and the regions about it. Everywhere he found that the slave-trade was rampant. In 1864 he returned to England. In 1865 he was sent out again by the British government and the Royal Geographical Society. Starting from Zanzibar he made his way overland to lake Nyassa and, rounding its southern end, then made his way north-west to lake Tanganyika. In January 1867 the natives carrying his medicine disappeared. Tortured by fever and dysentery the lonely man continued his wanderings, till on October 8, 1871, he reached Ujiji on the north-east side of lake Tanganyika, at the end of his resources.

For some years he had lost all touch with the outer world and expeditions from England and America were sent to look for him. The American expedition, led by a young journalist, Stanley, found Livingstone at Ujiji on October 13, 1871. Together they explored the north end of lake Tanganyika and then turned west till they reached Unyamweze, 200 miles west of the lake. There Stanley left Livingstone in March 1872, amply supplied with stores, and returned to the coast to send him bearers to carry them. They reached Livingstone in August, and with them he turned south to explore the smaller lakes which lie to the south-west of Tanganyika. In the swamps east of lake Bangweolo, which he reached in January 1873, his incredible powers of endurance were beginning to fail. In April, unable to walk further, he was carried in a litter to a village in Ilala some 50 miles south of lake Bangweolo. There on the morning of May 1, 1873, he was found by his native followers dead on his knees in the attitude of prayer. They buried his heart under a tree, and carried his body with all his papers and instruments for close on 1000 miles to Zanzibar. No greater tribute has ever been paid by Africans to a leader. In April 1874 his body was laid in Westminster Abbey.

This amazing odyssey had covered some thirty years. For most of it Livingstone had travelled alone with native companions and had shown powers of physical endurance unequalled in human records. No labours ascribed to the heroes of epics were so great as the toils which this solitary traveller faced. No pilgrim in sober reality has ever so deserved the title of Mr. Steadfast. What he saw was noted in journals with the scrupulous care of a trained scientific observer. They revealed, as nothing had yet done, the continuing tragedy of the slave-trade in Africa. Their first result was to start a movement to send missionaries to the regions he had traversed, and to open them up to legitimate trade. At the time of his death in the early 'seventies these movements were gaining impetus in England, America and also in Germany.

NOTES

[1] Scott Keltie, *The Encyclopaedia Britannica*, 11th edition, Livingstone.

[2] Livingstone, *Missionary Travels and Researches in South Africa*, p. 39.

CHAPTER XLVII

EGYPT

WHILST Livingstone was at work opening the dark continent from the south, events were in train at its north-eastern extremity which were destined to change the relative positions of Europe, Asia and Africa.

Nelson's victory at the battle of the Nile had made it impossible for Napoleon to realise his project for connecting the Mediterranean and the Red Sea by a canal through the isthmus of Suez.[1] When he drove the Turks into the sea at Aboukir in 1799, Mehemet Ali, a young Albanian officer, was saved from drowning in the gig of the British admiral Sir Sidney Smith. In the years of confusion which followed Mehemet Ali rose to be Pasha of Egypt, a position to which he was formally raised by the Sultan in 1806. Like Peter the Great he conceived the idea of constructing the industrial and military system of Egypt on Western lines. He then went on to create for himself an Egyptian empire which he governed as Khedive under the nominal suzerainty of the Sultan of Turkey. By 1823 his armies had conquered a part of the Sudan and had founded Khartum. In 1848 Mehemet Ali resigned in favour of his son, Ibrahim, who died in four months, bequeathing the Khedivial throne to his son Abbás I. The murder of Abbás I. in July 1854 brought to the throne his uncle Said, an intimate friend of the Frenchman Ferdinand de Lesseps. As Khedive, he gave Lesseps a concession to construct the Suez Canal. Port Said, where the work was started, records his name.

Lord Palmerston opposed the project for the reasons which had led the arch-enemy of England to conceive it. His opposition delayed the work, but, none the less, the canal was opened to traffic on November 17, 1869. The voyage from England to India was reduced by nearly 5000 miles. The routes to China and Australia were greatly shortened and most of the ships which used the canal were British.

On the death of Said in 1863, his nephew Ismail had become Khedive. The capital used to construct the canal had in part been provided by Egypt, and in raising this capital the Khedive discovered how easy it was to borrow from European financiers. A habit of wild extravagance was developed by Ismail, which by 1875 had brought his treasury to the verge of bankruptcy. Disraeli, now in power in England, had realised Palmerston's mistake, and seized the opportunity to correct it by buying from Ismail his shares in the Suez Canal for £4,000,000. This gave the right to the British to appoint one-third of the directors. The incident is a classic example of British reluctance to cross bridges (even land bridges) until they are reached.

The financial troubles of Egypt were due in part to Ismail's ambition to extend his empire south of Khartum to include the sources of the Nile. In 1862 Speke, starting from Zanzibar, had reached the point where the Nile issues from lake Victoria Nyanza. He had then made his way northwards to Gondokoro, the highest point on the Nile which boats from Egypt could reach. At Gondokoro he met Sir Samuel Baker and supplied him with information which enabled Baker to find lake Albert Nyanza which Speke had missed. In 1871 Ismail engaged Baker to conquer the country south of Gondokoro and to open the lakes to navigation. He was followed in 1874 by 'Chinese' Gordon, who in 1875 had steamers plying on lake Albert Nyanza.

In 1876 Ismail suspended the payments due to his foreign creditors, but agreed to create a commission of the public debt, on which France, Austria and Italy appointed members. In 1877 was added a British commissioner, Major Baring, afterwards Lord Cromer. In the same year Gordon was made governor-general of the Sudan, where he took the most vigorous steps to suppress the slave-trade. In 1878 Ismail was forced to agree to entrust the government of Egypt to three ministers, Nubar Pasha, an Armenian, Blignières, a Frenchman, and Sir Rivers Wilson. Ismail intrigued with the army to get rid of the ministers and restore his autocracy. Matters were brought to a crisis by Bismarck, who threatened to intervene in the interest of German bond-holders. England and France were thus forced to join Germany in moving the Sultan of Turkey to depose Ismail and appoint his son Tewfik as Khedive. This was in 1879, and when Ismail quitted Egypt Gordon resigned and left the Sudan.

In 1881 the Egyptian army mutinied and forced Tewfik to dismiss his ministers, and to appoint their leader Arabi Pasha as minister of war. On June 11, 1882, the Christians in Alexandria were massacred. The British fleet in the harbour bombarded Arabi's batteries, but the French refused to take part in the action and sailed away. British troops were landed to protect the lives of the foreigners.

There were now in Egypt two rival authorities, the Khedive and the army headed by Arabi. The British government invited the French to join in a military expedition to suppress Arabi and establish the rule of Tewfik. The French Chamber, in fear of Germany, refused to vote the money. On July 20, 1882, the British government announced its intention of acting alone, to restore the Khedive's authority and secure the canal. When the British expedition under Sir Garnet Wolseley reached Alexandria,

Arabi had drawn up his troops to oppose their landing at Aboukir. On August 18 the British fleet suddenly steamed away to Port Said, and made its way down the canal as far as Ismailia. There Wolseley landed his troops and marched through the desert on Cairo. The Egyptian army had moved from Aboukir to meet them and blocked the way with trenches at Tel-el-Kebir. On September 13 (1882) they were driven from this position by Wolseley. The troops in Cairo surrendered when the British advance guard entered the city. On September 19 a decree was issued in Tewfik's name disbanding the army. In September 1883 Sir Evelyn Baring was appointed as agent and consul-general.

We have seen what troubles awaited England when she seized the Cape of Good Hope, in order to safeguard her route to the East. She was now led by the same motive to assume control of the Suez Canal when it superseded the Cape route. From the northern, as from the southern extremity of the African continent, she found herself dragged into the distant interior by forces she vainly tried to resist.

Gordon, by tireless journeys and the sheer force of his personal influence, had created some semblance of rule in the vast regions which stretched from Wadi Halfa at the second cataract to the Nile sources on the equator. His successors were powerless to restrain the militant tribes, whose only form of trade was in slaves. These tribes had found a religious leader who gave them the kind of organisation which Mahomet had once given to the tribes of Arabia. According to Moslem tradition, Mahomet declared that one of his descendants would establish justice on earth and would bear the title of al-mahdi, an Arabic word which means 'he who is guided aright'. At the head of the negroid tribes in the Sudan there appeared a leader accepted by them as the Mahdi. To deal with this movement some British officers were sent under General Hicks. In September 1883 Hicks and his staff, when leading an expedition in Kordofan, were lured into the desert and slaughtered. Rejecting Baring's advice, the British government decided that Egypt must abandon the Sudan. In January 1884 Gordon was commissioned to evacuate the troops and officials. In February he reached Khartum, but by May was cut off from Egypt by the hordes of the Mahdi. The British government was slowly forced by the rising anger of public opinion to attempt his rescue. In October (1884) Wolseley began his march up the Nile. On January 27, 1885, Sir Charles Wilson, in command of the steamers approaching Khartum, learned that the city had just fallen and that Gordon was killed.

It was then decided to leave the Sudan to its fate, and Lord Cromer devoted himself to the task of restoring order and prosperity in Egypt. He abolished forced labour, improved irrigation and by 1888 had balanced the budget. He had now begun to create an Egyptian army under British officers. In March 1896 the Italian army was destroyed at Adowa by the Abyssinian emperor Menelik. The Khalifa (successor) who had now succeeded the Mahdi was threatening Wadi Halfa, the point on the Nile at the second cataract to which the Egyptian government had withdrawn. Sir Herbert Kitchener at the head of Egyptian troops was ordered to push the frontier 250 miles to the south at Dongola, which he occupied in September 1896. Two years later a further advance was made by British as well as by Egyptian troops. On September 2, 1898, the Khalifa's hordes tried to arrest Kitchener's march on Khartum at Omdurman, and were mowed down by machine-gun fire. On September 4 Kitchener's forces held a religious service near the spot where Gordon was killed in Khartum. The Egyptian and British flags were hoisted together over the city.

Here Kitchener was met by the news that Major Marchand and 5 other Frenchmen with 100 native followers had made their way to the upper Nile from French Senegal, the most western point on the African coast. They had hoisted the French flag at Fashoda 300 miles to the south of Khartum. Kitchener reached Fashoda on September 18 and for a time England and France were in measurable distance of war. The French yielded to Lord Salisbury's firmness, and eventually Marchand was ordered to haul down the Tricolour. He made his way across Abyssinia to French Somaliland opposite Aden, and thus completed a journey of west to east of over 4000 miles, equal in length to the distance from Cape Town to Cairo. The words 'Remember Fashoda' continued to embitter the relations of England and France for a number of years.

One year after this incident the Khalifa and his leading chiefs were brought to bay in the wilds of Kordofan by Sir Reginald Wingate and killed in battle. Thereafter the Egyptian and British flags waved over the Nile and its sources, other than the tributary stream which flowed from the mountains of Abyssinia. Lord Cromer endeavoured in vain to persuade the British authorities to complete arrangements with the Emperor for controlling the waters which rose in his territories.

NOTE

[1] See above, p. 452.

CHAPTER XLVIII

THE SCHLIEFFEN PLAN

By a strange coincidence Japan appeared on the world stage as a national state at the same time as Italy and Germany, in the year 1871. Relieved at last from internal convulsions these three peoples were now free to apply to the work of production the knowledge of physical forces acquired in the previous century. That Germany was able to advance more rapidly than Italy or Japan was due to various conditions, physical and human. Their country was richly stored with coal and iron, and its people equipped with the qualities required to exploit those resources—drive, diligence, an aptitude for science and the discipline born of military habits. With internal frontiers and tariffs abolished they were free to create a system of transport on a national scale. With Atlantic ports they were able to build a mercantile marine and a navy to make it respected on the seas. But the largest factor of all was Bismarck, a man great enough to see that peace was the first requisite of the empire he had used war to create. France, from which he had torn two provinces, he did not attempt to conciliate. His policy was to keep her in weakness and isolation. With the Austrian Empire it was otherwise. In the generous peace which Bismarck had made on the morrow of Sadowa he had laid the foundation of a close friendship between the German and Austrian Empires.

In 1872 the emperors of Russia and Austria were invited and came to Berlin, ostensibly to recognise the title of Emperor assumed by William I. in the previous year. The result was a close understanding between the three empires. In 1873 Victor Emmanuel came from Italy to visit Berlin. In 1874 the British ambassador wrote that "our relations with Germany were never better, more cordial or more satisfactory than at present".

In 1875 the peasantry of Bosnia and Herzegovina rose in rebellion against Turkey. The struggle rapidly spread to Montenegro, Serbia and Bulgaria. This Slavonic rising was overwhelmed by the Turkish armies, which in 1876 massacred some 20,000 Bulgarian Christians. In 1877 Russia entered the lists to rescue her kindred, drove the Turkish armies back and, by April 1878, was encamped before Constantinople. She there dictated the Treaty of San Stefano which, had it stood, would have given her the mastery of the Balkan peninsula. This neither England nor Austria were prepared to accept. Europe was on the brink of war when in June 1878 Bismarck succeeded in bringing the powers into conference at Berlin. There Russia was brought to accept a modification of the Treaty of San Stefano which satisfied Austria and England.

The Tzar descried the Congress as "a coalition of Europe against Russia under the leadership of Prince Bismarck". That statesman realised that the part he had played as president of the Congress had lost him the friendship of Russia. If Germany were attacked by Russia on the east, France would at once enter into the struggle to recover her lost provinces. So in 1879 he made a secret alliance with Austria to resist any attack made by Russia on either of them. If Austria or Germany were attacked by a power other than Russia (*i.e.* France) and such power were supported by Russia, whether in arms or only by mobilisation, then Austria and Germany would combine for their mutual defence. In 1882 this arrangement for central Europe to defend its eastern and western flanks became the Triple Alliance when Italy was drawn into its terms.

Austria was thus insured against an attack from Russia. But Austria might also take the initiative and attack Russia. Bismarck saw that the fear of such an attack might impel Russia to seek an ally in France, and so defeat his policy of keeping France in isolation. So in 1887 he contracted another alliance with Russia herself, in which he undertook that Germany should come to her aid if Austria attacked her.

Bismarck could work these feats of diplomacy because he had given the German Empire a constitution which made him its real ruler. The Reichstag elected by manhood suffrage had no power to dismiss the chancellor and was, as Wilhelm Liebknecht said, "but the figleaf of an autocracy". Only the emperor could dismiss the chancellor, and Bismarck knew that with William I. on the throne his own position as the real ruler of Germany was secure. In 1888 William I. and his invalid son died, and there came to the throne a young successor resolved to rule in his own person and brook no mayor of the palace. In 1890 Bismarck was dismissed, and the reinsurance treaty which bound Germany to defend Russia against an Austrian attack was allowed to lapse.

A movement had now started in Russia to develop her vast natural resources by applying the powers of mechanisation. Factories sprang into being. The iron and coal fields were linked by a railway. In 1891 the project of linking the Baltic and Black Seas with the Pacific by the Trans-Siberian railway was started. Russia was in desperate need of capital and, rebuffed at Berlin, turned to Paris, where her overtures were greeted with rapture. A treaty which laid the foundation of the Franco-Russian Alliance which Bismarck had feared was signed in 1891. In 1894 it ripened into a military convention which bound Russia and France to come to each other's assistance with powerful armies if either were attacked by Germany. French money, meanwhile, was poured into Russia.

Germany was now faced by the prospect of a war with France, in which armies from the east larger than her own would attack her in the rear. The plans of the general staff in Berlin were framed to meet this contingency. The Russian millions could only be mobilised slowly when war broke out. The German plans were, therefore, laid to invade France and destroy her armies in the first few weeks of the war. She would then be free to turn to the east and destroy the slowly gathering masses from Russia with her vastly superior technique. But to paralyse France before the Russian attack could mature the German armies must march through the low countries of Belgium. The German plan, prepared by the chief of the staff, Count Alfred von Schlieffen, proposed to ignore the fact that in 1832 Prussia had guaranteed the frontiers of Belgium against invasion.

Thus in 1894 the five leading powers of Europe were ranged into two opposing camps. We must now turn to consider how it was that this great collision, when it happened twenty years later, was not confined to Europe, but, as in the eighteenth century, swept all the continents into the struggle.

CHAPTER XLIX

THE PARTITION OF AFRICA

On their way to the coast the bearers of Livingstone's body met a British expedition under Cameron which had started too late to save him. They firmly refused to bury his body, as Cameron desired, and continued their way to Zanzibar. Cameron went on to Ujiji, where he found and preserved Livingstone's papers. He then went on till he reached the Atlantic coast south of the Congo in 1875, the first European to cross central Africa.

Stanley, meanwhile, had started from Zanzibar in 1874 to explore the Congo and reached its mouth in 1877. On his return to Europe Leopold II., king of the Belgians, engaged his services and sent him back to the Congo. There, in the next few years, he laid the foundations of the Congo Free State. The vast territories drained by the Congo were to be organised as an independent state, not annexed to Belgium, but under the personal sovereignty of Leopold. The idea was designed to avoid the jealousies aroused and the compensations claimed for new territory annexed by a sovereign state. The missionaries also believed that under the beneficent leadership of Leopold they could safeguard the natives from exploitation. In France and Germany his project was watched with the closest attention; for along the African coast the struggle for trade had developed apace in recent years. In 1840, when Livingstone sailed for South Africa, Hamburg merchants had started to sell German goods at African ports. A few years later the Basel Missionary Society began to send German missionaries (who also traded) to the west coast. Very soon after Livingstone died there were 60 German factories between Portuguese Guinea and British South Africa, and also some 100 missionary stations. Throughout this period, when central Europe was distracted by wars, Germans had left the Fatherland in millions to settle, for the most part, in North America, Brazil and Australia, under alien flags, where a language other than theirs was spoken. Societies were formed in Germany to direct the movement and to keep the emigrants in touch with the Fatherland.

After 1871, when the German states (other than Austria) were at last merged in a national union, "all the scattered energies of Germany in the direction of colonisation, as in other directions, were united into one strong current".[1] It quickly gathered a force which Bismarck recognised. In 1883 he asked the chambers of commerce at Hamburg, Bremen and Lübeck to say that steps should be taken to promote German trade, especially in Africa. Their replies pointed to annexations.

Next year their advice was applied to the African coast north of the Orange river. The British regarded this region as coming 'within their sphere', but government policy was still ruled by the principle expressed in 1865 when a House of Commons committee had resolved "that all further extensions of territory or assumption of government or new treaty offering any protection to native tribes would be inexpedient".[2] In deference to the views of Sir Bartle Frere, when governor of the Cape, Walfisch Bay and 15 miles round it was annexed in 1878. Further than this the British government refused to go unless or until the Cape government would accept all financial responsibilities. While the British and Cape governments were debating this question at leisure, Bismarck in 1884 occupied and annexed the coast on either side of Walfisch Bay, as far north as Angola and as far south as the Orange river. At the same time he hoisted the German flag over Togoland and the Cameroons north of the equator. He then tried to annex the coast between Natal and Delagoa Bay; but the British government, now thoroughly startled, sent a man-of-war which hoisted the Union Jack at Santa Lucia Bay in December 1884.

Up to now the Liberal government in London had assumed that the powers of Europe would accept and apply the principle of non-annexation which England had imposed on herself. The determined action of Bismarck shattered this dream. Portugal realised the importance of asserting titles which were centuries old and of making the most of them. She proposed a conference, which met at Berlin at the end of 1884, in which the United States and every country in Europe but Switzerland joined. In 1885 a general act was signed by all the powers in Europe, which recognised the Congo Free State and settled the principle that annexations in Africa, to be valid, must be based on effective occupation by the power which annexed.

The results which followed this general act in the course of ten years can be seen at a glance by comparing the political map of the continent as it was before the Conference of Berlin with the map as drawn at the close of the century. The aims which led to these vast annexations largely defeated each other. Portugal hoped to unite Angola with Mozambique by annexing the country between them explored by Livingstone. Germany hoped to annex these regions and so to unite her possessions north of the Orange river with German East Africa. North of the equator France was hoping to connect the territory she annexed on the western coast with French Somaliland at the mouth of the Red Sea. The British aspired to control a chain of territories stretching from Egypt

MAPS SHOWING AFRICA:

(1) Before Partition

(2) After Partition

(*Overleaf*)

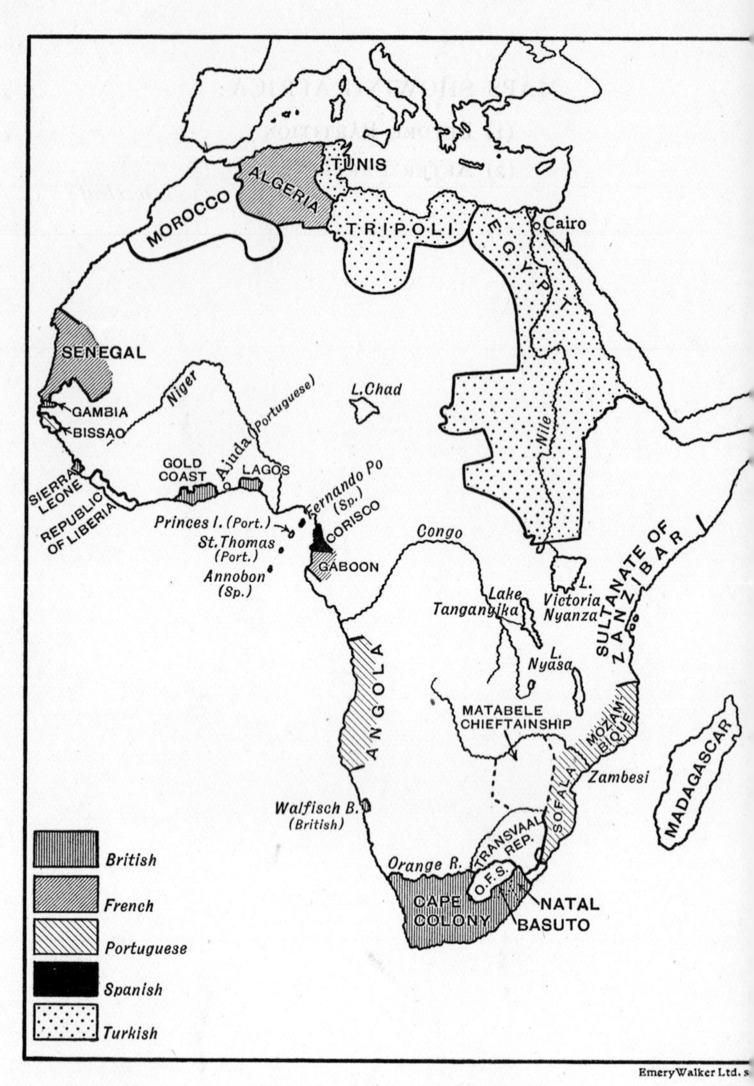

AFRICA BEFORE PARTITION, 1876

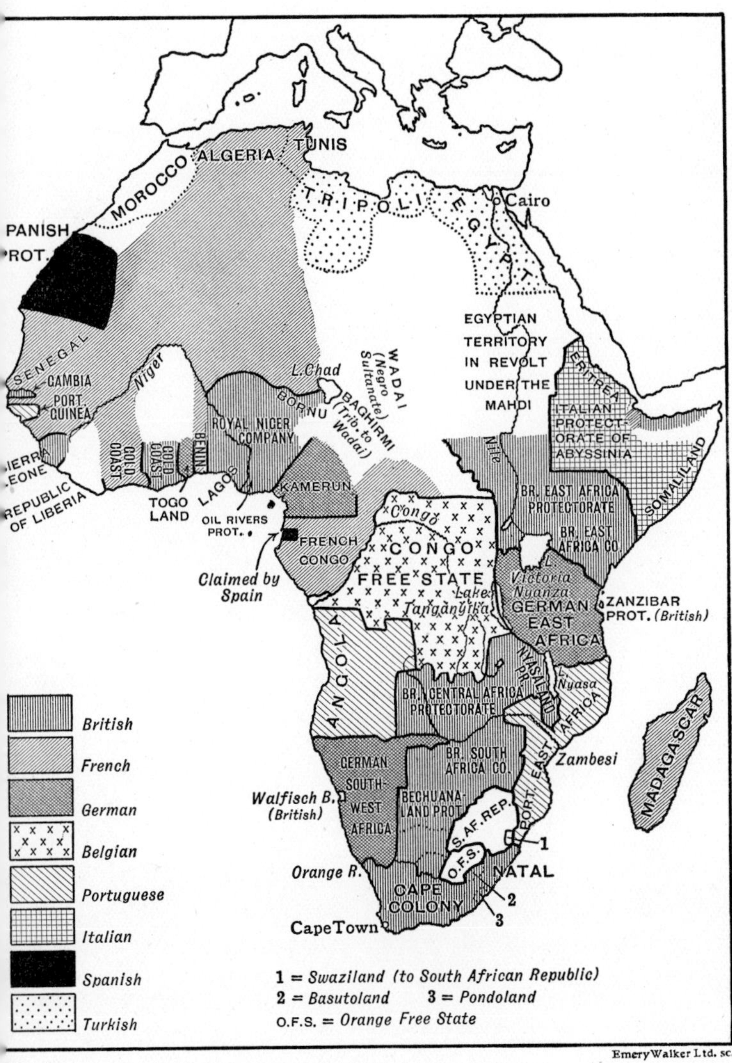

AFRICA AFTER PARTITION, 1893

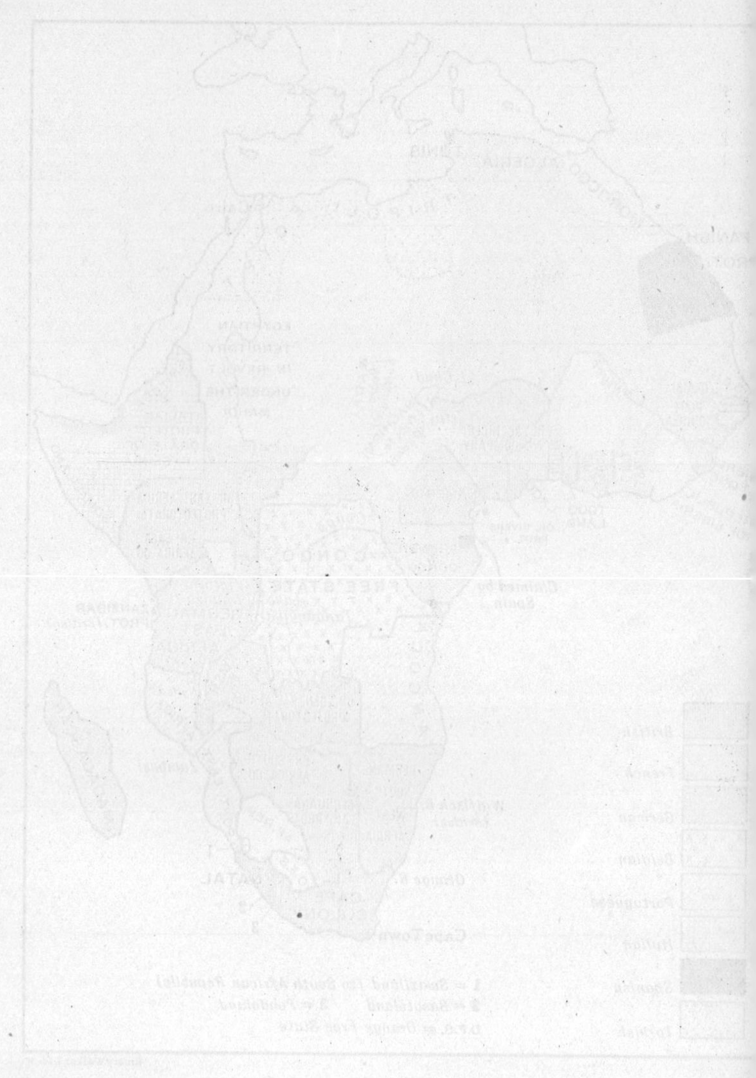

south to British Bechuanaland and the Cape. By the end of the century these ambitions had all defeated each other. Yet the whole continent had been parcelled out to one or other of the powers of Europe except Liberia and Abyssinia. The Congo Free State was practically Belgian. Even Abyssinia was recognised by the powers as an Italian protectorate, and was so shown on the maps before 1896, when Menelik asserted his independence at the battle of Adowa.

The cause which first set in motion this rapid partition of a whole continent by the powers of Europe was the horrors of the slave-trade in the interior as revealed by the travels of Livingstone. That motive was reinforced and obscured by two others. One was anxiety to secure new markets for products which the mechanised industries of Europe were now pouring out in exchange for raw materials. But stronger still was the non-economic passion for power and dominion which, as Mr. Cole has observed, is stronger in men than the motive to obtain the necessaries of life.[3] The greed for trade and passion for power led to appalling crimes, especially in the Congo Free State, until it was stripped of its international and philanthropic pretensions. When responsibility for its government was openly assumed by a national state, the Belgian government, the ruthless oppression of the natives was stopped, and its system of government will now bear comparison with the best in tropical Africa.

Divided as the civilised world was and is into national states, no other alternative to partition was possible. While no thoughtful observer will argue that the African natives are receiving justice at the hands of their white rulers, he will also admit that their present conditions are definitely better than those which Livingstone revealed. From coast to coast the stronger tribes were free to raid the weaker for slaves to be sold to the Arab traders, a condition which must have led to the final destruction of the whole race had it continued. And worse must have followed, had no civilised governments assumed the task of policing these regions and of checking the slave-trade and the slave-hunting wars which it provoked. As in Swaziland, unscrupulous Europeans would have debauched the chiefs, and acquired control of the tribal lands and the native resources. A civilised government could only control its nationals by assuming control of the regions they were trying to exploit.

No civilised state is entitled to think with much satisfaction of its work for the last fifty years in Africa. The things they have left undone have been worse than the things they have done, as they usually are in human affairs. In one respect the course of events had dealt hardly with the African people as compared with the Indian. The contact of Europe with India led to the final establishment of a paramount government for the whole peninsula, a government which could look at the problems of its diverse peoples as a whole, and in course of time give them a sense of unity. In Africa, a much larger country, with a people more uniform but fewer in numbers, there is no government to see or consider their interests as a whole or direct them along the path to national union and ultimate self-government.

NOTES

[1] Scott Keltie, *The Partition of Africa*, p. 166.

[2] The Royal Institute of International Affairs, *Information Department Papers*, No. 18, p. 6.

[3] See above, p. 510.

CHAPTER L

PARTITION OF THE SOUTHERN PACIFIC

THE activities of German traders had also extended to the islands of the southern Pacific. In the year that the German Empire was proclaimed at Versailles, the Hamburg South Sea Trading Company established a station on the Duke of York island just north of New Guinea, and from it supplied its plantations in Samoa with Kanaka labour. Their activity aroused fears in Australia that the German Empire might annex New Guinea.

In 1883 the German press started to urge the Emperor to annex. In alarm, the government of Queensland called on Lord Derby to annex New Guinea, and, before receiving an answer, hoisted the Union Jack on the island. Lord Derby refused to recognise their action, but in 1884 agreed to proclaim a protectorate over the southern coast of New Guinea. Three weeks later Germany annexed the northern coast and the islands known as New Britain. A scramble followed on the lines marked out for partitioning Africa. Spheres of influence were first delimited by Germany, France and Great Britain, and before the close of the century the islands scattered about the Pacific were annexed by one or other of these powers, or else by the United States. Germany secured the islands to the north and east of New Guinea and also Samoa. The French possession of the Marquesas and Society Islands and of New Caledonia was confirmed. Hawaii and a small island close to Samoa were annexed to the United States of America. A Franco-British condominium was established in the New Hebrides. The rest of the islands scattered about the southern Pacific came under the British flag.

The most important result of these annexations was the impetus given to the movement to create a national government for Australia. The domestic need, which Lord Grey had foreseen, of some government competent to deal with the continent as a whole had long been felt. But the movement was always stifled by colonial legislatures whose vision was bounded by their local and vested interests. Till the German Empire came into the field in 1884 the colonial assemblies, like that in Cape Colony, assumed an almost exclusive influence of the British power in the regions about them. The German annexations disturbed this dream and provided the impetus required to surmount the local jealousies which had blocked the way to a federal union. These jealousies were not overcome till, at the instance of Sir Harry Parkes, the premier of New South Wales, a national convention was created, composed of delegates sent by the electorates themselves, and not by the local legislatures. In the years 1897 and 1898 this convention, meeting at Adelaide, Sydney and Melbourne, produced the constitution of the Australian Commonwealth, which in 1899 was ratified by an act of the Imperial parliament. The Commonwealth of Australia was proclaimed and came into being on the first day of the twentieth century.

CHAPTER LI

INDIA FROM THE MUTINY TO THE GREAT WAR

In the quarter of a century which followed the Mutiny the administrative system of India was steadily improved. The educational system inaugurated by Wood and Dalhousie had produced an army of Indian subordinates who could speak English and were trained to execute the orders of their British superiors. At the Indian universities the landowners were able to educate their sons for the service and also for professions, especially law. The literature and history of England were the basis of their studies and led them to desire for India the principles of self-government which England had developed.

In England, meanwhile, the views of John Bright had begun to influence the Liberal party. In 1880, when Gladstone came to power at the head of a substantial Liberal majority, Lord Ripon was appointed as governor-general with instructions to make some attempt to introduce a representative system in the sphere of local government. A brief account of his measures in *The Oxford History of India* is worth quoting, if only for the light it throws on the attitude of the author, who was serving at the time as a magistrate in the North-West Provinces.

The name of the Marquess is chiefly remembered for a series of Acts passed in 1883–5 introducing the so-called scheme of local government, based on the creation of District Boards and subordinate bodies, modelled more or less closely on the English system of County Councils and Rural District Boards. At the same time, the powers of Municipal Boards were extended and the Government of India intimated that the chairman of a municipality should be a non-official, whenever possible. The supreme Government recognised the fact that one general system could not be imposed upon all provinces. A large discretion necessarily was left to local governments and administrations concerning the manner in which the new institutions should be constituted and operated.

The degree to which the elective principle has been introduced varies greatly in different parts of India. The practice of appointing to office by popular election, which is not in accordance with the general sentiment, is difficult to work in a country where caste is the predominant institution, and the electors are sharply divided by differences in race, religion, traditions, and other respects.

The District Boards are concerned primarily with local roads, but are expected to take an interest in education, sanitation, famine relief and several other departments.

The actual working of the Boards has hardly justified the hopes of Lord Ripon. He avowed that "it is not primarily with a view to improvement in administration that this measure is put forward and supported. It is chiefly desirable as a measure of political and popular education. His Excellency in Council has himself no doubt that, in the course of time, as local knowledge and local interest are brought to bear more freely on local administration, improved efficiency will, in fact, follow." Perhaps.[1]

The statement that Ripon in 1883 modelled his reforms on the English councils which were not created till 1888 shows how little impression the events in the outer world can make on the mind of an official absorbed in the interests of India.

With traditional loyalty the British officials took the new councils under their wing and threw themselves into the task of making them work. The magistrate usually acted as chairman of the board, and with infinite patience laboured to persuade its members to do with equal efficiency things which previously would have been done by virtue of a simple command from himself. The general result achieved at the cost of much additional labour was no great loss in efficiency and no great gain on the part of elected members in capacity for making their own decisions. In some provinces the electoral system was so hedged with safeguards and restrictions as to have no practical effect in training electorates. In the larger municipalities there was more inefficiency and corruption, and also more training in the art of self-government.

An attempt was also made by Ripon to put Europeans in India on a footing of equality with Indians before the law. The story of his failure is best told by a qualified eye-witness:

But side by side with the ancient India, scarcely touched with the breath of Western civilization, there were also symptoms of India's new reaction to the British *raj*. It was not that aspect of India that I had gone out to study, but I found myself directly confronted with it in the turmoil of the Ilbert Bill. India had enjoyed more than five-and-twenty years of unbroken peace at home since the storm of the Great Mutiny, but the memories of terrible excesses on the one side and of fierce repression on the other were still smouldering and they flickered up suddenly when, in the third year of his Viceroyalty, Lord Ripon brought in a measure, technically termed the Criminal Procedure Code Amendment Bill, which at once provoked an extraordinary outburst of racial passion. Ripon had been sent out by Mr. Gladstone to initiate a more liberal policy towards Indians than that pursued by his predecessor, Lord Lytton, who had been Disraeli's nominee. But the Ilbert Bill, to which the Viceroy himself had not originally attached great importance, was far less an integral part of his programme of Indian reforms than a normal outcome of administrative necessities, which required the extension to Indian magistrates in rural districts of the powers to try Europeans with which, whether Europeans or Indians, they were already invested in the three great Presidency towns of Calcutta, Madras and Bombay. Englishmen chose, nevertheless, to see in this measure a dangerous invasion of their rights, and when Lord Ripon's supporters dared to suggest that Indian rights had also to be taken into consideration, the leading European organ in Calcutta, *The Englishman*, replied with the characteristic statement that "the only people who have any right to India are the British; the so-called Indians have no right whatever". Into the details of the controversy there is no need for me to enter now. I had neither the knowledge nor the inclination to go into them at the time, but what I saw and what made a lasting impression on me was the revelation of intense racial bitterness. Englishmen denounced the Bill as a deliberate attempt to "put the native on the *gaddi*", and Indians denounced all opposition to it as a shameless repudiation of Queen Victoria's great Proclamation of 1858. The revolt of the Europeans was not confined to the unofficial community, but found aiders and abettors amongst British officials in all the public services. In the heat of the moment a scheme was even concocted in Calcutta for seizing the Viceroy and putting him forcibly on board ship for deportation out of India. The storm had somewhat subsided by the time I reached Calcutta, for the Viceroy, though appointed from England by a powerful Liberal government with a large majority in the House of Commons behind it, had been driven to whittle down all the chief provisions of the Bill under such pressure of angry European opinion in India that Indians had some excuse for describing it as sheer lawlessness. But the atmosphere was still electric, and though I had certainly no pro-Indian bias, it came as a severe shock to me when at a large men's dinner party my host, who was a prominent member of the English community, after proposing the health of the Queen Empress as "the first loyal toast" went on to propose "Damnation to the Viceroy" as a second loyal toast.

The echoes of the storm reverberated in England, but the Parliamentary debates proceeded for the most part on the usual party lines. The shrewdest comment of all was a cartoon in *Punch* which represented Lord Ripon as a Mahout driving an Indian elephant with a group of Anglo-Indians in the howdah behind him, who were shaking their fists at him and seemed on the point of laying violent hands upon him. The cartoon was called "The Anglo-Indian Mutiny: a bad example for the elephant". One immediate result could hardly have been foreshadowed with greater prescience. The success of the Europeans' agitation against the Ilbert Bill was an object-lesson to the Indians in the power of organized agitation for political purposes, and their reply to it was the foundation in the following year of the Indian National Congress as an organization through which, in default of regular representative assemblies, the Western-educated Indian could make his voice heard not only in India but in England, and, for the first few years at least, made it heard with a greater regard for lawful forms and methods than Anglo-Indians had shown in their campaign against the Ilbert Bill.[2]

Sir Valentine Chirol goes on to suggest that government would have been wise to have recognised the Congress and encouraged it to develop on constitutional lines. This might, perhaps, have been done if the agents of England on the spot had believed, as did Munro at an earlier date, that the people of India might, in course of time, learn to govern themselves. The Mutiny had combined with the mechanisation of India to dismiss that idea to the region of dreams. One wonders whether Munro himself would have persevered in this faith, had he known an India where a third of the whole population depended for their very existence on the punctual working of mechanical equipment. The system imported from Europe worked because it was supervised by some hundreds of Englishmen whose standards of public duty, efficiency and faculty for decision were produced by institutions in which they and their ancestors were bred. So tremendous were the risks of catastrophe in a mechanised India that British officials shrank from transferring the ultimate power of direction to Indian hands. The duty of making final decisions was too little imposed on Indians, and Englishmen came to regard them as naturally incapable of facing the ordeal. They developed a distrust of the principles inspiring the polity which had made them more capable of decision than Indians. To have treated the Congress as the germ of a parliament would only have been possible to rulers strong in the faith of Munro. In result it became a platform for asserting the demand for self-government rather than a training ground for practising the qualities needed for the task.

The impact of British ideas on Indian society was thus complicated by the opposite and no less powerful influence to which the English were subject in India. They tended to acquire a certain distrust of the principles underlying the society by which they themselves were produced. The policies which appealed to them were such as England could not follow to the end without renouncing the law of her being. The West in adjusting its relations to the East was hampered by the tendency of its representatives to lose their grasp of its own essential ideas.

The era in Indian administration which began in 1848 was closed by Lord Curzon, whose energy and ardour for administrative reform rivalled Dalhousie's. He left his mark on every department and, like Dalhousie, an heritage of unrest to those who followed him, which took the form not of risings but of organised murder. In 1905, the year that Lord Curzon left India, a Liberal government came to power in England with an overwhelming majority. Morley, as Secretary of State for India, decided to meet the demand for constitutional reform on the part of educated Indians who did not believe in anarchy. By an Imperial Act in 1909 he provided that a certain number of members might be elected to the Indian legislatures. Indian spokesmen were thus given the right to criticise their rulers without being made in any degree responsible for the conduct of government. Morley had failed to realise the effect of a system which gave Indians every scope for finding fault, and scarcely any for providing remedies. He could not allow himself to hope that the people of India could in any real sense adopt the principles of government developed in the West.

If it could be said that this chapter of reforms led directly or indirectly to the establishment of a parliamentary system in India, I, for one, would have nothing at all to do with it.[3]

When such was the verdict of the greatest living exponent of Liberalism, Englishmen accepted the view of that small body of their countrymen who had given their lives to the government of India. They did not inquire how it could be reconciled with the principles of the polity into which India was incorporated.

NOTES

[1] *The Oxford History of India*, p. 756.
[2] Sir Valentine Chirol, *Fifty Years in a Changing World*, pp. 221-3.
[3] *House of Lords Debate*, December 17, 1908.

CHAPTER LII

FROM WAR TO UNION IN SOUTH AFRICA

THAT the rapid partition of Africa and Polynesia was accomplished without a war was largely due to the experienced sagacity of Salisbury and Bismarck. In a wider view it was due to the fact that Great Britain had an undisputed control of the seas. Bismarck himself had no desire to dispute that control and was fully content with an army which allowed him to dominate Europe. Yet though the partition of Africa had led to no rupture of peace at the time, it had set in train the events which were destined to close the epoch that since Trafalgar had localised wars to continents. The storm which has blackened the skies of the world was heralded by a cloud no bigger than a man's hand in South Africa.

The Gladstone government of the 'eighties had tried to cling to the traditional policy of non-annexation, if only because its predecessor, the Beaconsfield government, had begun to challenge it. In the Transvaal the emigrant Boers had failed to establish a stable government. On the south-east they were threatened by the Zulus, but the burghers were slow to respond to the call for military service and refused to pay their taxes. In 1877 the Transvaal pound fell to one shilling and the state was bankrupt. Sir Bartle Frere then commissioned Theophilus Shepstone to annex the Transvaal, and crushed the Zulu power at the cost of several disasters and £5,000,000.

Paul Kruger, meanwhile, was heading a movement to cancel the annexation, and visited London twice for the purpose. His efforts were supported by Gladstone in speeches which in 1880 brought the

Conservative government down and carried the Liberal government to office. The Boers then rose in rebellion and in February 1881 defeated and killed Sir George Colley at Majuba. Mr. Gladstone had already decided to cancel the annexation and refused to allow this disaster to affect his decision. The Republic was recognised once more, and in 1884 the title of 'The South African Republic' was conceded. In Kruger the burghers had found a ruler able to rule and one they were willing to obey.

Since his first encounter with Livingstone Kruger had been trying to cut the route which the great explorer had opened to the north. As the terms under which the Transvaal Republic was recognised precluded its western extension, parties of Boers were sent into Bechuanaland to establish independent republics called Goschen and Stellaland.

It was in these years that Cecil Rhodes, a diamond digger in Kimberley, was turning his mind to the regions which Livingstone had opened to the north. He had made his fortune and got himself elected by the diggers to the Cape Assembly. In 1884 the German annexation of the coast north of the Orange river opened his eyes to the need for resolute action. Through his efforts Sir Charles Warren was sent out with a force which reached Bechuanaland in 1884, dissolved the two mushroom republics and proclaimed a British protectorate over the region between the Transvaal and the German colony. "That young man", said President Kruger, who had met Rhodes with Warren, "is going to cause me trouble".[1]

In the following year gold-bearing reefs were discovered in the Transvaal which were soon to make the poorest state in South Africa the richest. Johannesburg, named after the president (Stephanus Johannes Paul Kruger), sprang into being. In a few years the mines had attracted an alien community (uitlanders) equal in number to the burghers.

Rhodes, meanwhile, had lost no time in exploiting the road he had opened to the north. In 1887 he sent emissaries to negotiate concessions with Lobengula, the Matabele chief. In 1889 he obtained the charter which enabled the British South Africa Company to exploit these concessions and administer the country. The sphere assigned to the Company was soon extended as far north as the southern shore of Lake Tanganyika. In 1890 England and Germany signed the treaty which secured to Great Britain the protectorate of Zanzibar, what is now Kenya and also Uganda. In return the Germans acquired the island of Heligoland off their coast and German East Africa with a boundary marching with the boundary of the Congo Free State. The dream of Rhodes that the British dominions might extend from the Cape to Egypt was thus frustrated. His own activities in Rhodesia had already defeated the German project of uniting German South-West Africa with German East Africa and also the Portuguese claim to the regions explored by Livingstone between Angola and the Mozambique.

In that same year, 1890, Rhodes had become prime minister of the Cape and, like Grey, had realised that, large as the Cape Colony was, it was only a fragment of a larger whole. The construction of railways to the gold-fields was fast increasing that unity. The Cape and Natal were both pushing their lines to the Transvaal frontier to secure their share of this traffic. The Transvaal was pushing a line to Delagoa Bay, which would rob both the Cape and Natal of most of the traffic for which they were competing. This was only one of a number of questions which inflamed the relations of the Cape Colony, Natal, the Orange Free State and the Transvaal, and compelled Great Britain to interfere whenever a crisis was reaching the flash-point. The relation of the white to the black population was the greatest of all these questions. They could only reach their solution when the people on the spot, whether British or Dutch, had established one government which could rule South Africa at least so far as the Zambesi. It was this which Rhodes had in mind when he spoke of eliminating the imperial factor. He saw that South Africans must govern themselves; he was also resolved that they should remain under the British flag, as Canada and Australia had done. The separate flags of the two republics presented an obstacle which he tried and failed to get round.

Flags are the flowers of sovereignty and the seed they shed takes root with amazing rapidity. The effect which the sense of separate statehood had on the minds of the emigrant farmers north of the Orange river, in the course of a few decades, is indeed significant. By 1880 the Transvaal burghers were ready to die for the right to statehood which England had recognised in 1852. Kruger, like Rhodes, was conscious that in South Africa there was no permanent room for separate sovereignties and flags. The tenacity with which he and his burghers clung to the title of 'South African Republic' is evidence of the fact. It was natural that the view of the farmer president, who could scarcely read and write, should be narrower than that of Rhodes with his Oxford training. Kruger thought of South Africa ruled by his own people, as the Transvaal was ruled. The sudden access of wealth helped to convert his dream to an aim. Rhodes thought of South Africa ruled, as the Cape was ruled, by British and Dutch together, irrespective of race. He earned and enjoyed the confidence of his Dutch electorate, until he lost it by crimes into which he was led by impatience. But even when he had lost it, he still thought of South Africa as destined to be ruled by the Dutch no less than the British. In 1900 when the British had again annexed the Transvaal and Kruger was in flight, he spoke as follows to a chauvinist meeting in Cape Town:

You think you have beaten the Dutch! But it is not so. The Dutch are not beaten; what is beaten is Krugerism, a corrupt and evil government, no more Dutch in essence than English. No! The Dutch are as vigorous and unconquered to-day as they have ever been; the country is still as much theirs as it is yours, and you will have to live and work with them hereafter as in the past. Remember *that* when you go back to your homes in the towns or in the up-country farms and villages: let there be no vaunting words, no vulgar triumph over your Dutch neighbours; make them feel that the bitterness is past and that the need of co-operation is greater than ever; teach your children to remember when they go to their village school that the little Dutch boys and girls they find sitting on the same benches with them are as much part of the South African nation as they are themselves, and that as they learn the same lessons together now, so hereafter they must work together as comrades for a common object—the good of South Africa.[2]

While head of the Cape government, Rhodes devoted a great part of his time to establishing in Rhodesia the rule of the Chartered Company, of which he was chairman. Meanwhile the cosmopolitan community on the Rand, excluded from all political rights, was growing more restless. As all prospects of managing Kruger faded, Rhodes, who suffered from heart disease and knew that his days were numbered, began to think of how to displace Kruger and bring to power in the Transvaal some leader with whom he could work. With this object in view he got into touch with leaders on the Rand, who resented the burdens imposed on the mining community, but had little grasp of his wider aims. He thus promoted a revolution which, as he thought, would compel the Imperial government to intervene to restore order in the Transvaal. To render this intervention effective he quietly gathered under Dr. Jameson, his closest confidant, such forces as he controlled in Rhodesia and the Cape at Pitsani, in the region from which Livingstone had started on his travels.

As the movement developed on the Rand, Jameson realised that its leaders were at sixes and sevens. Some of them, caring little for the aims of Rhodes, meant only to found another republic in closer sympathy with the mining interest.

Jameson, conscious of his own power of handling men when face to face with them, believed he could straighten out matters if once he could get to Johannesburg. He telegraphed to Rhodes that the only way to save a fiasco was for him and his force to go there as quickly as possible. Rhodes, seeing the folly of the step he proposed, telegraphed back a peremptory refusal. Jameson afterwards said that on reading this telegram he thought to himself:

> Rhodes is the Prime Minister of the Cape, and of course as such he cannot make himself responsible for a proposal to invade the Transvaal Republic. It is up to me to take this responsibility on myself. And like a damned fool I never saw that I could not do this thing without involving Rhodes himself.[3]

His plans were defeated by a squalid miscarriage. The man entrusted with the task of cutting the telegraph line from Pretoria to the Rand got drunk and failed to blow up a bridge. A powerful commando reached the western extremity of the Rand in time to capture Jameson and his followers before they could reach Johannesburg. Next day the German Emperor telegraphed to Kruger congratulating the Transvaal that "without appealing to the help of friendly powers" he had repelled the raiders. A German warship was sent to Delagoa Bay.

In England public opinion was deeply shocked by Jameson's outrage. In this crisis Kruger had appeared at his best. He spared the raiders and handed the leaders over to the British authorities. Jameson was tried in England and condemned to imprisonment. But the future reactions of British and Dutch throughout South Africa were profoundly embittered. Rhodes had betrayed the confidence of the Dutch he had laboured so long to earn. In the Transvaal the temper of the burghers was too gravely exasperated to allow of any substantial reforms on the gold-fields, and the Emperor's telegram had convinced them that if matters came to a struggle with England the German Empire would be fighting on their side.

On the news of Jameson's capture Rhodes had resigned in disgrace. His leadership passed to Milner, who was sent to South Africa as high commissioner and took up the uitlanders' cause. In 1899 he met Kruger to discuss their grievances at Bloemfontein and, when the conference failed, measures were taken to strengthen the British forces in the Cape and Natal. The Transvaal and Orange Free State had entered into a close alliance, and in September, Kruger decided to take the initiative, believing that the foreign powers, or at any rate Germany, would support him in arms. Steyn, the president of the Free State, who did not share his confidence, was overborne. In September 1899 an ultimatum was launched from Pretoria and Boer commandos from the Transvaal and Free State invaded Natal and the Cape Colony. Majuba and the Jameson raid were fresh in their memories, and the spirit in which they marched is described by one of them, the heroic son of a former president of the Free State, who was Kruger's Secretary of State at the time:

> Looking back, I think that war was inevitable. I have no doubt that the British Government had made up its mind to force the issue, and was the chief culprit, but the Transvaalers were also spoiling for a fight, and, from what I saw in Pretoria during the few weeks that preceded the ultimatum, I feel sure that the Boers would in any case have insisted on a rupture.[4]

In this, as in so many other wars, could anyone undertake to pronounce who was the 'aggressor'?

Kruger, who had twice visited England, knew well enough that in a long struggle the two republics were no match for the British power. But in Europe and America Jameson's outrage had inflamed public opinion against Great Britain. The Emperor's telegram had sufficed to convince him that if once the struggle began, Germany would be able to mobilise the powers of Europe to intervene on his side. Of the deeper issues which divided Europe he knew little or nothing. Had the powers of Europe united against England their joint navies might perhaps have challenged her supremacy at sea. Such proposals confronted France and Russia with the question what their own position would be if the ruin of British power left them face to face with the German and Austrian Empires. The truth was forced on the German Emperor's mind that, unsupported by the Russian and French navies, that mighty engine of power, the German army, was confined to Europe.

In the British Dominions, as in Europe and America, public opinion had been outraged by the Jameson raid; but when war broke out, and the German attitude had shown that more than the grievances of the uitlanders was at stake, they joined in the struggle and sent contingents.

The efforts of the little republics, supported by rebellions in the Cape Colony, were prolonged and heroic. In Botha, Smuts and Hertzog they had found young leaders destined to prove their capacity in peace as well as in war. In 1902 they accepted a peace at Vereeniging which established governments under the British Crown in the place of the two republics. In 1905 a Liberal government came into power in England, which established responsible government in the two Crown Colonies. Scarcely eight years after the surrender at Vereeniging the Boer generals were ruling a Union which included the Cape and Natal as well as the Transvaal and Orange Free State.

As Sir George Grey had foreseen, the policy of dividing a country naturally one—a social and geographical unit—into separate sovereignties lay at the root of its troubles. After the war these troubles at once revived. The disfranchisement of rebels in the Cape had enabled the British to secure a majority with Dr. Jameson as their leader. Natal was British, as always. The officials who ruled in the two Crown Colonies were British as well. Yet conflict between the inland and coast colonies was only suppressed and kept in abeyance by the personal authority of the high commissioners, Milner and Selborne. To those in touch with the situation it was plain that the moment elective governments were in power in the Transvaal and Free State, disputes over customs, railways and native policy would rapidly move to a crisis. The only alternative to another struggle was to place all the four colonies under one government, and to merge their electorates in one. By ending the question of flags the Peace of Vereeniging had removed the one insuperable obstacle to this course. But the Jameson raid and the war had raised a difficulty almost as great in the passions they inflamed. For nearly three years the Boers and their leaders had held the whole British Empire at bay; but, in the end, had been overwhelmed and forced to surrender. Within five years the men who signed that surrender were ruling the former republics as ministers under the British Crown. To unite South Africa now meant that those leaders would rule the British, not only in the former republics, but also in Natal and the Cape Colony. But unless such a union were effected the Dutch and British would ere long be ranged in the field fighting each other once more.

The South African question had not been solved by the grant of self-government to the conquered republics, as Liberals in England imagined.

The solution was reached by asking the question what British interests in South Africa were. The war had been fought to retain South Africa in the British Empire. But for what in truth did the British Empire stand? After deep searchings of heart the answer reached was that the so-called empire stood, not for 'dominion over palm and pine', but for the government of men by themselves. British interests meant that a British minority must submit to be ruled by a Boer majority, which had lately yielded in arms to the might of the whole British Empire.

In the Transvaal, Botha was great enough to realise that he could only unite South Africa by winning the confidence of the British minority. He succeeded so far as to make some of them feel that the risk of trusting him was less than the risk of continued disunion. They turned to Jameson, now the one man in South Africa who could swing the British as a whole. Jameson was no longer prime minister in the Cape. His health had never recovered from the raid and imprisonment which followed it. "Do you realise", he said, "that the man you are asking to lead you is the man who has committed the greatest crime in South Africa?" The objection suggested its own answer. He did what was asked of him in a spirit of reparation. His devotion to Rhodes led him to do what he knew that Rhodes would have done had he been there. When brought into contact with Botha that devotion was soon transferred to the Boer leader and was richly returned. Botha, when prime minister of united South Africa, wept when he heard that Jameson had been forced by ill-health to resign the leadership of the party opposed to him. The strange devotion of the Boer and British leaders to each other, and the greatness common to both, had made possible what seemed to the world a political miracle.

NOTES

[1] Sarah Gertrude Millin, *Rhodes*, p. 73.

[2] Basil Williams, *Cecil Rhodes*, pp. 319, 320.

[3] Kerr and Curtis, *The Prevention of War*, p. 92. Published by the Yale University Press.

[4] Deneys Reitz, *Commando*, p. 15. Faber & Faber, 2nd Impression, 1929.

CHAPTER LIII

PROBLEMS RAISED BY THE GROWTH OF RESPONSIBLE GOVERNMENT

THE train of thought which had made it possible to construct a national state in South Africa from the ruins left by the war was destined to affect the structure of the British Empire as a whole. The great schism completed and acknowledged by the Treaty of Paris in 1783 had left England in possession of Canada, of important islands in the West Indies and also a commanding position in India. Within five years she had founded a convict settlement in Australia to replace the facilities she had lost in America. The protracted struggle with France which followed had added further possessions, including the Cape, Mauritius, Ceylon and Singapore. These she retained, not through any desire to extend her dominions, but only to secure her sea-routes to India and the East. The long depression which followed these wars had led numbers of people from the British Isles to seek new homes in Canada, Australia, New Zealand and South Africa. These colonies were allowed to govern themselves in accordance with the principles of the Wakefield school, as propounded in Durham's report. Their relations with the government in London were attended by constant friction, which never led to a rupture because it was assumed that sooner or later they would wish to sever their connection with England. As a rule their demands were conceded, though tardily. Turgot's remark that "colonies are like fruits which only cling till they ripen" was often on the lips of English officials and statesmen, and ever in the back of their minds.

In the early eighties this well-established view was unexpectedly challenged in a course of lectures delivered at Cambridge by the Regius Professor of History, Seeley. The significant feature, as he saw it, in the history of the last three centuries was what he called 'the expansion of England', the extension of English dominion, ideas and institutions to a great part of the temperate regions which discoverers had opened to Europe. The American colonies were in the main founded by people seeking to escape from the established system of religion in England, which had then tried to monopolise their trade. Their secession was really due to these two causes, neither of which applied to the colonies since developed by England.

The American colonies, having seceded, had founded a state on the federal principle, which by reason of its vast area was destined to become greater and far more powerful than the British Isles. On the opposite side of the globe was Russia, also by reason of its area destined to become more powerful than a state limited to the British Isles. If England remained as she was between two states of such magnitude she must rapidly decline to the level of a secondary power. That the German Empire, which had come into being scarcely a decade before Seeley delivered his lectures, was a factor in the situation escaped his notice.

Arguing to the future, from the past, as he saw it, Seeley declined to accept the conclusion that England was destined to lose her position in the world. Steamships, cables and railways had now brought the peoples of England, Canada, South Africa, Australia and New Zealand nearer each other than the peoples of the thirteen American States had been, when they created the American Commonwealth a century before. These communities were closely connected by race, language, ideas, institutions and religion. Following the example of the American states they could now be united in a federal union. The idea of 'England' was capable of expansion so as to include all the self-governing countries under the British crown.

These lectures, published in 1883 under the title *The Expansion of England*, gave a strong intellectual impetus to the wave of imperialism which, before the close of the century, led to vast annexations in Africa and the Pacific ocean. The idea of the Empire as a beneficent power, spreading the blessings of civilisation to races which could not govern themselves, was carried to a wide circle of readers by the writings and poems of Rudyard Kipling, a young journalist born and largely brought up in India. The value attached to a common flag, and the status of British citizen enjoyed by close on a quarter of the human race was enhanced by Seeley and Kipling. Yet Seeley's idea of a federal union made no progress whatever. On the contrary, it awakened suspicions in the colonies that the movement was really intended to revive the deeply resented and fast-diminishing power of 'Downing Street' to interfere with the claim of colonial electorates to manage their own affairs.

Seeley, who had never been in the colonies, failed to realise that responsible government was creating a national sense distinct from that of Great Britain. When he published his book, Canada had already gone far on that road. From the time of Lord Durham the maritime provinces, Quebec, Ontario and British Columbia were equipped with powers to manage their own affairs. They, like the states to the south of them, found that a number of neighbouring governments and electorates are incapable of handling interests which are common to them all. The creation of a federal government in 1867 had given the inhabitants of British North America the power to control their domestic interests from ocean to ocean. The free exercise of that power, especially in creating communications, was fast developing a national feeling, a sense of Canadian patriotism. In Australia the same process was only arrested by delay in following the Canadian example. When at last in 1900 a federal government was created for Australia, the sense of nationalism at once began to find its expression. It was not till Richard Jebb had travelled through these countries and had published in 1905 his book, *Studies in Colonial Nationalism*, that people in England began to realise that the self-governing parts of the British Empire were developing a national sense distinct from their own.

In 1910 the union of the Cape Colony and Natal with the Transvaal and Orange Free State committed South Africa to the same destiny as Canada and Australia. The idea of an England expanding to include these vast regions on opposite sides of the world passed to the limbo of forgotten things. Canada, Australia, South Africa and even New Zealand were now clearly predestined as the homes of national states. It came to be recognised that in course of time these peoples would severally assume a sovereignty as complete as that of Great Britain herself.

The ideas which had moved the British in South Africa to support the project of a national union so soon after the war began to affect current conceptions of the British Empire as a whole. It came to be seen as a system designed to promote the government of men by themselves, rather than as one designed to maintain 'dominion over palm and pine'. The idea was developed in different directions. We have seen how in 1908 the great apostle of nineteenth-century Liberalism had scouted the notion that the people of India could ever enjoy responsible government. The belief that responsible government, as developed in England, was a system peculiar and appropriate only to the white races was almost unquestioned even in Liberal circles. In their own interest the vast majority of mankind must submit to be governed by the races of Europe. To provide such disinterested government was the primary function of the British Empire. This idea had been crystallised in Kipling's phrase, 'the white man's burden'. A belief shared by the prophets of creeds so different as Morley and Kipling now began to be openly challenged. An idea of the Empire was advanced as a system whose primary function it was to equip all who came under its rule for the task of governing themselves. The vision that Indians and Africans in time might learn to govern themselves and come to rank with the self-governing Dominions began to emerge. The Empire came to be seen as the great nursery of national states, coloured as well as white. The change of outlook was reflected in terminology. It was from this time that the British Empire came to be known as the British Commonwealth.

In another direction this doctrine was pressed to its logical conclusion with ruthless severity. That Dominion electorates must control their own domestic affairs from first to last had now been recognised and accepted even in England. But what of external relations—relations controlled by a government responsible only to a British electorate, which also accepted the burden of defending the Commonwealth as a whole? So long as the wealth of the British Isles sufficed to maintain a fleet which could dominate every ocean no question was raised. But after the South African war the rapidly growing wealth and ambitions of the German Empire visibly threatened this position. The British government had been driven to suggest that Dominion governments should begin to make contributions to the common defence. Some response was made; but the growth of Dominion nationalism was marked by the fact that Canada and Australia declined to contribute to the cost of British defence, and decided to organise separate fleets of their own.

From time to time these questions were discussed at imperial conferences. The movement started by Seeley's book had led to the first of these conferences, when premiers from all the colonies were assembled in London to celebrate the fiftieth year of Queen Victoria's reign in 1887. A second met in 1897, after the Jubilee held to celebrate the longest reign in English history, an event which marked the spring-tide of imperial enthusiasm. It was at this conference that Joseph Chamberlain realised that colonial states-men would have nothing to do with Seeley's idea of organic union with England, and began to accept their alternative idea of uniting the Empire by a system of tariffs. The spontaneous share taken by the colonies in the South African war led to a third conference in 1902, and it then became a recognised institution. A fourth was held in 1907, a fifth in 1909 and a sixth in 1911. At this last conference the ques-tion of foreign affairs thrust themselves into the fore-ground. For the first time the secretary of state for foreign affairs, Sir Edward Grey, gave the assembled premiers, in secret, a full exposition of the whole foreign position.

For the first time also attention was drawn to the fact that the so-called self-governing Dominions had no control of foreign affairs. The question was raised by Sir Joseph Ward, the premier of New Zealand. To his crude proposal for transferring the control of foreign affairs to an imperial council on which the Dominion governments would be re-presented, the British prime minister, Mr. Asquith, replied:

It would impair if not altogether destroy the authority of the Government of the United Kingdom in such grave matters as the conduct of foreign policy, the conclusion of treaties, the declaration and maintenance of peace, or the declaration of war, and, indeed, all those relations with Foreign Powers, necessarily of the most delicate character, which are now in the hands of the Imperial Government, subject to its responsibility to the Imperial Parliament. *That authority cannot be shared*, and the co-existence side by side with the Cabinet of the United Kingdom of this proposed body—it does not matter by what name you call it for the moment—clothed with the functions and the jurisdiction which Sir Joseph Ward proposed to invest it with, would, in our judgment, be absolutely fatal to our present system of responsible government.[1]

For the moment this question was thus left in the air. But to those who believed that the British Commonwealth must in the end stand or fall by the principle of self-government, the upshot was difficult, but clear. The line which divided domestic from foreign affairs was unreal. A Dominion could not achieve self-government in the real sense of that word unless or until it achieved control of external affairs and with it the right to say whether the Dominion was at war, apart from the government of Great Britain. To assert this right was to place the Dominion in the same position as the American colonies when they had declared their independence. The only alternative was for the British and Dominion electorates to establish a government responsible to them all, charged with the issues of peace and war. The difficulty could not be met, as Seeley had proposed, by a national state on the largest scale, modelled on the United States. The existence of the Dominions ranking with countries like England or America as nations must be recognised. The British Commonwealth, to endure, must develop a conception new in the experience of mankind, an organic polity large and flexible enough to embrace in one commonwealth national states on the largest scales, divided by oceans one from another.

NOTE

[1] *Minutes of the Proceedings of the Imperial Conference of 1911*, Cd. 5745, p. 71.

CHAPTER LIV

PARTITION IN ASIA

In his great book, *The World Crisis*, Mr. Winston Churchill writes:

> In the year 1895 I had the privilege, as a young officer, of being invited to lunch with Sir William Harcourt. In the course of a conversation in which I took, I fear, none too modest a share, I asked the question, "What will happen then?" "My dear Winston," replied the old Victorian statesman, "the experiences of a long life have convinced me that nothing ever happens." Since that moment, as it seems to me, nothing has ever ceased happening. The growth of the great antagonisms abroad was accompanied by the progressive aggravation of party strife at home. The scale on which events have shaped themselves, has dwarfed the episodes of the Victorian Era. . . .
>
> I date the beginning of these violent times in our country from the Jameson Raid in 1896. This was the herald, if not indeed the progenitor of the South African War.[1]

It was but three decades before this war that the German people had attained to national union. Freed at last from the shackles imposed by their own disunion, they had used to the full the power to control physical forces which had sprung from the growth of freedom elsewhere. Their habit of military discipline had enabled them to use these powers with unparalleled effect. In one generation the German Empire was producing wealth on a scale which rivalled and threatened to surpass the wealth produced by the Anglo-Saxon commonwealths. Her goods were on every market, the ships which carried them on every sea. The means to sustain the unquestioned predominance of her army were richly provided. In Europe the German voice was decisive. The war in South Africa forced her rulers to realise that the power which their army gave them was limited to Europe so long as Great Britain controlled the seas. Their resolve to challenge that control ended the century in which wars were localised to continents, and opened the epoch in which a pistol-shot fired in the Balkans, a fracas in Mongolia or a rising in Spain might send a fire to rage through every continent, to be quenched, perhaps, in the ashes of civilised life.

The year after the Jameson raid events took place in the Pacific, which looked, for the moment, as though China was destined to share the fate which had overtaken the African continent. That this did not happen was due to the fact that Japan had appeared on the stage equipped as a national state at the same moment as Germany. In 1871 the hermit empire had emerged from its cell to find the nations of Europe encamped on all the shores of its ocean, and on most of its islands. They were dominant in China and fast reducing to ruins her ancient order and civilisation. The Japanese saw that while their islands were locked in mediaeval seclusion the people of Europe had been learning to harness the forces of nature. They were quick to recover the ground they had lost. In 1871 a mission was sent to Europe and America to "study the institutions of civilised nations, adopt those most suited to Japan, and gradually reform our government and manner, so as to attain the status equal to that of civilised nations". The event was to prove how easy it is to learn the secrets of physical control when once discovered; and how much more difficult it is to acquire control of human forces.

This did not appear to be so at the outset. The commission returned in 1873 to find that disputes over Korea, the Liuchiu Islands and Formosa had already brought Japan to the verge of war with China. Okubo, the head of the commission, convinced the Emperor that if Japan now attempted to conquer Korea both would become the prey of Russia. He was sent to Peking in 1874 with secret instructions to effect a settlement, and this he accomplished with the aid of the British minister, Wade.

A breathing-space was thus obtained. In the course of the next twenty years the Emperor's government succeeded in dissolving the feudal system and in founding a scheme of education which is now as comprehensive as any in the world. Industries were mechanised and a mercantile marine brought into being. An army was organised under German, and a navy under British, advisers. By 1894 the Japanese rulers felt themselves strong enough to try conclusions with Korea and China. In a few months they had utterly defeated the Chinese navy, and Li Hung-Chang was suing for peace at Shimonoseki. In April 1895 he had signed a treaty in which China agreed to give Japan extraterritorial rights, to renounce her suzerainty over Korea, to pay an indemnity of £40,000,000, and to cede to Japan Formosa, the Pescadores and also the Liaotung Peninsula which commands both the coast of Korea and the maritime approach to Peking. A note was at once addressed to Japan by Russia, France and Germany forbidding the cession of the Liaotung Peninsula. Remembering the wise counsels of Okubo, Japan obeyed, though with bitter resentment, and bided her time.

In the following year, 1896, Li Hung-Chang went to St. Petersburg to represent China at the coronation of the Tzar Nicholas II. He there conceded to Russia the right to connect the Siberian railway with Vladivostok across Manchuria, and made a defensive alliance with Russia against Japan.

Russia, with the virtual control of north Manchuria, could now continue her glacial movement to the south, until all China was absorbed in the Russian Empire. Perceiving this, the German government resolved to seize the first opportunity of staking a claim to a share of the prey. In China defeat by Japan had further weakened the tottering fabric of order. Missionaries scattered throughout the country were an easy target for popular resentment. In November 1897 two German missionaries were murdered in Shantung.

The German admiral von Diedrichs at once entered the harbour of Kiaochow and seized the city of Tsingtao, which lay inside it. Terms were exacted which secured to the Germans the virtual control of Shantung. In December the Russians countered this move by seizing the Liaotung Peninsula, with Port Arthur at its southern extremity. England, a few months later, secured the lease of Weihaiwei, and France of Kwang-chow, a port to the south-west of Canton.

Meanwhile the United States had declared war upon Spain, and on May 1 Admiral Dewey destroyed the Spanish squadron in Manila Bay. The German government, which had hoped to secure the Philippines from Spain, ordered von Diedrich to Manila to assert their claims. A conflict was only averted by the British admiral Chichester, who made it plain that his fleet would support Admiral Dewey. In July the Americans annexed Hawaii, as well as the Philippines, to secure their position in the Pacific.

As the Chinese realised what had been done by the foreigners on their coast a passion for vengeance began to spread through the inland regions. The movement took shape in the Boxer Rising, which had for its motto, 'Cherish the Dynasty and exterminate foreigners'. The Emperor's mother, who had seized the power from her well-meaning son, placed herself at the head of the movement. In June 1900 she ordered the foreign legations to leave Peking. On his way to protest against this order the German minister was murdered. The foreign legations had then to fight for their lives till August 14, when an international force of Japanese, Russians, British, Americans, French, Austrians and Italians entered Peking and raised the siege.

The rescue was mainly the work of Japan, but its fruits were quickly gathered by Russia. China was now prostrate, and Russia hastened to seize the whole of Manchuria and to connect Port Arthur with the Siberian railway at Harbin. She could now take Korea whenever she chose to do so, and Japan would then lie at her mercy. For Korea means more to Japan than Belgium to England. The Japanese saw they must fight before and not after the Russians had seized and fortified the coast of Korea. Even so, the struggle would be hopeless if the German fleet supported the Russians, and Japan was fighting alone.

In this predicament the Japanese government turned to England. The war in South Africa was still in progress and British resources were seriously strained. She was seeking a general settlement of questions at issue with Russia, in Persia, India and China, more especially the question of the open door to her trade in Manchuria. Finding she made no progress with Russia, she turned to Japan. On January 30, 1902, England and Japan signed a treaty of alliance, which bound each of them to aid the other if attacked by more than one power. A combination of western powers could no longer coerce Japan as in 1895. She was free to settle her quarrel with Russia alone. In February 1904 the war broke out and, to the world's astonishment, the Russians were beaten by land and sea. By September 5, 1905, Russia had signed a treaty, which recognised the paramount interest of Japan in Korea and ceded the Liaotung Peninsula and the railway as far north as Changchun.

NOTE

[1] Winston Churchill, *The World Crisis*, vol. i. pp. 25, 26.

CHAPTER LV

LENIN

THE Russian autocracy was profoundly shaken by the Japanese victories. In 1905 its very existence was threatened by risings which spread from St. Petersburg and Moscow to the shores of the Pacific. For the moment the Imperial government was saved by the guns of General Dubassov, which mowed down the rebel workers in the streets of Moscow.

In the wings of the stage had been waiting a figure, obscure at the time, but destined to take a leading rôle in a later act. In that district of London where Marx had laboured there had gathered in 1903 some fifty exiles from Russia. They were all people whose eyes were fixed on the goal to which Marx had pointed, but were closely divided as to his methods. Some of them thought that the Communist aim should be reached through the medium of popular institutions. Others held that Engels and Marx had been right when insisting that force must be used to its utmost limit by a dictator, backed by the workers organised as a class, to destroy every one who stood in their way. The leading exponent of this view was a man disguised under the name of Meyer, who was living at the time at 30 Holford Square, near the Euston Road. His real name was Ulianov; but he figures in history as Lenin, a nom-de-plume borrowed from a brother hanged in 1887 for the part he had taken in a plot to murder the Tzar. The group was so evenly divided that resolutions were passed by narrow majorities in opposite directions. Defeated on general principles, Lenin moved that the final direction of the party should be vested in a body outside Russia and thus rest in the hands of the exiles, of whom he was one. He carried this motion by 25 votes against 23. The bare minority, which included Trotsky, seceded and were known as the Mensheviks, which means the minority. The section which followed Lenin were known as Bolsheviks, or the majority. The name is a paradox, for their ultimate strength was due to the truth which Lenin had learned from Engels and Marx, that where force is in question in a mechanised world a minority will rule—that organisation is stronger than numbers.

In 1905 Lenin was leading the rebellion in Moscow, which was quelled by Dubassov. Lenin knew how to read the lessons of failure and apply them later with resounding success. When the rising had failed he escaped to Kuokolla in Finland.

> To this town, thirty miles from the capital, his staff followed him. Illegality was proclaimed the supreme law. From here he listened, watched, convinced and commanded. Near by a class was set up for instructing picked men in the art of street fighting. Short courses were held for training others to act as the general staffs of armed bands. He wrote:
>
> "The Japanese War introduced the use of hand grenades; a munition factory has put an automatic rifle on the market. . . . We can and must make use of the advance of military technique, teach the militant workers to make bombs wholesale, help them and our own fighting squads to accumulate stocks of explosives, detonators and automatic rifles." [1]

Ere long Lenin was driven from Finland to seek an asylum in Switzerland. He had now grasped the idea that the factory workers in St. Petersburg and Moscow were strong enough, if properly organised and mobilised at the opportune moment, to destroy the Byzantine autocracy and to put in its place the proletarian dictatorship conceived by Engels and Marx. The Communist revolution could then be extended from Russia to the world at large. Unlike

Trotsky, passion for personal power was never allowed to obscure the selfless aim which he had in view. The driving force of the Russian revolution when it came was largely due to the fact that Lenin was able to impart this spirit to others.

NOTE

Valeriu Marcu, *Lenin*, p. 147.

CHAPTER LVI

THE UNITED KINGDOM OF GREAT BRITAIN AND IRELAND

THE defeat which Japan inflicted on Russia started the national states of Europe down a rapidly steepening slope, till they lost control of their own movements and plunged into war. The failure of Pitt's attempt to settle the relations of Great Britain to Ireland was one of the factors which hastened the catastrophe. The Irish Catholics had accepted the Union on the understanding that they would now be allowed to send Catholics to represent them in the parliament of the United Kingdom. The refusal of George III. to allow Pitt to redeem this pledge had made the Union stink in their nostrils. In 1829 the pledge was redeemed, but too late. When their leader Daniel O'Connell was at last admitted to parliament he gave the Irish the repeal of the Union as their watchword. The idea that their place in the system was only to be used as a means to get out of it became a tradition. As the population of England grew, while that of Ireland declined, the Irish retained a representation out of all proportion to their relative numbers or wealth. But their strength in parliament was little used to secure legal or social reforms for themselves. They never became incorporate in the larger unit as Wales and Scotland had done.

The abuses of the Irish land system continued to yield periodic harvests of agrarian crime. Repressive measures, to which government was forced to resort, further tended to alienate feeling. Besides the reform of abuses, Ireland, like India, was in need of constructive measures. But paternal administration was contrary to the theories of an age dominated by the Manchester school. The peasantry remained backward, ignorant and reckless. A progressive extension of large grazing farms restricted the area available for cultivation. Potatoes were their staple, and relying on a crop subject to disease, which cannot be stored for more than one season, the population had increased by 1848 to over 8,000,000. With the failure of the crop in that and the following year the people perished by thousands. Then began a migration to America, Canada, Newfoundland, Australia and New Zealand. The poison of the Irish question was felt wherever the English tongue is spoken except, perhaps, in South Africa. The population was reduced to about 4,000,000, and the migratory habit thus created has since kept it at about that level.

While the policy of union failed in Catholic Ireland, with the Protestants of the north-eastern counties it met with definite success. As the soil was poor, so the native inhabitants were few and easy to displace from the part of Ireland most exposed to attack from Great Britain. The colonists had brought their customs with them, and by sheer force of character imposed them on the landlords. The 'Ulster custom' meant that tenants were entitled to compensation for improvements. By encouraging good farming it served the interests of landlord as well as of tenant. The principal industry, however, was textile, and the Union once for all settled the quarrel of the Irish weavers with those of Great Britain. The industrial revolution which began to make itself felt at the time of the Union tended to favour manufacture at the cost of farming, especially when free trade was adopted for the whole United Kingdom. Free trade meant that workers in the factories were to be fed from the cheapest food raised on the virgin lands of America. In the second half of the nineteenth century the profits of agriculture in the United Kingdom were reduced to a minimum. Prices favoured the industrial as compared with the agricultural districts of Great Britain. The manufactures of Ulster flourished while farming languished in the rest of Ireland, where depopulation was intensified by defects in the land laws.

Religion served to increase the contrast. In the eighteenth century autonomy for Ireland meant the rule of the Protestant minority. The Catholic emancipation reversed this position. Under the Union the north-eastern counties of Ireland were thus bound to Great Britain by ties of business and religion as well as of race. In the course of the nineteenth century they became in effect as much part of the United Kingdom as Scotland or Wales.

The close of the civil war in America released from the northern army thousands of Irishmen who had gone to America after the famine. In 1865 they started the Fenian Brotherhood under James Stephens, who announced that the flag of the Irish Republic should be raised in Ireland that year. The Habeas Corpus Act was suspended and the insurrection was quelled; but in 1866 an officer in charge of Fenian prisoners in Manchester was murdered. In 1868 Gladstone was returned to power with a large majority. In 1869 he disestablished the Irish Church and in 1870 passed a Land Act which entitled tenants to compensation for improvements and gave them facilities for buying their land.

In that year (1870) Isaac Butt, the leader of the Irish party at Westminster, founded an association to secure for Ireland a federal arrangement by which matters of imperial concern were to be left to the imperial parliament, while Ireland was to be given a national legislature through which to control her own domestic affairs. This proposal was given the name of Home Rule. Session after session resolutions were moved by Butt in favour of these proposals, without success. In these debates two Irish members, Biggar and Parnell, saw that it was possible for the Irish members to bring the business of parliament to a standstill by obstruction. When Gladstone came to power in 1880 these obstructive tactics were in full swing. Drastic changes in procedure were made to enable parliament to function at all.

Agricultural depression had led to a movement in Ireland to pay no rent. In October 1881 Parnell was imprisoned as a suspect. On May 2, 1882, he was released on giving a promise to assist in pacifying the country. On May 6 Lord Frederick Cavendish, who had just taken office as chief secretary, was murdered in Phoenix Park with the under-secretary Burke. Parnell denounced the crime, but he and his party opposed the bill introduced to deal with Irish crime which was only carried on July 1, 1882, by suspending the whole of his party. When the Crimes Act was due to expire in 1885 the Liberal cabinet was divided on the question whether to renew it. Their failure to save Gordon had greatly reduced their majority. On June 8, 1885, Parnell ordered his followers to vote with the opposition on a bill imposing new taxes on beer and spirits. Mr. Gladstone resigned and a government was formed by Lord Salisbury, who dissolved parliament in November (1885). Gladstone appealed to the country to give him a majority, independent of Irish members, and Parnell called on Irish voters in Great Britain, as well as in Ireland, to cast their votes against him. At the general election Gladstone won 335 seats as against 249 Conservatives elected to support Lord Salisbury. The Nationalist Irish held the balance with 86 members. Gladstone let it be known that he was prepared to "deal in a liberal spirit with the demand for Home Rule". In January 1886, supported by the Irish vote, he beat the government on the Address. Though abandoned by some of his leading colleagues he formed a government pledged to Home Rule.

The Tory Hotspur, Lord Randolph Churchill, at once crossed to Belfast and attended a demonstration of more than 70,000 Orangemen. In a speech at the Ulster Hall he told the Orangemen that if a Home Rule Bill were passed

> there will not be wanting to you those of position and influence in England who would be willing to cast in their lot with you and who, whatever the result, will share your fortunes and your fate.[1]

A few days later in a published letter he said:

> Ulster at the proper moment will resort to the supreme arbitrament of force; Ulster will fight, Ulster will be right; Ulster will emerge from the struggle victorious, because all that Ulster represents to us Britons will command the sympathy and support of an enormous section of our British community.

Thus from the outset the issue was reduced to the plane of physical force—not only in Ireland.

In June the House of Commons rejected the measure by 30 votes, for Gladstone had lost the support of some of his own party. He was beaten at the general election which followed, and Lord Salisbury returned to power with a clear majority. At the Irish Office Mr. Balfour, while enforcing law and order, embarked on the policy of 'killing Home Rule by kindness'. Money was freely expended on relieving congested districts, and on light railways and harbours. The Irish people at last began to enjoy the kind of prosperity which might have reconciled them to the union had it been brought to them earlier. Parnell was accused by *The Times* of condoning the murders in Phoenix Park, on the strength of letters which proved on inquiry to be forgeries. The prestige which this victory brought him was quickly neutralised by his appearance as a co-respondent in the Divorce Court. Catholic opinion was outraged and his struggle to retain the leadership of his party was closed by his death in 1891.

Throughout this period business in parliament was increasingly hampered by the tactics of the Irish members. In 1892 Mr. Gladstone was returned to office with a majority of 40, including the Irish vote. The second Home Rule Bill was passed by the Commons but thrown out in the Lords. Mr. Gladstone then retired from office and Lord Rosebery, who succeeded him as prime minister, declared that the conversion of England as the 'predominant partner' must precede the concession of Home Rule to Ireland. In June 1895 the Liberal government fell. At the general election which followed the Unionist party was returned to power with a clear majority of 152. They remained in office till 1905, the year in which Russia acknowledged defeat by Japan.

The Unionist party had now been split by the issue of Tariff Reform, which Chamberlain raised in 1903. In 1905 Mr. Balfour, who succeeded Lord Salisbury as prime minister, resigned. A Liberal government was formed by Campbell-Bannerman, which in January 1906 swept the country at a general election by an overwhelming majority.

The factor which made this majority so large was the introduction of Chinese labourers to work the Witwatersrand mines. The measure had greatly intensified the reaction against imperialism which followed the South African war. It placed in power a government committed to a wide and costly programme of social reform. In the House of Commons the Liberal government had a majority so large as to make them independent even of the Irish members. Yet for four years a Conservative majority in the House of Lords was able to frustrate most of the reforms which the House of Commons had passed. In 1909 the House of Lords threw out the budget which proposed the taxation of unearned increment on land values and licensed houses. Parliament was dissolved and in February 1910 a general election gave the Liberals a majority so reduced that henceforward they had to depend on the Irish vote and the Labour party. A bill was then passed by the House of Commons which deprived the House of Lords of the right to reject a finance bill or any other public bill thrice passed by the lower house in the course of two successive sessions. The enactment of this measure would mean that thereafter Home Rule for Ireland could be passed over the vote of the House of Lords.

The Parliament Bill was thrown out in the Lords and in December 1910 the government again appealed to the country, which returned them to power in the same strength as before. In August 1911 the Parliament Bill was passed by the Lords, under the threat that if they rejected it a sufficient number of Liberal peers would be added to their number to pass it.

Lord Rosebery's doctrine that Home Rule must await the approval of the predominant partner was now renounced by the Liberal government, and in 1912 they introduced a bill for giving an Irish executive and parliament exclusive control of Irish affairs. Specified Imperial interests were reserved to the control of the Imperial parliament, in which Ireland was still to be represented by 42 members. With grave searchings of heart the cabinet had decided that Ulster, as well as the rest of Ireland, should be placed under the Dublin parliament.

The conflict between the electorate and conservative and capitalist interests entrenched in the House of Lords was now threatening to undermine the respect for law which the British people had developed through long centuries of responsible government. A series of strikes, notably in the coal-mining and transport industries, had fostered a tendency in the minds of the working class to resort to direct action. This tendency was spread to wider circles by a militant movement of women to obtain the vote by the use of violent methods. Before the Home Rule Bill was published the Ulster Protestants had declared their intention to refuse to recognise a Dublin parliament, and in defiance of the act when passed to set up a provisional government of their own. In the autumn of 1912 half a million Irish Protestants bound themselves by a solemn and religious covenant to resist the application of the Home Rule Bill to Ulster. Bonar Law and other Conservative leaders in England approved their action. In the autumn session of 1912 the debates on the Home Rule Bill were marked by open violence in the House of Commons. In 1913 the Bill was passed by the House of Commons, rejected in the Lords and passed again by the House of Commons.

Meanwhile the Ulster Protestants, led by Sir Edward Carson, were drilling and arming. When parliament met in 1914 to pass the bill for a third time and enact it over the vote of the House of Lords, the movement had spread to England. The Ulster covenant was widely signed. In the park of an English peer volunteers were drilling to support the resistance threatened in Ulster. An opposing movement began to develop in southern Ireland, where appeals to physical force found a ready response. In November 1913 volunteers to the number of 100,000 were enrolled by Professor MacNeill and began to drill. Mr. Redmond, the Irish Nationalist leader, endeavoured to secure control of the movement by placing himself at its head.

In March 1914 the attitude of officers in command of the British forces at the Curragh, when ordered to protect military stores in the north of Ireland, made it doubtful whether the army itself would support the government. In April 35,000 rifles and 3,000,000 cartridges were clandestinely landed at Larne and distributed to the Ulster volunteers. The situation had become so critical that on July 21 the King summoned a conference of party leaders to Buckingham Palace.

> My intervention at this moment [he said] may be regarded as a new departure, but the exceptional circumstances under which you are brought together justify my action. For months we have watched with deep misgivings the course of events in Ireland. The trend has been surely and steadily towards an appeal to force, *and to-day the cry of civil war is on the lips of the most responsible and sober-minded of my people.*

The conference failed, and five days after the King had uttered this ominous warning blood was shed.

In Ireland a cargo of arms landed at Howth was received by a body of volunteers. They were stopped on the way to Dublin by police and a company of soldiers. In the affray which followed three of the volunteers were killed and thirty were wounded.

The Ulster leaders had now laid their plans to arrest the British officials in Belfast, and to set up a provisional government of their own on receipt of a telegram from Sir Edward Carson. He had written this telegram and was on his way to despatch it, when a note from Mr. Asquith reached him to say that war between England and Germany was now merely a question of hours. The message was never despatched.[2] The fact that in July 1914 England was nearer to civil war than she had been since Charles I. raised his standard at Nottingham in 1642 is now almost forgotten.

NOTES

[1] Winston Churchill, *Lord Randolph Churchill*, vol. ii. p. 65.

[2] Sir Edward Carson told me this after the outbreak of war.

CHAPTER LVII

EVENTS LEADING TO WORLD WAR

THE war which engaged the armies of Russia in eastern Asia had affected the balance of power in Europe from its outset. France, immediately driven to look for support nearer home, had turned to Great Britain, who after the war in South Africa was feeling the danger of isolation. In April 1904 an agreement was signed by which England was given a free hand in Egypt in return for allowing the French a free hand in Morocco.

The idea that such ancient rivals as France and England could support each other came as a shock to the German government. As Russia was paralysed by successive defeats in the East and by risings at home, Berlin determined to break the stalk of the Anglo-French understanding before it could ripen. In March 1905 the Emperor went to Tangier to assert the German claim to a voice in the settlement of Morocco. In June France was threatened with war if Delcassé, who had made the agreement with England, continued in charge of foreign affairs. Delcassé retired and arrangements were made for a conference over Morocco which took place at Algeciras in 1906. In England the Liberal government had come into power; but the Germans had made it so plain that their object was to end the *entente* between England and France, that the new foreign minister, Sir Edward Grey, gave the fullest support to the French at the conference. It forced the Liberal cabinet to realise that England might be driven to come to the aid of France, if attacked by Germany. The general staffs in London and Paris were authorised to discuss what military measures the two countries should take to aid one another in such an event.

In England public attention was now drawn to the rapid growth of the German navy. Since 1871 the German government, backed by the strongest army in Europe and profoundly influenced by the military outlook of its general staff, had been able to make its will effective on the continent of Europe whenever it chose to do so. The Jameson raid, 1896, the seizure of the Philippines by America in 1898, the Boer war and the conference of Algeciras had successively proved that the power of Germany to speak the last word in international affairs was limited to Europe by the maritime power of Great Britain.

In these years the mechanised industries of the German people were fast outstripping the productive power of Great Britain. That Germany might in a few decades be able to build a fleet which would make her will as decisive across the seas as it was in Europe was no idle vision. The experience of the Jameson raid led to the first German Navy Law, published in 1897 and passed in the following year. This programme was accelerated from time to time, till after the Boer war the threat it involved to British security was realised at the Admiralty in London. It was not till after the conference of Algeciras in 1906 that public opinion in Great Britain awoke to the danger. At that moment a government had come into power committed to large and expensive reforms at home. The cost of increasing the navy to meet the German threat was a serious obstacle to its programme. Repeated efforts were made to reach an agreement with Germany to limit naval expenditure. Berlin would listen to none of them. Though parliament and the electorate were torn by faction and the country was moving to a constitutional crisis, there was general agreement that, whatever the cost, the navy must be kept strong enough to resist any attack which the German fleet could make on the shores and commerce of the British Isles. The British and German peoples embarked on a race for maritime power, the one to maintain its lead, the other to overtake it.

When Russian ambitions in the East were defeated, her attention was turned once more to the Balkan peninsula. England, embarrassed by the war in South Africa, had tried in vain to settle the questions which had long embittered her relations with Russia, in Persia and China. In 1907 the Russian bureaucracy realised the mistake it had then made. In August an Anglo-Russian agreement was reached over Persia, Afghanistan and Tibet. In three years the growth of German power by land and sea had thrown England into the arms of France and Russia, her two traditional rivals. Had peace been maintained for the first third of the twentieth century, as it was for the last third of the nineteenth, Germany by now would be rivalled in wealth only by the United States, so high is the vigour and intelligence of her people and their natural capacity for production. Her manufactures, by sheer efficiency, would have won a predominant place in the markets of the world, more especially in those countries which lay between her borders and the Persian Gulf. No government, not even that of America, is solely controlled by the question of wealth. The degree to which the policy of a government is controlled by questions of bread and butter is mainly determined by the nature of the polity behind it. Where a country is ruled by civilians, who can be removed from office by a wide electorate, the question of livelihood will bulk more largely than questions of power and prestige. Such a system, moreover, instils in the minds of those who conduct it a habit of compromise.

The opposite is true of a government based on military power rather than on votes. Soldiers are accustomed by the nature of their training to give and obey orders rather than to reason about them. Questions of honour, prestige or power count with them more than questions of industry or finance. There is little in their training to foster the habit of compromise. They naturally tend to think that physical force is the dominant factor in human affairs.

In Germany, Bismarck was strong enough to control the soldiers; but after his time the general staff had become the ruling power, as it was in Austria. Such a government was very impatient when it found that across the seas its will was not, as in Europe, the decisive factor. It was set on creating the naval power which would make it decisive, and with patience would have succeeded; but its Austrian ally, which was also ruled by the military mind, brought matters to an issue too soon.

Before 1903 Alexander Obrenovitch, king of Serbia, had been friendly to Austria. In that year he was murdered by officers, Serbian Nationalists who hated the Austrians, and Peter, the head of the rival dynasty of Karageorgevich, was placed on the throne. From that moment the general staff at Vienna was set on destroying 'this nest of conspirators'.

In July 1908 a revolution broke out in Turkey. Its authors were former students of Roberts College, founded by an American mission in Constantinople. When the mission had asked for leave to found a second college in Adrianople, the Sultan Abdul Hamid had shrewdly replied that to grant it would ruin the foundations of his throne. The ideas introduced by the first college had already accomplished that work. Its pupils had formed a committee in Paris, which in 1908 had moved to Salonika and there undermined the loyalty of the Turkish army in Macedonia. In July the army revolted, and the

Young Turks forced the Sultan to accept a constitution.

The Austrian government at once realised the danger that a Nationalist government in Constantinople might claim to administer Bosnia and Herzegovina, which under the Treaty of Berlin were administered by Austria, but still formally belonged to the Turkish Empire. In September the Austrian chancellor, Aehrenthal, met Isvolsky, the Russian minister, at a castle in Bohemia and agreed that the powers should be asked to sanction the annexation of Bosnia and Herzegovina to Austria, and also the passage of Russian warships from the Black Sea to the Mediterranean. The closure of the straits had prevented Russia from using her Black Sea fleet in the struggle with Japan. London and Paris at once objected to the opening of the straits and in October, Aehrenthal announced to the powers that Austria had annexed Bosnia and Herzegovina, whose kindred people, the Serbians, were hoping to incorporate in their kingdom. In March 1909 the German government, determined to stand by Austria, demanded from Russia an unconditional acceptance of the annexation. Russia, too weakened to resist, accepted the ultimatum and, for the moment, swallowed her resentment.

Meanwhile, further trouble was brewing in Morocco, and in April 1911 the tribes near Fez revolted against the Sultan. Europeans in Fez were in danger and a force was sent by the French to protect them. In July a German gunboat, the *Panther*, was sent to Agadir, a port on the Atlantic coast of Morocco, and the German press began to demand a coaling station in these regions. This at once roused British anxieties. A speech at the Mansion House by Mr. Lloyd George, the most pacifist member of the ministry, made it clear that England would stand by the side of France. The German demand for the whole of the French Congo was withdrawn, and Germany accepted a strip of French territory between the Cameroons and the Belgian Congo in return for conceding the French a free hand in Morocco. In Germany the agreement gave a fresh impulse to the movement for enlarging the fleet with corresponding reactions in England.

In September 1911, while Germany, France and England were engaged on resolving the Agadir question, Italy declared war upon Turkey and sent an army to occupy Libya. This blow to Turkey encouraged the Christian peoples and states of the Balkan peninsula to combine in attacking the Nationalist government. In October 1912 Serbia, Bulgaria and Greece declared war, and in six weeks had driven the Turkish armies back to the gates of Constantinople. But in 1913 the allies quarrelled over the spoil and Bulgaria attacked Serbia and Greece. Roumania came to their aid, whilst the Turks marched back to Adrianople and occupied the country to the east of it from the Black Sea to Gallipoli. Bulgaria, which Austria regarded with friendship, was utterly beaten and crippled, while Serbia emerged victorious from the struggle with her power and ambitions immensely increased. The general staff in Vienna made up its mind that no time was too soon to humble Serbian pretensions.

The opportunity came quickly. On June 28, 1914, the heir to the Austrian throne was murdered at Sarajevo by a Bosnian fanatic, whom Vienna believed was the agent of Serbian conspirators who had murdered King Alexander in 1903. Austria, counting on German support as in 1908, resolved to impose conditions on Serbia which would mean, if accepted, that Serbia had renounced her status as a sovereign state. On July 23 the ultimatum was launched, and the general staff proceeded to mobilise the forces required to seize Belgrade if its terms were refused. The slower process of mobilising her vast armies for war was also started by Russia. Acting on British and Russian advice the Serbian government at once accepted seven of the ten conditions imposed by the ultimatum; but on July 28 Austria declared war on Serbia. The Russian order for mobilisation was immediately countered by the mobilisation of the German army. The German government believed that Great Britain was paralysed by the Irish crisis. In vain did Sir Edward Grey endeavour to revive the concert of Europe by gathering the leading powers to a conference. Germany was in dread of the millions which Russia could gather, however slowly, and pour on her eastern frontiers. War with Russia meant, as she knew, war with France. On August 1 she declared war upon Russia, and the Schlieffen plan began to operate. On August 2 she occupied Luxemburg, and served an ultimatum on Brussels demanding free passage for German troops through Belgian territory. England replied with an ultimatum requiring Germany to respect the neutrality of Belgium. On August 3 Germany declared war on France.

The invasion of Belgium by Germany brought into action against her a power which, given time, could create and equip forces more dangerous to the Empires of central Europe than the millions of peasants which Russia, with her low powers of mechanisation, could never hope to arm and equip. It spread a war, which the German staff had thought would leave them the masters of Europe in a few weeks, to all the continents. It brought into action against them the human and industrial resources of Canada, Australia, New Zealand, South Africa and India, of the British Commonwealth as a whole, which included one-fifth of the habitable world. It closed the seas and confined the centre of Europe to its own resources. It lifted the war from the scale of a struggle for mastery in Europe to a struggle for mastery throughout the world. In Europe Turkey and Bulgaria sided with Germany, while Italy, Roumania and Greece sided against her. Outside Europe the majority of states were drawn into the struggle against Germany; in Asia Japan, China, Arabia and Siam; in Africa Liberia; in America the United States, Bolivia, Brazil, Cuba, Ecuador, Guatemala, Haiti, Honduras, Nicaragua, Panama, Peru, Uruguay. Before the close of this war all the continents, most of the sovereign states of the world and a vast majority of human beings were directly involved in the struggle.

CHAPTER LVIII

THE GREAT WAR

THE German plan for destroying the armies of France in a few weeks was now brought into operation. So vast were the numbers involved that the tiny forces of Belgium and England seemed scarcely to count as a factor, and no attempt was made by the German navy to impede the crossing of the small army of 90,000 men which England threw into France in the first few days.[1] For several weeks the German armies continued to advance first to the west, and then in an encircling movement to the south with a force which seemed irresistible. By September 5 they had crossed the Marne not many miles to the east of Paris, but were now beginning to lose their coherence. Under the direction of Joffre the French armies and the small British force suddenly attacked. The German armies were forced to retreat across the Marne, from which they retired in good order to the parallel line of the river Aisne. This strong defensive position they were able to hold. But the German plan of destroying all enemy forces in the west in the first few weeks of the war had failed. It was now destined to last for over four years, and to spread to the greater part of the world.

From the outset the invasion of Belgium had brought to the surface the secular issue, the struggle between political systems based on authority, and systems based on the rights of peoples to govern themselves. It was this which brought the self-governing countries of the British Empire to throw their weight into the struggle, and falsified German hopes of India. In the light of after events it is plain that Germany could have retrieved her initial failure on the Marne if the forces of the whole British Empire had not been thrown into the scale in the earlier years of the war. That troops from all parts of the British Empire came to the aid of France in holding a line of trenches, which ran from the North Sea to the Swiss frontier, was due to the conviction that the German conquest of France and Belgium would be the prelude to a suppression in every part of the world of institutions which had sprung from England. It was this which frustrated the German hopes, after their first failure at the Marne, of conquering Europe and then combining its forces to destroy the maritime power of England. That power which closed the supplies of the world to Germany, but kept them open to her enemies, was in the end the determining factor. That this would be so had become plain by the end of the year 1916. By that time the German staff had made up their minds that the conquest of Europe was still possible, if by the unrestricted use of the submarine they could destroy all merchant ships, those of neutrals as well as of their enemies, which were bringing supplies to nourish the Allied forces against them in Europe. In the spring of 1917 it became clear to President Wilson that if matters took their course the Allies would be forced to make a peace which would leave Germany predominant in Europe. On April 2 he declared war on Germany.

In that month alone 875,000 tons of merchant shipping was destroyed by the German submarines. Great Britain had only six weeks of food available. Had destruction at this rate continued, England would have been forced by starvation in the course of the summer to sue for peace. The danger was met by the organisation of the convoy system, which was rendered effective by the aid of American and Japanese warships.

When America entered the war events were happening in Russia which promised to relieve the central Empires from all fears in the east. They would then be free to concentrate most of their forces in one final effort to destroy the British, French and Italian armies in the west, before America could come to their aid. In March 1917 the government of the Tzar, sapped by every form of corruption to which great autocracies are prone, suddenly collapsed. The downfall of this ancient Byzantine regime was appropriately started on December 29, 1916, by the murder of the monk Rasputin, the evil genius of the Emperor and Empress, planned and executed by members of their own family. In March 1917 starving crowds began to riot in the streets of Petrograd. Troops sent to suppress them fraternised with the rioters, and on March 15 the Tzar was forced into abdication. A provisional government was formed by the Liberal leaders in the Duma, a government pledged to continue the war.

The soldiers, meanwhile, were deserting in thousands from the front, intent on escaping the horrors of war, and also on getting back to their villages to seize a share in the land. As in 1905, committees of soldiers, workers and peasants were formed which were known as soviets. Communists saw in the general confusion the first stage of the world revolution which Marx had foretold. Their exiled leaders hurried to Petrograd; from Siberia Stalin and Kamenev, from America Trotsky. Lenin, however, was marooned in Geneva; for the Provisional government in Russia had advised the Allies to refuse to allow him to cross their frontiers. So he turned for help to a government at war with his own.

The German staff, which allowed him to pass through their country in a sealed railway-carriage, thought of him indeed as a dangerous microbe, but had no idea of the infection which he would spread in Russia to their own ultimate detriment and danger.[2]

With Zinoviev he passed through Sweden to Finland and entered Russia by sledge. Such was his haste that he boarded a train to Petrograd, accepting the risk of arrest on arrival. The Provisional government, willing to wound, was afraid to strike. Lenin was met on the platform by his soviet friends and carried in triumph to a palace where the Petrograd soviet had established its headquarters. Within twenty-four hours he was urging the soviets to destroy the Provisional government, assume control of the revolution, seize the factories and land and make peace with the Germans. Many of those who had hailed his return were shocked by these drastic proposals.

The Provisional government denounced him as a traitor and ordered his arrest. Their decision was taken when the chance of giving effect to it had passed. As Lenin had rightly seen, the soldiers were deserting the front, not only to escape the horrors of war, but also to reach their villages in time to seize for themselves a share of the land. The workers in towns were no less eager to seize the factories from the owners. These hungering masses, by their sheer multitude, were able to conceal him, whilst he, with the aid of Trotsky, was at work transforming the soviets into a genuine organisation. Cells were formed in the army, the navy, the post office, telegraphs and railways. Trotsky, who now began to reveal his genius for military organisation, was forming the War-Revolutionary Committee and creating a force in Petrograd properly furnished with arms and provisions.

Kerensky, meanwhile, was quarrelling with Kornilov, the commander-in-chief at the front. By November, Lenin and Trotsky were ready to strike, and struck. In twenty-four hours their forces were masters of Petrograd, the ministers were surrounded in the Winter Palace and Kerensky had fled. The palace was stormed and the ministers were arrested. On November 7 Lenin emerged from his hiding and openly appeared at the Smolny Institute where the soviet had made its headquarters. He immediately issued the following proclamation:

> The Provisional Government is deposed. The authority of the State has passed into the hands of the organ of the Petersburg Soviet of Workers' and Soldiers' Deputies—the Military Revolutionary Committee, which now stands at the head of the Petrograd proletariat and garrison. The cause for which the people have struggled, immediate conclusion of a democratic peace, abolition of landlord property rights over the land, labour control over production, creation of a Soviet Government—that cause is securely achieved. Long live the Revolution of Workmen, Soldiers and Peasants! War-Revolutionary Committee of the Petersburg Soviet of Workers' and Soldiers' Deputies.[3]

Kerensky, before his fall, had arranged for elections to return a constituent assembly. When Lenin seized the government in Petrograd these elections were actually in progress and even he was unable to stop them. The result showed that, despite their success, the Bolsheviks were still a minority, for they only polled 9,000,000 votes out of 32,000,000. In January 1918 Lenin was faced by a representative assembly in the Taurida Palace in which he could count on no more than 180 votes in a total of 580. Lenin, in readiness for their meeting, had brought to Petrograd a regiment of Latvian communists and a force of marines in whose loyalty to the soviets he could trust. From the Central Committee of soviets he obtained a mandate to suppress the assembly. With this document in his hand he went to the Taurida Palace and instructed the officer commanding his troops to enforce the decree of dissolution. Seeing no hope of resistance, the members dispersed to their homes. The constituent assembly vanished from history. Its fate made it clear that Lenin, as ruler of Russia, was as firmly attached to the methods as well as the aims of Marx as when he divided the meeting of exiles that had gathered in 1903 in a small upper chamber in London.

Lenin, who never lost time, at once commissioned Trotsky to negotiate peace with Germany at Brest-Litovsk. For the moment the Germans were military masters of the situation and, had they chosen to occupy Petrograd, the Soviet government could not have stopped them. A Bismarck would have seen a potential ally in a country which lay at his mercy. But Bismarck left no successors, and Ludendorff was set on exacting the most onerous terms which the Russians could be forced to accept in time to allow him to concentrate his forces for a shattering blow on the western front in the spring. By March he had forced the Soviet government to accept a treaty in which they agreed to yield half a million square miles of territory, with a population of 66,000,000 (more than a third of the people in Russia), and to pay a heavy indemnity. Lenin was wise enough to gamble on the chance that the terms could not be enforced if once his own power was firmly established in Russia. That he made the soviets accept them speaks volumes for the influence he had acquired already.

The Treaty of Brest-Litovsk was signed on March 3, 1918. The defection of Russia enabled the Germans to concentrate their forces on the western front.

In the spring of 1918 the British and French armies were only saved from destruction by a hair-breadth. At the critical moment a breakdown of transport, due to want of lubricants and of rubber for tyres, helped to bring the German advance on Amiens to a standstill: for the whole world had been organised to limit the central Empires of Europe to their own resources. American troops were now arriving and were used to reinforce the British and French wherever the bulging lines were in danger of breaking. At the end of a battle which lasted for weeks the German advance came to a standstill on a line too long for their dwindling numbers to hold. In July one further effort was made by the Germans; but the French counter-attacked on the ground where the battle of the Marne had been fought. In August the British followed suit to the east of Amiens. The Allies had now gained the initiative and henceforth were free to strike where they chose. The Germans on the defensive were pinched by hunger and began to lose heart. Throughout September they were forced back in a series of battles with tremendous slaughter on both sides. The example of Russia began to react on Germany and her allies.

On September 29 Bulgaria surrendered and signed an armistice, and the German government then decided to sue for peace. Their appeal to President Wilson was announced to the Reichstag on October 6 and reached Washington on the following day. It proposed to accept as a basis of peace the 14 points which President Wilson had enunciated in his message to Congress on January 8, 1918. Wilson replied on October 8, refusing to request an armistice unless the German armies were prepared to retire to their own frontiers. He further inquired whether the Chancellor was speaking for the Kaiser or the Reichstag. On October 12 the Chancellor replied, agreeing to evacuate foreign territory and asserting that he spoke for the Reichstag and the German people. On this same day a German submarine sank the packet-boat *Leinster* in the Irish Sea and more than 400 British and Americans on board her were drowned. On the 14th President Wilson replied, drawing attention to this outrage, and also to the wanton destruction of property in the Belgian and French territories from which the Germans were retiring. He plainly intimated that, if he were asked to deal with the military masters and the monarchical autocrats of Germany now, he must demand not peace negotiations but surrender.

To this 'terrible note', as the Chancellor described it, a reply was sent on October 27 in submissive terms, saying that the German government awaited proposals for an armistice. On October 30 President Wilson replied, agreeing to take up the question of an armistice with the Allies which must give them unrestricted power to enforce the terms of peace.

This correspondence was then submitted by President Wilson to the Allied council in Paris. On November 5 the President was able to transmit to the German government the following memorandum:

The Allied Governments have given careful consideration to the correspondence which has passed between the President of the United States and the German Government. Subject to the qualifications which follow, they declare their willingness to make peace with the Government of Germany on the terms of peace laid down in the President's Address to Congress of January 8, 1918, and the principles of settlement enunciated in his subsequent Addresses.

They must point out, however, that Clause 2, relating to what is usually described as the freedom of the seas, is open to various interpretations, some of which they could not accept.

They must therefore reserve to themselves complete freedom on this subject when they enter the Peace Conference.

Further, in the conditions of peace laid down in his Address to Congress of January 8, 1918, the President declared that the invaded territories must be restored as well as evacuated and freed, and the Allied Governments feel that no doubt ought to be allowed to exist as to what this provision implies.

By it they understand that compensation will be made by Germany for all damage done to the civilian population of the Allies and their property by the aggression of Germany by land, by sea, and from the air.[4]

The President added that he was in agreement with the interpretation set forth in the last paragraph of this document. He further added that Marshal Foch had been authorised to receive representatives of the German government and to communicate to them the terms of an armistice. It was signed at Spa at 5 A.M. on November 11, and the cease-fire was sounded on both sides at 11 A.M. that day. In the meantime, the German navy had mutinied at Kiel, and mutinies were fast spreading to the army. On November 9 the Kaiser had fled to Holland.

NOTES

[1] Cruttwell, *A History of the Great War*, p. 6.
[2] *Ibid.* p. 425.
[3] Broad and Russell, *The Way of the Dictators*, pp. 242, 243.
[4] *A History of the Peace Conference of Paris*, vol. i. pp. 457, 458. Oxford University Press.

CHAPTER LIX

BASIC TERMS OF PEACE

THE Great War, like the wars which followed the French Revolution a century before, was a war waged to exhaustion. In the course of that century mechanisation had vastly increased the number of human beings who inhabit this planet. When the crisis came it inflicted suffering on enormously greater numbers, and also made the process of exhaustion far more rapid. In the British Empire alone more than 9,000,000 were enlisted, and of these one in every three suffered death, wounds or imprisonment at the hands of their enemies. In France, Italy, Russia and the central Empires the sufferings endured were proportionately greater. Nearly 13,000,000 combatants are thought to have lost their lives in the actual struggle. The number of civilians who perished by hunger, massacre or disease was several times greater.

By the victors the war was fought to a finish in the genuine belief that so and not otherwise they could end the conditions which had led to such vast calamities. The war, in their view, had been forced on the world by autocracies in Europe, which placed the virtual control of policy in the hands of military leaders, of the general staffs in Berlin and Vienna, of men like "Conrad von Hotzendorf, the Chief of the Austrian Staff, who presented his master with a proposal for war every spring with the regularity of an almanac".[1] The Allied peoples were nerved to their final efforts by ideas which their leaders expressed in phrases, "a war to end war" or "to make the world safe for democracy".

When the great German advance had been checked in the summer of 1918 the Allies were fully prepared to continue the war through another winter till the following spring, when America would be able to throw her millions with decisive effect on the western front. The sudden collapse of the central Powers in the autumn of 1918 was the greatest surprise of the war. The victors were suddenly faced with the task of reconstructing the world on the basis which President Wilson had outlined in his 14 points. In these the idea that nations must in future govern themselves was fundamental. The idea of nationalism, and, indeed, of national self-government, ignored by the Congress of Vienna, was now in the forefront.

> The achievement of Lloyd George and Clemenceau in lifting up the hearts of their peoples and sustaining their resolve was of incomparable value . . . their supreme importance lay in an unrivalled power of convincing their countrymen by example, precept, and the fire of the spirit that the war must and could be won somehow.[2]

Milner, a colleague who weighed his words, ranked Lloyd George as a minister in war greater even than Chatham.[3] The victory of the Allies was, he believed, due in the main to his "incomparable drive".[4] The future historian who views these events with a measure of detachment denied to contemporaries will, I believe, endorse these judgments. Had he shown the same courage in leading public opinion in making the peace as he showed in winning the war, as he showed once more in making the Irish Treaty, the world might be different from what it now is. He will figure in history, I think, as one great as a man can be without principle, on a level, therefore, lower than that where men like Chatham, Washington or Lincoln will stand.

As the bugles were sounding the cease-fire, Lloyd George was deciding to dissolve the parliament elected eight years before and to hold a general election. The task of reconstructing the framework of human society shattered by the war must, he felt, be approached with a fresh mandate from public opinion behind him. From the nature of the case public opinion at the moment was highly abnormal and subject to violent gusts of passion. In a few months the country had passed from the fear of imminent defeat to a victory more overwhelming than the wildest optimists had dreamed. Restraints which the government had exercised over the press were suddenly relaxed. A cry of vengeance went up. Candidates were everywhere asked whether they would see to it that Germany should be made to pay for the costs of the war. The question was pressed on the prime minister himself and received no clear and emphatic reply. On December 28 Mr. Lloyd George was returned to power with a majority of 262. In the words of Mr. Fisher, a member of his cabinet, the electorate

> were angry, vindictive, unquiet. They wanted redress and safety. No statesman in a democratic age, however independent, can prevail against the clear and passionate wishes of his countrymen. Clemenceau would have ceased to represent France, Orlando would have ceased to represent Italy, if they had not worked for the weakening of the enemy powers, and for the better protection of their respective states. Lloyd George had received an emphatic mandate from his constituencies that the enemy must be made to pay. . . . Of all these statesmen, the one most naturally prone to take a liberal view of the situation, the British Prime Minister, was the most clearly committed to a course of retribution.[5]

This view, that a democratic leader must elicit and follow public opinion, rather than seek to guide it at the risk of his own position, explains, I believe, the utter ruin of the Liberal party in this century. To the questions put to him in the course of this election Mr. Lloyd George might have replied by quoting the terms for stopping the war which he himself had given the enemy on October 5. These terms were

> that compensation will be made by Germany for all damage done to the civilian population of the Allies and their property by the aggression of Germany by land, by sea, and from the air.

He might have said "in the face of that promise I cannot undertake to make the enemy pay for the whole cost of the war. We entered this war on the plea that Germany had treated her guarantee of Belgian neutrality as a scrap of paper. If you wish to end this war by treating the promise I made to limit compensation as no more than a scrap of paper, you must send someone else than me to tear it up at the Peace Conference." My personal conviction is that had Mr. Lloyd George made such a clear and emphatic statement he would have secured a majority greater than that which he got. Nor can I imagine any other political leader in the face of such a statement by the minister who, as every one felt, had led the country to victory, going to the Peace Conference with a mandate to make Germany pay for the war.

If Mr. Lloyd George had asked for and got a mandate from the British electorate to interpret strictly the terms upon which the Allies had agreed to suspend hostilities, he could certainly have counted on President Wilson's unwavering support. They together would have governed the situation. The globular sum required to compensate civilians for the damage done to their persons and property in the devastated areas, and also by aircraft and submarines, was one which experts could have computed. It would almost have come within the capacity of the vanquished countries to find the money. Such a settlement made at Paris would not have created the uncertainties which rendered impossible the task of reconstructing the system of production, trade and finance which the war had broken in pieces.

NOTES

[1] Cruttwell, *A History of the Great War*, p. 4.
[2] *Ibid.* pp. 627, 628.
[3] In an unreported speech at a small dinner at the Claridge's Hotel at which the author was present.
[4] Milner used these words in a private conversation with the author, after Lloyd George's fall from power.
[5] Fisher, *A History of Europe*, vol. iii. p. 1158.

CHAPTER LX

THE CONFERENCE OF PARIS

In his 14 points Wilson had stated in general terms the hopes which inspired the British and American resolve to fight the war to a finish. The fullest expression was to be given to the instinct of nationalism which the Congress of Vienna had sought to ignore. Poland must be restored and the Austrian and Turkish Empires dissolved into national states. Such states must, where possible, be given access to the sea. Governments must be controlled by the people they governed. Relations between sovereign states must in future be controlled with the full knowledge of the peoples concerned. Barriers to trade between nations were to be removed. Armaments must be reduced to a level sufficient to enable each state to protect its own frontiers, but not to threaten those of its neighbours. The interest of peoples unable to govern themselves must be considered in deciding which of the sovereign states were to govern them in future. As a means to these ends and also to secure the peace of the world,

> a general association of nations must be formed under specific covenants for the purpose of affording mutual guarantees of political independence and territorial integrity to great and small States alike.

The French had only been saved from utter destruction by the aid of British and American armies. They presumed, therefore, that the peace to be made must always assure them that help, if ever their frontiers were threatened again.

On January 19 the victorious nations assembled in Paris essayed the task of embodying these ideas in treaties of peace which the vanquished nations would then be called on to sign. The British delegates were confronted by President Wilson with the terms which the Allies themselves had framed on October 5. They were subject, however, to intensive pressure from members of parliament who had promised at the recent election that the cost of the war should be wrung from the enemy. The delegates from the British Dominions, who wished to tell their several electorates that Germany would be made to pay the costs of the war, were equally pressing. Suggestions were made to President Wilson that the matter might be compromised if his government would agree to remit the vast sums which America had loaned to the Allies. The President refused to consider the suggestion. In the end the problem was solved by persuading President Wilson to construe the terms, which the Allies had framed on October 5, into meaning that the sums required to pension the wounded and dependents of combatants killed in the war could be reckoned as damage to civilians.[1]

The amount required to meet these charges was one which defied calculation at the time. It was, in any case, one which the vanquished countries ruined by the war could not by their utmost exertions yield. It was, therefore, left to a Reparations Commission, on which the United States was invited to serve, to decide two years later what Germany could afford to pay. On the night that the treaty was signed Lord Milner remarked with ominous foresight that the Allies would in the end get more had they asked for less.

The victors were not content with forcing these terms on the vanquished. They further required that Germany should admit that the terms were just. The chapter of the treaty which dealt with reparations was, therefore, prefaced by the following Article (231):

> The Allied and Associated Governments affirm and Germany accepts the responsibility of Germany and her allies for causing all the loss and damage to which the Allied and Associated Governments and their nationals have been subjected as a consequence of the war imposed upon them by the aggression of Germany and her allies.

No expedient could have been more effective in defeating the end for which it was designed. The enforcement of their signature to this Article has done more than anything else to convince the people of Germany that the war was, in fact, imposed upon them by the will of malignant enemies.

These terms, had it been possible to enforce them, would have crippled the power of Germany for a century and, by the French, were intended to do so. But a century is but a breathing-space in the life of a nation. So provisions were added which it was hoped would render Germany for a time unable, and in the end unwilling, to renew her quarrel with France. The German army was limited to 100,000, about the size which a state no larger than Belgium was able to maintain. Conscription was forbidden. It was thought that when once the German people had enjoyed freedom from compulsory service they would never wish to return to it. The Germans were also forbidden to fortify or even to occupy with troops their western frontiers. In all sincerity this measure of disarmament was imposed on Germany as the first step in the process of general disarmament which the 14 points had foreshadowed. It was represented as such in the letter addressed to the German delegates which presented the draft of the treaty they were called upon to sign.

The Austro-Hungarian Empire had dissolved itself. Its constituent nations established themselves as sovereign states. The Slavs in the south were annexed to Serbia, which assumed the title of Yugo-Slavia. The eastern part of Hungary was annexed to Roumania. Bohemia was detached from Austria and established as Czechoslovakia, which also included a slice of Hungary. The Austria which survived these reductions was a minor state with a population rather over 6,000,000 which was solidly German in language and race. The reasons which led Bismarck to exclude these Germans from the national union he created were now completely removed. That the German and Austrian republics would wish to unite was apparent. Such a union would be in accord with the principles which inspired the 14 points. But the French were firmly opposed to a union which must add to the future strength of the German Republic. It was, therefore, forbidden in terms of the treaties.

The German colonies were placed under mandates, mostly entrusted to Great Britain, British Dominions and France, to the bitter disappointment of Italy, whose delegates for a time quitted the Conference. Palestine was entrusted to England to be opened to the Zionist movement as a home for the Jews. Syria was entrusted to France and Mesopotamia to England.

The number of sovereign states in the world was raised by the Conference of Paris from 54 to 67, counting in that number the British Commonwealth as one international sovereignty. It was realised, however, that this multiplication of national states would tend to increase rather than diminish the danger of war. The growing unity of the human race, imposed by mechanisation, had to be recognised and the recognition expressed in some system. The sovereignty of states had somehow to be reconciled with the need for controlling human society as a whole. The experience of the British Commonwealth and its imperial conference seemed to suggest how this could be done. There were those who thought that some arrangement for a frequent or continuous conference of the governments of the world, at a specified centre equipped with a permanent secretariat, was the furthest step which could be taken for the present.

Such modest proposals were far from contenting a public opinion appalled by the horrors which had overtaken mankind. The smaller states, especially the neutrals, were urgent in demanding some measure of future security stronger than any they could hope to provide for themselves. The result was the Covenant of the League of Nations, strongly moulded by American ideas under the leadership of President Wilson, the outlines of which are too familiar to require description here. By Article 10—

> The Members of the League undertake to respect and preserve as against external aggression the territorial integrity and existing political independence of all Members of the League. In case of any such aggression or in case of any threat or danger of such aggression the Council shall advise upon the means by which this obligation shall be fulfilled.

The provisions of Article 16 must also be quoted at length:

> Should any Member of the League resort to war in disregard of its covenants under Articles 12, 13 or 15, it shall *ipso facto* be deemed to have committed an act of war against all other Members of the League, which hereby undertake immediately to subject it to the severance of all trade or financial relations, the prohibition of all intercourse between their nationals and the nationals of the covenant-breaking State, and the prevention of all financial, commercial or personal intercourse between the nationals of the covenant-breaking State and the nationals of any other State, whether a Member of the League or not.
>
> It shall be the duty of the Council in such case to recommend to the several Governments concerned what effective military, naval or air force the Members of the League shall severally contribute to the armed forces to be used to protect the covenants of the League.
>
> The Members of the League agree, further, that they

will mutually support one another in the financial and economic measures which are taken under this Article, in order to minimise the loss and inconvenience resulting from the above measures, and that they will mutually support one another in resisting any special measures aimed at one of their number by the covenant-breaking State, and that they will take the necessary steps to afford passage through their territory to the forces of any of the Members of the League which are co-operating to protect the covenants of the League.

Any Member of the League which has violated any covenant of the League may be declared to be no longer a Member of the League by a vote of the Council concurred in by the Representatives of all the other Members of the League represented thereon.

These provisions were clearly designed to maintain the structure of human society as established in treaties of peace by the Conference of Paris. It was realised, however, by the British and American delegates that the onerous and humiliating conditions imposed on the conquered peoples would have to be modified when the passions raised by the war had begun to subside. At the instance of President Wilson it was, therefore, provided in Article 19 that—

The Assembly may from time to time advise the reconsideration by Members of the League of treaties which have become inapplicable and the consideration of international conditions whose continuance might endanger the peace of the world.

By these and other provisions of the Covenant functions were imposed on the League of Nations which were those of a world government. Its opening words clearly implied that international law was henceforward established as the paramount law of mankind. It remained for experience to prove whether the League was endowed with the powers necessary to discharge the functions imposed upon it; whether, in fact, the powers required by a world government could be based on a covenant made between sovereign states.

The Covenant was incorporated as the first chapter of the treaty of peace. In the great hall at Versailles, where the German Empire was proclaimed in 1871, the delegates of the German Republic were required to sign the treaty.

NOTE

[1] *A History of the Peace Conference of Paris*, vol. v. pp. 372, 373. Oxford University Press.

CHAPTER LXI

FROM VERSAILLES TO LOCARNO

On the same day the British and American governments signed treaties with France, undertaking to defend her against aggression. The British treaty was to become effective only when Congress had endorsed the American treaty. These three treaties were designed to relieve France, Belgium and the small states, enlarged or brought into being by the Conference of Paris, from the fear that Germany might do again what she had done in 1914. The treaties as signed were no more than a programme. Henceforward it rested with sovereign governments to decide, either by action or refusal to act, whether the peace of the world would in fact be secured.

If the Senate at Washington ratified the treaties, the United States would then be morally committed to war in Europe, at any time in the future, if Germany threatened the frontiers of Belgium or France. Such committal in advance was certainly contrary to the spirit if not to the letter of the American constitution. Within nine months it was clear that the Senate would refuse to ratify either of the treaties. On this refusal the conditional promise of England to guarantee French security fell to the ground.

In a war which was largely fought on her own soil France had endured unparalleled sufferings. She had only been saved from utter destruction by the aid of the Anglo-Saxon peoples. On the morrow of victory her fears were suddenly revived by refusal to give her a firm promise of that aid in the future. Fears like curses render men blind, and accomplish the very evils they threaten. She now fell back on the hopeless project of maintaining her armed supremacy in Europe and of keeping Germany crippled and in permanent subjection; and this she essayed to do by enforcing the terms of the Treaty of Versailles to the letter and even beyond the letter. The fatal provisions of the Treaty, which entitled the conquerors to exact from Germany the uttermost farthing, was a weapon in the hands of France. The British had counted on American support on the Reparations Commission for the policy of scaling down to reasonable figures the amount which Germany would be called on to pay. Deprived of American support alike on the Reparations Commission and in the Councils of the League, the influence of France was for the moment dominant, and the British and French governments rapidly drifted into antagonism. As the British saw, the German Republic could only meet the sums it was asked to pay under the Treaty if, and when, its industries were helped to recover some measure of prosperity. As Mr. Bonar Law, the British prime minister, said to M. Poincaré:

> You can try to get your money, and a small amount it will be in any case. You can try by seizing what you can get your hand on now, but you cannot do the two things. You cannot at the same time seize what you can get and leave German credit a chance of recovery.[1]

This was in January 1923 when the French and Belgian governments had decided to occupy with troops the Ruhr basin, which holds 80 per cent of the coal and iron production of Germany and 10 per cent of her population.

In the view of competent observers the occupation of the Ruhr inflicted on Germany sufferings greater than the civil population had endured through any corresponding period during the war. On September 27 the German Republic agreed to withdraw the passive resistance it had organised to counter the armed intervention. The British government was at last able to persuade the French to agree that a committee under the presidency of an American banker, General Dawes, should examine the German capacity to pay and devise arrangements whereby the payments should be made. In April 1924 the Reparations Commission had adopted the plan recommended by the Dawes Committee. An international loan to enable Germany to restore her currency, which had finally lost its value during the occupation, was heavily over-subscribed.

Meanwhile the French had begun to realise that their action in the Ruhr was not only provoking a passion of hatred in Germany, but also alienating the sympathies of Great Britain. In June Poincaré resigned and his place was taken by Herriot, who immediately got into touch with the Labour government which was now in office in London. The fact was faced that the Treaty of Versailles was increasing armaments instead of reducing them. France and her allies in Europe were armed to the teeth to enforce its provisions. The general insecurity was delaying the recovery of trade. But even Herriot made it plain that France and her allies, Poland, Czechoslovakia, Yugo-Slavia and Roumania, must continue to arm, unless they could count on the British also as allies if ever the need arose to enforce on Germany the provisions of the Treaty of Versailles. The position was expressed in the phrase that the victorious nations in Europe could not consider disarmament unless they were first given security. Under French inspiration, an agreement was framed at Geneva, called the Protocol, for strengthening and extending the Covenant of the League. Amongst various and elaborate provisions it contained the words:

In accordance with paragraph 3 of Article 16 of the

Covenant the signatory States give a joint and several undertaking to come to the assistance of the State attacked or threatened.[2]

The Protocol, as approved by the League Assembly, was then submitted to the various governments for ratification. By this time a Conservative government had come into power in England with Austen Chamberlain as foreign minister.

To France the Protocol was valuable only if it meant that should Germany at any time in the future attack her, then England was committed in advance to support France and her allies in arms. In 1919 Great Britain had been prepared to do this if America was similarly pledged. By the Protocol she was asked to give this pledge without the American pledge. The position was brought home to English public opinion by the fact that the self-governing Dominions firmly refused to give such a pledge, so far as they themselves were concerned. It was not America only, but the new world as a whole, that refused to redress the balance of the old. The British government recognised that if it accepted the Protocol it could not count on the resources of the British Commonwealth; but only on those of the United Kingdom. Its reaction was that of the American Senate to the Articles of the Covenant in 1920. In 1925 the British government refused to commit its electorate to war in advance of future conditions which it could not foresee. To do so would mean that the national government of Great Britain had renounced its control of the issues of peace and war. The control of its foreign affairs would have passed from London to Geneva, to whatever power there was dominant, which would in effect have been France. The Protocol was destroyed by the British refusal to endorse it. The victorious states and especially France refused to reduce the arms which defended their frontiers, unless, or until, those frontiers were guaranteed by the navy and army of Great Britain.

In Germany a number of publicists, who had realised during the war the importance of studying foreign affairs, had established an institute for the purpose. The Ruhr occupation had led them to examine the motive which caused the French to inflict such miseries on their country. They reached the conclusion that the motive was legitimate fear in the minds of the French that if Germany were ever allowed to recover her strength, she would use that strength at once to exact vengeance from France. The key to the problem must, therefore, be found in some measure designed to relieve the French from their fear of invasion. These ideas were conveyed to Stresemann, the foreign minister who was then in office, a realist in the true sense of that word. He let Chamberlain know that Germany would consider a voluntary pledge to accept her western frontiers as final, and not to resort to war to alter her eastern frontiers. With these proposals Chamberlain approached Briand, who was now the foreign minister in France. This led to a conference at Locarno in October 1925 between the foreign ministers of Great Britain, France, Germany, Belgium and Italy. The British were willing to pledge themselves to war against any power which sought to violate the frontiers which divide Belgium and France from Germany. The French struggled in vain to secure the extension of this guarantee to the frontiers of their allies east of Germany, to get in effect what the British had refused to give under the Protocol. In December a series of treaties were signed at Locarno which committed England to armed intervention against any power which sought to violate the frontier dividing Germany from France and Belgium. This pledge applied to Great Britain alone, and the other self-governing members of the British Commonwealth have always refused to endorse it. The demilitarised zone of the Rhineland, as prescribed in the Treaty of Versailles, was accepted in terms by Germany. She thus renounced of her own free will any claim to fortify her western frontiers against the French.

In January 1926 Cologne was evacuated by British troops and in the following September Germany was admitted to the League of Nations.

NOTES

[1] King-Hall, *Our Own Times*, vol. i. p. 127.
[2] Noel Baker, *The Geneva Protocol*, p. 221.

CHAPTER LXII

RESPONSIBLE GOVERNMENT IN INDIA

IN this same year, 1926, an Imperial Conference was held. Its conclusions reduced to explicit form the changes wrought by the war and the so-called peace which followed it in the structure of the Commonwealth which now included one-fourth of mankind. The inclusion of India and Ireland as fully qualified members of the Conference was one of these changes.

When the war broke out the German government had hoped for, and the British government had feared, a rising in India. The German hopes were frustrated and the British fears were allayed by the ruthless invasion of Belgium. That tiny but all-important fraction of the Indian peoples who could read and write, had learned English and were capable of political thought and expression, were quick to realise what the fate of their country would be under German rule. The Nationalist leaders in British India joined with the princes in uniting the country in support of Great Britain. A considerable part of the Indian army was sent to Europe to endure unspeakable sufferings during the winter in the trenches of Flanders. As the war dragged on and spread to Asia, it was realised that Indian troops could be better employed for dealing with the critical position in Mesopotamia.

The attack by the empires of central Europe on Serbia, Belgium and France, which had brought Great Britain into the war, had forced her to state the issue for which she was fighting, as the right of nations to govern themselves. She had called upon India as well as the Dominions to join the struggle in defence of this right. When India had answered this call and had poured out her treasure and blood to support the cause of self-government, leaders of Indian opinion could scarcely do otherwise than ask what England herself would do, if the cause of self-government prevailed, to extend its blessings to India. Opinion has moved so quickly in the last twenty years that it is not easy to realise now the practical difficulty raised by this question. With rare exceptions, officials who had given their lives to the study of Indian conditions, honestly believed that self-government as practised in England or the Dominions was out of the question for a country like India. This belief was by no means confined to officials in India, whose experience makes them cautious in outlook and slow to adopt novel opinions, nor yet to Conservatives in England. The belief that responsible government was a system which none but the peoples who sprang from Europe could hope to attain prevailed so strongly, even in Liberal circles, that a shock such as that which the war gave to the fixed ideas of the British people was needed to change it.

It must further be added that the Nationalist leaders in India themselves shrank from the burden of responsible government. Whilst they asked that elective legislatures should be freed from all official control, and be given unlimited power to alter the law and control supply, they wished the executive power in the government of India and the provinces to remain where it was, in executives responsible to the viceroy. In a word they desired the system, which in the eighteenth century had paralysed government in the American colonies and in Ireland, and in the nineteenth had led to the same results in Canada till Lord Durham exposed its dangers. The government of India endorsed these ideas, but Mr. Austen Chamberlain, the secretary of state for India, refused to sanction proposals which had always led to a deadlock of government and revolution in the previous experience of the British Commonwealth.

The task of deciding what should be done was faced by Montagu, who succeeded Chamberlain in 1917. This decision which broke from all the traditions that had previously governed the relations of East and West, was curiously announced on August 20, 1917, as an answer by Montagu to a question put in the House of Commons:

> The policy of His Majesty's Government, with which the Government of India are in complete accord, is that of increasing the association of Indians in every branch of the administration and the gradual development of self-governing institutions with a view to the progressive realization of responsible government in India, as an integral part of the British Empire. They have decided that substantial steps in this direction should be taken as soon as possible, and that it is of the highest importance, as a preliminary to considering what these steps should be, that there should be a free and informal exchange of opinion between those in authority at Home and in India. His Majesty's Government have accordingly decided, with His Majesty's approval, that I should accept the Viceroy's invitation to proceed to India to discuss these matters with the Viceroy and the Government of India, to consider with the Viceroy the views of Local Governments, and to receive the suggestions of representative bodies and others. I would add that progress in this policy can only be achieved by successive stages. The British Government and the Government of India, on whom the responsibility lies for the welfare and advancement of the Indian peoples, must be judges of the time and measure of each advance, and they must be guided by the co-operation received from those upon whom new opportunities of service will thus be conferred and by the extent to which it is found that confidence can be reposed in their sense of responsibility. Ample opportunity will be afforded for the public discussion of the proposals which will be submitted in due course to Parliament.

We now know that this momentous pronouncement was written in its final form by Lord Curzon, who, when some years later he saw the results, confessed that he himself had not fully realised what the words 'responsible government' would be construed to mean.

In 1918 Mr. Montagu and Lord Chelmsford produced a report in which they advised that certain powers should be transferred from the provincial executives to ministers responsible to elective legislatures. Powers suggested for transfer were local self-government, education, public health, agriculture, public works, excise and taxation correlative thereto.

These proposals, which came to be known as dyarchy, were drafted into a bill which, when presented to parliament, was referred to a joint committee of both Houses. The practice of submitting Indian affairs to a parliamentary inquiry, which had given its members direct knowledge of Indian problems in the days of the British East India Company, was thus revived. The bill was passed into law in 1919. It contained a provision that at the end of ten years a further inquiry should be held by parliament, to show how the Act had worked. At the end of a decade an exhaustive inquiry was made by a commission which was sent to India under Sir John Simon. It reported in 1930 and became the subject in the following year of a conference in London of British representatives with Indian princes and political leaders. From this conference issued proposals for the establishment of full responsible government in the provinces and for their inclusion in a federal union, which should also include the native states. These proposals were embodied in a white paper, which again was submitted for detailed inquiry by a joint committee of both Houses in 1933. Its report, issued in 1934, was drafted into a measure which passed into law in 1935. This new constitution brings India within measurable reach of the goal of full responsible government proposed in the pronouncement made on August 20, 1917.

During the war India had been given a place along with the self-governing Dominions in the Imperial Cabinet. At the Conference of Paris she appeared on a footing of equality with them, and since the war has been recognised as a full and equal member of the Imperial Conference.

CHAPTER LXIII

THE IRISH FREE STATE

THE appearance of the Irish Free State in 1923 as a full member of the Imperial Conference was destined to have a profound effect on the constitution of the British Commonwealth. In order to explain how this happened it is necessary to recall the course which events in Ireland had taken since England declared war on Germany on August 4, 1914.

Exactly two weeks before that date King George V. had uttered his ominous warning, "to-day the cry of civil war is on the lips of the most responsible and sober-minded of my people". This terrible and unmistakable fact had largely encouraged the German and Austrian governments to believe that the crisis in Europe could be handled by them without interference from Great Britain. This belief was falsified by the ruthless invasion of Belgium, the small country of Catholic people. The support of Nationalist Ireland in a war against Germany was instantly pledged by Redmond. The troops which had recently fired on an Irish crowd were greeted with cheers in the streets of Dublin. The order to establish a provisional government in Belfast which Carson had in his pocket was never despatched. He ordered his volunteers to prepare for battle in Belgium and France. The rifles with which they were armed were used in battle with the Germans who had made them.

Events, however, were soon to show that Redmond and the Nationalist members of parliament had lost their control of the Irish masses. In 1905 Arthur Griffith had founded Sinn Fein, an organisation which rejected Home Rule as conceived since the time of Isaac Butt, and sought to revive the position created in 1783, when the British parliament had for ever disclaimed all right to legislate for Ireland. Sinn Fein, literally construed, means 'we ourselves', and its implications are 'mind your own business, and leave us to ours'. Its nearest English equivalent is 'self-determination'. With no conscious control of their own affairs a great mass of the Irish people had developed an extreme particularism, which made them blind to the paramount issues of the war.

The methods which Griffith adopted resembled those which Gandhi has followed in India, methods which did not appeal to that section of Irishmen who, like the Fenians, wished for an Irish republic and believed only in physical force as the means to that end. These extremists had joined MacNeill's volunteers by thousands.

On September 25, when Redmond appealed for volunteers to fight in France, MacNeill and his party expelled him from the corps. Part of them followed Redmond and part MacNeill. Redmond would have offered to send his followers to the front if he had thought they would go. He offered them to the government for home defence and his offer was refused. It is hard to see what else the government could have done. To find soldiers for the front was a question of life or death for the country and its allies. Carson could scarcely have maintained his offer of troops for the front had it been understood that Nationalist regiments raised to enforce Home Rule on Ulster were to remain in Ireland intact as recognised forces of the Crown, while those raised to resist Home Rule were perishing at the front. This did not, however, prevent Redmond from appealing to his countrymen to confirm the grant of Home Rule by enlisting in the British army.

To begin with this appeal, backed by the heroic example of his brother, met with considerable response. In April 1915 Redmond believed that 25,000 Nationalist volunteers had enlisted, and that 250,000 Irishmen were with the colours.

In September the Home Rule Act received the royal assent, but an Act was passed suspending its operation until after the war. In May 1915 the Coalition government was formed in response to the voice of public opinion, which demanded that all parties should unite for the conduct of war. Redmond refused office, doubtless believing that if he accepted, more of his followers would secede to MacNeill. Carson accepted, and his inclusion in the cabinet was quoted in Ireland as proving that the Coalition government henceforward went into definite alliance with Ulster against Nationalist Ireland. In January 1916 conscription was imposed on Great Britain. Its application to Ireland was successfully opposed by Redmond, who would otherwise have lost the whole of his following.

In the early months of this year the episode connected with the name of Wolfe Tone was repeated. Sir Roger Casement, an Ulster Protestant, had retired on a pension at the close of a very distinguished career in the British consular service. After the outbreak of war he had found his way to Berlin. In the early months of 1916 he arranged to bring to Ireland a cargo of rifles in a German submarine to arm MacNeill's volunteers for a general rising at Easter. On April 20, 1916, Casement was captured by the British on the Irish coast. On learning his failure, MacNeill tried to call off the rising planned for Easter, and to a great extent succeeded. One group, however, broke away and coalesced with others not under MacNeill's control. The first of these groups was led by Pearse, the second by Connolly, a Labour leader in Dublin. Pearse never expected the rebellion to succeed, but believed that his own death would convert Ireland to the republican cause. Events proved that his reading of Irish psychology was sound. Connolly, a man of admitted ability, had, with Larkin, led the Dublin strike in 1913. After its failure he formed a body called 'the Citizen Army', largely composed of retired soldiers. His aim was a workers' republic, and his followers were socialists first and nationalists afterwards.

On Easter morning, April 24, 1916, Pearse and Connolly seized the General Post Office and other public buildings, proclaimed a republican government and shot at sight all who resisted them. Everyone in uniform was a mark for the rebels. Wounded and defenceless soldiers from France were, it was said, among the victims. On April 27, Sir John Maxwell was sent to Ireland with plenary powers. On the 29th the leaders surrendered. Sporadic risings in various parts of Ireland were easily suppressed.

In the three weeks following the rebellion the leaders were tried by court-martial and 14 were executed. At the front discipline required that soldiers absent from duty should be shot. To leave unpunished men who had conspired with the enemy to slay their own loyal compatriots was out of the question. The number executed was moderate, but the moral effect in the eyes of the world was largely destroyed by a demented officer who shot Skeffington, a pacifist whose only crime had been opposition to recruiting. The executions, coupled with this story, sent a flame of anger through the whole Irish world. In Canada, recruiting amongst Irishmen came to a standstill, and an Irish minister in Queensland declared that while the Germans had shot only their enemies, like Miss Cavell, the British had been guilty of shooting their friends.

An attempt was now made by Lloyd George to patch up the situation. Redmond and Carson agreed that Home Rule should come into immediate effect for the 26 counties, the 6 north-eastern counties to stay as they were till after the war. Meanwhile, the Irish members were to remain at Westminster. A refusal of Conservative members in the cabinet to accept this last provision wrecked the agreement and ruined the position of Redmond in Ireland. Sinn Fein had long been pouring contempt on the constitutional methods of the Nationalist party, and in Ireland their attitude was now felt to be justified by the failure of the Redmond-Carson agreement. In 1914 Sinn Fein had been on the verge of extinction. In 1916 its adherents were still few, though contributions from Irish Americans had begun to strengthen it. But in England a false idea was created that the Easter rising was the work of Sinn Fein, a mistake which had the effect in Ireland of bringing the whole revolutionary movement under its aegis. It now modified its previous plan of ignoring the British government and embarked on a policy of armed resistance. Control of the organisation passed to leaders who had taken part in the Easter rising who got into touch with the German secret service.

When America came into the war a further attempt was made to deal with the situation by summoning an Irish convention under the chairmanship of Sir Horace Plunkett. Though Sinn Fein refused to participate the convention was held; but in April 1918 had to report the failure of members from the south to reach an agreement with those of Ulster. Nothing could be done to release large forces in Ireland to come to the aid of their comrades in France who were now fighting 'with their backs to the wall'.

The end of the war in November 1918 was at once followed by a general election throughout the

United Kingdom. All the Nationalist members but 7 lost their seats. Avowed supporters of Sinn Fein were returned to the number of 73. The Unionist north elected 26 members.

On January 21, 1919, the Sinn Fein members met at the Mansion House, Dublin, and proclaimed the independence of Ireland. Murders of the Irish police had already begun. By the end of the year it had proved impossible to recruit further police in Ireland. On January 1, 1920, a recruiting office was opened in London. Men who had served in the war were enlisted and sent to Ireland in numbers greater than could for the moment be clothed as policemen. They arrived in Ireland dressed in khaki with black Glengarry caps: so the Irish called them 'the Black and Tans', after the hounds for which Limerick is famous.

The police were backed by 50,000 British troops under General Macready. Still matters were going from bad to worse. Columns paraded the country districts, and when they were ambushed exacted reprisals by burning the neighbouring farms and cottages. Bands of Sinn Feiners countered these measures by burning the country houses belonging to Unionist landlords. Property to the value of millions of pounds was consigned to the flames. Life and property alike were at the mercy of pistol and torch. In the course of the year 1920 the murders of 182 police, 54 soldiers and 46 civilians were officially reported. Police were unable to emerge from their barracks except in force. In extensive districts government ceased to function at all and Sinn Fein began to adjudicate civil and criminal suits in courts of their own. In July 1920 the government decided to meet this challenge. The Black and Tans were now some 13,500. To those were added some 1500 auxiliaries who were all ex-officers of the army, navy or air force. They were chosen for courage and fierceness shown in the war, and allowed to believe that any methods they used to suppress the rising would receive official support. That they copied the murderous and incendiary tactics of Sinn Fein is scarcely surprising. The death of some of their comrades was quickly avenged by the murder of the mayor of Limerick. A bomb killed one of their number in Cork, and that night the principal business streets of the city went up in flames. From this method of meeting crime with crime public opinion in Great Britain recoiled with abhorrence.

In the course of this year, 1920, the British government was preparing a measure, which was destined to lead to a constitutional settlement. The crux of the problem was that 6 counties of Northern Ireland refused to come under a Home Rule government in Dublin and would fight rather than do so. It was now proposed to give Home Rule to 26 counties of Southern Ireland, and also to the 6 counties of Northern Ireland, each with a government of their own. The two legislatures were each to send 20 members to a joint council to administer railways, fisheries and animal diseases. The two legislatures could, if they chose, agree to increase the powers of this council, and so convert it little by little into a federal government of Ireland. This measure was passed into law on December 23, 1920. The elections were fixed for May 1921, but in Southern Ireland no contested elections took place. Four moderates were nominated for Trinity College. For the other 124 seats Sinn Fein candidates were returned unopposed. They refused to function under the Act, but regarded themselves as Dail Eireann, the parliament of an Irish Republic. To the 52 seats in Northern Ireland were elected 40 Unionists, 6 Republicans and 6 Nationalists.

Meanwhile the struggle continued with increasing ferocity throughout the country. On June 22, 1921, the King himself opened the parliament of Northern Ireland at Belfast, and seized the occasion to

> appeal to all Irishmen to pause, to stretch out the hand of forbearance and conciliation, to forgive and to forget, and to join in making for the land which they love a new era of peace, contentment and goodwill.[1]

In both islands public opinion was now sick and ashamed of the frightful excesses practised on both sides, and Mr. Lloyd George was quick to follow the King's initiative. He was able to persuade the Sinn Fein leaders to agree to an armistice and to send delegates to a conference with cabinet ministers in London, which met in October.

In demanding an Irish Republic, Sinn Fein was asking for something which the British government and parliament, if they agreed to it, could not deliver, even at a time when their power in the world was greater than ever before or since. Ulster would have fought to the death to resist it, and Ireland would at once have been plunged into civil war. From every part of the world, from the United States no less than the British Commonwealth, thousands of Catholic and Protestant Irishmen would have flocked to join the contending forces in Ireland. The landing of volunteers and munitions at northern and southern ports could only be stopped if the British fleet were used to maintain a blockade, to keep the ring whilst Catholics and Protestants in Ireland slaughtered each other, an expedient that no responsible statesman could contemplate for a moment. At the root of the problem was a state of mind divorced from realities, which led the Irish to demand what the British in the plenitude of their strength were powerless to grant. This state of mind could only be cured, and that very slowly, by giving the Irish every power to manage their own affairs, which the British parliament could deliver as well as concede. To deliver the

6 Protestant counties was not in their power, and on this they were adamant from the outset. Arthur Griffith, who led the Irish spokesmen, was quick to see that if a republic for the 26 counties was granted, the hope of uniting Ireland would be dead for ever, and ceased to press this demand. The British on their side saw that a state of mind in the Irish people which nothing but the discipline of freedom could cure, was in the long run a greater danger to British security than the active sympathy of Irish rebels with any power at war with England. It was realised that the Union had failed not only to solve the problem of governing Ireland, but had also impaired the power of the British to govern themselves. By organised opposition the Nationalist members had clogged and delayed the business of parliament. At critical junctures they had held the balance of power between the parties, and had used their position to the full. They had brought the United Kingdom to the verge of a civil war. This state of affairs had helped to encourage the central Empires to plunge the world into war, which alone averted what might well have proved in the end a greater catastrophe to the cause of freedom. That Great Britain at last secured Home Rule for herself was the most important result of the Irish Treaty. The significance of this fact can be realised if we imagine what the state of this country would now be if since 1921 there had been at Westminster some 70 Nationalist members bent on impeding the business of parliament, and often holding the balance between the parties. Conservative critics of the Irish Treaty are slow to remember that its signature made Conservative governments with moderate majorities possible in England.

On December 21, 1921, the Treaty was signed which gave the 26 counties the same status as Canada, under the name of the Irish Free State.

In the summer of 1923 the Irish Free State was admitted to the League of Nations on the proposal of Great Britain, and Irish ministers took their seats in the Assembly at Geneva. Mr. Cosgrave, the President of the Irish Free State, took part in the Imperial Conference, which, during the autumn, was held in London.

NOTE

[1] *The Round Table*, No. 44, September 1921, p. 766.

CHAPTER LXIV

SOUTH AFRICA DURING AND AFTER THE WAR

When the Union in 1910 had given South Africa the same status as the Dominion of Canada, or the Commonwealth of Australia, the Nationalists had taken the line which Wolfe Tone had argued for Ireland in the days of Grattan. They had urged that if England went to war the Union government should proclaim its neutrality. On this issue Hertzog had broken with Botha and left his cabinet. After the war the following story was told by de Villiers (familiarly known to his friends as Japie), at the time when he held the post of chief justice, to another member of the South African bench. The chief justice himself had fought in the South African war. His story was that some of those who had signed the Peace of Vereeniging had done so subject to a reservation, explicit amongst themselves, that a treaty signed under duress could not be regarded as binding if ever future events should give them the chance of reversing its terms. When the war broke out in 1914 they waited on Botha and urged that here was the chance they had looked for to recover their independence. Botha, with his usual patience, heard them to the end, and then said, "Gentlemen, I could not answer your arguments if it were not for one thing which you have not mentioned—my word, which I pledged at Vereeniging. And the reasons why I must keep it are set forth in this book." He lifted a copy of the Bible which lay on his desk.

It is always difficult to say how far a story told like this, even by men with judicial training, exactly records what was done and said. But whatever the truth of this story may be, it reflects the character of Botha not merely as known to his friends, but also as shown by his whole record. He was beyond measure the greatest man I have ever been privileged to meet, and this I say as one who opposed him in the Transvaal legislative council, honestly, but sometimes wrongly. To appreciate fully the inborn sincerity of Botha one has to recall the Homeric standards of the primitive society in which he grew up. Botha could read and write, but never did either if he could help it and, therefore, owed little to education in the narrower sense of that word. His greatness lay in his own unerring instinct for values, in his judgment of men and the qualities which lift some men above others, and also of military and political situations. This sureness of judgment had made him realise the priceless value of truth in handling men. By unswerving faith to a treaty he had signed under duress he united two races who had long fought with each other, and died their ruler. His fidelity and political insight gave to this world-wide commonwealth foundations deeper than those which his military genius had once shaken. In a book like this there is little room for digression, but this one leaf I must spare to lay on his grave.

Turning a deaf ear to the tempters, Botha and Smuts offered to help the Imperial government in whatever way might be most acceptable, and were asked to deal with the German forces in South-West Africa. Orders were instantly sent from Cape Town to General Beyers, who commanded the defence force stationed at Potchefstroom. But Beyers and his German wife were already in league with the enemy and Beyers suborned de la Rey. Since the Boer war the old general had been under the influence of van Rensburg, an ignorant soothsayer whose influence over him the Germans had probably secured in their interest; for de la Rey's prestige on the veldt was second only to Botha's. Beyers had arranged to take de la Rey in a motor from Pretoria to Potchefstroom to use his authority to induce the defence force to side with the Germans. When crossing the Rand de la Rey was killed by an accident too strange and improbable even to be used by a writer of crude sensational fiction. Some police in search of motor bandits summoned the car to stop, and, when it refused, fired at the tyres. One bullet which glanced off the road killed de la Rey. This accident enabled Botha and Smuts to reach Pretoria from Cape Town in time to call on the commandants who had served with them in the Boer war to join them in suppressing the rebellion which Beyers was leading. A Boer rebellion was suppressed by Boers loyal to Botha, and Beyers was drowned in the Vaal when trying to escape capture. But this civil war started a cleavage which was destined to yield momentous results after Botha died.

Having settled accounts with his own people, Botha called on the British to join his loyal commandos in attacking the Germans. When this second struggle was fought to a finish Botha ordered his officers to use the utmost consideration in accepting the German surrender. "I too have known", he said to them, "what it means to surrender when beaten."

It was words like these that he used in vain to his colleagues at the Conference of Paris (1919), and had the Treaty of Versailles been framed in accordance with views like his the world would now be a happier place than it is. But the strain, never broken for twenty years, had worn out his strength, and three months after the peace was signed he was dead. Had he survived some years he might well have healed the terrible rift which the civil war of 1914 had left in the ranks of his people.

His successor, Smuts, was called on to deal with another rebellion, this time in Johannesburg. A large number of Boers, with republican sympathies, had now found employment in the mines. In the heterogeneous ranks of Labour some British communists, in direct touch with the Third International in Moscow, were actively working. The belief was spread that the Chamber of Mines meant to remove the colour bar and displace Europeans. In March 1922 a dangerous outbreak took place. General Smuts rushed to Johannesburg and with great courage and resolution suppressed the rising, in which nearly 800 people were killed and wounded.

When the country went to a general election two years later the Labour party were moved by a deep resentment against General Smuts. Under Colonel Creswell they made a pact with the Nationalists led by General Hertzog, who still remembered with bitterness the action of Botha and Smuts in suppressing the rising of 1914. The Nationalists won 63 seats, the Labour party 18, the South African party 53, and one Independent was elected. On June 24, 1924, General Hertzog became prime minister. The inclusion in the cabinet of Colonel Creswell was a safeguard that no attempt would be made to sever the British connection as long as he stayed there. The Nationalists were further faced by the fact that any attempt to proclaim a republic would involve the country in civil war. With the burden of office on his shoulders General Hertzog came to view the position much as Botha and Smuts had viewed it.

CHAPTER LXV

THE COMMONWEALTH OF NATIONS AFTER THE WAR

Mr. Asquith in 1911 had told the Imperial Conference that

the authority of the Government of the United Kingdom in such grave matters as the conduct of foreign policy, the conclusion of treaties, the declaration and maintenance of peace, or the declaration of war, and, indeed, all those relations with Foreign Powers, necessarily of the most delicate character, which are now in the hands of the Imperial Government, subject to its responsibility to the Imperial Parliament . . . *cannot be shared*[1] [with Dominion governments and parliaments].

These words must now be reviewed in the light of after events. In the Great War defeat of the Allies was averted by a number of countries, which successively threw themselves into the struggle at critical junctures. Failure of any one of these countries to act at the critical moment might have changed the result of the war in favour of Germany. Had Great Britain not intervened when she did, the German armies would have mastered France. The long line from the North Sea to the Swiss frontier could not have been held if help had not come from the British Dominions and India, as fast as men could be trained and ships could carry them. The collapse of Russia would have spelt defeat for her allies if America had not come to their help in time.

The landscape, as Mr. Asquith had seen it, was changed when both the Dominions and India were throwing their strength into the war. Their ministers were included in a cabinet created by Mr. Lloyd George. The idea that this cabinet could be made responsible to a parliament elected by the Commonwealth as a whole was under discussion. In 1917 an imperial conference was held at a stage in the war when the German power appeared unbreakable. Its view was recorded as follows:

The Imperial War Conference is of opinion that the readjustment of the constitutional relations of the component parts of the Empire is too important and intricate a subject to be dealt with during the war, and that it should form the subject of a special Imperial Conference to be summoned as soon as possible after the cessation of hostilities.

It deems it its duty, however, to place on record its view that any such readjustment, while thoroughly preserving all existing powers of self-government and complete control of domestic affairs, should be based upon a full recognition of the Dominions as autonomous nations of an Imperial Commonwealth, and of India as an important portion of the same, should recognise the right of the Dominions and India to an adequate voice in foreign policy and in foreign relations, and should provide effective arrangements for continuous consultation in all important matters of common imperial concern, and for such necessary concerted action, founded on consultation, as the several Governments may determine.[2]

If Lansdowne's advice had been followed the war would have been ended leaving the German army and navy intact. What the effect would have been on the future relations of the self-governing states of the Commonwealth is a question we need not pursue. In the following year the German morale suddenly collapsed. By the end of that year her fleet had surrendered, her armies were broken, the Allies were encamped on the Rhine and their statesmen were summoned to Paris to settle the terms of peace. A number of countries had secured a voice in the Peace Conference by declaring war on the central Empires, without contributing much to the fighting line. The Dominions and India had pledged all their resources. They had thrown great armies into the struggle under generals like Currie, Monash, Russell, Botha and Smuts, which had played no secondary part in the final issue. Their statesmen had sat in the cabinet of the Empire, and had shared in the conduct of the war. When the Allied governments met to settle the terms of peace in Paris, it could scarcely be argued that a conference which included the spokesmen of China and Haiti, should be closed to those statesmen. Dominion ministers and those of India were admitted to the conference side by side with those of Great Britain. They signed the treaties and took their place on the League of Nations on the same footing as the spokesmen of national states like Belgium or Serbia.

In 1919 and for ten years afterwards it was felt that the British Commonwealth was now free from all serious menace from without. The Dominions had established their position as national states, not only in the eyes of Great Britain, but also in those of the world at large. The effect can be seen in the speech made by General Smuts to the Union parliament at Cape Town in September 1919 on his return from the Conference of Paris.

> Until last year British Ministers had signed all documents and dealt with all matters affecting the Dominions. But a change had come about in Paris when representatives of the Dominions had, on behalf of the King, for the first time signed the great documents on behalf of the Dominions. The change was that in future the representatives of the Dominions should act for the Dominions. This precedent had now been laid down for the future. The British Constitution was most elastic, and the precedent might bring about the greatest changes. Where in the past British Ministers could have acted for the Dominions, in future Ministers of the Union would act for the Union. The change was a far-reaching one which would alter the whole basis of the British Empire. In future all parts of the British Empire stood exactly on the same basis.[3]

When the Imperial Conference met in October 1926 there were sitting at the table ministers of two governments, the Irish Free State and the South African Union, members and supporters of which had, during and after the war, been closely connected with those who had striven to separate their countries from the British Commonwealth. On the other hand, actual experience of office, both in Ireland and South Africa, had brought their spokesmen who sat in the Conference to realise how difficult it was for countries like theirs to enjoy the verities of freedom in isolation. The Irish and South African members of the Conference were thus at one in hoping to secure some agreed pronouncement which would strengthen their hands in dealing with the extremists who were pressing for republican independence. On the other hand, ministers from Australia and New Zealand were profoundly averse to any pronouncement which might further weaken the ties which united the self-governing states to each other.

To handle these delicate issues a committee was appointed with Lord Balfour as chairman. It produced a report which the Conference adopted. Its tenor may be seen from the following extracts:

We were appointed at the meeting of the Imperial Conference on October 25, 1926, to investigate all the questions on the Agenda affecting Inter-Imperial Relations. Our discussions on these questions have been long and intricate. We found, on examination, that they involved consideration of fundamental principles affecting the relations of the various parts of the British Empire *inter se*, as well as the relations of each part to foreign countries. For such examination the time at our disposal has been all too short. Yet we hope that we may have laid a foundation on which subsequent Conferences may build.

II. Status of Great Britain and the Dominions.—The Committee are of opinion that nothing would be gained by attempting to lay down a Constitution for the British Empire. Its widely scattered parts have very different characteristics, very different histories, and are at very different stages of evolution; while, considered as a whole, it defies classification and bears no real resemblance to any other political organisation which now exists or has ever yet been tried.

There is, however, one most important element in it which, from a strictly constitutional point of view, has now, as regards all vital matters, reached its full development—we refer to the group of self-governing communities composed of Great Britain and the Dominions. Their position and mutual relation may be readily defined. *They are autonomous Communities within the British Empire, equal in status, in no way subordinate one to another in any aspect of their domestic or external affairs, though united by a common allegiance to the Crown, and freely associated as members of the British Commonwealth of Nations.*

A foreigner endeavouring to understand the true character of the British Empire by the aid of this formula alone would be tempted to think that it was devised rather to make mutual interference impossible than to make mutual co-operation easy.

Such a criticism, however, completely ignores the historic situation. The rapid evolution of the Oversea Dominions during the last fifty years has involved many complicated adjustments of old political machinery to changing conditions. The tendency towards equality of status was both right and inevitable. Geographical and other conditions made this impossible of attainment by the way of federation. The only alternative was by the way of autonomy; and along this road it has been steadily sought. Every self-governing member of the Empire is now the master of its destiny. In fact, if not always in form, it is subject to no compulsion whatever.

But no account, however accurate, of the negative relations in which Great Britain and the Dominions stand to each other can do more than express a portion of the truth. The British Empire is not founded upon negations. It depends essentially, if not formally, on positive ideals. Free institutions are its life-blood. Free co-operation is its instrument. Peace, security, and progress are among its objects. Aspects of all these great themes have been discussed at the present Conference; excellent results have been thereby obtained. And, though every Dominion is now, and must always remain, the sole judge of the nature and extent of its co-operation, no common cause will, in our opinion, be thereby imperilled.

Equality of status, so far as Britain and the Dominions are concerned, is thus the root principle governing our Inter-Imperial Relations. But the principles of equality and similarity, appropriate to *status*, do not universally extend to function. Here we require something more than immutable dogmas. For example, to deal with questions of diplomacy and questions of defence, we require also flexible machinery—machinery which can, from time to time, be adapted to the changing circumstances of the world. This subject also has occupied our attention. The rest of this Report will show how we have endeavoured not only to state political theory, but to apply it to our common needs.[4]

It was agreed in 1923 that any of the Governments of the Empire contemplating the negotiation of a treaty should give due consideration to its possible effect upon other Governments and should take steps to inform Governments likely to be interested of its intention.

This rule should be understood as applying to any negotiations which any Government intends to conduct, so as to leave it to the other Governments to say whether they are likely to be interested.

When a Government has received information of the intention of any other Government to conduct negotiations, it is incumbent upon it to indicate its attitude with reasonable promptitude. So long as the initiating Government receives no adverse comments, and so long as its policy involves no active obligations on the part of the other Governments, it may proceed on the assumption that its policy is generally acceptable. It must, however, before taking any steps which might involve the other Governments in any active obligations, obtain their definite assent.

Where by the nature of the treaty it is desirable that it should be ratified on behalf of all the Governments of the Empire, the initiating Government may assume that a Government which has had full opportunity of indicating its attitude and has made no adverse comments will concur in the ratification of the treaty. In the case of a Government that prefers not to concur in the ratification of a treaty unless it has been signed by a plenipotentiary authorised to act on its behalf, it will advise the appointment of a plenipotentiary so to act.[5]

We went on to examine the possibility of applying the

principles underlying the Treaty Resolution of the 1923 Conference to matters arising in the conduct of foreign affairs generally. It was frankly recognised that in this sphere, as in the sphere of defence, the major share of responsibility rests now, and must for some time continue to rest, with His Majesty's Government in Great Britain. Nevertheless, practically all the Dominions are engaged to some extent, and some to a considerable extent, in the conduct of foreign relations, particularly those with foreign countries on their borders. A particular instance of this is the growing work in connection with the relations between Canada and the United States of America which has led to the necessity for the appointment of a Minister Plenipotentiary to represent the Canadian Government in Washington. We felt that the governing consideration underlying all discussions of this problem must be that neither Great Britain nor the Dominions could be committed to the acceptance of active obligations except with the definite assent of their own Governments. In the light of this governing consideration, the Committee agreed that the general principle expressed in relation to Treaty negotiations in Section V (*a*) of this Report, which is indeed already to a large extent in force, might usefully be adopted as a guide by the Governments concerned in future in all negotiations affecting foreign relations falling within their respective spheres.[6]

The fact that the British government had negotiated the Locarno treaties without consultation with, though with the full knowledge of, the Dominion governments, was condoned by the following resolution:

The Conference has heard with satisfaction the statement of the Secretary of State for Foreign Affairs with regard to the efforts made to ensure peace in Europe, culminating in the agreements of Locarno; and congratulates His Majesty's Government in Great Britain on its share in this successful contribution towards the promotion of the peace of the world.[7]

This report, in fact, did no more than cross the *t*'s and dot the *i*'s of the statement which General Smuts had made to his parliament in Cape Town when he returned from the Conference of Paris in September 1919. Canadian and Australasian ministers could accept it as providing an agreed and authoritative picture of the Commonwealth as it is: Irish and South African ministers could present it to their followers as the Magna Carta of commonwealth liberties.

In sections not quoted above the Balfour report had recognised that under the law the Dominions were still bound by such statutes as the Colonial Laws Validity Act, by the Merchant Shipping Act, by the reservation of bills for approval in London and by limitation of their powers of extraterritorial legislation. The Balfour report, therefore, proposed a special sub-conference to consider these matters, which met in London in 1929 and reported in the following January. The report was approved by the Imperial Conference which met in 1930, and embodied in the Statute of Westminster which was passed into law by the British parliament on December 3, 1931. In this statute the British parliament renounced all future right to legislate for the self-governing Dominions except at the instance of their own governments. Henceforward Great Britain and the self-governing Dominions were to be united in constitutional law only by the fact that the same monarch would officiate as head of each of these self-governing states.

Looking back to the state of public opinion as it was in the year 1914 the changes wrought by the Balfour report, and those in the status of India and Ireland, would have been unthinkable, had it not been for the shock given to established ideas by the war and events which sprang from the war. Its effect in forcing this change of outlook on the people and government of England, and in opening their eyes to the meaning of their own institutions—to the infinite range of that meaning, may in the end prove to outweigh the more evident mischiefs wrought when the passions of war were let loose.

The British Commonwealth now includes no less than six separate sovereignties. The governments of the United Kingdom, of the Irish Free State, of Canada, of Australia, of New Zealand and of South Africa are each responsible for the conduct of foreign affairs to their several electorates. In the metaphysical view of General Smuts these sovereign communities are united by a common allegiance to the Crown, which in that sense is common to them all; but as an executive officer the King must act as the head of six separate states. But the movement towards complete independence cannot be limited to these six. In course of time India and Ceylon, Burma and Palestine will claim and acquire control of their foreign affairs. A day will come when the British West Indies will wake from their insular torpor and break the bonds of their obsolete constitutions. They will find that self-government can only be attained by joining together in one Dominion which will presently demand equality with the others. In a future, perhaps more remote, negro Dominions will emerge in tropical Africa and start on the path which the peoples of India and Ceylon are now treading. If the sovereignties under the Crown should be more than doubled, we may well consider what kind of unity in foreign affairs a dozen or so sovereign states, diverse in race and scattered all over the face of the globe, will succeed in maintaining.

NOTES

[1] *Minutes of the Proceedings of the Imperial Conference of 1911*, Cd. 5745, p. 71.

[2] *The Round Table*, No. 27, June 1917, p. 446.

[3] *Ibid.* No. 43, June 1921, p. 540.

[4] *Ibid.* No. 66, March 1927, pp. 430, 431.

[5] *Ibid.* pp. 437, 438. [6] *Ibid.* p. 441. [7] *Ibid.* p. 444.

CHAPTER LXVI

THE GREAT DEPRESSION

ON May 14, 1927, *The Times* remarked in a leader:

> After the years of storm a certain routine, almost an inertia, of peace is being re-established. The state of Europe in 1927 is certainly immeasurably better than it was in 1923.[1]

The prospect of a general disarmament was in sight. At Geneva a commission was at work preparing a general agreement on the subject. Mr. Kellogg was drafting a unilateral treaty by which governments were to renounce war as an instrument of national policy and bind themselves never again to seek the settlement of conflicts one with another except by pacific means. On August 27, 1928, this Pact was signed at Paris by 15 governments. By the end of 1931, 45 other states had adhered to it.

Locarno seemed to have mended the mischief done at Versailles. With the aid of British and American capital German industry had begun to revive. Money lent from America with the utmost freedom enabled the people of Europe to buy the products of her farms and factories, and also to pay the interest on loans made in the war. At the close of 1928 Mr. Hoover as secretary of commerce at Washington was able to report that

> business in nearly all branches was on a level rarely, if ever before, attained . . . and the standard of living of the masses of the people remained higher than anywhere else in the world.[2]

The value of shares rose so rapidly that a fever of speculation set in. The profits of speculation were attracting money from Europe, till securities reached imaginary values.

In less than a year from Hoover's announcement the bubble had burst and the gamblers were rushing to cut their losses. On October 24, 1929, over 13,000,000 shares were sold at a loss on the Stock Exchange of New York. Investors were seized with a panic and this sudden and violent collapse of values in the richest and most prosperous community in the world immediately checked and reversed the revival of trade which had followed Locarno. Confidence was everywhere shattered and producers restricted the plans they had laid for development. The value of raw material sank and in vast quantities became unsaleable. The check to prosperity made itself felt on the farms, the mines and the factories of every continent. Millions of workers who lost their employment shivered and starved, while barns and warehouses bulged with the raw materials of clothing and food which could not be sold. And as the depression deepened cyclones began to develop which travelled from one state to another, and everywhere left destruction in their track. The British and American bankers, who after Locarno had advanced considerable sums on short terms to revive German production, began to call in their money. In the first week of July 1931, 100,000,000 marks were withdrawn and before the end of that month every bank in Germany but the Reichbank was closed by decree. Two months later the rapid shrinkage of London reserves had compelled England to suspend payments in gold. By the end of September Denmark, Norway, Sweden and Egypt had also been forced off the gold standard. In the next few years a number of governments were obliged to reduce the value of their currencies. By February 1933 the cyclonic depression was sweeping across the United States with redoubled force. When President Roosevelt assumed office in March all but 11 of the 48 States suspended the payment of private debts, banks were everywhere crashing and closed, the financial system was at a standstill, and a large proportion of that opulent people were faced by starvation. Action of some sort to deal with the crisis was everywhere forced on governments by public opinion. A few examples will serve to illustrate the expedients adopted.

The American people owed their unexampled prosperity for over a hundred years to the great constitutional act which had given government, peace and free trade to an area richly stored with natural resources which was larger than western Europe. They thought it was due, however, to protective tariffs which the natural advantages of their vast and productive country had enabled them to maintain. They now endeavoured to relieve the depression by raising the tariffs still higher, by a measure passed into law in June 1930 which bears the names of two members of Congress, Hawley and Smoot. The effect of this measure was to make it impossible for their creditors abroad to sell in America the goods to purchase the dollars required to enable them to repay the money they owed to American creditors. In June 1931 President Hoover was forced to propose a moratorium on debts due from foreign states to America. The payments were never resumed. By November 1933 every government in Europe which owed money to the U.S.A., including Great Britain, had defaulted with the minor exception of Finland.

The financial fidelity of England had been her most cherished tradition. Her default on the debt which she owed to America made it easy for more impoverished countries to follow her example. A number of governments suspended payment on obligations due to their creditors. In America the default became final at the moment when her own domestic finances were plunged into chaos. The political reactions there were profound. The American people began to regret the part they had taken in the war. Stringent precautions were taken to ensure that in any future struggle in Europe no further aid would be rendered to her former associates. The measures designed for their own economic recovery were taken henceforward with less regard to any reactions they might have on the rest of the world. At the World Economic Conference of 1933 it transpired that the central banks of England, France and the U.S.A. had agreed on a plan to stabilise exchange which the Conference was prepared to adopt. The American delegates approved the proposal, but it did not happen to suit the domestic programme which their government was considering at the moment. The proposal was instantly vetoed by Washington, and the World Economic Conference was forced to adjourn with nothing achieved.

The expedient of raising tariffs to protect their own markets was not confined to America. In 1932 it was followed by England. By agreements made at Ottawa the practice of protecting British producers inside the Commonwealth, including its dependencies, was established. The open door in the British dependencies, which contained one-fifth of the world's population, was a thing of the past. Elsewhere the raising of tariffs became general, for countries which sought to maintain the value of their currencies quickly found that the goods they produced were undersold at home and abroad by the goods produced by countries where currencies were cheapened. Each country was forced to protect the industries which employed its people by all sorts of restrictions. Imports were rationed by quotas. Restrictions on foreign exchange were imposed, which made it impossible for the merchants of one country to obtain payment for goods supplied to another. Nations were driven to exchange their goods by the clumsy and primitive method of barter. International trade sank to a fraction of its former volume. Harbours were cluttered with rusting ships.

As to the steps which governments ought to have taken to arrest the crisis and restore prosperity economists expressed many and different opinions; but most, if not all of them, would agree that the crisis would have passed and the trade and prosperity of the world would have recovered better and sooner than it has, if every government could have abstained from action of any sort. But this the tortured condition of public opinion in every country, in each of upwards of 60 sovereign states, would not allow. These states acted like so many men on a foundering ship who, by each thinking first of their own individual safety, diminish the general chance of escape and increase the common disaster. That millions of suffering people should come to feel that Marx and Engels were genuine prophets and to see in the methods they preached the only path to salvation was a natural consequence. But to grasp the political effects of the great depression we must turn for a moment to events which had taken place in Russia during the war, events which were one of its major results.

NOTES

[1] King-Hall, *Our Own Times*, vol. ii. p. 436.
[2] *Ibid.* p. 444.

CHAPTER LXVII

BOLSHEVISM

THE reader must hold in mind the thesis which Marx and Engels had launched on the world some 70 years before Russia was plunged into anarchy by the war. In Book II., Chapter XXXVIII., I described that thesis, and have further suggested that Engels and Marx were profoundly, though unconsciously, influenced by the Prussian environment in which they grew up. They had taught that the world revolution they prophesied must be achieved by force. In every country the proletariat armed and organised by a dictator must destroy the capitalists, abolish private property and seize and operate the whole machinery of production. When once personal gain had ceased to operate as the motive power of production, the need for force in human affairs would vanish and with it the need for national states with governments based upon force. An order of society, which secured to each of its members their due share in the fruits of their common endeavour, would give full play to the instincts of men to serve society. Such a change, however, could never be effected by constitutional means, for the reason that capitalists who controlled governments would resist it by force. They and their governments must be destroyed by force.

This creed was held by Lenin with a faith fervent as that which inspired the followers of Islam. A fanatic who is also a master of action, who never forgets his ultimate goal, but yet knows when to retreat as well as advance if that will help him to reach it, is a formidable leader. In Russia at the close of the war there was everything to encourage the methods which Engels and Marx had enjoined. The Tzarist government, which had fallen in ruins, had long accustomed its subjects to violence. The world was drenched in blood by the war, and men in millions were used to killing. The victorious Allies justified Marx's prophecies by pouring in troops and munitions to aid the propertied classes in destroying the communist regime. To those who had seen the collapse on the eastern front in the war the task may well have seemed easy. The lessons of the French Revolution were forgotten, for Denikin and Koltchak were restoring the land to the landlords as they advanced.

In Russia Trotsky now did what Carnot had done in the French Revolution. The peasant soldiery flocked to his banners, ready to die rather than yield the land they had seized. As the White armies advanced so the Red forces increased. In January 1920 Koltchak's armies surrendered in Siberia, and a month later the admiral and his prime minister faced a firing squad at Irkutsk. In April Denikin, forced back into the Crimea, resigned his command in favour of Wrangel, who won an initial victory. By July Soviet armies had driven the Polish invaders out of the Ukraine, had entered Poland and were threatening Warsaw. Every government in Europe trembled for fear that the Russian Revolution might sweep from the east, as the French Revolution had swept from the west. But the Soviet armies invading a hostile country began to encounter the difficulties which had baffled Koltchak and Denikin. Pilsudsky, aided by French munitions and military advice, was able to cut the Russian communications. By the end of August Pilsudsky had crippled the Russian invasion and had taken some 60,000 prisoners. The battle of the Vistula was described by Lord D'Abernon as "the eighteenth decisive battle of the world". It forced the Soviet government to concentrate their energies on the task of consolidating their own position in Russia. In

October they were able to drive Wrangel and his army from the Crimea.

In the first three years of their rule, whilst the Bolshevik government was fighting invading armies, the internal struggle in Russia, confused by all sorts of cross currents, was proceeding apace. In August 1918 Lenin was seriously wounded and barely escaped with his life. The would-be assassin was a Jewess and a social revolutionary; but the outrage, none the less, enabled the Bolshevik government to inaugurate a reign of terror. An order was issued announcing that "the bourgeoisie must be brought under control and mass terrorism instituted. The universal watchwords must be Death or Victory." An extraordinary commission to combat counter-revolution, speculation and sabotage, known as the Cheka, was placed under the control of Dzerzhinsky. He was charged to fight the enemy within whilst Trotsky was fighting the enemy without.

The real number of people who perished in this terror will never be known. One estimate puts it at more than 1,500,000. But whatever the true figure, the butchery vastly exceeded anything accomplished in the course of the French Revolution. In the general condition of anarchy which prevailed it is likely that more were slaughtered by plunderers and private enemies than by the Cheka. In considerable numbers the wealthier people had escaped from Russia in the earlier days of the revolution. The class which suffered most heavily were the intelligentsia, including those who had earned their living by technical knowledge and skill, the people who in civil society correspond to officers, the sergeants and corporals in an army. Some hundreds of thousands of these were butchered. More than the rich, it was men of this numerous and intelligent class who were seized with terror when the Bolshevik government called on the proletariat of every country to follow their example.

CHAPTER LXVIII

FASCISM

In the summer of 1917, when the Russian soldiers began to desert the trenches, the Socialist party were inciting the troops in Italy to follow their example. The appalling disaster of Caporetto in the following autumn was largely the fruit of their propaganda. With the help of the Allies the Austrian advance into Lombardy was checked. The Italian morale was restored and a year later, on the eve of the Armistice, the Italian army with the help of a British division broke through the Austrian lines, seized their headquarters at Vittorio Veneto and forced their government to sue for peace. But the pride which Italians felt in this victory was speedily quenched by the treatment she met at the hands of her Allies. She had hoped for an empire in Asia Minor. Her claims to the coast of Dalmatia were strongly opposed by President Wilson, and the African colonies taken from Germany fell to the share of England and France. The Italian delegates withdrew from the Conference and only returned because they were warned that the treaty of peace would be signed in their absence.

The people of Italy felt that the fruits of victory had turned in their mouth to ashes. They had lost 632,000 killed in the war: 2,000,000 more of their men had been wounded. The value of their currency had fallen by 70 per cent. Food and fuel were costly and scarce. The decision to enter the war began to be thought of as the greatest mistake in Italian history. The head of the government, Nitti, described the proposal to celebrate the funeral to an 'unknown soldier' as an 'inglorious reminder' and refused to authorise it.

The Socialists raised their heads once more and openly insulted men who had fought in the war. In this temper of bitter disappointment the people of Italy went to a general election. In November 1919 the Socialists captured 150 seats, and entered parliament strong enough to create a deadlock. Government was paralysed and the country was moving headlong to anarchy. The Socialists controlled one-fourth of the local authorities, and used their power to plunder the propertied classes. Land was seized and given to peasants. Strikes were the order of the day. 'Eviva Lenin' became a popular cry and communist leaders were taking their orders from Moscow. Red guards appeared, murders were rife and a veritable terror was established which the government was powerless to repress. In August and September 1920 the workers began to seize the iron and steel factories. Had they found in their ranks a leader like Lenin he would, at this juncture, have seized the reins from the nerveless government. The creation of a second communist state would have raised the movement to the international plane as projected by Marx. In all probability this would have happened when the workers were seizing the factories, if the Socialists had not already expelled from their ranks the one leader who was capable of doing in Italy what Lenin was doing in Russia.

This man was Benito Mussolini, the son of a radical blacksmith at Forli. Trained as a teacher, he had gone to Switzerland, where he fraternised with exiles from Russia and published articles so violent that the Swiss police had put him over the frontier. In 1911 the Italian government had imprisoned him for inciting workers at Forli to tear up a railway which was carrying soldiers to the Libyan war.[1]

A different side to his character was revealed when

the young agitator was called to his period of service as a conscript in the army. In the ranks of the Bersaglieri, the shock troops of Italy, he began to realise the importance of discipline in the life of a people and also to see that in discipline lies the key to power. His officers found in him a docile and highly efficient soldier.

Released from the army, he crossed into Austrian territory, where his nationalist feelings were roused by seeing Italians ruled by their ancient oppressors. He was soon deported for writing "an article maintaining that the Italian border was not at Ala, the little town which in those days stood on the old frontier between our Kingdom and the old Austria".[2]

From Austria he went to Forli and there established a paper. The name which he gave it, *The Class War*, shows that nationalist feeling was not yet uppermost in his mind. The paper succeeded so well that in 1912 he was called to edit the *Avanti*, the principal Socialist journal in Italy. His articles quickly secured him a leading position in the Socialist party.

At the outbreak of war he was greatly impressed by the fact that the Socialist members in the German Reichstag supported the war credits. Their conduct led him to suspect that Marx had been wrong in thinking that workers in any great crisis would forget their national feelings and combine as a class. In his articles he urged that Italy should ignore the Triple Alliance and refuse to declare war on the side of Austria, a policy that suited the pacifist creed of his party. But when presently the *Avanti* began to urge that Italy should enter the war against her former allies, the editor was made to resign and expelled from the party. "You cannot", he told the meeting which expelled him on November 4, 1914, "forbid me my Socialist faith, or prevent me from continuing to work for the cause of Socialism and the revolution".[3]

This formal divorce from the Socialist party was fraught with momentous results. In the next few weeks he had found the means for starting a paper of his own, *Il Popolo d'Italia*. Through its columns he advocated war as necessary to "create an atmosphere more propitious to the realisation of the demands of the working class. . . . To-day it is war; to-morrow it will be the revolution".[4] The entry of Italy into the war on May 22, 1915, was largely due to its influence. In September he went to the front and was quickly promoted to the rank of corporal for courageous and exemplary conduct. On February 23, 1917, he was terribly wounded, but survived unspeakable tortures to leave hospital on crutches in August. He at once resumed the direction of *Il Popolo d'Italia*.

We have seen how Italian society was thrown into utter confusion by the disappointment which followed the war. With a government almost as feeble as Kerensky's had proved, the country seemed to be moving straight to a communist revolution. The professional and salaried classes, technicians and shopmen, as well as capitalists and owners of land, saw themselves threatened with the fate which was overtaking men of their kind in Russia. Young men of this type who had served in the war understood the methods of organised force better than men who worked in factories, and were even more ruthless in temper. A counter-revolution began to develop on lines which Marx had scarcely foreseen. The communist gangs began to encounter bands of ex-soldiers armed with bludgeons, revolvers and knives. These bands, which were known as *squadre*, surpassed their opponents in the violence of their methods.

Mussolini himself had organised one of these bands in Milan.

On the 23rd of March, 1919, I laid down the fundamental

basis at Milan, of the "Italian Fasci di combattimento"—the fighting Fascist programme. . . .

I prepared the atmosphere of that memorable meeting by editorials and summons published in the *Popolo d' Italia*. Anyhow, the ones that came were not numerous. . . . After two days of discussion, fifty-four persons signed our programmes. . . .

I did not favour any bureaucratic, cut-and-dried organisation. It was thought wise that in every big town the correspondent of the *Popolo d'Italia* should be the organiser of a section of the "Fasci di combattimento" with the idea that each group should become a centre of Fascisti ideas, work and action.[5]

Mussolini had made up his mind to smash the Socialist party which had turned him out of its ranks and had hopes of enticing the bulk of their followers into his own. He had still to decide whether his final appeal should be made, as Lenin and Trotsky had made it, to a sense of class in the proletariat, or to the feelings of nationalism which Garibaldi, Cavour and Mazzini had fanned to a flame in the previous century. He was trying, in fact, to ride both horses together. With D'Annunzio he was planning the raid which that poet made on Fiume on September 12, 1919. Some of the braves who followed D'Annunzio were drawn from the ranks of the Fascists, and funds to maintain their hold on Fiume were raised through *Il Popolo d'Italia*. At this very time Mussolini and some of his Fascists were standing as candidates in the general election, on a programme designed to outbid the Socialist party.

Its chief points were the dissolution of the monarchy and senate; the abolition of all titles of nobility; the confiscation of church property; workers' control of factories and industries; and the formation of a Constituent Assembly which should be the Italian section of an International Constituent Assembly of Peoples.[6]

The workers refused to swallow the bait. Of the 346,000 votes which were cast at the general election in November 1919 the Fascists polled no more than 4000. Mussolini and all of his candidates were defeated.

This rebuff determined the form which the Fascist creed was to take. The former editor of *The Class War* and *Avanti* conquered his instinct to appeal to the class from which he had sprung. The keynote of his movement, henceforth, was loyalty to the nation as a whole, raised to the point of fanaticism. The long ages through which foreigners and priests had ruled in Italy had bred in her people a sense of inferiority. Her national union was only achieved by the aid of France, England and Germany, which had then treated her as a secondary power. It had not removed the sense of inferiority which had kept the masses indifferent to public interests and ruined her popular institutions. Apart from the heroes of the *risorgimento* there was little in modern history for Italians to remember with pride. So the future dictator began to turn their minds to the age before the Italian people had bowed their necks to the northern barbarian, to memories of Rome and her Empire, rather than Italy.

> It is destiny that Rome again takes her place as the city who will be the directress of the civilization of all Western Europe. Let us commit the flame of this passion to the coming generations; let us make out of Italy one of the nations without which it is impossible to conceive the future history of humanity.[7]

Mussolini had thus made up his mind to combat, in the cause of imperialism, the doctrines which Marx had preached. He was none the less ready to follow the methods which Marx had prescribed. His electoral failure had encouraged his soldierly instinct to regard organised force as the basis of power. A dictatorship based on a whole nation might prove as effective as one based on a single class.

In the years of anarchy which followed the election, Mussolini was getting in touch with the *squadre* and was linking them up with the Fascist party he had founded at Milan under disciplined control. Through *Il Popolo d'Italia* he directed their movements throughout the country. His superlative gifts as a leader began to be recognised. He had grasped the power which a small minority can wield, if they understand and submit to military discipline. The Socialist masses, who greatly outnumbered the Fascists but had found in their ranks no one to discipline or direct them, were increasingly cowed. In the course of two years Mussolini had made such way that he and 34 Fascists were returned to parliament at the general election of November 1921. Their leader acquired a national position and also the chance of displaying his superb gifts as an orator. His speeches attacking the ministers were addressed over their heads to the nation. His increasing control of the turbulent *squadre* gave him an influence out of all proportion to the number of his party in the Chamber. Capitalists who had found the government unwilling or powerless to protect them were now coming to see a possible saviour in the ex-Socialist leader, who knew how to fight his former associates with their own weapons. They began to supply the thing he most needed at this juncture, funds to arm and equip the organised forces behind him.

Directed by Mussolini the Fascists were seizing control of the local authorities. These forcible seizures were not confined to those which the Socialists controlled. Mussolini decided when the moment had come to extend this treatment to the national government. In October 1922 he ordered the Fascist legions to march on Rome. Some 50,000 disciplined men in four columns, led by Bianchi, de Bono, De Vecchi and Balbo obeyed his call and converged on Civitavecchia a little to the north of Rome. Mussolini controlled their movement from

Milan. On October 28 the columns occupied Rome. Martial law was proclaimed by the government, but the King disallowed the edict. On October 29 Mussolini was summoned to Rome and received the royal commission to form a government.

The first use which he made of the legal authority placed in his hands by the King reveals the capacity of a born leader for taking risks. He ordered the Fascist columns to evacuate Rome within twenty-four hours. The order was obeyed.

On November 16 he summoned the Chamber and told them:

> I could have made of this dull and grey hall a bivouac for corpses. I could have nailed up the doors of Parliament and have established an exclusively Fascist Government. I could have done these things, but at least for a time I did not do them.[8]

His methods, though somewhat less summary, were, in the end, no less effective than Lenin had used in suppressing the constituent assembly in Russia. In 1923 he established a system whereby the party which polled a majority of votes secured two-thirds of the seats in the Chamber. The change was strongly opposed by Matteotti, the Socialist leader. His fate was like that of Thomas à Becket. Some angry words which Mussolini had written in *Il Popolo d'Italia* were read by de Bono and some Fascist gangsters as a hint to remove the turbulent Socialist. Like Henry II. Mussolini was gravely embarrassed. Though the murderers were lightly punished, he took measures to control the criminal elements in his party, and ere long recovered from the grave discredit which the murder had brought on himself. By 1928 he had made constitutional changes which vested absolute power in the Fascist Grand Council, over which he presided. It was then decreed that a list of 400 candidates for election to the legislature should be framed by the Council and submitted to the electorate for acceptance and rejection as a whole. The popular election was reduced to the merest formality by the absolute control of the press which the Fascist regime had acquired. Every paper unwilling to act as the mouthpiece of government was suppressed. The wireless station which enabled millions in all parts of the country to hear the voice of one speaker was even more potent as an instrument of authority in the hands of a ruler endowed with the gifts of an orator. As the organisation of the Fascist party was strengthened, their numbers were strictly limited. All other political parties were suppressed. Their leaders were imprisoned or driven into exile beyond the frontiers. The Fascist creed and no other was taught in the national schools. From the age of seven children were drilled and prepared for service in the national forces.

Some years of vigilance were required to enable Mussolini to assert his absolute control of the gangster elements which had helped to establish his power. The swift and dramatic call on his followers to evacuate Rome when the King had placed the government in his hands was the key to his final success in this task. In the course of the next four years he had purged his party of every recalcitrant member, and received its unquestioning obedience.

Mussolini was proving, meanwhile, that he knew how to use the power he had grasped. He showed a capacity for administrative work on a level with that of Napoleon and Caesar. Augustus in founding the Roman Empire had assumed in his own person the offices of tribune, consul, quaestor and aedile. Mussolini outbid this example; for he was, at one moment, minister of the interior, of foreign affairs, of war, of the army, of the air force, of the guilds and of colonies. Elective local authorities were replaced by *podestas* appointed by himself. Every organ of the national life was infused with his vigour. Efficiency was promoted and corruption repressed. The budget was balanced and the currency reformed. Roads were constructed, marshes were drained and public works were organised on a scale which recalled the splendours of ancient Rome. Capital and land were left in the hands of private owners to show that Fascism had nothing in common with the Marxian programme it was fighting. No attempt was made to eliminate class distinctions, but classes were treated as organs of the national state. Whilst strikes were forbidden the state dictated the wages which employers must pay. Industries were organised as corporations, not owned, but closely controlled by the state. As a further challenge to the Marxian creed the quarrel which had separated church and state since the national government had occupied Rome and dethroned the Pope was now composed. Mussolini was strong enough to recognise the Vatican as an international state, with the Pope as its sovereign. The crucifix was restored to the national schools. By conceding this shadow of international sovereignty Mussolini had grasped the substance of power. In a moral crisis the will of the secular despot was destined to prove decisive.

Mussolini had seen that the failure of Italians to sustain the rôle of a first-class power had been due to their own slackness and indifference. He has drilled them into efficiency by the application of military discipline to every department of civil life. And military organisation is from its nature swift to produce striking results. In a few years he has made the people of Italy feel that they stand second to no other in the world. They lift their heads and serve the state as never before since the early days of Imperial Rome. The failure of that majestic regime to beget in its subjects those qualities which make for abiding greatness was a longer and more instructive story than the rise of Caesarism.

NOTES

[1] King-Hall, *Our Own Times*, vol. i. p. 164.
[2] Benito Mussolini, *My Autobiography*, p. 30. Published by the Paternoster Library.
[3] Broad and Russell, *The Way of the Dictators*, p. 82.
[4] *Ibid.* p. 83.
[5] Benito Mussolini, *My Autobiography*, pp. 72-7.
[6] Broad and Russell, *The Way of the Dictators*, p. 85.
[7] Benito Mussolini, *My Autobiography*, p. 128.
[8] *Ibid.* p. 185.

CHAPTER LXIX

NAZISM

EXCEPT for the few years during which Napoleon was master in Europe the German people had never submitted to foreign rule or contracted a sense of inferiority. Had Bismarck believed, like Cavour, in popular government he might well have established that system in the home of the Reformation. But Bismarck was the product of a state which had risen to power by the military methods of Frederick the Great. On all but a fringe of the German people he imposed a system of government which made them the dominant power in Europe, and gave full play to their industry and gift for organisation. When he fell from power the amazing growth of its commerce was bringing the German Empire into the current of world affairs, where its rulers, less cautious than Bismarck, were to find that their will was not so decisive as in matters affecting Europe alone. The impatience of military rulers and their incapacity to measure the forces they challenged, ranged the greater part of the world against them in war. The plan to eliminate France from the conflict in a few weeks suddenly miscarried at the Marne. The German retreat was redeemed from any appearance of a rout by incomparable discipline. The high command had almost complete control of the information which reached, not only the troops, but the people behind them. To persuade the people, and still more the troops, that this first failure to reach Paris was no more than a temporary check was a task made possible by the almost unbroken record of military success on every front for close on four years.

Throughout those years the German soldiers were far more accustomed to victory than defeat. As the stocks of food and of raw materials dwindled they were the last to feel the effects. The final retreat, which began in August 1918 and never became a rout, demoralised starving civilians in Germany to a far greater extent than the men in the line, whose retreats had so often been followed by victorious advances. They had not been told how rapidly the early success of the submarine war on shipping had turned to failure. They were still holding the richest districts of France, and nearly the whole of Belgium when the news reached them that the government was suing for peace, that their war-lord was expelled from his throne and country at the word of an American president, that an armistice was signed which deprived them of all their weapons. They had presently to hear that the most humiliating peace in history had been signed and accepted by a government of Socialists and Jews. In the autobiography of Adolf Hitler we can see how men like himself, who had fought and endured all the horrors of the war, felt that their efforts had been betrayed by civilians behind the lines and not, as we now know, by a failure of nerve in the high command.

Hitler, as everyone knows, was an Austrian. His father, a cobbler, had risen a step in the social ladder when he somehow secured a post in the customs. That "hash of nations",[1] the Austro-Hungarian Empire, was a hotbed of racial antagonisms, and the young Hitler developed a stronger contempt for the Slavs and a more extravagant pride in his German blood than if he had grown to manhood in the German Empire itself. He lived in sight of its frontiers and yearned to belong to it.

The death of his parents had left him homeless and, when 17 years of age, he went to Vienna, where he hoped to enter the professional class, first as an artist and then as an architect. Poverty stood in his way. To earn his living he hired himself as a bricklayer's labourer, but lost his job on refusing to join the trade union. The incident gave a definite bent to his mind. In Vienna he also came into touch with the anti-Semitic movement and conceived an inveterate hatred of Jews.

In 1912 he left the Habsburg Empire, for which he conceived a profound contempt, and crossed the frontier to Munich. He was there when war was declared and on August 3 petitioned King Ludwig for leave to join a Bavarian regiment, which was granted the same day. He went to the western front and fought in the trenches throughout the war, was wounded, awarded the Iron Cross and, like Mussolini, rose to the rank of corporal. One is tempted to ask why a man with this record, who was afterwards destined to rule Germany, was never raised to commissioned rank. The answer might help to explain why the military empires were beaten at their own game of war by the allied democracies.

When the Armistice was signed Hitler was lying in hospital blinded by mustard gas. When discharged he went to join the reserve battalion of his regiment at Munich, to find it in the hands of a soldiers' council. He retired in disgust to a camp at Traunstein, but returned to Munich in the following March (1919).

When the Armistice was signed the King of Bavaria had fled. His place was taken by Socialist governments. A movement was set on foot (which the French were supporting) to detach the southern states from the Reich. The secessionist government in Munich was forcibly suppressed by bands of ex-soldiers or *Freikorps* led by General von Epp.

In the later years of the war the general staffs on either side had found it necessary to employ intelligence officers to watch trends of opinion which might weaken the discipline or morale of the ranks.

Von Epp and the soldiers who suppressed the Communist government in Munich were accustomed to such semi-political work. With the warning of Russia before them they were deeply concerned to prevent the soldiers from drifting into the Communist ranks. von Epp seems to have lighted on Hitler as a man suitable for work of this kind.

A few days after the liberation of Munich I was summoned to attend a Commission to inquire into the revolutionary events in the 2nd Infantry Regiment. That was my first incursion into more or less pure politics.

A few weeks after that I was ordered to attend a "course" for members of the Defence Force. The intention underlying this was to supply the soldier with definite principles to guide his thoughts as citizens of a State.[2]

It was in this work that Hitler began to be conscious of his gift as a speaker and to dream of founding a party of men who had fought in the war to retrieve the ruin brought on his country, as he believed, by Jews and democrats. He had studied the writings of Marx and was placing his own interpretation upon them, convinced that a Jew's real meaning must always be sought not in, but between, the lines that he writes. Throughout the pages of his autobiography runs the amazing idea that the Communist movement is really a deep-laid plot to enable Jewish capitalists to control and exploit mankind.

At this period he was influenced by the lectures of one Gottfried Feder, who drew a distinction between two kinds of capital, international Jewish exploitive loan capital and national productive capital. "The latter was purely the final outcome of creative labour", the former "owed its existence exclusively to speculation".

Thus the State's duty towards capital was comparatively simple and clear It merely had to see that capital remained the servant of the State and did not contemplate obtaining control of the nation. In taking this attitude the State could confine itself to two objects: maintenance of efficient national and independent administration on the one hand, and of the social rights of the workers on the other.[3]

These words explain why he afterwards described his followers as National Socialists.

One day I received orders from my Headquarters to go and find out what was going on in a society which was apparently political, and which was to hold a meeting during the next few days, under the name of the "German Workers' Party"; Gottfried Feder was to speak at it. I was to go to the meeting and have a look at the people, and then make a report.[4]

At the meeting Hitler learned that its founders were two obscure individuals, Drexler, a locksmith, and Harrer, a journalist. He listened to Feder's address, and when he sat down a professor got up to speak and suggested that the young party should aim at detaching Bavaria from Prussia and joining with Austria. Hitler sprang to his feet and delivered a flood of invective which, before he sat down, had driven the professor to fly from the room.

The speech had clearly made an impression. A few days later the committee sent him a postcard to say that his name was enrolled in the German Workers' Party and asked him to meet them. He attended the meeting to find that the so-called party had

no programme, not a leaflet, nothing at all in print, not even a miserable rubber stamp; but obviously plenty of faith and good intention. . . .

Fate seemed to be beckoning me. I should never have joined one of the existing great Parties, and I shall explain my reasons more precisely. In my eyes it seemed an advantage that this ridiculous little band, with its handful of members, had not stiffened into an 'organisation', but still offered the individual a real opening for personal activity. There was work to be done, and the smaller the Movement was, the sooner could it be pulled properly into shape. It was still possible to determine the character, objective and methods of this society, and that was quite impossible in the case of the existing great parties.

The longer I turned it over in my mind, the more the conviction grew in me that some small Movement such as this one might pave the way for the national resurrection, but that the political parties in Parliament never would, for they clung far too closely to obsolete conceptions or had an interest in propping up the new *régime*. For what had to be proclaimed here was a new theory of the world, and not a new election cry.

After two days of agonised meditation and questioning, I finally made up my mind to take the step. It was the decisive turning point of my life Retreat was neither possible nor desirable.

That is how I became a member of the German Workers' Party, and was given a provisional ticket of membership, bearing the number 'Seven'.[5]

Drexler and Harrer were powerless as robins to cope with a cuckoo hatched in their nest. Hitler at once insisted on frequent meetings, summoned by postcards typed by himself. At the first 7 people appeared; at the next 11; then 13, 23, 34. He then decided to risk the party funds on a notice in the *Münchener Beobachter* (the "Munich Observer"), an ultra-patriotic and anti-Semitic paper. One hundred and eleven people came to this meeting and Hitler was allowed to address them himself. He dwelt on the sufferings of Germany, the malice of the Allies, the treachery of Marxists and Jews, the iniquities of the Peace. The effect of his eloquence is shown by the fact that the audience contributed 300 marks. Demobilised soldiers began to join the party in numbers and Harrer and Drexler were rapidly pushed into the background.

In February 1920 Hitler once more decided to stake the whole funds of the movement on a meeting, this time in a hall large enough to hold nearly 2000 people. Now for the first time guards of ex-soldiers were organised to suppress interrupters. The opening speech of Dr. Johannes Dingfelder left the audience cold. Then Hitler followed on the theme 'Germany waken'. Germany must be saved from the wrongs done her by France, the Allies, the 'November criminals'.

In a few minutes interruptions hailed on me and there were violent scenes in the body of the hall; a handful of faithful war comrades and a few other adherents engaged the disturbers and managed to restore quiet after a bit.[6]

Hitler then proceeded to read the programme prepared by Feder—union of all Germans in a greater Germany, the abrogation of the Treaty of Versailles, the return of the German colonies, the purging of Jews from the nation, abolition of unearned incomes, confiscation of war profits, nationalisation of trusts, old-age pensions, the destruction of departmental stores in the interest of small shop-keepers, confiscation of land for public purposes, the cancellation of mortgages, and the penalty of death on usury, the substitution of German for Roman law, educational reform, protection of mothers and children, abolition of child labour, physical development for youth, a national army, exclusion of Jews from the press, and national control of the press, the common interest before self, a strong centralised unitary state.

The applause began to drown the interruptions and hooting, and finally, when I had explained the 25 points, I had before me a hall full of people united in a new conviction, a new faith, a new will. A fire had been kindled, from the glow of which the sword was to emerge, destined to restore freedom to the Germanic Siegfried and life to the German nation.[7]

It was after this meeting at which the twenty-five points of the programme were announced and expounded by Hitler that he changed the name of the party to National Socialist German Workers' Party. At the end of this year (1920) he was able to buy the *Münchener Beobachter*. The 60,000 marks for the purpose were obtained from von Epp by one of his officers, Captain Röhm, who was No. 60 in the list of the German Workers' Party. As Hitler meant to appeal to the German people as a whole he changed the name of the paper to *Völkischer Beobachter*. There is in the English language no single equivalent for the word 'Völkischer'. It includes ideas which appeal to nationalist sentiment but also to radical feeling. Its choice illustrates the genius of Hitler for attracting the widest possible circle. This paper filled in the Nazi movement the part which *Il Popolo d'Italia* was playing in Italy.

All over Germany, and especially in Bavaria, discharged and often homeless soldiers, like Hitler himself, had formed themselves into *Freikorps* like the *squadre* in Italy. Their members were now drawn in ever-increasing numbers into the Nazi party, of which Hitler was now the recognised leader. The manner in which Mussolini and Hitler rose to power in the same way at the same time was due to similar conditions in either country produced by the war and the so-called peace which followed it. How and when the two movements came into touch is a question which cannot at present be answered. It must have been at an early date, for the question of redeeming the Germans in the southern Tyrol from Italian rule has never been raised in the Nazi programme.

In 1922 Göring, the most brilliant of the airmen who survived the war and a man of wealth, came to Munich to attend a course at the university. He there met Hitler, made large contributions to his funds and undertook to organise the storm troops (S.A.).

The march on Rome in 1922, which raised Mussolini to power, inspired the ambitions of Hitler to follow his tactics. Mussolini's example had already been copied by the Marquis de Estella in Spain. The Ruhr had been occupied by the French, and the mark began to fall, until by the end of the year it was worthless. Black troops were quartered in Germany and the sense of humiliation was deeper than that which its people had felt at the time of the Armistice. The Nazis were raising the cries, 'Up in arms against Red Berlin', 'Never rest till the criminals of November 9, 1918, are overthrown', 'The pigsty in Berlin must be cleaned out'. By the autumn their members had risen to 70,000. Ludendorff joined in the movement and leading industrialists began to finance it.

At this time General von Kahr, together with General von Lossow, who commanded the Bavarian reichswehr, and Lieutenant von Seisser at the head of the Munich police, ruled in Bavaria as a kind of triumvirate. On November 8, 1923, von Kahr was addressing a mass meeting in Munich when Hitler suddenly entered surrounded by Nazi storm troopers. He leapt onto a table, fired two shots in the air to secure attention and announced that a national revolution had broken out and that no one must leave the hall. He then requested Kahr, Lossow and Seisser to join him in an anteroom while Göring addressed the meeting.

In the anteroom Hitler asked the triumvirate to join him in a march on Berlin, and threatened to shoot them and then commit suicide if they refused. They finally agreed and returned to the hall, where Hitler announced that President Ebert would be deposed, or else he and his confederates would perish in the attempt to establish a national government. Ludendorff, who was present, threw himself into the movement and marched next morning arrayed in a top-hat and frock-coat with Hitler, Göring and Röhm at the head of the storm troopers. In the course of the night the triumvirate had taken measures to suppress the movement they had promised to support. The Nazi column was met by police and troops who opened fire and killed eighteen of them. The soldiers were careful to miss Ludendorff, who was easily distinguished by his civilian costume. Hitler, Göring and Röhm, who were by him, probably owed their lives to this fact.

Göring escaped; but Ludendorff, Hitler and Röhm were arrested and tried with some others. The state of public opinion, inflamed by the Ruhr occupation, reduced the trial to a farce. Hitler used the court as a platform from which to address the German people.

> The future of Germany means the annihilation of Marxism. . . . Our movement was not founded to secure seats in parliament and stipends; our movement was founded to change the destiny for Germany in the eleventh hour. . . . Who is born to be a dictator will not be pressed, but must himself press forward. . . . Who feels himself called to rule a people has not the right to say: When you want me or send for me, I will come. He has the duty to do. . . . I carry the responsibility all alone. I cannot concede that I am guilty, but I concede my deed.[8]

On April 1, 1924, Ludendorff was acquitted. Hitler was sent to the fortress of Landsberg, given a comfortable room there, treated with every consideration and released by the end of the year. He employed these months in writing *Mein Kampf*, which became in the Nazi movement as sacred as the Koran in Islam, or the writings of Marx in the Third International.

His imprisonment also gave him leisure to reconsider the tactics he had copied from Mussolini. He now seems to have realised the folly of any course which might lead to an armed conflict between his following and the Reichswehr. He foresaw that the small regular army would agree with his aims, and would readily support him if once he obtained the legal right to command their obedience. He could then with ease abolish the Republic and establish himself as dictator. He none the less relied on the organised force of ex-soldiers drawn from the lower middle class to fight the communist movement, and help him to win seats in the Reichstag.

Marx was wrong in his forecast that the salaried class would be drawn into the wage-earning class and merged in the proletariat. Improvements in mechanisation tend to reduce the number of manual workers and to increase the number of those required to direct them, to keep the accounts and to advertise and market the products of industry.[9] Before the war this salaried and shopkeeping class in Germany had never succeeded in forming a political party. The trade unions had enabled the manual workers to establish a formidable party in bitter opposition to the ruling and propertied classes, whose arrogance had led the country to war and defeat. As prices were raised by inflation the unions had also helped them to secure a rise in wages. The class to which Hitler appealed had not been able to secure a corresponding rise in their salaries and were suffering even greater privations than the classes above and below them. Besides the salaried class were numbers of young men like Hitler himself, who were trained only to war and its ways, such men as the British government had enrolled in the Black and Tans. Hitler, like Mussolini, had seen that Marx and Lenin could be fought with their own weapons. If manual workers could create a dictatorship so also might young men of his class, so many of whom had served like himself as corporals or sergeants in the ranks. All that was needed was one of themselves who knew how to lead them. And it so happened that the closely organised proletariat had failed to produce any one with the qualities of a leader. Had the German Marxians found a Lenin, the constant riots which distracted Germany for nearly ten years would quickly have grown into civil war, in which blood would have flowed like water. As it was, leadership and discipline was all on the side of the Nazis, and when men appeal to physical force to decide political issues leadership and discipline are more potent than numbers in a mechanised world. "It never troubles a wolf how many the sheep be."

As recent events have shown in Russia, a movement based on physical force has its own internal problem to face. Hitler, like Mussolini, had sought to gather the largest possible following by appealing to socialists as well as to nationalists. In Prussia the Nazis were extreme in their socialism. They began to view with suspicion the attitude of Hitler, tempered, no doubt, by concern to secure contributions to the funds of the party from the propertied class. In December 1925 two brothers, Gregor and Otto Strasser, assembled at Hanover the leaders of districts (*Gauleiters*) in northern and western Germany. The cry was raised 'We will not be governed by the Munich Pope'. Feder, who was sent by his leader to watch the proceedings, reported the gathering as 'anti-Hitler'. In May 1926 a further meeting was held at Bamberg. Gregor Strasser returned to the charge, bringing with him his secretary, Dr. Paul Joseph Goebbels. Hitler had arranged that his own partisans should attend this meeting in predominant numbers. Goebbels, seeing how things were going, deserted Strasser and transferred his allegiance to Hitler. On May 22 the meeting adopted a declaration that the twenty-five points were unalterable. The open dispute whether the party should stand for more or less socialism was closed on the surface. It was also during this period that Röhm differed from Hitler as to the rôle of the storm troopers. Röhm had resigned his command in the force and had gone to Bolivia to take part in the struggle with Paraguay. These quarrels continued to smoulder till in June 1934 they were quenched in blood.

In May 1924, a month after Hitler was sent to

Landsberg, an election was held. The Nazis decided to try their fortunes in alliance with Count Reventlow's party. To the general astonishment they polled nearly 2,000,000 votes and secured the election of 32 members to the Reichstag, including Ludendorff, Röhm and Feder. At the end of the year 1924 another election was held; but this time the Nazi vote was more than halved, and they only secured the election of 14 members. The adoption of the Dawes plan by the Reparations Commission in April 1924 had been followed by the rapid investment of British and American capital in German industries, which had greatly relieved the distress created by the Ruhr occupation and the flight from the mark. In December 1925 the Treaty of Locarno, signed in London, did even more to revive prosperity. The German government joined the League, which for the next few years seemed destined to realise the hopes of its founders. Throughout these years of hope and prosperity the Nazi party, under the inspired leadership of Hitler, increased, but not at a pace to alarm public opinion at home or abroad. The growth in the number of its members was as follows:

1925 . . .	27,000
1926 . . .	49,000
1927 . . .	72,000
1928 . . .	108,000
1929 . . .	178,000[10]

At the close of this last year the panic suddenly broke in New York and rapidly spread to the rest of the world. British and American bankers began to recall the loans they had made to the German banks. By 1931 the numbers of unemployed had risen from under 2,000,000 in 1929 to more than 4,500,000 and, again, to over 6,000,000 in 1933. The effect on the growth of the Nazi party is shown by the following figures:

1929 . . .	178,000
1930 . . .	389,000
1931 . . .	862,000
January 1932 . . .	920,000
June 1932 . . .	1,200,000[11]

The return of depression accomplished the doom of the Weimar Republic and threw the game into Hitler's hands. In the field of domestic affairs the Social Democrats had a notable record. They had thrown themselves into the task of fighting the physical diseases which war and starvation had left in their train. They had very greatly improved the system of education and extended the social services. As with all such measures, when properly organised, the results were slow to mature. Most of the splendid social reforms which foreign visitors now admire are the fruits of measures conceived and effected by popular governments under the Weimar Republic.

In March 1930 Müller, the last socialist chancellor, resigned. His successor, Brüning, the leader of the Centrists, was afterwards described by Hindenburg as "the best since Bismarck". In July Brüning was defeated in the Reichstag and a general election was fixed for December 14. With daemonic energy Hitler threw himself into the contest. He recalled Captain Röhm from Bolivia and gave him command of the storm troopers. The electoral campaign was conducted with a violence greater than the Fascists had used in Italy. The Nazis polled more than 6,400,000 votes. They secured 107 seats in the Reichstag and were now second in strength only to the 143 seats held by the Social Democrats. Before this election the Nazis had been "regarded in the German and foreign press as an insignificant group of fanatics".[12] The world was now to find itself faced with a second and enlarged edition of Mussolini in central Europe.

The Centrum party which followed Brüning had

won but 68 seats and was fourth on the list, for the Communist members were 77. But Brüning remained in office and, with Hindenburg's consent, ruled by emergency decrees under Article 48 of the constitution.

The elections of 1930 were followed by heavy withdrawals of foreign capital. On July 14, 1931, all banks in Germany but the Reichsbank were closed by decree. In March 1932 Hindenburg's tenure of office as president lapsed. He agreed to seek re-election, and Hitler decided to stand against him. Brüning conducted an active campaign in Hindenburg's favour, and the speeches he made secured his return to office. In the final result Hindenburg was elected with 53 per cent of the votes cast. Hitler was second on the list of candidates with 36·8 per cent of the votes.

Brüning, however, was determined to break up the bankrupt landed estates in East Prussia, and the Junkers had made up their minds to drive him from office before he could carry his measures. With Hindenburg safely elected as president once more, they felt that their hour had come, and General von Schleicher, a master of intrigue, was employed to persuade the president that Brüning must go. On Sunday, May 29, Brüning was summoned to the presence of Hindenburg, who read from notes in his hand a series of complaints against his ministry. Brüning replied, and after nearly an hour's discussion put the question, "Do you wish me to resign?" Hindenburg answered, "It is against my conscience to keep a Cabinet which is so unpopular; it must go as soon as possible. But you must remain as Foreign Minister in a new Government, as Stresemann did. That is your duty." Brüning replied, "I, too, have a conscience and it forbids me, at a moment when the State is in peril, to change my mind every day."[13]

The cabinet met and decided to resign. Early next day the American ambassador informed Brüning that Herriot had agreed to consider proposals for disarmament which Brüning had made at Geneva and Tardieu had refused to discuss. The American ambassador had been told to persuade him to return to Geneva as soon as possible, for there was every prospect of his speedy success. Schleicher got wind of this message and cleverly managed that Brüning should have no chance of informing Hindenburg before his dismissal had taken effect. For Brüning had always looked for success in the field of foreign affairs for holding his own with the German people. The agreements which closed at Lausanne the disastrous chapter of reparations were his work. But as with the Social Democrats, the fruits were gathered by those who threw him from power.

On May 31 Papen was named chancellor, with General von Schleicher as minister of war. The Reichstag was dissolved and a general election announced for July 31, at which the Nazis secured 230 seats and became the largest party in the Reichstag. The country, meanwhile, was plunging towards utter confusion. Blood was freely shed in the streets in fights between Nazis and Communists. Murders were of almost daily occurrence. Behind the scenes industrial magnates, Junkers and Nazi leaders were involved in a network of plots and counter-plots, the stories of which recall the age of the Borgias. A slight revival of trade in the autumn of 1932 seemed to be turning the scale against Hitler. The industrial magnates began to withhold their subscriptions to his party, which fell into dire financial straits. The moment had come, so Papen appears to have thought, for another general election. It was held in November 1932. The Nazi vote was reduced by 2,000,000 whilst the Communist vote was increased by 750,000. But as 90 per cent of the total votes were cast against Papen's government, Schleicher decided that Papen must go and manœuvred him into resigning. Hindenburg vetoed Hitler's offer to form a government supported, as Brüning had been, by presidential decrees. On December 4 Schleicher himself was called to the office of chancellor and Gregor Strasser deserted Hitler to support him. Papen, determined to have his revenge on Schleicher, was at work bringing the industrialists and Hitler together. In view of the fact that Hitler had now parted with his Socialist colleague, Gregor Strasser, 4,000,000 marks were provided to save the Nazi treasury from impending bankruptcy. Schleicher was threatening to expose scandals into which a Reichstag commission was looking. It seems that money which the Reichstag had voted to relieve agricultural distress had found its way into landowners' pockets. On January 28 Hindenburg sent for Schleicher and asked him to withhold a statement on the subject which a Reichstag committee was demanding. Schleicher refused and resigned. On January 30, 1933, Hitler became chancellor with Göring in his cabinet. Papen became vice-chancellor, Hugenberg minister of economics and von Blomberg minister of defence. On February 1 the Reichstag was dissolved and new elections ordered for March 5.

On February 27 the Reichstag building went up in flames. Whilst the fire was burning the broadcasting stations and the press were informing the German people that this was the first act of a Communist rising to be followed by the looting of Berlin, a Communist terror and civil war throughout Germany. Hitler proclaimed his purpose to save the nation. "It will be my principal task", said Göring, "to extirpate Communism from our people. Let me tell the Communists my nerves have never given way up to now, and I feel strong enough to repay their criminal activities in kind."[14] Within twelve hours of the fire the Nazi government had seized and monopolised an exclusive control of the press as well as the wireless stations. When the general election took place on March 5 the voters had heard and read no view of the situation but that which the Nazi government had given. Of the votes polled 43·9 per cent were cast for the Nazis. Of the 647 deputies elected 288 were Nazis. Though the largest party they had failed to secure a clear majority.

On March 21 the Reichstag met at the Kroll Opera in Berlin. It was asked to consider an 'Enabling Act' which empowered the cabinet to enact whatever laws it might choose without reference to the Reichstag. The measure was opposed by Otto Wels on behalf of the Socialists. A vote was taken amid shouts from the Brown Shirts, who surrounded the building. The Enabling Act was passed into law by 441 votes to 94.

The utter collapse of the Social Democrats was possibly due to the fact that their leaders were worn out by the work they had done for years to restore the fabric of national life under conditions imposed by the Treaty of Versailles. They had seen the ruin to which a regime based on authority had led, and were trying to establish in Germany a system based on consent. Like liberals elsewhere, they too often forgot that even a government based on electoral majorities must enforce the law when persuasion has failed. Their destroyer had not committed the opposite error. He had read the lesson of his own failure in 1923 and seen the wisdom of giving the face of violence a mask of legality with holes for its eyes. The Enabling Act passed by the Reichstag legalised an absolute despotism. With the Nazi regime in control of police and the army there was nothing to check the zeal of his Brown Shirts. Communists, Socialists, Jews, all who had raised their voices against them were swept into concentration camps.

> At the height of the Terror 20,000 inhabitants of Germany were, at the lowest computation, living behind the wire in conditions which remain a perpetual reproach to the governors of a supposedly civilised community.[15]

Henceforward Hitler could appeal to popular votes with safety. When he chose to do so in November (1933) almost 90 per cent of the votes cast were given in his favour.

With a stroke of the pen Hitler was now able to do what Bismarck himself had not dared to attempt. The governments of the states were deprived of all independent powers, and the German Reich lost all traces of its federal structure. It became a unitary and highly centralised despotism which claimed to control its subjects on every side of their lives.

This 'totalitarian' claim, pressed with German vigour and thoroughness, was soon to bring the Nazi regime into conflict with the Catholic and Protestant Churches. Its hatred of Jews helped to divorce it from the Christian religion itself. It now began to revert to Hegel's idea, which identified God with the national state, an idea which took popular shape in reviving the pagan cult of tribal deities.

On the field which ended our own civil wars the Royalist general surrendered his sword with the words, "Now gentlemen you can do as you please —unless you choose to fight with each other". By 1934 the Nazis had mastered and suppressed all organised movements opposed to them. Relieved from external pressure the cleavage between nationalists and socialists, conservatives and radicals, which Hitler had closed on the surface in 1926, began to reopen. Mixed with this issue was the question whether the Reichswehr, the regular army of 100,000 men controlled by Junker and conservative interests and commanded by von Blomberg, should swallow the Brown Shirts, or whether the 2,500,000 Brown Shirts commanded by Röhm should swallow the Reichswehr. Extremists to the left of the Nazi party were beginning to look to Röhm as their leader. Hitler was alive to the evident danger that the Brown Shirts headed by Röhm might do with him what he, through their agency, had done to others. With this danger in view he had formed a bodyguard dressed in black shirts, whose personal devotion to himself he could trust.

In the spring of 1934 Hitler and von Blomberg had agreed to support each other as against the ambitions of Röhm. In discussing plans for disarmament, Hitler, on April 16, had offered the British government to deprive the Brown Shirts and other para-military organisations of their arms. This offer decided the Nazi extremists and Röhm to remove Hitler from power, and seize control of the state and the Reichswehr whilst the Brown Shirts still had arms in their hands. Hitler, Göring and Goebbels got wind of the plot. Their plans were laid to remove the conspirators before they could strike.

In framing the list of those to die it is fairly safe to conjecture that this modern triumvirate unconsciously followed the precedent set two thousand years before and rendered immortal by Shakespeare.

> *Antony.* These many then shall die; their names are prick'd.
> *Octavius.* Your brother too must die; consent you, Lepidus?
> *Lepidus.* I do consent.
> *Octavius.* Prick him down, Antony.
> *Lepidus.* Upon condition Publius shall not live,
> Who is your sister's son, Mark Antony.
> *Antony.* He shall not live; look, with a spot I damn him.

It was even so that these modern triumvirs decided that former brothers in arms must die. But when blood is to flow like water, why spare former enemies public or private? It is most unlikely that the hundreds destined to perish were all connected with Röhm's conspiracy.

On June 29 the *Völkischer Beobachter* published an article by General von Blomberg in which he said that the Reichswehr stood once more on firm ground, since the upheaval of June 1933 had given them back the foundations without which an army could not exist. The article concluded:

The warrior community of the trenches which Adolf Hitler has made the basis of the new national community becomes the starting point of the great tradition which the armed forces, as heirs of the old Army, have taken over.[16]

Through the small hours of Saturday, June 30, Hitler and Goebbels flew to Munich, surprised Röhm, Heines and other Nazi leaders in bed, and ordered their execution with a number of confederates. In Berlin Göring was busy. At 1.30 P.M. Gregor Strasser was kidnapped by storm troopers and, according to his brother, was beaten and trampled to death in a wood. A car full of men in plain clothes drove up to the door of General von Schleicher, rang the bell and shot the late chancellor and his wife as they opened the door. The mutilated body of General von Kahr, who, together with General von Lossow and Lieutenant von Seisser, had fooled Hitler at Munich in 1923, was found in a swamp. His two confederates escaped from the country. Papen was saved by the intervention of Hindenburg; but some of his personal staff were shot.

For several days the firing parties drawn from the Black Shirts continued their work. The bodies of some of the victims were burned and the ashes sent to their relatives by post. On one of these packets was the number 238; but the total number of those who perished is unknown. The Brown Shirts were given a month's leave without arms or uniforms. Two out of three were dismissed, and the force reduced to 800,000. The organisation, which had mastered all others by violence, had learned that violence could be used to its utmost expression by its leader to enforce his authority. Such expedients impose themselves on systems which try to find a permanent basis in physical force. As my pen records how Hitler destroyed Strasser and Röhm, Tomsky has died by his own hand and Stalin is sending Zinoviev, Kamenev and others of his former comrades to the shambles in Moscow.

In this hour I was responsible for the fate of the German nation; thereby the supreme court of the German people, during these twenty-four hours, consisted of myself.[17]

Such were the words in which Hitler explained his conduct to the Reichstag on July 13. On July 12 Göring had said in a public speech:

The action of the State leadership in those days was the highest realisation of the legal consciousness of the people. . . .

I have clearly said to you that the rule of the law must be assured. There can be only one concept of the law: namely, the one laid down by Der Führer. . . . The law and the will of Der Führer are one.[18]

Never in history has the rule of law been rejected in more unequivocal words, or the principle of tyranny proclaimed so directly. A month later, when the aged Hindenburg died, Hitler claimed that the powers of the president should now be combined in his own person with those of chancellor. In the plebiscite taken the claim was approved by close on 90 per cent of the voters. As the secretary of the chancellory announced:

There is no need for a constitution regulating the conduct of affairs of State; at any rate, there is no need for a written constitution. One thing suffices in the National-socialist State: a fanatical will, based on faith in the principle of leadership and loyalty to Der Führer and those whom he leads, to possess a German State which will unite all Germans in a national and social community. . . .

Herr Hitler has joined the functions of the President with those of the Chancellor and holds the joint offices for the period of his life.[19]

NOTES

[1] Adolf Hitler, *My Struggle*, p. 20. Published by the Paternoster Library.
[2] *Ibid.* pp. 93, 94.
[3] *Ibid.* p. 95.
[4] *Ibid.* p. 98.
[5] *Ibid.* pp. 100, 101.
[6] *Ibid.* p. 142.
[7] *Ibid.* pp. 142, 143.
[8] Schuman, *Hitler and the Nazi Dictatorship*, pp. 41, 42.
[9] *Ibid.* p. 101.
[10] *Ibid.* p. 72.
[11] *Ibid.* pp. 72, 73.
[12] *Ibid.* p. 131.
[13] John W. Wheeler-Bennett, *Hindenburg*, pp. 392, 393. Macmillan & Co.
[14] Broad and Russell, *The Way of the Dictators*, p. 55.
[15] *Ibid.* p. 62.
[16] *Bulletin*, vol. xi., No. 1, p. 19.
[17] Schuman, *Hitler and the Nazi Dictatorship*, p. 459.
[18] *Ibid.* pp. 301, 302.
[19] *Ibid.* p. 469.

CHAPTER LXX

MANCHURIA

In the Great War the belligerent states, whose very existence was threatened, were driven to assume control of the national life in all its aspects. The totalitarian regimes are attempts by leaders, inured to the habits of war, to establish on a permanent footing a system of government devised for the purpose of war. The model erected in Italy was widely copied in countries which had not developed the habits required for responsible government. At one time or another a regime of this kind was established in Spain, Turkey, Poland and Greece, and in most of the Balkan and Baltic states. On the opposite side of the world the Japanese Empire was by its nature and history disposed to a system of government based on the sword.

We have seen how the Emperor Meiji ended the reign of the Shoguns and the power of the Daimyo, and attached to himself and his throne the loyalty of their feudal retainers. His achievement enabled his people to reveal their genius for organisation. In one generation they created the army and navy which broke the power of Russia, and gave them a permanent footing on the continent in Korea and the Liaotung Peninsula. But as with Rome in ancient days, the occupation of conquered countries beyond the sea helped to establish the standing army as a power with an outlook and policy of its own not fully controlled by the government at home.

In China, Dr. Sun Yat Sen, a Cantonese trained at Hongkong, had long been preparing a revolution. In 1911 he brought to an end the last of the numerous dynasties which had ruled China for thousands of years. In hopes of uniting the country he accepted the most powerful minister at Peking, Yuan Shih-kai, as first president of the Chinese Republic. Yuan was hoping to use his position as a step to the throne, in the hopes of founding a new dynasty.

When the war broke out in 1914 Yuan, supported by President Wilson, proposed that hostilities should be excluded from Chinese waters and territories. Japan refused to agree, and sent an ultimatum to Germany demanding the cession of Kiaochow and her rights in Shantung. On August 23 Japan declared war and seized Kiaochow. While the powers of Europe were at war with each other, Japan, with her feet in Shantung, felt herself free to do as she pleased with China. In January 1915 she demanded rights from Peking which were meant to secure her the same position in China as England had acquired in Egypt. Wilson, learning what was afoot, notified China and Japan that Washington would not recognise such an agreement if made. The agreement was none the less forced on the Chinese, with certain modifications, and embodied in two treaties signed on May 25, 1915.

In February 1917 the cause of the Allies was gravely imperilled by the submarine menace. In return for destroyers to patrol the Mediterranean they agreed to support the claims of Japan in Shantung. After America entered the war she also agreed to recognise that 'Japan had special interests in China'. In August 1917 China declared war on Germany in order to secure a voice in the final settlement. When the war came to an end Yuan was dead and the south of China had broken away from the north with a rival government in Canton. These two governments agreed to send a joint delegation to Paris. Their position was gravely weakened by China's internal divisions, and President Wilson, intent on securing the adhesion of Japan to the League of Nations, agreed to recognise her right to retain Tsingtao and the economic concessions which Germany had lost in Shantung. The Chinese delegates refused to sign the Treaty of Versailles; but secured admission to the League of Nations by signing the Treaty of St. Germain.

The treatment accorded to China at Paris was one of the reasons which led the Senate to reject the Treaty of Versailles. In America public opinion was demanding a stronger navy, for relations with Japan were now seriously strained. Before launching his naval programme President Harding decided to call an international conference to discuss limitation of naval armaments and the settlement of affairs in the Far East. Great Britain, prompted by Canada, decided not to renew her alliance with Japan if an all-round settlement of the Far East, to which the United States was a party, could be secured. The conference opened at Washington in November 1921 and there Shidehara accepted a drastic revision of the treaties which his country had forced on China in 1915. He also agreed to withdraw the Japanese forces which were still in Shantung to the town of Tsingtao. The nine Powers represented at Washington, the U.S.A., Belgium, the British Empire, China, France, Italy, Japan, Holland and Portugal signed a treaty which bound them all to respect the sovereignty of China and the open door to trade in that country. While Shidehara remained in office the arrangements were observed in the spirit as well as in the letter.

China, meanwhile, was in chaos. In the north, authority had passed on the death of Yuan to the general in each province who commanded the strongest army. In the south, Sun Yat Sen, rebuffed as a visionary by the British and American governments, turned for help to Soviet Russia. Two able

Russian advisers were sent to Canton. The one, Borodin, a master of Bolshevist propaganda, created round Sun Yat Sen the kind of legend which in Russia had grown round the name of Lenin. The legend was greatly enhanced by the death of Sun in 1925. The other adviser, Galens, a soldier of high capacity, established a military institute at Canton. At the head of it he placed the young Chiang Kai-shek, who had served as secretary to Sun Yat Sen.

In July 1926 the Cantonese armies started their march to the north under Chiang Kai-shek. By September he had reached the Yangtze and had occupied Hankow. In March 1927 the Nationalist forces had seized Nanking. In June the Cantonese leaders discovered that Moscow had ordered Borodin to establish a Communist government to take their place. Borodin and Galens fled for their lives, and relations with Moscow were severed. At the end of 1927 Chiang Kai-shek proclaimed Nanking as the capital of China.

In that year Shidehara resigned. His place was taken by Tanaka, who reflected the views of the militant faction.

In the spring of 1928 Chiang Kai-shek crossed the Yangtze, hoping to reach Peking before three northern war-lords could seize it, Yen Hsi-shan from Shansi, Feng-husiang from Honan and Chang Tso-lin from Manchuria. On May 8 his advance was stopped at Tsinan by Japanese forces landed at Tsingtao. The Chinese army was driven back with considerable bloodshed, and its route to Peking was blocked. The Japanese ordered Chang Tso-lin to return with his troops to Manchuria. He obeyed, and as his train was passing on June 3 under the bridge which carried the Japanese railway over the Chinese line at Mukden an explosion occurred which killed him. In July 1929 Tanaka was forced to resign by debates in the Japanese diet, in which his opponents alleged that the murder of Chang Tso-lin had been planned by Japanese officers. For the next two years his Liberal successors were trying to control the Japanese officers in their relations with the Young Marshal Chang Hsüeh-liang, who had taken the place of his father Chang Tso-lin.

The wave of anger which passed over China, and led to a boycott of Japanese goods, was strong enough for the moment to force the generals striving for the mastery of Peking to abate their rivalry. On July 7, 1928, Chiang Kai-shek, who had made his way to Peking, attended a ceremony with Yen Hsi-shan and Feng-husiang to announce to the spirit of Sun Yat Sen that China was now united under the government of Nanking. It was formally recognised as the government of China by the U.S.A. on July 25, and also by Great Britain and most of the powers in the following December.

The appearance of unity attained by Nanking was illusory. For years China, north and south of the Yangtze, was distracted by civil wars. The government at Nanking was fighting for its life, first with the war-lords and then with the Communists, a movement which sprung from the same agrarian causes as the Taiping Rebellion. In the north the Young Marshal was picking a quarrel with Soviet Russia, arresting her consuls and dismissing Russian officials from the railway administration. Russia applied for redress to Nanking and threatened to recover her rights by force. The U.S.A., Great Britain and France then hastened to remind Russia and China that both of them, in signing the Kellogg Pact, had agreed to renounce the use of war as an instrument of policy. In the autumn of 1929 Russia, without declaring war on China, sent General Galens with 3000 Soviet troops to assert her rights in Manchuria. The forces sent by the

Young Marshal to meet them were scattered like chaff. In December 1929 he agreed to recognise all the claims of the Soviet government.

The example which Russia had set was not lost on the Japanese army. In the course of the next two years the collapse which began in New York had begun to affect both Japan and Manchuria. In 1929 Japan's export of raw silk was worth 780,000,000 yen, of which silk to the value of 755,000,000 yen went to America. By 1932 these figures had sunk to 382,000,000 and 362,000,000.[1] The fall in prices destroyed the profits of the railways owned by Japan in Manchuria. Their traffic was further reduced by the competition of railways built by the government of Manchuria with money borrowed from Japanese banks, the interest on which was now in arrears. A fall in the value of Manchurian currency was also attracting the traffic from the Japanese to the Chinese lines. The government of Chang Hsüeh-liang evaded the settlement of disputes, which were numbered by hundreds. Koreans settled by Japan were murdered by Chinese peasants. On August 17, 1931, the Japanese war office reported that on June 17 Chinese soldiers in Mongolia had murdered one of their officers, Captain Nakamura.

The Japanese army had now resolved to seize control of foreign affairs from the powerful commercial interests which supported the policy of Shidehara. With this end in view they set out to secure the support of the peasants, from whom the rank and file of the army were drawn. On September 9 *The Times* correspondent in Tokyo reported that a squadron of six army planes, in a flight round the Japanese Alps, had dropped 100,000 leaflets calling on the nation to awake to the danger threatening Japanese rights in Manchuria. On September 15 came the rumour of troubles in the British navy, followed by heavy withdrawals of gold from London, which drove the pound off the gold standard. The moment had come to follow the example which Russia had set in northern Manchuria. On September 18 the Japanese high command announced that the South Manchurian railway had been cut near Mukden by Chinese soldiers. Japanese forces at once seized the town, burned the barracks and shot a number of Chinese soldiers. At the same time strategic points in various parts of Manchuria were occupied by Japanese forces with a swiftness which showed that plans had been fully prepared for such an emergency.

When all this happened the Young Marshal Chang Hsüeh-liang was away on a visit to Peiping. General Honjo, who commanded the Japanese army, had his furniture and personal effects packed into cases and sent after him. Early in October General Honjo proclaimed in Mukden that the rule of Marshal Chang Hsüeh-liang was no longer recognised in Manchuria. The Japanese government announced that this proclamation was made without their authority. General Honjo ignored the announcement and proceeded to seize and administer the whole of Manchuria.

In China south of the Wall the boycott of Japanese goods, which had started in 1928, was immediately tightened and carried to the furthest extremes. At Shanghai the shops refused to sell food to Japanese residents. Labourers in Japanese factories struck, and Chinese clerks refused to serve in Japanese offices. Frequent clashes occurred in the streets. On October 8, 1931, the Japanese consul-general warned the mayor of Greater Shanghai that unless protection was given to Japanese residents he would take his own measures.

By the end of the year Japanese business was completely paralysed, and on January 20, 1932, the consul-general served five specific demands on the mayor of Greater Shanghai. On the following day

Admiral Shiozawa threatened to enforce them. The Japanese navy was itching to emulate the achievements of the rival service in the north. On the night of January 28-29 Japanese planes bombed the railway station at Chapei. Marines were sent by the admiral from the International Settlement to occupy the ruins. They met with a check; for the Nineteenth Army, which had just arrived from Canton, held the position with surprising tenacity.

On February 1 Japanese warships shelled Nanking, and the Chinese government moved beyond their reach to Loyang.

In recent years Russian and Japanese forces had scattered the armies of China like chaff, wherever they met them. In defending the narrow streets of Shanghai and the country beyond, which is seamed by canals and embankments, the Chinese were showing a power of resistance which Shiozawa had not foreseen. This fact was quickly realised by the naval authorities in Tokyo, who called on the war office to send a division without delay. By the end of February four divisions, fully equipped, had been sent to Shanghai. From the International Settlement to the forts at Woosung, which command the mouth of the Whangpoo river where it empties into the Yangtze, the fighting raged till the whole of this populous district was laid in ruins. By March 3 the Japanese troops had forced the Chinese back and were holding a line some twenty miles west of the Whangpoo. At this juncture the Japanese and Chinese commanders were brought together by American, British and other European officers in Shanghai. On April 27 an armistice was concluded and signed on May 5, under which the Japanese agreed to withdraw their forces from the Chinese territory they had occupied.

In the meantime the Japanese army was extending its hold over Manchuria. 'A self-governing guiding board' was established at Mukden. It consisted of local Chinese officials closely controlled by Japanese officers. On February 18 a 'Declaration of Independence' was published, and Mr. Pu Yi, the dethroned Emperor of China, was appointed to figure as chief executive of the state to which the name of Manchukuo was given. (He was afterwards given the title of Emperor.) The country was occupied by Japanese troops up to the Amur river and thus brought into dangerous contact with the frontiers of Soviet Russia. In January 1933 Japanese troops seized first the province of Jehol and then the passes through the Great Wall immediately south of Jehol. From these strategic positions they could penetrate Inner and Outer Mongolia and so threaten the Soviet frontiers from the south. They could also threaten Peiping and dominate the provinces of China proper south of the Wall.

The seizure of Manchuria by the army in the autumn of 1931 had forced Shidehara to realise that his government had lost all control of the military forces. On December 10, 1931, he resigned, and three days later a new government was formed by Inukai. On February 7, 1932, Inouye, the minister of finance, was murdered. On February 20 the Seiyukai or Conservative party was returned at a general election by a clear majority of 136. On March 6 Baron Dan, the leading financier of Japan, was also murdered. On April 16 a Japanese National Socialist party was consciously formed on the Fascist and Nazi models. On May 15 a band of young naval officers and students of the military academy, wearing their uniforms, murdered Mr. Inukai, the prime minister, and bombed five important buildings in Tokyo. On the following day the *Asahi* published an article inspired by the naval and military high commands, which ran as follows:

> The fact that no military officers were involved in yesterday's incidents shows that the leaders retain the

confidence of all ranks, but as the young officers are aware of the country's sufferings, it is doubtful if discipline could be maintained if the high officers were associated with the politicians who lack the country's confidence. The nation should therefore get rid of corrupt party governments and demand a strong national government able to cope with the present situation. The Army cannot approve a continuation of the Seiyukai Cabinet nor a party coalition.[2]

On May 26 a new ministry was formed by Admiral Saito, a former governor-general of Korea.

Throughout the period under review the reader must hold in mind that the government of Japan in its dealings with foreign powers knew that it could not control its own naval and military forces. It was they, in fact, which controlled the government, members of which had reason to know that their lives hung by a thread.

When the Japanese army seized Mukden on September 18, 1931, the Council and Assembly of the League of Nations were in session at Geneva. On the following day China appealed to the League under Article 11 of the Covenant, which merely prescribes that "any war or threat of war, whether immediately affecting any of the Members of the League or not, is hereby declared a matter of concern to the whole League, and the League shall take any action that may be deemed wise and effectual to safeguard the peace of nations". The Council, which, under this Article, is called on to deal with the matter, considered the appeal on September 22. On September 30 it requested the recall of the Japanese troops, and the government of Japan concurred in the resolution. The record of these proceedings was sent to the State Department at Washington. Mr. Stimson at once replied that his government were "in whole-hearted sympathy with the attitude of the League of Nations" and that they would "dispatch to Japan and China notes along similar lines". He added that his government had "already urged cessation of hostilities and a withdrawal from the present situation of danger".[3]

General Honjo, as we have seen, ignored these proceedings, with which his own government had concurred.

M. Briand, the president of the Council, now proposed that as the Kellogg Pact as well as the Covenant was in question, the U.S.A. should be asked to send a representative to sit with the Council. The opposition of Mr. Yoshizawa, the Japanese member, to this proposal was overruled. The invitation was sent and accepted. On October 16 Mr. Prentiss B. Gilbert, the American consul at Geneva, took his seat on the Council.

At this time the Institute of Pacific Relations was holding a conference at Shanghai, and its Chinese and Japanese members were there brought into friendly relations. In their private discussions the idea was mooted of sending an impartial commission to Manchuria to report on the facts. This idea was conveyed by the Japanese members to their government, which in its grave embarrassment welcomed any suggestion which would make for time. On November 21 Mr. Yoshizawa was instructed to propose to the Council that the League of Nations should send a commission of inquiry to the spot. Mr. Stimson strongly approved the proposal. On December 10 the Council appointed nationals of five powers as a commission with Lord Lytton as chairman, which arrived at Mukden in the following April.

Meanwhile the Japanese army continued to ignore the promise made by their government on September 30 to withdraw their troops to the railway zone. Their intention of severing Manchuria from China, as a puppet state subservient to Japan, became so plain that Mr. Stimson felt constrained to declare that such intentions were contrary to the Washington Treaty, in which the integrity of China and the open door were guaranteed by the nine Powers which signed it. He therefore drafted a note addressed to both China and Japan, which President Hoover approved, declaring that his government would refuse to recognise any arrangements which contravened the principles laid down in the Washington Treaty or the Kellogg Pact.

On January 5, 1932, he read the draft to the British and French ambassadors at Washington. On January 7 he delivered the notes to the Japanese ambassador and the Chinese chargé d'affaires and handed copies to the representatives of the six other powers which had signed the Nine Powers Treaty. On January 8 he published the notes.

In October 1929, when Mr. MacDonald had conferred with President Hoover at his Rapidan camp, they had published an announcement agreeing to regard the Kellogg Pact "as a positive obligation to direct our national policy in accordance with its pledge". As Mr. MacDonald was still prime minister in 1932, Mr. Stimson expected that the British government would support his action. He had not thought it necessary to learn before delivering, and also publishing his note to Japan, how the British government itself would regard it. On January 11, to his utter disappointment, the press was informed by the foreign office in Whitehall, that as full assurances had been given by the Japanese government of maintaining the open door, "His Majesty's Government have not considered it necessary to address any formal note to the Japanese Government on the lines of the American Government's note, but the Japanese Ambassador in London has been requested to obtain confirmation of these assurances from his Government".

The contents of this communiqué [says Mr. Stimson] were such as to be taken by most readers, including—what was most important—the Japanese government, as a rebuff to the United States. It stated in substance that, in view of former statements by Japanese representatives Japan would adhere to the Open Door policy and would welcome participation and co-operation in Manchurian enterprise, the British government did not consider it necessary to address any formal note to Japan on the lines of our note but had requested the Japanese Ambassador in London to obtain confirmation of these earlier assurances of his government. Its omissions were the most important feature of the communiqué. It was entirely silent as to the preservation of the sovereignty, independence and integrity of China, the Kellogg-Briand Pact, and the assertion of the principle of the non-recognition of the fruits of unlawful aggression. It thus ignored entirely the questions of world peace and China's integrity which we had deemed the most important features not only of our note, but of the previous three months' negotiations in which we had been supporting the efforts of the League of Nations and the British government. The communiqué dealt solely with the single problem of continuing trade relations with Manchuria.[4]

The governments of France, Holland and Belgium at once followed the line which the British government had taken in failing to support the American initiative. The unity of America with the powers of Europe in condemning the breach of China's integrity, which Mr. Stimson had laboured to sustain, was thus destroyed. His subsequent efforts to restore it were also rebuffed.[5]

Throughout this crisis the British government was firmly resolved to take no step which might conceivably lead to hostilities with Japan. One primary object of the Washington Conference had been to avoid a ruinous race in naval construction between Great Britain, the United States and Japan, and this object had been secured by an agreement designed to make each of the three navies immune from attack in their own waters. For this reason alone Great Britain was in no position to fight Japan in the Pacific. Apart from this, since the Great War she had followed the policy of reducing her armaments in the vain hope of encouraging Europe to disarm. She was, moreover, in the deepest trough of the great economic depression. Her resolve to avoid a war with Japan was shared by the other great powers with seats on the Council of the League.

By the smaller and more numerous powers the crisis was viewed from a different angle. If a naval war broke out in the Far East, it would scarcely involve countries like Sweden, Czechoslovakia, Switzerland or the South American republics. By minor powers the League of Nations was valued for the collective security it promised to the integrity of their frontiers. They viewed with utter dismay the refusal of Great Britain and the leading powers on the Council to endorse the American policy of warning Japan that no violation of China's integrity would be recognised. They therefore insisted on raising the question for discussion in the Assembly, a body in which they had voices and votes. So strong was the feeling at Geneva that the British foreign minister, Sir John Simon, found it expedient to move a resolution which endorsed in terms the policy which Mr. Stimson had proposed and he himself had rejected on January 11. On his motion the Assembly declared on March 7, 1932, "that it is incumbent upon the members of the League of Nations not to recognize any situation, treaty, or agreement which may be brought about by means contrary to the Covenant of the League of Nations or to the Pact of Paris".[6]

The policy which Mr. Stimson proposed in January was thus in the end adopted and adhered to by the League and Great Britain herself. But the manner in which the Stimson proposal had been first rebuffed, though little noticed in England, made a lasting impression on the whole American people. It widened a rift in Anglo-American relations which was presently destined to grow, till America was swept by a passion to avoid all possible contact with world affairs and to treat their continent as though it belonged to a separate planet. Since the Treaty of Versailles no British decision in foreign affairs was fraught with such far-reaching results as the answer published on January 11, 1932, to Mr. Stimson's proposal.[7]

The motion passed by the League Assembly was immediately brought to the test by the Japanese army. On March 12, 1932, 'the Minister for Foreign Affairs of Manchukuo' informed the governments of the seventeen countries which had consular officials in Manchuria, and also to the governments of thirty-five other countries, that the provinces of Manchuria and Jehol had "united themselves to establish an independent Government severing their relations with the Republic of China and have created 'Manchukuo', the State of Manchuria, on March 1st, 1932".[8] The communication went on to request that the governments addressed would formally recognise this position.

The report of the Lytton commission which reached Geneva on September 22, 1932, followed the lines laid down in the resolution which the League Assembly had passed on March 7. While refusing to countenance any proposal for detaching Manchuria from the sovereignty of the Chinese Republic, it advised the creation of a special regime designed to safeguard the rights of Japan in that country.

Throughout the protracted discussions which followed Japan refused to accept any solution which did not recognise the independence of the state of Manchukuo from China. When on February 24, 1933, the Assembly by a unanimous vote refused to recognise the independence of Manchukuo, Mr. Matsuoka, the Japanese delegate, hinted that Japan would withdraw from the League. Mr. Stimson supported the attitude of the League, and on March 27 Japan gave formal notice of intention to leave it.

NOTES

[1] Grigg, *The Faith of an Englishman*, p. 60. Macmillan & Co.
[2] *Survey*, 1932, p. 428.
[3] *Ibid.*, 1931, p. 484.
[4] Henry L. Stimson, *The Far Eastern Crisis*, pp. 101, 102.
[5] *Ibid.* pp. 162-4.
[6] *Survey*, 1932, p. 553.
[7] On this passage an American friend, who has intimate knowledge of the facts, has sent me the following comment: "In all fairness to the British Government and Sir John Simon, I would bring in somewhere an explanation of the difference, apparently, in fundamental concept, the British official concept apparently having been that nothing short of a show of force, sanctions or something positive, would stop Japan, whereas the principle on which Mr. Stimson was apparently proceeding was that a solidarity of adverse world opinion might be effective."
[8] *Survey*, 1932, p. 554.

CHAPTER LXXI

COLLAPSE OF SECURITY

THE example set by Japan in quitting the League was quickly followed by Germany. In 1925, when the Treaty of Locarno was signed and Germany had agreed to enter the League, the Council decided to appoint a 'Preparatory Commission' on which the U.S.A., Russia and Germany were represented 'for determining the questions which should be submitted to a preparatory examination with a view to a possible conference for the reduction and limitation of armaments'.[1] This conference did not meet till February 1932, when the world was plunged in economic depression and Japan was defying the League. In the previous year Germany had launched a battleship which conformed to conditions imposed by the Treaty of Versailles, and yet was a match for warships of far heavier tonnage. The French Chamber replied with a vote of £19,000,000 for completing the chain of fortifications on their eastern frontiers; and plans were laid for strengthening the British and French navies.

Throughout this conference France, supported by the Little Entente and Poland, argued that they could not disarm unless they were first assured that if war were afterwards threatened they should have on their side forces strong enough either to prevent it, or at any rate to secure victory for themselves. If Great Britain and the U.S.A. were not willing to pledge themselves in advance to fight on their side, then an international force must be created strong enough to coerce an aggressor. Great Britain and the U.S.A. were opposed to giving any such guarantees, until a genuine movement towards disarmament had first been accomplished. Brüning asserted in firm though moderate terms the German case for equality of status. He was now making a last effort to blanket the sails of the Nazi movement, and in January 1932 had announced that Germany would pay no more reparations. In order to help him Great Britain proposed a conference to consider the question at Lausanne; but when this Conference met in June (1932) Brüning had just been forced to resign and Papen was chancellor. The Lausanne Conference relieved Germany of further obligation to pay reparations.

Papen then proposed that the German claim to equality of status should be settled by direct negotiations with France. But the pitch was queered by aggressive speeches made by Schleicher, his minister of war, by Herriot's reply to those speeches and a British statement supporting the French position. When the Disarmament Conference resumed its meeting in September (1932) the Germans refused to attend, on the ground that in so far as the ex-Allied powers had failed to disarm they had broken the disarmament clauses of the Treaty of Versailles, and had thus released Germany from her undertakings in that respect. In December (1932), however, Ramsay MacDonald convened at Geneva a meeting of representatives of the U.S.A., Great Britain, France, Germany and Italy, which declared "that the principle of equality of rights in a system which would provide security for all nations should be embodied in the Convention containing the conclusions of the Disarmament Conference".[2] In the light of this declaration Schleicher, who had now succeeded Papen as chancellor, agreed that the German delegate should rejoin the Disarmament Conference. When the Conference reopened on February 2, 1933, Hitler had succeeded Schleicher as chancellor and before the end of the month Japan had given notice of withdrawal from the League. A plan submitted by Great Britain for the reduction of armaments was the basis of discussion. On May 17 (1933) Hitler, in a conciliatory speech, agreed to accept the British draft as the basis of a treaty.

On June 12, 1933, the World Economic Conference was opened in London. It was wrecked in less than a month by President Roosevelt's refusal to take part in proposals for the stabilisation of currencies.

On October 14 a speech was made by Sir John Simon at the Disarmament Conference in which, to meet the views of the French, he announced certain modifications in the plan for rearmament proposed by the British. The reduction in existing armaments was to be postponed for four years, during which the machinery for inspection of armaments by the League should be given a trial. In the meanwhile Germany was to be forbidden to rearm. Hitler immediately withdrew the German delegate from the Conference and on October 19 announced the withdrawal of Germany from the League. In a plebiscite taken on November 12 his action was approved by 95·1 per cent of the valid votes cast.

He now assumed a conciliatory attitude and on December 18, 1933, proposed a ten-year non-aggression pact with France, Poland and her other neighbours, provided that Germany was allowed to fortify her eastern and western frontiers, and that the Reichswehr be converted into an army of 300,000 men conscribed for one year. To these proposals the French returned an unconciliatory answer on January 1, 1934. In that month an arrangement was published whereby Germany and Poland agreed to suspend their disputes for ten years. On January 30, the anniversary of the Nazi revolution, Hitler once more declared his pacific intentions as instanced by the Polish agreement, offered to settle by direct negotiation all questions outstanding with France, promised if that were done, to accept the spirit as well as the letter of the Locarno Treaties; but insisted once more on Germany's claim to equality of status. He thanked Great Britain for certain proposals which Sir John Simon had addressed to governments, members of the Disarmament Conference, on January 28. These proposals Sir John Simon had framed after consultation with Signor Mussolini in Rome. They abandoned the position which Sir John Simon had taken at Geneva on October 14, 1933, and went far towards accepting the Führer's latest proposals. In France these British proposals were greeted with anger and the French attitude stiffened when in February 1934 Barthou became foreign minister. It was common knowledge that Germany was rearming in defiance of the Treaty of Versailles. The German estimates published on April 10, 1934, showed an increase of one-third on military establishments; but Hitler had now offered to limit her number of military aircraft to 50 per cent of the military aircraft of France.[3] On April 17, M. Barthou refused to pursue the negotiations for a settlement with Germany which Sir John Simon had proposed on January 28, and asked that the Disarmament Conference should resume its work. This refusal is always described in Germany as the French "No" to Hitler's proposals to limit his armaments.

On May 29, 1934, the General Commission of the Disarmament Conference met at Geneva. Sir John Simon and M. Barthou made speeches which openly divided the Conference into opposing camps—those who wished for disarmament first and were ready to make concessions in order to secure the co-operation of Germany, and those who wished the powers who feared Germany to make an agreement for their common security before discussing the question of disarmament. Great Britain was supported by

America, the Scandinavian states, Switzerland and Spain; France by Russia, Turkey, the Little Entente and the Balkan bloc. The deadlock was thinly masked by a compromise resolution planned by Mr. Norman Davis, the American spokesman, and on June 11 (1934) the Conference adjourned *sine die*. On June 9 Mr. Eden said to his constituents:

> We have in no sense solved the main difficulties of the European situation, which consist in the present relations of the chief powers of Continental Europe. Unless they can be improved there will be no disarmament agreement, no political entente, and in consequence no extension of international trade recovery in Europe. . . . This is the problem which European statesmanship has so far singularly failed to solve.[4]

Until 1933 their common hostility to France had led the Germans and Russians to regard each other with friendly feelings. The fall of the Weimar Republic and the rise to power of a government in Germany openly hostile to the Communist regime was forcing Russia into the arms of France. Her eastern frontiers were openly menaced by the Japanese army which had seized and was holding Manchuria in defiance of the League. On May 18, 1934, Litvinoff and Barthou met at Geneva and framed proposals for an 'Eastern Locarno' by which Russia, Poland, the Baltic states, Czechoslovakia, Germany and France should all agree to resist any attempt to violate frontiers east of Germany. Russia was to enter the League. Italy approved these proposals, which were warmly greeted by both parties in the English parliament on July 13, 1934. On July 21 the Soviet government informed Berlin of its readiness to accept them. Yet, only a fortnight before, the executive committee of the Comintern in Moscow had issued a manifesto declaring its intention to destroy the Nazi regime and establish in its place a "German Soviet Republic under Communist leadership fraternally allied to the U.S.S.R." This document, entitled 'Programme of Emancipation for the German Working Class', outlined plans for the creation of a German Red Army to be linked up with communist elements in Poland and other countries.[5] It is not to be wondered, therefore, that Hitler received these proposals coldly, declining to enter on military engagements with other powers, so long as those powers refused to recognise Germany's claim to equal rights in the matter of military armaments.

For the moment these new proposals were overshadowed by the news of the massacres at Munich and Berlin and then on July 25 of the murder of Dr. Dollfuss by Nazis in Vienna. Mussolini promptly announced his intention of preventing the inclusion of Austria in Germany, and moved strong military forces up to the Brenner and the Carinthian frontiers. Hitler, wise enough not to accept the challenge, now turned his attention to securing the return of the Saar to Germany. This depended on the issue of the plebiscite fixed for January 13, 1935. The Nazi excesses and conflict with the Catholic Church had raised some doubt whether the inhabitants of the Saar might not after all prefer to remain outside the German Reich.

On September 18, 1934, the Soviet government was admitted to the League with a permanent seat on the Council. On January 13, 1935, an overwhelming majority of residents in the Saar voted for reunion with Germany and thereby greatly enhanced the power and prestige of the Hitler regime.

Since the Conference of Paris in 1919 the relations of France with Italy had been seriously strained. Mussolini's action in threatening to protect Austria against absorption by Germany had now created warmer relations. When Barthou was murdered on October 18, 1934, Laval, who took his place at the foreign office, had applied himself to the task of settling the various disputes which had long estranged the two countries.

These cool relations had their origin in the promises made to Italy when she entered the war in 1915.[6] At the Peace Conference Italy had asked that the status of Italians in Tunis should be placed by the French on a more satisfactory footing, for the rectification of the frontiers of Libya with access to lake Chad, for the cession of Jibuti and the French railway which led from that port to Addis Ababa, for the cession by England of the port of Kismayu and the Juba river at the southern extremity of Italian Somaliland. This cession England had made to Italy in 1924; but except for a rectification of frontiers which allowed no access to lake Chad, France had refused to meet the Italian demands. In the Danube basin France was set on maintaining the frontiers fixed in the Peace Treaties, while Italy supported the Hungarian claim for revision. So strained were relations that both governments had massed troops on the Franco-Italian frontier. France was now feeling the need of these troops on her eastern frontiers to meet the growing menace of Germany.

On January 4, 1935, Laval met Mussolini at Rome. On January 8 cordial agreements were announced covering all the points at issue. On the question of armaments it was stated:

> The French and Italian Governments, referring to the Declaration of equality of rights of December 11th, 1932, have found themselves in agreement in their recognition that no country can modify by unilateral act its obligations in the matter of armaments, and that in the case of this eventuality being established they should consult each other.[7]

This was a clear notice to Germany that Italy was now ranged on the side of France in the matter of disarmament, and also that France and Italy would be free to employ elsewhere the large forces which had faced each other on their common frontier. This agreement meant the transfer of 200,000 French troops from the Italian to the German frontier.

When the terms of the Franco-Italian settlement came to be studied, it looked as though M. Laval had obtained all he could ask in return for exceedingly moderate concessions. As after events were to show, Mussolini believed that Laval had promised to give him a free hand in the great African enterprise for which he was now preparing.

The glorious past with which Mussolini had sought to connect the Fascist regime was Imperial Rome, and not that of Cavour and the Risorgimento. He had always aspired to create for Italy an empire comparable to that of the Caesars, and had not forgotten that before the disastrous defeat of Adowa, Abyssinia had been marked on African maps as an Italian protectorate.

The Abyssinian Empire had now been admitted as a fully self-governing state to the League of Nations. This admission of a barbarous and primitive state to the League was fraught with momentous results for the League itself, and the curious train of events which led to this step must be briefly narrated.

In January 1922 the *Westminster Gazette* published appalling accounts of the Abyssinian slave-trade and its horrors from the pens of two English observers. The matter was taken up by the Anti-Slavery Society and the government was plied with questions in parliament. On June 5, 1923, Mr. Charles Roberts told the Society that "The Foreign Office has not given us very much help. . . . They may think . . . that we may be suspected of ulterior designs against the independence of Abyssinia."

In fact this conjecture was sound. The French, who were hoping to secure for their nationals commercial or mining concessions in the Abyssinian Empire, had seen in the agitation against the slave-trade a movement which might possibly lead to a British protectorate over the country. In order to checkmate any such project, and also to strengthen their influence with the Emperor, the French government encouraged him to apply for admission to the League. When the matter came up at Geneva in September 1923 Mr. Edward Wood, on behalf of the British government, questioned whether Abyssinia was a state fit for admission to the League. The Italian spokesmen in the Assembly at first supported this view; but half-way through the proceedings they suddenly changed their attitude, and did everything possible to outbid the French in supporting the Abyssinian request. The Abyssinian Empire was admitted to membership in the League on the joint proposal of France and Italy.

In 1928 Mussolini, who was still absorbed in the task of restoring his country to order at home, made a twenty years' pact of friendship and arbitration with the Abyssinian Empire. The depression which started the following year was ere long to confront him with a growing problem of unemployment. By 1932 the Manchurian incident had shown how easy it was for a highly militarised country to flout the League and ignore treaties such as the Kellogg Pact. In 1933 Abyssinia was brought to his mind as a field for a similar exploit by de Bono, one of the four who had led the march on Rome.

One day I said to the Duce, "Listen, if there is ever a war down there, and if you think me worthy and capable, you ought to give me the honour of conducting it". The Chief looked me straight in the eye and said at once, "Certainly". I added: "You don't think me too old?" "No," he replied, "because there is no time to be lost. . ."

From that moment the Duce had the idea clearly in his mind that the question was going to be decided not later than 1936.

By the end of 1934 the Duce had himself drawn up a document entitled "Directives and Plan of Action for Solving the Italo-Abyssinian Question". It was very secret and only five copies were made.[8]

De Bono was appointed high commissioner for Eritrea and Somaliland. On December 5, 1934, some fighting took place between Italian and Abyssinian forces at Walwal. The Emperor, Haile Selassie, had already appealed to the League for redress, when in January 1935 the Duce announced his agreement to stand by France in affirming that "no country can modify by unilateral act its obligations in the matter of armaments".

On February 3, 1935, the British government issued a statement supporting this last declaration in terms, adding "that French and British Ministers were agreed that the general settlement with Germany should deal simultaneously with the organization of security; equality of rights in a system of security; an agreement replacing Part V of the Versailles Treaty; and the resumption by Germany of her place in the League". "We hope too", said M. Laval, "that Germany will respond to the pressing call we are making to her."

The materials of war and number of troops which Italy was passing through the Suez Canal were now beginning to claim public attention. On February 22, 1935, the British government reminded Italy of the agreement of December 13, 1906, in which England, France and Italy had promised to maintain the integrity of Abyssinia and not to intervene "without the understanding of the others". Two days after this 5000 more Italian troops were embarked for Africa.

In the meantime arrangements had been made for Sir John Simon and Mr. Eden to visit Berlin and discuss with Herr Hitler the proposals outlined in the British statement made on February 3. On

March 16, 1935, before this visit could be made, the German government announced the reinstitution of compulsory military service, with a view to increasing the German army in time of peace to 36 divisions. In a statement given to the press it was said that this was "a decisive event in German history, namely, the first great liquidation measure of the Versailles dictate, through which the essential shame of this Treaty is finally extinguished". On March 18 the British government protested against this announcement as a "further example of unilateral action, which, apart from the issue of principle, is calculated seriously to increase uneasiness in Europe". On March 21, 1935, France followed suit and also Italy, which declared that "in any eventual future negotiations it will not be able simply to accept as ready-made situations of fact those which have been determined by unilateral decisions that annul engagements of an international character".

Next day Italy informed the League Secretariat that "the despatch of troops to Africa was dictated by the necessity of providing for the safety of the colonies, especially in view of the military measures taken on a much larger scale by Abyssinia".

On March 24 Simon and Eden arrived in Berlin for a visit which lasted two days. In these conversations Hitler claimed for the German army a maximum force of 550,000 men, for her navy 35 per cent of the British tonnage, and parity in the air with Britain and France, unless the Soviet air force was further increased. He raised objections to the proposals for mutual military assistance contained in the Eastern Pact. He saw in the growing strength of Russia a threat of immediate attack on Germany, the only real bulwark against communism, and the far-reaching designs of the Third International. In the previous September he had said:

If a single country in Western or Central Europe

succeeded to Bolshevism the poison would spread till it infected the oldest and finest civilizations. By waging war on Bolshevism Germany, as often before in her history, is fulfilling a European mission.

These conversations showed how embittered the mutual relations of Russia and Germany had grown since the Nazi regime had come to power. It could scarcely be otherwise, since its leader had written in *Mein Kampf*:

Fate itself seems to wish to give us our direction. When fate abandoned Russia to Bolshevism it robbed the Russian people of the educated class which once created and guaranteed their existence as a State. The Germanic element may now be regarded as entirely wiped out in Russia. The Jew has taken its place. It is as impossible for the Russian to shake off the Jewish yoke by his own strength as it is for the Jew to keep control of the vast Empire for any length of time. His character is not that of an organizer, but of a decomposing leaven. The immense Empire will one day collapse. . . .

The present-day rulers of Russia have no intention of entering into any alliance for a long period. . . .

The menace which Russia suffers under is one which perpetually hangs over Germany. Germany is the next great objective of Bolshevism. . . .[9]

One can see why Russia had hastened to strengthen her armed forces since the author of these words had become the absolute ruler of Germany. This rapid expansion of Russian arms made it easy for Hitler to convince his people that Bolshevist armies would overrun them unless they themselves were armed to the teeth. And, indeed, the Comintern manifesto of July 7, 1934,[10] had given him ample reason for saying so. Henceforward the French proposal of an Eastern Locarno was reduced to the character of arrangements for mutual defence between France and Russia, with all the possible results to which the previous alliance of Russia with France had led. It is said that the Foreign Office in London, when consulted by France, replied that they saw no legal objection to such an alliance. This, at any rate, is clear, that nothing was said to remind Paris that the German staff would once more revert to the Schlieffen plan, if war with Russia meant war with France, an event which would then involve England in terms of the Locarno Treaty.

On March 26, 1935, the British ministers left Berlin, Simon for London, Eden for Moscow. He was there received with open arms. At a banquet M. Litvinoff said that his visit was not merely a beginning of co-operation between their two countries, but also a pledge of its continuation. He concluded by drinking the health of King George, of the British people and of Mr. Eden himself.

On April 11, 1935, Mussolini, Flandin, Laval, MacDonald and Simon met at Stresa to consider the situation. Their conclusions, which were of a general nature, were published on April 14 and concluded with the words:

> The three Powers, the object of whose policy is the collective maintenance of peace within the framework of the League of Nations, find themselves in complete agreement in opposing, by all practicable means, any unilateral repudiation of treaties which may endanger the peace of Europe, and will act in close and cordial collaboration for this purpose.[11]

This concord of Italy, France and England was henceforward described as the Stresa front.

On April 15, 1935, the League Council met, as requested by France, to consider "the decisions of the German Government relating to armaments". It further decided that consideration of the Abyssinian appeal should be postponed to the ordinary session in May. On April 16 the Council of the League on the motion of England, France and Italy passed resolutions condemning the action of Germany in repudiating the Treaty of Versailles, and creating a committee to frame

> measures to render the Covenant more effective in the organization of collective security, and to define in particular the economic and financial measures which might be applied should, in the future, a State, whether a member of the League of Nations or not, endanger peace by unilateral repudiation of its international obligations.

Denmark abstained from voting, but otherwise these resolutions were passed by unanimous vote, with the enthusiastic support of Litvinoff. The news was greeted with anger in Germany.

On May 2 (1935) a pact was signed in Paris which, if ratified by the French legislature, would bind France and Russia to help each other if either were "threatened with, or in danger of, aggression on the part of any European State", without waiting for any ruling or action by the Council of the League.

On May 3 the German press uttered a warning note. In repudiating the enforced terms of the Treaty of Versailles, Germany had proclaimed her intention of observing the Treaty of Locarno, into which she had freely entered. If France were to invalidate the treaty in practice through some one-sided agreement the responsibility could not be placed on Germany.

On May 16 (1935) Czechoslovakia adhered to the Franco-Russian Pact.

On May 21 (1935) Hitler reviewed the position of Germany in a speech to the Reichstag. He promised to observe freely negotiated treaties, like Locarno, *so long as the other partners stood by it*, but added that "as a result of the military alliance concluded between France and Russia without doubt an element of legal insecurity has been introduced into the one clear and really valuable mutual treaty of security in Europe—the Locarno Treaty".

A decree was issued fixing the period of active

service for the army, navy and air force at one year.

In the House of Commons on May 22 Mr. Baldwin welcomed Herr Hitler's speech as a positive contribution to peace.

On June 7 M. Laval became prime minister, retaining the portfolio of foreign affairs. On the same day Mr. Baldwin replaced Mr. MacDonald as prime minister, Sir Samuel Hoare went to the foreign office, and Mr. Eden became minister for League affairs. On June 18, 1935, England and Germany signed an agreement which settled the relative strength of their navies—the only agreement for limiting armaments reached since the Washington Treaty of 1922 ended (for its duration) the race for maritime power, which, more than anything else, had created the alignment of force which had led to the Great War. In France it was urged that England in making this agreement had now condoned the conduct of Germany in repudiating the Treaty of Versailles by unilateral action. Such action the British government had condemned in terms two days after the reimposition of conscription was announced in Berlin. It was further said that the Anglo-German agreement had destroyed the Stresa front.

NOTES

[1] King-Hall, *Our Own Times*, vol. i. p. 279.
[2] *Ibid.* vol. ii. p. 286.
[3] *Bulletin*, vol. xi. No. 17, p. 567.
[4] *Ibid.* vol. x, No. 26, p. 812.
[5] *Ibid.* vol. xi. No. 20, p. 663.
[6] See p. 718.
[7] *Bulletin*, vol. xi. No. 14, p. 475.
[8] Review in *The Times Literary Supplement* of *La Preparazione e Le Prime Operazioni*. By Emilio de Bono, Maresciallo d'Italia. Rome: Instituto Nazionale Fascista di Cultura.
[9] Chap. xiv. of the English edition quoted in the *Bulletin*, vol. xi. No. 20, pp. 660-1.
[10] See p. 772.
[11] *Bulletin*, vol. xi. No. 21, p. 720.

CHAPTER LXXII

ABYSSINIA

For reasons other than the Anglo-German agreement, the Stresa front was now in serious danger. The official agenda of the Stresa Conference was confined to the question of German rearmament. Abyssinia had, none the less, been discussed by the British and Italian members of the Conference in informal conversations. The question then, as the British ministers thought, was mainly confined to the frontier incident at Walwal, and was in the hands of the League Council, which was meeting to deal with it immediately after the Stresa Conference. In these conversations the British ministers got the impression "that the prospects of a peaceful settlement were brighter". "It was the volume of the reinforcements sent to East Africa that in May began to create concern."[1]

In the year preceding the general election which took place in the autumn of 1935 the League of Nations Union in England was collecting millions of answers to a questionnaire which crystallised public opinion in favour of peace, and also of treating the Covenant as the necessary means to that end. The wide response to the questionnaire visibly affected the government's policy. In their speeches, ministers gave the impression that whilst they might be trusted to keep the country out of war, they would also see to it that, so far as in them lay, the powers of the League would be exercised to the full, as they had not been exercised in the case of Japan.

In pursuit of this policy Eden visited Rome on June 23, 1935, and explained to the Duce the grave concern which his government felt at the turn events were taking as regards Abyssinia. Their attitude was not dictated by British interests, but solely by their obligations as members of the League; for only through the League could England play her full part in maintaining the peace of Europe. As evidence of British good faith he offered to cede to Abyssinia a strip of land in Somaliland which would give her independent access to the sea. The offer was not accepted. On July 6 Mussolini, addressing 5000 Black Shirts, said: "We have entered upon a struggle which we as a Government and a revolutionary people have irrevocably decided to carry to its conclusion". On July 21 the *Echo de Paris* published an interview in which the Duce said that the moment of decision had come. He knew the risks and the difficulties; he had reflected, weighed and prepared with minute care. All he could say was that Italy was sure of imposing her will. "The nation will have to make a great effort. After that it will occupy a great place in the world."

There were other leading journals in Paris which at this time were voicing the views of the Duce and were definitely under his influence, attacking Great Britain almost as strongly as the papers in Italy. It was obvious also that Fascist organisations in France, like the Croix de Feu, were mobilised in the Italian interest. How well the *Echo de Paris* was apprised of the Duce's intentions was shown when this journal wrote on August 19, 1935:

The breach is complete and total. It may be asked whether Mussolini has not abandoned his idea of avenging Adowa, and now wants to add to his prestige the military success of founding a colony in Abyssinia. If that is his will, no force can stop him.

In September the Italian troops will move on Addis Ababa. France ought to stay close by Britain's side, but neither must she lose contact with Rome, because it is desirable to see that Italy, in revolting against the disciples of peace, does not join Germany in the camp of trouble-makers.

These last words exactly express the double plan which M. Laval was trying to follow.

By September 4 the machinery of the League had helped to settle the Walwal dispute; yet this settlement in no way affected the course of events. Italian forces continued to pour through the Suez Canal.

On September 11 the Assembly met at Geneva and Sir Samuel Hoare opened the proceedings with a speech "reaffirming the support of the League by the Government that I represent, and the interest of the British people in collective security". But collective security, he added,

> means much more than what we commonly call sanctions. It means not merely Article 16, but the whole Covenant. It assumes a scrupulous respect for all treaty obligations. . . . The obligations of the Covenant remain, their burden upon us has been increased manifold. But one thing is certain. If the burden is to be borne, it must be borne collectively. If risks for peace are to be run, they must be run by all . . . on behalf of His Majesty's Government I can say that they will be second to none in their intention to fulfil, within the measure of their capacity, the obligation which the Covenant lays upon them. The ideas enshrined in the Covenant and, in particular, the aspiration to establish the rule of law in international affairs . . . have become a part of our national conscience. . . . The League stands, and my country stands with it, for the collective maintenance of the Covenant in its entirety, and particularly for steady and collective resistance to all acts of unprovoked aggression. . . . There, then, is the British attitude towards the Covenant. I cannot believe that it will be changed so long as the League remains an effective body, and the main bridge between the United Kingdom and the Continent remains intact.

The British lead was followed with enthusiasm by the spokesmen of Norway, Belgium, Holland and Sweden. On September 13 M. Laval endorsed the British position and added:

I have spared no effort for conciliation. I maintain the hope that the Council may, within a short space of time, be able to discharge its task of conciliation. . . . I persist in refusing to think that it is without hope.

It must be realized that there is no discrimination between France and the United Kingdom in the effective search for such a pacific solution. . . . We are all bound by a solidarity which will determine our duty. Our obligations are inscribed in the Covenant. France will not fail to discharge them.

On behalf of South Africa Mr. te Water pointed to the danger that if Italy conquered Abyssinia she might militarise the natives and so force militarisation on the whole African continent. The interest with which the peoples of Asia were watching the issue was stressed by the Aga Khan.

Mussolini's reply was conveyed to the world in two interviews, one published in the *Morning Post*, the other in the *Matin*, on September 17. In the *Morning Post* he said:

On January 29th I had the British Government informed that the Italian Government invited the British Government to consider specific agreements for a harmonious development of the Italian and British interests in Ethiopia. I was ready to table my case—I wanted to do that. The British Foreign Minister answered evasively. In face of that silence there was only one way left. And I took it.

He added that after Stresa, the attitude of the British government "revealed its inclination to block off every demand of Italy for satisfaction". And he had, therefore, decided to go straight ahead. In the *Matin* he said, Italy

will go quite straight in what she thinks to be the path of right and that of her vital necessities. It was believed at first that I was playing a game of poker. There can be nobody to-day who still doubts that the unshakable decision of the people is such as has been openly stated.

Referring to the long-standing friendship with Britain, he added:

"We find it monstrous that a nation which dominates the world refuses us a wretched plot of ground in the African sun. Many times and in every way I have given the assurance to Great Britain that her interests in Abyssinia would be scrupulously safeguarded. But the interests for which she is so strongly opposing us are other interests and she does not say so."

Never from their side, he went on, would come any hostile act against a European nation; "but if one is committed against us, well, it means war. Italy does not want it, but she is not afraid of it."

On October 3, 1935, General de Bono formally proclaimed the opening of hostilities and ordered his troops to invade Abyssinia. The unequal contest between an army equipped with every device of mechanisation and hordes of primitive natives began. The Abyssinians had on their side every difficulty which a tropical climate and a mountainous country can oppose to invaders; but events were to prove that against such difficulties the internal combustion engine and command of the air is now the decisive factor.

On October 7 the Council of the League decided that Italy had violated her obligations under Article 12 of the Covenant. On October 10 a co-ordinating committee was set up, which proposed that members of the League should cease to buy Italian goods, and also place an immediate embargo on the export to Italy of arms, munitions and implements of war, and on loans and credits to Italy. But the list of excluded goods did not include iron and steel, coal, cotton, wool, copper, lead, zinc or petroleum, the primary necessity of a modern mechanised army. A Canadian proposal to include these commodities in the list was approved to come into operation "as soon as the conditions necessary to render this extension effective had been realised", *i.e.* the U.S.A., Germany and other states outside the League should also agree to withhold these supplies. Broadly speaking, these proposals were accepted by all the states, members of the League, other than Austria, Hungary, Albania, Paraguay and (in part) Switzerland.

On November 2, after the co-ordinating committee had fixed the date for the application of sanctions, M. Laval made a statement in which he said that they must seek as quickly as possible for an agreed solution of the conflict. Sir Samuel Hoare added that conversations were taking place between Rome, Paris and London on the possibility of such a settlement. M. van Zeeland's suggestion, that the British and French governments should be given a sort of moral mandate from the committee to mediate on behalf of the League, received tacit consent.

On November 14 the general election was held in Great Britain which gave the National government a working majority of about 250. The electorate clearly felt that the National government could be trusted to protect Abyssinia through the League without involving the country in war with Italy.

Public opinion was now strongly demanding an embargo on oil, the one sanction which Mussolini most feared. Its imposition was resisted by M. Laval who thought, not without reason, that Mussolini would refuse to consider his proposals for a settlement if once the embargo on oil were imposed.

To the House of Commons on December 5 Sir Samuel Hoare said that "the delay in considering the oil embargo had been due to the French political situation only, and was unavoidable". He therefore urged concentration on "finding a basis of settlement and making it possible for the world to return to normal life". They must make a particular effort to surmount the difficulties "in the course of the next few days and weeks". On December 7 Mussolini replied in a speech to the Chamber. The situation, he said, had slightly improved in the last few hours, but added: "The Italian people listen to words, but judge by facts. Now the fact which is announced for December 12th, *i.e.* the embargo on petrol, is such as gravely to prejudice the development of the situation." On that same day Sir Samuel Hoare visited M. Laval in Paris. On December 8 a statement was issued saying that the two ministers had

> sought the formulas which might serve as a basis for a friendly settlement of the Italo-Ethiopian dispute. There could be no question at present of publishing these formulas. The British Government has not yet been informed of them, and once its agreement has been received, it will be necessary to submit them to the consideration of the interested Governments and to the decision of the League of Nations. . . . We are both satisfied with the results which we have reached.

Sir Samuel Hoare, who was seriously overstrained, then left for a rest in Switzerland and on December 9 Mr. Baldwin informed parliament that the draft proposals had reached London and were receiving "urgent consideration". On December 10 they were forwarded to Rome and Addis Ababa, but their general nature had by now been disclosed in Paris and telegraphed to the London press. This disclosure came as a painful surprise not merely to public opinion, but also to most of the cabinet ministers. On December 13 they were published and three days later the Emperor declared

> that the act by us of accepting even in principle the Franco-British proposals would be not only a cowardice towards our people, but a betrayal of the League of Nations and of all the States which have shown that they could have confidence up to now in the system of collective security.
>
> These proposals are the negation and the abandonment of the principles upon which the League is founded. For Ethiopia they would consecrate the amputation of her territory and the disappearance of her independence for the benefit of the State which has attacked her. They imply the

definite interdiction for her own people to participate usefully and freely in the economic development of about a third of the country, and they confide this development to her enemy, which is now making its second attempt to conquer this people.

. . . the security of other weak or small States would be made doubtful if such a recompense should be accorded to a State condemned as the aggressor.

In England public opinion endorsed this view and saw in the draft proposals a betrayal of the pledges which the government had made at the general election and at Geneva. Sir Samuel Hoare returned to London and on December 18 his resignation was announced. He explained his conduct to the House of Commons next day. They had reached a turning point, he said, about a fortnight ago, when it was clear that a new situation was about to be created by the question of the oil embargo.

"From all sides", he went on, "we received reports that no responsible Government could disregard that Italy would regard the oil embargo as a military sanction or an act involving war against her. . . . We had no fear as a nation whatever of any Italian threats. If the Italians attacked us we should retaliate, and, judging from our past history, we should retaliate with full success. What was in our minds was . . . that an isolated attack of this kind launched upon one Power without, it may be—and I shall refer to this subject again in a minute—without, it may be, the full support of the other Powers, would, it seemed to me, almost inevitably lead to the dissolution of the League."

In these circumstances he had gone to Paris, and it was in an atmosphere of threatened war that the conversations began. It was also an atmosphere in which the majority of the member States—indeed, the totality of the member States—appeared to be opposed to military action. It was a moment of great urgency. He did not feel justified in proposing any postponement of the oil embargo unless it could be shown to the League that negotiations had actually started. It was a moment when no member State except Britain had taken any military precautions.

Lastly, it was a moment when it seemed to him that

Anglo-French co-operation was essential if there was to be no breach at Geneva. For two days he had discussed with M. Laval, not terms to be imposed on the belligerents, but proposals that might bring the two parties into the same room, and might make subsequent negotiation possible.

The proposals were neither British nor French, but were simply the only basis on which peace seemed remotely possible—the minimum basis on which the French Government were prepared to proceed. "I felt that the issues were so grave," he went on, "and the dangers of the continuance of the war so serious, that it was worth making the attempt and that it was essential to maintain Anglo-French unity."

. . . . . .

Other States had done their best, but up to the present they had taken no military precautions. Britain alone had done so. "There is the British Fleet in the Mediterranean, there are the British reinforcements in Egypt, in Malta and Aden. Not a ship, not a machine, not a man has been moved by any other member State. Now that negotiations have failed, we must have something more than these general protestations of loyalty to the League . . . without this active co-operation it will be impossible to have more than an unsatisfactory peace. You cannot have a 100 per cent peace if you have only got 5 per cent co-operation that goes to the making of it."

. . . . . .

It was "a choice between the full co-operation of all the member States and the kind of unsatisfactory compromise that was contemplated in the suggestions which M. Laval and I put up".

Sir Samuel Hoare was followed by Mr. Baldwin, who said, "It is perfectly obvious now that the proposals are absolutely and completely dead". He felt that the question of the future of the League and the risk that by adhering to it they "found themselves standing alone to do what ought to be done by everybody", was one on which every member of parliament would have to do a lot of hard thinking. To the peers Lord Halifax said that the real mistake the government had made was that "of not appreciating the damage that, rightly or wrongly, these terms would be held by public opinion to inflict upon the cause we were pledged to serve".

Meanwhile, at Geneva, Mr. Eden had said that His Majesty's Government had no wish to pursue these proposals further, and the Council resolved that "in view of the preliminary character of these suggestions . . . the Council does not consider that it is called upon to express an opinion in regard to them at present". The Abyssinian delegate said that his government could not believe that the Ethiopian people would now be abandoned to an enemy. He pressed the Council to send a commission of inquiry to his country and also to give it financial aid. On January 21 both these requests were refused.

On January 3 *Il Popolo d'Italia* had said that the situation was now one which called for "inexorable action. Italy must strike and knock down the bloody slave-traders." The *Stampa* wrote that "the war must now be without quarter; an eye for an eye, and a tooth for a tooth". In the light of after events it is plain that the Duce, with sanctions running against him and the risk of an oil embargo hanging like a sword over his head, had decided to use every weapon which might hasten the end, regardless of all international conventions.

For the purpose of assessing the dues for transit through the Suez Canal the nature of cargoes have to be disclosed to the Suez Canal Company. From these returns the British war office knew that poison gas was being conveyed in large quantities to the theatre of war.

On March 3, when the spring offensive was opening, an urgent appeal was made by the League to both belligerents "for the immediate opening of the negotiations within the framework of the League and in the spirit of the Covenant with a view to the prompt cessation of hostilities". On April 2 Italy agreed to negotiate. It had now been reported, however, that Italian aircraft were showering poison gas on the Abyssinian troops with destructive effect. On March 23 the League had asked the Italian government for any observations they might wish to make regarding the use of poison gas. On April 3 the Emperor appealed once more to the League, urging that Italy had agreed to negotiate merely in order to postpone the imposition of the oil sanction. Since the League appeal of March 3 the Italians had "redoubled their barbarity, employing instruments of war and methods prohibited by international treaties signed by Italy". As the competence of the League to deal with the question of poison gas was challenged by Italy, the League on April 8 appointed three jurists to report on the matter. But in Abyssinia Italian aircraft laden with poison gas were doing their work more rapidly than the League machinery could move. Whilst the jurists were debating, the morale of the Abyssinian troops was utterly broken by a weapon they were powerless to resist. According to the account which the Emperor gave to the League Assembly on June 30,

> special sprayers were installed on aircraft by the Italians so that they could vapourize over vast areas a fine death-dealing rain. Groups of 9, 15 and 18 aircraft followed one another so that the fog issuing from them formed a continuous sheet. In order to kill off systematically everything living the aircraft passed over again and again; these fearful tactics succeeded, and the deadly rain made all those whom it touched fly, shrieking with pain.

On May 2 the Emperor and his family fled from his capital, which was then pillaged by his own troops, whose conduct appeared to justify the doubts expressed at Geneva in 1923 whether Abyssinia was a state fit for admission to the League of Nations. The foreign legations and Europeans were in imminent danger, but most of them were saved by taking refuge in the British compound, which sheltered some 2000 people of 23 nationalities. On May 5 the Italian troops entered Addis Ababa and order was restored.

Reporting the news to a crowd in Rome, Mussolini said:

> I announce to the Italian people and to the world that the war is finished. I announce to the Italian people and to the world that peace is re-established. . . . But it is strictly necessary that I should add that it is our peace, the Roman peace, which is expressed in this simple irrevocable, definite proposition: Abyssinia is Italian—Italian in fact because occupied by our victorious armies, Italian by right, because with the sword of Rome it is civilization which triumphs over barbarism, justice which triumphs over the slavery of 1,000 years.

When the 16th Assembly of the League opened on June 30 the Emperor appeared in person and said that a certain government, when Ethiopia had appealed to the League, had considered that the situation in Europe required them to retain the friendship of Italy. The price paid was the abandonment of Ethiopian independence to Italian greed. This secret agreement, contrary to the obligations of the Covenant, had exerted a great influence over the course of events. The question before the League was its own existence.

NOTE

[1] Quotations in this chapter are taken from the *Bulletin*.

CHAPTER LXXIII

DEMOCRACY, BOLSHEVISM AND FASCISM IN CONFLICT

M. Herriot had viewed with growing distrust the efforts of his colleague M. Laval to preserve the Stresa front at the cost of the League's authority. When the Hoare-Laval proposals to conciliate Italy were consigned to the scrap-heap M. Herriot had forced M. Laval to resign. His place was taken by M. Sarraut with M. Flandin as foreign minister. In February he brought the Pact which the French and Soviet governments had signed on May 2, 1935, before the Chamber for ratification. The German press reasserted the view that the Pact was in fact an alliance between France, Czechoslovakia and Russia against Germany, and contrary to the spirit of Locarno. It was, they added, encouraged by London.

On February 27, 1936, the Soviet Pact was ratified by the Chamber in Paris. In an interview published by the Paris *Midi* next day Hitler pleaded for friendlier relations with France:

> Let the French give great thought to what they are doing (in the Pact). They are allowing themselves to be dragged in the diplomatic game of a foreign Power which is only seeking to bring about among the nations of Europe a disorder from which she alone will reap the benefit.[1]

On March 4 the Foreign Affairs Committee of the Senate recommended the approval of the Pact. On March 7 Hitler convened the Reichstag and informed it that Germany was no longer bound by the Treaty of Locarno, and that German troops had been ordered to occupy the demilitarised zone of the Rhineland.

In a speech to the House on March 9 Mr. Eden made it clear that his government did not share the German view regarding the Franco-Soviet Pact, and that Germany's action had profoundly shaken confidence in the trustworthiness of any future obligations she might undertake. On March 12 the Senate in Paris completed the ratification of the Soviet Pact. On March 18 the representatives of England, France, Belgium and Italy met in London and agreed on measures to safeguard the situation created by the German repudiation of the Locarno Treaties. On March 20 M. Flandin told the Chamber that "the Stresa front could now be reconstituted, thanks to the opening of negotiations which, he said, should quickly bring about the cessation of hostilities in Abyssinia and of sanctions against Italy". The wish was, in truth, father to the thought, for Grandi was telling the Council of the League that Italy could not be expected to apply measures which would be incompatible with the position in which the states applying sanctions had placed her. On March 19 the Council declared that "the German Government has committed a breach of Article 43 of the Treaty of Versailles".

As the safeguards built at Locarno to buttress tranquillity were falling in ruins, a storm was gathering in another quarter to threaten the peace of Europe. In 1934 Socialist risings in Spain had been crushed with ruthless severity by the moderate parties which controlled the Cortes. In the course of 1935 the moderates had quarrelled amongst themselves and had failed to produce any stable government. On January 7, 1936, President Zamora dissolved the Cortes and decreed a general election in February. On January 19, Sotelo, a former minister of finance, addressing an audience in Barcelona warned 'patriotic Spaniards' that unless they bestirred themselves after the elections "there would wave over Spain the Red Flag, the symbol of the destruction of Spain's past, her ideals and her honour". In fear of a Fascist dictatorship, the various parties to the left, socialists, communists and anarchists drew together in what was known as 'the Popular Front' and won the elections by a substantial majority. On February 29 a large demonstration was held attended by Companys, the Catalan leader released from prison. One speaker announced that he brought "salutation that will go straight to your hearts from the Soviet Union, whose sympathy was with you during the glorious gesture of the October revolt". On April 7 the Cortes dismissed President Zamora for dissolving the Cortes on January 7 on his own authority. His place was taken by Azaña, the prime minister. Meanwhile, the country plunged into chaos. On April 19 Sotelo charged the government with failure to govern and declared that since they had taken office 106 churches had been burned and 74 persons killed. He warned the cabinet of the progress of Red propaganda in the army, and said that the dictatorship of the proletariat might lead to a counter-attack to set up a totalitarian state. On April 24 an official welcome was given to 120 Spaniards who had fled to Russia in October 1934. On April 28 Miguel Madia, who had led that rising and had just been released and made Barcelona's chief of police, was murdered with his brother. On June 9 the cabinet decided to open an embassy in Moscow. On July 12 Lieutenant Castillo, a police officer, who in April had killed a Fascist, cousin of the Marquis de Estella, was shot. The following night some police revenged the death of their comrade by murdering Sotelo. On July 18 the army rose in revolt, led by troops in Morocco. Their commander, General Franco, declared that their aims were in no sense anti-republican, but that misrule and interference from Moscow had made it imperative to remove the existing government from power. The government replied by calling on the people to assert their constitutional authority, and the country was plunged into civil war.

While these events were in progress in Spain a general election was due in France. There also the rising terror of Fascism had brought the Socialist and Communist parties together in a popular front. The final results announced on May 4 revealed a decisive swing to the Left. The Front Populaire secured a majority of 144. On June 4 a government was formed with M. Blum, a socialist Jew, as prime minister. A spontaneous and widespread outbreak of strikes suggested the fear that Labour might follow the primrose path to the bonfire lighted in Spain. But the patience and firmness of Blum averted the danger.

Immediately after the military rising in Spain two Italian planes made a forced landing in French Morocco. It was found that the planes and some of their crew had belonged to the Italian air force. They carried equipment for war and the papers found on them showed that their destinations were Ceuta and Melilla. It was widely believed that arms, munitions and trained combatants were finding their way from Germany to support the Insurgents. In France the supporters of M. Blum were clamouring for supplies to be sent to the government in Spain. Firmly refusing to adopt such a course M. Blum appealed to the British and Italian governments for "the rapid adoption of rigid observance of an agreed arrangement for non-intervention in Spain". He was heartily supported by England and similar appeals were made to Russia, Germany and Portugal. Non-intervention was adopted 'in principle' and an international committee was established in London to give effect to this policy.

On August 11 the Soviet government lowered the

age for calling recruits to the colours. The German reply soon followed. On August 24, 1936, a decree was issued by Hitler extending the period of active compulsory service in the army, navy and air force from one to two years. In the press the change was traced back to Barthou's rejection of the German disarmament proposals in favour of an alliance with Russia. The real difficulty, said the *Frankfurter Zeitung*, was no longer Versailles but was connected with the Popular Front projecting over France, which brought with it obligations and friendships disturbing to Franco-German relations. The German press was also attacking Russia for "intervening in Spain to spread Communism, and France for 'double-dealing' in putting forward 'a very dubious non-intervention proposal,' while at the same time permitting the delivery of French arms to the Spanish government". On August 27 the Russian ambassador arrived in Madrid and was warmly welcomed.

On September 9 the Nuremberg rally was used to denounce Bolshevism. Herr Hess said:

> A number of nations had recognized that the civilisation of the world was a great community bound together by fate in face of Bolshevism. The delegates of those nations to the Rally were particularly welcome, above all those of the Fascist Party of Italy which was, beside the Nazi Party, the most important anti-Bolshevist organisation.

On September 12 the Führer, addressing a Labour Front Congress, said:

> "We need rubber, therefore we will put German industry in a position to make German rubber. We need petrol. We will get it from the German soil." He then referred to Russia, where "life is fine for the bureaucrats, but not for the workers . . . while Russia has eighteen times as much territory as we have, Bolshevism cannot feed its people. What failures they are! If I had the Ural Mountains with their incalculable stores of raw materials; Siberia with its

vast forests; or the Ukraine, with its tremendous wheat fields, Germany, under National-Socialism, would be swimming in plenty."

Speaking two days later, he said:

Democracy disintegrated the European States and rendered them incapable of appreciating the danger. It formed the channel along which Bolshevism poured its poison into the different countries. He thought it possible that "Popular Fronts" or "similarly disguised Coalition Governments" would arise and endeavour to eliminate the last existing power of resistance to Bolshevism in these nations. If they succeeded Europe would relapse into a "sea of blood and grief".

On September 20 the *Völkischer Beobachter* reported that 200 Soviet aeroplanes, manned by Russians, had reached Barcelona. Next day it was stated in Rome that, until Italian relations with France and Great Britain had been completely clarified, it would be difficult to open negotiations for a new agreement to replace Locarno.

On October 14 the King of the Belgians addressing his cabinet supported their proposal for extending the period of military service to eighteen months: "We must follow", he said, "a policy exclusively and entirely Belgian. That policy should aim resolutely at placing us outside any disputes of our neighbours." Next day it was stated in Brussels that the government were rightly interpreting the wishes of their people in seeking to avoid for the future commitments which would automatically involve them in a Franco-German war. Since March 7 the Locarno Treaty had ceased to exist, and this had altered their position. The foreign minister added, "remember Abyssinia, which was led to believe that by basing her defence on the policy of collective security she would be saved". In Italy "the King of Belgium's speech was held by the press to justify the view that, given the unsettled and fluid condition of Europe, no conference of the Locarno Powers should be called until after the most careful preparation". In Germany Dr. Rosenberg said "that the return of Belgium to neutrality showed that the world was realizing that an alliance between France and Russia, as it existed in 1914, was a different matter from the Franco-Soviet Pact". On October 19 "statements in Rome as to Count Ciano's visit to Berlin included the comment that the two countries found a natural basic affinity in their political régimes, and that there was a convergence of interests upon many fundamental European problems". On October 10 General de Llano, one of the Insurgent leaders in Spain, "declared that Russia was aiding the Madrid Government and warned the Soviet that the insurgents had received offers of thousands of men from certain foreign Powers, which would be accepted if Russian propaganda in Spain and further political chicanery did not cease". On October 15 Stalin informed the Spanish Communist party that the "workers of the U.S.S.R. would merely fulfil their duty in rendering the revolutionary masses of Spain every possible assistance".

* * * * * *

In this chapter our narrative has ceased to rely on the work of historical writers, even in the form of the *Survey of International Affairs*. As we near the present we have perforce to depend on the work of contemporary journalists. The state of international relations at the moment of closing this story can be best conveyed, if the reader will call up his last reserve of patience and run his eye through the following extracts from *The Bulletin of International News* for the closing months of the year 1936: or at least let him read my analysis of these extracts in the Table of Contents.

On October 21—

The commander of the insurgents' air forces, speaking to the foreign press at Salamanca, said the chief danger of the war leading to international trouble was from Russia, since Russian material was pouring into Barcelona.

On the same day—

At a Hitler Youth demonstration, attended by Count Ciano, the leader of a Fascist Youth organization which was represented announced the launching of a joint Italo-German scheme for the training of youth leaders.

On October 23—

The *Börsen Zeitung*, referring to Count Ciano's conversations with Ministers in Berlin, said that the "movement in which the world, our part of it especially, finds itself goes back to the attack which, with the tolerance of many Western European States, is being made from the East against our civilization".

On October 24 Herr Hitler received Count Ciano, who afterwards inspected the Brown House at Munich.

The Government issued a statement announcing the recognition of Italy's Empire of Abyssinia.

On October 24—

Mussolini, speaking at Bologna, said that in only seven months they had conquered an empire, but they needed far more than that entirely to occupy and pacify it. He continued: "I hold out a great olive branch to the world. This olive branch springs from an immense forest of 8 million bayonets, well-sharpened and thrust from intrepid young hearts."

Signor Gayda, writing in his paper, discussed the Locarno problem and made it clear that Italy had assented to Herr Hitler's thesis that the Franco-Soviet Pact was deliberately aimed at Germany. He added that Italy was "inclined to see in it also a possible threat to herself. She is suspicious of any connection between a new Locarno Treaty and the League, and she maintains that she cannot become a co-guarantor with Great Britain until that country has cleared up her military and political intentions towards Italy."

On October 25—

Count Ciano made a statement to a press gathering which referred to the determination of the two Governments to co-operate in the interests of peace. This joint activity was based not only on common interest but on the "supreme obligation of Germany and Italy to defend their civil institutions".

. . . . .

They had also "agreed to recognize the fact that the National Government of General Franco is supported by the firm will of the Spanish population in the larger part of the national area, where it has succeeded in re-establishing order and civil discipline in contrast with the anarchical conditions prevailing there hitherto. At the same time we have once more confirmed the principle of non-intervention in Spanish affairs, as well as the maintenance of the international obligations entered into in that spirit. . . .

Further, they had "renewed the firm determination of the Italian and German peoples to defend with all energy the sacred inheritance of European civilization in its great institutions based on family and nation. In this spirit we have decided . . . to further the cultural relations between Germany and Italy".

On the same day (October 25)—

Reports from the Bosphorus showed that 12 Soviet vessels had passed there since October 1st, which were believed to be carrying war materials as well as food supplies, etc., for Spain.

It was on this day that—

It was pointed out in semi-official circles in Brussels that, by Article 1 of the Locarno Treaty, Belgium was, by implication, placed on terms of equality with the Great Powers, and now that Germany was rearmed and had militarized the Rhineland, while collective security had collapsed and France had developed a system of alliances —which tended "to divide Europe into two such antagonistic pro-French and anti-German groups as it was the aim of Locarno to dissolve"—Belgium could no longer shoulder the same responsibilities as before.

On November 9 at the Lord Mayor's banquet Mr. Baldwin

spoke with deep concern of the movement going on for rearmament, "an inconceivable folly for those of us who have the responsibility of governing the great countries in Europe". If the nations of Europe devoted for too long their care to arms and forgot the conditions of their people, there would grow discontent and despair. Indeed, he added, if armaments continued, they did not necessarily mean war, but they made it more likely.

War would mean all over Europe a degradation of the life of the people; it meant in the end, anarchy and world revolution.

In Britain they were looking to their defences; "and quite right too", and he went on: "I am prepared to devote all our efforts, whatever it may cost in men and money, to do what is necessary, but I am conscious all the time of the folly of all of us. I say the defence of this nation is inevitable in world circumstances and we are determined to leave no stone unturned to do all that we may consider necessary."

On November 10—

The discovery of a foreign plot to build up a Fascist organization was announced (in Moscow), and several foreign residents were reported to have been arrested. They were stated to include five Germans, as well as Poles, Austrians and Swedes.

On November 14 the German Government

formally denounced Part 12 (Section 2, chapters 3 and 4, and Section 6) of the Treaty of Versailles, relating to the internationalization of the Rhine, Danube, Elbe, Oder, Moselle and Niemen, and to the Kiel Canal.

On the same day—

The Government forces launched an offensive on all the insurgent positions round Madrid, and both sides claimed successes.

Reports from insurgent sources stated that two Russian vessels had arrived at Barcelona with war materials; also that 100 Russian bombing and fighter planes of the latest type had just arrived for the Madrid forces, besides tanks and anti-aircraft guns.

On November 17 in the House of Lords—

Lord Lothian asked for a precise declaration of the Government's attitude towards the League, as to whether they had in view Mr. Churchill's conception of it, for that meant fighting anywhere and everywhere in Europe to preserve the *status quo*, unless it were altered by League methods. Were they to go to war to maintain a Europe consisting of 26 Sovereign States armed to the teeth, to maintain the existing system in all circumstances? If that was not the Government's policy they should say plainly what they would fight for.

He did not think that the proper way to preserve the British Commonwealth was to accept responsibility all over Europe.

He also said it was difficult to understand what the Franco-Soviet Pact meant. The German General Staff was saying, "Can you assure us that if there is a war in the East we shall not be attacked in the West? If we have to face a war on both frontiers we must begin in the West."

On the same day (November 17)—

It was stated in Moscow that the Japanese Foreign Minister had informed the Soviet Ambassador that the Japanese Government and "a third party" had been discussing ways and means to combat Communism.

Semi-official comment on the news included the remark that the third party was Germany, and that the version of the agreement describing it as anti-Communist was merely a screen for the real agreement, which provided for co-ordination of action by Japan and Germany in case one of them should be at war with a third Power.

M. Litvinoff was reported to have told the German Ambassador that the majority of the Germans arrested had already confessed to the charges made against them.

On November 18 Italy refused to support France in protesting against Germany's denunciation of the

'Waterway' articles of the Treaty of Versailles. On the same day (November 18) Mr. Baldwin speaking at Glasgow said that in 1934 the government could not have got a mandate for national rearmament. Germany's action of March 7 last, the reintroduction of conscription, and the Abyssinian war had convinced large sections of the British people that rearmament was essential.

On that day (November 18) the German and Italian governments recognised the government of General Franco in Spain. General Franco announced that Germany and Italy,

> with Portugal and Spain, form the bulwark of culture, civilization and Christianity in Europe. This moment marks the peak of the life of Spain no less than the life of the world.

On November 19 nine 'Trotskyist wreckers' were placed on trial in Russia, including Stickling, a German, alleged to have confessed that he came to Russia to wreck the Soviet system according to a plan devised abroad.

On the same day (November 19) Mr. Eden, referring to foreign intervention in Spain, said to the House of Commons, "so far as breaches are concerned I wish to state categorically that I think there are other Governments more to blame than either Germany or Italy". On November 20 speaking at Leamington he said:

> British arms would never be used in a war of aggression, and they would never be used for a purpose inconsistent with the League Covenant or the Kellogg Treaty, but "they may", he went on, "and if the occasion arose they would be used in our own defence and in defence of the territories of the British Commonwealth. They may, and if the occasion arose they would, be used in the defence of France and Belgium against unprovoked aggression in accordance with our existing obligations. They may, and if a new Western European settlement can be reached they

would, be used in defence of Germany were she the victim of unprovoked aggression by any of the other signatories of such a settlement."

On the same day, November 20, Signor Gayda wrote

that it must be said very clearly, and without any useless turn of phrase, that Italy "is not prepared to see planted in the Mediterranean, on Spanish soil, a new centre of the Red revolution, a new base of Communist political and military operations".

Italy and "other strong and decided nations of Europe" were determined to prevent the grave error by which the Mediterranean had been opened to Soviet warships (by Montreux) from becoming the starting point of the absolutely irreparable destruction of European order. In undertaking this the anti-Communist defence of Italy, Germany and Japan would not be passive only, but "will assume such forms of reaction, though not offensive forms, as may be imposed by the aggressive initiative of the Soviets and of their Communist Committees".

On November 20, 2000 French volunteers joined the government militia in Barcelona.

On November 21 General Faupel, an officer qualified by special experience to advise on military operations in Spain, was sent by Hitler to represent him at Franco's headquarters. On the same day, November 21, the 12th International Brigade arrived in Madrid to form with the 11th a six-battalion division under the command of General Kleber, an officer in the service of the Soviet government.

On November 22 the *Völkischer Beobachter* described the Moscow arrests as "an international challenge". On November 24 four more Germans were arrested in Russia. On November 25 the Soviet government commuted the death sentence passed on Stickling to ten years' imprisonment. On the same day (November 25) an agreement with Japan against the Communist International was signed in Berlin by Herr von Ribbentrop and the Japanese ambassador.

In a statement to the Official News Agency, Herr von Ribbentrop said the Agreement was an epoch-making event, a turning point in the defensive struggle of all nations loving order and civilization against the forces of subversion.

Japan would never permit the spread of Bolshevism in East Asia, Germany formed the bulwark against this pest in the heart of Europe, and Italy would hold high the anti-Bolshevist banner in the South. He was convinced that the countries which had not yet realized the danger would one day be grateful to the Führer.

Count Mushakoji said Germany and Japan were the countries against which the resolutions of the 7th Congress of the Comintern were specially directed, and he was convinced that, acting together as guarantors of peace in the East and West, they would contribute, by the Agreement, to the pacification of the world.

While the Japanese-German agreement was welcomed in Rome it was pointed out that the understanding reached in Berlin by Count Ciano needed no amplification, and the paucity of Italian interests in the Pacific made it unnecessary for Italy to proceed beyond the establishment of the identity of views with Japan on the subject of Communism.

On the same day (November 25)—

The extraordinary Congress of Soviets, convened as a constituent assembly to pass the new Constitution, opened in Moscow, and the 2,050 delegates were addressed by Stalin, who called the Constitution "an indictment of Fascism inspiring all civilized people fighting for democracy against Fascist barbarism".

On November 26—

The Premier of the Ukrainian Republic, speaking in the Congress, accused Germany and Japan of preparing a "holy crusade against the Soviet Union", and warned the Nazis that marching into the Ukraine was more difficult than marching into the Rhineland. If they dared to approach the Soviet borders the Red Army would strike them a blow such as had never been seen in history, and he exclaimed "Hitler will not see our Ukrainian garden".

Izvestia, referring to the German-Japanese Agreement, said it was concluded against other countries as well as Russia. "Each of its participants", it stated, "sees in it a weapon for its aggressive conquering schemes; Japan, a weapon for the establishment of her monopoly of rule in Eastern Asia and the Pacific; and Fascist Germany a weapon for the conquest of Europe and the Near East. These are the real contents of the deal, which futilely drapes itself in ideological garments."

On the same day (November 26)—

M. Delbos received the Russian and Portuguese Ambassadors and was believed to have made an earnest appeal to both of them for a drastic reduction, if not a complete cessation, of the supplying of arms to the belligerents in Spain.

M. Potemkin was reported to have replied that his Government would be only too glad to take part, with Italy and Germany, in a joint return to real, as opposed to theoretical, non-intervention, but that they could not give an example in the faint hope that the Fascist countries would follow it.

The Portuguese Ambassador was reported to have observed that the existing largely moral support of Portugal would not be withdrawn unless Russia refrained from further activity in the Peninsula.

On November 27 an announcement was made in Japan that its government recognised Italy's rule in Abyssinia and that Italy recognised Manchukuo.

On the same day, November 27, the Spanish foreign minister sent a note to the secretary-general of the League requesting that the Council should be summoned to examine the situation in Spain in virtue of Article 11, paragraph 2 of the Covenant.

On November 28, speaking in Congress, M. Litvinoff said:

Fascism was ceasing to be an internal affair with the countries professing it. It had been this in Italy at first, but this had changed "after Mussolini's Fascism had been polished up by lessons from Berlin—it then became fertilized with the theories of German National-Socialism".

He referred to the great assistance given to the Spanish insurgents by both Germany and Italy, especially in the air, and said the German and Italian aeroplanes were in the hands of German and Italian pilots.

On the same day (November 28) M. Delbos

let it be known that he would announce publicly, in the near future, that France was prepared to assume the same obligations towards Great Britain as those publicly assumed on behalf of Britain by Mr. Eden in his speech of November 20th.

On November 29—

It was considered in Rome that a meeting of the League Council in consequence of the Spanish request for this would create "a grave and dangerous situation", which might again raise the question of Italy's membership.

The request was described as one of the usual Soviet manœuvres for causing confusion and the danger of war in Europe.

On the same day (November 29)—

The head of the Leningrad Communist Party made a speech in which he said: "Round us are small countries which dream of great adventures, or allow great adventurers to manipulate their territory. We are not afraid of these little countries, but if they do not mind their own business we shall be compelled to open our borders, and it will be too bad if we are compelled to use the Red Army on them."

On November 30 several hundred volunteers arrived in Barcelona from France, including Frenchmen, Germans, Italians, Hungarians, Austrians, Belgians and Poles. On December 1—

Reports were current that a body of Germans, estimated at 5,000 in number, had landed at Cadiz and passed through Seville on the way to the insurgent front.

Two contingents of French volunteers, numbering 4,000 men, were also reported to have landed at Barcelona.

On the same day, December 1, the All Union Congress in Moscow adopted in principle the draft of the new constitution. A commission was set up to embody in the text the amendments approved by Stalin.

* * * * * *

In the early weeks of December the world was amazed by news that Edward VIII. had renounced the throne of the British Commonwealth, in favour of his brother George VI. To deal with the crisis an act of parliament had to be passed in a few hours which, under the Statute of Westminster, required the concurrence of Dominion governments and the subsequent endorsement of their several parliaments. The swiftness and ease with which this crisis was surmounted revealed the strength of the bond which unites the Commonwealth. Though Mr. de Valera seized the occasion to eliminate the Crown from internal affairs of the Irish Free State, the legislation he passed through the Dail maintained the position of the Crown in external affairs. By its own act the Dail recognised the Irish Free State as part of the British Commonwealth, and the status of its citizens as British subjects in international law. The British democracies were, in fact, drawn closer together by a crisis which came as an utter surprise to most of their citizens. The decision with which they met it was in truth their answer to the challenge which dictators continue to hurl at the constitutional system for which they stand. How it helped to revive the courage of the smaller nations in Europe, who still adhere to that system, is shown in a recent speech of the Swedish foreign minister, Sandler. He refused to accept the view that the world's future depends on the issue of a struggle between Communist and Fascist dictatorships.

"By so doing", he said, "we leave no room for democracy and force ourselves to choose between brutalities of different colours. Not upon street fighting in Madrid does the fate of democracy in the world depend. No: the future of democracy depends upon the manner in which democratic States manage their own affairs, and upon their determination to defend themselves against material and ideological attacks."[2]

In an interview given to *The Times* correspondent the prime minister Hansson dotted the *i*'s and crossed the *t*'s. Self-government, he urged, was not a miraculous gift to be had for the asking. It has to be won, and when won, has then to be guarded like a treasure by continuous effort. Its security depends on deeds, not words, on capacity to adapt ourselves to changed conditions, and to sacrifice prejudices to the common good. We must strengthen our governments and show the dictators "who boom their policies and achievements upon a dazed world" that democracies are capable of initiative and decision. In Sweden national defence was no longer a party question. Sweden welcomes proposals for strengthening economic contacts with Scandinavian states, with Holland, Belgium and Switzerland—to mention only the smaller countries. Such a move to strengthen the smaller states, who do not wish to join the Fascist or Communist camps, should have the support of the British Commonwealth.

Such words are felt like a wholesome breeze in an atmosphere reeking with the turgid breath of dictators.

NOTES

[1] Quotations in this chapter are taken from the *Bulletin* except where otherwise stated.

[2] *The Times*, December 19, 1936.

CHAPTER LXXIV

RECAPITULATION

In Book I. we saw how the Kingdom of God was first conceived in the Hebrew mind, and traced the stages through which it developed. In the day of Jehovah the children of Israel were to vanquish the nations around them and bring them under his rule. When the Greek and Roman Empires had developed their overwhelming power the idea had passed to a transcendental plane in the minds of the Chasidim, afterwards known as the Pharisees.[1] The Lord himself, they conceived, would consume the world in fire and make it anew by a second act of creation. In that day of judgment he would sift out the righteous and send the wicked to eternal perdition. In a new heaven and a new earth, redeemed from all sin and from death, he would reign for ever, and sorrow and sighing would flee away. Jews with a spiritual outlook thought in this way in the time of our Lord. The Zealots, largely drawn from the peasants, still clung to the primitive idea of a physical conquest aided by miraculous power.

The mind of Jesus went far beyond these conceptions. To him reality was of the nature of spirit—the supreme personality—God, who created the world as the home of creatures he had made in his likeness. He, like the author of Genesis, held that the work of God's hands was good, though he saw the existence of evil, and made no attempt to explain it. The infinite duty of men to God was to him inseparable from their infinite duty one to another—each to all. He believed that men, though imperfect, could be brought to perfection, to the likeness of God. With the Greeks he saw that the social structure in which they grew up was the principal means to that end. Men would grow to perfection in so far as they learned to base their relations one to another on the laws of God, on the infinite duty of each to all. Their sense of duty and their knowledge how to discharge it would increase in so far as the system which governed their lives evoked and exercised their sense of duty and also their minds. The Kingdom of God as conceived by Jesus would, in fact, when realised, be a commonwealth, though the language he spoke contained no word to convey that idea.

Priests, whose authority he challenged, destroyed him before his essential idea had seized the minds of his simple followers. They had grasped some sides of his teaching and were able to set in motion the greatest revolution in thought, and the most far-reaching change in the structure of human relations, which the world has seen before or since. But under the guidance of Paul their minds reverted to the transcendental ideas of the Pharisee sect in which he was bred. Christ, they believed, would return, clothed with the power of God to destroy this world, to banish those who rejected his teaching to endless punishment and to rule the faithful minority in a new dispensation, a Kingdom of God redeemed from all evil. His followers, here in this world, were merely the germ of that Kingdom. Persecutions, first by the Jews and then by the Roman Empire, encouraged the idea that this world was the Kingdom of Satan, which must be destroyed before the Kingdom of God could come into being. The idea that men must first establish the Kingdom of God amongst themselves in this physical world, as a necessary step to its future existence in time and space, had not entered their minds, was beyond their range. To men of those times the Empire of Rome was the world, and a world-polity. St. Augustine saw it as the City of

Satan destined to early destruction. The Church sheltered the few who would live in the Kingdom of God when their master Christ had returned to destroy and remake the universe. St. Augustine stamped on the Christian mind that attitude which Rousseau described more than fourteen centuries after his time when he wrote:

> The Christians' country is not of this world. . . . If the state flourishes, he scarcely dares to enjoy the public felicity. If the state declines, he blesses the hand of God which lies heavy on his people.[2]

The followers of Christ had completely reverted to the concept of authority which he had challenged, the challenge which led to the cross. The Kingdom of Heaven, as they conceived it, was indeed a kingdom based on divine authority, an idea which was powerfully fostered by the Roman Empire in which they lived. When the Church, the city of God with its transcendental ideas, coalesced with the Roman Empire, the City of Satan, which none the less was the last defence which stood between civilisation and chaos, the problems which arise from the dual conception of church and state began to impose themselves on the world.

The attempt to solve that problem by creating the Holy Roman Empire as an instrument for the secular government of the world, whilst the Church wielded the spiritual power, proved a disastrous failure, for the basic reason that human affairs cannot be so divided. In the endless conflicts between emperors and popes neither Empire nor Papacy developed the attributes of a genuine government such as had ruled in the days of the Caesars. Chaos, maintained in central Europe and Italy till near the close of the nineteenth century, was the fruit of those conflicts. The seclusion which arrested the growth of Japan till the same period was another result of the dream that the Papacy was destined to rule the world.

That dream was in truth destroyed when the real dimensions of the world beyond Christendom were realised by the work begun by Henry the Navigator. By that time there had come into being in England and the Netherlands polities which were not based on the principle of authority, but, all unconsciously, on those which Christ had seen as the true relation of men to God and of men to each other. Those polities had undermined the habit of obedience to Rome. England and Holland together refused to recognise the papal claim to confine the newly discovered world to Catholic rule. From that struggle England emerged the strongest power on the high seas, and behind her fleet developed the freedom of thought and action implicit in her laws. Her people were learning to think of themselves as the state, a feeling developed even more strongly in those of them who founded self-governing colonies in America. By virtue of freedom the English were foremost in achieving that second and greatest conquest of nature, by which men are learning to harness her forces to their use.

Meanwhile the claims of pope and emperor to universal authority had come to be treated as the figment they were and always had been. In Spain, in France, in Austria, Prussia and Russia powerful monarchies had come into being, each based on authority, which they claimed to derive, not from emperor or pope, but direct from Heaven itself, as attested by the principle of heredity. As Louis XIV. boasted, "L'état, c'est moi". The autocrat was the state, and as such could own and govern parcels of territory like landed estates scattered through various parts of Europe. The kings by divine right fought one another to enlarge and extend their possessions, little troubled by the suffering which their wars inflicted on millions of people.

In the eighteenth century the American revolution dealt a final blow to the remnants of kingly authority in England. In America it brought into being a great republic which unmistakeably governed itself—in which, beyond question, the people themselves were the state. This idea laid hold on the French like flame, destroyed the monarchy and swept across Europe. But the French had yet to acquire the habits of mind which enabled the people of England and those of America to govern themselves. Internal order was restored only by a military despotism, which soon developed the typical vices of hereditary despotism. But, none the less, when this period of convulsion was ended, the idea that the people and not its rulers were the state had come to stay, not only in France but throughout Europe. The empires and kingdoms as reconstructed at the Congress of Vienna were mainly composed of territories contiguous to each other, surrounded by one frontier. The preposterous claim that the monarch is himself the state had received its death-blow. The system of national states as we know them to-day came into being, and helped to promote the devotion of the subject to his state, even where its ruler was a despot. At the same time the last remnants of the old idea of a universal authority for human society were banished to the limbo of forgotten things. That idea died with the Holy Roman Empire, and the Holy Alliance signally failed to revive it.

All this was happening in an age when the conquest of natural forces by man was profoundly changing the structure of human society. The change made itself felt in two conflicting and even different directions. On the one hand, the growing use of mechanical power was tending to make every part of the human race dependent on every other. Science was imposing the need of unity on men much faster than men were able to respond to that need. On the other hand, it increased the importance of existing governments. At the close of the eighteenth century the functions of government were thought of as limited to the maintenance of order. By the end of the nineteenth science had forced government to invade every department of human life. The state had become of greater importance to the life of each citizen. The demands which it made on him were also greater. Those two facts, the second no less than the first, tended to increase the sense of devotion in the citizen to his state. The sovereignty of states, which rests not on force but devotion, was raised thereby to a higher power. In accordance with Hegel's philosophy the national state was identified with God. The Great War revealed a stronger devotion in masses of men to their national states than was ever seen in the world before.

Mechanised power has thus helped to promote the authority of law and a sense of obedience to law within the authority of states, which has largely enhanced the power of governments. But between those states and their governments there is no law. Where their interests conflict the dispute must in the end be decided by the will of the stronger as expressed in war. At the same time occasions of conflict are immensely increased by the fact that mechanised power is making every part of mankind, every national state, more dependent than ever on all the others. Whilst governments are able, as never before, to order affairs within their sovereignty in accordance with justice and right, between these national governments there is nothing but anarchy. The world lives in fear of impending war, which ever grows deeper. To an ever-increasing degree each state is driven to spend its resources on weapons of war, and to train its subjects to use them.

The evils which Marx saw and attacked were

mainly the result of this international anarchy. In his blood was a deep aversion to the territorial state. Like St. Augustine he looked on the state as essentially evil. In his view the mechanisation of industry had merely enabled a capitalist minority to seize the power of exploiting the majority, which before was monopolised by the privileged classes. Church and state were controlled by capitalists for the purpose of exploiting the proletariat. To cure these evils the proletariat must rise and destroy by force the state, the church, the institution of private property and all classes above them. In the classless society which would then remain, force and the state, which in Marx's view is founded on force, would both be unnecessary. Force must be used once for all to end the necessity of using force in human affairs. The doctrine of Marx was no less dogmatic than the traditional religions to which it was opposed. It threatened with destruction all who refused to accept its tenets.

The capitalist states, as Marx prophesied, would plunge the world into war, and in doing so give the workers the chance of destroying them. His foresight seemed to be justified by the Great War and the Russian revolution. But Marx had failed to foresee the reactions which his own methods were destined to yield. In central Europe the classes threatened with destruction adopted those methods in self-protection. Experience and training acquired in war enabled them to organise force with greater effect than the communists. In a mechanised age, organisation counted for more than numbers. Against the world communist movement which centred in Moscow, the dictators, who led the militarised classes in central Europe, rallied their forces in the name of nationalism. In Italy and Germany the creed of nationalism was raised to its highest power. Dictatorships based on military power sprang into being in countries where habits of self-government had taken no root. The movement then quickly reacted on Russia itself, where the dictatorship has now been driven to rely on nationalist feeling, and is studious to promote it. So far the Marxian creed, which aimed at producing a communist world society in which government based on force would cease to be necessary, has indeed established a communist regime from western Europe to the shores of the northern Pacific and the frontiers of India and China. But in this regime there is still nothing to show that a ruthless use of force can produce a state of affairs in which the exertion of force becomes unnecessary. The Soviet Republic (so called) is a state which requires the unlimited obedience of its subjects, and exacts that obedience with severity more ruthless than rulers claiming divine authority have dared to use. In the nations beyond its frontiers fear of its violent methods has produced a spirit of nationalism more dogmatic, aggressive and dangerous than ever existed before. A great part of human society is now organised in national states, ruled by despots, who are teaching their subjects that a nation must live for itself alone, that nothing counts in this world but force, that war is a thing desirable in itself.

The idea that force can avail to eliminate force from human affairs was not confined to the communists. It has also inspired the dream that war could be ended once for all by fighting one war to an end and winning it. The hopes that we cherished in the hours of victory were expressed by President Wilson in his 14 points, which victors and vanquished agreed to accept as the basis of peace. In a speech at Milan on November 1, 1936, Mussolini, in a characteristic outburst, stamped on their grave. We must wipe the slate clean, he said, of

all the illusions and conventional falsehoods which still

constitute the remains of the great shipwreck of the Wilsonian ideologies.

> One of these illusions has crashed, the illusion of disarmament. No one wishes to disarm first, and to expect that all should disarm together is impossible and absurd. . . . Another illusion that we reject is that which passes under the name of collective security. Collective security has never existed, does not exist, and will never exist. A virile people realises its collective security within its own frontiers and refuses to entrust its destinies to the uncertain hands of third parties. Another commonplace which must be rejected is that of indivisible peace. Indivisible peace could only mean one thing—indivisible war. But the peoples refuse, and rightly refuse, to fight for interests which do not concern them.

The League of Nations, he added, is faced with this dilemma either to renew itself or to perish, and "as it is difficult to see how it can renew itself, it can, so far as we are concerned, tranquilly perish".

Can this brutal challenge be answered? As a record of sheer frustration what chapter in history compares with that which the nations have written for themselves since the war? They had seen the horrors inseparable from war in a mechanised age and had sought to end them by virtue of compacts between sovereign and national states. The fact must be faced that to-day the attempt has failed. The world has almost ceased to believe that written compacts have any binding effect on the national states that sign them. Nor is this true of dictators only who openly flaunt their belief that nothing counts in human affairs but naked force and national interest; for two ancient empires, the one in Asia, the other in Africa, have been left to their fate at the hands of aggressors by all the nations who signed the Covenant and entered the League. The Locarno Treaties and the Kellogg Pact are a dead letter. No state in the world as it is to-day is prepared to depend on the League for its safety. The smaller democracies, like the strongest dictatorships, are beating their pruning-hooks into swords and their ploughs into spears, preparing the earth for a harvest of blood. The belief that force is the only factor which counts in human affairs is invading the field of our own Commonwealth and threatening its order. As I write these words I see in the daily paper a picture of the place where the Prince of Peace was born, the church of the Nativity at Bethlehem, surrounded by soldiers with arms in their hands.[3] In the story told in these pages I can point to no time which appears so fraught with disaster to the human race as a whole as the present, the moment at which I am bringing this book to a close.

If I thought that its pages must end on a note of fear and despair I would burn them before they were printed; "*For fear is nothing else but a betraying of the succours which reason offereth*".[4] My thoughts revert to that scene when he that was born at Bethlehem, despised and rejected of men, was scourged and condemned to the death of a slave and a criminal. From that moment of utter despair there sprang the movement which has gone some way to create, and in the ages before us will bring to fulfilment, the Kingdom of God upon earth, the Divine Commonwealth, a human society based on the laws of God, on the one abiding reality, the infinite duty of men to God, of one to another.

Of all the lessons brought to my mind in the long task of framing this narrative the deepest is this, that apparent failure, when faced with courage and examined by reason, is the road to superlative triumph. That, I believe, is the true meaning which underlies all that has happened since the dawn which broke upon Easter Day. The spirit of Christ rose from his grave. It moved and yet moves the souls of men to face and accomplish the task which he set them.

Death and the pain which war inflicts upon men are not the essential evils with which they are threatened, but their own fear and failure to use to the full such powers as they have. Pain and death are not the ultimate evil which the study of medicine seeks to remove. Rather they have the value of symptoms that force to their notice diseased conditions which diminish their strength for the work they are called on to do, and impel them to study and deal with their causes. So the menace of war is a sign which points to a deep, though far less obvious, mischief in the state of mankind. We have thought to abolish the risk of war by a system of covenants and pacts between sovereign states. The visible failure of this experiment is needed to make us inquire once more whether the scale of values we accept is a true one. It drives us to reconsider the question—What is the ultimate end which men in their lives on this earth should pursue?

This was the question raised in the closing chapter of Book I. The answer suggested is implicit in the words of our Lord, "Seek ye first the Kingdom of God, and all things else shall be added unto you". The end and object of human society is to increase in men their sense of duty, one to another, and not, as a British statesman has told us, to raise the standard of living. The souls of men, as our Lord believed, were endowed by their Father, God, with an infinite capacity for growing to perfection. Illumined by Greek thought he had seen that, of all the things which mould and develop the minds of men, the social and political structure in which they grow up is the strongest. He was trying to convince the world that men can grow to perfection, but only in so far as they mould their relations one to another on the principle that each man owes an infinite duty to God, and therefore to all his fellows.

The organisation of tribal society into sovereign

states, a necessary step to that end, will block its final achievement if the sovereignty of national states is regarded, as it now is, by leaders in church and state as the last word in human development. We have now reached a stage in the growth of civilisation which cannot go further, and is doomed to go back, until we discover the means of passing from the national to the international state, to the state in the truest and fullest sense of that word. We can, I believe, discover those means if, feeling the awful danger of war, we do not allow our fears to betray the succours which reason offers. Since that distant age, when a knowledge of good and evil dawned on the minds of creatures living in forests and caves, they have gone from strength to strength. Human nature has made immeasurable strides since our Lord showed in his own person how divine it can be. But it cannot advance further till men learn to think of the scheme of human relations which he conceived as one to be brought from the realm of dreams to the earth in which they live, to be made incarnate in the flesh and blood of a living society. That is the world situation, as I see it, to-day.

NOTES

[1] See p. 98.
[2] See p. 365.
[3] *The Daily News and Chronicle*, December 21, 1936.
[4] The Apocrypha, Wisdom of Solomon, xvii. 12.

BOOK III

AN ATTEMPT TO APPLY THE GUIDING PRINCIPLE SUGGESTED IN BOOK I TO THE WORLD POSITION AS STATED IN BOOK II

CHAPTER I

THE KEY TO CONFUSED SITUATIONS

In 1935 the Dean of St. Paul's met a friend whose work kept him in touch with students throughout the world, and asked him what was their outlook on life at that time. His friend replied that young men were distraught by fear of two things—of finding no work through which they could earn a living, and of wars in which national governments would send them to fight and destroy one another. A whole generation which has learned how to use the forces of nature to meet its needs is oppressed by a fear that it will not be free to employ those forces for increasing its welfare, but may have to use them for mutual destruction.

In reviewing this situation there is, I suggest, at any rate one conclusion which issues with practical certainty. The dangers and difficulties under which the world as a whole is labouring, and which overshadow the mind of the young who have still the greater part of their lives to live, spring from one central cause. In the course of a few generations human beings have learned to control physical forces without acquiring a like measure of control over themselves and their relations one to another. Every serious effort to understand the present sense of ill-being which pervades human society leads the inquirer to this conclusion. One might shrink from repeating this truism were it not that its vital importance is so commonly disregarded in practice. Sir Josiah Stamp, whose main business in life is directing a vast system of mechanisation, went so far as to say that it would not matter if no important discovery in the region of physical science was made for the next twenty years. Yet those who have to organise study know how much more easy it is to raise funds to equip physical laboratories than it is to raise funds to promote social research. An officer employed to dispense funds for research in America told me that his greatest difficulty lay in the fact that the best minds were attracted to physical science.

For all this there are two closely connected reasons. Physical facts can be measured and stated with far greater precision than facts in the sphere of human relations. Conclusions reached are more easy to prove, and also yield practical results which are definite and often dramatic. Physicists live to see the results of their work issue in men flying, or in hearing and seeing each other from opposite sides of the world. The effect of all these discoveries on human relations is immense; but it cannot be measured and stated with anything like the precision attained in presenting physical data. Inductions from human data cannot be proved with the same exactitude; nor do they issue in rapid spectacular shape like the physical inventions which impress even children and savages. And yet the conclusions which issue from the study of human relations are in the end potent as those which come from the study of physical data. The ideas of Moses, Jeremiah, Plato, Aristotle, Paul, Augustine, Adam Smith, Kant, Marx or Whitehead do, in the long run, affect the course of human affairs as deeply as those of Copernicus, Harley, Newton, Faraday or Einstein.

The study of physical nature belongs to the realm of knowledge. The study of human relations must go beyond the frontiers of knowledge and enter the realm of wisdom. It discredits itself when it tries to reach its conclusions merely by a patient collection and analysis of facts. The collection of facts about human relations is essential, and often demands more labour and a greater expenditure of money than collection of physical data. But a study of human phenomena which relies on methods which yield such spectacular results when applied to physical data ends in a parody of the thing which it apes.

Physical science is from its nature departmental, even when it tries to consider what the physical universe is as a whole. Human science to fulfil its object must be catholic in the literal sense of that word. It must study human relations in all their departments; but it misses its final purpose when it fails in the effort to think of life as a whole. It should never cease to consider what is the end to be sought in all these diverse activities, or to have in its mind some answer to that question. For human activity proceeds by devising means to an end; but the means, as we handle them, tend to obscure the end and to be mistaken for ends in themselves. This defect of the human mind will be found to vitiate every department of life. What we call professionalism is the chronic disease of all the professions. The bedside manner developed by doctors, the unction of parsons or the over-refinement of lawyers are cases in point. Another is the failing of public servants which Dickens described as red-tape, which means that officials have come to think more of the methods of office than of the service which their office should render the public. Admiral Mahan has been quoted as saying that a military leader whose strategy is sound can afford to commit tactical blunders; but no tactical skill will save a military leader whose strategy is wrong. Commanders of regiments and warships, and even of armies and fleets, become so absorbed in the technical task of manœuvring their units that they lose sight of the ultimate aim of the war. They are mere tacticians. The strategist is the leader who never forgets the ultimate aim of the war.

Mahan's observation is as true when applied to all the activities of peace, and most of all in the field of politics. How many of those who direct the fortunes of states have envisaged and kept in mind the end which they ought to attain for the people whose life they direct?

The Covenant was a plan for preventing war. The project of equipping the League with police of its own, Locarno, the Kellogg Pact and a number of similar plans proposed and some of them realised, had the same object in view. Yet the sense of general security has declined. Throughout the world men everywhere feel that they live in a structure which some crime like the murder at Sarajevo, some despot drunk with excess of his own power or distraught by terror of losing it, or even some mere accident, may bring crashing about their heads. They are so possessed with a sense of impending disaster that they cannot apply their minds to the tasks of providing clothing and bread for themselves and their children.

In my own experience in South Africa, India and Ireland, I have met with problems which seemed to move in a vicious circle. Ingenious and elaborate plans for solving them had been found to lead nowhere. Reasons for doing this or that were so evenly balanced as to paralyse decision; or those who were forced to act acted at random. The one sure way to escape from such vicious circles is, I suggest, to leave aside the discussion of practical plans in all their intricacy until you have reached some clear view of the ultimate object you ought to attain. When you feel that your mind has grasped the end you are seeking, then look at the plans proposed in the light of that view. Test them by asking how far they are genuine means to the end as you see it. The sense of frustration produced by their detail will vanish. The ultimate object, when clearly viewed, will itself suggest plans of a similar nature, though usually plans which require more courage.

This method of approaching practical problems was in fact brought to my mind, or rendered explicit, by an incident which I here propose to relate.

In 1908 Lord Morley, a man of advanced democratic ideas, had remarked when explaining his scheme for Indian Reforms in the House of Lords: "If it could be said that this chapter of reforms led directly or indirectly to the establishment of a parliamentary system in India, I, for one, would have nothing at all to do with it".[1] The ideas expressed in these words still held the field when I visited India some years later, and was taken by Sir Valentine Chirol to the camp of a senior officer engaged on a tour of inspection. For several weeks we were able to see how our host administered a great division of one of the provinces, with the sense of pleasure one feels in watching a craftsman who is master of his tools. What impressed us most was the ease and rapidity with which he decided the questions laid before him by subordinate officers.

One early morning our host led us to the top of a great dam which had just been built where a river emerged from the hills. Turning his back on the valley which was slowly filling with water, the commissioner pointed to the jungle which covered the plains below us and was now to be cleared and brought under crops. "Here", he said, "is a difficult decision I have to make. There are two ways in which we can clear and settle this country. If we parcel it out to zemindars (landlords) they will get it cleared and settled by tenants in a very short time. If we try to settle the ryots (cultivators) ourselves it will take much longer. I have to confess that I find myself quite unable to decide which of these two plans to follow, and I want your opinion." To this I replied that I had no opinion to offer. Even if

I had one, the views of a man who had been in India a few weeks could have no value for one who had spent his life there. "None the less", said our obstinate host, "I mean to have your opinion. I want to see how the question strikes a mind that comes perfectly fresh to it." He was greatly in earnest, and I felt it discourteous to refuse. So I said: "If you will give me some more information I will try to form an opinion, but I still believe that it can have no value. Let me think what questions I ought to ask you." "That is fair", said our host. "If you ask me questions, I will try to answer them."

Greatly puzzled, I thought for some time and at length said: "The question which occurs to me is so general that I almost shrink from putting it. For several weeks we have watched you at work and have seen what the British administration is doing in India. It is giving the people a justice more effective and purer than any they have known in the past. It is combating plague and famine. It is teaching them new methods of agriculture and protecting the ryot from usury. In villages and towns it is introducing sanitary methods. In the schools it is giving them genuine knowledge. Throughout the country it is keeping the peace. Now the question I have to ask is this: Are these and the other benefits which our rule confers the ultimate end which it has in view? Or is it looking to something beyond these things, to enabling the people to provide these benefits for themselves?" After pausing for some time the commissioner replied: "Your question is a fair one; but I have to confess that I am not prepared with an answer. I will give you an answer, but we must postpone further discussion until I am able to give it."

The subject was not referred to again till late that evening when we sat round the camp-fire. The commissioner then returned to it. "I have been thinking all day of the question you put me this morning, and now I find myself able to answer it. I think that we ought to be looking beyond the immediate things that you see we are doing. We must make it our aim to enable the people of India to manage these things for themselves and, in the end, to do without us. After thinking over the matter all day I can see no other answer to be given than this. Now, what is your next question?" "My next question", I said, "is whether in the light of your long experience the zemindari or ryotwari system of land-tenure is most likely to fit the people who live under it to manage their own affairs?" With no hesitation our host replied: "The ryotwari system, of course".

This practical question as to how an area of land should be settled with human beings had baffled this experienced officer for months, possibly for years. The real question he had overlooked, and left unsettled in his mind, was not a question of detail but of ultimate values. When persuaded to turn from the question of policy and answer first the question of values which lay behind it, he was able at once to decide his policy in the light of his own answer. Many years after, when the Round Table Conference was meeting in England, the answer he gave to my second question was strongly confirmed. I happened to meet Mr. Iyengar, editor of the *Hindu*, and asked him if I was right in thinking that the Montagu-Chelmsford reforms had succeeded better in Madras than elsewhere. If so, what did he think was the reason. "Yes", he replied, "they succeeded better in Madras because of the ryotwari system established there by Sir Thomas Munro".

I have thus been led to believe that a path through the thickets of life can always be found by first deciding what is the ultimate goal we are trying to reach. When our purposes cross each other, let us look to the nature of our purpose to see what it is, before we devise plans to avoid thwarting each other. If in the process we find one purpose beyond all others worthy of attainment, we shall then find the question how to avoid thwarting each other easier to answer.

The most obvious truths are often the most neglected. Emerson remarked that while curious and exceptional things interest the talented mind, genius fastens on those which are common. On the very day that I read this remark of Emerson, Simpson, the state entomologist, a gifted American, called to advise me how to cope with white-ants which were ruining my trees. We spent a thrilling hour together, at the close of which Simpson remarked, "The trouble of my profession is that entomologists spend so much of their time on the rarer insects. The really important insects are the commoner species like termites and house-flies." A few days later he died of enteric, an immeasurable loss to science and South Africa; but his parting remark riveted Emerson's saying in my mind. The most obvious methods are those we neglect. We cannot expect much from the medicines prescribed by a doctor who has not paused to diagnose the malady he is treating. We must learn to state problems before we discuss their solutions. Having stated the problem we must also consider what is the end at which we are aiming in trying to solve it.

Of the first Book of this volume a friendly reviewer remarked that the task essayed was "really no less than that of defining the *summum bonum*, the end and purpose of human existence, and of stating the process by which it may be achieved". Other reviewers described the book as 'ambitious', a word which suggests that so great a theme should only be handled by minds of the highest order. To this my answer must be that the question is one which stands to be answered by every rational man for himself.

Failure to consider and answer it explains why so much discussion of world affairs leads to so little result. Counsel is darkened by argument leading nowhere, for the simple reason that the disputants have never really considered where they are trying to go. What is the practical use of discussing the state of the world as a whole unless there is some agreement as to what the purpose of life on this earth should be? To answer that question we must dare to consider what life is, and what are the ultimate realities. We can reach and express our conclusions, each for himself, without presuming to say that we know the end and object of life, that we know what life and reality are. Before we begin to talk of knowing we do well to consider what knowledge is and what are its limitations. I dare to assert that plans for reforming society have little value when framed by people who have not sought to answer these questions or are not prepared to state what answers they find.

We are told by the churches that divine revelation has answered these questions, or has answered them enough for practical purposes. The human mind, it is held, cannot answer such questions for itself. A sufficient knowledge for practical guidance has, therefore, been given through supernatural channels. The truth was conveyed in visions or otherwise to the minds of prophets and was placed on record in their writings for the guidance of men. The divine authority of these men was often attested by their visible power to work miracles. The belief of St. Paul in the teaching of Jesus was finally based on belief that the person of Jesus had risen from the grave, and had made himself known after physical death on the cross to himself and to many disciples. It was clear to St. Paul that, were he convinced that Jesus in person had not made himself known to his followers after death by supernatural means, the faith that he preached would be worthless.

In Book I., I have argued that miracles did not in fact happen, and most of the orthodox criticism has fastened on that point. But as yet no critic has grappled with the major point that I raised, which was this. Even if miracles did happen in fact could they afford evidence to prove the teaching of those who worked them? Can the ultimate problems of life be resolved by anything which happens in the world of phenomena? This question can be answered by taking an instance—the moral sense. In men is an instinct which tells them that the difference in acting this way or that is of infinite importance. So strong is this instinct with many that they choose to obey it, even when doing so means torture and death to themselves. Men have even done so when they believed that death was the end of existence itself. Now is or is not this instinct valid? Is it based on the truth, or is it an illusion? That is, I submit, the supreme enigma, the ultimate question, which each must in some way or other answer for himself. But can we find the answer in anything which could happen in the world of events? Can anyone picture and describe an event supernatural or natural which would settle that question once for all and place it for ever beyond dispute? If God himself should appear every day to all men and affirm the infinite difference of right from wrong, we should soon be disputing whether it was really God who appeared, and whether God existed at all. We should find men who doubted, and rightly doubted, the evidence of their senses, who found in their minds something which questioned that evidence as final. And the same thing would happen if one rose from the dead to warn us that the consequence of acts to ourselves was not ended with life on this earth.

And he said, I pray thee, therefore, father, that thou wouldest send him to my father's house; for I have five brethren; that he may testify unto them, lest they also come into this place of torment. But Abraham saith, They have Moses and the prophets; let them hear them. And he said, Nay, father Abraham: but if one go to them from the dead, they will repent. And he said unto him, If they hear not Moses and the prophets, neither will they be persuaded if one rise from the dead.[2]

As the being called man attained to humanity he came to realise that life is a riddle. He is faced by the question how to live it, and still in his childhood craves to be given some final answer which he cannot mistake and none can dispute. He shrinks from the truth that the writers who told the stories of Elijah and Job had begun to divine.

And, behold, the Lord passed by, and a great and strong wind rent the mountains, and brake in pieces the rocks before the Lord; but the Lord was not in the wind: and after the wind an earthquake, but the Lord was not in the earthquake: And after the earthquake a fire, but the Lord was not in the fire: and after the fire a still small voice. And it was so, when Elijah heard it, that he wrapped his face in his mantle, and went out, and stood in the entering in of the cave.[3]

So also with Job when he pleads and demands that an answer to the riddle of life shall be given him in some unmistakable form. But "God vouchsafes to Job no revelation . . . whatever help is to be obtained is to be had, not through an oracle, but by the exercise of Job's own thought".[4] The unpalatable truth, bitter in the mouth, but sweet in the belly, was dawning on the minds of those who had told these stories. In the parable of Dives and Lazarus it becomes explicit. The truth by which we are to live is to be sought by each for himself. We can find great help in the teaching of those that are wiser than ourselves; but we alone can decide who are the wise and what in their teaching is false or true. The return of one of them from the dead could help in no way to decide whether the thing that he told us was true. Our own conscience and mind, inseparable faculties, are the final oracle. With them we must read the world about us and make up our minds what it is, in order to know how we should live in it.

This belief that an answer to the riddle of life, which we cannot find for ourselves, is revealed in some supernatural way is one natural to man in his childhood. The growth of humanity from childhood to manhood, from superstition to genuine faith, is the theme of recorded history, the inner meaning of civilisation.

NOTES

[1] *House of Lords Debate*, December 17, 1908.
[2] Luke xvi. 27-31.
[3] 1 Kings xix. 11-13.
[4] See p. 39.

CHAPTER II

A CONFESSION OF FAITH

In the previous pages I have argued that action in public affairs cannot be discussed to advantage unless we have in our minds some clear conception of the object with which we propose to act. We are thus driven to state the answer we give to the riddle of life. I have further argued that the answer to this riddle cannot, from the nature of the case, be revealed by supernatural means—that it must be furnished by each for himself from his own conscience and mind. I cannot, therefore, evade the ordeal of stating my own answer for what it is worth.

To begin with I am conscious of a world in which I exist with others like me; that what I do affects them, and what they do affects me. I am also aware of a feeling common to us all that what we do, or else leave undone, is a matter of infinite importance. I am constantly feeling that, whilst I should like to do one thing to please myself, some inner voice is urging me to do something else for the sake of others. I also know that all normal men, to a lesser or greater degree, experience this conflict of motive. I myself and others are constantly failing to obey this voice; but none the less, having failed, we feel that we have failed in something of infinite importance. On the other hand, I know of innumerable cases in which men have sacrificed life itself and with it the very power of enjoyment, in order to achieve what they thought was their duty. They were acting as though some goal, other than their own pleasure, were the end and object of life. Were they under a mere illusion? Were they right in accepting good and evil as valid distinctions, as something other than pleasure and pain?

In making this choice between two opposite views we can, I submit, derive some guidance from reason applied to experience. This at least is plain, for all practical purposes, that if everyone acted on the theory that right is no better than wrong all human affairs would fall into chaos. If pleasure, not duty, is the end and object of life, then pleasure itself is unattainable. If everyone, on the other hand acted on the theory that right and wrong are valid distinctions, and that all conduct must be governed by a sense of duty, a state of society would be reached in which happiness would be raised to the highest possible level. If men were to act as though pleasure alone were the sole motive of conduct, society would cease to exist. Human beings would revert to the level of brutes, with this difference, that reason would give the strong a greater power than that of the brutes of inflicting misery on the weak. It would also expose the weak to suffering more poignant than beasts endure. Human beings would end by destroying each other and cease to exist. If all men could act at all times as though their sense of duty were paramount, society would cease to depend on restrictions. Freedom would develop to an ever-increasing degree. And with freedom men would acquire an ever-increasing control of nature, of physical forces and conditions. The physical pains to which we are heirs would be steadily diminished. The capacity in men of discerning the path of duty, and also the will to follow it, would be always improving.

In facing this inexorable choice which everyone must make, whether consciously or otherwise, we can each of us find in our own reason and experience substantial ground for deciding to base our lives on the faith that right and wrong are valid distinctions of infinite importance. It is, I submit, reasonable to assume that the difference of right and wrong is a real one, and to act, or try to act, in that faith. And assuming that the infinite difference of good and evil is based on reality, what then do I mean by reality itself? What kind of thing must a universe be, in which good and evil are valid distinctions of infinite importance? Are the things which I touch and see the realities, or is there behind them something more real, of which tangible things are the outward expression?

There is in fact something of which I am more keenly aware than I am of the things which I touch and see. I am conscious of the earth and of what there is in it, of the air which surrounds it, and of heavenly bodies in the space beyond. I am conscious, too, of my own body and limbs. But I know that this body does not comprise what I call myself. When I die it will cease to be "I" and will presently dissolve and return to the earth, water and air from which it was made. My own personality, of which I am vividly conscious, is something else and more than this body in which for the moment it finds its expression. If I do not know *what* I am, at least I know *that* I am. I believe also that millions of others exist like myself. I can see their bodies and hear their voices, and so learn what is in their minds. From these sights and sounds I infer that in these bodies are personalities like my own. These invisible personalities seem the most important things in the universe. I consider the things which I touch and see merely as affecting these personalities. If I care about meat and drink, housing and clothes, it is only because I find that such things are needed to keep in repair the body in which my own personality and those of others for the present exist. That impalpable essence, my own personality, is something of which I am more conscious than I am of the things which I touch and see, including my own body and limbs. In plain words we know of things which are not material, which we call spiritual. From matter we distinguish our minds or souls.

But which of the two is the ultimate reality in the universe? Are our minds merely a way in which matter behaves under certain conditions, or is mind the basic reality and matter a mere expression of mind? We are now certain that in so many million years matter, as we know it on this earth, will no longer serve as the vehicle of life. The history of man on this planet must end and cease to exist. If matter is the ultimate reality, matter will continue. But all our lives and what we did in them, and the consequence of our acts as affecting others, will have no kind of ultimate result. Its unimportance will, in fact, be infinite. If matter is the ultimate reality, our sense of the infinite difference of right from wrong is a sheer illusion.

This brings me back to my previous point. If human life were based on belief that the pleasure of each is his only good and his sense of duty a figment, then life would rapidly cease to be human. The law of the jungle, the negation of law—anarchy, would result. As I do not see how anyone can prove that matter is the ultimate reality—that our sense of right and wrong is illusion—I cannot myself understand how anyone in reason can base his life or call on others to base their lives on that belief. If the mere possibility of mistake is admitted, the results of action based on mistake of this order are beyond measure disastrous. On the other hand, if we assume that our sense of right and wrong is valid and based on the truth, then, if we have made a mistake, that mistake is of no final importance. If matter is the final reality, then nothing is of final importance. When life has ceased to exist and only matter remains, then human experience will be ended and vanish. What happened to men, what they did to each other, or how they lived, could have no after-effects, should life again recur in the universe.

In assuming that right and wrong are valid distinctions, as in fact most people assume, I am thus led to a further assumption. A universe in which this is so cannot cease to exist when our bodies have ceased to exist, when the wandering planet on which they have lived has returned to its parent sun and reverted to gas and flame. The final reality must belong to the same order of things as my own personality, and not to the same order of things as my body and limbs, as the visible and tangible world about me. The things which I touch and hear and see must themselves be expressions of something akin to that essence, my own personality. In my judgment of human beings I feel that the greatest are those in whom personality is carried to the highest. I am, therefore, led to suppose that the final reality behind the universe is personality carried to its highest degree, expanded to an infinite power. I cannot deny to this personality any qualities of goodness or greatness in the persons I know or of whom I have knowledge. I can only suppose that He has those qualities to an infinite degree. If so, some clue to His nature will be found in trying to see what is best in men as we know them; and in trying to grasp what that best is.

I must here pause to remark that while I assume that good and evil are valid distinctions, I cannot undertake to describe in general terms wherein that difference consists. When called on to act I must make up my mind for myself what is the right action as distinguished from the wrong. I can try to recognise goodness when I see it, and also evil. But I cannot hope to explain what they are, or, indeed, to say why evil should exist in the universe at all. Whenever we try to see what this universe is, we come in the end to insoluble riddles, because our human intelligence is limited. We have glimpses of reason, but have not powers of reason to the full. I will give as an instance a simple and often quoted example, our idea of unity, expressed in the figure 'one'. Yet having conceived the idea of unity and expressed it as 'one', as the atom of number, the indivisible unit, we find that our minds are dividing this atom into halves, quarters, and an infinite number of fractions. From our notion of unity we cannot exclude the idea of endless divisions. And so in the moral world our acceptance of good and evil as valid distinctions presents an insoluble riddle. But these limits to human thought do not excuse us from the task of forming some view, of making some guess, as to what the universe is, and what is our place in it. We have all to act, and our action affects others as well as ourselves. With what end in view are we to act? If we cannot know with absolute certainty we can still guess and act on the guess. Our life in the main is based on guesswork, from hour to hour and day to day. I know for certain that two added to two makes four, that two sides of a triangle will always be greater than the third. But outside this world of abstractions I know little for certain. I cannot know with absolute certainty that the sun will set to-night or rise to-morrow. A wandering comet might enter the solar system and destroy it. Yet all my experience leads me to guess that night and day will follow each other, and I base my actions on that belief. Except in the sphere of mathematics we act on a faith that is less than knowledge. Man in his childhood is ever craving an absolute knowledge which, could he attain it, would annihilate faith.

Though I cannot attempt to explain the mystery of evil, or the freedom of men to do evil or good, I treat them as facts. And from these assumptions I go on to infer that reality is something akin to my own personality, to all personalities that I know of, which contains what is best in them all and more without measure. When we meet personality carried to the highest degree we tend to describe it as 'genius'. By this word we imply some instinct and capacity to create, to bring into being something that did not exist before. It is so in music, in literature, art, and in all the fields of human activity. Our deepest instincts, our faculties at the highest, are constructive. "The end of man", as Carlyle said, "is an act not a thought". The problem of life, which we cannot evade, is to know how to act. Then, if personality, as we know it at its highest, is creative, we have reason to assume, as the writer of Genesis assumed, that ultimate reality, God, is supremely engaged in the work of creation.

There is something surely in the instinct of men to call themselves creatures. What else can this word imply than creations of some personality higher than themselves? If we think of God as goodness personified, as personality on the infinite scale, we are led to suppose that supreme reality would call into being further realities akin to himself. Such creatures would not be akin to himself unless they also were endowed with the faculty of creation. Their end and object must also be to construct, to bring into being on their own initiative what was not in being before. They could not resemble God or partake of his nature unless they could act on their own initiative. They must be free to create, to abstain from creation, to hinder its process. "And there shall be beautiful things made new for the surprise of the sky-children."[1] Truly. But best of all are the beautiful things that the sky-children make for themselves, and their highest delight is achieved in the making. Though I cannot say what goodness is, I feel that it must be something creative. Though I cannot say what evil is, or why it should exist, I feel that it is something which spoils or impedes creation.

Construction by intelligent beings implies a purpose and plan. I cannot conceive a creative God not inspired by a purpose, with no plan in his mind. If he calls into being creatures to join in his work of creation, I think that he means that these creatures should grasp enough of his purpose to join in his work. Could they see the whole of it from first to last, it is hard to see what power of initiative would remain to them. To me it seems he assigns us the task of divining the meaning of things with faculties which cannot indeed grasp the whole of an infinite purpose, but are yet sufficient to join in the work. I think we can now begin to discern a purpose running through the history of man, which can help us to see how to fit in our work with that purpose.

In the book of Genesis God is conceived as creating the world as the home of his creatures. These creatures he fashions, much as a potter might fashion an image from clay; but then, with a power denied to the potter, he breathes on the clay and in spires it with a life derived from his own. In the last century science has supplied a more rational and interesting view of the process. We can now see better what the universe is, and more of the stages by which it came to its present condition. We know this earth as a speck of dust in the universe on which, as nowhere else perhaps, physical conditions permitted the existence of life. As to what life is, or how it came to appear, when physical conditions permitted its existence, we know no more than the author of Genesis knew. But science has led us to believe that living things were not each fashioned by the hand of the great artificer. Beginning from forms hard to distinguish from crude matter, they developed in process of time one from another. The latest and highest development was man. In the course of aeons the animal slowly developed a brain, which was capable of seeing and thinking of himself as distinct from others. As the creature became conscious of himself as a person, as something distinct from the world and from other persons about him, he reached the stage of humanity. He began to realise that the things which he did affected others as well as himself. He slowly became aware of an instinct which moved him to act in the interest of others rather than of himself. He became conscious of good and evil, of right and wrong. As his power of doing as well as of seeing what was right developed, so human society began to exist. He began to imagine ways of making the world about him better. He was more able to achieve what he thought of, even though it meant a sacrifice of himself. He had not merely to choose like a judge between opposite courses. His imagination, the essential creative faculty, began to conceive new and difficult ideas for bettering those about him. He was sometimes able to bring these ideas to fruition at a cost to himself.

I cannot attempt to show how these faculties of seeing himself as distinct from others, of divining the interest of others as higher than his own, and of seeing how to promote it, were implanted in his mind. I can only describe the process by saying that, as men rose from the level of animals to be men, God was revealing his own nature to man—a supreme exercise of creative power, because he thereby called into being creatures capable of creating things which were new in the spiritual world. All human knowledge and all right action proceed, I believe, from divine revelation, which enabled men to reveal and create for themselves.

We do not believe now, like the author of Genesis, that God created the universe and the beings who live in it in six different stages by separate acts. We believe that the earth and the heavenly bodies have been brought to the stage they have now reached by the operation of physical laws through periods of time too great to measure. We believe that some hundreds of millions of years ago this earth had reached physical conditions which permitted the existence of that invisible, intangible factor which we call life. We do not know, or think that we know, what life is, or how it began on the earth. We accept its existence and beginning as facts. We believe that, having begun, life grew to an ever-increasing diversity by laws more complex and harder to grasp than mechanical laws, but just as fixed in their operation, and therefore rightly described as laws. In the process of time creatures developed, endowed with perception—fishes, insects, reptiles, birds and mammals. They are creatures endowed with knowledge in its most rudimentary form. But their actions are still governed by their own instincts and desires. They have no essential power of choice. But the process of growth continued till one branch of the mammals had developed reason. By reason we mean a capacity which enables a man to divine certain aspects of reality which a beast cannot grasp. A man can grasp mathematical truths, more or less of them, according to the power of his reason. All normal men can see and agree that two sides of a triangle are greater than the third. Such an aspect of truth could not be explained to an animal. It is fair to say that animal differs from human intelligence as the noises made by a monkey differ from human speech. The degree in which creatures are able to express their ideas to each other is the rough measure of those ideas.

Reason also enables a man to see and think of himself as something distinct from the world about him and from others who inhabit that world. The dawn of reason means that the conscious animal has become self-conscious. The man is aware that his conduct affects the lives of others, as their conduct affects his own. He finds that he cannot at all times do what he likes without inflicting some injury on others. He is conscious of an instinct which suggests that he ought to think of their needs and desires rather than his own. He begins to distinguish good and evil as something different from the pleasures and pain which govern the actions of animal life. Together with reason he develops a 'conscience', a sense of freedom to choose what is good for others rather than do what would please himself.

I cannot recall any definite moment in my own childhood when I suddenly realised a sense of duty as something which I ought to obey. Nor do I think that there was one definite moment in the childhood of man when the moral sense which made him something more than an animal entered his being. One can only say that as the growth of intelligence reaches a certain stage the creature becomes aware of some other standard of conduct than his own desire to achieve pleasure or escape pain. He begins to discern a distinction of good from evil, of right from wrong. He becomes conscious of freedom to choose what is better or worse by some other standard than that which distinguishes pleasure and pain. If the ultimate reality behind the universe is spirit, not matter—is something of the nature of our own personalities raised to the infinite scale, a being engaged on the work of creation—God, I can only regard this knowledge of good and evil, this sense of freedom to choose between them, as a revelation of God to his creature, nay more as an incarnation of God. I can best describe what has happened by saying that God has made men in his own likeness. Men join in the work of creation so far as they see and also choose, so far as they conceive and also achieve, what is good in itself. One who had mastered his own desires and did what was right regardless of mental and physical anguish, would thus be divine. From the records we have I believe that Jesus of Nazareth was such a man, wholly divine and not less divine because he was human. When such a man had lived and died and his life and death were on record, creation had passed to a higher plane. "Be ye perfect as your Father also is perfect" is in form a command, but in substance a promise. With that promise in mind, I am not prepared to assert that no human being will ever again master, as Jesus mastered, the mysterious principle of evil in our nature. I am not prepared to say that no other creature who lives on this earth will ever attain to the plane that he reached. The human race is still in its infancy, but a new chapter in its history was opened when one had shown in his life and death what man might hope to become in his prime. My faith is that as men obey the commands of Christ to create a system of society ordered in accordance with the laws of God, that system will bring into being men in his likeness. Others will grow to the stature of Christ, till a time will come when such are the rule and not the exception. The second coming of Christ may be true in a sense fuller than early Christians conceived.

In the view I take, this sense of a difference of right from wrong, of freedom to choose the better or worse, is of the nature of divine revelation. It was one implanted, little by little, by God in his creatures, with increasing strength in each generation. It was this sense which turned his creatures from beasts into men "made in the likeness of God". To the mind of each normal child this revelation is given, and with it a power of reason which, patiently used, suffices to tell us enough of the world we live in to find the path that our steps should tread.

NOTE

[1] Keats, *Hyperion*.

CHAPTER III

THE DOCTRINE OF AUTHORITY EXAMINED

In his infancy man conceived the forces of Nature as personalities and called them gods. He thought of the world as largely controlled by beings inspired by the faculties and passions of men, but with power much greater than men can possess. Superstition and paganism are the product of those long aeons during which one man could convey his ideas to another only by the transitory medium of speech. So long as speech was the only vehicle of thought the notions which entered the minds of men could not be brought to the test of effective criticism. We may safely assume that before the invention of writing men had been born with minds powerful as those of Moses, Isaiah, Gautama, Confucius or Mahomet. Their words no doubt raised the ideas of those who heard them to a higher plane. But their teaching, transmitted from one generation to another, would be changed and distorted in the process as stories are changed and distorted in course of transmission from mouth to mouth. Some improvement was doubtless achieved when men learned to express their thoughts in poems which others could memorise. Yet reason could not begin to produce a rational philosophy or religion till men could leave their thoughts on record. When the words spoken by Moses, or the words which men thought he had spoken, could be put into writing, a new epoch had opened. Readers could then see his ideas for themselves and also discuss them with others. They could thus be brought to the test of reason and conscience in each new generation. Conscience and reason could begin to suggest what was false and must be discarded, and what must be added to make the residue truer.

The Mosaic writings depicted Yahwe, the god of the Hebrews, as different in certain important respects from the gods worshipped by neighbouring tribes, such as Baal or Nebo. Moses conceived the new and creative idea that Yahwe was deeply concerned with the way in which one Hebrew dealt with another. He could not be satisfied like Baal or Nebo merely by rites or by offerings of food. To secure his favour Hebrews must learn to deal rightly one with another. The Hebrews were thus led by Moses to think of their own conscience as the law ordained by their god Yahwe. They thought of Yahwe as the spirit of rightness, as justice personified. The Hebrew began to conceive him as something of the order of his own personality, an invisible and intangible essence, as something belonging to the order of spirit rather than to the order of matter. He developed a feeling that Yahwe was a being who could not be known through the senses. No attempt must be made to depict him in visible or tangible form. To reduce Yahwe to the form of a graven image or to worship him in any visible shape was wrong in itself.

The Hebrew had thus achieved the idea that a man should behave towards his god as one good man would behave to another. One human being might serve another by offering him food when he was hungry. But no good man would think of trying to please another by killing his own child and by placing its roasted flesh before him. The fact that he offered his friend the dearest of all his possessions could not make that offering pleasing to a righteous friend. To offer a god the life and flesh of one's own child was to place that god on a lower level than human beings. To men who had once thought of God as the source from which their own moral sense was derived the idea of human sacrifice was impossible.

It is clear from the Pentateuch that some Hebrew or Hebrews had seen that if the difference we feel between good and evil is based on realities, then those realities must belong to the order of spirit rather than matter. Our own personalities are something more real than our tangible bodies. The final reality behind the universe must be something akin to our personalities.

These golden ideas were mixed with and largely obscured by heaps of traditional dross. But a time had arrived when the art of writing could preserve results of genuine thought. New thinkers with exceptional powers of mind were able to start from the point at which the older thinkers had stopped and continue their work of extracting truth from the ore of tradition. In the books of Exodus, Leviticus, Numbers and Deuteronomy we see what priestly scribes centuries later believed that Moses had taught. Their profession in life was conducting the ritual of sacrifice prescribed by tradition. In all sincerity they believed that Moses, divinely inspired, had prescribed this ritual in detail. In time thinkers arose outside the priestly profession who dared to assert that a spiritual god could not really delight in the burning flesh of calves and fatlings. There were others, like Jeremiah, who began to perceive that a god, such as Moses conceived Yahwe to be, must be something more than the best and most powerful of gods. Such a being must be the only God, and others like Baal and Nebo no gods at all.

This line of thought led on to conclusions which the national pride of the Hebrew was slow to accept. If Yahwe were the only God in the universe, was it possible to hold that the Hebrew people were his only concern? In so far as other peoples conformed to his law, was he not also their God? Must not his kingdom also be open to all nations and kindreds and peoples and tongues? The majestic conception which the name Jehovah conveys to our minds had developed by successive efforts of thought from the narrower idea of a tribal deity conveyed by the name of Yahwe.

It was later still that the further conclusion began to develop which first appears in the book of Job, and reached its fullest development in the saying of Jesus that God "is not the God of the dead, but of the living".[1] The ultimate reality cannot be real in any valid sense of that term unless it exists beyond the limits of time and space. A reality which comes to an end and ceases is no reality. If God is reality he must be eternal, and so must the principle of righteousness which he embodies. But if this principle is eternal what meaning can it have for creatures who exist only in time and space? Can the difference of right and wrong be of infinite importance to men, as they feel it to be, if their personalities cease to exist at the moment of physical death? If human beings are capable at all of sharing the righteousness which is God, their personalities must like his have an existence beyond the limits of time and space. If our personalities are real in any intelligible sense of that word, they cannot cease to exist when the bodies, through which we here express ourselves to each other, return to the dust out of which they were made. If our own personalities are not real there is no reality. There is no basis from which to infer an ultimate reality behind the material universe. There is no God. The conception of God as the ultimate reality beyond the limits of matter, as something eternal, involves the idea that our own personalities are also eternal. If our sense of the difference of right from wrong is valid and true, we cannot evade the conclusion that God is the God of the living and not of the dead.

Such, I think, was the faith which reached its fullest expression in the teaching of Jesus, a faith developed by powerful Hebrew thinkers by the aid of writing, because when thoughts could be written one thinker could begin where another left off. By this process emerged a conception of final reality as personality on the infinite scale which, with all its manifest difficulties, affords the best answer to the riddle of life. But these Hebrew thinkers, and those they taught, did not themselves regard this conception as a product of thought. To them the Mosaic idea of Yahwe appeared too majestic for human conscience and thought to conceive. It must, they assumed, have been told to Moses by Yahwe himself in so many words. This led to the story that Moses had learned what he taught in conversations with Yahwe himself in the clefts of Horeb.

The human race, still in its childhood, craves for certainty. The idea of direct revelation satisfied this craving. No one had seen, as yet, that if this craving were satisfied, if final answers to the riddle of life could in fact be vouchsafed, then the freedom of men to choose between right and wrong was illusory. The discovery that human knowledge of reality can never be more than a guess, a guess which each must make for himself, was reserved for the Greek thinkers. It never occurred to the Hebrew prophets that God could have left human beings to think out for themselves the faith which was needed to guide their actions. The great conceptions of God and his ways which entered their minds they regarded as oracles, of which they were only the vehicle or mouthpiece.

The invention of writing itself did much to promote this idea. The people who practised the art and knew how it worked were few. To the vast majority it seemed a mystery or indeed a species of magic. A story told in Australia may help the reader to realise how writing impresses the primitive mind. In a district bordering on the central deserts a native runner was employed to carry the mailbags to the houses of lonely settlers. Some tobacco together with an invoice was sent in one of these bags, but when it was opened the tobacco was gone. The runner charged with the theft at once admitted it. He explained with some bitterness that he knew that "that little devil piece of paper (the invoice) would tell on him if it could". So he took the precaution of putting the invoice in the hollow of a tree, flattering himself that it could not then see what he did when he stole the tobacco. This is, of course, an extreme illustration. To the primitive mind the magic and mysterious art of writing practised by priests was invested with notions of sanctity.

The teaching of Moses was, I suppose, transmitted by word of mouth from one generation to another for a number of centuries before it was reduced to writing by priests. Ideas and stories when transmitted by word of mouth grow like a snowball, and alter their shape. When, at last, the tradition was reduced to writing this process of growth and change was stopped. The great conceptions which Moses propounded had not been lost. They were, however, embedded in a mass of legend, folklore and ritual prescriptions, unconsciously added by men who repeated one to another what they thought and believed that Moses had taught. When all this tradition had been inscribed in five different books, the Hebrew world came to believe that Moses himself had written the Pentateuch. In the popular mind they came to be looked on as sacred writings. Ere long the belief developed that Moses had written what God himself had told him to write. They were all true and equally true. In these writings God had revealed answers to the riddle of life which the human mind could never have found for itself.

A belief that ultimate truths could only be known in this way became firmly embedded in the Hebrew mind.

In process of time there were born to the race others like Moses, with a keener moral sense than their fellows and exceptional powers of mind. They reached conclusions which lay beyond those which Moses had reached. They proclaimed that the God of Israel as revealed in the Pentateuch could not really be satisfied by exact and punctual performance of the ritual prescribed in its pages. He could only be satisfied by the just and righteous dealing of one man with another, by the right treatment of the weak by the strong. They also began to see and to say that such a God as Moses described could not be merely the God of the Hebrews. He must be the only God, the God of the whole universe, the God of the Gentiles as well as of the Jews. Their teaching was recognised by the conscience of many who heard it as true. But these prophets themselves were by no means immune from the powerful influence of tradition. So clear were these great ideas to their minds that they thought and said that God himself had told them these truths. They themselves were merely the mouthpiece of oracles. When their teaching was placed on record by themselves or others, it claimed to rank as an oracle or message from God. In course of time the books of the prophets were subject to the same psychological influence as the books of the law, the books which claimed to record the teaching of Moses. The books of the prophets were presently ranked as the word of God.

In this way grew the idea that men cannot find for themselves the truths without which they cannot govern their conduct through life. They can only know these truths in so far as God himself chooses to reveal them through the minds and mouths of selected teachers.

Let us try to see what this theory involves. We now believe that man came into being by the long, slow and gradual process whereby the brain in the animal kingdom became capable of reason. Little by little the creature grew to be conscious of himself as distinct from others. He found that his conduct affected their welfare, and there dawned in his mind an instinct which told him that he ought to aim at their welfare rather than his own. His reason began to suggest that, if he did this, it would be right, and, if he did that, it would be wrong. In all probability the creature had experienced this sense and had, therefore, been human for at least a million years before he acquired the art of recording his thoughts in writing. The theory of direct revelation unconsciously assumes that God waited to reveal himself and his ways to men till men had at last invented the difficult arts of writing and reading. Had Moses existed in palaeolithic times the message he received from God would have vanished in the mists of tradition through the thousands of years which passed ere the age of writing began. The truths that he seems to have uttered barely survived the few generations which passed before men were able to put into writing the growing mass of tradition in which they were still preserved. The theory that God reveals to men through chosen prophets truths which human reason could not discover for itself cannot in fact operate for long before the age of writing. It was only when men had learned to write as well as to speak the truths which God chose to reveal to them that these truths could survive to govern the conduct of after generations.

On the theory outlined above, ultimate verities are revealed by God only through the utterances of men chosen for the purpose. In the version of this theory which orthodox Christians follow the final revelation was made by God himself, who, for the purpose, became incarnate in the man Jesus of Nazareth. "The revelation was made once and for all in Christ. The Church is the witness and guardian of that revelation."[2] But teachers who claim to be prophets by no means agree; and how is a man to decide which are the prophets through whose mouths or pens God has chosen to reveal his truth? The Catholic replies that the Church is commissioned by God to answer such questions. And when men are in doubt as to what the inspired teachers meant, the Church is there to decide through its mouthpiece the Pope. When some British officers had been killed in Dublin, an Irish lady said to me, "I refuse to call this murder till the Pope tells me it is." The moral judgment she was free to exercise was still, in her view, subject to be overruled by the word of God expressly revealed through the mouth of the Catholic Church. But why did she think that the Catholic Church, as opposed to all other Churches, had been chosen by God as his mouthpiece? This, at least, is clear, that all men are not agreed in accepting the dogma of Papal infallibility. The Catholic accepts that dogma only because in the verdict of his own conscience and reason it is true. The voice of God as expressed through his own conscience and reason, and not the voice of the Church, is his final criterion. And so with the Protestant fundamentalist, who holds that ultimate truth is revealed not by the Church, nor yet in the Koran, but only in Scripture. In the last analysis there is nothing but his own conscience and reason to tell him that the Bible and not the Koran is the word of God.

The doctrine of authority, however we look at it, cannot be made to stand on all-fours. Any number of men in their senses will agree that two and two make four, that two sides of a triangle are greater than a third. On mathematical points we all agree in so far as our reasons are competent to grasp the questions involved. So certain are these laws that astronomers are able to predict the movement of heavenly bodies to a nicety. The human mind constantly craves to be equally certain about the meaning of life. The doctrine of authority, that essential truths about life and God cannot be reached by men for themselves but must be revealed through supernatural means, is really the product of this craving. The theory ignores the fact that this craving for certainty could not be satisfied without destroying in men the freedom which makes them men and more than the animals. Men are free only because each man is left to judge in the light of his own reason and conscience what the ultimate verities are. In making that judgment it will help him to study what others have thought and said on the subject. But he must judge for himself who are the thinkers who think most deeply, and also how far what they have said is true. If he cannot judge for himself how far what Moses and the prophets wrote was true, a man returned from the grave cannot help him to judge.

But why should he face this irksome task from which the human spirit recoils? The answer is that he cannot escape from action, and so from deciding how to act. Such decisions, unless taken by instinct, as an animal takes them, involve finding answers to questions which never can be answered with certainty. Unless he is prepared to answer such questions for himself he abandons his human status and reverts to a life on the plane of the beasts.

The secular conflict of church and state has its roots in the doctrine of authority. The Catholic Church, divinely inspired, pronounces that Jesus forbade divorce, except for the cause of adultery and that persons divorced may not marry again. The experience of centuries under changing social conditions reveals a number of evils to which the rigid enforcement of this ordinance leads. Commonwealths try to redress these evils by revising the law of marriage. But the Catholic Church cannot admit that a law, which it holds was divinely ordained, can ever be changed in the light of experience. Man could never discover for himself what was right or wrong in this matter; so the truth was revealed by God and ordained as a law which may not be changed.

It is of such claims that I use the word 'authority' in this chapter. I am fully aware that many beliefs upon which I act are based on 'authority', in another sense of the word. I try to be clean partly because I believe that disease is due to bacteria too small for the eye to see. To verify this belief I should have to work in a laboratory. I have not had time for such work and am satisfied to accept the teaching of biologists, who have spent their lives at the microscope. Most of the English people believe in the rule of law for similar reasons. They have had no leisure for the special studies which enable a few of us to say why we think that the rule of law is essential to human welfare. But whenever men come to believe that they know truths about life, which God has revealed by supernatural means at definite historical dates because men could never discover those truths for themselves, another situation arises. If all men could hold that belief in identical form the whole of human society would be organised in one church and state. Church and the state would be one and the same, and would take the form of a universal autocracy. The ideal of the Catholic Church would be realised. In practice this has not happened and will not happen. Various bodies hold various beliefs, which they each believe are divinely inspired. Such bodies are always in tacit conflict, which may break into open and physical conflict. Such bodies must come into conflict with states based on the principle of the infinite duty of each of its members to all.

In the first part of this book it was argued that the Kingdom of God as preached by Jesus was an organisation of human society ordered in accordance with the laws of God. It is equally true to describe this conception as an organisation of human society based on realities. The laws of God, the realities, have to be learned from experience by the use of human intelligence and conscience. In a polity so ordered there is room and need for organisations in which men gather for communion with God and one with another. But where such an organisation claims to possess supernatural knowledge of truths which human reason could not divine, it must in the end bring its members into conflict with a polity based on belief that men have an infinite duty to each other, a belief which must in the last resort be brought to the test of reason and conscience.

The world is still crowded with people who crave for certainty. There are now other creeds than the Catholic Church and Islam which appeal to this craving and demand an absolute acceptance of some authority which may not be questioned. The kind of people who in past generations found the asylum they needed in the Roman Church and in Islam are now drawn in increasing numbers to the Communist party or that of the Nazis, which demand absolute acceptance of the doctrines propounded by Marx or Hitler. The Communists, Nazis and the Catholic Church are in mortal conflict one with another, and the claim to authority ends by dividing and not by uniting the world. Yet the authoritarian doctrine leads to similar methods and institutions. In a censorship and control of the press which restricts even artistic criticism can be seen realised in the twentieth century the principle of the Index Expurgatorius. The Cheka and the Gestapo revive the methods of the Holy Inquisition. The trials they stage and the executions which follow them are a modern counterpart of the *auto-da-fé*. That name in itself reminds us how the principle of authority has robbed the word 'faith' of its true meaning and virtue.

> Do men gather grapes of thorns, or figs of thistles? Even so every good tree bringeth forth good fruit; but the corrupt tree bringeth forth evil fruit. . . . Therefore by their fruits ye shall know them.[3]

So principles work themselves out to their practical issues with inexorable logic. "In the long run what any society is to become will depend on what it believes, or disbelieves, about the eternal things."[4]

NOTES

[1] Mark xii. 27.

[2] I am here quoting verbatim a comment made by a gifted priest of the Roman Catholic faith, to whom an earlier draft of this book was submitted for criticism.

[3] Matthew vii. 16-20.

[4] Gore, *Jesus of Nazareth*, p. 250. The Home University Library.

CHAPTER IV

FAITH

My faith, then, is that my sense of the difference of right and wrong is valid, that final reality is God, a spirit personal in an infinitely higher degree than my own personality, and therefore supremely creative; and that God, having endowed his creatures with reason, conscience, imagination and freedom, set them to discover, little by little, what the universe is, and called them to join in the task of making it better and greater.

Do I mean by this that when God had created man in his likeness he cut himself off from communion with men? My answer is 'No'; for I myself am aware of communion with God. I have said that I do not believe that, when I am subject to doubts, God intervenes in some supernatural way to set them at rest. If I pray to be shown with absolute certainty that my sense of right and wrong is valid, I do not believe that my prayer will be answered. I must form my own judgment on the matter, and must act on that judgment. If I ask to be told whether the ultimate reality in things is of the nature of matter or spirit, I shall not be told; I shall find myself left to judge from the answer I have given to the previous question.

Whether life has a meaning is the same question put in another form, which must be answered by every thinking man for himself. I can prove that the angles contained by a triangle are together equal to two right angles, and no rational man will dispute my conclusion. But I cannot prove that life has a meaning or purpose. I know highly intelligent people who believe it has neither; but they cannot prove what they say; and I also observe that their practical lives are not based on that theory. I have at least one kindly and dutiful friend who thinks that he holds that view. I think that in time all reasonable men will come to agree that the ultimate riddle of life cannot be answered with certainty. But I also suggest that no responsible person who takes this view would dare to base his conduct on the theory that life has no meaning or purpose, still less to persuade others to do so. The result would be seen in unspeakable chaos, the utter destruction of human society, the rapid extinction of man himself. The only practical course is to assume that life has a meaning, that right and wrong are valid distinctions, that ultimate reality is of the nature of spirit not matter, something endowed to an infinite degree with all that is best in our own personalities. Such reality we speak of as God and, if life has a meaning, then God has a purpose. But if we believe that life has a meaning and that God has a purpose, we must also construct some view as to what that meaning and purpose are. If the meaning and purpose are infinite we cannot expect to grasp them as a whole. But we have to act; and cannot escape from action, and our action will all be at random unless we judge for ourselves what the meaning of life and the purpose of God are. The power of my mind is smaller than his, less than the power of the torch which I carry to guide my footsteps at night as compared with the light of the sun. Yet the torch, when I press the button and throw its glimmer on the ground at my feet, reveals enough of the infinite universe to enable me to guide my footsteps aright. Our glimmering reasons, properly used, do, I suggest, suffice to guide us on the pathway of life. Our first duty is to keep them charged, and with lamps which will glow as brightly as possible.

If we stake our lives on the faith that life has a

meaning and God a purpose, we must not shrink from the effort of framing the best guess that we can as to what is the meaning and what the purpose. To guess at the purpose we must look at experience so far as we know it. Now human experience in its largest aspect is history. We must do our best to form some idea what the purpose of God through history has been.

The trained historian is disposed to smile at any attempt to interpret the meaning of history as a whole. At least he would think that only a scholar like Acton who had given his whole life to the study of history should ever attempt it. But Acton himself would have said, like Newton before him, that the more one knows the better one knows how much there is that one does not know. So deeply absorbed was Acton's life in the task of collecting knowledge that he left his work on freedom unwritten and the plan of a history for others to write. What we have done will abide after us; but what we have known will perish with us, unless we have told it to others and written it down; and to teach and write are deeds in themselves. It is better to enter the kingdom of action halt and blind, than having both hands and both eyes to drift into everlasting futility. More knowledge of history perished with Acton than any one mind has ever acquired. All life consists in making decisions on inadequate information. The man who delays decision and waits to act till he feels that his knowledge is complete will leave such knowledge as he has on the scrap-heap. The busy politician, whose task is the making of history, cannot escape from the duty of guessing what his limited view of history means. The historian can help him by getting on record his better informed judgment. That is valuable material for men of action, but material only. They must in the end judge for themselves.

I believe that I see enough of the purpose of God to guide me in practice. I think that I help others as well as myself by trying to state as well as I can what I think I see. I believe that the meaning and purpose of life is creation. I think the supreme Creator has brought into being creatures who can join in the work of creation because he has given them power of discovering for themselves some knowledge of what he is and how he is working. He has given them freedom to use or neglect this power, to attempt or neglect the work of creation, without which they would only be blind mechanical instruments in his hands. He has, in a word, given them something of his own power to originate things for themselves. He means them to develop this power to the full, to use their reason and conscience to the utmost capacity. But this they could not do if he intervened to set things right when they go wrong. I do not believe that God intervenes at given moments to deflect the course of events which human activity has produced. I believe that he means men to judge for themselves what is better or worse, by seeing and feeling the results of what they have done. I do not believe that at given moments he intervened to reveal secrets the answer to which human intelligence could not discover. I think that he set us to seek the answers, to keep on seeking, and to judge what they are, better and better, the more we study the results of our answers. "Seek, and ye shall find; knock, and it shall be opened unto you."[1]

Does all this mean that God, having planted in man some sparks of his own nature, reason and conscience, the power to distinguish good and evil, the creative faculty, had then no further succour to give him? Does it mean that God and man are so much apart that no intercourse between them is possible? My answer to that question lies in my view of God as supreme personality.

To me the reality of which I am fully and directly aware is my own personality. Through my senses I am conscious of other personalities in the world than my own. Some of them seem better than others, to have nobler qualities than others, to be higher personalities. The highest thing I see in them is a passion to do good to others rather than themselves, a passion which is best described as love. The records of history lead me to believe that in one man at any rate, Jesus of Nazareth, this passion was completely developed. In his teaching and life and death I see personality at its highest, a man who had so mastered his own desires that his whole being was devoted to the welfare of others. His life is the crown of human experience. It enabled men thereafter to grasp what human personality at its highest can be. If final reality is something of the nature of my own personality raised to the infinite scale, the personality of Jesus is the highest clue that men have to the nature of God. He told us that God is love, and our reason and conscience respond to the thought. But his life and death make us see, as nothing else can, what that formula means. If God is love he must desire beyond all things communion with men, with the creatures he loves. I believe that, because I desire above all things communion with those that I love. In the love of others I find the best corrective of evil in myself. I was born with little or no sense of honesty or truth, but I loved others in whom the sense of honesty and truth was greater than my own. I learned to feel the horror of lies by seeing that those I loved abhorred a lie. I learned to dislike uncleanness by witnessing the love of purity in others. "And I, if I be lifted up from the earth, will draw all men unto myself."[2] Advice that friends have given me, sermons I have heard, books I have read, have helped at times. But of this I am sure that a much stronger force for good in my life has come from feeling the goodness in people I knew, or of whom I have heard and read, most of all, the supreme goodness of Jesus of Nazareth.

My view is that when God had bestowed on his creatures reason to discern right from wrong, freedom to choose between them, imagination, power to create, he meant them to use these faculties to divine reality as the necessary basis of further creation. If once I decide to direct my practical conduct by a faith that my sense of right and wrong is valid and true I shall see what is best in men as the key to reality. I shall think of reality as the best that I know in men, raised to the infinite scale. The more fully I grasp this idea and act on it, the more closely do I come into touch with reality and therefore into communion with God. It rests with man to establish with God a communion which God always and utterly desires. I believe this communion with final reality, with absolute though invisible goodness, is as real as the intercourse I enjoy with people better than myself. I know by experience the effect on myself of personal contact with friends better than myself. I know, too, the effect of hearing and reading of lives better than my own, pre-eminently that of Jesus of Nazareth. When I think of reality as all such goodness personified in the highest degree, and worship it as such, I am in direct communion with that reality. I am in his company. He draws me nearer his infinite heights than the best of my human friends, the persons I know through my senses. It is this that I mean by worship and prayer, and the influence they have on my life.

When Moses conceived the Hebrew God, Yahwe, as the spirit of righteousness, he realised and taught that any attempt to depict him in visible form was a sin. The legends which grew round the name of Moses fell away from this great conception. They tell us how Moses conversed with God in the clefts of

Horeb, and so desired to get some glimpse of his infinite person that God allowed Moses to see his back.[3] The story shows how little the scribes who recorded Mosaic tradition had grasped the significance of his teaching. This was left to prophets, especially to the writer who gave us the story of Elijah. It is not through our senses, or through things we can grasp through our senses, that we talk with God. "The still, small voice" which every man hears, though not with his ears, is the voice of God. To interpret its meaning is a task for man's own constructive reason, which is light from the mind of God, through which he can get a glimpse of reality.

I believe that a man can in his soul have such direct and immediate intercourse with God as he himself wills to have, and through it draw nearer to God and become more like him. So far as we get into touch with reality, we create further reality. But men get into nearer touch with reality by doing good as well as by seeking to apprehend what goodness is. I have known people who had no intellectual belief in God and who thought that men ceased to exist when they died, but whose lives were devoted to the service of others. In my view such people by doing good, and obeying a moral sense which they do not seek to explain, have established contact with one side of reality. They acquire a real communion with God, whom they do not recognise, and through that communion become more like him. Communion with God through our own souls is only one form of contact with reality, though an all-important form. The effort in men to think and act in obedience to the voice of duty within them is itself communion with God, even for those whose minds are unable to conceive reality as something personal like themselves, though infinitely more so—in other words, to believe in God.

"Religion", says Whitehead, "is solitariness; and if you are never solitary, you are never religious".[4] There must be direct communion of the several creature with the Creator, prayer. Yet religion cannot exist in the full sense of the word unless men also enter into communion with God in communion one with another. For the sense of religion to develop there must be churches, organised churches, and public worship. The emphasis laid by the Catholic Church on worship as adoration is tinged by the Hebrew conception of God as an oriental monarch. In the teaching of Jesus, God is conceived as a father, and men as his children, brethren one with another. The word 'adore' can also be used of the members of a family who 'worship' each other, and, because they so feel, take intense delight in each other's society. The essence of this feeling is a sense of devotion which leads each member of a family to forget himself and think only of his parents and brethren. Such feelings will find their expression in a large variety of symbols and forms. Those in whom the æsthetic sense is more highly developed will find that music and art can be used to express them. Those to whose minds abstract thought rather than sense appeals, may prefer to gather in bare walls to unite in extempore prayer and to listen to sermons. Men view reality as they view a mountain from different sides, and there must be various kinds of worship to suit the different orders of mind. But in all genuine worship one element is supreme. "God is Spirit: and they that worship him must worship in spirit and truth."[5] The essential feature of worship, private or public, is the recognition of reality as belonging to the order of spirit. To 'recognise' in the true sense of the word is to translate belief into action, to create a human society on the basis of reality, to establish the Kingdom of God upon earth.

NOTES

[1] Matthew vii. 7.
[2] John xii. 32.
[3] Exodus xxxiii. 23.
[4] Whitehead, *Religion in the Making*, p. 7. Cambridge University Press.
[5] John iv. 24.

CHAPTER V

PRINCIPLE REALISED IN PRACTICE

THE view of reality argued in the previous chapters may now be summarised briefly before we go on to see where it leads us in practice. I believe that reason and conscience and a sense of freedom to choose between right and wrong are qualities implanted by God in his creatures, an act of creation whereby he made men in his own likeness. But having revealed himself in this way to every creature worthy to be called a man, he committed to man the immense task of discovering for himself little by little the nature of reality, of joining with him in the work of creation by enlarging the sphere of reality. I do not believe that when, centuries before the Christian era, man had devised for himself the art of writing and for less than a century after that era, God intervened specially to reveal to mankind truths which they could not discover for themselves. I think that any idea that in some supernatural way God will reveal to a man what he ought, or ought not, to do in particular cases is a cardinal error. Such teaching encourages men to evade their primary duty of using and training their reason and practical judgment which God has given to men as their guide. Nor do I think that when things go seriously wrong with the world God intervenes to set them right. I think he has laid that task wholly on men themselves, and leaves them to learn from their own mistakes how to avoid them. The calamities we bring on ourselves are signposts which mark wrong turns we have taken. "Whom the Lord loveth he chasteneth"—through the agency of Nature herself. I do not believe in miracles, either as evidence of divine revelation or changing the course of events brought about by Nature or human action. God is not a *deus ex machina*. I think he has given us faculties which enable us to picture what he is like, what reality is. By employing these faculties we come to know him, not only in the sense that we know a fact, but also in the sense that we know a friend and enjoy his society. By using my reason to imagine what God must be as personified goodness and love, I associate with God, as with a friend better than myself. I am drawn to him and partake of his nature and strength. I see him as a person immeasurably greater than the greatest of men, and therefore creative; as one who by the law of his nature would bring into being creatures to share in his work of creation, who could therefore think and will for themselves.

To contrast the society in which we live in all its complexity with the lives led perhaps for a million years by our ancestors in caves and holes in the earth, in a state little removed from that of the beasts, is to get some glimpse of the work of creation on which man is engaged. But here let us note how far the task of further creation depends on knowledge of what is already created. This alone makes writing of all inventions the most momentous. Writing is the great repository in which all that is worth preserving in human thought can be stored and treasured so long as society exists to use it. So vast is the storehouse, and so rich and varied its contents, that priceless treasures are at times overlaid and buried by the mere mass of less valuable matter which is afterwards lodged in the vaults. In his recent lectures Dr. Scott Lidgett [1] has shown how Isaiah, and still more Jesus, rose from the vision of God as a monarch, which prevails in the Old Testament, to the vision of God as a father, which prevails in the New Testament. The transition from God conceived as personified power, however righteous the power, to God conceived as personified love was of all contributions to human thought the most precious and fruitful. As Dr. Scott Lidgett points out, the idea was quickly forgotten and Christendom reverted till recent times to thinking of God as embodying power divorced from love, as a sovereign rather than a father.

The same has happened to much that was best in Greek as well as in Hebrew thought. The Greeks approached their problems of life from a standpoint widely removed from that of the Hebrews. The children of Israel lived in a part of the world and a state of society controlled by powerful monarchies. It was hard for them to think of God otherwise than as a king. The insight of genius can at times transcend experience, as in Isaiah, who was able to picture God as inspired by feelings more loving and tender than any human monarch had shown. Yet Hebrew thought in the Old Testament seldom gets far from the idea of sovereignty and power as the dominant aspect of Jehovah. Greek thought developed in surroundings where kingly power was felt mainly as a distant menace, a menace which Greek valour in the Persian wars was able to repel and hold at a distance. For the first time in human experience a kind of government was realised in Greek cities which did not depend on kingly authority. To the Hebrew mind it was natural to think of duty, as the duty of obedience to a sovereign God. It was this duty of obedience to a supernatural authority which united the children of Israel. The end and object of life was comprised in obeying divine commands as conveyed and expressed through the mouths of the prophets. In a city like Athens such ideas were impossible, and thinkers were forced to approach the problem of life from a different angle. To them duty was first and foremost a human relation. It was this in men which made them something more than the beasts. It was this which bound them together in a city or state for the good of which each member was expected to live and work, and if need be to die. The fulfilment of duty, the attainment of goodness, was the end and object of life.

The Greek saw clearly enough that this end could not be attained by a man living in isolation. He must live in an organised society, however small, which he called a πόλις or state, the city in which the Greek citizen lived. To his fellow-citizen in this state he owed an unlimited duty. From this it followed that the state could make on each of its members an unlimited claim. It could call on the citizen to die if necessary, and therefore to sacrifice everything in life. The citizen was bound to obey that call; but with one exception. The state itself was merely a number of human beings, and liable to err. It might, therefore, command the citizen to do something which he felt was utterly destructive of goodness, the end and object of the state itself. In that extreme case the citizen must, for the sake of his fellow-citizens, refuse to obey their mandate, and must face all the consequences involved to himself. This, however, was clear, that the citizen, in all that he did, must study the interests of his fellow-citizens wherever those interests came into conflict with his own. His real good could be attained only by seeking the good of others.

In actual fact men often fail to act in accordance with this principle. To a great extent they act as though the interests of others were subordinate to their own. They are constantly choosing the worse rather than the better. The existence of evil, however hard to explain, is a fact to be faced. In a world where everyone was perfectly free to do as he pleased the morally unfit would survive, the worse would tend to destroy the better. In the primitive family this tendency is curbed by the natural authority of the head of the family—the father. As the family grows this parental authority can be stretched, to a certain extent, to ensure sufficient obedience to the chief or head of a tribe. When one tribe has conquered and subdued a number of others the idea of kingship begins to emerge. The power of the conquering chief is accepted as proof of his supernatural authority, and the state in its crudest form appears as monarchy.

The improved security which a monarch maintains enables his subjects to develop a life better on the whole than is possible under tribal conditions. This is so because the will of the monarch is law; and law is essential to order for two practical reasons. The worse man must be restrained from killing the better at will. The subject must also contribute some of his wealth to the general costs of the state. If this were left to the option of each, the more loyal subjects would be ruined by having to furnish what the less loyal subjects failed to contribute. The king invokes the loyalty of those who believe in his supernatural authority to enforce his behests. But apart from this question of willingness to obey, there is also the factor that men honestly differ as to what they should do, if only because the knowledge of each is narrowly limited.

We can see this at once, if we think what discipline means to an army. A thousand men with arms in their hands are powerless as a body, so long as each soldier acts on his own initiative. The situation is changed if they come to regard one of their number as authorised to command the rest. If some of them refuse to obey his authority, that authority will still be effective if others in sufficient numbers obey his orders to arrest and, perhaps, to execute mutineers. But even if all the thousand are perfectly ready to obey the leader, they still cannot move as a body this way or that, right or left, backwards or forwards, except at his orders. He must decide for them which way to move, and convey his decisions in words of command they can hear. So government is necessary to order for more than one reason. It is necessary because some men are less ready than others to put the general interest before their own. It is also necessary to save people from acting at cross-purposes. They cannot know how to act in the general interest unless a certain amount of direction is given them from without.

Monarchy depends on the primitive belief that the monarch is clothed with divine authority and also with knowledge divinely inspired as to how he should govern. It depends on the loyalty of the subject to the king. A monarch can rule, so long as he has subjects enough willing to enforce his commands on rebels. But the system rests on foundations which do not go down to the ultimate rock of realities. It is founded on powdered rock, which is sand. There are elements of truth in the principle of authority, but truth in so broken and pulverised a form that it cannot support an enduring structure. No student of history could argue that kings on the whole have decided practical questions more wisely than men of average ability. A human mind will judge not better but worse, if it falsely conceives that God himself has revealed its ideas and prompted its wishes. It is dangerous, indeed, for a mere man to mistake his own mind for the mind of God. The pages of history allow us to see how this notion affected a somewhat ridiculous monarch, King Frederick William IV. of Prussia.

> The royal crown seemed to him surrounded by a mystic radiance, which became for him who wore it the source of a divine inspiration not vouchsafed to other mortals. He said once, in 1844, to Bunsen: 'You all mean well by me, and are very skilful in executing plans; but there are certain things that no one but a king can know, which I myself did not know when I was Crown Prince, and have perceived only since I became King'.[2]

The effect on a people who accept such a theory of government is also sufficiently plain. The Germans as a people are in vigour and intellect admittedly second to none. The military empire, established by Frederick William's successors, at the height of its power was brought to ruin by lack of political judgment in those who controlled it. Just before the catastrophe von Bülow, the German chancellor, described his people as "political asses", and history will write him down as a flagrant example of his own criticism. Once more Germany is seeking salvation in the leadership of "a man sent from God."

The notion that any enduring structure of society can be founded on man's duty to God is a dangerous quicksand, until we have grasped the truth rendered explicit by Jesus, that man's duty to God can only be rendered in so far as each man renders his duty to men. Our duty to God and our duty to our neighbour are aspects of a whole, as inseparable as the convex and concave sides of an arc. And who are a man's neighbours but all those who stand in need of man's help? The enduring society must be one founded on man's duty to man, as the only means of rendering man's duty to God. The first system of society which sank its foundations down to this bed-rock was the Greek Commonwealth. Too slight and imperfect to survive long, it revealed to mankind a secret which, once found, was preserved in the literature of Greece. So preserved it can never be finally lost.

In the Greek Commonwealth the unlimited devotion of each citizen to his fellow-citizens was presumed. He was called on to render, if necessary, life itself for the sake of his fellow-citizens. The right of the Commonwealth to demand an unlimited sacrifice of each to all was presumed. Yet the citizen did not exist for the sake of the state. In the last analysis the state existed for the sake of the citizens. And this was so because goodness is more important to a man than his physical life. It is in man's interest to die for the benefit of others rather than to live for the benefit of himself. This explains what the Greeks meant by saying that the state exists for the sake of goodness.

Men cannot, however, serve each other so long as each is left to judge for himself what he ought to do at every moment. In this respect the commonwealth is faced by exactly the same difficulty as the monarchy. Men are not all good or equally good. A large number of citizens will constantly fail in their duty. The commonwealth, to exist, must be able to use force where necessary to exact from the citizen a minimum of duty. The use of force by the commonwealth is involved in the principle that an infinite duty is owed by each to all. The unlimited claim of the commonwealth on the citizens to obey it rests on that principle. If each owes an unlimited duty to the state, the duty of using force when called on to do so is clearly included. To this a thinker like Tolstoy objects that the use of compulsion is always wrong, and bases his view upon certain commands which he thinks that Jesus uttered. He supposes for instance that when Jesus commanded Peter to put up his sword on one special occasion he meant to prohibit the use of force in all human affairs. Did he really think that when Jesus cleansed his Father's house, the usurers yielded to moral persuasion? The Quaker objection to the use of force is, I suppose, prompted by the constant and flagrant abuse of force in human affairs. But those who accept the assumption that an increase of goodness in men is the end and object of life cannot accept the dogma that force is never permissible, because a general and continuous increase of goodness is possible only in a state of society so organised that those who are better control those who are worse, by force when necessary. They are driven back on the principle stated by Admiral Mahan: "The function of force in human affairs is to give moral ideas time to take root." It is not even true to say that the state could exist without force if all its citizens were perfectly virtuous, unless we also assume that they all were perfectly wise, and could always agree on every point. As noticed above, a regiment of men, however obedient, cannot move this way or that except in obedience to the orders of a leader. In a state there must be authority to tell men how to act and when.

In a monarchy the commands come from the king, normally expressed in the laws which he makes. In the Greek Commonwealth there was no king, but none the less there was sovereign authority expressed in the laws made by the citizens. The law was paramount and every citizen was bound to obey it. The officers appointed under the law were bound no less. To improve the law in the interests of the citizens themselves was the primary duty of citizens, their highest function. Their intellect as well as their conscience was exercised in the task. It was thus that the commonwealth existed in the fullest sense for the sake of promoting goodness in its members. The whole system depended for its working from hour to hour, and from day to day, on calling into active play the sense of duty in each to all.

When the Greeks conceived that the state exists for the sake of goodness—to improve the quality of its own members—they had reached a truth of primary importance to the future of mankind. They had realised how far the growth of a human mind depends, not merely upon what it is taught, nor even upon the example of others, but also upon the structure of society in which it grows up. Let us take a simple example. Suppose that two twin brothers are born in Russia as like as two twins can be, and that soon after their birth one is taken to the United States and is there reared as an American citizen whilst the other remains in Russia. Let us further suppose that they do not again meet till both are thirty years old. One can then imagine how great the difference between the two brothers will have become. It will in the main be that which two widely differing polities have impressed on their two similar natures, a difference as great as that impressed by two different seals on two pieces of exactly similar wax. Had both the brothers remained in Russia, or had both been taken to the United States, they would have remained as like each other as twins usually are.

The Greeks were the first to realise how largely the structure of society determines the character of those who grow up in that structure. They realised the importance of the mould into which the metal of human souls, while still fluid and plastic, is run. Of the manifold ways of improving men they saw, as the most important, the improvement of the social structure in which they grew up. This far they saw, that the structure of the state, to mould the character of its members aright, must be based on reality. Such reality they conceived was goodness, not pleasure, that instinct in men which made them men, that sense of duty which prompted them to see their own good in seeking the good of others than themselves. This instinct they saw as the vitalising principle of the state, which alone held it together, and endowed it with the qualities of a living organism. Their life in cities, protected by seas and mountains, had enabled them to realise states which applied this principle to groups consisting at most of some thousands of citizens. These groups were small enough to meet and discuss what was best for the group as a whole, to embody conclusions reached in laws, to which every citizen was expected or made to conform. They did not see how the principle could ever be brought to apply to groups of citizens too large to meet for discussion, or to frame laws in this way. They saw the commonwealth as an institution peculiar to Greeks, but they never saw how to apply it even to Greece as a whole. Mankind at large, the barbarian world, was beyond the range of this principle. So Aristotle thought, as Ezekiel had thought that the care of a righteous God was limited to the Hebrews. The Gentiles were beyond it.

A greater than Aristotle or Ezekiel was needed to grasp the essential link which connected the Hebrew and Greek conceptions. The fatherhood of God meant the brotherhood of man, the brotherhood not merely of Jew with Jew, or Greek with Greek, but of Jew with Greek, of man with man. The sense of duty in men to each other was what bound them together and bound them to God. This, not pleasure, was the ultimate element of value in life. To increase and perfect this sense as the principle of life was the end and object of human existence. But this could not be done merely by teaching or preaching, nor yet by example, nor yet by prayer or intercourse with God. The structure of human society itself must be based on the laws of God, on realities. The supreme task was to bring into being an order of society in which the infinite duty of each to all was fully expressed, applied, and called into exercise.

The task of seeing what this idea would mean in practice remained to be thought out in the light of experience by future generations of men. A vast project of creation was outlined by Jesus and left to those who followed him to realise. We have now better ideas of what creation means than men had in his day. We no longer see the world and the forms of life which people it, each fashioned in turn by the hand of a master craftsman. We now see no definite moment in time when man appeared on the earth as distinct from the animals. And so it is with the institutions which man is called to create for himself in partnership with God. The Kingdom of Heaven, the City of God, the divine commonwealth, the fabric of society bound together by the infinite duty of each to all, is not to be realised as the author of Genesis thought that order issued from chaos. It was something which dawned in the world without observation. It was first reduced to practice in Greece, on a tiny and wholly inadequate scale, by men who did not at all realise what they had done. In course of time when they came to examine it they got some glimmering of the principle which inspired its working. They also began to realise its marvellous reactions on the characters of those who worked it. But they did not see that the principle which inspired it was universal and could not in the end be limited to Greeks, still less to units so small as the Greek cities. Its essential idea, as grasped and expressed by Jesus, was smothered and obscured by the Roman Empire. A thousand years after his time it began to emerge again, in Alpine communes, in Italian cities, but also on the national scale in England. A group larger than a city, a whole nation, began to evolve a polity based on the infinite duty of men to each other. As in Greece men did it, not knowing at all what they did, not clearly discerning the principle which inspired their own creation. The principle was carried in the minds of emigrants accustomed to its working, and reproduced in distant parts of the world. Its gradual effect on the character of the people who governed themselves in this way attracted the notice of peoples who still lived under monarchies. They also aspired to govern themselves, though not always with equal success. Still in one way and another a number of national commonwealths came into being.

We have seen how priceless treasures of thought get buried and lost to sight in the vast and ever-increasing store-house of human records. The idea of God as a father rather than a sovereign which was given to the world in its fullness by Jesus was largely lost and only recovered in the nineteenth century.

The great Greek conception that goodness is the end and object of life, that the state exists to enable men to realise and perfect the goodness in them, has been lost to sight in much the same way.

It is clearly of vital importance that each generation should go through the great store-house of human thought, see what is there, and judge for itself what is really important and worth preserving. Happily the art of writing, rendered more efficacious by the art of printing, preserves from destruction the profoundest conceptions that have once dawned on the human mind. But writing and printing also preserve less valuable products of thought in ever-accumulating masses. The museum of literature grows so vast that we spend our time in its chambers lost in wonder and curiosity. This indestructible store-house of treasures is defeating its own object unless we compel ourselves to value the contents. We are apt to get lost in the interest of knowing what this man or that man has thought. Our primary business is to think for ourselves how far what he thought was the truth. We cannot evade this task. Our thinking can never be done for us once for all. Each generation must judge for itself what is more or less true in recorded thought. And in making this judgment each must remember the inexorable need which drives him to judge. We can none of us evade the necessity of action. Our mere inaction is affecting the lives of others. How to act, not how to think, is the ultimate problem of life. We are driven to thought because we find that thought is the only guide for action. Each man in each generation must employ this as his test in taking stock of the heritage of thought. When we ask ourselves which conceptions are truer than others, we must in the last resort be thinking how these conceptions will operate as a guide to our conduct, and therefore as a guide which we recommend others to follow.

If, indeed, it behoves us to make these judgments it also behoves us to express them as clearly as lies in our power. So far as we state with clearness the aspects of truth which we think we see, so far do we make it easier for those who follow us to test the value of what we have said. I sometimes wonder whether writers who puzzle their readers have thought out what they are trying to say. Is anything worth saying unless we can make it intelligible? A man who has grasped one real aspect of truth is in no real danger of thinking he has grasped the truth on all its sides. He views it as a glimpse of the infinite, of something too great for his limited human mind to grasp as a whole. The glimpse he sees as a flash-light which shows him at least where better to plant his feet on the ground before him. But the sense of so much beyond the ray that he cannot understand is itself a reason why he should keep his flash-light steady and clear, so that others can see what its limits are.

It is for this reason that I find myself driven to say in the plainest words I can find what I think are the truest conceptions in the whole range of recorded thought, so far as I know it. Nor shall I be troubled by the charge of repeating it if by doing so I succeed in making it clear to others what I mean. My own personality, and other personalities, these impalpable beings which think and act and know, are the only realities of which I am sure. I believe that reality as a whole is something of that kind, of which our own personalities are the outcome and creation. This supreme personality, I believe, is invested with all our faculties to an infinite degree. I think that God is goodness in personal form, and that men are of him and like him in so far as they achieve goodness. The end and object of human life is to be like God, to achieve more goodness and in doing so to join in his ceaseless work of creation. I think this idea of God was mainly reached through Hebrew conceptions. For both Hebrew and Greek, goodness finds its creative expression in the conduct of men to each other; they came to see that, in serving each other, men serve God and become like him. The Greeks were the first to realise clearly that this could only be done in so far as men were organised for mutual service, on the principle of the infinite duty of each to all. They showed in fact that a state so organised on the scale of a city could raise the life of its citizens to a plane higher than men had reached before. In modern times we have shown that the principle need not be limited to a city but can be made to apply to nations as wholes. We have seen that this can be done where a people have developed a certain degree of loyalty one to another. We have also seen how a commonwealth by exercising that sense of mutual loyalty tends to develop it, and so strengthen the working of the commonwealth.

All this has not prevented the nations of the world from falling into disastrous conflict one with another. The suffering which nations have inflicted on each other has gravely deranged the whole order of human society. It has made more difficult the working of commonwealths, has led men to doubt their value as institutions, and to great confusion of thought. Men have fallen into thinking and acting as though material things were the end and object of life. The explicit doctrine that matter, not spirit, is the ultimate reality has obtained such vogue that one of the greatest nations has now organised its life on this basis, and is calling on others to follow its lead.

NOTES

[1] Scott Lidgett, *The Victorian Transformation of Theology*. Epworth Press.

[2] Von Sybel, *The Founding of the German Empire*, vol. l. pp. 113, 114. Quoting from *Preusz. Jahrbücher*, IV. vol. 63, p. 528.

CHAPTER VI

THE GUIDING PRINCIPLE IN ITS APPLICATION

In Book III., Chapter I., I dared to suggest that a key can be found to confused situations, if we pause to consider what is the end we are trying to attain. To know the end we must first decide in our own minds how we conceive the nature of reality. And if we decide that reality is of the nature of spirit, something of the nature of our own personalities seen at their highest, we have then to ask why it is that institutions based on that principle have so miscarried, have failed so far to rescue the world from confusion.

The answer, I suggest, to this problem is that we still have a long way to go in reducing to practice our guess at the nature of reality—the principle that the duty which each man owes to all his fellows has no limits. In ancient Greece men learned to apply that principle to the government of cities; but the word 'all' was limited to a mere handful of citizens. They denied that such loyalty could be rendered effective in a group too large to be gathered in one meeting. So this loyalty of the citizen to the city meant that the cities fought one another and were constantly seeking to injure each other. The unlimited duty of each individual to his city was at times called into play to enable that city to injure and destroy others outside it.

In the modern world the principle has been raised to a higher power. It has now been applied not to thousands, but millions. In America more than a hundred million are organised as one commonwealth, and the organisation is effective. When it entered the Great War its government immediately asserted the right to send each and all of its citizens to face torture and death. The conscription it ordered was effective, and why? Because in America a sufficient number of citizens were not only prepared to face death when ordered to do so, but were also prepared to enforce those orders on others less loyal to the state than themselves. The American Commonwealth was effectively based on the principle of the infinite duty of each to all. But that 'all' is still but a section of human beings, though a large one. The American citizen is taught to think of American interests as paramount, as the Englishman is also encouraged to think of his own national interests as the final criterion of political decisions. If British and American interests clash, the loyalty of each to his nation may be called into play, as it was in the war of 1812. Two commonwealths may evoke the loyalty of their citizens to injure each other.

As a matter of fact, we feel that a British-American war is very unlikely. Nor are we in great fear of a war between countries like France, Switzerland, Belgium, Holland, Denmark, Norway or Sweden. The fear of war which overshadows the world in fact arises from those countries which up to the Great War were ruled by autocracies based on divine right which depended largely, as all such governments must, on organised force. The idea of force as the ruling factor in human affairs was so ingrained in the minds of their subjects that, when they had lost their faith in divine authority, they felt and acted as though force was the final sanction and the dominant factor in human affairs. They found it difficult to grasp a system of government based on the duty of men to each other, which used force, but only in so far as might be needed to maintain the system, 'to give moral ideas time to take root'.

The spirit which inspired the Marxian creed was revolt against the manifest injustice endured by the great majority under the existing order. Marx seems to have thought that, if the existing order could once be destroyed, with all that it stood for, the classes, religion, the state and especially property, the need for force in human affairs would vanish. If private property were abolished men all over the world could be trusted to behave justly to one another. But he could not conceive that the change he desired could be effected except by a final and consummate use of force. The proletariat must, to begin with, appoint dictators, authorised to organise and exercise force in a manner more ruthless than tsars or kaisers had ever attempted. His creed was adopted and his plan of campaign closely followed in Russia. But neither Marx nor Lenin had realised how the classes they threatened in western countries could adapt these methods in their own defence. In Italy and Germany dictatorships sprang into being with nationalism based on force as a creed opposed to communism. Their example was quickly followed by countries in Europe where self-governing institutions had taken no root. A great part of Europe and Asia is now ruled by autocracies based on force. Their antagonisms one with another and also to the commonwealths threaten the peace of the world.

If society consisted only of commonwealths, the danger of war would, I think, be remote. If it came to consist entirely of dictatorships based on force, whether communist or fascist, the constant outbreak of wars, liable to involve the world as a whole, would, I believe, be inevitable. If this view is broadly correct (and I think that most trained observers would agree with it) I cannot resist the conviction that the main security for the maintenance of peace is the character and outlook developed by people who have long had the experience of governing themselves, that the greatest danger to peace arises from the irresponsible temper and outlook developed under autocracies which, from their nature, come to regard their own power as the one object of all policy. Why is it that the efforts of leaders in the more enlightened countries to banish the fear of war from the world so utterly fail to achieve what they seek? The course of events will not, I predict, be released from the vicious circle in which they are moving till the practical statesmen who seek to direct them have begun to ask themselves anew what is the ultimate goal they are trying to achieve for those they rule. The essential evil is not, I submit, war and the miseries and evil which it brings in its train, nor is peace the essential good.

To regard peace as the end and object of policy in international affairs is, I believe, as great a mistake as it is to regard the maintenance of order as the end and object of domestic policy. War between states and disorder within them are the visible symptoms of a malady deeper than the sufferings they inflict, a malady which cannot be cured merely by anointing the sores it produces. The essential disease is a failure in the system to develop in men the sense of duty they owe to each other. The ultimate remedy lies in raising the standard of moral health in every locality and every department of human society. There is, I suggest, no public question, however local, which cannot, and should not, be brought to this test. In a previous chapter I have shown how an irrigation problem in India deserves to be handled from this standpoint. Let me now illustrate this point by a problem familiar to English readers.

A century ago the application of steam power to production in factories and to transport enlarged that recognised evil the slums. The worst feature of slums was, I suggest, the segregation of rich and poor in separate communities, where they lost sight of their duty one to another. We are trying to remedy this evil at a cost enormously greater than would have been needed to prevent its development. The internal combustion engine applied to transport is now creating a different problem. To provide suitable roads for the motor hundreds of millions of pounds have been spent on improving their surface and making them safe for the faster traffic which modern conditions require. The defective state of the law has made it profitable for landowners to build the houses which people need along the frontage of these roads. The children who live in them run straight from their doors or gates into arteries of traffic far more dangerous than the main line of a railway. The danger is greatly enhanced by the fact that the vehicles serving the houses have to stand in the road itself, narrowing and confusing the passage available for traffic, and obscuring the view alike to pedestrians and drivers. In a road so fringed with houses five people on the average are killed where one only was killed before the houses were built. It has also been shown .that the cost of providing public services, schools, playing grounds, churches, etc., is enormously greater for 10,000 people housed along main roads than if they were housed in a properly planned community, a little removed from the main artery of traffic. In result vast profits are reaped by the landowner and speculative builder. The loss falls on those at whose cost the road has been built, and also on those who are housed along it. This process is fast converting the main roads through England into long, continuous streets. From the millions who pass along them the beautiful countryside is concealed by houses. These manifold evils have led to a public outcry for a change in the present law and for housing the people in properly planned townships.

My suggestion is that all such problems can and should be brought to the test of one final question—how will the change proposed affect the people to whom it is applied, in diminishing or increasing their sense of duty one to another? To put the same question in another way, how will the change proposed affect their capacity for governing themselves? The answer is scarcely open to dispute. Ten thousand people housed in a garden city like Welwyn are physically able to control their own local affairs. They develop a sense of community, a regard for the public need and a habit of putting it before their own several desires. The same number of people housed in a thin line for miles up the Great North Road can develop no sense of community. Their local interests must be cared for by some much larger unit, by the county or the government itself, which means, in fact, by some external bureaucracy. Their sense of duty to each other cannot be developed by exercise in respect of their local affairs.

Where care has been taken to enable people to manage their own local affairs a sense of public duty will develop little by little, which in time will make itself felt in wider political fields. A people so organised will vote with a deeper sense of their public duty at national elections. The parliaments and governments they elect will reflect that temper. Majorities will grow more careful not to assert their power unreasonably over minorities. They develop the faculty of seeing the public interest as a whole, and also the habit of putting it before their own. In the international field a people so disciplined will be less ready to press national claims to the point of war than a people who are trained only to blind obedience to one ruler.

The particular cases of social reform here cited may serve to remind us how much more there is in the process of fitting a people to govern themselves than questions of franchise—of giving them votes. No public question is so small or so local that it cannot be handled in a way to accustom each person in the locality to consider the public interest as his own.

The principle of the commonwealth is a catholic principle in the truest and fullest sense of the word. It calls upon all the children of men by every act which affects their mutual relations to contribute something to the structure of human society as a whole, to the temple of God and man upon earth. The Indian or Chinese peasant who urges his neighbours to remove filth through the agency of the village council is bringing a little nearer the day when the growing volume of spiritual life will issue in a commonwealth wide enough to include first his nation and then all human beings, and establish the rule of law for them all. In the meetings of neighbours who have gathered in the evening to discuss how the village can be drained, or cleaner water can be brought to its homes, I think that our Lord would see an expression of the principle he typified in the consecration of food and drink.[1] The importance of any activity, however local and detailed in character, which tends to exercise faculty in men for serving each other cannot be overstated. It was once said of England that she saved herself by her exertions, and by her example saved the world. But the same can be said of every self-governing community. The success they achieve is not confined to themselves. One of the strongest factors in extending and improving local self-government throughout the world has been the fifty years' record of the London County Council. On the continent of Europe the system of government maintained in Switzerland is perhaps the most formidable menace to the despotisms which surround it. The development of national commonwealths, in accordance with the principle of their being, and in all their internal organs, is a vital means for extending that principle to the rest of the world in which it is denied. If the organisation of human society as one commonwealth is the true goal of human endeavour, the establishment throughout the world of local self-government and of national commonwealths is a necessary step to that goal.

Here I would urge is a guiding principle which can be applied by all who grasp it to public affairs in all their aspects, at all times and in all parts of the world. When building a dam it does not suffice to consider its value as insurance against famine in years of drought. To make two blades of grass spring up where only one sprang before, or to give every peasant a fowl in his pot, are means to an end, not ends in themselves. To enable more people to be born and live is itself but a means to an end. "Man shall not live by bread alone, but by every word which proceedeth out of the mouth of God." On the lips of the Master the language of philosophy was rendered in words which minds too simple to know what philosophy means could grasp. Ultimate values are things of the spirit and not material. They can be achieved in so far as men can believe this is so. The people who will live on the irrigated area ought to be settled in such manner that they may learn by exercise to develop their sense of duty one to another. So also with town planning. It is not enough to keep the main roads open to traffic, to reduce the danger to life on them, to enable people to live under healthier conditions and at lower cost. Beyond all this is the paramount object of enabling neighbours to see and discharge their mutual duties. By so doing and not otherwise the end and object of human life is attained. To bring this about is the business of government. The ultimate objects which states exist to achieve are not things material but things of the spirit.

There is, I submit, infinite scope for developing the internal structure of states in such manner as to exercise ever more fully the sense of duty men have to each other. But this of itself will not suffice. In states which remain fractions of human society, however large, the infinite duty of each to all can never be fully realised. We can see this when the principle was first reduced to political terms in the civic commonwealths of Greece. I, personally, cannot agree with the view constantly urged by scholars that life has never been lived at so high a level as in Athens. It is true that Athens produced monuments of thought, literature and art seldom if ever surpassed. They remain with us to-day, an imperishable evidence of her greatness. That greatness lies in the germs of truth they contained, but time was needed to develop these germs and apply them to facts. Implicit in Greek ideas was a principle fatal to slavery. Yet the greatest of Greek philosophers accepted slavery as an institution. Athenian life was based on it. Athenian citizens regarded the infinite duty of each to all as propounded by Pericles and Socrates as limited to themselves. In dealing with other democracies they recognised no right but the might of the stronger. Their failure to conceive the principle of the commonwealth on a national scale accomplished the ruin of Greece. Had the Greeks achieved a national commonwealth and held their own against Rome in the west as they held their own against Persia in the east, history would have followed a different course and the state of human society would, I believe, be far in advance of what it now is. But they knew not the day of their visitation. The achievement of the national commonwealth was postponed for ages till at length it was realised in England.

In the modern world the principle has been applied to a country as large as the United States. In course of time it was realised that its implications could not be squared with the maintenance of slavery, and slavery was abolished in America at a vast expenditure of lives and money. In countries like these has developed a definite sense of duty to the world at large. We can easily imagine a Russian or German statesman using the arguments which Athens applied to Melos.[2] We cannot imagine a recognised British or American statesman daring to argue crudely that in international affairs the only criterion is the might of the stronger. In his own country public opinion would condemn him. A long experience of self-government on the national scale has raised the sense of duty in men to each other to a plane much higher than was ever reached in the cities of Greece. The national commonwealth has done much to promote the sense of duty in men to each other. But that growth must always be checked and remain within certain limits so long as our institutions reflect the principle that the duty we owe is owed to the people of our own race, or to those resident in a certain territory. Let us hold in mind the warning given by our own conduct after the war. The principle of the commonwealth was certainly at stake in the war, and we were its champions. None the less, the bitter experience of war, ending in absolute victory for ourselves, bred in our minds a passion for power which made us forget the principle for which we had fought. We and our Allies used our power to exact from Germany a promise to pay sums of money which she could not have paid had she tried her utmost.

In Germany defeat had an opposite effect. They perceived as the source of all their misfortunes the system of authority with military power as its idol, to which they had submitted. At last the people of Germany renounced the principle of government by divine right, and to the best of their ability adopted the principle of self-government. The Weimar Republic produced leaders like Ebert, Rathenau, Stresemann, Brüning, Braun and Severing who compare favourably with the von Bülows and Bethmann-Hollwegs of the German Empire.

In their treatment of the Weimar Republic the dominant motive of all the victors was to exact reparations. The policy of France as expressed by Poincaré was to keep Germany as a beggared outcast from civilised nations. The policy had the effect of associating constitutional government in the German mind with the utmost extremes of poverty and national abasement. It rendered impossible the task in which the republican statesmen exhausted their efforts or gave their lives. It threw back a great part of the German people onto their traditional belief that power is the end and object of national life, an end for which it is worth sacrificing all the principles which make for freedom.

This policy defeated the particular objects at which it was aimed. A mere fraction of the money which the Germans were obliged to promise has, in fact, been collected. That fraction was enormously exceeded by the loss to the victors themselves, brought about by the derangements it involved in the system of international exchange. The disarmament provisions of the Treaty of Versailles are to-day a dead letter. Universal conscription is again established in Germany. Her factories are working overtime to equip the whole nation with every conceivable kind of weapon. This menace to peace is everywhere checking the growth of trade and general prosperity. The war, fought and won to make the world safe for democracy, has led to a second birth of despotism, which now pervades Europe and Asia in a form more dangerous and extreme than before.

The alternative course would have been to regard the establishment of a system in Germany under which its government was really responsible to the people of Germany themselves as the major interest of the world at large. In order to do this it would have been necessary rapidly to revise the Treaty of Versailles. The victors would have had to forego their claim to indemnities much sooner than they did. They must have disarmed or relaxed the disarmament clauses. Had their principal object been the establishment of the regime of responsible government in Germany itself, I can see no reason to doubt that that regime would be in existence to-day, and Germany would be sitting at the Council of the League. The people of Germany would have come to believe in that system as best for themselves. They would also have been given a sufficient experience in learning to work it. It is difficult to think that a policy directed to strengthening the Weimar Republic could have yielded dangers so great as those which a policy of keeping it shackled and weak have produced.

In the years which followed the war the statesmen who controlled the affairs of the victors would have described such a policy as wholly unpractical. Even in the light of after events I think they would say so still, and in one sense of the word 'practical' they would, I think, have been right. The public opinion of the peoples they govern would not allow them to do what in the interests of those people themselves was so obviously wise. The institutions of a national commonwealth, however great and however highly developed, do not suffice to reveal to its citizens the interests of human society as a whole. Nor can they clearly reveal to the people of one nation how inseparably its interests are bound up with those of human society as a whole. We are always trying to saddle the blame for whatever goes wrong on this person or that, or on whole bodies of persons. We argue as though the calamities of the world could all be avoided if only men could be better, and behave better than they do. In this we are right, but the major fact we so constantly overlook is this: in a world where even the best people cannot in fact do what is best there is something dangerously wrong with the system under which they are trying to do heir best. The defect, not only in statesmen, but in the great masses of people whose opinion determines the action of statesmen, is largely due to the system which moulds their minds. To preach good conduct is of little avail unless at the same time we alter the system to one which makes men see for themselves what goodness is and also inclines them to follow its dictates. Human nature cannot begin to realise its full possibilities until we have achieved a commonwealth which knows no limit but that of human society and renders all men obedient to laws common to all in things which affect them all. And when it is achieved the endless task will still remain of improving its quality.

I must not be thought to depreciate the efforts which statesmen are making to avert war, wherever the peace of the world is threatened. My argument is that their efforts will in the end fail and that human society will be engulfed in calamities worse than any yet known so long as prevention of war is sought as the goal of policy and crown of achievement. The tactical steps designed to prevent war should be conceived as means, but only one of the means, to be followed in the effort to attain human welfare. The wider policy needed to attain that end can only be conceived by men who have seen wherein human welfare consists, and do not shrink from saying what they have seen and what they seek. In the last analysis, a growth in the disposition of men to serve others than themselves, a constructive unselfishness, is the end to be sought. In so far as that one end is attained peace and all other blessings of life will ensue.

This threadbare platitude leads to the practical question to which I have ventured to suggest an answer which is far from threadbare. By what means is this virtue in human beings to be fostered, this final end of all human endeavour to be sought?

By each for himself in communion with God and his fellows, through churches and schools, and a great variety of institutions. But my answer is that the most potent of all these means will be the framework of society in which these various institutions are knit together. The virtue in human beings will grow in so far as that framework is designed to exercise and promote it. A state which disposes the minds of its members gathered in one locality to regard their duty to others as in any way limited to those who live in that area cannot develop their sense of duty in the highest degree. In a world divided into national states the growth of virtue in men, however developed in those states, must be arrested at a certain point. Wars and the miseries they bring in their train are a sure indication that in public affairs men have ignored the real end of human existence and have shrunk from the task of finding and applying the practical means of attaining that end.

NOTES

[1] See p. 158. [2] See p. 75.

CHAPTER VII

FROM THE NATIONAL TO THE INTERNATIONAL COMMONWEALTH

Most people who speak our language believe that the principle of the commonwealth under which they live will spread to the world at large, that in course of time all nations will somehow or other acquire the art of self-government. They would see nothing fantastic in a forecast that sooner or later the world will be covered by national commonwealths. But if they are asked to conceive a world in which all these national states are incorporated in one commonwealth to which every human being in the last resort owes his allegiance, they feel at once that they are asked to enter the realms of fantasy. They think of the national commonwealth contained by one frontier or coast as the last word in human development. The idea of the national state imprisons their minds. They can no more conceive a genuine commonwealth of nations than a Greek in the time of Aristotle could conceive a national commonwealth which contained all the cities of Greece. This profound belief in the national commonwealth as the last word in political construction is a gulf in the minds of men which has to be bridged before we can move to a higher level of civilisation than that we have reached.

What steps can be taken to change this outlook? How shall men be convinced that a government of the world responsible in an ever-increasing degree to those who are governed is a practical project, which can be achieved if they have it in view? I refuse to consider any ideal as deserving the name, unless I believe that it can and will be realised in practice. I must, therefore, endeavour to show how I think that a world commonwealth can be brought into being.

In discovering the practical steps to be taken our surest guide will be a grasp of the principle which unites a commonwealth and inspires it with life. If that principle is indeed an incipient instinct in men to act on motives which look to the good of others, and not to the satisfaction of their own needs and desires, we shall scarcely drift into thinking that a world commonwealth can be brought into being, at this stage at any rate, by anything in the shape of a world conference. The principle of the commonwealth is in being, but as yet far too weak and limited in scope to vitalise a world commonwealth and make it real. The national commonwealths which exist have strengthened their citizens' sense of devotion to each other, and have even helped to promote a habit of considering the interests of foreigners. Generally speaking, the feeling in commonwealths towards aliens is more generous than in authoritarian states. Yet, in every crisis this feeling is counteracted by the inexorable principle of national sovereignty. Whenever the interests of a commonwealth collide with those of another state, the claim of that commonwealth on its citizens to consider its interests and no others is usually paramount. This is one of the factors which make it so difficult for practical statesmen to think that the people they govern would ever consent to be merged in an international commonwealth.

Though I do not expect a system of government for the world to issue from a conference of statesmen appointed for the purpose by the national states of the world, I find myself able to picture, and at no very distant date, a federal commonwealth framed to include two or more of the national commonwealths in which the practice of responsible government is best understood. The next step to the ultimate goal in view is a commonwealth of nations, an international commonwealth in the real sense of those words. By this I mean a commonwealth which includes nations recognised as separate one from another, with distinctive national governments of their own. But I also mean a commonwealth which is a state in the genuine sense of that term, one in which these self-governing nations are all included, with a government competent to control those issues which national commonwealths cannot control, the issues of peace and war and all that relates thereto. Such a government must be responsible, not to the national governments which the commonwealth includes, but to the people they represent. That is the crux of the whole matter.

If such an international commonwealth were realised, and maintained its existence for a few generations, a change would quickly take place in the minds of its citizens. Their sense of devotion to the commonwealth as a whole would grow as the sense of loyalty in American States grew to the national commonwealth in which they were merged. The idea that supreme devotion can be rendered by men to some unit which is wider and more scattered than a national state would be proved in practice. The real obstacle which is barring progress to a world commonwealth is this deeply rooted obsession that the ultimate devotion which inspires men in the mass to dedicate their wealth and their lives to each other cannot, in fact, be rendered to any unit that is not of the nature of a national state. The actual creation of an international unit to which such devotion is effectively rendered would cut this obsession at its root. Its visible existence would convince an ever-increasing number of people that a commonwealth inclusive of all nations, a government of man responsible to man, is something more than a fantasy. In no great time the creation of a world commonwealth would come to be recognised by practical statesmen as the goal of all policy, the only structure of human society which can be regarded as finally based on realities. In international politics a principle of action would have been established to the test of which all policies could be brought.

The nations have moved forward and upwards to the brink of a canyon, and now stand in imminent danger of pushing each other into the chasm. The real chasm is in their minds. They cannot as yet conceive a loyalty of that kind which sustains a state and a government, other than a loyalty rendered to a national state. The realisation of one international state would be like a footbridge thrown over that canyon. If the bridge was a real one, however narrow, the nations would little by little find their way over it, to the infinite region beyond in which freedom, in the only complete sense of that word, can be realised.

It is needless to argue at any great length that a feat of political construction, more momentous and difficult even than that of the thirteen American States, must be the work of leaders who speak for nations in whose life the principle of the commonwealth is most fully expressed. There have been, and are in plenty, international states in the form of empires. The first international commonwealth must, from its nature, be the work of men who understand what the principle of the commonwealth means and how to apply it in practice. They must have acquired that knowledge in the government of national commonwealths, and be able to speak for the peoples they govern. These obvious remarks lead on to conclusions of vital importance. The task of releasing human affairs from the impasse to which they have come rests with those national states, and with the leaders of those states in which the principle of the government of men by themselves has been carried to its furthest point. In using these last words I am holding in mind the principle that self-government is real only in so far as the government it provides is real. There may be in central America states where every citizen is entitled to vote on reaching the age of puberty. Such a right is no proof that the state has attained the quality of a commonwealth. There must also be enough of these voters who are willing, not only to obey the law, but even to see that all others obey it. The first international commonwealth must from its nature be founded by states which have laid the foundation of effective self-government for themselves. They must be those national commonwealths which have carried self-government to the highest point which has yet been attained.

It is difficult to exaggerate, therefore, the responsibility which rests on the people of such states and on their leaders at this stage in the history of man. The difficult task of building a bridge whereby the nations at large can escape the obsession of nationalism of necessity rests with those which have reached the highest state of development. Until that is achieved no further advance in civilisation which is worth counting as such can, I think, be made. Nay more, I believe, that so long as the principle of national sovereignty is treated as the last word in political construction our present civilisation is threatened with dangers other, though greater, than those which overwhelmed Graeco-Roman civilisation. The national commonwealths alone can break that obsession by creating a sovereignty that is international and also effective. I am clear in my own mind that sooner or later man in the vast aeons of time which we now know that he has before him on this planet will achieve a government for himself. I am equally clear that if the first conscious steps to that goal are postponed for centuries, man is doomed in those centuries to pass through great tribulation. I do not believe that those sufferings are necessary. They can be prevented if steps to avoid them are taken in time.

CHAPTER VIII

THE LEAGUE OF NATIONS

THE principles which must in the end govern the structure of human society can only be discovered and tested by creating such institutions as the limited nature of public opinion allows. It is only when they are brought into operation that public opinion can begin to see, and that slowly, how far they are failing to realise the ends for which they were founded, and why. The League of Nations was the first unconscious acknowledgment by practical statesmen that national states are not the last word in human development, that the peoples who obey them are in fact but integral parts of a higher unity. It has proved the immense utility of an international machinery, and also the limits of that utility. It has rendered notable service in restoring to solvency bankrupt governments, in combating traffic in noxious drugs and white slaves and in throwing a flood of light on world conditions. It brings together in one place representative men from most of the world, and creates personal relations between them which are full of hope for the future. But its greatest service has been in revealing its own limitations, in its failure to achieve the primary object for which its founders designed it—collective security, the prevention of war by compacts between sovereign states. It has thus forced us to face the supreme question whether the maintenance of peace can be treated as the ultimate goal of human endeavour, the guiding principle of public policy. Its very failure is forcing the world to think once more what is the end and object of life.

The events which led to this great experiment were described in the previous Book. The military empires of central Europe had set out to destroy the smaller states on their eastern and western frontiers which lay in the path of their wider ambitions. When their power was shattered and the victors assembled in Paris to reconstruct the fabric of Europe, public opinion had reacted in the opposite direction. The principle of sovereignty vested in national states was treated as final and sacred. The number of sovereign states into which Europe was divided was increased. It was seen that these numerous states must come into conflict at times, if they exercised their sovereign rights to the full. To avert this danger the states of the world were to covenant one with another never to press their sovereign rights to the point of war, at any rate till they had tried all the methods of conciliation prescribed in the Covenant. Human society was thus to consist of a number of units, each and all of them organised on a principle different from that which governed their relations one with another. The national states existed in so far as the people who composed them were prepared to render a boundless devotion to the state as a whole. The claim of their governments to that boundless devotion was admitted. But these governments were to covenant one with another not to call on their subjects or citizens to enforce their will with arms on another state. They were also to covenant one with another to punish and coerce any member state which disregarded the compact.

The relation which combined people in states was a unilateral relation, the one-sided and absolute claim of the government to devotion, the one-sided and absolute duty of the subject to render it. The states were related to each other on the basis of compact, a bilateral and, indeed, multilateral relation.

We have now had time to see the result. While the unity and efficiency of the states, even of the states which did not exist before the war, has steadily increased, the relations of states to each other have sunk into ever-growing disorder. Never have men so hated the thought of war, for never before have so many of them known what it means. Yet never have men been less certain that they themselves may not live to see a war more widespread and terrible than the last.

We are now learning what national sovereignty means when carried to its practical conclusion in a highly mechanised world. Political thinkers are beginning to say, and almost to say with one voice, that the cause of civilisation is lost unless national states will agree to abandon some part of their sovereignty. Such remarks are becoming a common form in attempts to review the present state of human society. If sovereignty means anything it means the sole and exclusive claim of the state to command the obedience of its own citizens. How a government can abandon that sole and exclusive claim, without abandoning the claim to sovereignty itself, is seldom explained. If a government once concedes the right to the League of Nations to issue commands to its own subjects over its head it has merged its sovereignty in the League of Nations and is sovereign no longer.

Some thinkers, and even some statesmen who see where the principle of national sovereignty is leading, have suggested practical steps for restricting it. They urge that the League of Nations must have a 'police' of its own, a fleet, an army and an air force strong enough to enforce the Covenant on any recalcitrant member, just as a national government has police to enforce its law on rebellious citizens. But they shrink from stating the necessary consequence of their proposal. A League police must be recruited from subjects who owe allegiance to states which compose the League, from most if not all of them. Its members must all be pledged to obey, if necessary by giving their lives, the League of Nations, not the government of the national state to which they belong, if the two are at odds. The unlimited devotion of these men at any rate must be transferred from their national states to the League.

To have any effect such a force must be on a scale commensurate at least with any one of the national forces. Its cost will be comparable to that which the larger nations spend on their armaments. The League of Nations will require a budget comparable to that of one of the leading Powers.

At present its expenses are confined to the maintenance of its clerical staff at Geneva, the cost of commissions and incidental expenses. The League budget is smaller than those of many of the leading counties and towns in England. It is raised by voluntary contributions of the member states levied on the basis of an agreed assessment. A certain number of these states are in default, and the League budget is balanced by levying from all the others enough money to meet the deficits caused thereby. Though the burden on the wealthier states is slight, a constant pressure is exercised by their governments on the League secretariat to reduce its expenses. If instead of raising one or two millions a year the League had to raise a hundred millions or so to pay, equip and maintain an effective force of its own, a larger number of governments than at present would certainly fail to meet the demands levied upon them. The much heavier burden imposed on the states members who met the demands made on the budgets would be increased. The whole system would collapse for exactly the same reason that the financial system of the American Confederation collapsed after the War of Secession. The only effective remedy would be that applied in the present constitution of the United States. The League would have to be given power to go over the heads of the governments of the states and raise the revenues it needed by taxing their subjects, where necessary by distraint. To vest in the League power to levy and collect taxes from the subjects of sovereign states is to destroy their sovereignty, and at the same time to change its character from that of a league to that of an international state in the full sense of the term—a state with a government and a sovereignty of its own. Yet the fact remains that no one who has urged the creation of an international police on any effective scale has dared to suggest or, indeed, seen that the thing cannot be done, unless the League is given the constitution and powers of an international state.

The reason why they have not faced the necessary means to the end they urge is that they know full well in their hearts that the nations are not ready to take those means—not one of them is ready. And they are not ready because the system of national states, under which their peoples are born and bred, creates in the minds of those who grow up in them a sense that their ultimate duty is due to their national state, and not to the League to which that state is bound by the Covenant. So it was that America rejected the Covenant which her own president had fathered on the world. So it was that Manchuria and Abyssinia were led to their fate.

> Take up this mangled matter at the best:
> Men do their broken weapons rather use
> Than their bare hands.[1]

I do not think that a league of sovereign states can ever ensure the world against war. I am sure, none the less, that a league which makes no pretensions to powers which only a sovereign state can wield, can diminish the risks of war. In the heat of the Abyssinian crisis the Archbishop of York declared that it may "be necessary to have another great and horrible war to establish the efficacy of the League of Nations".[2] That earnest supporter of the League, Lord Grey, was perhaps a safer guide when he said, "I do not like the idea of resorting to war to prevent war". He had also said that without America the League would at best become "but a revived concert of the Great Powers of Europe, liable at any time to split into rival groups". In the light of Grey's words let us read once more those Articles of the Covenant which lured Abyssinia to her doom:

ARTICLE 10

The Members of the League undertake to respect and preserve as against external aggression the territorial integrity and existing political independence of all Members of the League. In case of any such aggression or in case of any threat or danger of such aggression the Council shall advise upon the means by which this obligation shall be fulfilled.

ARTICLE 16

Should any Member of the League resort to war in disregard of its covenants under Articles 12, 13 or 15, it shall *ipso facto* be deemed to have committed an act of war against all other Members of the League, which hereby undertake immediately to subject it to the severance of all trade or financial relations, the prohibition of all intercourse between their nationals and the nationals of the covenant-breaking State, and the prevention of all financial, commercial or personal intercourse between the nationals of the covenant-breaking State and the nationals of any other State, whether a Member of the League or not.

It shall be the duty of the Council in such case to recommend to the several Governments concerned what effective military, naval or air force the Members of the League shall severally contribute to the armed forces to be used to protect the covenants of the League.

The Members of the League agree, further, that they will mutually support one another in the financial and economic measures which are taken under this Article, in order to minimise the loss and inconvenience resulting from the above measures, and that they will mutually support one another in resisting any special measures aimed at one of their number by the covenant-breaking State, and that they will take the necessary steps to afford passage through their territory to the forces of any of the Members of the League which are co-operating to protect the covenants of the League.

Any Member of the League which has violated any covenant of the League may be declared to be no longer a Member of the League by a vote of the Council concurred in by the Representatives of all the other Members of the League represented thereon.

It was these Articles which led the United States to reject the Covenant, and thus to cripple the League from its birth. We are now faced by the fact that not one but all the states which signed the Covenant have broken their pledge in the letter as well as the spirit. These pledges are dead. No miracle can restore them to life. They are corpses hung round the necks of the nations that signed them and broke them, poisoning the life of the world and destroying the benefits to be gained from a league of nations in the true sense of that word, of a league, that is, which does not pretend to the attributes of a state. The only effective cure is to cut them away by a frank acknowledgment made in the light of bitter experience that in signing them we all made a mistake.

The League has failed in its primary duty of revising treaties made in the fevered temper which always follows a great war. I see no hope that the League can revise its own Covenant and am, therefore, forced to say what I think my own country should do, to deal with this mischievous situation.

I suggest that our first step should be to discuss with the other British Dominions the question how to establish a league of nations based on pledges which practical experience allows us to think can be kept. We have seen that nations are willing and able to send their leaders to one centre to discuss the affairs of the world in public as well as in private. Such discussion fosters the growth of a world opinion as opposed to merely national opinions. Experience has also shown that the nations are prepared to support an international secretariat as the necessary instrument of such discussion. We should also urge that a new covenant should omit pledges like those in Articles 10 and 16 which every member of the League has signally failed to discharge. As the Covenant stands Ireland, Canada, Australia, South Africa and New Zealand are all solemnly pledged in terms to preserve against external aggression the territorial integrity of Finland and Russia, of every state in western Europe but Germany, of almost every republic in Central and South America. To leave standing on paper a pledge which in fact lured Abyssinia to its fate, is to leave false coin in circulation, which debases the value of international credit. I feel little doubt that if we ourselves faced this position, the other British Dominions would face it with us.

I have no faith that the states now included in the League could ever succeed in framing a new covenant. They are too many in number and too diverse in their outlook. Such a change could only be effected in practice by a British initiative taken outside the League. I think that the British democracies would have to announce that at some future time they would give formal notice of leaving the League and at the same time invite the leading Powers, whose action in fact determines the peace of the world, to discuss the terms of a new covenant based, so far as possible, on the old, but omitting all pledges which experience has shown to be waste-paper. The declared intention of all the British communities to leave the existing League would in fact end its existence. The new league could then adopt at Geneva everything worth preserving. All the members of the old League would, I believe, in time adhere to the new league and take part in its counsels. I think that powerful states which hold aloof because they cannot subscribe to the pledges implied in such Articles as 10 and 16 would reconsider their position in a league freed from such pledges.

I do not suggest that a league, however reformed, will finally exorcise the danger of war. But I do believe that a league freed from automatic commitments would begin to prove a valuable instrument of peaceful diplomacy for revising obsolete treaties, and for bringing to light situations which, unless treated in time, drive nations to fight with each other. It would serve to remind the world of its growing unity, of its need for a government and international law in the real sense of those words. It would help men to realise that war is the product of anarchy and that anarchy is inseparable from a world cut up into sovereign states.

Though I think that a league of nations based on realities can do much to reduce the risks of war, I do not foresee any process whereby it can be moulded little by little into a genuine government of the world. Yet I have not shrunk, and I do not shrink, from upholding the creation of a world commonwealth, of a genuine government of mankind, as the practical goal of human endeavour. I believe that, unless conscious and effective steps are taken towards that goal, the level of civilisation we have now reached cannot be maintained. It is even in danger of falling in ruins, as it fell in the Dark Ages. But the project of a world government is not in sight till two or more commonwealths, more advanced than the rest, have recognised these truths, and by some immense spiritual effort have consciously merged their sovereignties in one international commonwealth. In order to do this they must create one government more competent than their separate governments to control the relations of the people it represents to the rest of mankind. That government must handle the issues of peace and war, and must have the forces necessary for that purpose. It must, therefore, have power to tax not the national states which compose it, but the citizens of those states. It must draw its authority to levy these taxes from the citizens themselves and not from their national governments.

Such an international state will not be established merely by the framing and acceptance of a federal constitution designed to accomplish these objects. It must prove its reality and efficacy to itself and the world. But if such a commonwealth were established and survived for some generations, the spirit which gave it reality would grow, as the spirit which now makes the United States the strongest national commonwealth in the world has grown. The transference of American loyalty from the state to the Union was a gradual process. Having adopted the constitution, they elected their president and members to Congress, they obeyed its laws and paid its taxes. All unconsciously as years went by they came to think of the Union rather than the State as the unit for which they were called on to live and to die. They awoke to the fact that the larger loyalty had raised their life to a higher plane, which was not consistent with slavery in their midst. In the end the great majority were found willing to devote their property and their lives to destroying slavery for the sake of the Union.

And so it will be with the first international commonwealth which survives for one or two generations. It will silently draw to itself the devotion of the peoples who agree to form it. They will recognise in time, and the world outside them will recognise, that their national life has not been impaired by the transfer of sovereignty to a larger unit, but has, in fact, been raised to a higher plane. The possibility of an international state composed of nations separated by oceans will have been demonstrated to the world. The gulf which at present exists in men's minds will have been bridged.

NOTES

[1] Shakespeare, *Othello*, Act I, Scene 3.
[2] *Survey of International Affairs*, 1935, vol. ii. p. 66.

CHAPTER IX

POLITICAL THOUGHT AND THE CHURCHES

THE previous chapters have led to the view of human society, divided into national states under no general direction, as checked in its onward and upward march by reaching the edge of a chasm, into which they must force each other unless the chasm is bridged in time. We have reached the further conclusion that the task of constructing a bridge whereby this dangerous chasm can be passed must from the nature of the problem rest with those national states which have reached a higher stage of political development than the rest, those which have best succeeded in applying the principle of the commonwealth to their own institutions. If so, the responsibility for (1) clear thinking, (2) readiness to act, and (3) decisive action, which rests on such national commonwealths, is great beyond measure.

I am trying to use the idea of responsibility in its strictest sense. Obligation is conditioned by power. Men are only responsible for doing what they are able to do. I have, therefore, put the responsibility for decisive action last. Matters have not reached that stage when leaders of national commonwealths, their representative statesmen, are able to act. There is not in the people they represent that public opinion which enables them to act. Their primary function is to express public opinion in action. They can guide public opinion in detail. But in larger matters of policy they cannot create public opinion, if only because the nature of their task denies them the time and also the detachment required for the thinking necessary to see what the wider issues are.

And this is especially true of the public opinion which is needed at great junctures in history to lift human affairs from one plane to another. The kind of thinking which Adam Smith did cannot be done by a minister who has to direct a public department, to control a parliament and to fight elections.

The public opinion which is needed to lift the course of human affairs to a higher plane must from its nature be religious in the truest sense of that word. It is for that reason that churches play an indispensable part in such movements. The abolition of slavery is a typical case in point. That negro slavery was incompatible with the relations of man to God and of men to each other, as expounded by Jesus Christ, became clear to most thoughtful Christians whose minds were not obscured by the fact that they owned slaves, or belonged to a slave-owning community. The public opinion which enabled statesmen to abolish the institution of slavery was created by Quakers and the Evangelical movement.

The abolition of slavery was a simple case, because all that was necessary at the moment was to abolish a definite institution regardless of cost, to forbid a particular practice. As Professor Huxley once said: "Before we can do right we must first know what it is right to do". In this negative case of slavery, the churches had no difficulty in knowing what was right. For them to create the opinion on which statesmen could act was merely a question of time and persistence.

The churches are now appealing to statesmen to abolish war. In doing so they voice an overwhelming mass of public opinion outside their ranks as well as within them. And statesmen have tried to respond. The League and the Kellogg Pact are among the results.

If the reasoning advanced in these pages is sound,

and naturally I think it is, to abolish war by a simple act such as was needed to abolish slavery is not possible. My contention is that war is not the essential evil, the real impediment which arrests the advance of civilisation. It is merely a symptom of a far more inveterate evil which can only be cured by definite and difficult acts of construction. To work out what those acts of construction should be is beyond the province and also the capacity of churches. In the case of slavery no great effort of mental construction was needed to guide the churches such as Adam Smith applied to another field of human activity. In this case, where national sovereignty is threatening to stifle human progress, some clearer and harder thinking must be done before those who create public opinion can know how to create it.

It is for this reason that I urge that clear thinking, readiness to act, and decisive action in the leading commonwealths is required to release human society from the deadlock in which it is fixed. The order in which I have put the crucial words is deliberate. I do not believe that the leading statesmen in the leading commonwealths can begin to release human affairs from their present impasse until bodies like churches have created the public opinion upon which they can act. But I do not think that churches can of themselves see how to create an effective and constructive public opinion until they are given some sound and definite idea of the kind of change which must be made in the social structure before men can rise to a higher level of civilisation. In the League of Nations the churches have felt that they had been furnished with such a constructive plan. They have done their best to strengthen the hands of statesmen in making full use of it. The immense volume of public opinion, in countries where government is responsible to public opinion, which supports the League is largely the result of their efforts.

In the light of actual experience can it still be argued that civilisation and its further progress can be maintained by virtue of a system based on no other foundation than compacts between national sovereignties? That question, I submit, has not as yet received the attention it deserves from political thinkers. By political thinkers I mean those who are free to see, think and declare what they feel to be true without regard to the effect that what they say may have on political programmes and parties. The life of such men centres for the most part, though not entirely, in universities. The circles of which I am thinking may be broadly described as academic.

The League of Nations was to a great extent the result of thought which came from those circles. To an overwhelming degree the influence of those circles has been used since the war to support and create the belief that human society must and can be stabilised on the basis of the Covenant.

I am forced to ask myself why is this so? I am not myself a trained political thinker. My walk in life has been mainly that of a political journeyman. As a young man I had to construct municipal institutions. In South Africa, India and Ireland I have been concerned with the structure of national governments. The mechanical necessities of these tasks have forced me once and again to consider what is the basic principle which unites a society in such manner as to render its members amenable to the rule of law. I have had to ask myself what law in the real sense of that term is. To these questions I have always found myself driven to the same answer, that the only factor that binds men together in the last analysis is a sense of duty one to another. I have also seen that where men are so bound together in organic unity their sense of duty deepens and grows with surprising rapidity. I have seen this happen in a town like Johannesburg. I have watched attempts to stabilise society in South Africa by elaborate compacts between its various governments and seen them break down in every direction. I have seen the opposite principle tried of establishing a government which could claim the unlimited devotion of all South Africans. In twenty-five years I have seen a growth in readiness to respond to that claim, greater than I hoped in the time, sufficient to offer assurance that the Union of South Africa is now established on lasting foundations. Since the Great War I have watched attempts to stabilise human society by virtue of compacts between its national states; and yet we see that the structure of human society is more precarious than ever it was before in time of peace. Even the system of international trade and finance as established before the war is being reduced to a system of barter between individual nations. The sense of uncertainty is affecting the life of every country, of every town, of every village community. The activities of men in their normal pursuits are so paralysed thereby that they are unable to exercise the power they have to produce and exchange the goods men need to support civilised life. Again I am driven to believe that this final attempt to relate national states to each other on a basis of compact is doomed to failure. I can see no hope for the future unless or until some conscious effort is made to unite human society on the basis of the infinite claim of society to unlimited devotion from each of its members.

I can only recall one political thinker of recognised authority, Benedetto Croce, who has clearly and firmly stated this view. I am, therefore, driven to ask myself why a view, which seems to my mind a truth of supreme importance, receives no support in intellectual circles, or, to speak more bluntly, why those circles provide no effective guidance for churches and practical statesmen.

The reasons, I think, are twofold. In the last century a professor of pure mathematics at Cambridge was wont to denounce applied mathematics as a degradation of the subject he taught. Universities, like every profession in life, are exposed to the subtle disease of professionalism. When doctors, clergy, soldiers or the members of any calling come to regard it as an end in itself and lose sight of the end for which it exists they injure their profession and their own value as professional men. The ultimate problem for all of us in our lives is how to act. Our thought is a guide to action—a means. As Carlyle has said, the end of life is not a thought but an act. A branch of knowledge pursued as an end in itself will lose its quality as a branch of knowledge. And this is pre-eminently true of political science. I have known a teacher of political science in a great university to argue that political theory, as he understood it, could have no relation to political practice. He expressly rejected the notion that political theory could ever be expected to afford any guidance to statesmen engaged upon practical politics. This explains, I think, why men experienced in public affairs, when they read the works of political theorists, find much that seems to have no relation whatever to facts of life they have handled. They are often expressed in a jargon which seems to have lost all touch with realities. I strongly suspect the value of every political theory which cannot in the end be grasped and applied by practical statesmen.

I have often been criticised on the ground that I treat human affairs as if they were subject to laws as binding as those which govern physical machinery. Spiritual facts cannot be weighed and measured with the same, or nearly the same, exactitude as physical facts. The element of free will, in which I profoundly believe, is one reason why principles cannot be applied in the sphere of human action with anything like the certainty and precision with which they are applied to physical nature. But are we then to say that human relations are not governed by principles in the long run? If not, is political science a genuine science at all? I firmly believe that it is, because I believe that by patient, intelligent and fearless study of fact, principles of life can be discerned. By observing those principles the lives of men can be raised to a higher plane; by ignoring them human affairs may be plunged in disaster. I believe that Milton was right when he spoke of truths "for the want of which whole nations fare the worse."[1] It is those truths that political thinkers should seek, and when they have found them, express in terms which those whose business it is to apply them can grasp. Political science is not merely a genuine science, but at this juncture of human affairs the most important of all the sciences. It is one which calls for the service of the best and most powerful minds. The task of helping the world across the gulf which arrests its progress lies in the first instance with political thinkers of recognised authority and not with statesmen or churches.

It is to the judgment of such thinkers that I venture to submit the propositions advanced in this book, and also the practical conclusions drawn from them. Can human beings ever be united in any lasting and permanent manner, except by virtue of a sense of duty, by an instinct which prompts them to put the interests of others before their own? Without such a sense of duty can compacts serve to unite them? Are states not bodies of men bound together by the principle that each member of the state owes an unlimited duty to all the others? Does not this principle mean the existence of a government in the state which claims an unlimited obedience from all its subjects? Is not the subject morally bound to render that obedience, except in the case where he feels that his government is so mistaken that to do so will work irreparable mischief to the state? I am here thinking of a case such as Socrates faced, and Christians are now facing in Germany, where the government forbids the citizen to utter what he thinks are truths "for the want of which whole nations fare the worse". This proposition means that there can be no right of rebellion; but there may be, and sometimes is, a duty to rebel. Must not the right of the government to this normal obedience mean that the government may call on the citizen to use force to impose its laws upon those who resist them? Could law, in fact, operate unless governments made this claim, and unless it were obeyed by its citizens? Can law in this sense of the word, therefore, exist outside the limits of a state? Is not international law, so called, something essentially different from the law which prevails in states? If the duty men owe to each other is the essential bond which unites states, should their governments not be rendered responsible to those of its citizens who have realised the sense of public duty to an adequate degree?

And now we come to questions the answers to which depend more on the reading of facts. Where a government is made in some genuine manner responsible to its citizens, and yet retains its reality as a government, does not their sense of duty to the state tend to increase? Is not the strongest sense of patriotism as a matter of fact produced in the most highly developed commonwealths? Is not the end and object of the state to increase this sense of duty in men to each other? Is not the state in the form of the commonwealth the most effective agency for developing this sense of duty in men in the mass? On the other hand, can a state limited to one section of human beings, and organised on the basis of the infinite duty of all its members to that section alone, fully develop their sense of duty to human beings outside that section? Must not national commonwealths—even in their most highly developed form—create a disposition in most of their citizens to regard their national interests as prior to the interests of society at large? Can the relations of groups of people each regarding their interests as primary be stabilised on the basis of compacts between their governments? Can a system of compacts between sovereign states from its nature be trusted to restrain them from using force against each other? Can the rule of law between nations ever be established on a basis of compact? Can a league of nations, however valuable as a stage in progress, and however highly developed as a contractual system, ever afford to human society the stability it needs? Can the state fulfil its essential function of increasing the sense of duty in men to each other, in the form of the merely national state? Can the sense of duty in men to each other be developed to its utmost capacity until they are organised in one state, subject to one law, in such manner that they are led to feel that their ultimate duty is owed to the human race as a whole, and not to one part of it? Have men any prospect of attaining a higher plane of civilisation than that reached, so long as they are organised under national sovereignties?

And now I come to questions which require some historical sense and experience of men in those who answer them. Can the national states of the world, even if all of them were commonwealths, ever be transformed by one act into a world state, so that all men owe their allegiance, in the last analysis, to a single sovereignty? Is it not in the nature of things that two or more, and those the most advanced commonwealths, would have to make a beginning by merging themselves into one international sovereignty?

If a world commonwealth is to be realised, must it not be by a gradual process, one national state after another deciding to merge its sovereignty in an international state which has come into being?

For the purpose I have in view, this long series of questions can, I think, be summarised in two. Can the progress of civilisation continue beyond the level it has now reached, or indeed maintain that level, unless or until the ultimate allegiance of all human beings is rendered to one sovereignty?

The second is a more practical question, though of equal importance.

Is the realisation of a world commonwealth conceivable unless or until two or more national commonwealths have succeeded in merging their national sovereignties into one international sovereignty?

I venture to submit these two questions to those thinkers who regard political theory as a necessary guide to political practice.

Clear unequivocal answers are too seldom given by political thinkers to questions like these. The reason, I think, is that their minds are influenced more than they realise by the attitude of mind from which practical statesmen can rarely escape. In the academic circles, to which I appeal, my first question, at any rate, would, I think, be dismissed as too academic to be worth considering. The idea of a world commonwealth would be treated as one which no body of people large enough to affect practical issues would consider. As to this I agree; but the willingness of men to take this or that particular step is, I submit, a question for the politician and not for political thinkers. The question, an opinion on which I am asking from trained and disciplined thinkers, is this. So long as people refuse all final allegiance to a sovereignty wider than national sovereignties, can they hope to rise to a higher plane of civilisation? Can a system of compact between these sovereignties, however developed, act as a real preventive of war and establish the rule of law between these sovereignties?

I believe that a clear pronouncement from intellectual circles on these questions would open the way for work which neither political thinkers nor politicians can do, which only churches and bodies like churches can do. At present the churches believe and preach that the evils inherent in national sovereignty can be cured by the League of Nations, on the principles embodied in the Covenant between those sovereignties. And in preaching this gospel they feel they are justified by the general teaching of political thinkers. But picture for a moment another situation. Suppose that a number of recognised and authoritative political thinkers were to teach that the League of Nations is at best no more than a palliative, so long as the principle of national sovereignty is assumed to be final, that no compact between governments can establish the rule of international law in the absolute sense of that word, that the first and essential step to be taken towards the establishment of international law is for two or more national commonwealths to establish one international sovereignty between themselves, the churches would then be able to begin the work which they only can do. If in national commonwealths churches were led to believe that the first duty of citizens in those commonwealths was not merely to support the Covenant, but to merge their own sovereignties in some wider international sovereignty, and that commonwealths by doing so would open to men a vista of hope which could in the course of time be realised, the hope of a structure of society based on realities, of a world ordered in accordance with the laws of God, then public opinion which would make such a change possible would slowly but surely come into being. The change that is needed is first and foremost a change in men's minds. The work of effecting that change is essentially work for the churches; but they cannot begin it till political thinkers have clearly said what the change should be. When once that change is effected the work of the practical statesmen begins. The materials upon which they can work have at last been prepared and brought to their hands.

NOTE

[1] Milton, *Areopagitica*, p. 35, edited by Edwin Arber. Constable & Co. Ltd., 1903.

CHAPTER X

THE DAY OF SMALL THINGS

As I write these pages the President of the British Association meeting at Norwich repeats the message of science to this generation. He foretells that our race has before it in this planet aeons of time; perhaps as long as those that covered the whole development of life in the past—that is to say, millions of years. As I read his words I feel joyfully sure that men will achieve a government of the world responsible to themselves before the first of those millions is passed, within centuries fewer than those since man became man. The human race is still in its early youth. I hold to this faith that through such a commonwealth the sons of men will one day rise to levels of virtue and happiness higher than those which seers and poets have figured in dreams of the Golden Age. A time will come when God, beholding his children on earth, will say: "These are they which came out of great tribulation."[1]

After tracing the growth of civilisation through the centuries which have passed since men learned how to record their doings this is the faith left in my mind. The stupendous advance achieved during that period has been the result of effort and thought, which became highly creative when men were able to read and criticise what others had thought before them, and also to compare what they were doing with what others had done. We have seen how great innovations in the outlook and structure of society were made in Palestine, Greece and England by communities which cannot have looked very important to their powerful neighbours at the time. We have also noticed periods when the progress of civilisation was delayed for centuries, because no one appeared at that time who was able to read the meaning of what had been done and also apply what he had read. I believe that the whole world would be other and better than it now is had the people of Athens seen how to apply the principles which inspired their commonwealth to the empire they created. The same, I think, may be said, if British policy in America had followed the counsels of Burke rather than those of Lord North.

In the second volume we saw how civilisation was raised to the plane it has now reached by the organisation of commonwealths on the national scale. In this volume I argue that it cannot now rise to a higher plane and may indeed decline, until men are able to realise a commonwealth on the international scale. But it does not follow that the high initiative needed to effect such a change can come from one of the major commonwealths. In the light of the past it may prove to lie with those which are relatively small and remote. The fable of Aesop, which tells how the lion caught in a net was released by the mouse, is a parable true of history.

I have argued that the first and critical step towards the realisation of an international commonwealth must be taken by two or more states which have carried the principle of the national commonwealth to its furthest expression: the fewer the easier. It would not matter how small the number might be, if the result was a genuine international commonwealth. Clearly this step would be least difficult for national commonwealths with a common language, with similar constitutions, whose security already depends on each other. I cannot, therefore, avoid the conclusion, to which the reasoning followed in these pages has led, that in the world as now ordered, either Australia, New Zealand, or both together, with Great Britain are the countries best able to construct the first foot-bridge across the gulf in men's minds which now prevents the world from passing from the national to the international commonwealth. But of this I am sure: the initiative would have to come from Australia or New Zealand. I cannot resist the conclusion that one or other of these minor commonwealths holds, though it does not know it, a key to the door which, until it is opened, imprisons the whole of mankind.

In saying this I am well aware that my readers will feel that I here enter the region of fantasy. It is just that feeling which attests the gulf in men's minds to which I am always referring. I will ask them, therefore, for once to give their fancy free rein, and to picture to themselves a federal union in which the Australian, New Zealand and British peoples had agreed to create a federal government for the purpose of controlling the relations of those countries to each other, and to the rest of the world. Such a government would have to include a legislature as well as an executive, a legislature empowered to impose and collect from the tax-payers the revenues required to enable the executive to discharge the international functions imposed on it.

In the past such proposals have always been met by arguments crystallised in Burke's aphorism, "*Natura obstat*"—geography stands in the way. To the League of Nations we owe it that this can no longer be said. If the Council and Assembly of the League can meet at one centre to transact business, in spite of all linguistic difficulties, there is no insuperable difficulty, so far as geography is concerned, in two or more states which use the same language creating an executive and legislature in one centre, with a secretariat like that of the League. The League was able to do this, and did it, because it renounced all claim to authority over the people who composed its constituent states. It treated the national sovereignties as final. It claimed no allegiance from individuals. This brings us back to the point that the real difficulty in creating an international commonwealth exists, not in the facts of nature, but only in the state of men's minds.

We are giving the rein to our fancy so far as to suppose that this difficulty has been surmounted by national commonwealths speaking the same language. We must also assume that the constitutional problems involved have been solved, that some distribution of voting power and the burden of taxation has been reached which the smaller nations have been willing to adopt. If all this happened, and the peoples in these widely separated countries recorded their votes and paid their taxes for two generations, certain results would, I think, be found to have followed. In the first place, the national governments in these three countries would have found themselves far better able to discharge the functions imposed on them, merely by reason of the greater security they enjoyed. In the second place, the sense of devotion in the minds of the people themselves to the federal authority would have grown, as it grew in the course of a few generations in America. If such an international state were created and continued to exist for two generations, any movement to disrupt it would be crushed by public opinion in the country in which that movement arose. The spiritual factor required to bind an international commonwealth in an indissoluble union would have come into being.

The United States was conceived as the nucleus of a commonwealth destined to include states other than those who founded it. "New States may be admitted by the Congress into this Union" were words written into the constitution. The terms of admission were wisely left to be settled whenever the occasion should arise. Here is a precedent to be followed wherever the first international commonwealth is called into being. It must from the nature of the case be founded as the nucleus of something destined to grow, as a state always ready to consider the inclusion of other states which from time to time may desire to join it. But no state should ever be admitted on terms which would tend to destroy its character as an international commonwealth.

A proposal to unite in one international commonwealth communities living on opposite sides of the globe, the commonwealths most remote from each other, as the first step to uniting all the peoples who inhabit this globe may seem paradoxical. But the very distance between them creates one of the major interests common to both. Their supreme interest in common consists in protecting the principle of freedom for which they stand. But inseparably connected with this is the heavy task of protecting the routes which connect them by sea and by air. Such an international commonwealth as I ask the reader to imagine would find its first material interest in safeguarding the routes on the maintenance of which its continued existence must always depend; the routes through the Mediterranean, the Suez Canal and the Red Sea.

I am holding in mind that other countries are vitally concerned in the maintenance of these routes, more especially Egypt and India. In course of time the millions of India will learn to govern themselves, but I also think they will only do this by a long and painful experience. It is easy to conceive, on the other hand, that the statesmen of India or Egypt might seek to enter an international commonwealth which controlled the route which connects the eastern and western hemispheres long before they have reached the stage of self-government which countries like England, Australia or New Zealand have attained. I can also conceive their accepting admission on terms which would not endanger the stability of the international commonwealth we are picturing, and which would not destroy its character as such. And if this were found possible, a step would have been taken towards the ultimate goal of incomparable value. A real international commonwealth in being, which included countries like India and Egypt, as well as countries like England, Australia and New Zealand, would once for all establish the idea of a world commonwealth including all nations and kindreds and peoples as the practical goal of human affairs. The impulse of other nations to join it would be greatly increased.

There are states in Europe as directly interested in the route from the west to east as India, Egypt, Australia, New Zealand or England herself. I am thinking of a country like Holland, and in a lesser degree Belgium, Denmark, Sweden, Norway and Iceland. I can scarcely conceive statesmen from all these countries with their various languages meeting in convention with those of England, Australia and New Zealand to found a new international commonwealth which would, among other functions, control the routes which connect the western and eastern hemispheres. But if England, Australia and New Zealand had once established a stable commonwealth which controlled that route, with or without the inclusion of India and Egypt, I can well conceive that Holland might wish to enter that commonwealth. I can also conceive her being admitted. And if something of this kind should happen, Belgium and the Scandinavian countries would quickly follow. That diversity of language would offer no insuperable obstacle has already been proved by the League of Nations. If, in spite of language difficulties, these nations can now transact their business in the Council and Assembly of Geneva, so could the business of a commonwealth be transacted in a polyglot cabinet and parliament. The inclusion of powers like France would then be in sight.

If an international commonwealth built from countries within the British Empire came to include countries in Europe which had never been part of that Empire, the most difficult stage in its growth to a world commonwealth, after its first foundation, would have been crossed. So the British Empire would have done its work and passed into history.

And, putting both Constitutions together, you will say that it was not the *Romans* that spred upon the *World*; But it was the *World*, that spred upon the *Romans*: And that was the sure Way of Greatnesse.[2]

When the British Commonwealth had been transformed into something which, beyond dispute, was an international commonwealth, the time would at last be in sight when the United States would become an integral part of it. I think that before this would happen South Africa, Ireland and Canada would have found their way into the international commonwealth. In doing so, Ireland might solve the problem of her own national unity. It may well happen that Canada may prove the bridge whereby the people of America may pass from national isolation to partnership in a world commonwealth. Whenever that happens the peace of the world will be finally secured. The more difficult nations would then be eager to join it, and the world commonwealth will be more than strong enough to contain and to mould them.

I think, too, that long before this had happened the countries which had merged their sovereignties in an international commonwealth would also have transferred their control of backward peoples to the government of that commonwealth. I can think of it controlling the natives of Africa, New Guinea and Java with a policy consciously directed towards fitting these peoples to govern themselves and to join in the government of the commonwealth as a whole.

Before a commonwealth had moved very far on the lines here rapidly sketched the danger of world wars would have become a thing of the past. Human society would have recovered at least the degree of stability reached in the nineteenth century, that transitory interval in which one national commonwealth was strong enough to control and police the maritime routes of the world. The world will never again see such control of the air as well as the sea by one national commonwealth. It may go through the terrible experience of seeing for a time such control exercised by a military despotism. But control by a despotism can have no permanence. The world will never again know the degree of stability it felt from 1815 to 1914 till some international commonwealth controls the main avenues through which the continents of the world have commerce with each other.

It is needless to develop this theme further. If a commonwealth such as I have here imagined had come into being, its gradual extension to include all the peoples of the world would be merely a question of time. Its influence would greatly accelerate the process whereby the peoples of Asia and Africa are learning to grasp and apply the principle of the commonwealth to their own institutions.

All this, of course, seems very remote; but it brings me back to the point with which I opened this chapter. We are now overshadowed by a sense of impending calamities which, if they befell, might plunge us back into centuries darker than those that followed the fall of ancient civilisation in Europe. I believe that these dangers are inherent in a world united by mechanisation, but divided into sovereign states, and can only begin to abate when men have learned to pass from the national to the international commonwealth. The most careful analysis I can make of this situation has led me to think that the peoples best able to set such a change in motion are the two minor commonwealths isolated in the southern hemisphere. I am bound to say where my argument has led me, however strange the conclusion may seem; for, should it perchance be a sound conclusion, Australia and New Zealand, either or both, have at this juncture of history an opportunity of serving human society which cannot be measured by their present size or position in the world.

NOTES

[1] Revelation vii. 14.
[2] Bacon, *Of the True Greatnesse of Kingdoms and Estates*.

CHAPTER XI

DOMINION STATUS

In the last chapter I have argued that the first international commonwealth in the real sense of that word must spring from the federal union of two or more nations versed in the art of self-government. This view is, I think, likely to meet with wider assent than some others advanced in these pages. Those who agree with it will, I believe, also agree that if any such step is possible at all in the course of the next century, it could only be taken by peoples included in the so-called British Commonwealth of Nations. That none of these nations, not even New Zealand, would at the present moment consider such a step is a fact that I face. And because I face it I must seek to explain it.

For the purpose of the argument I have throughout the previous pages spoken as though the Dominions were national commonwealths in the full sense of that word. Everyone knows that a vast majority of people in Ireland, in Canada, in South Africa, in Australia and even in New Zealand mean to develop as nations distinct from that in Great Britain. It is true that nearly everything has now been done which can be done by printing words upon paper to make them so. Step by step the position was established that the only law which governed them was the law they made through their own parliaments responsible to themselves. The end of this process has now been reached. By the Statute of Westminster the British parliament renounced its power to enact legislation which bound the Dominions, except on their own invitation. Of equal importance is the manner in which the Judicial Committee of the Privy Council, the authority from which there is no appeal, has interpreted the Act.

But have the Statute of Westminster and the subsequent ruling of the Privy Council really completed the status of the self-governing Dominions as national commonwealths? Let me put that question in another way. Is the status which these countries have now acquired such as to induce the attitude of mind in their peoples that the status of countries like the United States, Switzerland, Holland or France produces in the minds of their citizens? Can this ever be so until their governments have as openly and explicitly accepted the final responsibility for peace or war? The principle is now firmly established and recognised that a self-governing Dominion is not committed to sending one soldier to fight or to spending one pound or dollar on a war in which Great Britain is engaged except by consent of its own parliament. Yet while that position is fully accepted the question still remains unanswered whether, if Great Britain is involved in a war which threatens the peace of the world, the Dominions are also involved as belligerents.

To reverse this one-sided question may clear the issue. Is Great Britain committed to war if one of the Dominions is involved in a war which threatens the peace of the world? The question put in this way is at once felt to be academic, a question somewhat remote from the sphere of realities, or even a logical catch: for the only government in the British Empire which is paying serious attention to the task of preventing a world war is that of Great Britain. The Dominion peoples know it and feel it, and that knowledge and feeling unconsciously affects their habits of mind. The people of Great Britain are acutely aware that the slightest error of judgment on the part of their government may involve themselves and the whole world in a conflagration. In Ireland, Canada, Australia, New Zealand and South Africa the people have no such feeling in respect of their own governments.

I feel no doubt in my own mind that if Great Britain is again involved in a world war, the Dominions will act just as they acted in 1914. I have no doubts that their full strength will be thrown into the next great struggle, with results as decisive as in the past. But so long as human society is divided up into sovereign states, the first and most solemn duty of governments is to prevent the outbreak of war, a task which clearly involves an active, close and continuous study of world affairs. In countries like Switzerland, Belgium, Holland, Denmark, Norway and Sweden questions of foreign policy are treated as matters which call for supreme attention. The proportion of time devoted by governments and legislatures to discussing them shows that this is the case. They are fully equipped with the diplomatic machinery without which no government can be fully informed on the subject; and their taxpayers bear the cost.

At the Imperial Conference of 1911 Mr. Asquith affirmed in unequivocal terms that the British government could not share the responsibility for foreign affairs with Dominion governments. During and since the war that position was abandoned. After the war full and detailed information on foreign affairs has been transmitted by cable and mail from the Foreign Office to Dominion governments. In recent years responsible ministers in three Dominions have told me that these despatches were not circulated by the minister in charge of external affairs to his colleagues except in moments of crisis. When a crisis in foreign affairs compels these Dominion cabinets to consider their position, there is only one minister who brings to the subject a previous knowledge of foreign affairs other than that which an ordinary reader of the press would acquire. And this, I was told, was due to the fact that the electorates, to which they are answerable, take little interest in foreign affairs, except at a moment of crisis which threatens the world with war, or in some aspect of external affairs which directly affects their own livelihood.

When I look round the world, the only commonwealths I see which could take the initiative in relieving mankind from its present impasse in the century before us are self-governing Dominions. Yet I do not feel that, as things are, they will bring themselves to take it. I use the words 'as things are' because I can conceive them taking it as the result of some great catastrophe not so great as to rob them of all power of action, that is to say to destroy them as commonwealths. I think that this would have happened if the war had ended with a so-called peace which left the naval and military powers of the central empires in being, such a peace as in 1917 Lansdowne wished to see made. I think it may happen if the British commonwealths should experience and also survive another cataclysm as bad or worse than the Great War. But I write in the hope and presumption that such a catastrophe may be averted until the difficult step can be taken which alone, as I think, can prevent its certain recurrence sooner or later. I am, therefore, driven to ask what it is that deters these commonwealths from taking a step which they only can take, and which when taken by them will, I believe, enable the world to pass to a higher level of civilisation.

I am thus led to state a conclusion from which I have long shrunk. In spite of all that is said and written and of all appearances, the Dominions have not as yet acquired the character of national commonwealths, and cannot acquire it until they have accepted in unequivocal terms the responsibility for peace or war. They cannot do this, nor feel they have done it, until they have notified to the world at large that they are not involved in war till their own governments have officially declared that they are so involved.

The cabinet, parliament and electorate of a Dominion which had once come to this point would begin to take an interest in world affairs to which they cannot be brought in times of peace, so long as the present conditions exist. They would cease to be screened from the hard facts by direct contact with which men learn what those facts are. They would have to provide for themselves the diplomatic machinery without which no government can follow the course of foreign affairs. They would lose the habit of mind induced by a satellite position—the habit of mind which prevents them from seeing the key position which they hold at this juncture of human history.

This explains why I think that the first international commonwealth to come into being will be formed by the English-speaking communities most remote from each other. Of all these communities Canada will find it most difficult to achieve the status of a national commonwealth in the full sense of that word. Even if Canada reached the point of telling the world that the issues of peace and war were for her settled at Ottawa, and nowhere else, both she and the world would know that they still were, as a matter of fact, settled at Washington. The momentous task of founding the first international commonwealth must, I think, be achieved by peoples who have really known how it feels to depend on their own resources. The Dominions south of the line can, if they will, experience that feeling, and the task of initiating the first international commonwealth will, I believe, rest with them. If and when its stability was proved and also its capacity to include other democracies, those even of northern Europe, Canada would, I think, follow suit, and by doing so pave the way for its ultimate fusion with the great American Commonwealth. And whenever the people of North America add their strength to an international commonwealth the epoch of world wars in which we are now living will be finally closed.

CHAPTER XII

CONSTRUCTIVE RELIGION

I HAVE thus been led to conclude that in the world, as it now is, the first step from the national to the international commonwealth could only be taken by some of the self-governing nations under the British Crown. Critics may say that the picture I have drawn serves only to demonstrate the chimerical nature of my views. The reader, I feel, will allow that I have not sought to minimise the difficulties which stand in the way of the first step from the national to the international commonwealth. But the difficulties are not physical, as they were in the time of Burke. They are now spiritual difficulties—difficulties such as exist in the minds of men. They belong to that sphere in which it is true that "faith can remove mountains", and, because I believe that these words convey a vital truth in rhetorical form, I have tried to explain what I mean by the word 'faith': "In the long run what any society is to become will depend on what it believes, or disbelieves, about the eternal things".[1]

Such beliefs, I have urged, cannot be based on revelations attested or signed by miracles. "Verily I say unto you, There shall no sign be given."[2] If revelations could be so signed and attested there would then be no room for doubt and, therefore, no room for faith in the true sense of that word. I have not denied revelation as a fact. On the contrary, I can only describe the instinct which tells us that right differs from wrong, as a revelation by God to man. I have merely said that its truth cannot be attested by miracles, that it must be accepted as a matter of faith. I think that by giving us conscience and reason he led us on to discover his existence for ourselves, to know and adore him. I believe that Moses and the prophets divined the nature of God by flashes of insight, by intuitions deeper than those given to ordinary minds. Whence those visions of truth came, whether from within or without their minds, is not so important as the question whether their vision was truer than anything which the minds of men had before conceived. But the truth they spoke cannot be attested by thunders or earthquakes shaking the mountains on which they stood. I can only recognise their truths in so far as my own conscience and mind tell me that what they said was true. Here, in my judgment, were men whose thoughts went deeper and truer than those of men who had gone before them. I must listen with great attention to all they said, and do my best to grasp their meaning. This does not imply that all they said must be true. I must use my own judgment to winnow the grains of truth they produced from the husks of tradition in which it was grown.

The Hebrew prophets conceived the reality behind the visible and tangible universe as something of the nature of our own personalities raised to infinity. They thought of God as having created the world as we know it, with man in it; and here, I think, they were right. But in thinking that God had finished and ended the work of creation I think they were wrong. They thought of God as the spirit of righteousness whose laws men ought to obey. The spectacle of the powerful monarchs who ruled in the world about them coloured and also confined their conception of God. They thought of his laws as decrees of a monarch, and of man's disobedience as sin. The supreme importance of avoiding sin was uppermost in their minds. When they wrote in a code what they felt were the ten supreme commandments of God seven of the ten began with the words "Thou shalt not"—were couched in the negative vein.

While our Lord accepted much of their view his teaching went far beyond it. In his mind the Kingdom of God was not an order in which men, as the subjects of God, were mainly concerned with keeping his laws, with avoiding their breach. In his mind the work of creation had never ceased. It would always go on. Men were called to join as partners with God in making new things. The material world was the sphere in which men were called to cooperate with God in work of spiritual creation. The Kingdom of God on this earth was a system of society to be ordered by men themselves in accordance with the mind of God. In so far as men learned to see what the mind of God was, and based their relations on what they saw, the system they brought into being would shape those who lived under it in the likeness of God. His Kingdom *was* of this world, but also of the next. I think that our Lord saw this world as a field of preparation for worlds beyond, which men neglect at their peril. I do not believe that he taught that men can fulfil their duty to God in this world merely by avoiding sin, by helping others to avoid it, nor by any mere process of escape from the penalties of sin. Their fundamental task on this earth was the ordering of men's relations one with another in accordance with the mind of God—that is to say, on the basis of the infinite duty which each owes to God and his brethren the children of God.

In the first part of this book I tried to trace the influence which led Christians to think of the system conceived by the founder as something apart from human society as a whole. They missed his conception of this world as the workshop in which worlds beyond it are to be shaped. The church developed as something apart from the world, through which Christians escaped from the world, to something better beyond it. This led to a false and disastrous antithesis between church and state. The church is regarded, by Catholics at any rate, as something higher than the state and by its nature opposed to the state. How potent this view still is in the Catholic world can be seen from a book published since the first volume of *Civitas Dei* appeared, under the title of *Religion and the Modern State*:

> . . . The whole Christian tradition, and the prophetic tradition which lies behind it, are a standing protest against the injustice and falsehood of that which is commonly called civilization. The world which is the natural enemy of the Church is not a moral abstraction, it is an historical reality which finds its embodiment in the empires and world cities of history—in Babylon and Tyre and Rome. Wherever the city of man sets itself up as an end in itself and becomes the centre of a self-contained and self-regarding order, it becomes the natural enemy of the city of God.[3]

The reactions produced by such teaching can now be gauged by the millions who bow their knees in the temples erected by Marx and Hitler. In our hearts there is that which tells us that life and the world about us are good, with a goodness to be brought into being by ourselves. The communist stresses the material aspect of goodness, till he comes to deny the spiritual basis of life, and that life can persist beyond time and space. In a memorable broadcast Professor Toynbee utters a warning which Christians were wise to consider:

> The post-war Paganism also gives its converts directions for their conduct in practical life; and these directions are of the kind which human nature craves for; they are simple, and clear, and concrete, and confident. A believing Fascist or Communist can probably get more definite instructions than a believing Christian about how he is to behave here and now: whom to love, whom (in his case) to hate, what to fight for, what to worship.[4]

"Our Father which art in heaven, Hallowed be

thy name" is a prayer which assumes that spirit not matter is the essence of life. Then, first and foremost, the worshipper is directed to rivet his mind on the purpose of God, which is creative. "Thy kingdom come." The petition which follows is a specific warning against the idea that the Kingdom of God will be brought into being solely by the action of God himself. "Thy will be done, *In earth as it is in heaven.*" This can only mean, I submit, that the Kingdom of God will come, but only as we ourselves see and accomplish his will upon earth. We, the children of God and brethren, are called of our own free will to join with our Father in the work of creation, a work which can only go on in this world in so far as we join in it. How often the prayer "Thy will be done", shorn of the words which follow it, is narrowed on tombstones to express resignation, which at best is a negative virtue!

The prayer then proceeds to deal with things of importance, but important only in the second degree. "Give us this day our daily bread." God knows that men need the physical strength to accomplish his will and create his Kingdom on earth. They are right to secure and enjoy the material things which give them this strength, so long as they do not forget the end in the means. Quite late in the prayer comes the petition which accepts and affirms the point of view of the Old Testament. "And forgive us our trespasses, As we forgive them that trespass against us. And lead us not into temptation, But deliver us from evil." The avoidance of sin, forgiveness of sin, redemption from sin are essential. All this had been said before by the Hebrew prophets, and our Lord endorsed it. His own special contribution was the emphasis he laid on constructive aspects of conduct. To see and to do the will of God in this world (for we cannot do it until we see it) and so to create his Kingdom on earth is the first and foremost duty of man. He framed that prayer and bade his followers to repeat it, in order to remind them day by day that the service of God involves infinitely more than mechanical obedience to a code of laws. My criticism is that the churches have largely reversed the emphasis expressed by their founder in the order in which he framed these petitions. The second part of the Lord's Prayer has been treated as primary; part of the first has been almost forgotten, or misdirected and misunderstood.

In Protestant churches it is now usual to replace the ten commandments from the Old Testament by the two commandments which Christ is said to have uttered, and I have no doubt that he uttered:

> The Lord our God, the Lord is one: and thou shalt love the Lord thy God with all thy heart, and with all thy soul, and with all thy mind, and with all thy strength. The second is this, Thou shalt love thy neighbour as thyself There is none other commandment greater than these.[5]

Whether our Lord was the first to say this, or whether he was merely quoting words which Jewish Rabbis had used before him, is a question of no importance to those who believe that the final source of authority is in the conscience of men themselves. These words, if they mean anything, mean this, that every man owes an infinite duty to God and his children, his fellow-men.

All followers of Christ will agree that he said that, and meant that. Whether as a matter of fact he said it, is an interesting question of history, but one not so important as the question whether the saying is true. We are here faced by an aphorism which all who believe in conscience will feel to be true. All those who seek to determine their conduct by the view that our own personalities are the key to reality will accept this aphorism as truth. Christians, at any rate, will accept it as such. But I cannot read the records we have of our Lord's teaching without feeling that he clearly realised the dangerous tendency of human nature to leave such truths in the air. It was for this reason, I think, that he emphasised so strongly the importance of realising the Kingdom of God, of realising that Kingdom on earth. He was, I submit, calling on men to apply this principle to the lives they led. But a principle cannot be fully applied except by a system which men must create for themselves. When Jesus called upon men to create the Kingdom of God he was, I submit, calling upon them to create such a system. It was left for men to think and work out for themselves what that system would be.

It is for this reason that I have tried in these pages to think out for myself what a working system of human society would be, if framed to realise the principle of the infinite duty of each to all and also what practical steps we can take to create such a system. I am driven by reason and experience to believe that a system like this must, in the long run, mean the organisation of all human society in one commonwealth. I also see that a principle like this can only be realised little by little. It must first be realised for communities small as cities, before it can be realised for communities large as nations. It must be realised by nations before it can be realised for international commonwealths. Some international commonwealth or commonwealths must be realised before ever the final goal of the world commonwealth is in sight.

The great difficulty lies in moving from one stage to the next. It consists no longer in physical obstacles but only in human minds. The difficulty of so changing the minds of men, even in commonwealths most advanced, is hard to exaggerate. It is mountainous in size and as such can only be removed by faith. Because I feel that these mountains can only be moved by faith, I look with hope to repositories of faith, to churches which are based upon faith in the real sense of that word.

To leave the language of metaphor, I feel that when once the Protestant churches had learned to regard the creation of a world commonwealth as an all-important aspect of their work in realising the Kingdom of God, an international commonwealth in the English-speaking world would come into being in a few generations. A bridge would be thrown over the gulf in men's minds which now bars our progress to a higher civilisation. One bridge would suffice, but others would also, perhaps, be built on its model—the more the better. The task of merging two or more international commonwealths will not, I think, be so difficult as the task of creating the first international commonwealth. My hopes lie with the churches which are not bound by the chain of their past. Yet, strangely enough, the train of thought which runs through this book was first set in motion by reading long years ago the unfinished words found in the papers of a Catholic poet after his death:

THE KINGDOM OF GOD

"*In No Strange Land*"

O world invisible, we view thee,
O world intangible, we touch thee,
O world unknowable, we know thee,
Inapprehensible, we clutch thee!

Does the fish soar to find the ocean,
The eagle plunge to find the air—
That we ask of the stars in motion
If they have rumour of thee there?

Not where the wheeling systems darken,
And our benumbed conceiving soars!—
The drift of pinions, would we hearken,
Beats at our own clay-shuttered doors.

The angels keep their ancient places;—
Turn but a stone, and start a wing!
'Tis ye, 'tis your estrangéd faces,
That miss the many-splendoured thing.

But (when so sad thou canst not sadder)
Cry;—and upon thy so sore loss
Shall shine the traffic of Jacob's ladder
Pitched betwixt Heaven and Charing Cross.

Yea, in the night, my Soul, my daughter,
Cry,—clinging Heaven by the hems;
And lo, Christ walking on the water,
Not of Genesareth, but Thames![6]

NOTES

[1] Gore, *Jesus of Nazareth*, p. 250. The Home University Library.
[2] Mark viii. 12.
[3] Christopher Dawson, *Religion and the Modern State*, pp. 104-5.
[4] January 19, 1937.
[5] Mark xii. 29-31.
[6] Francis Thompson, *Selected Poems*, p. 130. Methuen & Co., 1911.

INDEX

Index of Names.—Names like America, Greece, Hitler, India, Napoleon, Rome are omitted from this Index as occurring too often to be useful, when indexed, in helping the reader to locate a reference.

Printed in Great Britain by R. & R. Clark, Limited, *Edinburgh.*

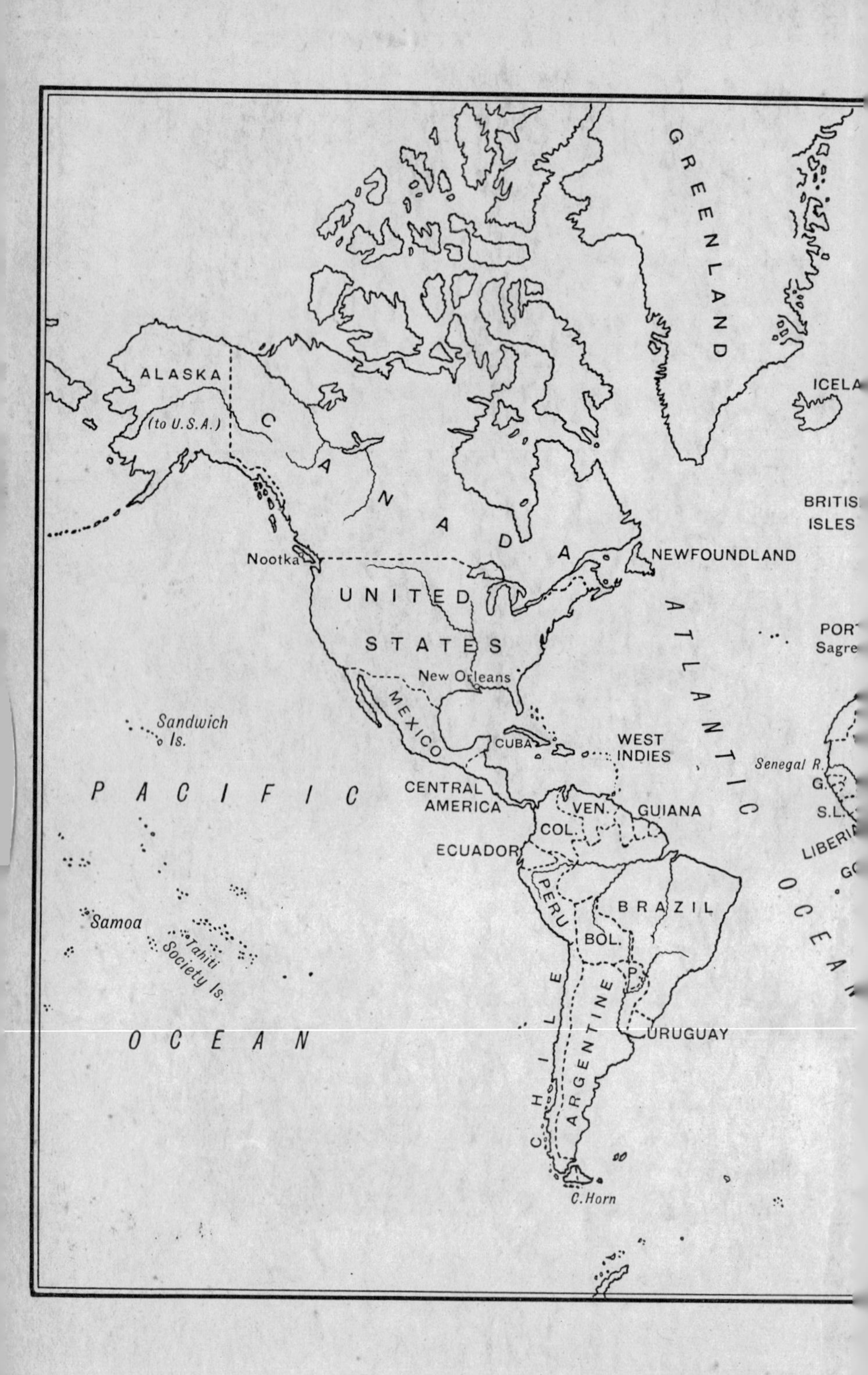
GREENLAND
ICELA
ALASKA
(to U.S.A.)
CANADA
BRITIS
ISLES
Nootka
NEWFOUNDLAND
UNITED
STATES
ATLANTIC
OCEAN
PORT
Sagre
New Orleans
MEXICO
Sandwich
Is.
CUBA
WEST
INDIES
Senegal R.
G.
S.L.
LIBERIA
PACIFIC
CENTRAL
AMERICA
VEN.
GUIANA
COL.
ECUADOR
PERU
BRAZIL
BOL.
Samoa
Tahiti
Society Is.
P.
CHILE
ARGENTINE
URUGUAY
OCEAN
C.Horn